Kontakte

6e

Kontakte

A COMMUNICATIVE APPROACH

ERWIN TSCHIRNER
Herder-Institut, Universität Leipzig
University of Arizona

BRIGITTE NIKOLAI
Werner-von-Siemens-Gymnasium, Bad Harzburg

TRACY D. TERRELL
Late, University of California, San Diego

Consultant:
NIKOLAUS EUBA
University of California, Berkeley

**McGraw-Hill
Higher Education**

Boston   Burr Ridge, IL   Dubuque, IA   New York   San Francisco   St. Louis
Bangkok   Bogotá   Caracas   Kuala Lumpur   Lisbon   London   Madrid   Mexico City
Milan   Montreal   New Delhi   Santiago   Seoul   Singapore   Sydney   Taipei   Toronto

McGraw-Hill
Higher Education

1 2 3 4 5 6 7 8 9 0 QPD / QPD 0 9 8

ISBN: 978-0-07-353533-3
MHID: 0-07-353533-8 (Student's Edition)
ISBN: 978-0-07-335509-2
MHID: 0-07-335509-7 (Instructor's Edition)

Editor-in-chief: *Michael Ryan*
Publisher: *William R. Glass*
Executive editor: *Christa Harris*
Director of development: *Scott Tinetti*
Development editor: *Paul Listen*
Editorial coordinator: *Margaret Young*
Marketing manager: *Jorge Arbujas*
Media producer: *Allison Hawco*
Managing editor: *Christina Gimlin*
Production editor: *Anne Fuzellier*
Art director: *Jeanne M. Schreiber*
Art manager: *Robin Mouat*
Design manager: *Violeta Díaz*
Interior designer: *Lisa Buckley*
Cover designer: *Laurie Entringer*
Photo research coordinator: *Nora Agbayani*
Photo researcher: *Inge King*
Illustrators: *Sally Richardson, Erik Watson, and Dave Bohn*
Production supervisor: *Tandra Jorgensen*
Media project manager: *Ron Nelms*
Production service: *The Left Coast Group, Inc.*
Compositor: *10/12 Californian by Aptara, Inc.*
Printer: *45# Pub Matte Plus by Quebecor World Inc.*

Cover: August Macke, Leute, die sich begegnen, 1914, watercolor. Photo © Blauel/Gnamm—ARTOTHEK.

Because this page cannot legibly accommodate all the copyright notices, page C-1 constitutes an extension of the copyright page.

Library of Congress Cataloging-in-Publication Data

Tschirner, Erwin P., 1956–
    Kontakte : a communicative approach / Erwin Tschirner, Brigitte
Nikolai, Tracy D. Terrell; consultant, Nikolaus Euba.—6th ed.
        p. cm.
    ISBN-13: 978-0-07-353533-3
    ISBN-10: 0-07-353533-8 (student's edition)
    ISBN-13: 978-0-07-335509-2
    ISBN-10: 0-07-335509-7 (instructor's edition)
1. German language—Grammar.   2. German language—Textbooks for foreign
speakers—English.   I. Nikolai, Brigitte.   II. Terrell, Tracy D.   III.
Title.
PF3112.T425   2008
438.2′421—dc22
                                                                2007038249

Contents

To the Instructor

Keeping Pace with the Profession: From Proficiency to the National Standards

Built on the foundation of five highly successful editions, the Sixth Edition of *Kontakte* offers a truly communicative approach that supports functional proficiency in all language skills. We believe that competent speakers must have an appropriate background knowledge of the communicative and cultural contexts in which language occurs. *Kontakte* places cultural competence, as an integral part of language learning, on a par with communicative competence by providing natural contexts within which students can acquire and practice language.

Moreover, *Kontakte* supports the National Standards, as outlined in *Standards for Foreign Language Learning: Preparing for the 21st Century* (1996; National Standards in Foreign Language Education Project, a collaboration of the ACTFL, AATG, AATF, and AATSP). The five "Cs" of Communication, Cultures, Connections, Comparisons, and Communities describe what students should know and be able to do as a result of their language study. *Kontakte* provides a solid foundation for their implementation.

Communication: Kontakte emphasizes communication in meaningful contexts in the target language. Throughout, students listen to and read comprehensible German and have ample opportunities to use German in autograph, interview, information gap, role-play, writing, and other personalized activities.

Cultures: The **Dialoge,** the **Kultur ... Landeskunde ... Informationen** boxes, the **Videoblick,** the **Videoecke,** and the **Lektüre** present various perspectives on the cultures of German-speaking people. Students listen to, read, and respond to texts and—in the video—to interviews with native speakers.

Connections: Chapter themes and activities encourage students to link their study of German with their personal lives and other subjects they are studying.

Comparisons: The **Situationen,** the **Kultur ... Landeskunde ... Informationen** boxes, the **Videoblick,** and the **Videoecke** lead students to make comparisons between their world and that of German-speaking people.

Communities: Through a number of activities, such as expanded **Nach dem Lesen** exercises, students have direct contact with the German-speaking world at home and abroad. The Online Learning Center website provides additional opportunities for contact with the German-speaking world.

New to the Sixth Edition

Throughout the review process, we received valuable input from instructors and students alike. As a result, we have undertaken a number of changes in the Sixth Edition, without altering the basic concept and approach of *Kontakte.*

- There are new and engaging vocabulary displays in many chapters.
- Chapter vocabulary has been revised with an eye to the *Frequency Dictionary of German* from Routledge (Jones and Tschirner, 2006).

- The **Kultur ... Landeskunde ... Informationen** boxes have been updated and revised as appropriate to reflect changes since the last edition.
- Several readings have been replaced with new readings that focus on contemporary German motion pictures, including *Das Leben der Anderen, Das Wunder von Bern,* and others.
- The page size has been increased in order to allow for a layout that is visually more pleasing and easier to read.
- Most photographs have been replaced to make the material more attractive for contemporary students.
- Several of the chapter opening paintings have been replaced with new art.
- The latest and final official spelling reform guidelines (August 1, 2006) have been implemented, with specific reference to Duden's recommendations in the 24th edition of *Die deutsche Rechtschreibung* (Dudenverlag: Mannheim, 2006).
- The *Blickkontakte* DVD program (formerly available on VHS) includes four new authentic video segments from German television programming.
- The *Kontakte Online Learning Center* has been thoroughly revised to reflect changes in the textbook, and now includes, free of charge, the video-based activities formerly available on the *Interactive CD-ROM*.

A Guided Tour of *Kontakte*, Sixth Edition

Each chapter has the following structure:

- **Situationen**
- **Videoecke**
- **Wortschatz**
- **Strukturen und Übungen**

Our guided tour presents an overview of the chapter structure and features of *Kontakte.*

Situationen

Colorful illustrations or photographs introduce vocabulary. Communicative activities support the acquisition of vocabulary and structures. Grammar cross-references tie activities to specific grammar points.

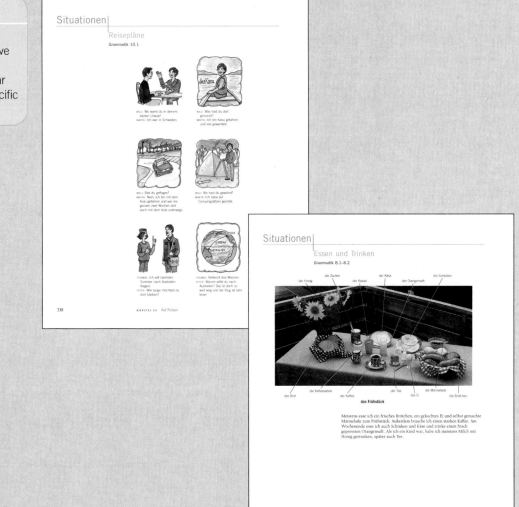

Situationen

Communicative activities form the core of *Kontakte.* Most activities are done with partners, small groups, or the whole class and incorporate both chapter vocabulary and structures.

Lektüre

Beginning in **Kapitel 1,** each chapter has two readings, along with pre- and post-reading activities that provide valuable linguistic input and support the development of reading skills. The readings appear in the **Situationen** sections.

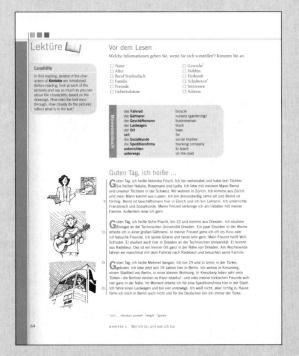

Situationen

Several recurring activity types provide for variety and stimulation: **Interaktion, Umfrage, Dialog, Informationsspiel, Interview,** and others.

Lesehilfe

This sidebar box offers background information on readings and tips to students for improving their reading skills.

Situation 4 | Ferienpläne

Melanie und Josef wollen beide einen Teil ihrer Ferien zu Hause in Regensburg verbringen, aber auch eine Reise machen. Was wollen sie wo machen? Können sie etwas zusammen machen? Hören Sie zu und ergänzen Sie die Tabelle.

NÜTZLICHE WÖRTER

die Ausstellung — exhibition
die Garage — garage
die Querflöte — transverse flute
sitzen — to sit

	Melanie	Josef	beide zusammen
in München			
zu Hause in Regensburg			
auf der Reise			

Lektüre

Vor dem Lesen

A. The following children's story is entitled "The Secret of the Kitchen Bench." Look at the drawings and—keeping the title of the story in mind—guess what the story will be about. Come up with possible answers to these questions:

Wer sind die Hauptpersonen? — *Who are the main characters?*
Wo findet die Geschichte statt? — *Where does the story take place?*
Wann findet sie statt? — *When does it take place?*
Was passiert? — *What happens?*

B. The following words are important for the story. Match them with the sentences or phrases explaining or paraphrasing them. Then find these words in the story and underline them.

1. _____ das Autodach — a. the lid of a container
2. _____ etwas Langes — b. the roof of a car
3. _____ nach draußen — c. directly
4. _____ der Deckel — d. a long object
5. _____ wach werden — e. to cause someone to awaken
6. _____ wecken — f. the opposite of falling asleep
7. _____ schnurstracks — g. outside the house

Lesehilfe

One approach to a short story is to focus on its global aspects—characters, place, time, and general action—before concentrating on detail. Read it several times at normal speed, resisting the urge to look up all new words. This serves two functions: (1) You understand the story more accurately because you never lose sight of the "big picture." (2) You learn vocabulary more effectively because you learn it in its full context.

112 KAPITEL 3 Talente, Pläne, Pflichten

Videoblick

Appearing once in each chapter, this video feature corresponds to the **Galerie** video clip found on the *Blickkontakte* DVD program and presents questions to activate students' background knowledge and reveal their schemata of interpretation.

Videoblick

Erste Berliner Fashion-Week

Deutschland ist einer der wichtigsten Modemärkte der Welt. Die erste deutsche Fashion-Week findet nun in Berlin statt.

- In welchen Städten gibt es viele Fashion-Shows?
- Gibt es viele Fashion-Shows in Berlin?
- Wie viele Modeschulen und Designer gibt es in Berlin?
- Wie oft soll die Berliner Fashion-Week stattfinden?

Fashion-Week in Berlin. Nach dem Vorbild von Paris, Mailand und New York.

Situation 11 | Frau Gretters neuer Mantel

Bringen Sie die Sätze in die richtige Reihenfolge.

_____ Von Kaufland. Er ist wirklich sehr schön.
_____ Finde ich ganz toll. Woher haben Sie ihn?
_1_ Guten Tag, Frau Körner.
_____ Ach, mein Mantel ist auch schon so alt. Ich brauche dringend etwas für den Winter.
_____ Guten Tag, Frau Gretter. Wie geht's denn so?
_____ Gehen Sie doch auch mal zu Kaufland. Da gibt es gute Preise.
_____ Danke, ganz gut. Wie finden Sie denn meinen neuen Mantel?

Situation 12 | Flohmarkt

Schreiben Sie fünf Sachen auf, die Sie verkaufen. Schreiben Sie auf, wer sie kauft und wie viel sie kosten.

MODELL: S1: Ich verkaufe meine Ohrringe. Brauchst du Ohrringe?
S2: Nein danke, ich brauche keine Ohrringe.
oder Zeig mal. Ja, ich finde deine Ohrringe toll. Was kosten sie?
S1: 2 Euro.
S2: Gut, ich nehme sie.

ZU VERKAUFEN	KÄUFER/KÄUFERIN	PREIS
1.		
2.		
3.		
4.		
5.		

Situationen 89

Kultur … Landeskunde … Informationen

Jugendschutz

Nicht in jedem Alter darf man alles. In Deutschland regelt das Jugendschutzgesetz, in welchem Alter Kinder und Jugendliche etwas dürfen oder können.

mit 13
- darf man in den Ferien arbeiten.
  aber: Die Eltern müssen es erlauben und die Arbeit muss leicht sein.

mit 15
- kann man mit der Arbeit anfangen.
  aber: Man darf nur 8 Stunden am Tag und 5 Tage in der Woche arbeiten.
- darf man im Restaurant Bier oder Wein trinken.
  aber: Die Eltern müssen dabei sein.

mit 16
- darf man von zu Hause wegziehen.
  aber: Die Eltern müssen es erlauben.
- darf man heiraten.
  aber: Die Eltern müssen es erlauben.
  und: Der Partner muss über 18 Jahre alt sein.
- darf man bis 24.00 Uhr in die Disko gehen.

mit 18
- darf man den Führerschein für ein Auto oder ein Motorrad machen.
- darf man ohne Erlaubnis heiraten.
- darf man wählen.
- darf man im Kino alle Filme sehen.
- darf man im Restaurant Alkohol trinken.
- darf man so lange in die Disko gehen, wie man will.
- darf man rauchen.

In Deutschland ist man mit 18 Jahren erwachsen.

Wie ist es in Ihrem Land? Machen Sie eine Tabelle.

Mit 13	Mit 15	Mit 16	Mit 18	Mit …

heiraten   wählen   Alkohol trinken
in die Disko gehen alle Filme sehen   Auto fahren
arbeiten   erwachsen sein   rauchen

118 KAPITEL 3 Talente, Pläne, Pflichten

Kultur … Landeskunde … Informationen

These short cultural readings offer insights into the German-speaking world. They are accompanied by activities that aid students in comparing and contrasting their own culture with that of the German-speaking countries.

Videoecke

The **Videoecke** feature corresponds directly to the interviews with native speakers of German found on the **Blickkontakte** DVD program, and provides activities that support listening/viewing comprehension.

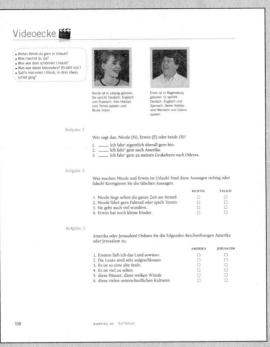

Strukturen und Übungen

Clear, concise grammar explanations and form-focused exercises provide a solid foundation for acquiring grammatical structures. Instructors may choose to assign these "blue pages" solely as homework, to incorporate them into the classroom experience, or do a combination of both.

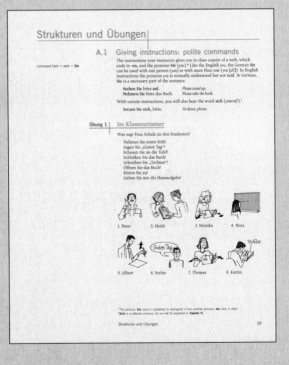

Wortschatz

Semantically-arranged lists contain all the newly introduced vocabulary in the chapter. Diacritical marks help students learn proper pronunciation.

Übungen

Following each of the grammar descriptions, these form-focused exercises practice the key grammatical concepts of the chapter.

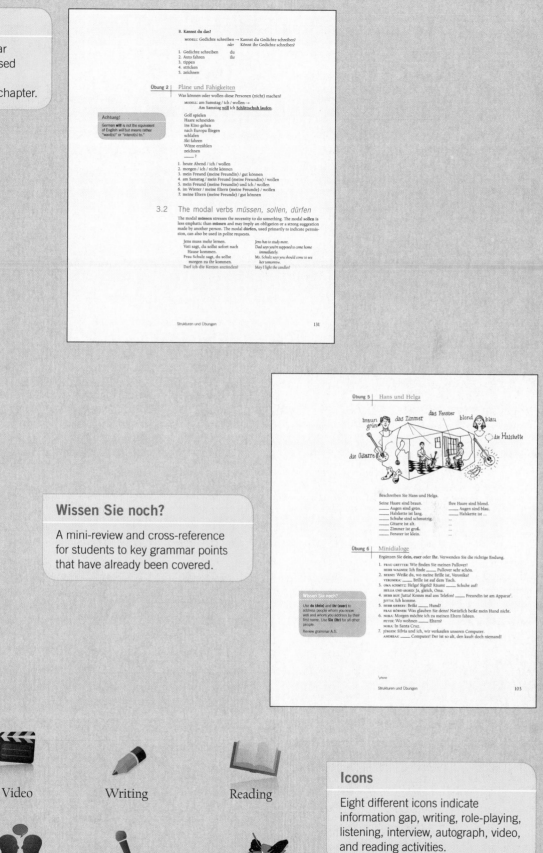

Wissen Sie noch?

A mini-review and cross-reference for students to key grammar points that have already been covered.

Icons

Eight different icons indicate information gap, writing, role-playing, listening, interview, autograph, video, and reading activities.

Listening   Video   Writing   Reading

Information Gap   Role Playing   Interview   Autograph

Exciting Multimedia Supplements for *Kontakte,* Sixth Edition

The Sixth Edition of **Kontakte** is accompanied by an array of multimedia supplements to support your instruction and your students' language learning needs.

Blickkontakte DVD Program

Available exclusively on DVD, the Sixth Edition of **Blickkontakte** offers the variety of authentic video materials that has won wide praise. As before, the Sixth Edition contains interviews with native speakers, filmed on location in Leipzig. Viewing and listening comprehension for the **Interview** segments are supported by the **Videoecke** feature in each chapter, consisting of photographs, interview questions, and viewing activities.

Fourteen selections from authentic German television broadcasts, called **Galerie,** correspond to the **Videoblick** feature found in each chapter of the main text. These were selected based on their accessibility, cultural and linguistic richness, and their interest to present-day students. Four selections are brand new to this edition. In addition to the **Videoblick** exercises, the *Instructor's Manual* contains overhead transparency masters and expanded activities that correspond to the **Galerie** segments.

Online Learning Center

An updated *Online Learning Center* website accompanies the Sixth Edition of **Kontakte.** This website offer students a wide variety of resources, including the complete *Audio Program,* additional vocabulary and grammar practice, cultural activities, the video-based activities formerly available on the *Interactive CD-ROM,* and much more. The audio, video, practice activities, and resources available on the *Online Learning Center* are offered free of charge to students.

Instructors will find digital color transparencies, the complete *Instructor's Manual, Test Bank, Audioscript,* links to professional resources, and other valuable tools on the Instructor's Center of the *Online Learning Center.* Access the **Kontakte** Sixth Edition *Online Learning Center* at www.mhhe.com/kontakte6.

The *Online **Arbeitsbuch*** is produced in collaboration with Quia™. This online version of the paper ***Arbeitsbuch*** offers students an integrated *Audio Program* and self-correcting and self-scoring activities. Instructors will find a sophisticated gradebook feature and tracking of student and class performance.

The *Kontakte* Program: Exceptional Instructional Materials

The instructional package of *Kontakte,* Sixth Edition, includes the following materials, designed to complement your instruction and to enhance your students' learning experience. Please contact your local McGraw-Hill sales representative for information on availability and costs of these materials. Available to adopters *and* to students:

- *Student Edition.* Full-color textbook with activities, grammar explanations and exercises, and helpful appendices.
- *Textbook Audio Program.* Corresponding to the Student Edition, this one-hour audio program contains the dialogues, selected texts from the **KLI** boxes, and readings. It is available free of charge on the *Online Learning Center.*
- ***Arbeitsbuch.*** A complete manual for further practice and acquisition of the four skills and cultural competence.
- Online ***Arbeitsbuch.*** This online version of the ***Arbeitsbuch,*** produced in collaboration with Quia™, offers the same outstanding practice activities as the paper ***Arbeitsbuch,*** with many additional advantages such as automatic feedback and scoring, and a gradebook feature for instructors.
- *Audio Program.* This seven-hour program, corresponding to the ***Arbeitsbuch*** and available free of charge on the *Online Learning Center* or for purchase on audio CDs, contains pronunciation practice and listening comprehension texts. It also includes the dialogues and narration series from the main text.
- *DVD Program.* The ***Blickkontakte*** video, now available exclusively on DVD, offers a variety of authentic video materials including interviews with native speakers of German and selections from authentic German television broadcasts.
- *Online Learning Center.* A web-based learning center with online activities and study resources for students, as well as a variety of resources for instructors.

Available to adopters only:

- *Instructor's Edition.* The main text containing margin notes with suggestions for using and expanding on the materials in the text, additional cultural information, teaching hints, and listening comprehension texts.

- *Instructor's Manual.* Available for download or viewing on the *Online Learning Center,* the *Instructor's Manual* provides a guided walk through **Einführungen A/B** and **Kapitel 1,** presents information on Natural Approach theory and practice, and offers hints and practical guidance to instructors. Included in the *Instructor's Manual* are transparency masters of the drawings in the main text as well as video activities for the authentic television footage on the ***Blickkontakte*** video.
- *Audioscript.* A transcript containing all the material recorded in the *Audio Program* is also available on the *Online Learning Center.*

- *Test Bank.* A collection of testing materials—thoroughly revised for the Sixth Edition—for assessing listening comprehension, vocabulary, grammar, reading, writing, culture, and oral proficiency.
- *Testing Audio Program.* Available on audio CD or on the *Online Learning Center,* this audio material accompanies the *Test Bank.*
- *Picture File.* Fifty full-color, 9" × 12" photographs taken exclusively for **Kontakte** in Germany, Austria, and Switzerland. Please note that the Picture File has not been revised for the Sixth Edition; instructors requesting a Picture File will receive a copy of the Fifth Edition Picture File.

The *Kontakte* Program: Exceptional Instructional Materials

The Natural Approach

Kontakte is based on Tracy D. Terrell's Natural Approach, which originally drew on aspects of Stephen D. Krashen's "Monitor Model" and its five hypotheses of instructed second-language acquisition. These five hypotheses are discussed in detail in the *Instructor's Manual* that accompanies **Kontakte.** The following are among the most important aspects of the Natural Approach as applied in this program:

1. **Comprehension precedes production.** Students' ability to use new vocabulary and grammar is directly related to the opportunities they have to listen to and read vocabulary and grammar in a natural context.

2. **Production needs to be acquired, too.** While comprehension activities need to take up a large amount of classroom time in early chapters and considerable amounts in later chapters as well, students need to be given numerous opportunities to express their own meaning in communicative contexts. Ideally, comprehension activities are topped off by speaking and/or writing, and production activities are introduced by listening or reading.

3. **Speech emerges in stages.** *Kontakte* allows for three stages:

   Stage 1. Comprehension: **Einführung A**
   Stage 2. Early speech: **Einführung B**
   Stage 3. Speech emergence: **Kapitel 1**

   The activities in **Einführung A** are designed to give students an opportunity to develop good comprehension skills without being required to speak much German. The activities in **Einführung B** are designed to encourage the transition from comprehension to an ability to make natural responses with short phrases. By the end of the **Einführung,** most students are making the transition from short answers to longer phrases and short sentences, using the materials of the **Einführung.** With the new material in each chapter, students will pass through the same three stages.

4. **Speech emergence is characterized by grammatical errors.** It is to be expected that students will make many errors when they begin putting words together into sentences, because it is difficult to monitor spontaneous speech. These early errors do not become permanent, nor do they affect students' future language development. We recommend correcting errors by expanding and rephrasing students' responses into grammatically correct sentences.

5. **Group work encourages speech.** Most of the activities lend themselves to pair or small-group work, which allows for more opportunities to interact in German during a given class period and practice in a non-threatening atmosphere.

6. **Students acquire language best in a low-anxiety environment.** Students will be most successful when they are interacting in communicative activities that they enjoy. The goal is for them to express themselves as best they can and to develop a positive attitude toward their second-language experience. The Natural Approach instructor will create an accepting and enjoyable environment in which to acquire and learn German.

7. **The goal of the Natural Approach is proficiency in communication skills.** Proficiency is defined as the ability to convey information and/or feelings in a particular situation for a particular purpose. Grammatical accuracy is one part of communicative proficiency, but it is not a prerequisite.

Acknowledgments

We would like to extend our heartfelt thanks to Nikolaus Euba, who reviewed the manuscript for the Sixth Edition and provided many valuable suggestions and comments. We are very grateful to Petra Clayton (Cuesta College) for her detailed and careful revision of the Fifth Edition *Arbeitsbuch.* Petra's enthusiasm for the teaching and learning of German is reflected in this revision. Thanks are also due to Silke Lipinski and Katharina Kley for their contributions to the textbook, the *Arbeitsbuch,* and the *Test Bank.* Further thanks are owed to Ulla Hirschfeld (Universität Halle) for her excellent work on the pronunciation and orthography sections in the *Arbeitsbuch* and for the pronunciation and spelling appendix in the main text.

We gratefully acknowledge our debt to the many instructors who over the past years have personally shared their experiences with us, especially James P. Pusack, Sue K. Otto, and the graduate student instructors at the University of Iowa. We are also grateful to Peter Ecke and the graduate student instructors at the University of Arizona. In addition, we would like to express our gratitude to the many members of the language teaching profession whose valuable suggestions contributed to the preparation of this new edition. We have learned tremendously from the loyal users of *Kontakte* and are always interested in hearing what they have to say. The appearance of their names does not necessarily constitute their endorsement of the text or its methodology.

Kenneth Scott Baker, *University of Missouri, Kansas City*

John Blair, *University of West Georgia*

Madelyn Burchill, *Concordia College, Moorhead*

Troy Byler, *Indiana University, Bloomington*

Muriel Cormican, *University of West Georgia*

Catherine C. Fraser, *Indiana University, Bloomington*

Astrid Gesche, *Queensland University of Technology*

Steve Grollman, *Concordia College, Moorhead*

Susanne Gross, *Australian National University*

Derek Hillard, *Kansas State University*

Ruth R. Kath, *Luther College*

Jürgen Koppensteiner, *University of Northern Iowa*

Douglas James Lightfoot, *University of Alabama*

Denise M. Meuser, *Northwestern University*

Susanne Rott, *University of Illinois at Chicago*

Frangina Spandau, *Santa Barbara City College*

Rudolph Strahl, *College of DuPage*

Barbara Taron, *Tulsa Community College*

Cynthia Trocchio, *Kent State University*

Meike Wernicke-Heinrichs, *Capilano College*

Special thanks to Dirk Hasenpusch and Stuart Cohen for their fine photographs. Our gratitude to Arden Smith, who painstakingly compiled the German-English and English-German end vocabularies; and to Elsa Peterson, who secured reprint permissions for the realia and readings.

The updated look of the interior of **Kontakte** is due to the artistry of Lisa Buckley. We thank Laurie Entringer for the imaginative cover. We also thank Chris Schabow from The Left Coast Group, Inc., whose fine work made our lives so much easier, and the editing, production, and design team at McGraw-Hill whose expertise helped transform manuscript into this book: Anne Fuzellier, Tandra Jorgensen, and Nora Agbayani. Nick Agnew, Jorge Arbujas, Rachel Dornan, and the rest of the McGraw-Hill marketing and sales staff, who so actively promoted **Kontakte** over the past years.

We continue to thank Eirik Børve and Thalia Dorwick, who launched the first edition; our first and second edition editors, Jeanine Briggs and Eileen LeVan, whose work is still found in the pages of this edition; our splendid third edition consultant, Dierk Hoffmann, who helped us improve the culture and grammar of **Kontakte,** and Catherine (Katy) Fraser, our consultant on the third and fourth editions who also revised the Test Bank of the fourth and fifth editions.

We would also like to express our enduring thanks to Gregory Trauth, editor extraordinaire of the third and fourth editions and best of friends. We still miss you, Gregory. Special thanks are due to our Development Editor, Paul Listen, whose amazing attention to detail and fine editorial eye have greatly enhanced the Sixth Edition. It has been a true pleasure to work with Paul.

Finally, we express our heartfelt gratitude to the McGraw-Hill World Languages editorial staff: Margaret Young, our Editorial Coordinator; Scott Tinetti, Director of Development; Allison Hawco, Media Producer; and Christa Harris, our Executive Editor, whose support and encouragement are deeply appreciated; and William R. Glass, our Publisher, whose guidance and experience helped bring this project to its successful completion.

To the Student

The Cast of Characters

The people you will read and talk about in **Kontakte** reappear in activities and exercises throughout the text. Some are American students, and others are from Germany, Austria, and Switzerland.

First, there is a group of students learning German at the University of California at Berkeley. Although they all have different majors, they are all in Professor Karin Schulz's German class. You will meet eight students in the class: Steve (Stefan), Heidi, Al (Albert), Nora, Monique (Monika), Peter, Kathy (Katrin), and Thomas. Each uses the German version of his or her name.

Little by little, you will be introduced to people who live in various parts of the German-speaking world. For example, in Göttingen, Germany, you will meet Silvia Mertens and her boyfriend, Jürgen Baumann. You will also get to know the Schmitz family. Rolf Schmitz, who is studying psychology at the University of California at Berkeley and who knows many of the students in Professor Schulz's German class, lives with his parents in Göttingen over the university holidays. He was born in Krefeld, a town near Düsseldorf, where his grandmother, Helene Schmitz, still lives. Rolf has twin sisters, Helga and Sigrid.

Rolf
Oma Schmitz   Helga   Sigrid

In Germany, you will also accompany an American student, Claire Martin, on her travels. Her best friends are Melanie Staiger and Josef Bergmann from Regensburg.

Claire   Josef   Melanie

In Berlin, you will meet Renate Röder, who is single and who works for a computer company. Renate travels a lot and speaks several languages in addition to German. You will also meet Mehmet Sengün. Mehmet came with his family to Berlin from Turkey when he was 10 and works as a truck driver.

Renate   Mehmet

In Dresden, you will meet Sofie Pracht, a student at the Technische Universität. Sofie is studying biology and wants to become a biologist. Her best friend is Willi Schuster, who is also a student at the TU Dresden. Marta Szerwinski, a friend of Sofie's and Willi's, comes from Poland but is currently working in Dresden.

Sofie   Willi   Marta

In the Munich neighborhood of Schwabing, you will meet two families: The Wagners and the Rufs. In the Wagner family, you will meet Josie and Uli, their son Ernst, and their daughters, Andrea and Paula. Jens Krüger, their cousin, comes to visit quite often, so you will meet him as well.

die Familie Wagner
Uli
Jens
Josie   Andrea

Paula   Ernst

The Wagners' neighbors are the Ruf family: Jochen Ruf, a writer who works at home and takes care of the children and household, and Margret, a businesswoman who is president of Firma Seide, which manufactures toys. They have two children: Jutta, who is a student at the Goethe Gymnasium (*high school*) with Jens Krüger, and Hans, her younger brother.

There are others in the neighborhood as well, such as Herr Günter Thelen and Herr Alexander Siebert, Frau Sybille Gretter, Frau Judith Körner, Michael Pusch—who is very taken with himself—and his girlfriend, Maria Schneider.

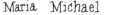

In Austria, you will get to know Richard Augenthaler, who is 18 and has just graduated from high school.

In Switzerland, you will meet the Frisch family, Veronika and Bernd and their three children. Veronika and Bernd live and work in Zürich, but they like to travel, and we will follow them on different occasions.

Getting Started with *Kontakte*

During your German course, you will be working primarily with two texts: The main text and the *Arbeitsbuch.* Both texts have been designed to provide you with ample opportunities to practice German in natural contexts. The following chart will give you an overview of these two books.

The Main Text

Book Element	What Is It?	How Will It Help?
Situationen (oral activities)	Oral activities done in class with instructor and classmates.	Give you opportunities to listen to and interact with others in German.
Lektüre, Kultur … Landeskunde … Informationen (reading, culture boxes)	Short readings and visuals on general interest or cultural topics relevant to the German-speaking world. For class or homework.	Allow you to acquire German and help you learn about the German-speaking world.
Videoblick, Videoecke (video view, video corner)	Video-based activities and exercises.	Allow you to hear and view a wide range of native speakers in authentic contexts.
Wortschatz (vocabulary list)	A list of the new words that appear in the **Situationen.**	For reference or review.
Strukturen und Übungen (grammar and exercises)	Explanations and examples of grammar rules followed by exercises, at the end of each chapter.	For self-study and for reference. Refer to the grammar when you edit your writing.
Appendices A, B	Part 2 of the **Informationsspiele and Rollenspiele.**	For use in the paired information gap and role-play activities.
Appendix C	Rules for the German Spelling Reform.	For quick reference.
Appendix D	Phonetics Summary Tables. A summary of German pronunciation and spelling.	For quick reference.
Appendix E	Grammar Summary Tables. Summaries of major grammatical points introduced.	For quick reference.
Appendix F	Verb charts: conjugation patterns of regular verbs and a list of strong and irregular weak verbs.	For quick reference.
Appendix G	Answers to single-response grammar exercises.	For checking your answers.
End vocabularies	German-English / English-German end vocabularies containing all the vocabulary used in **Kontakte.**	For reference.

The *Arbeitsbuch* (Laboratory Manual and Workbook)

Book Element	What Is It?	How Will It Help?
Hörverständnis (listening comprehension)	Authentic listening activities with short comprehension activities.	Provide you with more opportunities to listen to and acquire German outside of class.
Aussprache und Orthografie (pronunciation and spelling)	Recorded pronunciation and spelling exercises.	Introduce you to the sound system and spelling conventions of German.
Schriftliche Aktivitäten (written work)	Writing activities, coordinated with the chapter theme, vocabulary, and grammar.	Allow you to practice vocabulary and grammatical structures and to express yourself in writing creatively.
Kulturecke (cultural corner)	Activities that review key cultural points found in the corresponding chapter of the main text.	Help you identify, review, and remember the important cultural information of the chapter.
Answer Key	Answers to many of the recorded **Hörverständnis** and **Aussprache und Orthografie** exercises as well as to some of the **Schriftliche Aktivitäten** exercises.	Give you immediate feedback on comprehension, pronunciation and spelling, and written activities.

To the Student

Deutschland und Luxemburg
Einwohner
Deutschland: 82,5 Mio
Luxemburg: 480 000
Maßstab 2,0 cm = 100 km

DÄNEMARK

OSTSEE

NORDSEE

Flensburg

Helgoland

Kiel

SCHLESWIG-HOLSTEIN

Hiddensee

Rügen

Stralsund

Rostock

Greifswald

Güstrow

MECKLENBURG-VORPOMMERN

Neubrandenburg

Ostfriesische Inseln

Cuxhaven

Lübeck

HAMBURG

Hamburg

Schwerin

Prenzlau

Emden

Bremerhaven

Leer

BREMEN

Bremen

Lüneburg

BRANDENBURG

Oldenburg

DIE NIEDERLANDE

NIEDERSACHSEN

LÜNEBURGER HEIDE

Havel

POLEN

Ems

Weser

Osnabrück

Wolfsburg

BERLIN

Berlin

Oder

Hannover

Braunschweig

Brandenburg

Potsdam

Frankfurt

Bielefeld

Hameln

Magdeburg

Eisenhüttenstadt

Oder

Münster

TEUTOBURGER WALD

Bad Harzburg

SACHSEN-

Elbe

Paderborn

Göttingen

Wernigerode

Dessau

Wittenberg

Cottbus

NORDRHEIN-WESTFALEN

Essen

Dortmund

Kassel

Brocken

HARZ

ANHALT

Neiße

Ruhr

Fulda

THÜRINGEN

Eisleben

Halle

Leipzig

Görlitz

Krefeld

Düsseldorf

Saale

SACHSEN

Meißen

Dresden

Köln

Erfurt

Weimar

Aachen

Eisenach

Jena

Gera

Chemnitz

Bonn

Marburg

THÜRINGER WALD

Zwickau

Gießen

Suhl

ERZGEBIRGE

BELGIEN

Limburg

Fulda

Koblenz

HESSEN

RHÖN

Mosel

EIFEL

Wiesbaden

Frankfurt

Main

Bayreuth

TSCHECHIEN

RHEINLAND-

HUNSRÜCK

Mainz

PFALZ

Würzburg

LUXEMBURG

Worms

Luxemburg

Trier

Ludwigshafen

Mannheim

Nürnberg

BÖHMER WALD

FRÄNKISCHE ALB

Kaiserslautern

SAARLAND

Saarbrücken

Heidelberg

Rothenburg ob der Tauber

BAYERN

Rhein

Worms

Regensburg

BAYERISCHER WALD

Karlsruhe

BADEN-WÜRTTEMBERG

Straubing

Mosel

Stuttgart

Passau

Donau

Isar

FRANKREICH

VOGESEN

SCHWARZWALD

Neckar

SCHWÄBISCHE ALB

Tübingen

Ulm

Augsburg

Inn

München

Rottweil

Chiemsee

Freiburg

Friedrichshafen

BAYERISCHE ALPEN

Berchtesgaden

Konstanz

Lindau

Garmisch-Partenkirchen

Bodensee

DIE SCHWEIZ

Zugspitze

ÖSTERREICH

Landkarten

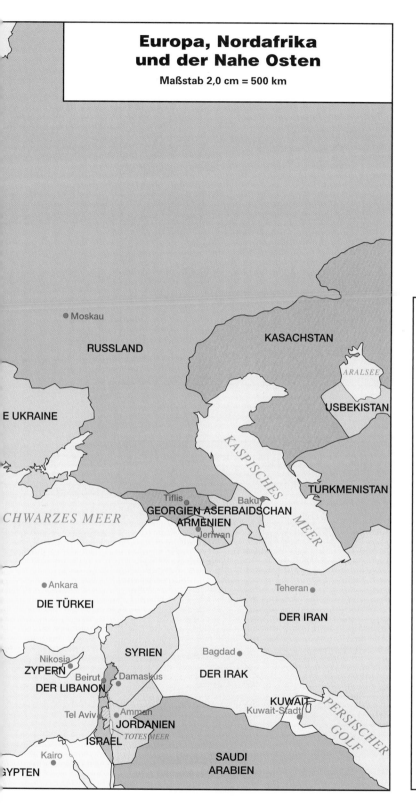

Europa, Nordafrika und der Nahe Osten

Maßstab 2,0 cm = 500 km

Moskau

RUSSLAND

KASACHSTAN

ARALSEE

E UKRAINE

USBEKISTAN

KASPISCHES MEER

TURKMENISTAN

Tiflis

Baku

GEORGIEN ASERBAIDSCHAN

ARMENIEN

CHWARZES MEER

Jerwan

Teheran

Ankara

DIE TÜRKEI

DER IRAN

SYRIEN

Bagdad

Nikosia

ZYPERN

DER IRAK

Beirut

Damaskus

DER LIBANON

KUWAIT

PERSISCHER GOLF

Kuwait-Stadt

Tel Aviv

Amman

JORDANIEN

TOTES MEER

ISRAEL

Kairo

SAUDI

GYPTEN

ARABIEN

EU-LÄNDER	EINWOHNER
Belgien	10,5 Mio.
Bulgarien	7,7 Mio.
Dänemark	5,4 Mio.
Deutschland	82,5 Mio.
Estland	1,3 Mio.
Finnland	5,3 Mio.
Frankreich	60,9 Mio.
Griechenland	11,1 Mio.
Großbritannien	60,4 Mio.
Irland	4,2 Mio.
Italien	58,8 Mio.
Lettland	2,3 Mio.
Litauen	3,4 Mio.
Luxemburg	0,5 Mio.
Malta	0,4 Mio.
die Niederlande	16,3 Mio.
Österreich	8,3 Mio.
Polen	38,1 Mio.
Portugal	10,6 Mio.
Rumänien	21,6 Mio.
Schweden	9,0 Mio.
die Slowakei	5,4 Mio.
Slowenien	2,0 Mio.
Spanien	43,8 Mio.
Tschechien	10,3 Mio.
Ungarn	10,1 Mio.
Zypern	0,8 Mio.
Gesamtbevölkerungszahl	490,9 Mio.

Österreich

Einwohner: 8,3 Mio

Maßstab 1,5 cm = 50 km

TSCHECHIEN

DEUTSCHLAND

Gmünd

Horn

Krems

Donau

Linz

WIEN

Sankt Pölten

Wien

OBERÖSTERREICH

Melk

Amstetten

NIEDERÖSTERREICH

Baden

Eisenstadt

Neusiedler See

Gmunden

Salzburg

Wiener Neustadt

Mariazell

Bad Ischl

Salzkammergut

Hallstatt

Liezen

STEIERMARK

Bruck an der Mur

BURGENLAND

Bodensee

Bregenz

Kufstein

Sankt Johann in Tirol

Salzach

Enns

Oberwart

VORARLBERG

Reutte

Wörgl

Bischofshofen

Zell am See

Radstadt

Sankt Georgen

Güssing

Feldkirch

Innsbruck

Kitzbühel

Bruck

SALZBURG

Arlberg

Landeck

TIROL

Mauterndorf

Mur

Graz

UNGARN

DIE SCHWEIZ

Osttirol
(zu Tirol)

Spittal an der Drau

Feldkirchen

Vintschgau

Lienz

SÜDTIROL

Meran

Drau

KÄRNTEN

Klagenfurt

Bozen

Villach

Wörther See

ITALIEN

SLOWENIEN

Rhein

SCHAFFHAUSEN

DEUTSCHLAND

Schaffhausen

Kreuzlingen

BASEL
(STADT)

Rhein

Thur

THURGAU

Basel

Liestal

Baden

Winterthur

Frauenfeld

Bodensee

FRANKREICH

Delemont

BASEL
(LAND)

AARGAU

ZÜRICH

St. Gallen

St. Margrethen

JURA

Aarau

Zürich

Herisau

AUSSER-
RHODEN

SOLOTHURN

Reuss

Appenzell

Zürichsee

INNER-RHODEN

Solothurn

Zug

SANKT

Biel

LUZERN

ZUG

Einsiedeln

GALLEN

Vaduz

ÖSTERREICH

J U R A

Luzern

SCHWYZ

Glarus

LIECHTENSTEIN

NEUCHÂTEL

Neuchâtel

Bern

Vierwaldstätter See

Stans

Schwyz

GLARUS

Chur

NEUENBURG

BERNER
OBERLAND

Sarnen

NIDW.

Braunwald

Klosters

Neuenburger See

Fribourg

OBW.

Altdorf

Davos

UNTERWALDEN

Engelberg

WAADT

BERN

Thun

Brienz

URI

Andermatt

Disentis

GRAUBÜNDEN

Lausanne

FREIBURG

Thuner See

Interlaken

Brienzer See

Jungfrau

Grindelwald

St. Moritz

Montreux

Jungfraujoch

Gstaad

Rhein

Rotten

Genf

Brig

TESSIN

**Die Schweiz
und Liechtenstein**

Einwohner

Genfer See

Sion

Bellinzona

Schweiz: 7,5 Mio

GENF

WALLIS

Locarno

Liechtenstein: 34 000

Zermatt

Maßstab 2,0 cm = 50 km

Matterhorn

Lugano

ITALIEN

Langensee

NIDW = NIDWALDEN
OBW = OBWALDEN

Kontakte

Heinrich Campendonk: *Junges Paar* (1915),
Colección Carmen Thyssen-Bornemisza, Madrid

HEINRICH CAMPENDONK

Heinrich Campendonk (1889–1957) was born in Krefeld, Germany and moved to Bavaria in 1911 to join famous artists like Franz Marc and August Macke in the group "Der Blaue Reiter." This painting is an excellent example of the artist's use of vivid colors and expressionist style. Campendonk is best known for his painted-glass windows in churches and public buildings.

Your goals in **Einführung A** should be to relax, listen to as much German as possible, and get to know your classmates. The focus of this chapter is primarily on listening skills; after you have heard German for several weeks, speaking it will come naturally to you.

Themen

Aufforderungen
Namen
Kleidung
Farben
Begrüßen und Verabschieden
Zahlen

Kulturelles

Vornamen
Farben als Symbole
Videoblick: Guten Tag und Auf Wiedersehen
So zählt man ...   So schreibt man ...
Videoecke: Persönliche Daten

Strukturen

A.1 Giving instructions: polite commands
A.2 What is your name? The verb **heißen**
A.3 The German case system
A.4 Grammatical gender: nouns and pronouns
A.5 Addressing people: **Sie** versus **du** or **ihr**

GOALS

Einführung A has 4 goals: **(1)** to convince students (sts.) that they will be able to understand the German you speak in class, **(2)** to help lower anxiety levels by letting them get to know their classmates, **(3)** to begin the binding of meaning to key words in the input, and **(4)** to help students learn to use a listening strategy of attending to key words and to context. All activities are designed to make the input comprehensible. You will use three principal techniques to provide comprehensible input that does not require the sts. to produce German words: **(1)** Total Physical Response (TPR), **(2)** descriptions of the sts. themselves, and **(3)** descriptions of pictures from your picture file (PF). Each technique is described in detail in the Instructor's Manual (IM). The IM also contains a "walk-through" with general descriptions and suggestions for *Einführung A–B* and *Kapitel 1*.

PRE-TEXT ORAL ACTIVITIES (1) Classroom commands: TPR (See also the IM). Introduce these actions in the first class session: *Stehen Sie auf, Setzen Sie sich, Laufen Sie, Schauen Sie* (hand above eyes to mime), *Singen Sie, Tanzen Sie, Nehmen Sie einen Bleistift usw.* In later class sessions add: *Hören Sie zu* (with hand behind ears), *Öffnen Sie das Buch* (use any book), *Schließen Sie das Buch, Schreiben Sie* (*Ihren Namen*) (in the air or on the board), *Lesen Sie* (as if reading a book), *Sprechen Sie* (blah! blah!). Finally, introduce the command *Sagen Sie* with short greetings: *Sagen Sie „Guten Tag". Sagen Sie „Auf Wiedersehen".* Have sts. shake hands and pretend to greet and say good-bye to each other. Then, have them say a short dialogue: *Guten Tag. Wie geht's? Gut, danke. Auf Wiedersehen. Auf Wiedersehen.* **(2) Names and descriptions of sts.:** (See the IM for suggestions on st.-centered input in Stage 1.) Write key nouns and adjectives on the board. Introduce the following words for people: *Professor, Professorin, Lehrer, Lehrerin, Student, Studentin, Mann, Frau;* and for physical appearance: *Schnurrbart, Brille, Kleidung* (*Rock, Jacke, Hose, Hemd, Schuhe, Pullover/Pulli*), and colors (*weiß, gelb, orange, rosa*). The particular words you introduce will depend on your sts. Other words and expressions you will probably use: *Wer ist ...? Wer hat ...? Wer trägt ...? Wie heißt ...? das, er, sie, ich, Sie, auch, aber, sondern, ja, nein, nicht, kein.* **(3) Numbers:** (See also the IM.) Introduce numbers by counting things in class for which sts. recognize the words: the number of men, women, total students, women with skirts, men with

beards. Then ask sts. to react to statements with numbers. **(4) Additional commands and vocabulary for using the text:** The sts. in Frau Schulz's 8:00 AM German class reappear frequently in all components of *Kontakte*. Review all commands from pre-text activity 1 and add the following commands (many from *Sit. 1*) if you have not already done so: *Schauen Sie nach oben / nach unten, Stehen Sie auf, Springen Sie, Gehen Sie, Laufen Sie, Halten Sie, Setzen Sie sich, Nehmen Sie einen Stift, Legen Sie den Stift weg, Nehmen Sie das Buch, Öffnen Sie das Buch, Lesen Sie, Lachen Sie, Schließen Sie das Buch, Sprechen Sie, Hören Sie zu, Singen Sie, Nehmen Sie ein Blatt Papier, Schreiben Sie, Geben Sie mir die Hausaufgabe usw.* Then, make the commands specific to a group and then to individuals: *Männer mit Brille: stehen Sie auf, setzen Sie sich; Frauen mit braunem Haar: gehen Sie an die Tafel, gehen Sie zurück an Ihren Platz, öffnen Sie das Buch, lesen Sie, schließen Sie das Buch usw.* **(5) Alphabet:** Write the letters of the alphabet on the board, or prepare a large alphabet chart (or cards) and place it in a location visible to all during the activity. After *z*, include the letters *ä, ö, ü,* and *ß.* Pronounce *ä, ö,* and *ü* as they sound (i.e., do not say *a-umlaut*, etc.) and the *ß* as *sz* (*es-zett*). Practice the letters of the alphabet several times. Then, give short dictations of well-known names, such as cars (*VW, BMW*) and cities (*Berlin, Wien*), and words from the chapter. Have sts. spell their names (first and last), first to you and then to a partner who writes them down. Introduce *Wie schreibt man das?* and *Wie, bitte?* During these first few weeks, reserve a few minutes each day to practice spelling. (Check the *Arbeitsbuch* to find out which sounds are practiced in which chapter.)

Situationen

Aufforderungen

Grammatik A.1

schreiben Sie   hören Sie zu   lesen Sie   stehen Sie auf   setzen Sie sich

Stefan   Nora   Peter   Frau Schulz   Albert   Heidi

Situation 1 | Aufforderungen

a.

b.

c.

d.

e.

f.

Vocabulary Display (page 6) A. Buchstaben. In this section, we introduce the International Phonetic Alphabet (IPA) to distinguish more clearly between how letters are spelled and how they are pronounced. Do not feel obligated to teach the IPA though. It is sufficient to pronounce the letters as you read them with your students. You may wish to point out the following: **(1)** The colon is used for lengthening, the apostrophe for showing stress. **(2)** [ɛ] and [e] both represent (German) **e**-sounds ([ɛ] is short with the lips more open and [e] is long with the lips more closed). Note that most Germans use a long *and* open sound–i.e., [ɛː]–to pronounce the letter **Ä**. **(3)** [j] is the sound that is usually spelled *y* in English, as in *young*. **(4)** [øː] is pronounced by saying [eː] while at the same time strongly rounding the lips. **(5)** [yː] is pronounced by saying [iː] while strongly rounding the lips. Note that [yː] refers to a vowel sound, not a consonant sound as is the case in English spelling. **(6)** [ɪ] refers to a short (German) **i**-sound with the lips slightly more open than with the long [iː]. **(7)** [ʏ] refers to a short (German) **ü**-sound with the lips slightly more open than with long [yː]. Note that [ˈʏpsilɔn] is stressed on the first syllable.

g.

h.

1. Geben Sie mir die Hausaufgabe!
2. Öffnen Sie das Buch!
3. Schließen Sie das Buch!
4. Nehmen Sie einen Stift!

5. Gehen Sie!
6. Springen Sie!
7. Laufen Sie!
8. Schauen Sie an die Tafel!

Situation 2 | Wer macht das?

Sit. 2. Briefly review letters *a–h* and numbers 1–8. Write numbers as words on the board and practice pronunciation. Explain task: *Sie hören acht Aufforderungen. Welche Nummer gehört zu welchem Bild?*

Hören Sie zu und schreiben Sie die Zahlen unter die Bilder.

a. ___3___   b. ___6___   c. ___2___   d. ___4___

Zum Beispiel: Nummer 1. Schreiben Sie „Heidi"! Zu welchem Bild gehört die Nummer 1? Richtig, zum Bild f. Point to drawing f. Ask students to work in pairs: *Arbeiten Sie mit einem Partner!* Read or play sentences twice in a row: *Ich lese Ihnen (spiele Ihnen) jetzt die Sätze vor. Hören Sie zu und schreiben Sie die Nummern zu den Buchstaben. Ich lese Ihnen alle Sätze zweimal vor.* Review activity by asking: *Nummer 2. Sagen Sie „a"! Zu welchem Bild gehört die Nummer 2? Richtig, zum Bild c.* Do the same for all sen-

e. ___5___   f. ___1___   g. ___8___   h. ___7___

tences. **Text for listening comprehension.** Nummer 1 – Schreiben Sie „Heidi"! Nummer 2 – Sagen Sie „a"! Nummer 3 – Hören Sie zu! Nummer 4 – Stehen Sie auf! Nummer 5 – Setzen Sie sich! Nummer 6 – Lesen Sie! Nummer 7 – Arbeiten Sie mit einem Partner oder einer Partnerin! Nummer 8 – Sagen Sie Ihren Namen!

B. Dialog. Presentation: *Das ist Heidi, das ist Stefan. Stefan fragt: „Wie heißt du?" Heidi sagt: „Heidi." Stefan fragt: „Wie schreibt man das?" Heidi sagt: „H-E-I-D-I. Und wie heißt du?"*

Receptive recall: *Wie heißt die Frau? Wie schreibt man das? Wie heißt der Mann? Wissen Sie, wie man das schreibt?* Practice the lines of the dialogue with your sts. a few times. Ask 5 sts. what their names are and how they spell them. Help them with their spelling if they have problems. Then ask sts. to turn to their classmates. Using the lines of the dialogue, they ask each of 5 classmates what his or her name is, how it is spelled, and write it down. *Nehmen Sie ein Blatt Papier! Nehmen Sie einen Stift! Stehen Sie auf! Fragen Sie fünf Personen: „Wie heißt du?" und „Wie schreibt man das?" Schreiben Sie die Namen auf! Bitte beginnen Sie!* As follow-up, ask 5 sts. what their neighbor's name is and how it is spelled.

Namen

Grammatik A.2–A.3

—Wie heißt du?
—Heidi.
—Wie schreibt man das?
—H-E-I-D-I. Und wie heißt du?

Heidi   Stefan

Buchstaben

Schreiben	Sprechen	Schreiben	Sprechen	Schreiben	Sprechen
A a	[a:]	J j	[jɔt]	L s	[ɛs]
Ä ä	[ɛ:]	K k	[ka:]	ß	[ɛs'tsɛt]
B b	[be:]	L l	[ɛl]	T t	[te:]
C c	[tse:]	M m	[ɛm]	U u	[u:]
D d	[de:]	N n	[ɛn]	Ü ü	[y:]
E e	[e:]	O o	[o:]	V v	[fau]
F f	[ɛf]	Ö ö	[ø:]	W w	[ve:]
G g	[ge:]	P p	[pe:]	X x	[Iks]
H h	[ha:]	Q q	[ku:]	Y y	['ʏpsilɔn]
I i	[i:]	R r	[ɛr]	Z z	[tsɛt]

Kultur ... Landeskunde ... Informationen

Vornamen

- Was sind häufige[1] Vornamen in Ihrem Land für Personen über 60 Jahre? für Personen um die 40? für Personen um die 20? für Neugeborene[2]?
- Welche Vornamen gefallen Ihnen[3]?
- Welche deutschen Vornamen gibt es auch in Ihrem Kurs?
- Welche deutschen Familiennamen gibt es in Ihrem Kurs?
- Möchten Sie einen deutschen Vornamen annehmen[4]? Welchen?

[1]*common* [2]*newborns* [3]*gefallen ... do you like* [4]*adopt* [5]*most popular*

Die beliebtesten[5] Vornamen in Deutschland 2006

Mädchennamen	Jungennamen
1. Marie	1. Leon
2. Sophie	2. Maximilian
3. Maria	3. Alexander
4. Anna/Anne	4. Lukas
5. Leonie	5. Paul
6. Lena	6. Luca
7. Emily	7. Tim
8. Johanna	8. Felix
9. Laura	9. David
10. Lea	10. Elias

Quelle: Gesellschaft für deutsche Sprache, e.V. (Wiesbaden).

Kultur ... Landeskunde ... Informationen (KLI). The *Gesellschaft für deutsche Sprache* publishes this list every year. Prepare activity by reading all questions and names. Ask sts. to work in groups of three to answer the questions. Follow up by asking sts. what their results are. Ask sts. if they want to adopt German names for the remainder of the semester and, if yes, which ones. Also use the list to practice pronunciation. **Comparison:** Some of the most popular names in the late 19th and early 20th centuries for girls were: Anneliese, Clara, Elisabeth, Frieda, Gisela, Helga, Irmgard, Luise, Marie, and Ursula. For boys: Ernst, Georg, Hans, Herbert, Joachim, Karl, Kurt, Paul, Werner, and Wolfgang.

Situation 3 | Wie heißt ...?

Sit. 3. Begin with *Darf ich vorstellen?* and then describe the characters: *Professorin Karin Schulz steht an der Tafel. Hier ist Thomas. Er hat langes Haar usw.* After introducing the characters, simply ask the questions listed in *Sit. 3.* Sts. answer with the name only or perhaps with *Er/Sie heißt ...* Then switch off the overhead and have sts. open their books and do the same activity in pairs. Give them only about 1 minute to do this.

1. Wie heißt die Frau mit dem Buch?
2. Wie heißt der Mann mit dem Stift?
3. Wie heißt die Frau an der Tafel?
4. Wie heißt die Frau an der Tür?
5. Wie heißt der Mann mit der Brille?
6. Wie heißt der Mann mit dem Schnurrbart?
7. Wie heißt die Frau mit dem Ball?
8. Wie heißt der Mann mit dem langen Haar?

Situation 4 | Interview: Wie schreibt man deinen Namen?

Sit. 4. Preparation 1: Practice spelling sts.' names. Ask 5–6 sts. to spell their names while you write them on the board. Tell sts. to ask one another what their names are and how they are spelled: *Arbeiten Sie mit einem Partner oder einer Partnerin. Fragen Sie ihn oder sie, wie er heißt oder wie sie heißt. Fragen Sie dann, wie man seinen oder ihren Namen schreibt. Wie fragt man, wie jemand heißt? Richtig: Wie heißt du? Und wie fragt man, wie man das schreibt? Richtig: Wie schreibt man das?* **Preparation 2:** Ask sts. to find people with the characteristics mentioned in *Sit. 4: Wer von uns trägt eine Brille?* etc. **Activity:** Ask sts. to get up and talk to people with the characteristics mentioned in *Sit. 4*, asking them what their names are and how they are spelled. Ask sts. to write down the names. **Follow-up:** Ask sts. what names they wrote down for each characteristic, and ask them to spell these names while you write them on the board.

MODELL: ein Student / eine Studentin mit Brille →
    S1: Wie heißt du?
S2 (*mit Brille*): Mark.
    S1: Wie schreibt man das?
    S2: M-A-R-K.

NAME

1. ein Student / eine Studentin mit Brille   _____
2. ein Student / eine Studentin in Jeans   _____
3. ein Student / eine Studentin mit langem Haar   _____
4. ein Student / eine Studentin mit einem Buch   _____
5. ein Student / eine Studentin mit Ohrring   _____
6. ein Student / eine Studentin mit kurzem Haar   _____

Kleidung

Grammatik A.4

der Hut die Krawatte

das Sakko das Hemd

der Anzug

Michael Pusch

die Jacke

die Hose

die Schuhe

Jens Krüger

die Bluse

der Rock

die Stiefel

Maria Schneider

das Kleid

der Mantel

Josie Wagner

Situation 5 | Kleidung

Wer im Deutschkurs trägt _____?

1. eine Bluse
2. einen Rock
3. eine Jacke
4. ein Kleid
5. Stiefel
6. ein Hemd
7. eine Hose
8. einen Hut
9. Sportschuhe
10. einen Pullover
11. eine Krawatte
12. einen Anzug

Stellen Sie zehn Fragen. Für jedes „Ja" gibt es einen Punkt.

MODELL: S1: Trägt Thomas einen Anzug?
       S2: Nein. Trägt Frau Körner einen Hut?
       S1: Nein.

Sit. 6. This activity is the first in a series of information-gap (IG) activities designed to create a genuine exchange of information in a controlled way. (See the IM for more ideas about using IG activities.) Sts. work in pairs. One st. works with the questions and drawing on this page, the other st. turns to the second half of the information-gap activity in Appendix A. They take turns asking each other up to 10 questions to find out what the people in their partner's drawing are wearing. For each *ja*, they get one point. The one with the most points after 10 questions wins. **(1) Preparation:** Practice pronunciation of all questions. Divide sts. into two groups, one working with the activity on this page, the other one working with the activity in Appendix A. An easy way to pair students off is to count 1, 2, 1, 2, etc. All twos turn to the appendix, and all ones work with the chart in the chapter. Remind students not to show their half of the activity to their partners. Explain the task to them. Alternatively, put sts. in groups of three, with two sts. completing the activity and the third st. keeping score. **(2) Activity:** Make sure sts. take turns, speak German, and don't look in one another's books. **(3) Follow-up:** Tell sts. what clothing each person is wearing, so that they hear a native-like pronunciation of the words of the activity again. *Thomas trägt eine Jeans, einen Pullover, ein Stirnband, eine Brille und Schuhe. Nora trägt ein Kleid, einen Hut, eine Jacke und Schuhe. Herr Siebert trägt eine Hose, ein Sakko, eine Krawatte, ein Hemd und Schuhe. Frau Körner trägt eine Bluse, einen Rock, einen Mantel und Stiefel.*

	THOMAS		NORA	
	JA	NEIN	JA	NEIN
einen Anzug	☐	☒	☐	☐
eine Bluse	☐	☐	☐	☐
eine Brille	☐	☐	☐	☐
ein Hemd	☐	☐	☐	☐
eine Hose	☐	☐	☐	☐
einen Hut	☐	☐	☐	☐
eine Jacke	☐	☐	☐	☐
eine Jeans	☐	☐	☐	☐
ein Kleid	☐	☐	☐	☐
eine Krawatte	☐	☐	☐	☐
einen Mantel	☐	☐	☐	☐
einen Pullover	☐	☐	☐	☐
einen Rock	☐	☐	☐	☐
ein Sakko	☐	☐	☐	☐
Schuhe	☐	☐	☐	☐
Socken	☐	☐	☐	☐
Sportschuhe	☐	☐	☐	☐
Stiefel	☐	☐	☐	☐
ein Stirnband	☐	☐	☐	☐
ein T-Shirt	☐	☐	☐	☐

? ? Thomas Nora Herr Siebert Frau Körner

*This is the first of many information-gap activities in **Kontakte.** Pair up with another student. One of you will work with the pictures on this page. The other will work with different pictures in Appendix A. The goal is to complete the activity speaking only German, while not looking at your partner's pictures.

Farben

Grammatik A.4

Situation 7 | Meine Mitstudenten

Schauen Sie Ihre Mitstudenten und Mitstudentinnen an. Was tragen sie?

NAME	KLEIDUNG	FARBE
1. Heidi	Rock	blau
2. _____	_____	_____
3. _____	_____	_____
4. _____	_____	_____
5. _____	_____	_____

Situation 8 | Umfrage: Was ist deine Lieblingsfarbe?

MODELL: S1: Ist deine Lieblingsfarbe blau?
      S2: Ja.
      S1: Unterschreib bitte hier.

UNTERSCHRIFT

1. Ist deine Lieblingsfarbe blau? _____
2. Trägst du gern schwarz? _____
3. Hast du zu Hause braune Socken? _____
4. Ist deine Lieblingsfarbe rot? _____
5. Trägst du gern gelb? _____
6. Hast du zu Hause ein grünes T-Shirt? _____
7. Ist deine Lieblingsfarbe lila? _____
8. Hast du zu Hause ein weißes Hemd? _____

Farben als Symbole

__Rot__ ist die Liebe[1]
__Weiß__ ist die Unschuld[2]
__Schwarz__ ist die Trauer[3]
__Blau__ ist die Treue[4]
__Grün__ ist die Hoffnung[5]
__Gelb__ ist der Neid[6]

KLI. Write the following color terms on the board: *blau, gelb, grün, rot, schwarz, weiß*. Ask sts. what the color blue symbolizes in English. Tell them that in German it symbolizes *Treue* (loyalty). Have sts. work in groups of three and write the color terms from the board in the spaces provided in the textbook. Tell them to start with the easy colors, e.g., red and black, and guess the rest. Follow up by asking: *Was ist die Liebe? Ja, rot ist die Liebe.*

[1]*love* [2]*innocence* [3]*grief, sorrow* [4]*loyalty* [5]*hope* [6]*envy*

Ich liebe Dich mehr...

...als meinen Teddybär!

Photo questions. *Wo sind diese Personen? Wie sehen sie aus? Was tragen sie? Wie alt sind sie?*

Samstags in der Stadt

Begrüßen und Verabschieden

Grammatik A.5

Guten Morgen!

Guten Tag!

Guten Abend!

Auf Wiedersehen! Wiedersehen!

Tschüss! Bis bald!

Situation 9 | Dialoge

1. Jürgen Baumann spricht mit einer Studentin.

   JÜRGEN: Hallo, bist du __neu__ hier?
   MELANIE: __Ja__. Du auch?
   JÜRGEN: Ja. Sag mal, __wie heißt du__?
   MELANIE: Melanie. Und __du__?
   JÜRGEN: Jürgen.

2. Frau Frisch ruft Herrn Koch an.

   HERR KOCH: Koch.
   FRAU FRISCH: Guten Tag, Herr Koch, __hier ist__ Frisch. Unser Videorekorder ist kaputt.
   HERR KOCH: __Gut__, ich komme morgen vorbei.
   FRAU FRISCH: Gut. Bis dann. __Auf Wiederhören__.

3. Jutta trifft ihren Freund Jens.

   JUTTA: Servus, Jens.
   JENS: Ach, __servus__, Jutta.
   JUTTA: Wo willst __du__ denn hin?
   JENS: __Ich__ muss zum Fußballtraining.
   JUTTA: Na, dann __viel Spaß__!
   JENS: __Danke__. Mach's gut, Jutta.

Guten Tag und Auf Wiedersehen

Sie sehen eine Reihe von Videoclips aus *Blickkontakte*, in denen sich Leute begrüßen oder voneinander verabschieden. Sehen Sie sich die Clips an, und schreiben Sie zu jedem Clip auf:

- Wer sind diese Leute: Mann oder Frau, jung oder alt?
- Begrüßen sich die Leute oder verabschieden sie sich?
- Welche Tageszeit ist es: Morgen, Mittag, Nachmittag, Abend, Nacht?
- Sagen sie **Sie** oder **du**?

Guten Tag. Quandt. Ich bin Paulines Mutter.

Videoblick. The video segment from *Blickkontakte* shows a number of situations excerpted from the popular German TV series *Unser Lehrer Dr. Specht*, in which people say hello or good-bye to each other. These situations are useful not only for introducing greetings and leave-taking but also to focus on the *Sie/du* distinction and to talk about clothes and colors. Detailed suggestions on how to use these video clips are provided in the video manual that accompanies the *Kontakte* video.

Situation 10* | Rollenspiel: Begrüßen

Sit. 10. Rollenspiel. This is the first of many role-plays in *Kontakte*. (See the IM). The role for student 1 (S1) appears here, the role for student 2 (S2) appears in Appendix B. **(1)** Set the scene as described in the role for S1. **(2)** Write the structure of the role-play on the board: *Begrüßung; Name; Alter; Verabschieden*. **(3)** Elicit possible greetings, questions, and how to say good-bye from sts. and write on board. Ask for appropriate responses to the greeting and leave-taking and for possible answers to the questions, and write them on the board as well. **(4)** Divide the class into 2 groups and assign one part of the role-play to each group. Ask sts. to practice the role-play in pairs. **(5)** Ask 2 or 3 pairs of sts. to perform their role-play in class. Provide feedback as to appropriateness and accuracy of language used after sts. have returned to their seats. The intention here is not to correct all or even most mistakes but rather to focus on a few phrases and sentences that are the most useful for all or most sts. in the context of this role-play. **(6)** Ask sts. to find new partners and to practice the role-play in pairs again. **(7)** Optional homework assignment: Ask sts. to write up their version of the role-play.

S1: Begrüßen Sie einen Mitstudenten oder eine Mitstudentin. Schütteln Sie dem Mitstudenten oder der Mitstudentin die Hand. Sagen Sie Ihren Namen. Fragen Sie, wie alt er oder sie ist. Verabschieden Sie sich.

Photo questions. *Welche Farben sehen Sie auf diesem Bild? Wo sind diese Personen? Was sagen sie? Wie sehen sie aus? Was tragen sie?*

Begrüßen

*This is the first of many role-playing activities in **Kontakte.** Pair up with another student. One of you takes the role of S1. The corresponding role for the other person (S2) appears in Appendix B.

Zahlen

Vocabulary Display
Introduction: *Wie viele Brillen sehen Sie? (Zwei.)*
Richtig, zwei. Zählen Sie bitte mit mir mit: eins,
zwei. Wie viele CDs sehen Sie? (Neun.) Richtig,
neun. Zählen Sie bitte mit mir mit: eins, zwei, drei ...
neun, usw. **Practice:** While pronouncing them, write
the numbers from 1 to 10 on the board or on an
overhead transparency. Point to these numbers in
quick, random succession, asking sts. to call out the
numbers you are pointing to. Do the same for numbers 11 to 20, 21 to 30, and 10 to 100 in steps of ten.
Present and review these numbers over the course
of several class periods while giving short number
dictations. **Game:** Sts. count to 100 (or however far
they get in, say, 2 to 3 minutes) using the following
procedure: **(1)** clap your hands; **(2)** tap your hands
on your knees; **(3)** say the next higher number.
Numbers with a 7 in them and multiples of 7 may
not be called out loud. Sts. snap their fingers
instead when they get to the "forbidden" numbers,
e.g., 7, 14, 17, 21, 27, 28, 35, 37, etc. When a st. calls
out one of these forbidden numbers by mistake,
everybody has to start over from the beginning.
Set up the game in German. **Point out:** *dreißig* is
spelled with *ß*.

0	null		20	zwanzig
1	eins		21	einundzwanzig
2	zwei		22	zweiundzwanzig
3	drei		23	dreiundzwanzig
4	vier		24	vierundzwanzig
5	fünf		25	fünfundzwanzig
6	sechs		26	sechsundzwanzig
7	sieben		27	siebenundzwanzig
8	acht		28	achtundzwanzig
9	neun		29	neunundzwanzig
10	zehn		30	dreißig
11	elf		40	vierzig
12	zwölf		50	fünfzig
13	dreizehn		60	sechzig
14	vierzehn		70	siebzig
15	fünfzehn		80	achtzig
16	sechzehn		90	neunzig
17	siebzehn		100	hundert
18	achtzehn			
19	neunzehn			

Situation 11 | Wie viele?

Sit. 11. Have sts. count the number of persons in
the class who fit the descriptions given in the
activity. Ask questions such as: *Wie viele Studenten*
und Studentinnen tragen eine Brille? Studenten und
Studentinnen mit Brille: Stehen Sie bitte auf!
(Fünf - John trägt eine Brille, Ann trägt eine
Brille, ...) Wie viele Frauen tragen eine Brille? (Drei.)
Sts. can say the number or hold up 2 fingers and
1 thumb. *Ja, drei Studentinnen tragen eine Brille.*
Und wie viele Männer?

Wie viele Studenten/Studentinnen im Kurs tragen ...?

eine Hose	_____
eine Brille	_____
eine Armbanduhr	_____
eine Bluse	_____
einen Rock	_____
Sportschuhe	_____

Kultur ... Landeskunde ... Informationen

So zählt man ...

eins, zwei, drei...

So schreibt man ...

1 7

eine Eins   eine Sieben

KLI. Use TPR to show sts. how to count in German. Use your hands as follows: **(1)** thumb up, **(2)** thumb + index finger, **(3)** thumb + index finger + middle finger, **(4)** thumb + index finger + middle finger + ring finger, **(5)** full hand, **(6)** full hand + thumb of other hand, and so on. Demonstrate how the number 1 and the number 7 are written in German. Use TPR: *Das ist eine Eins. Zeigen Sie die Eins.* Then use with *Sit. 12.*

Situation 12 | Informationsspiel: Zahlenrätsel

Sit. 12. *Das eine Bild zeigt ein Auto, das andere einen Teddybären.*

Verbinden Sie die Punkte. Sagen Sie Ihrem Partner oder Ihrer Partnerin, wie er oder sie die Punkte verbinden soll. Dann sagt Ihr Partner oder Ihre Partnerin Ihnen, wie Sie die Punkte verbinden sollen. Was zeigen Ihre Bilder?

SI: Start ist Nummer 1. Geh zu 18, zu 7, zu 29, zu 13, zu 60, zu 32, zu 12, zu 5, zu 14, zu 20, zu 11, zu 9, zu 3, zu 80, zu 23, zu 19, zu 4, zu 27, zu 8, zu 15, zu 35, zu 26, zu 2, und zum Schluss zu 17. Was zeigt dein Bild?

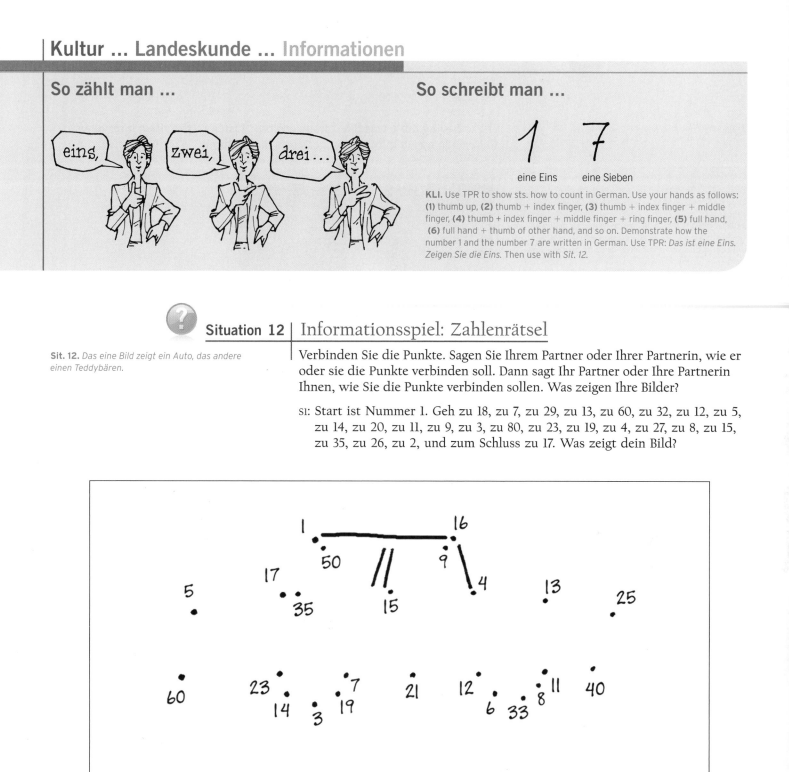

Videoecke

Aufgabe 1. Before watching the video let sts. speculate what the names of the people in the photographs might be. (1 = Juliane Ladstätter, 2 = Nicole Chibici-Revneanu, 3 = Sven Reschinski, 4 = Ayse Aydin). Ask them who might know Turkish and who might know Latin, Greek, and Hebrew. Then let them speculate whose favorite colors might be yellow and whose blue, and who might have lucky numbers and who not. Then play Interview A. Ask sts. to focus only on the person's name, the name of the city she/he comes from, her/his favorite color, and her/his lucky number. Ask sts. to write down these pieces of information or to check them in the chart. Play the same segment again, and ask sts. to focus on the languages. Play the segment a third time. When Juliane spells her last name (Ladstätter), ask sts. to write it down. You may wish to play the spelling part several times. When Juliane is asked what one says to greet people, ask sts. to write down her answer as well. Do the same for Interviews B–D. Note that Niki says how to say farewell at the end of the interview. She says *Pfiadi*, which derives from *Es führe dich Gott*.

Note. The interviews were filmed in Leipzig. That is why Juliane says that she is from Dresden, "some 100 km to the east." Sven and Juliane are from the *neue Bundesländer*, the former German Democratic Republic. That is why their first foreign language was Russian. Ayse, from the *alte Bundesländer*, had Latin as her first language and English as her second.

The following table was filled in incorrectly. Listen to the video interviews and decide which information goes in which column.

1.

2.

3.

4.

	A	B	C	D
Name	Niki	Sven	Ayse	Juliane
kommt aus	Dresden	Dormagen	Berlin	Graz
Fremdsprachen	Russisch, Englisch, Spanisch, Latein	Russisch, Englisch	Latein, Englisch, Türkisch	Englisch, Französisch, Spanisch, Latein, Griechisch, Hebräisch
Lieblingsfarbe	dunkelblau	gelb	gelb	blau
Glückszahl	keine	drei	sieben	keine

Aufgabe 2. Do this activity on a different day. Before playing the segment, you may wish to ask sts. to recapitulate what they know about the people in it before playing each interview.

Niki, Sven, Ayse, and Juliane describe where they come from in more detail. Match the place names with the additional information given in each interview.

1. _____ Dresden
2. _____ Dormagen
3. _____ Friedrichshain
4. _____ Graz

a. im Süden Österreichs
b. im Zentrum Berlins
c. die Hauptstadt von Sachsen
d. in der Nähe von Köln

Wortschatz. The *Wortschatz* follows each *Videoecke* section; it contains new words that have been introduced in the displays and activities in that chapter. These are the words sts. should recognize in a communicative context. Many of these words will be used actively by sts. in later chapters. Most words are grouped thematically to help sts. bind meaning to words. Note that all nouns are grouped by gender (feminine, masculine, neuter), with a separate listing for nouns used only in the plural. *Ähnliche Wörter* lists consist of true cognates and, in later chapters, of compound words with components that sts. will be able to recognize (e.g., *Spielplatz* from *spielen* and *Platz*). Advise sts. that if they have difficulty guessing the meaning of words in these lists, they can find the meanings in the German-English vocabulary at the end of the book.

Wortschatz

Aufforderungen — Instructions

arbeiten Sie mit einem Partner*	work with a partner
geben Sie mir	give me
gehen Sie	go, walk
hören Sie zu	listen
laufen Sie	go, run
lesen Sie	read
nehmen Sie	take
öffnen Sie	open
sagen Sie	say
schauen Sie	look
schließen Sie	close, shut
schreiben Sie	write; spell
setzen Sie sich	sit down
springen Sie	jump
stehen Sie auf	get up, stand up

Kleidung — Clothes

er/sie hat ...	he/she has . . .
hast du ...?	do you have . . . ?
er/sie trägt ...	he/she is wearing . . .
trägst du ...?	do you wear . . . ? / are you wearing . . . ?
eine Armbanduhr	a watch
eine Brille	glasses
eine Hose	pants
eine Krawatte	a tie
einen Anzug	a suit
einen Mantel	a coat; an overcoat
einen Ohrring	an earring
einen Rock	a skirt
ein Hemd	a shirt
ein Kleid	a dress
ein Sakko	a sports jacket
ein Stirnband	a headband
Stiefel	boots

Ähnliche Wörter†

er/sie trägt ... eine Bluse, eine Jacke; einen Hut; Schuhe, Sportschuhe

Farben — Colors

gelb	yellow
lila	purple
rosa	pink
schwarz	black

Ähnliche Wörter

blau, braun, grau, grün, orange [oraŋʒə], rot, weiß

Zahlen — Numbers

0	null	20	zwanzig
1	eins	21	einundzwanzig
2	zwei	22	zweiundzwanzig
3	drei	23	dreiundzwanzig
4	vier	24	vierundzwanzig
5	fünf	25	fünfundzwanzig
6	sechs	26	sechsundzwanzig
7	sieben	27	siebenundzwanzig
8	acht	28	achtundzwanzig
9	neun	29	neunundzwanzig
10	zehn	30	dreißig
11	elf	40	vierzig
12	zwölf	50	fünfzig
13	dreizehn	60	sechzig
14	vierzehn	70	siebzig
15	fünfzehn	80	achtzig
16	sechzehn	90	neunzig
17	siebzehn	100	hundert
18	achtzehn		
19	neunzehn		

Begrüßen und Verabschieden — Greeting and Leave-Taking

auf Wiedersehen!	good-bye
bis bald!	so long; see you soon
grüezi!	hi (*Switzerland*)
grüß Gott!	good afternoon; hello (*formal; southern Germany, Austria*)
guten Abend!	good evening
guten Morgen!	good morning
guten Tag!	good afternoon; hello (*formal*)
hallo!	hi (*informal*)
die Hand schütteln	to shake hands
mach's gut!	take care (*informal*)
servus!	hello; good-bye (*informal; southern Germany, Austria*)
tschüss!	bye (*informal*)
viel Spaß!	have fun

*The diacritic marks in the **Wortschatz** list are meant to help you learn which vowels are stressed. A dot below a single vowel indicates a short stressed vowel. An underline below a single vowel, double vowel, or diphthong (combination of two different vowels) indicates a long stressed vowel. Note that these markings are not used in written German but are provided here as an aid to pronunciation.

†**Ähnliche Wörter** (*similar words; cognates*) lists contain words that are closely related to English words in sound, form, and meaning and compound words that are composed of previously introduced vocabulary.

Personen — People

die **Frau**	woman; Mrs.; Ms.
die **Lehrerin**	female teacher, instructor
der **Herr**	gentleman; Mr.
der **Lehrer**	male teacher, instructor
die **Mitstudenten**	fellow (male) students
die **Mitstudentinnen**	fellow (female) students

Ähnliche Wörter

die **Freundin**, die **Mutter**, die **Professorin**, die **Studentin**; der **Freund**, der **Mann**, der **Professor**, der **Student**

Sonstige Substantive — Other Nouns

die **Tafel**	blackboard
die **Tür**	door
der **Stift**	pen
der **Bleistift**	pencil
Lieblings-	favorite
die **Lieblingsfarbe**	favorite color
der **Lieblingsname**	favorite name

Ähnliche Wörter

die **CD**, die **Schule**; der **Ball**, der **Fußball**, der **Kurs**, der **Deutschkurs**, der **Name**, der **Familienname**, der **Vorname**, der **Teddybär**, der **Videorekorder**; das **Auto**, das **Buch**, das **Telefon**

Fragen — Questions

heißen	to be called, be named
wie **heißen** Sie?	what's your name? (*formal*)
wie **heißt** du?	what's your name? (*informal*)
ich **heiße** ...	my name is . . .
was **zeigen** Ihre **Bilder**?	what do your pictures show?
welche **Farbe** hat ...?	what color is . . . ?
wer ...?	who . . . ?
wie **schreibt** man das?	how do you spell that?
wie **viele** ...?	how many . . . ?
wo **willst** du denn hin?	where are you going?

Wörter im Deutschkurs — Words in German Class

die **Antwort**	answer
die **Einführung**	introduction
die **Frage**	question
die **Grammatik**	grammar
die **Hausaufgabe**	homework
die **Sprechsituation**	conversational situation
die **Übung**	exercise
der **Wortschatz**	vocabulary
das **Kapitel**	chapter
stellen Sie **Fragen**	ask questions
tun	to do
unterschreib bitte **hier**	sign here, please
verbinden	to connect

Sonstige Wörter und Ausdrücke — Other Words and Expressions

aber	but
auch	also, too; as well
bitte	please
gibt es ...?	is there . . . ? / are there . . . ?
hübsch	pretty
kaputt	broken
mein(e)	my
mit	with
mit dem **kurzen Haar**	with the short hair
mit dem **langen Haar**	with the long hair
mit dem **Ohrring**	with the earring
mit dem **Schnurrbart**	with the mustache
nein	no
nicht	not
oder	or
schmutzig	dirty
sein	to be
sondern	but (rather/on the contrary)
trägst du gern ...?	do you like to wear . . . ?
viel	a lot, much
viele	many
von	of; from
zählen	to count
zu Hause	at home

Ähnliche Wörter

alt, **danke**, **dann**, **hier**, **in**, **neu**, **oft**, **so**, **und**

Strukturen und Übungen

A.1 Giving instructions: polite commands

command form = verb + **Sie**

Strukturen. The grammar explanations in *Ein-führung A* are meant to be used as "advance organizers" to help sts. understand your input. In general, sts. are not expected to be able to produce forms and structures that are explained in this chapter. All grammar points in *Einführung A* are presented again in later chapters. Marginal grammar notes provide sts. with rules of thumb and pointers to help them understand and learn the grammar concepts.

The instructions your instructor gives you in class consist of a verb, which ends in **-en,** and the pronoun **Sie** (*you*).* Like the English *you*, the German **Sie** can be used with one person (*you*) or with more than one (*you* [*all*]). In English instructions the pronoun *you* is normally understood but not said. In German, **Sie** is a necessary part of the sentence.

Stehen Sie bitte **auf.**	*Please stand up.*
Nehmen Sie bitte das Buch.	*Please take the book.*

With certain instructions, you will also hear the word **sich** (*yourself*).†

Setzen Sie sich, bitte.	*Sit down, please.*

A.1. *Aufforderungen.* The goal of A.1 is recognition of commands. Forms like separable prefixes and reflexive pronouns will be explained later.

Note. Answers to the *Übungen* are in Appendix G.

Übung 1 | Im Klassenzimmer

Was sagt Frau Schulz zu den Studenten?

Nehmen Sie einen Stift!
Sagen Sie „Guten Tag"!
Schauen Sie an die Tafel!
Schließen Sie das Buch!
Schreiben Sie „Tschüss"!
Öffnen Sie das Buch!
Hören Sie zu!
Geben Sie mir die Hausaufgabe!

1. Peter 2. Heidi 3. Monika 4. Nora

5. Albert 6. Stefan 7. Thomas 8. Katrin

---

*The pronoun **Sie** (*you*) is capitalized to distinguish it from another pronoun, **sie** (*she; it; they*).
†**Sich** is a reflexive pronoun; its use will be explained in **Kapitel 11.**

A.2 What is your name? The verb *heißen*

heißen = *to be called*
Wie heißen Sie? (*formal*)
Wie heißt du? (*informal*)

A.2. Point out the meaning of *Wie* in the question *Wie heißen Sie?* This is the sts.' first encounter with verb conjugation in German, so only the most useful forms are included here. The complete conjugations of *sein* and *haben*, and the first full conjugation of a regular verb (*kommen*) appear in *Einführung B*.

Use a form of the verb **heißen** (*to be called*) to tell your name and to ask for the names of others.

Wie **heißen** Sie? / Wie **heißt** du?*	*What is your name?*
Ich **heiße** ...	*My name is . . .*

heißen (singular forms)		
ich	heiße	*my name is*
du	heißt	*your name is*
Sie	heißen	
er	heißt	*his name is*
sie	heißt	*her name is*

Übung 2 | Minidialoge

Üb.2. *Minidialoge* appear frequently in the exercises. One way to use them is to assign them as homework and, in the next class, give the roles to sts. to perform. Familiarize sts. with the *er/sie*-form by using it in class. When taking attendance, ask: *Wie heißt Ihre Nachbarin? Heißt sie Anna?* etc. This procedure also helps sts. learn one another's names.

Ergänzen Sie[1] das Verb **heißen**: heiße, heißt, heißen.

1. ERNST: Hallo, wie _____ª du?
   JUTTA: Ich _____ᵇ Jutta. Und du?
   ERNST: Ich _____ᶜ Ernst.
2. HERR THELEN: Guten Tag, wie _____ª Sie bitte?
   HERR SIEBERT: Ich _____ᵇ Siebert, Alexander Siebert.
3. CLAIRE: Hallo, ich _____ª Claire und wie heißt ihr?
   MELANIE: Ich _____ᵇ Melanie und er _____ᶜ Josef.

A.3 The German case system

Case shows how nouns function in a sentence.

A.3. *Das deutsche Kasussystem.* Point out to sts. here that they will not need to know the reason for the endings on articles and adjectives to understand your speech. The context and your gestures will help them interpret what you say. Occasionally, a st. will insist on knowing the reason for every form. Avoid long grammar explanations in class. The forms will be explained when sts. are asked to produce them.

German speakers use a *case system* (nominative for the subject, accusative for the direct object, and so on) to indicate the function of a particular noun in a sentence. The article[†] or adjective that precedes the noun shows its case. You will learn the correct endings in future lessons. For now, be aware that you will hear and read articles and adjectives with a variety of endings. These various forms will not prevent you from understanding German. Here are all the possibilities.

der, das, die, dem, den, des	*the*
ein, eine, einen, einem, einer, eines	*a, an*
blau, blaue, blauer, blaues, blauen, blauem	*blue*

---

*The difference between **Sie** (*formal*) and **du** (*informal*) will be explained in Section A.5.
[†]Articles are words such as *the*, *a*, and *an*, which precede nouns.
[1]**Ergänzen** ... *Supply*

In addition, definite articles may contract with some prepositions, just as *do* and *not* contract to *don't* in English. Here are some common contractions you will hear and read.

in + das	= ins		*into the*
in + dem	= im		*in the*
zu + der	= zur	}	*to the*
zu + dem	= zum		
an + das	= ans		*to/on the*
an + dem	= am		*to/at the*

A.4 Grammatical gender: nouns and pronouns

A.4. *Genus: Nomen und Pronomen.* The two main points in this section are the notion of grammatical gender in German and the replacement of nouns by pronouns according to grammatical gender. Emphasize the usefulness of color-coded lists for learning gender. Use classroom objects and your PF (picture file) to help sts. bind articles to nouns and acquire correct pronoun substitution. The most frequent error in pronoun replacement is the use of *es* for all inanimate nouns. Articles and personal pronouns are discussed again in *Einführung B.*

masculine = **der**

neuter = **das**

feminine = **die**

plurals (all genders) = **die**

In German, all nouns are classified grammatically as masculine, neuter, or feminine. When referring to people, grammatical gender usually matches biological sex.

MASCULINE	FEMININE
der Mann	**die** Frau
der Student	**die** Studentin

When referring to things or concepts, however, grammatical gender obviously has nothing to do with biological sex.

MASCULINE	NEUTER	FEMININE
der Rock	**das** Hemd	**die** Hose
der Hut	**das** Buch	**die** Jacke

The definite article indicates the grammatical gender of a noun. German has three nominative singular definite articles: **der** (*masculine*), **das** (*neuter*), and **die**

	Singular	Plural
Masculine	der	die
Neuter	das	die
Feminine	die	die

der → er = *he, it*

das → es = *it*

die → sie = *she, it*

die (*pl.*) → **sie** = *they*

Note. You may need to point out the distinction in usage: *Haben* is used in a question about colors, *sein* in a statement.

Suggestion. You may wish to provide further clues to your sts.—e.g., nouns ending in *-er* are mostly masculine.

(*feminine*). The plural article is **die** for all genders. All mean *the*.

The personal pronouns **er, es, sie** (*he, it, she*) reflect the gender of the nouns they replace. For example, **er** (*he, it*) refers to **der Rock** because the grammatical gender is masculine; **es** (*it*) refers to **das Hemd** (*neuter*); **sie** (*she, it*) refers to **die Jacke** (*feminine*). The personal pronoun **sie** (*they*) refers to all plural nouns.

—Welche Farbe hat **der Rock?**	*What color is the skirt?*
—**Er** ist gelb.	*It is yellow.*
—Welche Farbe hat **das Hemd?**	*What color is the shirt?*
—**Es** ist weiß.	*It is white.*
—Welche Farbe hat **die Jacke?**	*What color is the jacket?*
—**Sie** ist braun.	*It is brown.*
—Welche Farbe haben **die Bleistifte?**	*What color are the pencils?*
—**Sie** sind gelb.	*They are yellow.*

Sometimes gender can be determined from the ending of the noun; for example, nouns that end in **-e**, such as **die Jacke** or **die Bluse**, are usually feminine. The ending **-in** indicates a female person: **die Studentin, die Professorin.**

In most cases, however, gender cannot be predicted from the form of the word. It is best, therefore, to learn the corresponding definite article along with each new noun.*

Übung 3 | Kleidung

Frau Schulz spricht über die Kleidung. Ergänzen Sie **er, es, sie** oder **sie** (Plural).

Frau Schulz:

1. Hier ist die Jacke. _____ ist neu.
2. Und hier ist das Kleid. _____ ist modern.
3. Hier ist der Rock. _____ ist kurz.
4. Und hier ist die Bluse. _____ ist hübsch.
5. Hier ist das Hemd. _____ ist grün.
6. Und hier sind die Schuhe. _____ sind schmutzig.
7. Hier ist der Hut. _____ ist rot.
8. Und hier ist die Hose. _____ ist weiß.
9. Hier sind die Stiefel. _____ sind schwarz.
10. Und hier ist der Anzug. _____ ist alt.

Übung 4 | Welche Farbe?

Welche Farbe haben diese Kleidungsstücke? Ergänzen Sie **er, es, sie** oder **sie** (Plural) und die richtige Farbe.

1. A: Welche Farbe hat Marias Rock?
   B: _____ ist _____.
2. A: Welche Farbe hat Michaels Hose?
   B: _____ ist _____.
3. A: Welche Farbe hat Michaels Hemd?
   B: _____ ist _____.
4. A: Welche Farbe hat Michaels Hut?
   B: _____ ist _____ und _____.
5. A: Welche Farbe haben Marias Schuhe?
   B: _____ sind _____.
6. A: Welche Farbe haben Michaels Schuhe?
   B: _____ sind _____.
7. A: Welche Farbe hat Marias Bluse?
   B: _____ ist _____.

*Some students find the following suggestion helpful. When you hear or read new nouns you consider useful, write them down in a vocabulary notebook, using different colors for the three genders; for example, use blue for masculine, black for neuter, and red for feminine. Some students also write nouns in three separate columns according to gender.

A.5 Addressing people: *Sie* versus *du* or *ihr*

A.5. *Jemanden ansprechen.* Sts. who have not encountered the formal/informal distinction in other
languages may need further explanation in class.

German speakers use two modes of addressing others: the formal **Sie** (*singular*
and *plural*) and the informal **du** (*singular*) or **ihr** (*plural*). You usually use **Sie**
with someone you don't know or when you want to show respect or social
distance. Children are addressed as **du.** Students generally call one another **du.**

Use **du** and **ihr** with friends, family, and
children. Use **Sie** with almost everyone else.

	Singular	Plural
Informal	du	ihr
Formal	Sie	Sie

Frau Ruf, **Sie** sind 38, nicht wahr?   Ms. Ruf, you are 38, aren't you?
Jens und Jutta, **ihr** seid 16, nicht wahr?   Jens and Jutta, you are 16, aren't you?
Hans, **du** bist 13, nicht wahr?   Hans, you are 13, aren't you?

Übung 5 | *Sie, du* oder *ihr*?

Üb. 5. Sts. should have no difficulty understanding
the meaning of the plural nouns. Plural forms of
nouns will be presented in *Einführung B.* **Item 5.**
The usage depends on the relationship between
the women. Explain that *Sie* would be used at first
but could later change to *du* if the women became
friends. This lends itself to discussion in class.

Was sagen diese Personen: **Sie, du** oder **ihr**?

1. Student → Student
2. Professor → Student
3. Freund → Freund
4. Studentin → zwei Studenten
5. Frau (40 Jahre alt) → Frau (50 Jahre alt)
6. Student → Sekretärin
7. Doktor → Patient
8. Frau → zwei Kinder

Gustav Klimt: *Margaret Stonborough-Wittgenstein* (1905), Neue Pinakothek, Munich

GUSTAV KLIMT

Gustav Klimt (1862–1918) was born in Vienna, Austria. His paintings are highly symbolic and very decorative. This painting of Margaret Stonborough-Wittgenstein nicely demonstrates the elegant—sometimes even decadent—style of *Jugendstil* art.

EINFÜHRUNG **B**

In **Einführung B**, you will continue to develop your listening skills and will begin to speak more German. You will learn to talk about your classroom, the weather, and people: their character traits, family relationships, and national origins.

Themen
Das Klassenzimmer
Beschreibungen
Der Körper
Die Familie
Wetter und Jahreszeiten
Herkunft und Nationalität

Kulturelles
So sehen sich die jungen Deutschen
Wetter und Klima
Videoblick: Das Wetter
Die Lage Deutschlands in Europa
Videoecke: Familie

Strukturen
B.1 Definite and indefinite articles
B.2 Who are you? The verb **sein**
B.3 What do you have? The verb **haben**
B.4 Plural forms of nouns
B.5 Personal pronouns
B.6 Origins: **Woher kommen Sie?**
B.7 Possessive adjectives: **mein** and **dein/Ihr**

GOALS
The purpose of *Einführung B* is to give sts. opportunities to make the transition from Comprehension to Early Speech. Continue to emphasize the development of the ability to comprehend German, but, at the same time, encourage sts. to begin to respond using single words and short phrases. In many activities throughout the text sts. will work in pairs or in small groups rather than having a strictly teacher-centered lesson. The semantic focus continues to be on identification and descriptions of common items and people in the sts.' environment.

PRE-TEXT ORAL ACTIVITIES
(1) Classroom commands. Use TPR to review classroom commands from *Einführung A*. Sample sequence: *Stehen Sie auf, öffnen Sie das Buch, schließen Sie das Buch, setzen Sie sich.* Repeat and recombine commands during the sequence. Narrow the size of the group participating in individual commands by giving selective descriptions: *Männer, die Jeans tragen, stehen Sie bitte auf, heben Sie die rechte Hand, setzen Sie sich.* **(2) Transition to Stage II:** Use the topics from *Einführung A* to make the transition from Stage I to Stage II. (See the IM for suggestions of the types of questions appropriate for Stage II activities.) Talk about numbers, clothes, and colors. Hold up fingers and ask either/or questions such as *Sind es fünf oder sechs?* Expand answers: *Ja, richtig, das sind fünf.* Create sequences using several types of questions: *Wer trägt ein weißes Hemd? (Robert.) Ja, das stimmt. Heute trägt Robert ein weißes Hemd.* (Use subject-verb inversion naturally to get the sts. used to both word orders.) *Trägt Tom eine gelbe Hose? (Ja.) Ja? Ist die Hose gelb? Nicht orange? Wirklich? Und welche Farbe hat Janes Bluse? Ist sie grün oder braun?*

Situationen

Grammatik B.1

Situation 1 | Das Klassenzimmer

Wie viele _____ sind im Klassenzimmer?

1. Studenten
2. Tische
3. Fenster
4. Lampen
5. Uhren
6. Türen
7. Bücher
8. Tafeln
9. Professoren/Professorinnen
10. Hefte

Situation 2 | Gegenstände[1] im Klassenzimmer

Sit. 2. Introduce new vocabulary and review old vocabulary by pointing and saying (or asking) *Das ist … (Was ist das?).* Review nouns by doing a TPR activity: *Zeigen Sie auf den Boden (das Fenster usw.)!* Then ask sts. to do *Sit. 2* in pairs: first, one st. asks all questions, then the other asks. This activity gives sts. the chance to produce the definite articles with nouns and to hear that adjectives in predicate position are not inflected.

MODELL: SI: Was ist grün?
        S2: Die Tafel und die Tür (sind grün).

1. weiß
2. schmutzig
3. sauber
4. neu
5. alt
6. klein
7. groß
8. grün
9. grau
10. _____

a. der Boden
b. das Fenster
c. die Tafel
d. die Uhr
e. der Schwamm
f. der Tisch
g. das Buch
h. die Tür
i. die Decke
j. _____

Beschreibungen

Grammatik B.2–B.3

Vocabulary Display
Presentation: *Das ist Michael Pusch. Er ist groß* (show with your hands that this means "tall," not "heavy," or contrast immediately with *klein*), *und er hat einen Schnurrbart. Herr Siebert steht neben Michael. Herr Siebert ist alt und er hat einen Schnurrbart und einen Bart usw.* **Receptive recall:** (covering up vocabulary above the characters but allowing their names to show) *Wer ist groß? Wer ist klein? Wer ist alt? usw.* When possible, ask about contrasting opposites (*groß/klein, alt/jung, usw.*). **Choral response. Productive recall:** *Wie ist Michael? Ist er groß oder klein? Und wie ist Jens? Ist er auch groß? Hat Michael einen Bart oder einen Schnurrbart? Was hat Herr Siebert? usw.* **Personalization:** *Wer im Deutschkurs hat blondes/ kurzes Haar? Wer ist klein/groß? usw.*

groß schlank — Michael Pusch

alt Bart — Herr Siebert

jung klein — Jens Krüger

langes, braunes Haar — Maria Schneider

kurzes, blondes Haar — Jutta Ruf

kurzes, graues Haar — Frau Körner

[1]objects

Situationen

27

Situation 3 | Im Deutschkurs

Sit. 3. Ask sts. to write a classmate's name for each description. If they don't know a name, they should go to that person and ask his or her name. It is usually easier to do this activity standing up so sts. are more inclined to move around. As a follow-up, ask the whole class: *Wer ist blond? Ja, Janet ist blond und Robert auch usw.*

Alternate Activity (AA). Have sts. write a description of someone in the classroom, using lists of words or phrases, and ask others to guess the identity.

1. Wer ist _____?
   a. blond
   b. groß
   c. klein
   d. schlank
   e. jung
   f. alt

2. Wer hat _____?
   a. braunes Haar
   b. graues Haar
   c. kurzes Haar
   d. langes Haar
   e. einen Bart
   f. blaue Augen
   g. braune Augen

Situation 4 | Interaktion: Wie bist du?

Sit. 4. Throughout *Kontakte,* new vocabulary is introduced both in the illustrations that begin each section and in the activities that follow them. Always make sure that students understand all the new words before asking them to work on their own or in groups. In *Sit. 4,* sts. first check the characteristics that apply to themselves. Next, each st. asks one male and one female st. what they are like: *Bist du fröhlich, traurig, konservativ, usw.?* The students questioned answer either *ja* or *nein,* according to what they have already checked. Those asking the questions should write down the name of the interviewee and check the boxes for which the answer is *ja.*

MODELL: S1: Bist du glücklich?
　　　　S2: Ja, ich bin glücklich.
　　oder Nein, ich bin nicht glücklich.

	ICH	MEIN PARTNER	MEINE PARTNERIN
glücklich	☐	☐	☐
traurig	☐	☐	☐
konservativ	☐	☐	☐
schüchtern	☐	☐	☐
religiös	☐	☐	☐
ruhig	☐	☐	☐
freundlich	☐	☐	☐
verrückt	☐	☐	☐
sportlich	☐	☐	☐

Photo questions. *Wie sieht der Mann / die Frau aus? Wie alt ist er/sie? Wie ist er/sie? (konservativ, schüchtern, sportlich)? Ist er/sie verheiratet? Hat er/sie eine große Familie? Warum ist er/sie froh/ traurig?*

Mir geht's gut.

Ach, wie traurig!

So sehen sich die jungen Deutschen

- Wie sehen Sie sich und Ihr Leben?[1]
  - ☐ Ich möchte Spaß haben.
  - ☐ Ich bin ehrgeizig[2].
  - ☐ Ich genieße[3] das Leben.
  - ☐ Ich bin verunsichert[4].
  - ☐ Ich bin egoistisch.
  - ☐ Ich bin überfordert[5].
  - ☐ Ich bin flexibel.
  - ☐ Ich bin aggressiv.

- Schauen Sie sich die Grafik an. Was sagen junge Deutsche?
  1. Wie viel Prozent der jungen Deutschen finden sich[6] vernünftig[7]?
  2. Wie viel Prozent der jungen Deutschen finden sich verantwortungslos[8]?
  3. Wie viel Prozent der jungen Deutschen finden sich selbstbewusst[9]?
  4. Wie viel Prozent der jungen Deutschen finden sich freundschaftsbezogen[10]?

[1]Wie ... What is your perspective on yourself and your life?
[2]ambitious [3]enjoy [4]insecure [5]overwhelmed
[6]finden ... consider themselves [7]sensible [8]irresponsible
[9]self-assured [10]focused on friendships

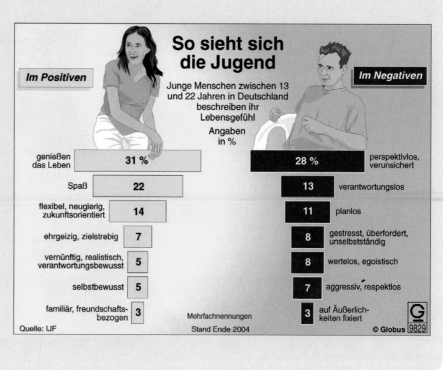

So sieht sich die Jugend

Im Positiven

Junge Menschen zwischen 13 und 22 Jahren in Deutschland beschreiben ihr Lebensgefühl

Angaben in %

Im Negativen

	Im Positiven		Im Negativen	
genießen das Leben	31 %	perspektivlos, verunsichert	28 %	
Spaß	22	verantwortungslos	13	
flexibel, neugierig, zukunftsorientiert	14	planlos	11	
ehrgeizig, zielstrebig	7	gestresst, überfordert, unselbstständig	8	
vernünftig, realistisch, verantwortungsbewusst	5	wertlos, egoistisch	8	
selbstbewusst	5	aggressiv, respektlos	7	
familiär, freundschafts-bezogen	3	auf Äußerlichkeiten fixiert	3	

Quelle: IJF   Mehrfachnennungen   Stand Ende 2004   © Globus 9829

Der Körper

Grammatik B.4

Vocabulary Display
Use TPR to introduce parts of the body. Begin with the hand: *Das ist die Hand. Das ist der Arm.* Add other parts one by one, repeating each new word several times: *Haar, Augen, Rücken usw.* Alternate with the touch command: *Berühren Sie den Arm. Berühren Sie Ihren rechten Arm mit Ihrer linken Hand. Berühren Sie das Bein.*

AA. *„Simon sagt"*: ask sts. to touch parts of their body, but this time precede (almost) every request with *„Simon sagt"*: *Simon sagt, berühren Sie die Augen. Simon sagt, berühren Sie die Nase usw.* If you give a command without first saying *„Simon sagt,"* any sts. who indicate the body part mentioned must sit down. Even adults enjoy this.

der Bauch
die Augen
die Ohren
die Nase
der Mund
das Gesicht
das Haar
der Kopf
die Schulter
der Rücken
der Arm
die Hand
das Bein
der Fuß
der Körper

MODELL: S1: Mein Monster hat fünf Beine und vier Arme.
S2: Das ist Momo.

Sit. 5. Preparation: First, describe all the creatures to sts. Then, describe one creature at a time in random order, and ask sts. to name the creature you are describing. **Activity:** Explain the task to sts. Working in pairs, one person chooses one creature without naming it, and describes it to his/her partner. If the partner correctly names the creature, he or she receives a point and the right to describe a creature. If the partner does not correctly name the creature, the st. describing gets a point and gets to describe another creature. Allow sts. 3-4 min. to do the activity in pairs and then ask them to describe creatures for you to guess.

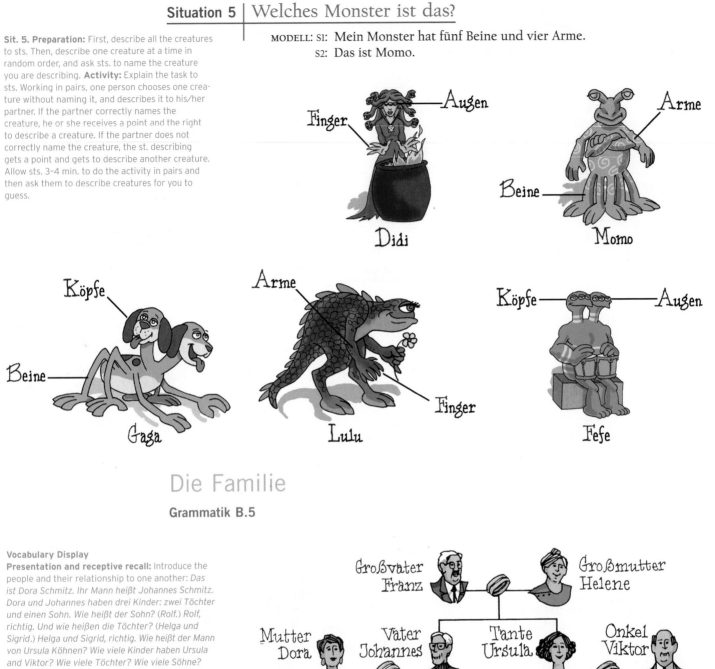

Die Familie

Grammatik B.5

Vocabulary Display

Presentation and receptive recall: Introduce the people and their relationship to one another: *Das ist Dora Schmitz. Ihr Mann heißt Johannes Schmitz. Dora und Johannes haben drei Kinder: zwei Töchter und einen Sohn. Wie heißt der Sohn? (Rolf.) Rolf, richtig. Und wie heißen die Töchter? (Helga und Sigrid.) Helga und Sigrid, richtig. Wie heißt der Mann von Ursula Köhnen? Wie viele Kinder haben Ursula and Viktor? Wie viele Töchter? Wie viele Söhne? Wie heißt die Tochter? Und die Söhne?* Introduce in a similar way (about 4-6 at a time): *Vater, Mutter, Onkel, Tante, Neffe, Nichte; Opa, Oma, Enkelkinder; Geschwister, Bruder, Schwester, Vetter, Kusine.* When working with the display at another time, you can introduce *Schwiegereltern, -vater, -mutter, -sohn, -tochter, Schwager, Schwägerin.* **Choral response:** Point to Helga and say: *Das ist Helgas Familie. Sigrid ist die Schwester. Wiederholen Sie bitte: die Schwester usw.* Students repeat only the family relationship. **Productive recall:** Similar to choral response. Pick a focal person (e.g., Dora Schmitz) and say: *Wer ist Johannes Schmitz? Johannes ist Doras _____ usw.* **Personalization:** *Schreiben Sie auf: den Namen von Ihrem Vater, von Ihrer Mutter, von einem Bruder (wenn Sie einen haben) usw.*

Dora und Johannes Schmitz sind verheiratet. Sie haben drei Kinder: einen Sohn und zwei Töchter.

Situation 6 | Interview: Die Familie

Sit. 6. (See the IM Walk-Through.)

1. Wie heißt dein Vater/Stiefvater? Wie alt ist er? Wo wohnt er?
2. Wie heißt deine Mutter/Stiefmutter? Wie alt ist sie? Wo wohnt sie?
3. Hast du Geschwister? Wie viele? Wie heißen sie? Wie alt sind sie? Wo wohnen sie?

Situation 7* | Informationsspiel: Familie

Sit. 7. This is the first information-gap activity in table form. As with previous information-gap activities, it is designed to create a genuine exchange of information in a controlled way. Sts. work in pairs. One st. works with the chart on this page, the other with the corresponding chart in Appendix A. Each has only half the information in the chart and must ask a partner questions to fill in the missing pieces. Model questions and answer pairs are given.

MODELL: S2: Wie heißt Richards Vater?
    S1: Er heißt Werner.
    S2: Wie schreibt man das?
    S1: W-E-R-N-E-R. Wie alt ist er?
    S2: Er ist ＿＿ Jahre alt. Wo wohnt er?
    S1: Er wohnt in Innsbruck. Wie heißt Richards Mutter?
    S2: Sie heißt ＿＿.
    S1: Wie schreibt man das?
    S2: ＿＿.

			Richard	Sofie	Mehmet
Vater		Name	Werner	Erwin	Kenan
		Alter	39	50	59
		Wohnort	Innsbruck	Dresden	Izmir
Mutter		Name	Maria	Elfriede	Sule
		Alter	38	47	54
		Wohnort	Innsbruck	Dresden	Izmir
Bruder		Name	Alexander	Erwin	Yakup
		Alter	15	27	34
		Wohnort	Innsbruck	Leipzig	Istanbul
Schwester		Name	Elisabeth	—	Fatima
		Alter	16	—	31
		Wohnort	Innsbruck	—	Izmir

To start the activity, pair sts. off by counting 1, 2, 1, 2, etc. All twos turn to the appendix, and all ones work with the chart in the chapter. Remind sts. not to show their half of the activity to their partners. Students alternate, asking questions for each person listed, moving vertically down the columns.
s2: *Wie heißt Richards Vater?*
s1: *Er heißt Werner.*
s2: *Wie schreibt man das?*
s1: *W-E-R-N-E-R. Wie alt ist er?*
s2: *Er ist 39 Jahre alt. Wo wohnt er?*
s1: *Er wohnt in Innsbruck. Wie heißt Richards Mutter?*
s2: *Sie heißt Maria.*
s1: *Wie schreibt man das?*
s2: *M-A-R-I-A. usw.*

Teach sts. phrases such as *Wie bitte? Noch einmal, bitte! Wie schreibt man das? Wie heißt das? Ich verstehe nicht. Danke.* to enable them to keep the complete interaction in German.

*This is an information-gap activity in table form. Pair up with another student. One of you will work with the following chart, the other with the corresponding chart in Appendix A. Different information is missing in each chart.

Wetter und Jahreszeiten

Vocabulary Display
Presentation: Use the overhead projector or your PF to introduce weather expressions. Then use a calendar to teach names of months and seasons. **Receptive recall:** Ask: *Welches Bild zeigt: Es ist heiß? usw.* Months and seasons: Ask: *Welche Jahreszeit haben wir im Januar? im Juli? usw.* **Choral response. Productive recall:** Cover the labels on the transparency and ask sts. what the weather is, which are winter months, in what season it is hot, windy, etc. Or bring in other pictures and ask: *Wie ist das Wetter?*

WIE IST DAS WETTER?

1. Es ist sonnig und warm.

2. Es ist sehr heiß.

3. Es ist kalt.

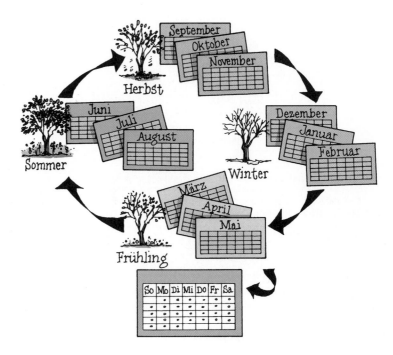

4. Es regnet.

5. Es ist kühl.

6. Es schneit.

7. Es ist windig.

Wetter und Klima

Wie ist das Wetter in Ihrer Stadt? Kreuzen Sie an.

Winterwetter in Berlin

	IM WINTER	IM SOMMER
sonnig	☐	☐
warm	☐	☐
(sehr) heiß	☐	☐
(sehr) feucht	☐	☐
mild	☐	☐
(sehr) kalt	☐	☐
viele Niederschläge[1] (Schnee/Regen)	☐	☐
windig	☐	☐
große Temperaturunterschiede[2]	☐	☐
geringe[3] Temperaturunterschiede	☐	☐

Deutschland hat ein gemäßigtes[4] Klima mit Niederschlägen in allen Jahreszeiten. Im Nordwesten ist das Klima mehr ozeanisch mit warmen, aber selten heißen Sommern und relativ milden Wintern. Im Osten ist es eher[5] kontinental. Im Winter liegen die Temperaturen im Durchschnitt[6] zwischen 1,5 Grad Celsius (°C) im Tiefland[7] und minus 6°C im Gebirge[8], im Juli liegen sie zwischen 18 und 20°C.

Ausnahmen[9]: Am Rhein ist das Klima sehr mild, hier wächst[10] sogar Wein. Oberbayern hat einen warmen alpinen Südwind, den Föhn. Im Harz sind die Sommer oft kühl und im Winter gibt es viel Schnee.

Wie sind die Temperaturen in Deutschland? Benutzen Sie die Tabelle.

	Sommer	Winter Tiefland	Winter Gebirge
in °C			
in °F			

Welche Gebiete[11] bilden Ausnahmen?

wo _____

Klima sehr _____ warmer _____ Sommer: _____

Winter: _____

Temperaturen in Fahrenheit und Celsius

Fahrenheit → Celsius

32 subtrahieren und mit 5/9 multiplizieren

°F	°C
0	-17,8
32	0
50	10
70 ~	21,1
90	32,2
98,6	37
212	100

Celsius → Fahrenheit

Mit 9/5 multiplizieren und 32 addieren

°C	°F
-10	14
0	32
10 ~	50
20	68
30	86
37	98,6
100	212

[1]precipitation [2]temperature variations [3]minor [4]moderate [5]more [6]im ... on average [7]lowlands
[8]mountains [9]exceptions [10]grows [11]areas

Das Wetter

Sie sehen einen Film über das Wetter in Bayern und in Thüringen.

- Ist es Winter oder Sommer?
- Wo ist es warm?
- Wo liegt Schnee?
- Wie wird das Wetter in den nächsten[1] Tagen?

The video segment describes one of the stranger days in German weather history, with summer weather–in winter–in Munich and ice and snow in Thüringen, only a few hundred kilometers to the north.

[1]here: *next few*

Es ist immer so bei uns in München.

Situation 8 | Dialog: Das Wetter in Regensburg

Sit. 8. Use this dialogue as an exercise in listening comprehension, following the steps outlined in *Sit. 9* of *Einführung A:* **(1)** Set the scene; **(2)** Play the dialogue several times while sts. fill in the blanks; **(3)** Ask sts. to check their answers in pairs or groups; **(4)** Write answers on the board.

Josef trifft[1] Claire an der Uni.

JOSEF: Schön heute, nicht?
CLAIRE: Ja, sehr __warm__ und __sonnig__ – wirklich schön!
JOSEF: Leider __regnet__ es so oft hier in Bayern – auch im __Sommer__.
CLAIRE: Ist es auch oft __kühl__ und __windig__ hier?
JOSEF: Ja, im __Frühling__. Und manchmal __schneit__ es noch im April.

Situation 9 | Informationsspiel: Temperaturen

Sit. 9. (See also the IM.) As in *Sit. 7*, one st. uses the chart on this page, the other st. uses the chart in Appendix A. Use the following steps: **(1)** Introduce the topic: *Wissen Sie, wie viel Grad Celsius 65 Grad Fahrenheit sind? Nein? Das werden Sie jetzt erfahren.* **(2)** Preteach vocabulary: Review numbers from 0 to 100 and introduce how to express negative numbers, e.g., *minus fünf.* **(3)** Set up activity: Practice the sample exchange. Remind sts. to use phrases such as *Wie bitte?* and not to look at each other's charts. Divide sts. into two groups and set a time limit of 2-3 minutes. **(4)** Follow-up: Ask students to convert additional Fahrenheit temperatures such as today's high and low temperatures. To convert Fahrenheit into Celsius, subtract 32 and multiply by 5/9.

MODELL: S1: Wie viel Grad Celsius sind 90 Grad Fahrenheit?
S2: _____ Grad Celsius.

°F	90	65	32	0	−5	−39
°C	32	18	0	−18	−21	−39

Sommer im Voralpenland

[1]*meets*

Herkunft und Nationalität

Grammatik B.6–B.7

Vocabulary Display
Presentation: Introduce countries by using the map on the overhead projector and saying: *Hugh Grant kommt aus Großbritannien. Er spricht Englisch.* [Juliette Binoche: Frankreich (*Schauspielerin*), Federico Fellini: Italien (*Regisseur*), Vladimir Putin: Russland (*Politiker*), Luciano Pavarotti: Italien (*Sänger*), *usw.*] Use names students will know and concentrate on those countries of most interest to sts.
Receptive recall: Ask either/or questions (*Kommt Jacques Chirac aus Spanien oder Frankreich?*) or make false claims (*Juan Carlos kommt aus Schweden, nicht wahr?*) **Productive recall:** *Woher kommt ___?* or *Wo spricht man Französisch? Deutsch? Spanisch? usw.* Alternatively, quiz sts. about capital cities: *Wie heißt die Hauptstadt von ___? Or* use directions (*Welches Land liegt westlich von Spanien?*) and other geographical features (*Welche Länder liegen in Skandinavien?*).
Personalization: Ask who has been to which country, who has come from where, or who has friends anywhere in Europe. Develop an association activity by using this information (see the IM) or by asking *Wer möchte mal nach Ungarn reisen? usw.*

 Situation 10 | Dialog: Woher kommst du?

Sit. 10. This dialogue lends itself to serving as a model for sts.' own interactions and to their moving from comprehension to production via a series of steps. The following steps are intended for use with the textbooks closed. **(1)** Set the scene: *Sie hören ein kurzes Gespräch zwischen Claire und Melanie. Claire und Melanie sind auf einer Party.* **(2)** Ask focus questions: *Ist Claire Deutsche? Woher kommt sie? Ist Melanie Deutsche? Woher kommt sie?* **(3)** Play the dialogue. **(4)** Ask sts. to tell you the answers to the focus questions. **(5)** Ask sts. to count the words in each sentence. **(6)** Divide sts. into two groups, assign 1 role to each group, and ask each group to repeat their lines. **(7)** Ask groups to repeat their lines from memory. **(8)** Ask 2–3 pairs of volunteers (1 from each group) to present the dialogue in front of the class. Instead of assuming their previous roles, however, they should change the lines of the dialogue to talk about themselves. **(9)** Sts. get up and work in pairs. While moving from one person to the next, they act out their personalized versions several times.

Claire trifft Melanie auf einer Party.

CLAIRE: Wie heißt du?
MELANIE: Melanie. <u>Und du</u>?
CLAIRE: Claire.
MELANIE: Bist du <u>Amerikanerin</u>?
CLAIRE: Ja.
MELANIE: Und <u>woher</u> kommst du?
CLAIRE: <u>Aus</u> New York. Und du?
MELANIE: Aus Regensburg. Ich <u>bin</u> von hier.

Situation 11 | Herkunft

Sit. 11. Practice model questions and answers with your sts. Also practice the character names. Then ask sts. to write 7 questions, based on information in the display: 2 questions with *woher,* 2 questions with *wer,* and 3 *ja/nein* questions. Sts. then get together in pairs to ask and answer their questions. As always, they should take notes about their partner's responses, and you should conclude with a brief whole-class follow-up.

MODELL: S1: Woher kommt Silvia Mertens?
S2: Sie kommt aus _____.
S1: Wer kommt aus Dresden?
S2: _____.
S1: Kommt Bernd Frisch aus Innsbruck?
S2: Nein, er kommt aus _____.

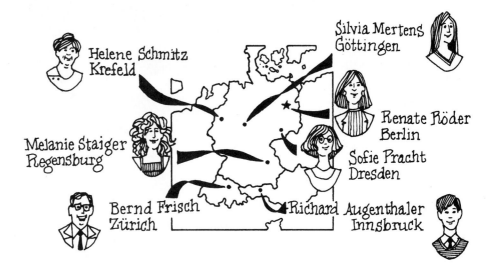

Situation 12 | Rollenspiel: Herkunft

Sit. 12. First set the scene: *Sie sind Studenten in Deutschland, und ich bin ein neuer Student / eine neue Studentin. Sie sind neugierig und stellen mir Fragen. Ich spreche über meine Familie und meine Freunde.* Brainstorm with students what questions one might ask. Write them on the board. Model pronunciation, have them repeat, and then answer the questions as they apply to you. Then have students work in pairs. S1 will work from here; S2 will turn to the appendix. Ask sts. to write down the answers.

S1: Sie sind ein neuer Student / eine neue Studentin an einer Universität in Deutschland. Sie lernen einen anderen Studenten / eine andere Studentin kennen. Fragen Sie, wie er/sie heißt und woher er/sie kommt. Fragen Sie auch, ob er/sie Freunde/Freundinnen in anderen Ländern hat und welche Sprachen sie sprechen.

Follow-up: Ask three to six students questions about themselves or about what they learned from their partners.

Kultur ... Landeskunde ... Informationen

Die Lage Deutschlands in Europa

Deutschland liegt mitten in Europa. Es grenzt an[1] Dänemark, _Polen_, Tschechien, Österreich, die _Schweiz_, Frankreich, Luxemburg, _Belgien_ und die Niederlande. Die Grenzen[2] Deutschlands sind _3 757_ Kilometer lang. Die längste Grenze ist die mit Österreich. Sie ist _815_ Kilometer lang. Die Grenze zu Dänemark ist nur _67_ Kilometer lang, die Grenze zu Polen _442_, zu Tschechien 811, zur Schweiz _316_, zu Frankreich 448, zu Luxemburg _135_, zu Belgien 156 und zu den Niederlanden _567_ Kilometer. Im Norden grenzt Deutschland an zwei Meere, die Nordsee und die _Ostsee_. Deutschland gehört[3] zur Europäischen Union. Welche Länder gehören noch zur Europäischen Union? Schauen Sie auf die Karte auf Seite 35.

[1]grenzt ... *has borders with* [2]*borders* [3]*belongs*

KLI. This text practices comprehension of numbers over 100 in addition to providing geographical information about Germany. Source: *Statistisches Bundesamt* **(1)** Establish the context by asking. e.g.: *Wo liegt Deutschland? Wo genau in Europa? Wie heißen seine Nachbarländer?* Wie viele Nachbarn hat Deutschland insgesamt? *Dazu hören wir jetzt einen Text.* **(2)** Read the text at least twice while sts. fill in the blanks. **(3)** Review sts. answers. **(4)** Follow-up: Ask sts. to group the neighboring countries according to whether they lie to the West, the South, the East, or the North. Additional questions: *Wie heißt das Meer zwischen Großbritannien und Deutschland? zwischen Schweden und Polen? Welche Länder gehören zur Europäischen Union?* Refer sts. to the map of Europe on page 35. At press time, there were ongoing negotiations with Turkey (*die Türkei*) and Croatia (*Kroatien*) about joining the EU.

Videoecke

Birgit, geboren in Munderdingen in der Nähe von Ulm, wohnt zur Zeit in München.

Ivo, geboren in Leipzig, macht gerade sein Abitur. Vater kommt aus Jugoslawien, Mutter aus Leipzig.

Aufgabe 1

Aufgabe 1. Before playing the video, ask sts. to speculate which statements might be true and which false. Then ask sts. to focus on statements 1, 2, 5, and 6 while playing the segment once. Ask sts. if all these answers are true. Then replay the segment while asking sts. to focus on statement 2. Play only until the answer is heard. Play answer several times to give your sts. the chance to come up with the correct answer. Do the same for statements 4 and 7. Play the whole segment again and ask sts. how long Birgit has been married (statement 6) and how old her daughter is (statement 7).

Listen to the interview with Birgit and decide if the following statements are true (**richtig**) or false (**falsch**). Correct any false statements.

	RICHTIG	FALSCH
1. Birgit hat zwei Schwestern.	☐	☐
2. Eine Schwester wird nächste Woche 32.	☐	☐
3. Birgits Mutter ist Hausfrau.	☐	☐
4. Birgits Großeltern leben noch.	☐	☐
5. Ihre Onkel und Tanten sieht Birgit nur selten.	☐	☐
6. Birgit ist verheiratet.	☐	☐
7. Birgit hat einen Sohn.	☐	☐

Aufgabe 2

Aufgabe 2. Discuss the caption that goes with Ivo's photo. Explain what *Abitur* means. Then work with the video the same way as with Birgit's interview.

Listen to the interview with Ivo and decide which of the following answers are correct.

1. Ivo hat	☐ drei Geschwister.	☐ vier Geschwister.
2. Ivos Mutter	☐ ist in Rente.	☐ hat ihre eigene Firma.
3. Ivo	☐ hat noch Großeltern.	☐ hat keine Großeltern mehr.
4. Ivo hat Verwandte in	☐ Italien.	☐ Jugoslawien.
5. Ivo ist	☐ verlobt.	☐ verheiratet.
6. Ivo	☐ hat Kinder.	☐ hat keine Kinder.

Wortschatz

Das Klassenzimmer	The Classroom
die Decke, -n*	ceiling
die Kreide	chalk
die Tafel, -n (R)†	blackboard
die Uhr, -en	clock
die Wand, ⸚e	wall
der Boden, ⸚	floor
der Schwamm, ⸚e	eraser (*for blackboard*)
der Stift, -e (R)	pen
der Bleistift, -e (R)	pencil
der Tisch, -e	table
der Unterricht	class; instruction
das Fenster, -	window
das Heft, -e	notebook

Ähnliche Wörter

die Lampe, -n; die Professorin, -nen (R); die Studentin, -nen (R); die Uni/Universität; der Professor, Professoren (R); der Student, -en (R); der Stuhl, ⸚e; das Buch, ⸚er (R); das Papier

Beschreibungen	Descriptions
er/sie hat ...	he/she has . . .
einen Bart	a beard
blaue Augen	blue eyes
blondes Haar	blond hair
kurzes Haar	short hair
er/sie ist ...	he/she is . . .
dick	large, fat
ernsthaft	serious
glücklich	happy
groß	tall; big
klein	short; small
nett	nice
ruhig	quiet, calm
sauber	clean
schlank	slender, slim
schön	pretty, beautiful
schüchtern	shy
traurig	sad
verrückt	crazy

Ähnliche Wörter

blond, freundlich, intelligent, jung, konservativ, lang, nervös, optimistisch, progressiv, religiös, sportlich, tolerant

Der Körper	The Body
der Bauch, ⸚e	belly, stomach
der Kopf, ⸚e	head
der Mund, ⸚er	mouth
der Rücken, -	back
das Auge, -n	eye
das Bein, -e	leg
das Gesicht, -er	face
das Ohr, -en	ear

Ähnliche Wörter

die Hand, ⸚e; die Schulter, -n; der Arm, -e; der Fuß, ⸚e; das Haar, -e

Die Familie	The Family
die Frau, -en (R)	woman; wife
die Nichte, -n	niece
die Schwester, -n	sister
die Tante, -n	aunt
der Mann, ⸚er (R)	man; husband
der Vetter, -n	male cousin
das Kind, -er	child
die Eltern	parents
die Großeltern	grandparents
die Geschwister	siblings

Ähnliche Wörter

die Kusine, -n; die Mutter, ⸚ (R) die Großmutter, ⸚; die Tochter, ⸚; der Bruder, ⸚; der Neffe, -n; der Onkel, -; der Sohn, ⸚e; der Vater, ⸚ der Großvater, ⸚

Wetter und Jahreszeiten	Weather and Seasons
der Frühling	spring
im Frühling	in the spring
der Herbst	fall, autumn
der Monat, -e	month
es ...	it . . .
ist 18 Grad Celsius	is 18 degrees Celsius
ist feucht	is humid
ist schön	is nice
regnet	is raining; rains
schneit	is snowing; snows

---

*Beginning with this chapter, the plural ending of nouns is indicated in the vocabulary lists. Refer to page 43 for explanation.
†(R) indicates words that were listed in a previous chapter and are presented again for review.

Ähnliche Wörter

der Januar, im Januar, der Februar, der März, der April, der Mai, der Juni, der Juli, der August, der September, der Oktober, der November, der Dezember; der Sommer, der Winter; Fahrenheit, heiß, kalt, kühl, sonnig, warm, windig

Länder, Kontinente, Meere	Countries, Continents, Seas
Deutschland	Germany
Frankreich	France
Griechenland	Greece
Österreich	Austria
Russland	Russia
Tschechien	Czech Republic
Ungarn	Hungary
Weißrussland	Belarus
die **Ostsee**	Baltic Sea
die **Schweiz**	Switzerland
das **Mittelmeer**	Mediterranean Sea

Ähnliche Wörter

Afrika, Ägypten, Albanien, Algerien, Amerika, Asien, Australien, Belgien, Bosnien und Herzegowina, Brasilien, Bulgarien, China, Dänemark, England, Europa, Finnland, Großbritannien, Holland, Irland, Israel, Italien, Japan, Jugoslawien, Kanada, Kroatien, Kuba, Liechtenstein, Marokko, Mexiko, Moldawien, Neuseeland, Nordirland, Norwegen, Palästina, Polen, Portugal, Rumänien, Schweden, Slowenien, Spanien, Südafrika, Südamerika, Tunesien; die Nordsee, die Slowakei, die Türkei, die Ukraine; die Niederlande (*pl.*), die USA (*pl.*)

Herkunft	Origin
der/die **Deutsche**, -n	German (person)
Ich bin **Deutsche/r.**	I am German.
der **Franzose**, -n / die **Französin**, -nen	French (person)
der **Österreicher**, - / die **Österreicherin**, -nen	Austrian (person)
der **Schweizer**, - / die **Schweizerin**, -nen	Swiss (person)

Ähnliche Wörter

die **Amerikanerin**, -nen; die **Australierin**, -nen; die **Engländerin**, -nen; die **Japanerin**, -nen; die **Kanadierin**, -nen; die **Mexikanerin**, -nen; der **Amerikaner**, -; der **Australier**, -; der **Engländer**, -; der **Japaner**, -; der **Kanadier**, -; der **Mexikaner**, -

Sprachen	Languages
Deutsch	German
Französisch	French

Ähnliche Wörter

Arabisch, Chinesisch, Englisch, Italienisch, Japanisch, Portugiesisch, Russisch, Schwedisch, Spanisch, Türkisch

Sonstige Wörter und Ausdrücke	Other Words and Expressions
das ist ...	this/that is . . .
das sind ...	these/those are . . .
dein(e)	your (*informal*)
ein bisschen	a little (bit)
genau	exactly
heute	today
Ihr(e)	your (*formal*)
kennen	to know
kommen (aus)	to come (*from*)
leider	unfortunately
manchmal	sometimes
noch	even, still
sehr	very
sonst	otherwise
sprechen	to speak
wann	when
was	what
welch-	which
wer	who
wie	how
wirklich	really
wo	where
woher	from where
wohnen (in)	to live (in)

Strukturen und Übungen

B.1. *Bestimmter und unbestimmter Artikel.* This section reviews the definite article and introduces the indefinite article. Mention that this form is the nominative, the first of the German cases that students will learn.

B.1 Definite and indefinite articles

Recall that the definite article **der, das, die** (*the*) varies by gender, number, and case.* Similarly, the indefinite article **ein, eine** (*a, an*) has various forms.

Das ist **ein** Buch. Welche
  Farbe hat **das** Buch?

This is a book. What color is the book?

Das ist **eine** Tür. Welche
  Farbe hat **die** Tür?

This is a door. What color is the door?

Here are the definite and indefinite articles for all three genders in the singular and plural, nominative case. There is only one plural definite article for all three genders: **die.** The indefinite article (*a, an*) has no plural.

der → ein
das → ein
die → eine
die (*pl.*) → ø

	Singular	Plural
Masculine	**der** Stift	**die** Stifte
	ein Stift	Stifte
Neuter	**das** Buch	**die** Bücher
	ein Buch	Bücher
Feminine	**die** Tür	**die** Türen
	eine Tür	Türen

Übung 1 | Im Klassenzimmer

Frau Schulz spricht über die Gegenstände im Klassenzimmer und die Farben. Ergänzen Sie den unbestimmten[1] Artikel, den bestimmten[2] Artikel und die Farbe.

Note. Answers to the *Übungen* are in Appendix G.

MODELL: FRAU SCHULZ: Das ist eine Lampe.
            Welche Farbe hat die Lampe?
      STUDENT(IN): Sie ist gelb.

1. Und das ist _____ᵃ Stift.
   Welche Farbe hat _____ᵇ Stift?
   Er ist _____ᶜ.

2. Und das ist _____ᵃ Stuhl.
   Welche Farbe hat _____ᵇ Stuhl?
   Er ist _____ᶜ.

3. Und das ist _____ᵃ Tafel.
   Welche Farbe hat _____ᵇ Tafel?
   Sie ist _____ᶜ.

*See Sections A.3 and A.4.
[1]*indefinite* [2]*definite*

4. Und das ist ____ᵃ Uhr.
   Welche Farbe hat ____ᵇ Uhr?
   Sie ist ____ᶜ.

5. Und das ist ____ᵃ Buch.
   Welche Farbe hat ____ᵇ Buch?
   Es ist ____ᶜ.

6. Und das ist ____ᵃ Brille.
   Welche Farbe hat ____ᵇ Brille?
   Sie ist ____ᶜ.

Übung 2 | Was ist das?

Üb.2. Assign for homework and/or use for oral work in class.

Herr Frisch spricht mit seiner kleinen Tochter.

MODELL: Ist das eine Decke? →
         Nein, das ist ein Bleistift.

1. Ist das eine Tür?

2. Ist das eine Uhr?

3. Ist das eine Lampe?

4. Ist das ein Tisch?

5. Ist das ein Stuhl?

6. Ist das eine Studentin?

7. Ist das ein Heft?

8. Ist das eine Tafel?

B.2. This is the first presentation of a full verb conjugation. Do not expect

sein = *to be*

sts. to be able to produce all these forms at this stage. As with most verb forms, the *ich-*, *du-*, and *Sie*-forms are usually the first to be acquired, because they are used most frequently in class. You can help your sts. become familiar with the other forms by using them in a natural communicative manner.

Suggestion. To practice plural forms, pairs of sts. can be designated as twins to respond in chorus. Other sts. can use the *ihr*-form when addressing the "twins."

Achtung!

NOT = **NICHT**

—Ist Jens groß?
—Nein, er ist **nicht** groß, er ist klein.

B.2 Who are you? The verb *sein*

Use a form of the verb **sein** (*to be*) to identify or describe people and things.

—**Sind Jutta und er** blond?   *Are Jutta and he blond?*
—Ja, **sie sind** blond.   *Yes, they are blond.*

Peter ist groß.   *Peter is tall.*
Das Fenster ist klein.   *The window is small.*

sein					
Singular			*Plural*		
ich	bin	*I am*	wir	sind	*we are*
du	bist	*you are*	ihr	seid	*you are*
Sie	sind		Sie	sind	
er		*he*			
sie }	ist	*she* } *is*	sie	sind	*they are*
es		*it*			

Übung 3 | Minidialoge

Ergänzen Sie das Verb **sein**: bin, bist, ist, sind, seid.

1. MICHAEL: Ich bin Michael. Wer _____ᵃ du?
   JENS: Ich _____ᵇ Jens. Jutta und ich, wir _____ᶜ gute Freunde.
2. FRAU SCHULZ: Das ist Herr Thelen. Er _____ᵃ alt.
   STEFAN: Herr Thelen ist alt?
   FRAU SCHULZ: Ja, Stefan. Herr Thelen ist alt, aber Maria und Michael _____ᵇ jung.
3. HERR THELEN: Jutta und Hans, wie alt _____ᵃ ihr?
   JUTTA: Ich _____ᵇ 16 und Hans _____ᶜ 13.
4. MICHAEL: Wer bist du?
   HANS: Ich _____ᵃ Hans.
   MICHAEL: Wie alt bist du?
   HANS: Ich _____ᵇ 13.

B.3 What do you have? The verb *haben*

haben = *to have*

B.3. This is the full conjugation of another useful irregular verb. (The forms of the regular verb *kommen* appear in *B.6*.) Verb conjugation is introduced gradually in the early chapters, because we want sts. to learn to understand and produce forms of these verbs through meaningful practice, without focusing too much on conjugation patterns or endings. You might want to have sts. play the roles in the *Minidialoge (Üb. 4)*.

The verb **haben** (*to have*) is often used to show possession or to describe physical characteristics.

Ich habe eine Brille.	*I have glasses.*
Hast du das Buch?	*Do you have the book?*
Nora hat braune Augen.	*Nora has brown eyes.*

haben

Singular			Plural		
ich	habe	*I have*	wir	haben	*we have*
du	hast	*you have*	ihr	habt	*you have*
Sie	haben		Sie	haben	
er		*he*			
sie	hat	*she* } *has*	sie	haben	*they have*
es		*it*			

Übung 4 | Minidialoge

Ergänzen Sie das Verb **haben**: habe, hast, hat, habt, haben.

1. FRAU SCHULZ: Nora, _____ᵃ Sie viele Freunde und Freundinnen?
   NORA: Ja, ich _____ᵇ viele Freunde und Freundinnen.
2. MONIKA: Stefan, _____ du einen Stift?
   STEFAN: Nein.
3. PETER: Hallo, Heidi und Katrin! _____ᵃ ihr das Deutschbuch?
   HEIDI: Katrin _____ᵇ es, aber ich nicht.
   PETER: Dann _____ᶜ wir zwei. Ich _____ᵈ es auch.

B.4 Plural forms of nouns

B.4. *Plural der Substantive.* The many plural forms are something new for most sts. There are few rules to reliably predict the endings. Acquisition will take place gradually as sts. have the opportunity to hear and use the nouns with their plural endings. The chart summarizes some common associations between gender and plural forms in German. Sts. should also use the *Wortschatz* lists to help them discover patterns in plural formation. Because the nouns in the *Wortschatz* have been grouped according to gender, the correspondences between gender and plural forms are more apparent.

Just as with English, there are different ways to form plurals in German.

Albert hat ein Heft. Peter hat zwei **Heft**e.	*Albert has one notebook. Peter has two notebooks.*
Heidi hat eine Kusine. Katrin hat zwei Kusine**n**.	*Heidi has one cousin. Katrin has two cousins.*

These guidelines help you to recognize and form the plural of German nouns.

1. Most feminine nouns add **-n** or **-en.** They add **-n** when the singular ends in **-e**; otherwise, they add **-en.** Nouns that end in **-in** add **-nen.**

eine Lampe, zwei Lampe**n**	eine Frau, zwei Frau**en**
eine Tür, zwei Tür**en**	eine Studentin, zwei Studentin**nen**

2. Masculine and neuter nouns usually add **-e** or **-er.** Those plurals that end in **-er** have an umlaut when the stem vowel is **a, o, u,** or **au.** Many masculine plural nouns ending in **-e** have an umlaut as well. Neuter plural nouns ending in **-e** do not have an umlaut.

MASCULINE (der)	NEUTER (das)
ein Rock, zwei R**ö**ck**e**	ein Heft, zwei Heft**e**
ein Mann, zwei M**ä**nn**er**	ein Buch, zwei B**ü**ch**er**

3. Masculine and neuter nouns that end in **-er** either add an umlaut or change nothing at all in the plural. Many nouns with a stem vowel of **a, o, u,** or **au** add an umlaut.

MASCULINE (der)	NEUTER (das)
ein Bruder, zwei Br**ü**der	ein Fenster, zwei Fenster

4. Nouns that end in a vowel other than unstressed **-e** and many nouns of English or French origin add **-s.**

ein Auto, zwei Auto**s**	ein Hotel, zwei Hotel**s**

The following chart summarizes the guidelines provided above.

Singular	Plural	Examples
ein _____er	no ending: some words add an umlaut where possible	ein Lehrer, zwei Lehrer ein Vater, zwei V**ä**ter
ein _____	add **-e**; masculine words often add an umlaut, neuter words do not	ein Rock, zwei R**ö**ck**e** ein Haar, zwei Haar**e**
ein _____	add **-er**; add an umlaut where possible	ein Mann, zwei M**ä**nn**er** ein Buch, zwei B**ü**ch**er**
eine _____	add **-n, -en,** or **-nen,** depending on final letter of the word	eine Lampe, zwei Lampe**n** eine Tür, zwei Tür**en** eine Freundin, zwei Freundin**nen**
ein(e) _____ *(foreign words)*	add **-s**	ein Hobby, zwei Hobby**s** eine Kamera, zwei Kamera**s**

Beginning with this chapter, the plural endings of nouns are indicated in the vocabulary lists as follows.

LISTING	PLURAL FORM
das Fenster, -	die Fenster
der Bruder, ⸚	die Brüder
der Tisch, -e	die Tische
der Stuhl, ⸚e	die Stühle
das Kleid, -er	die Kleider
der Mann, ⸚er	die Männer
die Tante, -n	die Tanten
die Uhr, -en	die Uhren
die Studentin, -nen	die Studentinnen
das Auto, -s	die Autos

Übung 5 | Der Körper

Üb. 5-6 can be illustrated and supplemented with objects in the classroom. Assign for homework or use for oral work.

Wie viele der folgenden Körperteile hat der Mensch[1]?

MODELL: Der Mensch hat zwei Arme.

Arm
Auge
Bein
Finger
Fuß
Haar
Hand
Nase
Ohr
Schulter

Übung 6 | Das Zimmer

Üb. 6. Model and encourage positive responses. Discourage sts. from using *nicht* in their answer. *Kein* is introduced in *Kapitel 2*.

Wie viele der folgenden Dinge sind in Ihrem[2] Zimmer? (ein[e], zwei, …, viele, nicht viele)

das Buch
das Fenster
die Lampe
der Stuhl
der Tisch
die Tür
die Uhr
die Wand

In meinem Zimmer ist/sind _____ Buch/Bücher, …

[1]*person* [2]*your*

B.5 Personal pronouns

B.5. *Personalpronomen.* This section reviews what sts. have previously learned about personal pronouns. Note that the plural pronouns *ihr* and *sie* are often the last to be acquired.

Personal pronouns refer to the speaker (first person), to the person addressed (second person), or to the person(s) or object(s) talked about (third person).

	Singular		Plural	
First person	ich	*I*	wir	*we*
Second-person informal	du	*you*	ihr	*you*
Second-person formal	Sie	*you*	Sie	*you*
Third person	er	*he, it*		
	es	*it*	sie	*they*
	sie	*she, it*		

Wissen Sie noch?

der → **er** = *he, it*
das → **es** = *it*
die → **sie** = *she, it*
die (*pl.*) → **sie** = *they*

Review grammar section A.4.

As you know, third-person singular pronouns reflect the grammatical gender of the nouns they replace.

—Welche Farbe hat **der Hut?**	*What color is the hat?*
—**Er** ist braun.	*It is brown.*
—Welche Farbe hat **das Kleid?**	*What color is the dress?*
—**Es** ist grün.	*It is green.*
—Welche Farbe hat **die Bluse?**	*What color is the blouse?*
—**Sie** ist gelb.	*It is yellow.*

The third-person plural pronoun is **sie** for all three genders.

—Welche Farbe haben **die Schuhe?**	*What color are the shoes?*
—**Sie** sind schwarz.	*They are black.*

Übung 7 | Welche Farbe?

Üb. 7. Remind sts. that while *haben* is used in the question, their response will use *sein: Welche Farbe hat der Hut? Er ist schwarz.*

Frau Schulz spricht über die Farbe der Kleidung. Antworten Sie!

1. Welche Farbe hat der Hut?
2. Welche Farbe hat das Hemd?
3. Welche Farbe hat die Hose?
4. Welche Farbe hat die Bluse?
5. Welche Farbe haben die Socken?
6. Welche Farbe hat das Kleid?
7. Welche Farbe hat der Rock?
8. Welche Farbe haben die Stiefel?
9. Welche Farbe hat die Jacke?
10. Welche Farbe hat der Mantel?

B.6 Origins: *Woher kommen Sie?*

kommen aus = *to come from* (a place)

B.6. The full regular conjugation of the present tense is presented here for the first time with *kommen*. Present-tense forms of other regular verbs will appear in *Kapitel 1*.

To ask about someone's origins, use the question word **woher** (*from where*) followed by the verb **kommen** (*to come*). In the answer, use the preposition **aus** (*from, out of*).

—Woher kommst du / kommen Sie?   *Where do you come from?*
—Ich komme aus Berlin.   *I'm from Berlin.*

kommen			
ich	komme	wir	kommen
du	kommst	ihr	kommt
Sie	kommen	Sie	kommen
er sie es }	kommt	sie	kommen

The infinitive of German verbs, that is, the basic form of the verb, ends in **-n** or **-en**. Most verbs follow a conjugation pattern similar to that of **kommen**.

Kommen Sie heute Abend?   *Are you coming this evening?*
Warten Sie! **Ich komme** mit!   *Wait! I'll come along.*

Übung 8 | Minidialoge

Üb. 8. Assign for homework and have the dialogues performed in class.

Ergänzen Sie **kommen, woher** und **aus** und die Personalpronomen.

1. MEHMET: Woher _____ᵃ du, Renate?
   RENATE: Ich _____ᵇ aus Berlin.
2. FRAU SCHULZ: Woher _____ᵃ Lydia?
   KATRIN: Lydia kommt _____ᵇ Zürich.
   FRAU SCHULZ: _____ᶜ kommen Josef und Melanie?
   STEFAN: Sie _____ᵈ aus Regensburg.
   FRAU SCHULZ: Und woher komme _____ᵉ?
   ALBERT: Sie, Frau Schulz, Sie kommen _____ᶠ Kalifornien.
3. FRAU SCHULZ: Kommt Sofie aus Regensburg?
   HEIDI: Nein, _____ᵃ kommt aus Dresden.
   FRAU SCHULZ: Kommen Josef und Melanie aus Innsbruck?
   STEFAN: Nein, sie _____ᵇ aus Regensburg.
4. ANDREAS: Silvia und Jürgen, kommt _____ᵃ aus Göttingen?
   SILVIA: Ja, _____ᵇ kommen aus Göttingen.

der → mein, dein, Ihr
das → mein, dein, Ihr
die → meine, deine, Ihre
die (pl.) → meine, deine, Ihre

B.7 Possessive adjectives: *mein* and *dein/Ihr*

The possessive adjectives **mein** (*my*), **dein** (*informal your*), and **Ihr** (*formal your*) have the same endings as the indefinite article **ein**. In the plural, the ending is **-e**. Here are the nominative forms of these possessive adjectives.

B.7. *Possessivadjektiv.* We have divided the introduction of possessive adjectives into 2 parts to make the acquisition of these forms easier. The 3 most frequently used forms are described here; they will serve as a reference point for learning the others, which will be introduced in *Kapitel 2.* Point out to sts. that German masculine and neuter forms, on the one hand, and feminine and plural forms, on the other hand, are often the same, as they are here.

	Onkel (*m.*)	Auto (*n.*)	Tante (*f.*)	Eltern (*pl.*)
ich	mein	mein	meine	meine
du	dein	dein	deine	deine
Sie	Ihr	Ihr	Ihre	Ihre

Achtung!

Note that the forms of **Ihr** are capitalized, just as **Sie** is, when they mean *your.*

—Woher kommen **deine** Eltern, Albert? *Where are your parents from, Albert?*
—**Meine** Eltern kommen aus Mexiko. *My parents are from Mexico.*

Wie heißt **Ihr** Vater, Frau Schulz? *What is your father's name, Ms. Schulz?*
Und **Ihre** Mutter? *And your mother's name?*

Üb. 9. Assign as homework, and have sts. perform the dialogues in class.

Achtung!

Just as in English, an *s* added onto someone's name in German indicates possession. In German, however, there is no apostrophe before the *s.*

Das ist Helga. Das ist Helgas Vater.
This is Helga. That is Helga's father.

Übung 9 | Minidialoge

Ergänzen Sie die Possessivpronomen.

1. FRAU SCHULZ: Wo sind _____ Hausaufgaben?
   PETER: Sie liegen leider zu Hause.
2. ONKEL: Ist das _____ᵃ Hund?
   NICHTE: Nein, das ist nicht _____ᵇ Hund. Ich habe keinen Hund.
3. LYDIA: He, Rosemarie! Das ist _____ᵃ Kleid.
   ROSEMARIE: Nein, das ist _____ᵇ Kleid. _____ᶜ Kleid ist schmutzig.
4. KATRIN: Woher kommen _____ᵃ Eltern, Frau Schulz?
   FRAU SCHULZ: _____ᵇ Mutter kommt aus Schwabing und _____ᶜ Vater kommt aus Germering.

Übung 10 | Woher kommen sie?

Üb. 10. Suitable for oral work in class or for a written homework assignment.

Beantworten Sie die Fragen.

1. Woher kommen Sie?
2. Woher kommt Ihre Mutter?
3. Woher kommt Ihr Vater?
4. Woher kommen Ihre Großeltern?
5. Woher kommt Ihr Professor / Ihre Professorin?
6. Wie heißt ein Student aus Ihrem Deutschkurs und woher kommt er?
7. Wie heißt eine Studentin aus Ihrem Deutschkurs und woher kommt sie?

Carl Spitzweg: *Der Bücherwurm* (1850), Museum
Georg Schäfer, Schweinfurt/Deutschland

CARL SPITZWEG

Carl Spitzweg (1808–1885) war ein sehr
volkstümlicher[1] deutscher Maler und
Autodidakt. Seine Bilder sind oft ironisch.
„Der Bücherwurm" ist ein gutes Beispiel[2] für
Spitzwegs humorvolle Perspektive.

[1]*popular* [2]*example*

KAPITEL **1**

Wer ich bin und was ich tue

In **Kapitel 1** you will learn to talk about how you spend your time: your studies, your recreational pursuits, and what you like and don't like to do.

Themen
Freizeit
Schule und Universität
Tagesablauf
Persönliche Daten

Kulturelles
Freizeit
Schule
Videoblick: Christkindl
Videoecke: Tagesablauf

Lektüren
Brief eines Internatsschülers
Guten Tag, ich heiße …

Strukturen

1.1 The present tense
1.2 Expressing likes and dislikes: **gern / nicht gern**
1.3 Telling time
1.4 Word order in statements
1.5 Separable-prefix verbs
1.6 Word order in questions

PRE-TEXT ACTIVITIES
Provide input by using yourself as a model: *Am Wochenende spiele ich oft Tennis. Ich spiele auch Karten mit meinem Freund Peter. Ich spiele gern Karten, aber Peter nicht. Er spielt gern Gitarre.* Mime the meaning of words sts. don't recognize. Make sure sts. understand the meaning of *gern: Ich tanze gern. Tanzen Sie gern, Melanie? (Nein.) Melanie tanzt nicht gern. (Ja.) Monika tanzt gern. usw.*

Review the present-tense forms that were introduced in the preliminary chapters with *sein, haben, heißen,* and *kommen.* In *Kapitel 1* the sts. need to understand and use many more present-tense forms. Note that regular present-tense forms are introduced in grammar Section 1.1, and verbs with separable prefixes and associated nouns in 1.5. It is unlikely, however, that you will be able to maintain this neat separation of categories within an activity when the focus is on meaning. Most sts. have no trouble with present-tense endings in German and quickly become accustomed to the variation of verb forms owing to person-number agreement. However, for those sts. with no prior foreign language experience, the concept of verb endings may take some time to grasp. In any case, sts. will not be able to use verb forms easily until they have had multiple opportunities to hear them used in communicative contexts.

GOALS
This chapter extends sts.' listening and speaking skills to exchange personal information. Sts. will continue to respond with single words, but short phrases will become increasingly common in their speech, and they will use more complete sentences in guided activities. They will learn to recognize and understand the various forms of the present tense, including verbs with separable prefixes.

Situationen

Vocabulary Display
First state the infinitive of each activity, then read the sentences and have sts. repeat: *wandern – Peter und Stefan wandern gern usw.* After pronouncing each activity, do an association activity. (See the IM for suggestions on using association activities in Stage III.) *Peter und Stefan wandern gern. Wer von Ihnen wandert gern? Heben Sie bitte die Hand.* Associate one st. with each activity. *Lisa wandert gern usw.* After going through all the activities, see if sts. can remember the names matched with each hobby: *Wer wandert gern? (Lisa.)* Then ask students to produce the sentences by asking: *Was macht Lisa gern? (Sie wandert gern.) usw.*

Grammatik 1.1–1.2

Peter und Stefan wandern gern.

Ernst spielt gern Fußball.

Jutta und Gabi spielen gern Karten.

Melanie tanzt gern.

Michael spielt gern Gitarre.

Veronika reitet gern.

Thomas segelt gern.

Herr und Frau Ruf gehen gern spazieren.

Situation 1 | Hobbys

Sit. 1. Preparation. Read through the situation. Ask sts. to repeat each line after you. Act out words unfamiliar to them, if they cannot guess (*reisen, kochen, reiten*). Next, sts. should individually read the exercise and write *ja* or *nein* next to every line as it applies to them. You then ask: *Was machen Sie gern in den Ferien? Wer von Ihnen reist gern? Heben Sie bitte die Hand! usw.* For items 3 and 4 ask: *Wessen Eltern ...?* and *Wessen Bruder oder Schwester ...?* (Most students will probably understand *wessen* immediately from context.) For 5 ask: *Was mache ich gern? Was glauben Sie?*

AA. *Sit. 1* can also be done as *Partnerarbeit*, where sts. ask each other what they or their families like to do. On an overhead or on the board, write appropriate questions for the responses in 1-5: **(1)** *Was machst du gern in den Ferien?* **(2)** *Was machst du gern im Winter?* **(3)** *Was machen deine Eltern gern?* **(4)** *Hast du einen Bruder? (Ja/Nein.) eine Schwester? (Ja/Nein.) Was macht er/sie gern?* **(5)** *Was macht unser Deutschlehrer / unsere Deutschlehrerin gern?* Model pronunciation and ask sts. to repeat. As they do so, answer the question for yourself. Then, have students work in pairs. 1 asks the questions, and 2 answers while 1 takes notes; then they switch.

Sagen Sie **ja** oder **nein**.

1. In den Ferien ...
   a. reise ich gern.
   b. koche ich gern.
   c. spiele ich gern Volleyball.
   d. arbeite ich gern.

2. Im Winter ...
   a. gehe ich gern ins Museum.
   b. spiele ich gern Karten.
   c. gehe ich gern Schlitten fahren.
   d. schwimme ich gern.

3. Meine Eltern ...
   a. spielen gern Tennis.
   b. spielen gern Golf.
   c. gehen gern ins Kino.
   d. singen gern.

4. Mein Bruder / Meine Schwester ...
   a. wandert gern in den Bergen.
   b. zeltet gern.
   c. boxt gern.
   d. spielt gern Gitarre.

5. Mein Deutschlehrer / Meine Deutschlehrerin ...
   a. geht gern auf Partys.
   b. reitet gern.
   c. geht gern ins Konzert.
   d. spielt gern Fußball.

Situation 2 | Informationsspiel: Freizeit

AA. Have sts. guess whether these statements are true for their instructor: *In meiner Freizeit schwimme ich gern; gehe ich ins Kino; telefoniere ich gern; koche ich gern; arbeite ich für die Uni; spiele ich Fußball; boxe ich gern usw.*

Sit. 2. This is one in the series of information-gap activities. (See the IM.) Model questions and answers are given. The corresponding chart is in Appendix A. To start the activity, sts. pair off by counting 1, 2, 1, 2, etc. All twos turn to the appendix, and all ones work with the section in the chapter. Remind sts. not to show their half of the activity to their partners. After 1 has completed the table, 2 then asks questions to elicit the information needed to fill in the table in the appendix. If sts. prefer, 1 can fill half the chart and then let 2 ask questions, then switch again to finish the task. Or else they can simply alternate asking questions for each person listed:
s1: *Wie alt ist Rolf?*
s2: *20. Wie alt ist Richard?*
s1: *18. Was macht Richard gern?*
s2: *Er geht gern in die Berge. Woher kommt Rolf? usw.*
One way to personalize this activity and recycle the vocabulary a few days later is to collect the same information presented in the chart from the sts. in the class. Ask each of them to hand in a slip of paper with their name, age, where they are from, and what they like to do, and then make up your own 2-part chart. Use this personalized *Informationsspiel* as a warm-up activity. Sts. will enjoy speaking about themselves and will learn more about each other.

MODELL s1: Wie alt ist Rolf?
s2: __20__.
s1: Woher kommt Richard?
s2: Aus __Innsbruck__.
s1: Was macht Richard gern?
s2: Er __geht gern in die Berge__.
s1: Wie alt bist du?
s2: _____.
s1: Woher kommst du?
s2: _____.
s1: Was machst du gern?
s2: _____.

	Alter	Wohnort	Hobby
Richard	18	Innsbruck	geht gern in die Berge
Rolf	20	Berkeley	spielt gern Tennis
Jürgen	21	Göttingen	geht gern tanzen
Sofie	22	Dresden	kocht gern
Jutta	16	München	hört gern Musik
Melanie	25	Regensburg	besucht gern Freunde
mein Partner / meine Partnerin			

Situation 3 | Interview: Was machst du gern?

MODELL: S1: Ich spiele gern Karten. Du auch?
S2: Ja, ich spiele auch gern Karten.
Nein, ich spiele nicht gern Karten.

1. Ich spiele gern Schach.
2. Ich wandere gern.
3. Ich gehe gern spazieren.
4. Ich reite gern.
5. Ich singe gern.
6. Ich spiele gern Volleyball.
7. Ich höre gern Musik.
8. Ich koche gern.
9. Ich tanze gern.
10. Ich lerne gern Deutsch.

Kultur ... Landeskunde ... Informationen

Freizeit

- Was machen Menschen in Ihrem Land in ihrer Freizeit?
- Was machen Sie in Ihrer Freizeit? am Wochenende? abends? in den Ferien?
- Was machen Ihre Eltern in ihrer Freizeit? am Wochenende? abends? in den Ferien?
- Wie viele Stunden Freizeit haben Sie am Tag?
- Sehen Sie sich die Grafik an. Was machen Deutsche öfter[1] als Sie? Was machen sie weniger[2] oft als Sie?
- Wie viele Stunden Freizeit haben Deutsche am Tag? Raten[3] Sie!

Die häufigsten Freizeitbeschäftigungen der Deutschen

täglich, in Prozent

Fernsehen	Entspannen[4]	Lesen	im Internet surfen	mit dem Hund rausgehen	Freunde treffen	Sport treiben	Gartenarbeit
74	46	38	14	14	6	6	6

[1]*more often* [2]*less* [3]*Guess* [4]*relaxing*

Situation 4 | Umfrage

Sit. 4. This is an autograph activity. (See the IM for suggestions on the use of autograph activities.) Sts. move around the classroom and try to find someone who can answer *ja* to a question in the activity. 1 asks 2 a question, and if 2 answers *ja*, he/she signs the line next to that activity. Once 2 answers *ja*, 1 moves on and asks a different person the next question. If 2 answers *nein*, 1 can then ask another question. Sts. try to get as many signatures as possible within a certain time limit, perhaps 5 minutes. The person who gets the most signatures wins.
Follow-up. Ask sts. about their responses. *Wer spielt gern Gitarre? Wer schwimmt gern?* Then address the person identified and ask for confirmation. *Schwimmen Sie gern, Katy?*

MODELL: S1: Schwimmst du gern im Meer?
 S2: Ja.
 S1: Unterschreib bitte hier.

UNTERSCHRIFT

1. Schwimmst du gern im Schwimmbad? _____
2. Trinkst du gern Kaffee? _____
3. Spielst du gern Gitarre? _____
4. Hörst du gern Musik? _____
5. Gehst du gern zelten? _____
6. Arbeitest du gern? _____
7. Gehst du gern joggen? _____
8. Tanzt du gern? _____
9. Spielst du gern Golf? _____
10. Machst du gern Fotos? _____

Schule und Universität

Grammatik 1.3

Vocabulary Display
Pronounce the subjects with the appropriate definite article and have sts. repeat. Sts. will have little difficulty understanding the subjects, but pronunciation may be a problem. Have sts. repeat in chorus. Then associate each subject with a st. *Wer studiert Kunst?* If no one studies a particular subject, make up a person's name and write it on the board (without a subject) and say *Michael studiert Kunst.* Go through all the subjects. Then go through the names asking: *Was studiert Michael?* (*Er studiert Kunst.*) You may wish to point out that all the subjects in this display are feminine, except for *der Sport* and *der Maschinenbau.*

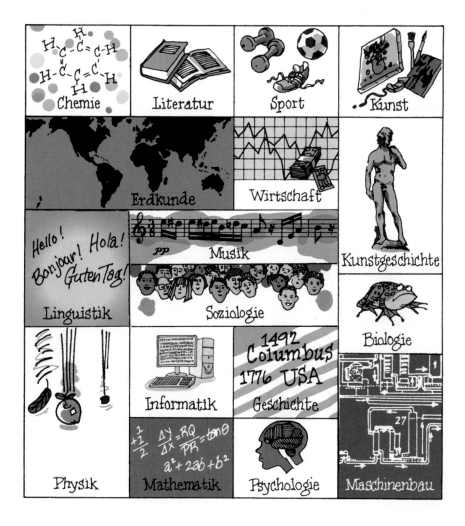

Situation 5 | Dialog: Was studierst du?

Sit. 5. (See the IM.) Set the scene and introduce the characters. Work either with sts.' books open or closed. With books closed, ask the following focus questions: **1.** *Woher kommt Rolf?* **2.** *Was macht er in den USA?* **3.** *Was studiert Stefan?* At the end, have sts. work in pairs to produce a similar dialogue.

Stefan trifft Rolf in der Cafeteria der Universität Berkeley.

STEFAN: Hallo, bist du __neu__ hier?

ROLF: Ja, ich __komme__ aus Deutschland.

STEFAN: Und was machst __du__ hier?

ROLF: Ich __studiere__ Psychologie. Und du?

STEFAN: __Chemie__.

Situation 6 | Wie spät ist es?

Sit. 6. Present ways to tell time using the overhead projector or a toy clock before doing the activity in class. Enliven your presentation and recycle verbs with commentary: *Es ist acht Uhr. Um acht Uhr gehe ich zur Uni. usw.*

AA. Point out the time difference between Germany and your time zone and ask sts. to calculate the current time in Germany.

Cultural note (Sit. 7.) Although this chart still represents a typical *Gymnasium* schedule for 5th to 10th grade, including breaks and regular school hours, several reforms induced by the poor results of the PISA study have brought about changes in the traditional structure of German schools. In many German states, sts. at the *Gymnasium* now graduate after 12 years instead of 13. Afternoon classes are also becoming more common. What has stayed the same is that two foreign languages are mandatory, besides German and math (*Lang-* or *Hauptfächer,* usually 4 periods per week). *Kurz-* or *Nebenfächer* such as history, biology, and physics are taught twice a week. Every student in a given grade takes the same courses.

S1: Wie spät ist es?

S2: Es ist _____.

1.   2.   3.   4.   5.

6.   7.   8.   9.   10.

Situation 7 | Informationsspiel: Juttas Stundenplan

Sit. 7. (See the IM.) Introduce days of the week and, if necessary, review the pronunciation of the academic subjects, before doing the activity. Model the question before having sts. work in pairs. The corresponding chart is in Appendix A.

MODELL S1: Was hat Jutta am Montag um acht Uhr?

S2: Sie hat Latein.

Uhr	Montag	Dienstag	Mittwoch	Donnerstag	Freitag
8.00–8.45	Latein	Mathematik	Deutsch	Biologie	Französisch
8.50–9.35	Deutsch	Englisch	Englisch	Latein	Physik
9.35–9.50	←		Pause		→
9.50–10.35	Biologie	Sozialkunde	Mathematik	Geschichte	Religion
10.40–11.25	Geschichte	Französisch	Physik	Mathematik	Deutsch
11.25–11.35	←		Pause		→
11.35–12.20	Sport	Musik	Erdkunde	Sport	Latein
12.25–13.10	Erdkunde	Deutsch	Kunst	Sozialkunde	frei

Kultur ... Landeskunde ... Informationen

Schule

- Wann beginnt in Ihrem Land morgens die Schule?
- Wann gehen die Schüler nach Hause?
- Wann und wo machen sie Hausaufgaben?
- Wann haben sie Freizeit?
- Welche Schulfächer haben Schüler?
- Welches sind Pflichtfächer[1]?
- An welchen Tagen gehen die Schüler in die Schule?

Schauen Sie auf Juttas Stundenplan (Situation 7).

- Wann beginnt für Jutta die Schule?
- Wann geht sie nach Hause?
- Welche Fächer hat Jutta?
- Wie viele Fremdsprachen hat sie?
- An welchen Tagen geht sie in die Schule?

Was meinen Sie?

- Wann und wo macht Jutta Hausaufgaben?
- Wann hat sie Freizeit?

KLI. (See also the IE notes for *Sit. 7.*) Ask sts., in small groups, to complete the first 7 questions about their own schools. Write the results in 1 column on the board. Then ask sts. to analyze the chart in *Sit. 7* (second set of questions) and write the results in a second column on the board.

Cultural note. Point out that while the word "student" is used for both school and university students in English, in German a distinction is made between *Schüler/in* (*Grundschule* [elementary school] through *Gymnasium*) and *Student/in* (university only).

Photo questions. *Wer sind diese Leute? Was machen sie? Wie alt sind sie? Was fragen sie? Welche Jahreszeit ist es?*

[1] *required subjects*

Große Pause an einem Gymnasium in Berlin

Situation 8 | Interview

Sit. 8. Model pronunciation and have sts. repeat. Have sts. guess the meaning of new expressions in context (*erster Kurs, nach Hause, ins Bett*). Ask sts. to think briefly about their answers and jot them down. Or else sts. could quickly draw their schedule in a manner similar to Jutta's. They then find partners, and 1 asks the questions while 2 answers. 1 records 2's responses. Afterward, ask sts. to mention 3 things they learned from their partners.

1. Welche Fächer hast du in diesem Semester? Welche Fächer magst du? Welche Fächer magst du nicht?
2. Wann beginnt am Montag dein erster (1.) Kurs? Welcher Kurs ist das? Wann gehst du am Montag nach Hause?
3. Wann beginnt am Dienstag dein erster Kurs? Welcher Kurs ist das? Wann gehst du am Dienstag nach Hause?
4. Arbeitest du? An welchen Tagen arbeitest du? Wann beginnt deine Arbeit?
5. Wann gehst du in der Woche ins Bett? Und am Wochenende?

Information. The study of foreign languages plays a major role in Germany. In most German states, sts. now start learning their first mandatory foreign language, usually English, in elementary school. All sts. study a foreign language for at least 5 years. At the *Gymnasium*, sts. must take at least 7 years of one foreign language and 5 years of a second foreign language, sometimes even a third. While Germany still has no official *Ganztagsschule*, afternoon classes are becoming more widespread at the secondary level. Sts. are expected to spend considerable time every day completing their homework at home.

Tagesablauf

Grammatik 1.4–1.5

Herr Wagner steht auf.

Er duscht.

Er frühstückt.

Er geht zur Arbeit.

Er geht einkaufen.

Er räumt die Wohnung auf.

Er geht im Park spazieren.

Er geht ins Bett.

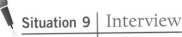

Situation 9 | Interview

1. Wann stehst du auf?
2. Wann duschst du?
3. Wann frühstückst du?
4. Wann gehst du zur Uni?
5. Wann kommst du nach Hause?
6. Wann machst du das Abendessen?
7. Wann gehst du ins Bett?

Situation 10 | Am Wochenende

Sit. 10. Pre-teach any unfamiliar vocabulary. Ask sts. to record answers for themselves using S, W, or V. After they have finished for themselves, have them compare their results with a partner: *Ich spiele sicher Computerspiele. Spielst du am Wochenende Computerspiele?* and record the partner's answers.

Was machen Sie am Wochenende sicher, wahrscheinlich, vielleicht?

S = sicher
W = wahrscheinlich
V = vielleicht

	ICH	PARTNER/PARTNERIN
1. Ich spiele Computerspiele.	_____	_____
2. Ich stehe spät auf.	_____	_____
3. Ich kaufe ein.	_____	_____
4. Ich lese eine Zeitung oder ein Buch.	_____	_____
5. Ich singe im Chor.	_____	_____
6. Ich höre Musik.	_____	_____
7. Ich arbeite fürs Studium.	_____	_____
8. Ich rufe Freunde oder meine Familie an.	_____	_____
9. Ich räume mein Zimmer oder meine Wohnung auf.	_____	_____
10. Ich gehe mit Freunden aus.	_____	_____
11. Ich gehe ins Kino.	_____	_____
12. Ich jobbe.	_____	_____

Situation 11 | Bildgeschichte: Ein Tag in Sofies Leben

Sit. 11. This is the first "narration series," a set of sketches that form a connected narrative. These series are included to give sts. a chance to hear and use verb forms and tenses and to practice narration in past, present, and future. Use the same approach as with the vocabulary displays, followed by an oral or written practice of narration. In this situation sts. practice separable-prefix verbs in a meaningful context. Note: Narration series are also on tape in the laboratory program. **Presentation** (transparency on overhead): *Das ist Sofie. Was macht Sofie an einem normalen Tag? Bild 1. Sofie steht um sieben Uhr auf. 2. Sie duscht. 3. Sie frühstückt. 4. Sie packt ihre Bücher ein. 5. Sie geht zur Uni. 6. Sie füllt ein Formular aus. 7. Sie geht zur Post. 8. Sie holt ein Paket ab. 9. Sie geht nach Hause. 10. Sie ruft ihre Freundin an. 11. Sie gehen zusammen aus.* **Receptive recall** (random order): *Welches Bild zeigt „Sofie geht zur Uni?"* (*Bild 5.*) *usw.* **Choral response.** **Productive recall** (normal sequence): *Was macht Sofie in Bild 1? usw.* **Personalization:** *Schreiben Sie auf, was auch Sie an einem ganz normalen Tag machen.* **Focus on narration:** Ask sts. to write down the sentences from memory (with the help of the drawings). Put sts. in groups of 3 to proofread one another's writing. Follow up by writing the story on the board, according to your students' dictation.

Situation 12 | Informationsspiel: Diese Woche

Sit. 12. (See the IM.) The corresponding chart is in Appendix A.

MODELL S1: Was macht Silvia am Montag?
S2: Sie steht um 6 Uhr auf.
S1: Was machst du am Montag?
S2: Ich _____.

	Silvia Mertens	Mehmet Sengün	mein(e) Partner(in)
Montag	Sie steht um 6 Uhr auf.	Er geht um 7 Uhr zur Arbeit.	
Dienstag	Sie arbeitet am Abend in einer Kneipe.	Er lernt eine neue Kollegin kennen.	
Mittwoch	Sie schreibt eine Prüfung.	Er singt im Männerchor.	
Donnerstag	Sie ruft ihre Eltern an.	Er geht einkaufen.	
Freitag	Sie geht tanzen.	Er hört um 15 Uhr mit der Arbeit auf.	
Samstag	Sie geht mit Freunden ins Kino.	Er räumt seine Wohnung auf.	
Sonntag	Sie besucht ihre Eltern.	Er repariert sein Motorrad.	

Lektüre

Lektüre. The reading in each *Lektüre* section is introduced by a variety of reading strategies and exercises. (See the IM for more on reading.) The most important strategies are explained in detail when they are first introduced. In later chapters, the skills are just practiced. Besides global strategies such as anticipating content, sts. are introduced to specific foreign-language reading skills such as contextual guessing or recognizing cognates and compounds. This reading is a letter that a boarding-school student writes to a friend about his daily routine at the school. **(1)** Establish the context by asking 2 or 3 sts. about their daily routines during the school week. Use questions like: *Wann stehen Sie während der Woche auf? Wann frühstücken Sie? Wann beginnt der Unterricht an der Uni? Wann machen Sie Mittagspause?* etc. **(2)** Focus sts.' attention on the *Lesehilfe* box next to the reading so that they have a feel for the text type. Then let sts. read *Vor dem Lesen* Part A and work on questions 1 through 7 with a partner while jotting down their answers. Wrap up by briefly discussing their answers. **(3)** Ask sts. to read through the text before they work on *Vor dem Lesen* Part B individually. Do a wrap-up on the board by sorting the words that they find into two lists: 1) words that are actually English, and 2) words that are cognates. **(4)** Explain *Arbeit mit dem Text* Part A and demonstrate the task in class. Ask sts. to read the sentence in line 7 and then guess what *von ... bis* means in this context. Proceed similarly with *Morgentoilette*. Let sts. read lines 4 and 5. Then you might want to help the guessing along by miming that you comb your hair, wash your face, and so forth. Assign the rest of the task and Part B of *Arbeit mit dem Text* as homework. Emphasize that sts. need to read the text at least one more time before they start on Part B. **(5)** Part C of *Arbeit mit dem Text* lends itself to groupwork in class after Part B has been completed. Explain the task, then ask sts. to work in groups of 2 or 3 and determine on what information from the text they base their inferences. Do a quick wrap-up in class before you assign *Nach dem Lesen* as homework.

Vor dem Lesen

A. Think back to when you were in the ninth grade and answer the following questions.

Welchen Tagesablauf haben Schüler in Ihrem Land in der 9. Klasse?

1. Wann stehen die Schüler und Schülerinnen während der Woche auf?
2. Wann frühstücken sie?
3. Wann beginnt der Unterricht?
4. Wann ist Mittagspause?
5. Wann ist der Unterricht zu Ende?
6. Wann essen die Schüler und Schülerinnen zu Abend?
7. Wann gehen sie ins Bett?

B. In the following text, underline the words that are English or that seem to be closely related to English. If you are unsure about a word that looks similar to an English word, look it up in the glossary in the appendices of this book. Then write it in the margin of the text next to the German word.

Before reading this text, look at its structure. Judging from the salutation at the beginning **(Liebe Ana)** and the greeting at the end **(Bis bald und alles Liebe Dein Felix)** you might guess that it is a letter. It is written by Felix to his friend Ana. Felix is a ninth-grade student at an **Internat** (boarding school). Apparently Ana has asked Felix what his day looks like, and he is telling her that in his letter.

Liebe Ana,

du hast mich in deinem letzten Brief nach meinem Tagesablauf gefragt. Er ist wahrscheinlich[1] auch nicht viel anders[2] als bei euch. Wir stehen während der Woche morgens sehr früh auf,
5 nämlich um 6 Uhr 55. Dann machen wir unsere Morgentoilette. Um 7 Uhr 20 versammeln wir uns zu einem kurzen Morgengebet[3].

Von 7 Uhr 20 bis 7 Uhr 40 haben wir Zeit zum Frühstücken. Ich bin meistens schon nach 10 Minuten fertig[4], weil[5] ich so früh noch gar keinen Hunger habe. Ich trinke nur eine Tasse Kakao
10 und esse ein Brötchen oder vielleicht nur ein halbes mit Marmelade. Danach gehen wir zum Unterricht. Der Unterricht beginnt bei uns um 7 Uhr 55. Immer nach zwei Schulstunden haben wir eine Pause. Nach der sechsten Stunde gibt es Mittagessen.

15 Das Mittagessen dauert von 13 Uhr 10 bis 13 Uhr 40. Bis 15 Uhr 30 haben wir dann Freizeit. Manche üben Klavier[6], treiben Sport, lesen, hören Musik oder verbringen[7] die Zeit mit ihren Freunden. Fernsehen dürfen[8] wir nicht. Um 15 Uhr 30 gibt es Tee und Kuchen. Ab 16 Uhr ist „Silentium". So nennen wir die Zeit, in
20 der wir unsere Hausaufgaben machen. Sie heißt Silentium, weil keine lauten Aktivitäten erlaubt sind, damit[9] wir ungestört unsere Hausaufgaben machen können. Wer[10] früher fertig ist, kann lesen oder mit Kopfhörer Musik hören, aber nicht laut.

Um 18 Uhr gibt es Abendessen und danach ist Abendfreizeit. Im
25 Sommer spielen wir oft Fußball oder fahren Inliner oder mit dem Skateboard. Im Winter spielen wir Brettspiele[11] oder am Computer, schreiben Briefe so wie ich gerade oder sehen fern. Um 21 Uhr müssen wir in unsere Zimmer und um 21 Uhr 30 müssen wir das Licht ausmachen[12]. Am Wochenende dürfen wir eine Stunde
30 länger aufbleiben.

So, jetzt müssen wir in unsere Zimmer. Ich schreibe morgen weiter.

Bis bald und alles Liebe

Dein Felix

Arbeit mit dem Text

A. You can guess the meaning of many words from context. Guessing from context is a very useful skill, especially when reading. Try to guess the meaning of the following words by looking at the sentences in which they appear. Some hints are provided.

1. **Morgentoilette** (line 5) HINT: the first things you do after getting up to get ready for the day
2. **von ... bis** (line 7) HINT: used to express time periods
3. **meistens** (line 8) HINT: used to express frequencies; related to English "most"
4. **Brötchen** (line 10) HINT: something to eat for breakfast on which you may put jam

---

[1]*probably* [2]*different* [3]*das Gebet prayer* [4]*finished* [5]*because* [6]*piano* [7]*pass* [8]*are allowed* [9]*so that*
[10]*Whoever* [11]*board games* [12]*das ... turn off the light*

5. **Mittagessen** (line 14) HINT: what you eat after six hours of school
6. **üben** (line 16) HINT: what you do with a piano to improve proficiency
7. **ungestört** (line 21) HINT: The reason for the silence is so that students may work _____; notice the prefix **un-**.
8. **Kopfhörer** (line 23) HINT: gadget that fits on your head for listening to music
9. **ausmachen** (line 29) HINT: what you do to the lights when you go to bed

B. What is Felix's day like? What does he do, and when? Read the text and match the activity to the time.

Was macht Felix wann?

1. __h__ 6.55 Uhr
2. __a__ 7.20 Uhr
3. __i__ 7.20–7.40 Uhr
4. __c__ 7.55 Uhr
5. __j__ 13.10–13.40 Uhr
6. __f__ 13.40–15.30 Uhr
7. __b__ 15.30 Uhr
8. __e__ 16.00–18.00 Uhr
9. __g__ 18.00–21.00 Uhr
10. __d__ 21.30 Uhr

a. Er macht sein Morgengebet.
b. Es gibt Tee und Kuchen.
c. Der Unterricht beginnt.
d. Er macht das Licht aus.
e. Silentium: er macht Hausaufgaben.
f. Er hat Freizeit.
g. Es gibt Abendessen und dann ist Abendfreizeit.
h. Er steht auf.
i. Er frühstückt.
j. Er isst zu Mittag.

C. **Zwischen den Zeilen lesen.**[1] When reading and listening, we usually understand more than what is being said. We come to conclusions based on particular information or indications. When we do this we are drawing inferences. What are possible answers to the following questions? On what information from the text do you base your inferences?

Was glauben Sie? Was steht im Text dazu?

1. Auf welche Art[2] von Internat geht Felix?
2. Wann schreibt er den Brief?
3. Wer ist Ana?

Nach dem Lesen

Schreiben Sie einem Klassenkameraden einen Brief auf Deutsch über Ihren Tagesablauf. Schreiben Sie ca. 100 Wörter. Vergessen Sie nicht die Anrede[3] und den Abschiedsgruß.

Liebe Ana / Lieber Felix
...
Viele Grüße / Herzliche Grüße / Alles Liebe
Deine Ana / Dein Felix

---

[1]Zwischen ... *Reading between the lines.* [2]welche ... *what kind* [3]*salutation*

Persönliche Daten

Grammatik 1.6

Vocabulary Display
The goal of this section is to introduce question forms. Ask sts. to scan the ID application form. Reassure them that they need not understand every word. They should try to figure out the meanings of the technical words from context. Ask questions such as: *Wie heißt die Frau? Wo wohnt sie? Welche Farbe haben ihre Augen? Wie groß ist sie? Wie alt ist sie? Wann ist sie geboren? Wo ist sie geboren?* Write questions on the board, and have sts. repeat them. Now personalize by asking similar questions: *Wo wohnen Sie? und Ihre Familie? Wo sind Sie geboren? usw.* Use an association activity to review sts.' answers: *Wo wohnt Claudia? Wie alt ist sie? usw.* If sts. seem ready to produce a few questions themselves, have them ask you your name, age, etc.

Antrag auf Ausstellung eines Personalausweises

Familienname: Ruf

geborene(r): Schuler

Vornamen: Margret

Geburtstag: 13. April 1969

Geburtsort: Augsburg

Staatsangehörigkeit: deutsch

Augenfarbe: blau, grau, (grün), braun   Größe 172 cm

München   Sonnenstr.   11
           Straße   Hausnummer

München, den 30.5.2008

Margret Ruf
Unterschrift des Antragstellers

Situation 13 | Dialog: Auf dem Rathaus

Sit. 13. (See the IM.) This dialogue provides a model for the interview that follows it. We suggest moving from comprehension to production via a series of steps. The following steps are intended for use with the textbooks closed. **(1)** Set the scene: *Melanie braucht einen neuen Personalausweis* (show picture of a *Personalausweis*). *Sie wohnt in Regensburg. Also geht sie auf das Rathaus in Regensburg* (show picture of a *Rathaus*). *Sie spricht mit einem Beamten.* **(2)** Ask focus questions: *Wie heißt Melanie mit Nachnamen? Was ist ihre Adresse? Was ist ihre Telefonnummer? Was ist sie von Beruf? Ist sie verheiratet?* **(3)** Play the dialogue. **(4)** Review sts.' answers. **(5)** Ask sts. to count the words in each sentence. **(6)** Divide sts. into two groups, assign one role to each group, and ask each group to repeat their lines. **(7)** Ask groups to repeat their lines from memory. To help sts. remember, write the first word or words of each question on the board. **(8)** Ask 2-3 pairs of volunteers (1 from each group) to present the dialogue in front of the class. Instead of assuming their previous roles, however, they should change the lines of the dialogue to talk about themselves. **(9)** Sts. get up and work in pairs. While moving from one person to the next, they act out their personalized versions several times.

Cultural note. In German-speaking countries, you are required to register with the local town administration when you take residence somewhere *(einen Wohnsitz anmelden)*. You must also inform them whenever you move *(ummelden/abmelden)* so that the government always has your current address. The *Einwohnermeldeamt,* or an administrative subdivision, also issues passports and ID cards.

Melanie Staiger ist auf dem Rathaus in Regensburg. Sie braucht einen neuen Personalausweis.

BEAMTER: Grüß Gott!

MELANIE: Grüß Gott. Ich brauche einen neuen Personalausweis.

BEAMTER: _Wie_ ist Ihr Name, bitte?

MELANIE: Staiger, Melanie Staiger.

BEAMTER: Und _wo_ wohnen Sie?

MELANIE: In Regensburg.

BEAMTER: _Was_ ist die genaue Adresse?

MELANIE: Gesandtenstraße 8.

BEAMTER: Haben Sie auch _Telefon_?

MELANIE: Ja, die Nummer ist 24352.

BEAMTER: _Wann_ sind Sie geboren?

MELANIE: Am 3. _April_ 1984.

BEAMTER: Was sind Sie _von Beruf_?

MELANIE: Ich bin Studentin.

BEAMTER: Sind Sie verheiratet?

MELANIE: _Nein_. Ich bin ledig.

Videoblick

Christkindl

In Süddeutschland und in Österreich bringt das Christkindl am Heiligen Abend die Geschenke. Viele Städte haben einen Christkindlmarkt[1]. Einer der bekanntesten Christkindlmärkte ist in Nürnberg. In diesem Video lernen Sie das Nürnberger Christkindl kennen.

- Wer spielt die Rolle des Nürnberger Christkindls?
- Wie alt ist diese Person?
- Was für Fragen stellen ihr die Kinder?
- Was sind ihre Hobbys?

Videoblick. The video segment focuses on holiday traditions, particularly on the Southern German and Austrian tradition of the Christ child and on various regional Easter traditions. The clip on the Christ child features views of the Christkindlmarkt in Nürnberg, one of the most famous Christmas markets in the world.

[1]Christmas market

Was braucht das Nürnberger Christkindl am dringendsten? Jawohl, warme Schuhe und gute Nerven.

Situation 14 | Interview: Auf dem Rathaus

Sit. 14. (See cultural note under *Sit. 13.*) Have sts. work in pairs. 2's book should be closed, and 1 should write down the information as 2 answers. Sts. might also need to ask: *Wie schreibt man Ihren Namen? Wie, bitte? usw.*

1. Wie heißen Sie?
2. Wie alt sind Sie?
3. Wo sind Sie geboren?
4. Wo wohnen Sie?
5. Was ist Ihre genaue Adresse?
6. Was ist Ihre Telefonnummer?
7. Was studieren Sie?
8. Sind Sie verheiratet?
9. Welche Augenfarbe haben Sie?
10. Welche Haarfarbe?

Situation 15 | Rollenspiel: Auf dem Auslandsamt

Sit. 15. *Rollenspiel.* This is one of many role-plays in *Kontakte*. (See the IM.) The role for student 1 (s1) appears here, the role for student 2 (s2) appears in Appendix B. **(1)** Set the scene as described in the role for s1. **(2)** Provide sts. with a model by working with the enactment of the role-play found in the workbook/lab manual. **(3)** Write the structure of the role-play on the board: *begrüßen; fragen und antworten; bedanken und verabschieden.* **(4)** Elicit possible greetings, questions, and how to say good-bye from sts. and write on board. Ask for appropriate responses to the greeting and leave-taking and for possible answers to the questions, and write them on the board as well. **(5)** Divide the class into 2 groups and assign 1 part of the role-play to each group. Ask sts. to practice the role-play in pairs. **(6)** Ask 2-3 pairs of sts. to perform their role-play in class. Provide feedback as to appropriateness and accuracy of language used, after sts. have returned to their seats. The intention here is not to correct all or even most mistakes but rather to focus on a few phrases and sentences that are the most useful for all or most sts. in the context of this role-play. **(7)** Ask sts. to find new partners and to practice the role-play in pairs again. **(8)** Optional homework assignment: Ask sts. to write up their version of the role-play.

s1: Sie sind Student/Studentin und möchten ein Jahr lang in Österreich studieren. Gehen Sie aufs Auslandsamt und sagen Sie, dass Sie ein Stipendium möchten. Beantworten Sie die Fragen des Beamten / der Beamtin. Sagen Sie am Ende des Gesprächs „Auf Wiedersehen".

Das Regensburger Rathaus

Sit. 16. Preview *Nützliche Wörter* and the information missing in the poster. Ask sts. to guess what the missing information might be. Write guesses on the board. Ask sts. to work in pairs. Read or play the complete text at least twice. Ask sts. to correct their guesses on the board. Read or play one last time asking sts. to knock on the table when they hear the following words: *Spitzname, Vollbart, Sonnenbrille, Narbe, Halstuch.* **Text for listening comprehension:** *Gesucht wird der Bankräuber Paul Steckel, bekannt unter dem Spitznamen Narben-Paule. Er ist 35 Jahre alt, sieht aber älter aus. Seine Haare sind mittelblond, zuletzt hatte er einen Vollbart. Seine Augen sind graublau. Er trägt oft eine Sonnenbrille. Besonderes Kennzeichen ist eine circa drei Zentimeter lange Narbe unter dem rechten Auge. Steckel ist einen Meter fünfundachtzig groß, schlank und spricht mit Berliner Akzent. Meistens trägt er eine schwarze Jeansjacke und Cowboystiefel, dazu ein Halstuch. Vorsicht, er ist bewaffnet!*

Schreiben Sie die fehlenden Angaben[2] in den Steckbrief.

NÜTZLICHE WÖRTER

der Bankräuber	*bank robber*
der Spitzname	*nickname*
besonderes Kennzeichen	*distinguishing feature*
die Narbe	*scar*
das Halstuch	*bandanna*
bewaffnet	*armed*

GESUCHT

Paul Steckel

Spitzname: _____-Paule

Alter: _____ Jahre, sieht älter aus

Haarfarbe: mittel_____, Voll_____

_____: graublau

Besonderes Kennzeichen: _____

unter dem rechten _____

Größe: _____ cm, schlank

Akzent: _____

Kleidung: meistens _____ Jeansjacke

und _____, dazu ein _____

[1]*Wanted* [2]*information*

Lektüre 📖

Lesehilfe

In this reading, several of the characters of ***Kontakte*** are introduced. Before reading, look at each of the pictures and say as much as you can about the characters, based on the drawings. Now read the text once through. How closely do the pictures reflect what is in the text?

Lektüre. This reading consists of three short first-person introductions of three of the characters in *Kontakte*.
(1) Establish the context, e.g., by asking 2–3 students to say as much about themselves as they can.
(2) Explain the prereading task, allow your students about one minute to complete the task, and discuss their answers briefly. Ask: *Welche Informationen geben Sie, wenn Sie sich vorstellen? Sagen Sie ja oder nein,* and read all options one by one.

Vor dem Lesen

Welche Informationen geben Sie, wenn Sie sich vorstellen[1]? Kreuzen Sie an.

☐ Name
☐ Alter
☐ Beruf/Studienfach
☐ Familie
☐ Freunde
☐ Geburtsdatum

☐ Gewicht[2]
☐ Hobbys
☐ Herkunft
☐ Schulnoten[3]
☐ Interessen
☐ Adresse

Miniwörterbuch	
das **Fahrrad**	bicycle
die **Gärtnerei**	nursery (gardening)
der **Geschäftsmann**	businessman
der **Lastwagen**	truck
der **Ort**	town
seit	for
die **Sozialkunde**	social studies
die **Speditionsfirma**	trucking company
unterrichten	to teach
unterwegs	on the road

Guten Tag, ich heiße …

Guten Tag, ich heiße Veronika Frisch. Ich bin verheiratet und habe drei Töchter. Sie heißen Natalie, Rosemarie und Lydia. Ich lebe mit meinem Mann Bernd und unseren Töchtern in der Schweiz. Wir wohnen in Zürich. Ich komme aus Zürich und mein Mann kommt aus Luzern. Ich bin dreiunddreißig Jahre alt und Bernd ist
5 fünfzig. Bernd ist Geschäftsmann hier in Zürich und ich bin Lehrerin. Ich unterrichte Französisch und Sozialkunde. Meine Freizeit verbringe ich am liebsten mit meiner Familie. Außerdem reise ich gern.

Guten Tag, ich heiße Sofie Pracht, bin 22 und komme aus Dresden. Ich studiere Biologie an der Technischen Universität Dresden. Ein paar Stunden in der Woche
10 arbeite ich in einer großen Gärtnerei. In meiner Freizeit gehe ich oft ins Kino oder ich besuche Freunde. Ich spiele Gitarre und tanze sehr gern. Mein Freund heißt Willi Schuster. Er studiert auch hier in Dresden an der Technischen Universität. Er kommt aus Radebeul. Das ist ein kleiner Ort ganz in der Nähe von Dresden. Am Wochenende fahren wir manchmal mit dem Fahrrad nach Radebeul und besuchen seine Familie.

15 Guten Tag, ich heiße Mehmet Sengün. Ich bin 29 und in Izmir, in der Türkei, geboren. Ich lebe jetzt seit 19 Jahren hier in Berlin. Ich wohne in Kreuzberg, einem Stadtteil von Berlin, in einer kleinen Wohnung. In Kreuzberg leben sehr viele Türken – die Berliner nennen es Klein-Istanbul – und viele meiner türkischen Freunde wohnen ganz in der Nähe. Im Moment arbeite ich für eine Speditionsfirma hier in der Stadt.
20 Ich fahre einen Lastwagen und bin viel unterwegs. Ich weiß nicht, aber richtig zu Hause fühle ich mich in Berlin auch nicht und für die Deutschen bin ich immer der Türke.

[1]*sich … introduce yourself* [2]*weight* [3]*grades*

(3) Explain the reading task *Arbeit mit dem Text*; ask your sts. to work in groups of 2–3 and fill in the table for Veronika Frisch. Briefly discuss afterward and assign Sofie Pracht and Mehmet Sengün for homework. Additional homework questions/tasks: *Welche Person finden Sie am interessantesten? Welche Fragen würden Sie dieser Person gern stellen? Schreiben Sie einen ähnlichen Text über sich selbst.* When sts. compose a similar autobiographical statement, tell them to start with creating a chart similar to the one in the reading task. An interesting variation of the composition task might be to ask sts. not to include their name. Collect the autobiographical statements the next class period, shuffle them, and return them in sets to sts. in small groups who have to figure out whom these statements are about.

AA. After the reading has been discussed, read "liar's" versions of the biographies to your students. Ask your students to knock on the table or to stamp their feet whenever they hear you read a "lie." For example, Veronika Frisch: *Guten Tag, ich heiße Rosemarie Frisch. Ich bin verheiratet und habe einen Sohn und zwei Töchter. Sie heißen Stefan, Natalie und Lydia. Ich lebe mit meinem Mann Kurt und unseren Kindern in Deutschland. Wir wohnen in Zürich. Ich komme aus Luzern und mein Mann kommt aus Zürich. Ich bin 34 und mein Mann ist 50. Bernd ist Professor hier in Zürich und ich bin Lehrerin. Ich unterrichte Spanisch und Geographie. Ich reise gern und spiele auch gern Tennis.*

Photo questions. *Wer sind diese Leute? Sind sie Deutsche? Wo wohnen sie? Was machen sie? Was findet man in diesem Laden?*

Note. When Berlin was a divided city, Kreuzberg was on the outskirts of West Berlin, close to the Wall. Now it is in the center of the reunited city, and its character has changed. For example, formerly low rents went up by as much as 80% and forced people to give up their businesses and apartments and move elsewhere.

Berlin-Kreuzberg, die türkische Hauptstadt Deutschlands

Arbeit mit dem Text

Was erfahren Sie über Veronika Frisch, Sofie Pracht und Mehmet Sengün? Vervollständigen Sie die Tabelle.

Name	Veronika Frisch	Sofie Pracht	Mehmet Sengün
Alter			
Geburtsort			
Familie/Freunde			
Wohnort			
Beruf			
Studienfach			
Freizeit			
Sonstiges[1]			

Nach dem Lesen

Stellen Sie sich vor.[2] Schreiben Sie einen kurzen Text. Kleben[3] Sie ein Foto auf das Papier oder zeichnen[4] Sie ein Selbstporträt. Hängen Sie Ihre Texte im Klassenzimmer an die Wand.

[1]*other information* [2]*Stellen … Introduce yourself.* [3]*Glue* [4]*draw*

Videoecke

- Was studierst du?
- Gibt es da interessante Seminare?
- Wann beginnen deine Seminare?
- Wann stehst du da auf?
- Was machst du dann?
- Was machst du mittags?
- Was machst du in deiner Freizeit?
- Und was machst du dieses Wochenende?

Uli kommt aus Marburg (Hessen). Ihre Hobbys sind Musik, Sport, Lesen, Reisen und Briefe schreiben.

Michael kommt aus Magdeburg (Sachsen-Anhalt). Seine Hobbys sind Angeln, Basteln und Lesen.

Aufgabe

Aufgabe. (1) Describe Uli or Michael. Ask sts. to listen to your description and to decide which of the two you are describing. Start with *Diese Person liest gern*. Then provide another piece of information. **(2)** Discuss the interview questions with your sts. **(3)** Ask sts. to read through the statements and to guess to whom these statements might apply. **(4)** Play Uli's interview once. Collect students' answers (without correcting them) and write them on the board or on an overhead transparency. Play Uli's interview again and ask for corrections. Then play Michael's interview and ask if anybody has changed his or her mind. **(5)** Play Uli's interview again and ask sts. to clap their hands when they hear one of the numbered statements from the list. Stop the recording and ask for the statement number. Do the same with Michael's interview.

Student interviews. (1) Ask sts. to jot down their own answers to the interview questions. **(2)** Pair sts. to interview each other. Ask them to jot down their partner's answers. **(3)** Follow up by sampling a few of the answers given in the interviews.

Uli oder Michael? Welche Aussagen treffen auf Michael zu, welche auf Uli? Schreiben Sie U (Uli) oder M (Michael) neben die folgenden Aussagen.

1. _____ studiert Ostslawistik und Deutsch als Fremdsprache.
2. _____ studiert Humanmedizin.
3. _____ hat keine interessanten Seminare.
4. _____ steht um halb sieben auf.
5. _____ geht ins Bad, duscht, zieht sich an und frühstückt.
6. _____ isst mittags in der Mensa.
7. _____ ruht sich aus, wenn er Zeit hat.
8. _____ singt im Chor, macht Sport und besucht Veranstaltungen in der Gemeinde.
9. _____ liest gern und geht gern angeln.
10. _____ geht dieses Wochenende mit Freunden angeln.
11. _____ geht auf eine Wochenendfreizeit mit ihrer Gemeinde.

Wortschatz

Freizeit — Leisure Time

lesen (R)	to read
er/sie liest	he/she reads
Zeitung lesen	to read the newspaper
liegen	to lie
in der Sonne liegen	to lie in the sun
reisen	to travel
segeln	to sail
spielen	to play
wandern	to hike
zelten	to camp

Ähnliche Wörter

die Gitarre, -n; die Karte, -n; die Musik; die Sonnenbrille, -n; der Ball, -e (R); der Fußball, -e (R); der Kaffee; der Volleyball, -e; das Foto, -s; das Golf; das Hobby, -s; das Schach; das Squash; das Tennis; boxen; hören; kochen; reiten; schwimmen gehen; singen; tanzen; windsurfen gehen

Orte — Places

die Arbeit	work
zur Arbeit gehen	to go to work
der Berg, -e	mountain
in die Berge gehen	to go to the mountains
in den Bergen wandern	to hike in the mountains
das Kino, -s	movie theater, cinema
ins Kino gehen	to go to the movies
das Meer, -e	sea
im Meer schwimmen	to swim in the sea
das Rathaus, -er	town hall
auf dem Rathaus	at the town hall
das Schwimmbad, -er	swimming pool
ins Schwimmbad fahren	to go to the swimming pool

Ähnliche Wörter

die Party, -s; auf eine Party gehen; die Uni, -s (R); zur Uni gehen; auf der Uni sein; der Park, -s; im Park spazieren gehen; das Bett, -en; ins Bett gehen; das Haus, -er; zu Hause sein; nach Hause gehen; das Konzert, -e; ins Konzert gehen; das Museum, Museen; ins Museum gehen

Schule und Universität — School and University

die Erdkunde	earth science; geography
die Geschichte	history
die Kunstgeschichte	art history
die Informatik	computer science
die Kunst	art
die Lehrerin, -nen (R)	female teacher, instructor
die Prüfung, -en	test
die Schülerin, -nen	female pupil
die Sozialkunde	social studies
die Wirtschaft	economics
der Lehrer, - (R)	male teacher, instructor
der Maschinenbau	mechanical engineering
der Schüler, -	male pupil
der Stundenplan, -e	schedule
das Auslandsamt, -er	center for study abroad
das Fach, -er	academic subject
das Stipendium, Stipendien	scholarship
das Studium, Studien	university studies
die Ferien (pl.)	vacation

Ähnliche Wörter

die Biologie, die Chemie, die Linguistik, die Literatur; die Mathematik; die Musik; die Pause, -n; die Physik; die Religion; die Soziologie; der Kurs, -e (R); der Sport; das Latein; das Semester, -; lernen; studieren

Persönliche Daten — Biographical Information

die Farbe, -n	color
die Größe, -n	height
die Narbe, -n	scar
die Staatsangehörigkeit, -en	nationality, citizenship
die Unterschrift, -en	signature
der Beruf, -e	profession
was sind Sie von Beruf?	what's your profession?
der Familienstand	marital status
der Geburtstag, -e	birthday
der Personalausweis, -e	(personal) ID card
der Spitzname, -n	nickname
der Wohnort, -e	residence
das Alter	age
ledig	unmarried
verheiratet	married

Ähnliche Wörter

die Adresse, -n; die Augenfarbe; die Haarfarbe; die Nummer, -n; die Hausnummer, -n; die Telefonnummer, -n; die Person, -en; die Präferenz, -en; der Name, -n (R); der Familienname, -n (R); der Vorname, -n (R); geboren; wann sind Sie geboren?

Tagesablauf — Daily Routine

die Woche, -n	week
in der Woche	during the week

der **A**bend, -e	evening	**a**n·rufen	to call up
der T**a**g, -e	day	**au**f·hören (mit)	to stop (doing something)
den g**a**nzen Tag	all day long	**au**f·räumen	to clean (up)
		auf·stehen	to get up
der M**o**ntag	Monday	**au**s·füllen	to fill out
der D**ie**nstag	Tuesday	**au**s·gehen	to go out
der M**i**ttwoch	Wednesday	**ei**n·kaufen (gehen)	to (go) shop(ping)
der D**o**nnerstag	Thursday	**ei**n·packen	to pack up
der Fr**ei**tag	Friday	f**e**rn·sehen	to watch TV
der S**a**mstag	Saturday	er/sie sieht f**e**rn	he/she is watching TV
der S**o**nntag	Sunday	k**e**nnen·lernen	to get acquainted with

das W**o**chenende, -n — weekend
am W**o**chenende — over the weekend

Sonstige Verben — **Other Verbs**

		arbeiten	to work
fr**ü**h	early	bes**u**chen	to visit
sp**ä**t(er)	late(r)	bl**ei**ben	to stay, remain
		br**au**chen	to need; to use
um w**ie** viel Uhr ...?	at what time ... ?	d**u**schen	to (take a) shower
w**a**nn?	when?	fl**ie**gen	to fly
um halb dr**ei**	at two thirty	fr**ü**hstücken	to eat breakfast
um s**e**chs (Uhr)	at six o'clock	k**au**fen	to buy
um sieben Uhr zw**a**nzig	at seven twenty	m**ö**gen	to like
um Viertel vor v**ie**r	at a quarter to four	ich m**a**g	I like
um zwanzig nach f**ü**nf	at twenty after/past five	du m**a**gst	you like
welcher Tag ist h**eu**te?	what day is today?	spaz**ie**ren gehen	to go for a walk
wie sp**ä**t ist es?	what time is it?	s**u**chen	to look for
wie viel **U**hr ist es?	what time is it?	unterschr**ei**ben	to sign

Ähnliche Wörter

die Sek**u**nde, -n; der Mom**e**nt, -e; im Mom**e**nt

Ähnliche Wörter

beg**i**nnen, repar**ie**ren, tr**i**nken

Sonstige Substantive	**Other Nouns**
die T**a**sche, -n	bag; purse; pocket
die W**o**hnung, -en	apartment

Sonstige Wörter **Other Words**
und Ausdrücke **and Expressions**

der Br**ie**f, -e	letter
der Ch**o**r, ⸚e	choir

g**e**rn	gladly, with pleasure
wir s**i**ngen gern	we like to sing
ihr(e)	her
s**ei**n(e)	his
s**i**cher	sure
wahrsch**ei**nlich	probably

das **A**bendessen, -	supper, evening meal
das H**a**lstuch, ⸚er	bandanna
das Mot**o**rrad, ⸚er	motorcycle
Mot**o**rrad fahren	to ride a motorcycle
das Z**i**mmer, -	room

Verben mit trennbaren	**Verbs with Separable**
Präfixen	**Prefixes**

ab·holen	to pick (somebody) up (from a place)
an·kommen	to arrive

Strukturen und Übungen

1.1 The present tense

1.1. *Präsens: regelmäßige Verben.* This section introduces more regular verbs in the present tense. Verbs that change their stem vowel appear in *Kapitel 2.* We do not expect sts. to use all endings correctly in speech at this stage. The *ich-, du-,* and *Sie*-forms are likely to be acquired first. Include the other forms in your input, too, so sts. can become familiar with them.

One German present-tense form expresses three different ideas in English.

Ich spiele Gitarre.

$\begin{cases} \text{\textit{I play the guitar.}} \\ \text{\textit{I'm playing the guitar.}} \\ \text{\textit{I'm going to play the guitar.}} \end{cases}$

Most German verbs form the present tense just like **kommen (Einführung B).**

Wissen Sie noch?

ich	-e
du	-st
er/sie/es	-t
wir	-en
ihr	-t
Sie, sie	-en

Review grammar B.6

spielen			
ich	spiele	wir	spielen
du	spielst	ihr	spielt
Sie	spielen	Sie	spielen
er sie es	spielt	sie	spielen

Note. You might wish to point out to sts. that Appendix F summarizes verb conjugations. Appendix E contains summaries of other important grammar points.

Gabi und Jutta **spielen** gern Karten.

Gabi and Jutta like to play cards.

Verbs whose stems end in an s-sound, such as **-s, -ss, -ß, -z (-ts),** or **-x (-ks),** do not add an additional **-s-** in the **du**-form: **du tanzt, du heißt, du reist.**

—Wie **heißt du?**
—**Ich heiße** Natalie.

What's your name?
My name's Natalie.

Verbs whose stems end in **-d** or **-t** (and a few other verbs such as **regnen** [*to rain*] and **öffnen** [*to open*]) insert an **-e-** between the stem and the **-st** or **-t** endings. This happens in the **du-, ihr-,** and **er/sie/es**-forms.

Reitest du jeden Tag?

Do you go horseback riding every day?

reiten			
ich	reite	wir	reiten
du	reitest	ihr	reitet
Sie	reiten	Sie	reiten
er sie es	reitet	sie	reiten

Übung 1 | Was machen sie?

Note. Answers to the *Übungen* are in Appendix G.

Üb. 1. This is the first example of an exercise in which there are restrictions of both a grammatical and a semantic kind as to what combinations are possible. First, sts. need to select a verb that agrees in person and number with the subject at hand. Then, they need to select an object that makes sense to use with the verb selected during the first step. This two-step approach is based on the following two goals: **(1)** to sensitize sts. to paying attention to word endings; and **(2)** to focus sts. on meaning even during grammar exercises by making it difficult to come up with correct sentences without understanding what they mean. Work with the first two or three sentences as sample sentences in class.

Kombinieren Sie die Wörter. Achten Sie auf die Verbendungen.

MODELL: Ich besuche Freunde.

1. ich	lernen	Freunde
2. ihr	besuche	ins Kino
3. Jutta und Jens	studiert	Spaghetti
4. du	hört	ein Buch
5. Melanie	reisen	gut Tennis
6. ich	kochen	nach Deutschland
7. wir	lese	in Regensburg
8. Richard	spielst	Spanisch
9. Jürgen und Silvia	geht	gern Musik

Übung 2 | Minidialoge

Üb. 2-3. Assign the next two exercises for homework. In class have pairs of sts. read the dialogues aloud. Sts. must choose the subject pronoun in *Üb. 2* and the verb ending in *Üb. 3*.

Ergänzen Sie das Pronomen.

1. CLAIRE: Arbeitet Melanie?
   JOSEF: Nein, _____ arbeitet nicht.
2. MICHAEL: Schwimmen _____ gern im Meer?
   FRAU KÖRNER: Ja, sehr gern. Und Sie?
3. MEHMET: Was machst _____^{a} im Sommer?
   RENATE: _____^{b} fliege nach Spanien.
4. CLAIRE: Woher kommt _____^{a}?
   HELGA UND SIGRID: _____^{b} kommen aus Krefeld.
5. JÜRGEN: _____^{a} studiere in Göttingen. Und _____^{b}?
   KLAUS UND CHRISTINA: _____^{c} studieren in Berlin.

Übung 3 | Minidialoge

Ergänzen Sie die Verbendungen.

1. CLAIRE: Du tanz_____^{a} gern, nicht?
   MELANIE: Ja, ich tanz_____^{b} sehr gern, aber mein Freund tanz_____^{c} nicht gern.
2. FRAU SCHULZ: Richard geh_____^{a} im Sommer in den Bergen wandern.
   STEFAN: Und was mach_____^{b} seine Eltern?
   FRAU SCHULZ: Seine Mutter reis_____^{c} nach Frankreich und sein Vater arbeit_____^{d}.
3. JÜRGEN: Wir koch_____^{a} heute Abend. Was mach_____^{b} ihr?
   KLAUS: Wir besuch_____^{c} Freunde.

1.2 Expressing likes and dislikes: *gern / nicht gern*

verb + **gern** = *to like to do something*
verb + **nicht gern** = *to dislike doing something*

1.2. *Gern* and *nicht gern* do not correspond directly to any English forms, but sts. usually have no difficulty using them in simple sentences.

To say that you like doing something, use the word **gern** after the verb. To say that you don't like to do something, use **nicht gern.**

Ernst spielt **gern** Fußball.	*Ernst likes to play soccer.*
Josef spielt **nicht gern** Fußball.	*Josef doesn't like to play soccer.*

I	II	III	IV
Sofie	spielt	gern	Schach.
Willi	spielt	auch gern	Schach.
Ich	spiele	nicht gern	Schach.
Monika	spielt	auch nicht gern	Schach.

The position of **auch/nicht/gern** (in that order) is between the verb and its complement.*

Übung 4 | Was machen die Studenten gern?

Üb. 4–5. Assign for homework, which may be written. Follow up in class with questions to sts. about their own likes and dislikes.

Bilden Sie Sätze.

MODELL: Heidi und Nora schwimmen gern.

Heidi/Nora

Monika / Albert
1.

Heidi
2.

Stefan
3.

Nora
4.

Peter
5.

Katrin
6.

Monika
7.

Tee
Albert
8.

*The complement provides additional information and thus "completes" the meaning of the verb:
ich spiele → ich spiele Tennis; ich höre → ich höre Musik.

Übung 5 | **Und diese Personen?**

Sagen Sie, was die folgenden Personen gern machen.

MODELL: Frau Ruf liegt gern in der Sonne. Jutta liegt auch gern in der Sonne, aber Herr Ruf liegt nicht gern in der Sonne.

1. Frau Ruf   Jutta   Herr Ruf
2. Jens   Ernst   Jutta

3. Jens   Jutta   Andrea
4. Michael   Maria   die Rufs   die Wagners

1.3   Telling time

Ask the time in German in one of two ways.

Wie spät ist es?   *What time is it?*
Wie viel Uhr ist es?

Es ist eins.
Es ist ein Uhr.

Es ist drei.
Es ist drei Uhr.

Es ist Viertel vor elf.
Es ist zehn Uhr fünfundvierzig.

Es ist Viertel nach elf.
Es ist elf Uhr fünfzehn.

vor = *to*
nach = *after*

Es ist zehn (Minuten) vor acht.
Es ist sieben Uhr fünfzig.

Es ist zehn (Minuten) nach acht.
Es ist acht Uhr zehn.

The expressions **Viertel, nach, vor,** and **halb** are used in everyday speech. In German, the half hour is expressed as "half before" the following hour, not as "half after" the preceding hour, as in English.

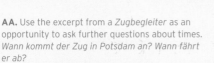

halb = *half, thirty*
halb zehn = *half past nine, nine thirty*

Es ist halb zehn.   *It is nine thirty (halfway to ten).*

The 24-hour clock (0.00 to 24.00) is used when giving exact or official times, as in time announcements, schedules, programs, and the like. With the 24-hour clock only the pattern [(*number*) **Uhr** (*number of minutes*)] is used.

AA. Use the excerpt from a *Zugbegleiter* as an opportunity to ask further questions about times. *Wann kommt der Zug in Potsdam an? Wann fährt er ab?*

Ankunft	km	Abfahrt	Anschlüsse
14.22 Potsdam Stadt		**14.24**	
	↓	14.43	Wildpark 14.49 Werder (Havel) 14.56 (204)
	24	*E* 15.01	Wustermark 15.39 Nauen 15.57 (204.4)
			S-Bahnanschlüsse (Taktverkehr) bestehen in Richtung: Wannsee – Westkreuz – Charlottenburg – Zool Garten (Ⓢ 3)

Der Zug geht um vierzehn   *The train leaves at two twenty-four p.m.*
Uhr vierundzwanzig.

Übung 6 | Die Uhrzeit

Üb. 6. For oral work in pairs.

Wie spät ist es?

MODELL: Es ist acht Uhr.

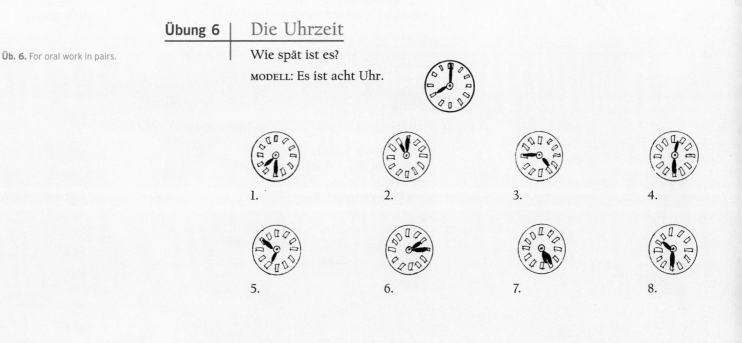

1.   2.   3.   4.

5.   6.   7.   8.

1.4 Word order in statements

1.4. *Wortstellung in Aussagen.* The placement of the verb in second position when the subject is not the first element appears to be a simple rule, but it is acquired relatively late. Early mastery of this rule in speech is not expected.

In English, the verb usually follows the subject of a sentence.

SUBJECT	VERB	COMPLEMENT
Peter	takes	a walk.

Even when another word or phrase begins the sentence, the word order does not change.

	SUBJECT	VERB	COMPLEMENT
Every day,	Peter	takes	a walk.

In statements, verb second.

In German statements, the verb is always in second position. If the sentence begins with an element other than the subject, the subject follows the verb.

I	II	III	IV
SUBJECT	VERB		COMPLEMENT
Wir	spielen	heute	Tennis.

	VERB	SUBJECT	COMPLEMENT
Heute	spielen	wir	Tennis.

Übung 7 | Rolf

Üb. 7. Assign as homework or do in class. If assigned as homework, explain to sts. what the task is beforehand. The verb-second rule is practiced for reading purposes only. Identifying the subject is an important technique when reading. However, we do not practice this rule for speaking purposes at this stage, since it is very unlikely that sts. will profit from it this early in their acquisition of German.

Unterstreichen[1] Sie das Subjekt des Satzes. Steht das konjugierte Verb vor[2] oder nach[3] dem Subjekt?

1. <u>Rolf</u> kommt aus Krefeld.   *nach*
2. Im Moment studiert er in Berkeley. _____
3. Seine Großmutter wohnt noch in Krefeld. _____
4. Samstags geht Rolf oft ins Kino. _____
5. Am Wochenende wandert er oft in den Bergen. _____
6. Außerdem treibt er gern Sport. _____
7. Im Sommer geht er surfen. _____
8. Er geht auch ins Schwimmbad der Uni.

Übung 8 | Sie und Ihr Freund

Üb. 8. Before assigning this exercise for written homework, explain the task and do a few sample sentences with your sts. Follow up in class by having sts. read their answers aloud. Combine with oral questions.

Bilden Sie Sätze. Beginnen Sie die Sätze mit dem ersten Wort oder den ersten Wörtern in einer Zeile. Beachten[4] Sie die Satzstellung[5].

MODELL: Heute (ich / sein _____) → Heute bin ich fröhlich.

1. Ich (studieren _____)
2. Im Moment (ich / wohnen in _____)
3. Heute (ich / kochen _____)
4. Manchmal (ich / trinken _____)
5. Ich (spielen gern _____)
6. Mein Freund (heißen _____)
7. Jetzt (er / wohnen in _____)
8. Manchmal (wir / spielen _____)

[1]Underline [2]before [3]after [4]Pay attention to [5]word order

1.5 Separable-prefix verbs

1.5. *Verben mit trennbaren Präfixen*. In this chapter, sts. will mostly need to use the structure with the prefix at the end of the sentence. Infinitive forms will be used in *Kapitel 2*. Point out that this is the first encounter with *Satzklammer*, a characteristic feature of German sentence structure. The next example of *Satzklammer* occurs with the modal *möchte* in *Kapitel 2*.

Many German verbs have prefixes that change the verb's meaning. They combine with the infinitive to form a single word.

stehen	*to stand*
gehen	*to go*
kommen	*to come*
aufstehen	*to stand up*
ausgehen	*to go out*
ankommen	*to arrive*

In statements, verb second, prefix last.

When you use a present-tense form of these verbs, put the conjugated form in second position and put the prefix at the end of the sentence. The two parts of the verb form a frame or bracket, called a **Satzklammer,** that encloses the rest of the sentence.

Claire <u>kommt</u> <u>an</u>.

Claire <u>kommt</u> am Donnerstag <u>an</u>.

Claire <u>kommt</u> am Donnerstag in Frankfurt <u>an</u>.

Here are some common verbs with separable prefixes.

abholen	*to pick up, fetch*
ankommen	*to arrive*
anrufen	*to call up*
aufhören	*to stop, be over*
aufräumen	*to clean up, tidy up*
aufstehen	*to get up*
ausfüllen	*to fill out*
ausgehen	*to go out*
einkaufen	*to shop*
einpacken	*to pack up*
kennenlernen	*to get acquainted with*

Übung 9 | Eine Reise in die Türkei

Mehmet fliegt morgen in die Türkei. Was macht er heute? Ergänzen Sie die folgenden Wörter: **ab, an, auf, auf, auf, aus, aus, ein, ein.**

1. Er steht um 7 Uhr _____.
2. Er räumt die Wohnung _____.
3. Er packt seine Sachen[1] _____.
4. Er ruft Renate _____.
5. Er füllt ein Formular _____.
6. Er holt seinen Reisepass _____.
7. Er kauft Essen[2] _____.
8. Abends geht er _____.
9. Er geht ins Kino. Der Film hört um 22 Uhr _____.

[1]*things* [2]*food*

Übung 10 | **Was machen die Leute?**

Üb. 10. Use in class or as homework.

Verwenden Sie die folgenden Verben.

abholen
ankommen
anrufen
aufräumen
aufstehen
ausfüllen
ausgehen
einkaufen
einpacken
kennenlernen

MODELL: Frau Schulz kauft ein paar Lebensmittel ein.

1.

Rolf

2.

Thomas

3.

Heidi / Thomas

4.

Albert

5.

Peter / Monika

6.

Peter / Monika

7.

Frau Schulz

8.

Stefan

9.

Katrin   Rolf

1.6   Word order in questions

1.6. *Wortstellung in Fragesätzen.* Word order in German questions is generally not a problem for English-speaking learners. Students will already have heard many yes/no questions as well as questions beginning with a question word.

In **w**-questions, verb second.

When you begin a question with a question word (for example, **wie, wo, wer, was, wann, woher**), the verb follows in second position. The subject of the sentence is in third position. Any further elements appear in fourth position.

I	II	III	IV	
Wann	beginnt	das Spiel?		When does the game start?
Was	machst	du	heute Abend?	What are you doing this evening?
Wo	wohnst	du?		Where do you live?
Welches Fach	studierst	du?		Which subject are you studying?

Here are the question words you have encountered so far.

wann	*when*
was	*what*
welcher*	*which*
wer	*who*
wie	*how*
wie viel(e)	*how much (many)*
wo	*where*
woher	*from where*

Questions that can be answered by *yes* or *no* begin with the verb.

Tanzt du gern?	*Do you like to dance?*
Arbeitest du hier?	*Do you work here?*
Gehst du ins Kino?	*Are you going to the movies?*

Übung 11 | Ein Interview mit Marta Szerwinski

Üb. 11. Students need to change the form and order of the words. Assign as written homework. Follow up in class with oral pair work.

Schreiben Sie die Fragen.

MODELL: du + heißen + wie + ? → Wie heißt du?

1. du + sein + geboren + wann + ?
2. du + kommen + woher + ?
3. du + wohnen + wo + ?
4. du + haben + Augenfarbe + welch- + ?
5. du + sein + groß + wie + ?
6. du + studieren + ?
7. du + studieren + Fächer + welch- + ?
8. du + arbeiten + Stunden + wie viele + ?
9. du + machen + gern + was + ?

Übung 12 | Noch ein Interview

Üb. 12. Assign for homework. In class, ask sts. to interview someone who plays Sofie, or else play the role of Sofie yourself.

AA. After doing the exercise with the given responses, sts. could be encouraged to make slight variations in both questions and answers.

Stellen Sie die Fragen.

1. —Ich heiße Sofie.
2. —Nein, ich komme nicht aus München.
3. —Ich komme aus Dresden.
4. —Ich studiere Biologie.
5. —Er heißt Willi.
6. —Er wohnt in Dresden.
7. —Nein, ich spiele nicht Tennis.
8. —Ja, ich tanze sehr gern.
9. —Nein, ich trinke kein Bier.
10. —Ja, Willi trinkt gern Bier.

*The endings of **welcher** vary according to gender, number, and case of the following noun. They are the same endings as those of the definite article. Therefore, **welcher** is called a **der**-word.

(M)	(N)	(F)	(Pl)
welch**er** Name	welch**es** Alter	welch**e** Adresse	welch**e** Studienfächer

Joachim Heuer: *Die rote Geige* (ca. 1979),
Kunstsammlung, Universität Leipzig

Chapter opening artwork: You may wish
to contrast the more naturalistic paintings
of *Einführung B* and *Kapitel 1* with the more
expressionistic style of Campendonk in *Einführung
A* and Heuer's modernist still life here.

Suggestion: Use Heuer's painting as a starting
point to introduce *Besitz und Geschenke*. Questions
you might ask include: *Welche Gegenstände sehen
Sie auf dem Bild? Welche Farben haben sie? Wo
stehen die Gegenstände? Sehen sie natürlich
aus? Was ist ungewöhnlich? Was sehen Sie im
Hintergrund? Welche Fragen haben Sie an das Bild?*

JOACHIM HEUER

Joachim Heuer (1900–1994) wurde in Dresden geboren, wo er auch bis zum Ende
seines langen Lebens als Künstler[1] tätig war. Er war ein Maler, der wegen[2] seines
Stils und seiner Einstellung[3] zur Kunst in der ehemaligen DDR nicht anerkannt[4]
wurde.

[1]*artist* [2]*because of* [3]*attitude* [4]*recognized*

2

Besitz und Vergnügen

In **Kapitel 2** you will learn to talk more about things: your own possessions and things you give others. You will also learn how to describe what you have and don't have and to give your opinion on matters of taste or style.

Themen
Besitz
Geschenke
Kleidung und Aussehen
Vergnügen

Kulturelles
Der Euro
Videoblick: Erste Berliner Fashion-Week
Vergnügen
Videoecke: Hobbys

Lektüren
Ringe fürs Leben zu zweit
Film: *Im Juli*

Strukturen
2.1 The accusative case
2.2 The negative article: **kein, keine**
2.3 What would you like? **Ich möchte ...**
2.4 Possessive adjectives
2.5 The present tense of stem-vowel changing verbs
2.6 Asking people to do things: the **du**-imperative

GOALS
The focus of *Kapitel 2* is the sts.' immediate environment outside the class: things they have, things they would like to have, and what they like to do. The suggested additional activities provide further chances for talking about daily activities, as a review of the topics from *Kapitel 1*.

PRE-TEXT ACTIVITIES
Bring in pictures of items found in the sts.' environment. First identify and talk briefly about the items, then pass each picture to a different st. Ask: *Wer hat den/das/die* _____? Then ask another st.: *Was möchten Sie haben? Den* _____, *das* _____ *oder die* _____? (If sts. ask, point out that *der* changes to *den* in these sentences.)

Situationen

Besitz

Vocabulary Display   **Grammatik 2.1–2.2**

Introduce vocabulary as usual: presentation, receptive recall (*Wo steht der Schrank? Links, rechts oder in der Mitte?*), choral response, productive recall, personalization: *Schreiben Sie auf, was alles in Ihrem Zimmer ist!* (See the IM for suggestions on introducing vocabulary.)

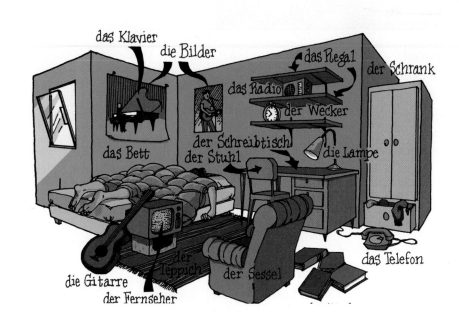

Situation 1 | Hast du einen Schlafsack?

Sit. 1. In this activity, sts. use the accusative forms *einen/ein/eine* and *keinen/kein/keine*. The masculine is stressed in this interaction, since it is the only gender that changes in the accusative. Demonstrate the model question and answer. Use the overhead projector to point to the item mentioned. Then repeat the model with 1–2 other items from the list. Make sure sts. understand the meaning of all new words before they work in pairs. Cover the labels on the transparency, and ask *Was ist das?* The response to this question will be in the nominative, and it may be necessary to point this out. Have sts. alternate asking and answering. You may want to point out that *kein* will have the same ending as *ein* in their responses. Afterward, to make sure that sts. understand the relationship between the definite and indefinite articles, you could ask: *Welche Sachen/Dinge im Bild sind maskulin/feminin/neutrum? Wie wissen Sie das?*

MODELL: s1: Hast du einen Schlafsack?
　　　　　s2: Ja, ich habe einen Schlafsack.
　　　　　　　Nein, ich habe keinen Schlafsack.

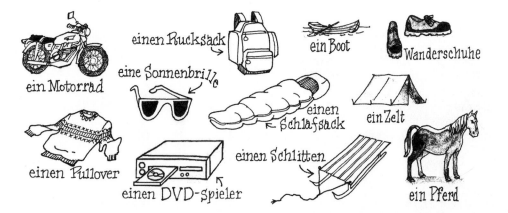

Der Euro

Fragen Sie Ihren Partner oder Ihre Partnerin.

1. Wie heißt die Währung[1] in dem Land, in dem du geboren bist?
2. Welche Münzen gibt es, z. B. 1-Cent-Münzen, 2-Cent-Münzen?
3. Welche Geldscheine gibt es, z. B. 1-Dollar-Scheine, 2-Dollar-Scheine?
4. Welche Farbe haben die Geldscheine?
5. Welche Bilder und Symbole gibt es auf den Geldscheinen und Münzen?

Lesen Sie den Text zum Thema *Euro* und beantworten Sie die Fragen zum Text.

1. Wie viele Länder hat die EU? In wie vielen Ländern der EU gilt der Euro als gesetzliches Zahlungsmittel? In welchen Ländern der EU gilt er noch nicht?
2. In welchen weiteren Ländern ist der Euro gesetzliches Zahlungsmittel?
3. Welche Rolle spielt der Euro in der Schweiz?
4. Was sieht man auf den Euro-Scheinen, was auf den Euro-Münzen? Sind alle Euro-Scheine und -Münzen in allen Ländern gleich?
5. Was zeigt die deutsche und die österreichische 10-Cent-Münze und was die deutsche und österreichische 2-Euro-Münze?

Seit dem 1. Januar 2002 gibt es in Deutschland und in elf anderen Ländern der Europäischen Union (EU) den Euro. Der Euro ist gesetzliches Zahlungsmittel[2] in Deutschland, Österreich, Finnland, Belgien, Luxemburg, Italien, Frankreich, Spanien, Portugal, Irland, Griechenland und in den Niederlanden. Die EU-Länder Dänemark, Schweden, Polen und Großbritannien behalten vorerst[3] ihre alten Währungen. Neun andere EU-Länder – Estland, Litauen, Slowenien, Zypern, Lettland, Malta, die Slowakei, die Tschechische Republik und Ungarn – wollen der Eurozone beitreten[4], sobald die notwendigen Bedingungen dazu erfüllt sind[5].

Neben den 12 Ländern der Eurozone ist der Euro in 12 weiteren Ländern die offizielle Währung. In den drei europäischen Kleinstaaten Andorra, Monaco, und San Marino und im Vatikanstaat, und auch in den vier Ländern des ehemaligen[6] Jugoslawiens, nämlich im Kosovo, in Montenegro, in Kroatien und in Serbien, ist der Euro gesetzliches Zahlungsmittel, dazu in allen vier französischen Überseegebieten: Französisch-Guayana, Martinique, Guadeloupe und Réunion. Die Schweiz ist nicht Mitglied[7] der EU und auch nicht Mitglied der Eurozone. Trotzdem[8] akzeptiert man fast überall in der Schweiz neben[9] der eigenen Währung, dem Schweizer Franken, auch den Euro.

Ein Euro hat 100 Cent. Der größte Geldschein ist der 500-Euro-Schein und die kleinste Münze ist die 1-Cent-Münze. Neben 1-, 2-, 5-, 10-, 20- und 50-Cent-Münzen gibt es auch 1- und 2-Euro-Münzen. Die Scheine sind in allen Ländern gleich[10]. Sie zeigen auf einer Seite Brücken[11] und auf der anderen Seite Fenster und historisch wichtige Portale. Der 5-Euro-Schein zeigt z.B. eine Brücke und ein Portal im klassischen Stil und der 50-Euro-Schein eine Brücke und ein Fenster aus der Renaissance.

Eine Seite der Münzen ist ebenfalls in allen Ländern gleich. Sie zeigt die Länder der Eurozone. Die andere Seite ist von Land zu Land verschieden[12]. Die deutschen 10-, 20- und 50-Cent-Münzen zeigen z.B. das Brandenburger Tor und die 1- und 2-Euro-Münzen den deutschen Adler[13]. Alle acht österreichischen Münzen haben ein anderes Motiv, die österreichische 10-Cent-Münze z.B. zeigt den Stefansdom[14] und die 2-Euro-Münze die österreichische Pazifistin Bertha von Suttner.

500 Euro

50 Euro

10 Euro

10 cent   2 Euro

10 cent (D)   2 Euro (D)

10 cent (A)   2 Euro (A)

---

[1]*currency*   [2]*gesetzliches ... legal tender*   [3]*behalten ... will keep for the time being*   [4]*join*   [5]*sobald ... as soon as the necessary requirements have been met for that*   [6]*former*   [7]*member*   [8]*Nonetheless*   [9]*in addition to*   [10]*the same*   [11]*bridges*   [12]*different*   [13]*eagle*   [14]*der Dom cathedral*

KLI. Have sts. research the back of all Austrian coins and ask them how they would design the back of the German Euro coins. Raise the question of how a nation can be visually represented on coins or bills.

Situation 2 | Dialog: Stefan zieht in sein neues Zimmer

Sit. 2. (See the IM.) Establish the context: *Stefan studiert jetzt und er will nicht bei seinen Eltern wohnen. Er möchte im Studentenheim wohnen, aber er hat keine Möbel. Stefan trifft Katrin im Möbelgeschäft.* (Show a picture or explain.) Questions to focus attention: **(1)** *Was macht Stefan morgen?* **(2)** *Was braucht Stefan?* **(3)** *Was hat er schon?* **(4)** *Wie viel Geld hat er?* Questions for second reading: **(1)** *Was glaubt Katrin?* **(2)** *Was schlägt sie vor?*

Katrin trifft Stefan im Möbelgeschäft.

KATRIN: Hallo, Stefan. Was machst du denn hier?

STEFAN: Ach, ich brauche noch ein paar Sachen. Morgen ziehe ich in mein neues Zimmer.

KATRIN: Was brauchst du denn?

STEFAN: Ach, alles Mögliche.

KATRIN: Was hast du denn schon?

STEFAN: Ich habe einen Schlafsack, eine Gitarre und ... und ... und einen Wecker.

KATRIN: Das ist aber nicht viel. Wie viel Geld hast du denn?

STEFAN: So 30 Dollar.

KATRIN: Ich glaube, du bist im falschen Geschäft. Der Flohmarkt ist viel besser für dich.

STEFAN: Ja, vielleicht hast du recht.

Situation 3 | Informationsspiel: Was machen sie morgen?

Sit. 3. (See the IM.) The corresponding chart is in Appendix A. In this version, sts. must ask their partners the same questions that they ask about the characters in the book. To do this activity, sts. must clearly understand how to conjugate regular and separable-prefix verbs in 2nd- and 3rd-person singular. Model the first 4 questions using *Jürgen* as your subject and the last 4 questions using *du* as the subject, to make sure that sts. hear the correct pronunciation and to alert them to the separable-prefix verbs, which are not modeled in the example. Have the sts. repeat after you. It is more efficient for S1 to complete the entire chart and then allow S2 to ask questions. For additional speaking practice, ask sts. to switch partners and ask: *Was macht Ihr Partner / Ihre Partnerin morgen?* Sts. can list everything their partner plans to do the next day: *Morgen schreibt Ann einen Brief, sie lernt den Wortschatz auswendig und sie besucht einen Freund.* Your follow-up can be similar: *Ann, wer war Ihr Partner / Ihre Partnerin? Was macht er/sie morgen?* Ann must then answer as above or simply ask 3-4 sts.: *Tony, was machst du morgen?* or *Fred, sag uns bitte drei Sachen, die du morgen machst.*

MODELL: S1: Schreibt Silvia morgen einen Brief?

S2: Ja.

S1: Schreibst du morgen einen Brief?

S2: Ja. (Nein.)

	Jürgen	Silvia	mein(e) Partner(in)
1. schreibt/schreibst ... einen Brief	–	+	
2. kauft/kaufst ... ein Buch	+	+	
3. schaut/schaust ... einen Film an	–	–	
4. ruft/rufst ... eine Freundin an	–	+	
5. macht/machst ... Hausaufgaben	+	+	
6. isst/isst ... einen Hamburger	–	–	
7. besucht/besuchst ... einen Freund	+	+	
8. räumt/räumst ... das Zimmer auf	–	–	

Situation 4 | Interview: Besitz

Sit. 4. (See the IM for suggestions on using interviews.) First, set the scene by asking a few of the interview questions. Then model pronunciation of the interview questions. As sts. repeat, answer the questions as they apply to you, and encourage sts. to write down any of your answers that might help them to formulate their responses. You will need to review types of jewelry and perhaps write the vocabulary on the board. Some sts. may have unusual pets as well, so be prepared to supply other animal vocabulary to individual sts. Remind your sts. to write down their partner's answers, since afterward they will find new partners and discuss what they learned about the first interviewee.

1. Was hast du in deinem Zimmer? Was möchtest du haben?
2. Hast du wertvolle Sachen? DVD-Spieler, Auto, Computer, Handy? Was möchtest du haben?
3. Hast du einen Hund oder eine Katze? Möchtest du einen Hund oder eine Katze haben?

Geschenke

Grammatik 2.3

Vocabulary Display
In this section, sts. will learn to use *möchte* and acquire new vocabulary. Present new vocabulary, using yourself as an example: *Ich möchte eine Tasche; ich möchte keinen Koffer.* Or, to test receptive recall, bring in pictures of the items in the display, hand them out to sts. and ask: *Wer hat den Hund? das Videospiel? usw.*

der Hund • der Koffer • das Handy • die Kinokarte • der Film

die Tasche • die Kamera • das Videospiel • der Computer • das Geld

---

Situation 5 | Was möchten sie?

Sit. 5. Preparation: Take several pairs of pictures from the PF, including but not limited to the vocabulary in the sketch. Ask sts. which they think the characters would rather have: *Was möchte Herr Siebert/Jutta/usw.? _____ oder _____?* As you model the exercise, make sure to emphasize the articles so sts. will answer correctly without having to think about gender and accusative: *einen Hund oder eine Katze, ein Haus oder eine Wohnung?* Call on individual sts.; sts. should respond with one noun or the other—the entire sentence is not necessary. **Activity:** Ask sts. to work in pairs according to the model, asking about each character in the picture, not just about Herr Siebert.

MODELL: S1: Was möchte Herr Siebert?
      S2: Er möchte _____.

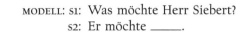

ein Auto • ein Surfbrett • ein Fahrrad • eine Katze • ein Haus

Herr Siebert • Jutta • Ernst • Josie • Herr Ruf

Photo questions. *Was für ein Geschäft ist das? Was möchte der Mann kaufen? Für wen?*

Auf der Suche nach dem coolsten Computerspiel

Situationen

83

Situation 6 | Dialog: Ein Geschenk für Josef

Sit. 6. (1) Set the scene by reminding sts. who Melanie, Claire, and Josef are and by telling them where Melanie and Claire are and what they are discussing. (Refer to the cast of characters in the preface if you wish.) **(2)** Preteach vocabulary: *schwierig, teuer, zusammen, welche Art.* **(3)** Ask sts. to open their books, and play the dialogue for them at least twice while they fill in the blanks. **(4)** Write sts.' answers on the board, or ask them to write their answers on the board, while making any necessary corrections. **(5)** Play the dialogue one last time for the benefit of sts. who did not get the right answers. **(6) Follow-up:** *Ist ein Songbuch ein gutes Geburtstagsgeschenk? Was wünschen Sie sich zum Geburtstag?*

Melanie trifft Claire in der Mensa.

MELANIE: Josef hat nächsten Donnerstag <u>Geburtstag</u>.
CLAIRE: Wirklich? Dann brauche ich ja noch ein <u>Geschenk</u> für ihn. Mensch, das ist schwierig. Hat er denn Hobbys?
MELANIE: Er <u>spielt</u> Gitarre und <u>hört</u> gern Musik.
CLAIRE: Hast du schon ein Geschenk?
MELANIE: Ich <u>möchte</u> ein Songbuch kaufen. Aber es ist ziemlich <u>teuer</u>. Kaufen wir es zusammen?
CLAIRE: Ja, klar. Welche Art Musik hat er denn <u>gern</u>?
MELANIE: Ich glaube, Soft-Rock und Oldies. Elton John, Céline Dion und so.

 Situation 7 | Zum Schreiben: Eine Einladung

Schreiben Sie eine Einladung zu einer Party. Benutzen Sie das Modell unten und Ihre Phantasie!

CALIGULA* PARTY

Wann: Mittwoch den 11. Juni – ab 20 Uhr.
Wo: Ludwig-Thomaheim – Neubau 5. Stock.
Wie: Im Kostüm der Epoche, mit eigenem Kissen, um darauf zu ruhen.

B.D.E.A. (Bring Deinen Eigenen Alkohol)
* Der wahnsinnige römische Kaiser

Situation 8 | Rollenspiel: Am Telefon

Sit. 8. *Rollenspiel:* The role for s1 appears here, the role for s2 appears in Appendix B. **(1)** Set the scene as described in the role for s1. **(2)** Provide sts. with a model by working with the enactment of the role-play found in the workbook/lab manual. **(3)** Write the structure of the role-play on the board: *Begrüßen; Erkundigen (nach Interesse und/oder Verfügbarkeit); Einladen; Zeit und Ort vereinbaren; Verabschieden.* **(4)** Elicit sample greetings, questions, etc. and write on the board. Ask for appropriate responses and also write on the board. **(5)** Divide the class into 2 groups and assign one part of the role-play to each group. Ask sts. to practice the role-play in pairs. **(6)** Ask 2–3 pairs of sts. to perform their role-play in class. Provide feedback as to appropriateness and accuracy of language used after sts. have returned to their seats. **(7)** Ask sts. to find new partners and to practice the role-play in pairs again. **(8)** Optional homework assignment: Ask sts. to write up their version of the role-play. **Sit. 8.** *Cultural note.* Tell your sts. about German telephone etiquette. When answering the phone, people usually say only their last name. At the end of their conversation, they say „*Auf Wiederhören.*"

S1: Sie rufen einen Freund / eine Freundin an. Sie machen am Samstag eine Party. Laden Sie Ihren Freund / Ihre Freundin ein.

Lektüre

Lesehilfe

Before starting to read, it is always useful to look at the complete text, the title, and any subtitles, accompanying pictures, tables, photos, or drawings, in order to get a general idea of what the text will be about. Look at this text, its title, subtitles and its accompanying pictures. Then write down what the main topic of the text probably is and what subtopics it suggests.

Lektüre: The text *Ringe fürs Leben zu zweit* was adapted from an authentic article in a journal. Newspaper articles generally have headings, sub-headings, themes, or logos that make it easier for readers to focus on particular topics and to find what interests them. Titles, subtitles, pictures, and visuals of all kinds also assist a reader in determining what a text is about. **(1)** Introduce the topic by drawing two interlocking wedding bands on the board and asking sts. what they associate with that. **(2)** The *Lesehilfe* box alerts sts. to look at the layout and visuals to get a general idea of what the text is about. Introduce the task and let sts. work in small groups. Do a quick wrap-up in class. **(3)** Explain that sts. need not understand every single word to understand a reading passage, before asking them to read the text quickly and work on *Vor dem Lesen* individually. This exercise again focuses on cognates, words whose spelling and meaning are similar in German and English. Further examples for German *k* or *z* corresponding to English *c* are *Kassette - cassette, Präferenz - preference, kochen - cook*. Collect the cognates that sts. underlined in the text and write them on the board. You may want to sort the words into nouns, verbs, and adjectives. Check whether they guessed the meaning correctly.

(continued on next page)

Vor dem Lesen

German and English are closely related languages and share many words. Sometimes the words look almost identical, with minor spelling variations such as German **k** or **z** for English *c*. Sometimes you have to use a little guesswork to see the English word in the German one, as in the word **Ägypter** (*Egyptian*). In the following text, underline the words whose meanings you think you can guess by knowing English.

Ringe fürs Leben zu zweit

Symbole ewiger[1] Liebe

Der Ehering symbolisiert ewige Liebe: er hat keinen Anfang und kein Ende. So wie der Ring kein Ende hat, soll auch die Liebe nie aufhören. Er signalisiert aller Welt: Dieser Mann / Diese Frau ist verheiratet. Jeder Ring kann zum Ehering werden. In Deutschland ist der Ehering oft ein einfacher goldener Ring. Zum Ehering wird ein Ring
5   durch die eingravierte Schrift. Auch auf sehr schmale Ringe kann man die Vornamen der Eheleute und das Hochzeitsdatum eingravieren.

Wenn[2] der Ring einmal am Finger ist, darf er nie[3] mehr herunter kommen. Wenn der Ring kalt wird, wird auch die Liebe kalt. Wenn der Ring zerbricht oder wenn er verloren geht, dann ist das schlecht für die Liebe.

Das Herz als Sitz der Liebe

10 Die alten Griechen und Ägypter trugen den Ehering am linken Ringfinger. Sie glaubten[4], dass eine Ader[5] von diesem Finger direkt zum Herzen führt. Sie glaubten, dass das Herz der Sitz der Liebe ist. Ein bekannter Kinderreim lautet:

Er (oder sie) liebt mich von Herzen,
mit Schmerzen[6],
15 *oder gar nicht.*

Wenn man wissen möchte, ob der Freund oder die Freundin einen[7] liebt, dann pflückt man eine Blume und reißt ihr nacheinander alle Blütenblätter ab[8]. Bei jedem Blütenblatt sagt man eine Zeile des
20 Reims. Das, was man beim letzten Blütenblatt sagt, gilt[9].

In Italien trägt man den Ring noch heute an der linken Hand. In Deutschland trägt man nur den Verlobungsring[10] an der linken Hand. Den Ehering
25 trägt man an der rechten Hand.

---

[1]*eternal* [2]*When, If* [3]*darf ... it must never* [4]*believed* [5]*vein, artery* [6]*pain* [7]*here: you* [8]*reißt ... plucks all its petals one at a time* [9]*is valid* [10]*engagement ring*

Arbeit mit dem Text

A. Guess the meaning of the following words by looking at the context of the sentences in which they appear. Some hints are provided.

1. **Ehering** (Zeile 1) HINT: **Ehering** is a compound of **Ehe** and **Ring.** Look at the drawing. What kind of rings are they? What might **Ehe** mean?
2. **Anfang** (Zeile 1) HINT: the opposite of the noun **Ende**
3. **aufhören** (Zeile 2) HINT: a verb similar in meaning to the noun **Ende**
4. **Eheleute** (Zeile 6) HINT: You already guessed **Ehe. Leute** means people; what might the combination of these two words mean?
5. **herunter** (Zeile 7) HINT: Because the second clause contains the phrase *must never*, **herunter** is probably the opposite of **am Finger.**
6. **zerbricht** (Zeile 8) HINT: What bad things can happen to a ring? The root of this word is **brich.** German **ch** is often English *k.* What English word is spelled *br__k* and is something bad?
7. **verloren** (Zeile 8) HINT: Ignore the prefix **ver-** and the **-n** for a moment. German **r** is sometimes related to English *s.* What verb is this?
8. **Herzen/Herz** (Zeile 11) HINT: What might be called the seat of love (line 12) and be connected to other parts of the body by a vein?
9. **Kinderreim** (Zeile 12) HINT: You know what **Kinder** means. If you pronounce **Reim,** it sounds like *rhyme,* which is its meaning. What might the combination of these two words mean?

B. Beantworten Sie die folgenden Fragen.

1. Warum symbolisiert ein Ring ewige Liebe?
2. Was signalisiert ein Ehering der Welt[1]?
3. Welche Ringe trägt man in Deutschland oft als Eheringe?
4. Was ist oft in Eheringen eingraviert?
5. Was passiert, wenn der Ring vom Finger herunter kommt? Was glauben viele Leute?
6. Was macht man in Deutschland, wenn man wissen möchte, ob der Freund oder die Freundin einen liebt?
7. Was trägt man in Deutschland an der linken Hand und was an der rechten Hand?

Nach dem Lesen

A. Gibt es in Ihrer Klasse unterschiedliche Traditionen und Kulturen? Sammeln Sie in Ihrer Klasse Antworten auf die folgenden Fragen.

1. Trägt man in Ihrer Kultur Eheringe? Wenn ja, an welchem Finger welcher Hand trägt man sie? Wenn nicht, wie signalisiert man, dass Menschen verheiratet sind? Oder signalisiert man es gar nicht?
2. Was macht man in Ihrer Kultur, wenn man herausfinden möchte, ob jemand einen liebt?

B. Was halten Sie von Symbolen, die zeigen, dass zwei Menschen miteinander durchs Leben gehen wollen? Finden Sie sie wichtig? Warum (nicht)?

[1]der ... to the world

Grammatik 2.4

Vocabulary Display. Presentation.
Was trägt Michael? Er trägt ein Unterhemd, eine Unterhose, Sandalen und Socken. Go over all four people.
Receptive recall. Cover up labels for clothing: *Wer trägt Ohrringe? Wer trägt ein Nachthemd?* Go over all items. **Choral response.** Practice pronunciation of new words with questions containing possessive adjectives: *Sprechen wir über Michael. Wiederholen Sie bitte! Wie findest du sein Unterhemd? Wie findest du seine Unterhose?* etc. **Productive recall 1.** Cover up labels: *Was trägt Michael?* etc. **Productive recall 2.** *Schreiben Sie auf, was diese vier Personen tragen. Schreiben Sie „Michael trägt" und ergänzen Sie die Kleidungsstücke. Achten Sie auf die richtige Form von „ein".* **Follow-up.** Write value judgments on the board such as: *Super. Sexy. Toll. Langweilig. Zum Gähnen. Hässlich. Todschick.* Write display items in four gender/plural columns with the headings: *seinen/ihren, sein/ihr, seine/ihre, seine/ihre.* Ask sts. to work in pairs asking each other *Wie findest du Michaels Unterhemd? Und seine Unterhose?* Alternatively, ask sts. to work in groups of 3 with 2 people asking each other questions and the third person keeping tabs on who likes what and on whether they use the correct form of the possessive adjective.

der Haarschnitt
der Ohrring
die Halskette
die Sporthose

Silvia

HELGA: Wie findest du ihren Haarschnitt?
SIGRID: Sieht gut aus!

das Piercing
der Schal
das Armband
das Nachthemd

Melanie

CLAIRE: Wie findest du ihr Nachthemd?
JOSEF: Klasse!

die Sonnenbrille
der Bademantel
die Handschuhe
der Gürtel

Rolf

SIGRID: Wie findest du seinen Bademantel?
HELGA: Nicht schlecht!

das Unterhemd
die Unterhose
die Socken
die Sandalen

Michael

JUTTA: Na, wie findest du seine Socken?
JENS: Hässlich!

Situation 9 | Interaktion: Wie findest du meine Sportschuhe?

Sit. 9. Preparation 1: (meaning-focused) *Ich trage heute … / Rob trägt heute …* Try to mention most of the items in the list. *Was tragen Sie? Lesen Sie die Liste in Sit. 9 und kreuzen Sie an, was Sie heute tragen.* **Part 1:** Sts. read the list individually and mark what they are wearing. **Preparation 2:** Introduce more descriptive adjectives in reference to your own clothing: *Wie finden Sie meine Schuhe? Wie finden Sie meinen Pullover? toll, schön, ganz nett, hässlich, furchtbar?* Then demonstrate the model with a student. **Part 2:** Sts. work in pairs to complete the chart.

1. Kreuzen Sie an, was Sie heute tragen.
2. Fragen Sie, wie Ihr Partner / Ihre Partnerin das findet.

> MODELL: S1: Wie findest du meine Schuhe?
> S2: Deine Schuhe? Nicht schlecht.

echt stark   klasse   Finde ich ganz toll!

super

voll süß   Steht/Stehen dir gut!   Sieht/Sehen gut aus!

	Was Sie heute tragen	Wie Ihr(e) Partner(in) das findet
meine Hose		
meine Schuhe		
mein Kleid		
meinen Schal		
meinen Gürtel		
mein Armband		
meine Halskette		
meinen Ohrring / meine Ohrringe		

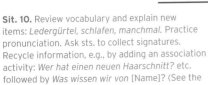

Situation 10 | Umfrage: Hast du einen neuen Haarschnitt?

Sit. 10. Review vocabulary and explain new items: *Ledergürtel, schlafen, manchmal.* Practice pronunciation. Ask sts. to collect signatures. Recycle information, e.g., by adding an association activity: *Wer hat einen neuen Haarschnitt?* etc. followed by *Was wissen wir von [Name]?* (See the IM for working with association activities.)

> MODELL: S1: Hast du einen neuen Haarschnitt?
> S2: Ja.
> S1: Unterschreib bitte hier.

UNTERSCHRIFT

1. Hast du einen neuen Haarschnitt?
2. Magst du Ledergürtel?
3. Trägst du heute eine Kette?
4. Findest du meine Hose schick?
5. Hast du ein Piercing?
6. Schläfst du im Schlafanzug?
7. Trägst du manchmal eine Brille?
8. Findest du mein Hemd / meine Bluse toll?
9. Trägst du gern einen Ring?
10. Hast du einen Sonnenhut?

Videoblick 🎬

Erste[1] Berliner Fashion-Week

Deutschland ist einer der wichtigsten Modemärkte[2] der Welt.
Die erste deutsche Fashion-Week findet nun in Berlin statt[3].

- In welchen Städten gibt es viele Fashion-Shows?
- Gibt es viele Fashion-Shows in Berlin?
- Wie viele Modeschulen und Designer gibt es in Berlin?
- Wie oft soll die Berliner Fashion-Week stattfinden?

[1]*first* [2]*fashion markets* [3] findet statt *takes place* [4]*example*

Fashion-Week in Berlin: Nach dem Vorbild[4] von
Paris, Mailand und New York.

Situation 11 | Frau Gretters neuer Mantel

Sit. 11. Have sts. reorder the lines of the dialogue, working in groups of 3. Then put the sts. into groups of 7 and hand out all the lines of the dialogue (each line written on a separate piece of paper) to each group, and ask sts. to line themselves up according to the correct sequence of their dialogue lines. Then ask each st. to read his or her line.

Bringen Sie die Sätze in die richtige Reihenfolge.

____5____ Von Kaufland. Er ist wirklich sehr schön.

____4____ Finde ich ganz toll. Woher haben Sie ihn?

____1____ Guten Tag, Frau Körner.

____6____ Ach, mein Mantel ist auch schon so alt. Ich brauche dringend etwas für den Winter.

____2____ Guten Tag, Frau Gretter. Wie geht's denn so?

____7____ Gehen Sie doch auch mal zu Kaufland. Da gibt es gute Preise.

____3____ Danke, ganz gut. Wie finden Sie denn meinen neuen Mantel?

Situation 12 | Flohmarkt

Sit. 12. Explain the activity and ask sts. to write down five items they want to sell. Then, write four columns on the board labeled *meinen/deinen, mein/dein, meine/deine,* and *meine/deine.* Ask sts. to tell you what they want to sell, and in which column to write the item. Practice model exchange with several items on the board. Model and make sure sts. understand the new vocabulary: *verkaufen, kaufen, brauchen, kosten, nehmen, zeig mal.* Ask sts. to find five different buyers by engaging in the model exchange and by writing down the names of the buyers. Encourage sts. to expand on the model, e.g., *Nein, ich brauche keine Ohrringe, aber ich finde dein T-Shirt toll. Verkaufst du es?* **Follow-up:** Ask who sold what to whom: *Was haben Sie verkauft? Wer hat es gekauft? Für wie viel hat er (sie) es gekauft?* Don't expect students to produce the present perfect forms yet. **Alternative.** Change the activity into a *Flohmarkt* role-play either by bringing a few small items to class yourself or by asking students to bring some.

Schreiben Sie fünf Sachen auf, die Sie verkaufen. Schreiben Sie auf, wer sie kauft und wie viel sie kosten.

MODELL: S1: Ich verkaufe meine Ohrringe. Brauchst du Ohrringe?
       S2: Nein danke, ich brauche keine Ohrringe.
          oder Zeig mal. Ja, ich finde deine Ohrringe toll. Was kosten sie?
       S1: 2 Euro.
       S2: Gut, ich nehme sie.

ZU VERKAUFEN	KÄUFER/KÄUFERIN	PREIS
1. _____	_____	_____
2. _____	_____	_____
3. _____	_____	_____
4. _____	_____	_____
5. _____	_____	_____

Lektüre: The *Lektüren* in some of the chapters introduce sts. to classic and recent films produced in the German-speaking countries. For this particular section, have sts. look at the movie poster and talk about it. Ask them questions such as: *Was assoziieren Sie mit den Personen auf dem Poster? Wie sehen sie aus? Was machen sie? Sind sie Freunde, Verwandte oder Fremde? Warum heißt der Film „Im Juli"? Was für ein Film kann das sein (Krimi, Liebesfilm, etc.)?* Collect sts.' answers on the board and by doing so create a possible story line with sts.' help.
Note. Fatih Akin, born in 1973, is the son of Turkish immigrants who came to Germany in the 1960s. Akin made his debut as a movie director in 1998 with his short film *Kurz und schmerzlos*, and has become very successful since then. His fourth movie, *Gegen die Wand* (2004), in particular, earned a lot of praise and received many awards. *Im Juli* is his second film, which is a road movie, romantic and funny. Daniel, the main character, falls in love with Melek, a Turkish woman, whom he even follows to Turkey. Convinced that Melek is the love of his life, Daniel does not notice that Juli, who has loved him for a long time, is the one. Juli's and Daniel's journey through Eastern Europe turns out to be an exciting undertaking as almost everything goes wrong: they fall into the river Danube, are involved in a car chase, and even end up in prison.

Vor dem Lesen

A. Beantworten Sie die folgenden Fragen.

1. Was sehen Sie auf dem Foto?
2. Warum heißt der Film wohl „Im Juli"?
3. Wer ist der Regisseur?
4. Wann startete der Film im Kino?

Im Juli

Regisseur: Fatih Akin

Schauspieler in den Hauptrollen:
Moritz Bleibtreu, Christiane Paul

Erscheinungsjahr: 2000

B. Lesen Sie die Wörter im Miniwörterbuch. Suchen Sie sie im Text und unterstreichen Sie sie.

Miniwörterbuch		
langweilig	boring
flippig	weird, funky
das **Pech**	bad luck
fahren	to drive
der **Liebeskummer**	love problems

Film: *Im Juli*

Der junge Lehrer Daniel (Moritz Bleibtreu) lebt in Hamburg und ist ein sehr langweiliger Typ. Nur die flippige Schmuckverkäuferin Juli (Christiane Paul) interessiert sich für ihn. In den Sommerferien trifft Daniel auf einer Party die Türkin Melek (Idil Üner). Sie ist auf dem Weg nach Istanbul. Daniel verliebt sich sofort in seine „Traumfrau". Pech
5 für Juli, die auch auf die Party kommt! Als Melek am nächsten Morgen in die Türkei fliegt, fährt Daniel seiner großen Liebe mit dem Auto nach – 2 700 Kilometer bis nach Istanbul. Auf der Autobahn trifft er Juli wieder. Sie will aus Liebeskummer einfach weg-trampen. Daniel nimmt sie in seinem Auto mit. Für Juli und Daniel beginnt eine wilde Odyssee und eine Reise in ein neues Leben. Am Ende ist Daniel ein anderer Typ: nicht
10 mehr der schüchterne und langweilige Lehrer, sondern ein cooler Lover und auch Juli ist keine traurige junge Frau mit Liebeskummer mehr.

Arbeit mit dem Text

Welche Aussagen sind falsch? Verbessern Sie die falschen Aussagen.

1. Daniel kommt aus Hamburg.
2. Auf einer Reise lernt Daniel die Türkin Melek kennen.
3. Juli liebt den langweiligen Daniel.
4. Daniel fährt mit dem Motorrad nach Istanbul.
5. Juli fliegt mit Melek in die Türkei.
6. Am Ende der Reise ist Daniel nicht mehr langweilig.

Nach dem Lesen

A. Suchen Sie weitere Informationen über den Regisseur Fatih Akin im Internet.

1. Woher kommt Fatih Akin?
2. Woher kommen seine Eltern?
3. Wie alt ist er?
4. Wie heißt sein erster Film?
5. Welche Preise haben seine Filme bekommen[1]?

B. Sehen Sie den Trailer zum Film im Internet an und gestalten Sie Ihr eigenes Filmposter.

[1]*received*

Vergnügen

Grammatik 2.5–2.6

Herr Wagner schläft gern.

Jens fährt gern Motorrad.

Sofie trägt gern Hosen.

Melanie lädt gern Freunde ein.

Mehmet läuft gern im Wald.

Ernst isst gern Eis.

Hans liest gern Bücher.

Natalie sieht gern fern.

Situation 13 | Interview: Was machst du lieber?

MODELL: S1: Schwimmst du lieber im Meer oder lieber im Schwimmbad?
S2: Lieber im Meer.

1. Isst du lieber zu Hause oder lieber im Restaurant?
2. Spielst du lieber Volleyball oder lieber Basketball?
3. Trägst du lieber ein Hemd (eine Bluse) oder lieber ein T-Shirt?
4. Fährst du lieber Fahrrad oder lieber Motorrad?
5. Schreibst du lieber Postkarten oder lieber Briefe?
6. Liest du lieber Zeitungen oder lieber Bücher?
7. Lädst du lieber Freunde oder lieber Verwandte ein?
8. Läufst du lieber im Wald oder lieber in der Stadt?
9. Fährst du lieber ans Meer oder lieber in die Berge?
10. Schläfst du lieber im Hotel oder lieber im Zelt?

Situation 14 | Umfrage: Fährst du jedes Wochenende nach Hause?

MODELL: S1: Fährst du jedes Wochenende nach Hause?
S2: Ja.
S1: Unterschreib bitte hier.

UNTERSCHRIFT

1. Fährst du jedes Wochenende nach Hause? _____
2. Schläfst du manchmal im Klassenzimmer? _____
3. Vergisst du oft wichtige Geburtstage? _____

4. Siehst du mehr als vier Stunden pro Tag fern? _____
5. Trägst du oft eine Krawatte? _____
6. Lädst du oft Freunde ein? _____
7. Liest du jeden Tag eine Zeitung? _____
8. Sprichst du mehr als zwei Sprachen? _____

 Situation 15 | Informationsspiel: Was machen sie gern?

Sit. 15. (See the IM.) The corresponding chart is in Appendix A.

MODELL: s1: Was trägt Richard gern?
s2: Pullis.
s1: Was trägst du gern?
s2: _____

	Richard	Josef und Melanie	mein(e) Partner(in)
fahren	Motorrad	Zug	
tragen	Pullis	Jeans	
essen	Wiener Schnitzel	Pizza	
sehen	Fußball	Gruselfilme	
vergessen	seine Hausaufgaben	ihr Alter	
waschen	sein Auto	ihr Auto	
treffen	seine Freundin	ihre Lehrer	
einladen	seinen Bruder	ihre Eltern	
sprechen	Italienisch	Englisch	

Kultur ... Landeskunde ... Informationen

Vergnügen

Was ist am Wochenende für Sie am wichtigsten[1]? Kreuzen Sie an:

Ausschlafen	☐
Fernsehen	☐
Sport	☐
Lesen	☐
Hobbys	☐
Freunde einladen	☐

Lesen Sie zuerst, was Deutschen am Wochenende am wichtigsten ist. Beantworten Sie dann die Fragen.

- „Glotze" ist ein anderes Wort für _____.
- In welchen vier Bereichen gibt es Unterschiede zwischen Männern und Frauen?
- Sind Hobbys wichtiger für Frauen oder für Männer?
- Wer liest lieber, Männer oder Frauen?
- Machen Sie dieselbe Umfrage in Ihrem Kurs. Wie ist das Resultat? Gibt es auch Unterschiede zwischen Männern und Frauen? Ist das Resultat typisch (repräsentativ) für Studenten?

[1]am ... *most important* [2]*excursions, outings* [3]*to experience* [4]*to nurture* [5]*to take it easy, be lazy* [6]*bars, taverns* [7]*to take care of, handle* [8]*Significant* [9]*differences* [10]*areas*

FOCUS-FRAGE

„Was ist Ihnen am Wochenende am wichtigsten?"
GLOTZE TOTAL
von 1300 Befragten* antworteten

Fernsehen	**49%**
Familienleben	**45%**
Ausschlafen	**44%**
Ausflüge[2] machen	**37%**
Natur erleben[3]	**35%**
Hobbys	**34%**
Lesen	**32%**
Partnerschaft pflegen[4]	**27%**
Faulenzen[5]	**26%**
Ausgehen/Kneipen[6]	**23%**
In Ruhe einkaufen	**19%**
Sport	**18%**
Kultur/Kino/Konzerte	**17%**
Reparaturen erledigen[7]	**16%**

Deutliche[8] Unterschiede[9] zwischen Männern und Frauen gibt es in den Bereichen[10] „Familienleben" (38 % zu 51 %), „Hobbys" (43 % zu 26 %), „Lesen" (24 % zu 39 %) und „Reparaturen" (28 % zu 6 %). Die alten und neuen Bundesländer unterscheiden sich am meisten bei „Familienleben" (43 % zu 52 %) und „Faulenzen" (29 % zu 17 %)

* Repräsentative Umfrage des Sample-Instituts für Focus
Mehrfachnennungen möglich

Situation 16 | Bildgeschichte: Ein Tag in Silvias Leben

Sit. 16. (See the IM for suggestions on using narration series.) *Sit. 16* contains stem-changing verbs and separable-prefix verbs and uses subject-verb inversion. Sentences: 1. *Silvia schläft bis acht Uhr.* 2. *Vor dem Frühstück läuft sie fünf Kilometer.* 3. *Heute trägt sie Jeans und eine Jacke.* 4. *Sie fährt mit dem Bus zur Uni.* 5. *Um zwölf Uhr isst sie in der Mensa.* 6. *Sie trifft Jürgen.* 7. *Jürgen lädt sie zum Abendessen ein.* 8. *Nach dem Essen geht sie nach Hause und sieht fern.* 9. *Dann liest sie noch eine halbe Stunde im Bett.* 10. *Um 12.30 schläft sie ein.* **Receptive recall:** *Welches Bild zeigt: Silvia fährt mit dem Bus zur Uni? (Bild 4.) Nach dem Essen geht Silvia nach Hause und sieht fern. (Bild 8.) Um 12.30 schläft Silvia ein. (Bild 10.) Vor dem Frühstück läuft Silvia fünf Kilometer. (Bild 2.) Heute trägt sie Jeans und eine Jacke. (Bild 3.) Mittags isst sie in der Mensa. (Bild 5.) Sie liest noch eine halbe Stunde im Bett. (Bild 9.) Sie trifft Jürgen. (Bild 6.) Silvia schläft bis 8 Uhr. (Bild 1.) Jürgen lädt Silvia zum Abendessen ein. (Bild 7.)* **Choral response. Productive recall:** *Was zeigt Bild 1?* usw. **Personalization:** Then ask sts. to work in small groups as they describe their day to one another.

AA. Have sts. describe Jürgen's day.

Videoecke

Aufgabe 1. (1) Preview the interview by focusing sts.' attention on the photos and captions: *Wer kommt aus Sachsen? Woher kommt Ulrike? Wer studiert Dolmetschen und Übersetzen? Wer studiert Erziehungswissenschaften?* Explain the subjects. **(2)** Read the sentence fragments out loud and explain unfamiliar vocabulary, e.g., *Lebenshaltungskosten, Brosche, Ölfarben, bummeln, Jahrhundert.* **(3)** Play Yvonne's interview once. **(4)** Ask sts. to complete the task in groups of three, and play the tape again. **(5)** Let sts. work in groups for 3–4 minutes. **(6)** Play the tape again. For each sentence ask sts. to knock on the table or to clap their hands when they hear the first part of the sentence. Stop the tape. Play the whole sentence and ask sts. what the second part was.

- Was für Hobbys hast du?
- Gehst du gern auf Partys?
- Was gehört zu einer richtigen Party?
- Gehst du oft ins Kino?
- Welche Filme guckst du gern?
- Gehst du gern einkaufen?
- Wofür gibst du das meiste Geld aus?
- Trägst du gern Schmuck?
- Besitzt du irgendwas Besonderes?
- Wie hast du das bekommen?

Yvonne kommt aus Rochlitz (Sachsen). Sie studiert Erziehungswissenschaften und Sozialpädagogik.

Ulrike kommt aus Berlin. Sie studiert Dolmetschen und Übersetzen Englisch–Spanisch, Journalistik und Deutsch als Fremdsprache.

Aufgabe 1

Was sagt Yvonne? Verbinden Sie die beiden Satzhälften.

1. Am Wochenende, wenn ich Zeit habe, _____
2. Ich gehe sehr gern auf Partys _____
3. Ich gehe sehr gern ins Kino, _____
4. Ich gehe sehr gern einkaufen _____
5. Das meiste Geld gebe ich für Lebenshaltungskosten aus _____
6. Ich trage sehr gern Schmuck, _____
7. Das ist eine silberne Brosche _____

a. aber meist nur zu besonderen Anlässen.
b. male ich Aquarelle oder mit Ölfarben.
c. nur momentan habe ich leider nicht viel Zeit.
d. und dann bummel' ich in Leipzig durch die Innenstadt.
e. und dann natürlich für Kleidung.
f. und die stammt aus dem 19. Jahrhundert.
g. von meinen Freundinnen.

Aufgabe 2. (1) Read the words and let sts. guess for what questions they may provide the answers. **(2)** Ask sts. to underline the words they hear as you play Ulrike's interview once. **(3)** Play Ulrike's interview again. This time ask sts. to knock on the table or clap their hands when they hear a particular word. Stop the tape after each word they hear. Also point out the words that are not in Ulrike's interview. Ask sts. where they heard these words before. Answer: In Yvonne's interview. **(4)** Ask sts. to complete the second part of *Aufgabe 2* in groups of three.

Student Interviews. (1) Ask sts. to jot down their own answers to the interview questions. **(2)** Pair sts. to interview each other. Ask them to jot down their partner's answers. **(3)** Follow up by sampling a few of the answers given in the interviews.

AA. As a follow-up, have sts. write a brief summary of each interviewee's comments.

A. Worüber spricht Ulrike? Unterstreichen Sie die Wörter, die Sie hören!

schwimmen
Fahrrad fahren
joggen
Inline skaten
tauchen
Ski fahren
Step-Aerobic
lesen
viele nette Leute
gute Stimmung
Spaß haben
Musik
tanzen
essen und trinken
Klamotten
weggehen
Action-Filme
Komödien
Krimis
Liebesfilme
Dramas
Horrorfilme
Ohrringe
Ring
Brosche
Kette
Tauchausrüstung

B. Ordnen Sie die Wörter den folgenden Kategorien zu: Hobbys, Party, Filme, Besitz.

Wortschatz

Besitz	Possessions
der **Fernseher**, -	TV set
der **Rucksack**, ⁼e	backpack
der **Schlafsack**, ⁼e	sleeping bag
der **Schlitten**, -	sled
der **Schmuck**	jewelry
der **Schreibtisch**, -e	desk
der **Wecker**, -	alarm clock
das **Bild**, -er	picture
das **Boot**, -e	boat
das **Fahrrad**, ⁼er	bicycle
das **Handy**, -s [hɛndi]	cellular phone
das **Klavier**, -e	piano
das **Pferd**, -e	horse
das **Surfbrett**, -er	surfboard

Ähnliche Wörter

die **Kamera**, -s; die **Kinokarte**, -n; der **CD-Spieler**, -; der **Computer**, -; der **DVD-Spieler**, -; das **Videospiel**, -e; der **Walkman**, **Walkmen**; der **Wanderschuh**, -e; das **Buch**, ⁼er (R); das **Songbuch**, ⁼er; das **Wörterbuch**, ⁼er; das **Radio**, -s; das **Telefon**, -e (R); das **Autotelefon**, -e

Haus und Wohnung	Home and Apartment
der **Schrank**, ⁼e	wardrobe
der **Sessel**, -	armchair
der **Stuhl**, ⁼e (R)	chair
der **Teppich**, -e	carpet
das **Regal**, -e	bookshelf, bookcase
das **Zimmer**, - (R)	room

Ähnliche Wörter

die Katze, -n; der Hund, -e; das Haus, ⁻er (R)

Kleidung und Schmuck — Clothes and Jewelry

die Halskette, -n	necklace
die Sonnenbrille, -n (R)	sunglasses
die Sporthose, -n	tights, sports pants
die Unterhose, -n	underpants
der Bademantel, ⁻	bathrobe
der Gürtel, -	belt
der Handschuh, -e	glove
das Armband, ⁻er	bracelet
das Nachthemd, -en	nightshirt
das Unterhemd, -en	undershirt

Ähnliche Wörter

die Jeans (pl.); die Socke, -n; der Pullover, -; der Pulli, -s; der Ring, -e; der Ohrring, -e (R); der Schal, -s; das Piercing; das T-Shirt, -s

Sonstige Substantive — Other Nouns

die Art, -en	kind, type
die Bibliothek, -en	library
die Einladung, -en	invitation
die Lust	desire
hast du Lust?	do you feel like it?
die Mensa, Mensen	student cafeteria
die Mitbewohnerin, -nen	female roommate, housemate
die Reihenfolge, -n	order, sequence
die Sache, -n	thing
die Stadt, ⁻e	city
die Stunde, -n	hour
die Tasse, -n	cup
die Telefonzelle, -n	telephone booth
die Zeitung, -en	newspaper
der Gruselfilm, -e	horror film
der Haarschnitt, -e	haircut
der Mensch, -en	person
Mensch!	Man! Oh boy! (coll.)
der Mitbewohner, -	male roommate, housemate
der Wald, ⁻er	forest, woods
im Wald laufen	to run in the woods
das Frühstück, -e	breakfast
das Geld	money
das Geschäft, -e	store
das Geschenk, -e	present
das Jahr, -e	year
das Studentenheim, -e	dorm

das Vergnügen	pleasure
das Zelt, -e	tent
die Verwandten (pl.)	relatives

Ähnliche Wörter

die Karte, -n (R); die Geburtstagskarte, -n; die Postkarte, -n; die Telefonkarte, -n; die Party, -s (R); die Pizza, -s; der Basketball, ⁻e; der Bus, -se; der Film, -e; der Flohmarkt, ⁻e; der Geburtstag, -e (R); der Kilometer, -; das Bier, -e; das Ding, -e; das Eis; das Fax, -e; das Hotel, -s; das Restaurant, -s; das Telegramm, -e

Verben — Verbs

an·schauen	to look at
aus·sehen, sieht ... aus	to look
es sieht gut aus	it looks good
ein·laden, lädt ... ein	to invite
essen, isst	to eat
fahren, fährt	to drive, ride
glauben	to believe
klingeln	to ring
laufen, läuft (R)	to run
lieben	to love
möchte	would like
recht haben	to be right
schicken	to send
schlafen, schläft	to sleep
Sport treiben	to do sports
stehen	to stand
das steht / die stehen dir gut!	that looks / they look good on you
treffen, trifft	to meet
treffen wir uns ...	let's meet ...
verkaufen	to sell
wissen, weiß	to know
ziehen	to move

Ähnliche Wörter

bringen; finden; gratulieren; kosten; sehen, sieht; vergessen, vergisst; waschen, wäscht

Adjektive und Adverbien — Adjectives and Adverbs

bequem	comfortable
billig	cheap, inexpensive
dringend	urgent(ly)
echt	real(ly)
einfach	simple, simply
falsch	wrong
ganz	whole; here: quite
grell	gaudy, shrill; here: cool, neat
hässlich	ugly
hübsch (R)	pretty

langweilig	boring
richtig	right, correct
schlecht	bad
schwierig	difficult
teuer	expensive
toll	neat, great
wertvoll	valuable, expensive
wichtig	important
ziemlich	rather
ziemlich groß	pretty big

Ähnliche Wörter
besser; schick

Possessivpronomen / Possessive Adjectives

dein, deine, deinen	your (*informal sg.*)
euer, eure, euren	your (*informal pl.*)
ihr, ihre, ihren	her, its; their
Ihr, Ihre, Ihren	your (*formal*)
mein, meine, meinen	my
sein, seine, seinen	his, its
unser, unsere, unseren	our

Präpositionen / Prepositions

an	at; on; to
am Samstag	on Saturday
am Telefon	on the phone
ans Meer	to the sea
bei	with; at
bei Monika	at Monika's
bis	until
bis acht Uhr	until eight o'clock

für	for
zu	to; for (*an occasion*)
zur Uni	to the university
zum Geburtstag	for someone's birthday

Sonstige Wörter und Ausdrücke / Other Words and Expressions

alles	everything
alles Mögliche	everything possible
also	well, so, thus
da	there
dich	you (*accusative case*)
diese, diesen, dieser, dieses	this; these
ein paar	a few
etwas	something
heute Abend	this evening
ihn	him; it (*accusative case*)
kein, keine, keinen	no; none
klar!	of course!
lieber	rather
ich gehe lieber …	I'd rather go . . .
mittags	at noon
morgen	tomorrow
natürlich	naturally
nie	never
niemand	no one, nobody
schon	already
vielleicht	perhaps
wenn	if; when
zusammen	together

Strukturen und Übungen

2.1 The accusative case

Wissen Sie noch?

Case indicates the function of a noun in a sentence.

Review grammar A.3.

nominative = subject
accusative = direct object

2.1. *Akkusativ*. The focus here is on the use of the accusative for direct objects. (The other major use of the accusative–with accusative prepositions–will be introduced later, in 6.2. Accusative pronouns are covered in 3.3.) The rule of thumb for sts. is to change the masculine singular ending to *-en*; all other forms stay the same. Encourage sts. to associate this ending with the masculine singular accusative, because it is the characteristic ending of this case.

The nominative case designates the subject of a sentence; the accusative case commonly denotes the object of the action implied by the verb, such as what is being possessed, looked at, or acted on by the subject of the sentence.

Jutta hat einen Wecker.	*Jutta has an alarm clock.*
Jens kauft eine Lampe.	*Jens buys a lamp.*

Here are the nominative and accusative forms of the definite and indefinite articles.

	Tisch (*m.*)	Bett (*n.*)	Lampe (*f.*)	Bücher (*pl.*)
Nominative	der	das	die	die
Accusative	den			
Nominative	ein	ein	eine	–
Accusative	einen			

Note that only the masculine has a different form in the accusative case.

Der Teppich ist schön. Kaufst du **den** Teppich?	*The rug is beautiful. Are you going to buy the rug?*

Übung 1 | Im Kaufhaus

Üb. 1. You can introduce the chart on the next page and allow sts. to hear accusative forms by creating sentences that they will judge true or false. Then assign the exercise for homework and have sts. check their answers against the answer key (Appendix G).

Was kaufen diese Leute? Was kaufen Sie?

MODELL: Jens kauft **den** Wecker, das Regal und den DVD-Spieler.

	Jens	Ernst	Melanie	Jutta	ich
der Pullover	–	–	–	+	
der Wecker	+	–	–	–	
die Tasche	–	+	+	–	
das Regal	+	–	+	–	
die Lampe	–	–	–	+	
die Stühle	–	+	–	–	
der DVD-Spieler	+	–	–	+	
der Schreibtisch	–	+	+	–	

Übung 2 | ## Ihr Zimmer

Was haben Sie in Ihrem Zimmer?

Üb. 2. Remind sts. to use indefinite (rather than definite) articles in the singular and no article in the plural. Have sts. tell a partner or the class what they have in their room.

MODELL: Ich habe einen/eine/ein/_____, ...

das Bett
das Bild / die Bilder
die Bücher
der CD-Spieler
der Fernseher
die Gitarre
das Klavier
die Lampe / die Lampen
das Radio

das Regal / die Regale
der Schrank
der Schreibtisch
der Sessel
der Stuhl / die Stühle
das Telefon
der Teppich
der Wecker
_____

2.2 The negative article: *kein, keine*

2.2. *Negativer Artikel: kein, keine.* Point out that, in general, *kein* is used to negate a noun that has either an indefinite article or no article and that, otherwise, negation is expressed using *nicht*.

Kein and **keine** (*not a*, *not any*, *no*) are the negative forms of **ein** and **eine**.

Im Klassenzimmer sind **keine** Fenster.	*There aren't any / are no windows in the classroom.*
Stefan hat **keinen** Schreibtisch.	*Stefan doesn't have a desk.*

The negative article has the same endings as the indefinite article **ein**. It also has a plural form: **keine**.

ein → kein
einen → keinen
eine → keine
[plural] → keine

	Teppich (*m.*)	Regal (*n.*)	Uhr (*f.*)	Stühle (*pl.*)
Nominative/Accusative	ein/einen	ein	eine	–
Nominative/Accusative	kein/keinen	kein	keine	keine

—Hat Katrin **einen** Schrank?	*Does Katrin have a wardrobe?*
—Nein, sie hat **keinen** Schrank.	*No, she doesn't have a wardrobe.*
—Hat Katrin **Bilder** an der Wand?	*Does Katrin have pictures on the wall?*
—Nein, sie hat **keine** Bilder an der Wand.	*No, she has no pictures on the wall.*

Vergleiche[1]

Wer hat was? Was haben Sie?

MODELL: Albert hat keinen Computer. Er hat einen Fernseher und eine Gitarre, aber er hat kein Fahrrad. Er hat ein Telefon und Bilder, aber er hat keinen Teppich.

	Albert	Heidi	Monika	ich
der Computer	−	+	−	
der Fernseher	+	−	−	
die Gitarre	+	+	−	
das Fahrrad	−	−	+	
das Telefon	+	+	+	
die Bilder	+	−	+	
der Teppich	−	+	+	

2.3   What would you like? *Ich möchte ...*

Use **möchte** (would like) to express that you would like to have something. The thing you want is in the accusative case.

Ich möchte **eine Tasse Kaffee,** bitte.   *I'd like a cup of coffee, please.*
Hans möchte **einen Fernseher**   *Hans would like a TV set for*
   zum Geburtstag.   *his birthday.*

Möchte is particularly common in polite exchanges, for example in shops or restaurants.

KELLNER: Was möchten Sie?   WAITER: *What would you like?*
   GAST: Ich möchte ein Bier.   CUSTOMER: *I'd like a beer.*

[1]*Comparisons*

Following are the forms of **möchte.** Note that the **er/sie/es**-form does not follow the regular pattern; it does not end in **-t.**

möchte			
ich	möchte	wir	möchten
du	möchtest	ihr	möchtet
Sie	möchten	Sie	möchten
er sie }möchte es		sie	möchten

To say that someone would like to do something, use **möchte** with the infinitive of the verb that expresses the action. This infinitive appears at the end of the sentence. Think of the **Satzklammer** used with separable-prefix verbs, and pattern your **möchte** sentences after it. Other verbs similar to **möchte** are explained in **Kapitel 3.**

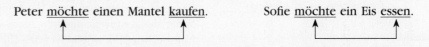

Peter **möchte** einen Mantel **kaufen.**   Sofie **möchte** ein Eis **essen.**

Übung 4 | Der Wunschzettel

Was, glauben Sie, möchten diese Personen?

MODELL: Meine beste Freundin möchte einen Ring.

das Auto	die Katze	der Ring
der Computer	der Koffer	die Rollerblades
der DVD-Spieler	das Motorrad	die Sonnenbrille
der Fernseher	die Ohrringe	die Sportschuhe
die Hose	der Pullover	der Teppich
der Hund	das Radio	der Videorekorder

1. Ich _____
2. Mein bester Freund / Meine beste Freundin _____
3. Meine Eltern _____
4. Mein Mitbewohner / Meine Mitbewohnerin und ich _____
5. Mein Nachbar / Meine Nachbarin in der Klasse _____
6. Mein Professor / Meine Professorin _____
7. Mein Bruder / Meine Schwester _____

2.4 Possessive adjectives

Use the possessive adjectives **mein, dein,** and so forth to express ownership.

—Ist das **dein** Fernseher?	*Is this your TV?*
—Nein, das ist nicht **mein** Fernseher.	*No, that's not my TV.*
—Ist das Sofies Gitarre?	*Is this Sofie's guitar?*
—Ja, das ist **ihre** Gitarre.	*Yes, that's her guitar.*

Here are the nominative neuter forms of the possessive adjectives.

Just as the personal pronoun **sie** can mean either *she* or *they*, the possessive adjective **ihr** can mean either *her* or *their*. When it is capitalized as **Ihr**, it means *your* and corresponds to the formal **Sie** (*you*).

	Singular	Plural
	mein Auto (*my car*)	**unser** Auto (*our car*)
	dein Auto (*your car*)	**euer** Auto (*your car*)
	Ihr Auto (*your car*)	**Ihr** Auto (*your car*)
	sein Auto (*his/its car*)	
	ihr Auto (*her/its car*)	**ihr** Auto (*their car*)

Note the three forms for English *your:* **dein** (*informal singular*), **euer** (*informal plural*), and **Ihr** (*formal singular or plural*).

Albert und Peter, wo sind **eure** Bücher?	*Albert and Peter, where are your books?*
Öffnen Sie **Ihre** Bücher auf Seite 133.	*Open your books to page 133.*

Possessive adjectives have the same endings as **ein** and **eine**.

ein → mein
eine → meine
einen → meinen
[plural] → meine

Possessive adjectives have the same endings as the indefinite article **ein**. They agree in case (*nominative* or *accusative*), gender (*masculine, neuter,* or *feminine*), and number (*singular* or *plural*) with the noun that they precede.

Mein Pulli ist warm. Möchtest du **meinen** Pulli tragen?	*My sweater is warm. Would you like to wear my sweater?*
Josef verkauft **seinen** Computer.	*Josef is selling his computer.*

Like **ein**, the forms of possessive adjectives are the same in the nominative and accusative cases—except for the masculine singular, which has an **-en** ending in the accusative.

Possessive Adjectives Nominative and Accusative Cases				
	Ring (m.)	Armband (n.)	Halskette (f.)	Ohrringe (pl.)
my	mein/meinen	mein	meine	meine
your	dein/deinen	dein	deine	deine
your	Ihr/Ihren	Ihr	Ihre	Ihre
his, its	sein/seinen	sein	seine	seine
her, its	ihr/ihren	ihr	ihre	ihre
our	unser/unseren	unser	unsere	unsere
your	euer/euren	euer	eure	eure
your	Ihr/Ihren	Ihr	Ihre	Ihre
their	ihr/ihren	ihr	ihre	ihre

Übung 5 | Hans und Helga

Üb. 5. For homework or oral work in class. Follow up by describing someone in the class and asking sts. to identify the person. Begin with clues that are not too helpful. Then have sts. do the same or describe volunteers.

Beschreiben Sie Hans und Helga.

Seine Haare sind braun.
_____ Augen sind grün.
_____ Halskette ist lang.
_____ Schuhe sind schmutzig.
_____ Gitarre ist alt.
_____ Zimmer ist groß.
_____ Fenster ist klein.

Ihre Haare sind blond.
_____ Augen sind blau.
_____ Halskette ist ...
...
...
...
...

Übung 6 | Minidialoge

Üb. 6. Assign for homework. Besides adding the possessive adjective, sts. need to choose the correct ending. Use this convention: The informal singular is used with a single first name, the informal plural with more than one first name, and the formal forms with *Herr* or *Frau*.

Ergänzen Sie **dein, euer** oder **Ihr**. Verwenden Sie die richtige Endung.

1. FRAU GRETTER: Wie finden Sie meinen Pullover?
   HERR WAGNER: Ich finde _____ Pullover sehr schön.
2. BERND: Weißt du, wo meine Brille ist, Veronika?
   VERONIKA: _____ Brille ist auf dem Tisch.
3. OMA SCHMITZ: Helga! Sigrid! Räumt _____ Schuhe auf!
   HELGA UND SIGRID: Ja, gleich, Oma.
4. HERR RUF: Jutta! Komm mal ans Telefon! _____ Freundin ist am Apparat[1].
   JUTTA: Ich komme.
5. HERR SIEBERT: Beißt _____ Hund?
   FRAU KÖRNER: Was glauben Sie denn! Natürlich beißt mein Hund nicht.
6. NORA: Morgen möchte ich zu meinen Eltern fahren.
   PETER: Wo wohnen _____ Eltern?
   NORA: In Santa Cruz.
7. JÜRGEN: Silvia und ich, wir verkaufen unseren Computer.
   ANDREAS: _____ Computer! Der ist so alt, den kauft doch niemand!

Wissen Sie noch?

Use **du (dein)** and **ihr (euer)** to address people whom you know well and whom you address by their first name. Use **Sie (Ihr)** for all other people.

Review grammar A.5.

---

[1]*phone*

Üb. 7. This is another example of an exercise type first introduced in *Kapitel 1, Üb. 1*, in which sts. need to pay attention to both grammar and meaning when selecting elements to construct sentences. Explain the task and do a few sample sentences with your sts. before assigning it as homework. First, sts. need to select a form of *verkaufen* that agrees in person and number with the subject at hand. Next, they need to choose an object in column 4 that is likely owned by the person in the subject position. Finally, they need to choose a form of the possessive adjective that agrees with the subject and that agrees with the gender number of the object selected from column 4. These objects are followed by their definite article in the nominative to remind sts. of their gender. You may wish to remind your sts. that no ending on the possessive adjective is associated with the neuter gender in the accusative case, etc.

Sie und die Studenten und Studentinnen in Frau Schulz' Deutschkurs brauchen Geld und organisieren einen Flohmarkt. Schreiben Sie Sätze. Wer verkauft was?

MODELL: Monika verkauft ihre CDs.

(Monika)	verkaufe	ihr	Computer (der)
Thomas	verkaufen	(ihre)	Ohrring (der)
ich	verkaufen	ihre	Wörterbuch (das)
Katrin	verkaufen	ihren	DVD-Spieler (der)
Peter und Heidi	(verkauft)	ihren	(CDs) (*pl.*)
wir	verkauft	mein	Bücher (*pl.*)
Stefan	verkauft	seine	Gitarre (die)
Nora und Albert	verkauft	seinen	Bilder (*pl.*)
Frau Schulz	verkauft	unsere	Telefon (das)

2.5 The present tense of stem-vowel changing verbs

2.5. *Präsens: Verben mit Vokalwechsel.* The presentation of stem-vowel changing verbs completes the introduction of the present tense of verbs that are not modals. (For modals see 3.1 and 3.2.) Point out that there are four patterns. Not all verbs with these vowels in the infinitive make these vowel changes (e.g., *machen* and *kaufen* do not); the changes are restricted to strong verbs, a term that will become meaningful to sts. only when the perfect tense has been introduced in *Kapitel 4*.

There are four types of stem vowel changes:
a → ä, au → äu, e → i, e → ie.

In some verbs, the stem vowel changes in the **du**- and the **er/sie/es**-forms.

—**Schläfst** du gern?   *Do you like to sleep?*
—Ja, ich **schlafe** sehr gern.   *Yes, I like to sleep very much.*
Ich **lese** viel, aber Ernst **liest** mehr.   *I read a lot, but Ernst reads more.*

These are the types of vowel changes you will encounter.

a → ä	fahren:	du fährst	er/sie/es fährt	*to drive*
	schlafen:	du schläfst	er/sie/es schläft	*to sleep*
	tragen:	du trägst	er/sie/es trägt	*to wear*
	waschen:	du wäschst	er/sie/es wäscht	*to wash*
	einladen*:	du lädst ... ein	er/sie/es lädt ... ein	*to invite*
au → äu†	laufen:	du läufst	er/sie/es läuft	*to run*
e → i	essen:	du isst‡	er/sie/es isst	*to eat*
	geben:	du gibst	er/sie/es gibt	*to give*
	sprechen:	du sprichst	er/sie/es spricht	*to speak*
	treffen:	du triffst	er/sie/es trifft	*to meet*
	vergessen:	du vergisst‡	er/sie/es vergisst	*to forget*
e → ie§	lesen:	du liest‡	er/sie/es liest	*to read*
	sehen:	du siehst	er/sie/es sieht	*to see*
	fernsehen:	du siehst ... fern	er/sie/es sieht ... fern	*to watch TV*

Jürgen **läuft** jeden Tag 10 Kilometer.   *Jürgen runs 10 kilometers every day.*
Ernst **isst** gern Pizza.   *Ernst likes to eat pizza.*
Michael **sieht** gern **fern**.   *Michael likes to watch TV.*

Achtung!

—Läufst du **gern** in der Stadt?   *Do you like to jog in the city?*
—Nein, ich laufe **lieber** im Wald.   *No, I prefer jogging in the forest.*

---

*Recall that verb stems ending in **-d** or **-t** insert an **-e-** before another consonant: **ich arbeite, du arbeitest**. Verb forms that contain a vowel change do not insert an **-e-**: **du lädst ein**. Verb forms without this vowel change, however, do insert an **-e-**: **ihr ladet ein.**
†Recall that **äu** is pronounced as in English *boy*.
‡Recall that verb stems that end in **-s, -ß, -z,** or **-x** do not add **-st** in the **du**-form, but only **-t.**
§Recall that **ie** is pronounced as in English *niece*.

Üb. 8-10. This sequence of exercises focuses first receptively on the meaning of verb endings (*Üb. 8*), before moving on to producing verb forms (*Üb. 9*), and finally, to contrasting the forms of the stem-vowel changing verbs. You may wish to alert your sts. to the fact that *machen* in *Üb. 9* is not a stem-changing verb. Use *Üb. 10* as an activity in class after having assigned it for homework: using the statement-question format of the assignment, sts. interview each other about their preferences.

Übung 8 | Minidialoge

Ergänzen Sie das Pronomen.

1. OMA SCHMITZ: Seht _____a gern fern?
   HELGA UND SIGRID: Ja, _____b sehen sehr gern fern.
2. FRAU GRETTER: Lesen _____a die Zeitung?
   MARIA: Im Moment nicht. _____b lese gerade ein Buch.
3. HERR SIEBERT: Isst Ihre Tochter gern Eis?
   HERR RUF: Nein, _____a isst lieber Joghurt. Aber da kommt mein Sohn, _____b isst sehr gern Eis.
4. SILVIA: Wohin[1] fährst _____a im Sommer?
   ANDREAS: _____b fahre nach Spanien. Und wohin fahrt _____c?
   SILVIA: _____d fahren nach England.

Übung 9 | Jens und Jutta

Ergänzen Sie das Verb. Verwenden Sie die folgenden Wörter.

machen (2×)
fahren (2×)
essen (3×)
sehen
lesen
schlafen

MICHAEL: Was _____a Jutta und Jens gern?
ANDREA: Jutta _____b sehr gern Motorrad. Jens _____c lieber fern.
MICHAEL: Was essen sie gern? _____d Jens gern Chinesisch?
ERNST: Jens _____e gern Italienisch, aber nicht Chinesisch. Und Jutta _____f gern bei McDonald's.
MICHAEL: Und ihr, was _____g ihr gern?
ANDREA: Ich _____h gern Bücher und Ernst _____i gern. Und im Winter _____j wir gern Schlitten.

Übung 10 | Was machen Sie gern?

Sagen Sie, was Sie gern machen, und bilden Sie Fragen.

MODELL: ich/du: bei McDonald's essen →
Ich esse (nicht) gern bei McDonald's. Isst du auch (nicht) gern bei McDonald's?

1. wir/ihr: Deutsch sprechen
2. ich/du: Freunde einladen
3. ich/du: im Wald laufen
4. ich/du: Pullis tragen
5. wir/ihr: fernsehen
6. ich/du: Fahrrad fahren
7. wir/ihr: die Hausaufgabe vergessen
8. ich/du: schlafen

[1]*Where*

2.6 Asking people to do things: the *du*-imperative

2.6. The formal *Sie*-imperative was introduced in *Einführung A. Kapitel 10* will complete the presentation of the imperative by adding the *ihr*- and *wir*-forms to a summary of all forms.

Use the **du**-imperative when addressing people you normally address with **du,** such as friends, relatives, other students, and the like. It is formed by dropping the **-(s)t** ending from the present-tense **du**-form of the verb. The pronoun **du** is not used.

Drop the **-(s)t** from the **du**-form to get the **du**-imperative.

(du) arbeitest →	Arbeite!	*Work!*
(du) isst →	Iss!	*Eat!*
(du) kommst →	Komm!	*Come!*
(du) öffnest →	Öffne!	*Open!*
(du) siehst →	Sieh!	*See!*
(du) tanzt →	Tanz!	*Dance!*

Verbs whose stem vowel changes from **a(u)** to **ä(u)** drop the umlaut in the **du**-imperative.

(du) fährst →	Fahr!	*Drive!*
(du) läufst →	Lauf!	*Run!*

Wissen Sie noch?

To form commands for people you address with **Sie,** invert the subject and verb: **Sie kommen mit. → Kommen Sie mit!**

Review grammar A.1.

Imperative sentences always begin with the verb.

Trag mir bitte die Tasche.	*Please carry the bag for me.*
Öffne bitte das Fenster.	*Open the window, please.*
Reite nicht so schnell!	*Don't ride so fast!*
Sieh nicht so viel fern!	*Don't watch so much TV!*

Übung 11 | Probleme, Probleme

Üb. 11. This exercise is divided into two sections to make the task more manageable. Sentences 1–5 go with a–e, 6–10 with f–j.

Peter spricht mit Heidi über seine Probleme. Heidi sagt ihm, was er machen soll.

MODELL: PETER: Ich vergesse alles. (1)
HEIDI: Schreib es dir auf! (e)

1. Ich vergesse alles.
2. Ich sehe den ganzen Tag fern.
3. Ich arbeite zu viel.
4. Ich bin zu dick.
5. Ich trinke zu viel Kaffee.
6. Ich esse zu viel Eis.
7. Mein Pullover ist alt.
8. Ich koche nicht gern Italienisch.
9. Das Wochenende ist langweilig.
10. Ich fahre nicht gern Auto.

a. Treib Sport!
b. Trink Cola!
c. Lies ein Buch!
d. Mach eine Pause!
e. Schreib es dir auf!
f. Fahr Fahrrad!
g. Iss lieber Joghurt!
h. Lade deine Freunde ein!
i. Kauf dir einen neuen Pullover!
j. Koch Chinesisch!

Übung 12 | Ach, diese Geschwister!

Üb. 12. Watch sts.' sentences closely for the position of *nicht* before the complements in the negative commands.

Ihr kleiner Bruder macht alles falsch. Sagen Sie ihm, was er machen soll.

MODELL: Ihr kleiner Bruder isst zu viel. → Iss nicht so viel!

1. Ihr kleiner Bruder schläft den ganzen Tag.
2. Er liegt den ganzen Tag in der Sonne.
3. Er vergisst seine Hausaufgaben.
4. Er liest seine Bücher nicht.
5. Er sieht den ganzen Tag fern.
6. Er trinkt zu viel Cola.
7. Er spricht mit vollem Mund.
8. Er trägt seine Brille nicht.
9. Er geht nie spazieren.
10. Er treibt keinen Sport.

Übung 13 | Vorschläge[1]

Üb. 13. Alert sts. to the separable-prefix verbs in sentences 4, 7, and 10.

Machen Sie Ihrem Freund / Ihrer Freundin Vorschläge.

MODELL: deinen Eltern einen Brief / schreiben →
Schreib deinen Eltern einen Brief.

1. heute ein T-Shirt / tragen
2. keine laute Musik / spielen
3. den Wortschatz / lernen
4. deine Freunde / anrufen
5. nicht allein im Park / laufen
6. nicht zu lange in der Sonne / liegen
7. dein Zimmer / aufräumen
8. heute Abend in einem Restaurant / essen
9. nicht zu spät ins Bett / gehen
10. früh / aufstehen

[1]*Suggestions*

Wer Jemandt hie der gern welt lernen Dütsch schriben und läsen
uß dem aller kürtzisten grundt den Jeman erdencken kan Do durch
ein Jeder der vor nit ein büchstaben kan der mag kürtzlich und bald
begriffen ein grundt do durch er mag von jm selbs lernen sin schuld
uff schribe und läsen und wer es nit gelernen kan so ungeschickt
were Den will jch vm nut und vergeben glert haben und gantz nüt
von jm zü lon nemen er sig wer er well burger oder hantwercks ge
sellen frouwen und Junckfrouwen wer sin bedarff der kum har jn dr
wirt drüwlich glert vm ein zimlichen lon · Aber die junge knabe
und meitlin noch den fronvasten · wie gewonheit ist · 1516

Ambrosius Holbein: *Ein Schulmeister und seine
Frau bringen drei Knaben und einem Mädchen
das Lesen bei* (1516), Kunstmuseum, Basel

AMBROSIUS HOLBEIN

Dieses Gemälde[1] von Ambrosius Holbein (1494–1519) entstand als
Aushängeschild[2] eines Schulmeisters. Das Schulmeisterschild zeigt einen Lehrer
und seine Frau, die drei Jungen und einem Mädchen das Lesen beibringen[3].

Chapter opening artwork: Ambrosius Holbein was a brother of the more famous Hans Holbein the Younger. This painting was used as a kind of advertising tool to attract potential students. At a time when schooling was a privilege, it would have been comparable to the signs craftsmen used to show the kind of service they provided. Humanist and Renaissance artists were discovering the bourgeois world as a motif for their works. The text above the picture reads roughly: *Ist jemand hier, der gern Deutsch schreiben und lesen lernen wollte aus dem aller einfachsten Grund, den sich jemand erdenken kann, und wer auch keinen Buchstaben kennt, der wird es bald können. Er kann es lernen, seine eigenen Schulden aufzuschreiben und zu lesen. Und ist einer so ungeschickt, dass er es nicht lernen kann, den habe ich vergebens gelehrt und nehme gar keinen Lohn von ihm. Wer immer es ist, Bürger oder Handwerksgesellen, Frauen und Jungfrauen, wer es nötig hat, der komme her und er wird treulich um einen günstigen Lohn gelehrt. Aber die jungen Knaben und Mädchen nach den Fronfasten, wie Gewohnheit ist. 1516.*

Suggestion: Use the painting as a starting point to review classroom vocabulary and to introduce some new words. *Was sehen Sie auf dem Bild? Wie viele Personen sind auf dem Bild? Wer ist der Mann auf der linken Seite? Wer ist die Frau auf der rechten Seite? Was machen die Kinder? Was ist das Zimmer? Was hat der Mann in der Hand? Was macht er damit? Ist das eine moderne Schule?*

[1] painting [2] signboard [3] are teaching

Talente, Pläne, Pflichten

In **Kapitel 3**, you will learn how to describe your talents and those of others. You will learn how to express your intentions and how to talk about obligation and necessity. You will also learn additional ways to describe how you or other people feel.

Themen

Talente und Pläne
Pflichten
Ach, wie nett!
Körperliche und geistige Verfassung

Kulturelles

Videoblick: Handys in der Schule
Jugendschutz
Schuljahr und Zeugnisse
Videoecke: Fähigkeiten und Pflichten

Lektüren

Das Geheimnis der Küchenbank (Ulrike Kaup)
Die PISA-Studie

Strukturen

3.1 The modal verbs **können, wollen, mögen**
3.2 The modal verbs **müssen, sollen, dürfen**
3.3 Accusative case: personal pronouns
3.4 Word order: dependent clauses
3.5 Dependent clauses and separable-prefix verbs

Situationen

Talente und Pläne

Grammatik 3.1

Peter kann ausgezeichnet kochen.

Rosemarie und Natalie können gut zeichnen.

Claire kann gut Deutsch.

Melanie und Josef wollen heute Abend zu Hause bleiben und lesen.

Silvia will für Jürgen einen Pullover stricken.

Sofie und Willi wollen tanzen gehen.

Situation 1 | Kochen

Sit. 1. (See notes to *Kapitel 2, Sit. 11.*) Be sure to set the scene before asking sts. to put the sentences in order. *Zwei Studenten sitzen in der Mensa / im Cafe / usw. und sprechen miteinander.* s1 *lädt* s2 *zum Abendessen / zum Kochen ein. Was kochen sie?* You might ask sts. to do this activity as a race and award an extra point, or a prize, to the pair that first places the sentences in the correct order. Have sts. finish by playing the roles, varying content as they wish. You may need to give sts. some guidance in replacing words–*Spaghetti, Chinesisch usw.*

Bringen Sie die Sätze in die richtige Reihenfolge.

    5   Spaghetti esse ich besonders gern.

    6   Dann komm doch mal vorbei.

    4   Nicht so gut. Aber ich kann sehr gut Spaghetti machen.

    3   Kannst du Chinesisch kochen?

    1   Kochst du gern?

    2   Ja, ich koche sehr gern.

    7   Ja, gern! Vielleicht Samstag?

    8   Gut! Bis Samstag.

Situation 2 | Informationsspiel: Kann Katrin kochen?

Sit. 2. The corresponding chart is in Appendix A. Establish the context and model pronunciation in the example given, and then pronounce the adverbs (*ausgezeichnet, fantastisch usw.*) and the activities in the chart, having the sts. repeat after you immediately: *Kann Katrin zeichnen? Wie heißt diese Frage, wenn Sie einen Partner fragen? (Kannst du zeichnen?) Richtig.*

For extra practice of the *du-* and *ich-*forms, sts. could switch partners and repeat the activity with someone new, omitting the questions about Katrin and Peter and simply questioning their partner. To wrap up the activity, ask 3-4 sts. to describe either what they can do or what their partners can do.

MODELL: s1: Kann Peter kochen?
s2: Ja, fantastisch.
s1: Kannst du kochen?
s2: Ja, aber nicht so gut.

[+] ausgezeichnet
fantastisch
sehr gut
gut

[0] ganz gut

[−] nicht so gut
nur ein bisschen
gar nicht
kein bisschen

	Katrin	Peter	mein(e) Partner(in)
kochen	ganz gut	fantastisch	
zeichnen	sehr gut	kein bisschen	
tippen	nur ein bisschen	ganz gut	
Witze erzählen	ganz gut	ganz gut	
tanzen	fantastisch	sehr gut	
stricken	gar nicht	kein bisschen	
Skateboard fahren	ganz gut	nicht so gut	
Geige spielen	ausgezeichnet	nur ein bisschen	
schwimmen	gut	nur ein bisschen	
ein Auto reparieren	nicht so gut	nicht so gut	

Situation 3 | Interview: Kannst du das?

Sit. 3. Ask sts. first to record answers for themselves using B, N, or K. After they have finished for themselves, have them compare their results with a partner: *Ich kann besonders gut Walzer tanzen. Kannst du das?*—and record the partner's answers.

Alternate Activity. Ask sts. to draw a grid with columns headed *besonders gut, nicht so gut, kein bisschen* and to fill in their personal preferences and weaknesses using the given expressions as a starting point, but expanding or altering with more personal information, e.g. *Tennis spielen, Hip-Hop tanzen* etc. Then interview a partner and record the results.

Was können Sie besonders gut, nicht so gut, kein bisschen?

B = besonders gut
N = nicht so gut
K = kein bisschen

MODELL: s1: Ich kann besonders gut tauchen. Kannst du das?
s2: Ich kann nicht so gut tauchen.

	Ich	Partner/Partnerin
1. tauchen		
2. Gitarre spielen		
3. ein Fahrrad reparieren		
4. Schlittschuh laufen		
5. Französisch		
6. singen		
7. Haare schneiden		
8. Walzer tanzen		
9. Tischtennis spielen		

Sit. 4. Remind sts. who Melanie and Josef are and where they live, and tell them what the context of the situation is. Play the audio (or read the text) several times while sts. jot down what Melanie and Josef plan to do during their vacation. Ask them to work in groups of three and to compare notes after each listening. In addition, you may wish to put the table on the board and to fill in any

information as it is provided by the sts. Do not volunteer any information; rather, play the audio again and provide them with one word or two or the first two or three letters of a word. When the table is complete, ask sts. what Melanie and Josef can do together. Finally, ask sts. which of Melanie's and Josef's activities they like and which additional plans they have for their next vacation. Focus on activities rather than on going places. **Text for listening comprehension:** *MELANIE: Ich freue mich schon auf die Ferien, denn da kann ich viel machen, wozu ich sonst keine Zeit habe. Ich will zum Beispiel nach München fahren und eine Ausstellung für Fotografie besuchen. Außerdem will ich tauchen lernen. Im Schwimmbad der Universität kann man einen Tauchkurs für Anfänger machen. Ich möchte viel Querflöte spielen, denn das macht mir großen Spaß. Im Sommerurlaub muss man natürlich auch verreisen, irgendwohin, wo man schwimmen und in der Sonne liegen kann. Ich weiß noch nicht genau, wohin ich fahren möchte, aber vielleicht hat Josef ja eine Idee. JOSEF: Ich will in den Ferien mindestens drei Wochen verreisen. Am liebsten möchte ich nach Italien fahren, irgendwohin ans Meer, wo man schwimmen und in der Sonne liegen kann. Ich möchte jeden Tag lange schlafen und abends in Straßencafés sitzen. Vorher muss ich allerdings noch die Garage aufräumen und mein Motorrad reparieren. Das wird sicher auch ein paar Tage dauern.*

Situation 4 | Ferienpläne

Melanie und Josef wollen beide einen Teil[1] ihrer Ferien zu Hause in Regensburg verbringen, aber auch eine Reise machen. Was wollen sie wo machen? Können sie etwas zusammen machen? Hören Sie zu und ergänzen Sie die Tabelle.

NÜTZLICHE WÖRTER

die Ausstellung	exhibition
die Garage	garage
die Querflöte	transverse flute
sitzen	to sit

	Melanie	Josef	beide zusammen
in München	Ausstellung für Fotografie		
zu Hause in Regensburg	tauchen lemen	Garage aufräumen	
	Querflöte spielen	Motorrad reparieren	
	schwimmen	schwimmen	√
auf der Reise	in der Sonne liegen	in der Sonne liegen	√
		lange schlafen	
		in Cafés sitzen	

Lektüre 📖

Vor dem Lesen

A. The following children's story is entitled "The Secret of the Kitchen Bench." Look at the drawings and—keeping the title of the story in mind—guess what the story will be about. Come up with possible answers to these questions:

Wer sind die Hauptpersonen?	*Who are the main characters?*
Wo findet die Geschichte statt?	*Where does the story take place?*
Wann findet sie statt?	*When does it take place?*
Was passiert?	*What happens?*

B. The following words are important for the story. Match them with the sentences or phrases explaining or paraphrasing them. Then find these words in the story and underline them.

1. __b__ das Autodach   a. the lid of a container
2. __d__ etwas Langes   b. the roof of a car
3. __g__ nach draußen   c. directly
4. __a__ der Deckel   d. a long object
5. __f__ wach werden   e. to cause someone to awaken
6. __e__ wecken   f. the opposite of falling asleep
7. __c__ schnurstracks   g. outside the house

Lesehilfe

One approach to a short story is to focus on its global aspects—characters, place, time, and general action—before concentrating on detail. Read it several times at normal speed, resisting the urge to look up all new words. This serves two functions: (1) You understand the story more accurately because you never lose sight of the "big picture." (2) You learn vocabulary more effectively because you learn it in its full context.

[1]*part*

Lektüre: The reading "Das Geheimnis der Küchenbank" is taken from a children's book entitled *Ein Vampir vom Flohmarkt* by Ulrike Kaup. Cultural knowledge of kitchen benches is important here. If sts. are unfamiliar with kitchen benches and how common they are in German homes, show them pictures of eating areas that have such benches. Point out how many are designed with lids that open for storing things. **(1)** The goal of the prereading activity is to anticipate content and orient oneself by looking at the title and illustrations of the text. Ask sts. to work on the questions in *Vor dem Lesen* Part A in small groups. Encourage them to guess and use their imagination when they try to come up with answers to the questions. **(2)** Part B lends itself to individual work, followed by a wrap-up later in class to check for the correct answers. While sts. find the words in the text and underline them they read the text for the first time. The intention here is to introduce the meaning of important new vocabulary from the text and practice guessing from context at the same time. If sts. have difficulties with this exercise, they might find it helpful to work by categories, i.e. start with the nouns, then the verbs, and then the adjectives. Sts. might also find the task easier if they look for recognizable cognates as parts of words. Making reference to the context in which the words appear will also help make some of the paraphrases clearer. **(3)** *Arbeit mit dem Text* Part A introduces the important concept of compound nouns in German. Rec- ognizing word parts and guessing what the whole compound may mean is a very important skill when working with unfamiliar texts. Have sts. work using the *Nützliche Wörter* list to come up with potential English equivalents. Then ask them to find the words in the reading. **(4)** Part B is designed to help sts. develop a global understanding of the text by focusing on the important aspects of the people, places, time, and action. The questions *wer, wo, wann,* and *was (passiert)* are a productive way to approach almost any reading. Before having sts. order the sentences, spend some time with the class working through the narrative structure. Write four words on the board, each as the head of a column: *Wer? Wo? Wann? Was?* Elicit responses and write them in the appropriate columns: *WER: Wer sind die Personen? Wie heißen Sie? Wie alt sind sie ungefähr? Was wissen wir über sie? WO: Wo findet die Geschichte statt? An wie vielen unterschiedlichen Orten findet die Geschichte statt? Welche sind sie? WANN: Zu welcher Zeit findet die Geschichte statt, z.B. heute? vor hundert Jahren? vor 1 000 Jahren? Wie viel Zeit vergeht vom Anfang der Geschichte bis zum Ende? An welchen Wörtern erkennen Sie das?* Once you have the *wer, wo,* and *wann* you can elicit the *was* by asking sts. questions about the characters, places, and times just written on the board: *Was macht der Papa? Wo macht er das? usw.* Once you have worked through the narrative structure as a class, the sts. will be ready to work on the plot sequence task in small groups or in pairs. Since sts. at this point cannot be asked to summarize a text, sentence ordering provides a simplified version of the reading. **(5)** *Nach dem Lesen.* Ask sts. to get together in small groups and brainstorm for ideas how the story could go on. Use the suggestions in this section to get them started. A written assignment of 100-150 words can be done as homework. **(6)** As a follow-up, you may want to read the actual ending of the story, or summarize it for the sts. (See the IM for the text of the rest of the story.)

Das Geheimnis der Küchenbank

Marie schaut zum Küchenfenster hinaus. Sie ist schon lange fertig mit Frühstücken. „Guck mal[1], Papa", ruft sie plötzlich. „Guck mal, was Mama und Raul vom Flohmarkt mitbringen!" Auf
5 dem Autodach ist etwas Langes festgeschnallt[2]. Es ist aus dunklem Holz und hat vier Beine, die in die Luft ragen. „Sieht aus wie eine Küchenbank zum Aufklappen", sagt Papa und stellt seine Kaffeetasse auf die Spüle.

10 Papa und Marie gehen nach draußen. Mit Mama und Raul tragen sie die Bank ins Haus. Mama ist schrecklich stolz. „Die Bank war ganz billig", sagt sie. „Nur den doofen Deckel kriegen wir nicht auf." „Der klemmt[3]", sagt Raul. „Das ist kein Problem", sagt
15 Papa. „Das repariere ich morgen, da habe ich Zeit."

In der Nacht wird Raul plötzlich wach. Da hat es doch gerade geklopft![4] Er hört es ganz deutlich. Kerzengerade sitzt er im Bett. „Marie", ruft er leise. Aber Marie hat das Klopfen auch gehört und liegt bis zur Nase unter der Decke[5]. Raul klettert aus dem Bett und weckt Papa und Mama. „Du hast bestimmt geträumt[6]", beruhigt
20 ihn Mama. „Jetzt klopft keiner mehr!" „Doch", flüstert Raul. „Da ist es wieder." Und jetzt hören Mama und Papa auch ganz deutlich, dass da einer klopft. Es kommt aus der Küche.

Mit einem Mal sind Mama und Papa hellwach. Papa springt aus dem Bett und marschiert schnurstracks in die Küche. Mama und Raul schleichen aufgeregt
25 hinterher. Da steht Marie auch auf. Und dann starren alle auf die Bank. Papa versucht noch einmal den Deckel hochzuklappen[7]. Doch der bewegt sich nicht. „Verdammter Mist", flucht Papa. „Vielleicht geht es damit", sagt Mama und gibt Papa einen Tortenheber[8]. Papa schiebt den

Tortenheber zwischen Deckel und Bank und versucht vorsichtig den Deckel anzuheben. Das Holz ächzt und knarrt. Dann ein Ruck und der Deckel springt auf. Im selben Moment hört man ein lautes Kreischen[9].

Vor Schreck lässt Papa den Tortenheber fallen. Ein bleiches[10] Gesicht sieht Papa an, dann Mama und Raul und dann Marie. Es hat zwei funkelnde Augen, einen blassen Mund und zwei blitzende Eckzähne. „Wahnsinn", flüstert Marie. „Ein klei- ner Vampir!" Langsam richtet sich der Vampir auf. Seine langen dünnen Finger umklammern eine leere Blutkonserve[11]. Er hält sie Papa unter die Nase. „Voll machen!", krächzt[12] er mit heiserer Stimme. „Pfui Teufel", sagt Papa. Aber er geht zum Kühlschrank und holt eine Flasche Kirsch-
45 saft[13]. Damit füllt er die Konserve. „Was soll das denn?", fragt Raul erstaunt. „Vampire trinken doch Blut!" „Ein Vampir, der eine Kü-chenbank mit einem Sarg verwechselt[14], trinkt bestimmt auch Saft", sagt Papa.

Gierig[15] setzt der Vampir die Konserve an die bleichen Lippen. Aber dann schüttelt er sich und spuckt den Saft in hohem Bogen wieder aus[16]. Direkt auf
50 Mamas Nachthemd. „Bingo", sagt Raul. „So eine Schweinerei!", schimpft Mama. Der Vampir schüttelt sich noch einmal. „Schmeckt wie Spülwasser", sagt er böse.

[1]*Guck ... Look* [2]*fastened* [3]*Der ... It's stuck* [4]*Da ... Something was knocking!* [5]*blanket, covers* [6]*dreamt* [7]*to open up* [8]*cake server* [9]*screech* [10]*pale* [11]*blood bag* [12]*croaks* [13]*cherry juice* [14]*eine ... confuses a kitchen bench with a coffin* [15]*Greedily* [16]*spuckt aus spits out*

„Will Teufelszeug! Dalli, Dalli!" Da weiß Papa Bescheid[1]. Ist vom Abendessen nicht noch eine halbe Flasche Rotwein übrig? Die holt Papa jetzt und schenkt ein[2]. Der Vampir nimmt einen Probeschluck[3]. Mama und Raul gehen in Deckung[4]. Doch diesmal

55 trinkt der Vampir die Konserve in einem Zug leer. „Er mag das Zeug", jubelt Raul. „Er hat nicht einen Tropfen übrig gelassen!" „So", sagt Mama, „jetzt, wo er satt ist, wird er hoffentlich Ruhe geben!"

Aus: Ulrike Kaup, *Ein Vampir vom Flohmarkt*

Arbeit mit dem Text

A. In German, there are many nouns that consist of two or more individual words. When you know the parts, it is relatively easy to guess what the compound means. What are the English equivalents of the following words?

1. die Eckzähne
2. der Flohmarkt
3. das Küchenfenster
4. der Kühlschrank
5. das Nachthemd
6. der Rotwein
7. das Spülwasser
8. das Teufelszeug
9. der Wahnsinn

NÜTZLICHE WÖRTER

die Ecke	*corner, edge*
der Floh	*flea*
die Küche	*kitchen*
der Sinn	*sense*
spülen	*to wash, rinse*
der Teufel	*devil*
der Wahn	*delusion*
das Wasser	*water*
der Wein	*wine*
die Zähne	*teeth*
das Zeug	*stuff*

B. **Die Handlung.** Die folgenden Sätze fassen die Geschichte zusammen[5]. Bringen Sie die Sätze in die richtige Reihenfolge.

___10___ Dann probiert Papa es mit Rotwein.
___7___ Der Vampir hat Hunger und möchte Blut trinken.
___11___ Der Vampir trinkt den Rotwein bis auf den letzten Tropfen aus.
___4___ Die ganze Familie geht in die Küche.
___9___ Doch der Vampir spuckt den Kirschsaft in hohem Bogen auf Mamas Nachthemd.
___6___ In der Bank sitzt ein kleiner Vampir und kreischt.
___3___ In der Nacht hört Raul ein Klopfen und weckt seine Eltern.
___2___ Mama und Raul bringen eine Küchenbank vom Flohmarkt mit.
___1___ Marie und Papa sitzen am Frühstückstisch.
___5___ Papa öffnet die Bank mit einem Tortenheber.
___8___ Zuerst probiert Papa es mit Kirschsaft.

Nach dem Lesen

The story goes on. How do you think it continues? What happens to the little vampire after having drunk all that wine? Come up with ideas on how the story might continue and then finish it.

Wie geht die Geschichte weiter? Schreiben Sie ca. 100–150 Wörter.

[1]weiß ... *Papa knows what to do*   [2]schenkt ... *pours (it) in*   [3]nimmt ... *here: tries a sip*   [4]gehen ... *take cover*
[5]fassen ... *summarize the story*

Pflichten

Grammatik 3.2

Jens hat schlechte Noten. Er muss mehr lernen.

Er darf nicht mit seinen Freunden Skateboard fahren.

Jutta muss in der Schule besser aufpassen.

Sie darf in der Stunde nicht mit ihrer Freundin reden.

Jutta muss nach der Schule ihre Hausaufgaben machen.

Videoblick

Handys in der Schule

Was ist in der Schule erlaubt? Was ist verboten?

- Wo gibt es Schummelhilfe[1] bei Klassenarbeiten[2]?
- Was kann man per SMS schicken[3]?
- Darf man in der Schule seinen Bauchnabel[4] zeigen?
- Wer hat mit Schulklamotten[5] keine Probleme?

This short clip focuses on two problem areas for school kids: the use of cell phones in school and rules of clothing. While teachers may collect cell phones before tests in German schools, they may not tell their students to cover their belly buttons.

[1]*cheating help* [2]*tests* [3]*per ... send as a text message* [4]*belly button*
[5]*school clothes*

Verboten – Handys in der Klassenarbeit

Situation 5 | Schlechtes Zeugnis!

Jens hat drei Fünfen im Zeugnis.

- Was muss er machen? Was darf er nicht machen? Kreuzen Sie an.
- Schreiben Sie dann noch eine Sache dazu, die er machen muss, und eine, die er nicht machen darf.
- Entscheiden Sie schließlich, was am wichtigsten ist (1), was weniger wichtig (2–9) und was am unwichtigsten (10).

Sit. 5. Tell sts. about the German grading system (see the KLI on *Schuljahr und Zeugnisse*, p. 126).
Preparation: First talk about Jens's report card: *In welchen Fächern hat Jens eine Eins? eine Zwei? usw. Ist Jens ein guter oder ein schlechter Schüler? Was muss er tun, um ein guter Schüler zu sein?* Sts. work in groups of 3-4, treating this situation as a problem-solving activity. You should establish the pattern for the conversation by asking the first 3-4 questions and demonstrating the use of *muss* and *darf: Darf Jens Freitagabend in die Disko gehen? Nein, er darf Freitagabend nicht in die Disko gehen. Jens hat ein schlechtes Zeugnis. Muss er Latein lernen? Ja, er muss Latein lernen. Er hat eine Fünf in Latein.* Encourage sts. to make up as many additional responses as possible for the last two items. Afterward, write the responses on the board, correcting the grammar if necessary.

Follow-up: *In welcher Klasse ist Jens? In welche Klasse kommt er? Welches Fach haben amerikanische Schüler nicht?* Have sts. look at the drawing of Jens on the previous page. Ask: *In welchen Fächern muss Jens mehr lernen?*

MUSS	DARF NICHT		WIE WICHTIG? (1–10)
☐	☐	in die Disko gehen	_____
☐	☐	Latein lernen	_____
☐	☐	den ganzen Tag in der Sonne liegen	_____
☐	☐	seine Hausaufgaben machen	_____
☐	☐	jeden Tag ins Schwimmbad gehen	_____
☐	☐	eine Woche nach Italien fahren	_____
☐	☐	Nachhilfe nehmen	_____
☐	☐	mit seinen Lehrern sprechen	_____
☒	☐	_____	_____
☐	☒	_____	_____

Situation 6 | Umfrage: Musst du neben dem Studium arbeiten?

Sit. 6. (See the IM for suggestions on working with autograph activities). Explain new vocabulary, e.g., *neben dem Studium, Tiere, bis Mittag* and practice pronunciation. Set up the task and give sts. about 5 min. to walk around and ask questions. Turn the follow-up into an association activity (see the IM) to practice the third-person singular forms of the modal verbs.

AA. Practice the modal *dürfen* by asking sts. what they are not permitted to do in class, at home, in the student cafeteria, in the dorms, etc.

MODELL: S1: Musst du neben dem Studium arbeiten?
S2: Ja.
S1: Unterschreib bitte hier.

UNTERSCHRIFT

1. Musst du neben dem Studium arbeiten? _____
2. Kannst du gut Auto fahren? _____
3. Musst du mal wieder deine Eltern besuchen? _____
4. Darfst du in deiner Wohnung Tiere haben? _____
5. Musst du heute noch Hausaufgaben machen? _____
6. Kannst du jeden Tag bis Mittag schlafen? _____
7. Musst du oft einkaufen gehen? _____
8. Darfst du schon Bier trinken? _____

Situation 7 | Dialog

Sit. 7. (See the IM for suggestions on presenting dialogues.) **(1)** Set the scene by reminding sts. who Rolf and Katrin are, where they are, and what they are discussing. **(2)** Preteach vocabulary: *stören; Viel Glück!* **(3)** Ask sts. to open their books; play the dialogue for them at least twice while they fill in the blanks. **(4)** Write sts.' answers on the board, or ask them to write their answers on the board, while making any necessary corrections. **(5)** Play the dialogue one last time for the benefit of sts. who did not get the right answers. **(6) Follow-up:** *Wer hat morgen (diese Woche noch) eine Prüfung? In welchem Fach? Müssen Sie noch viel lernen? usw.*

Rolf trifft Katrin in der Cafeteria.

ROLF: Hallo, Katrin, ist hier noch <u>frei</u> ?

KATRIN: Ja, klar.

ROLF: Ich hoffe, ich störe <u>dich</u> nicht beim Lernen.

KATRIN: Nein, ich muss auch mal <u>Pause</u> machen.

ROLF: Was machst du denn?

KATRIN: Wir haben morgen eine <u>Prüfung</u> und ich <u>muss</u> noch das Arbeitsbuch machen.

ROLF: <u>Müsst</u> ihr viel für euren Kurs arbeiten?

KATRIN: Ja, ganz schön viel. Heute Abend <u>kann</u> ich bestimmt nicht fernsehen, <u>weil</u> ich so viel lernen muss.

ROLF: Ich glaube, ich störe dich nicht länger. <u>Viel Glück</u> für die Prüfung.

KATRIN: Danke, tschüss.

Situation 8 | Stefans Zimmer

Sit. 8. Sts.' books are closed. Show both drawings on the overhead and establish the context. First ask sts. to find all items that are different. Write these items on the board. Then ask what has to be done to the items on the board. You might also ask sts. to imagine that their parents are coming to visit. Ask for individual responses about what needs to be done before they arrive: *Stellen Sie sich vor, Ihre Eltern kommen zu Besuch. Was müssen Sie machen, bevor Ihre Eltern kommen?*

Stefans Mutter kommt zu Besuch.

Das ist Stefans Zimmer.

So soll es sein.

Was muss Stefan machen?

den Tisch abräumen   die Kerzen anzünden   seine Kleidung aufräumen

das Bett machen

den Papierkorb ausleeren   den Boden sauber machen   die Pflanze gießen

das Bild an die Wand hängen   den Schrank zumachen   das Fenster zumachen

den Fernseher ausmachen   die Bücher gerade stellen

die Katze aus dem Zimmer werfen

Jugendschutz

Nicht in jedem Alter darf man alles. In Deutschland regelt das Jugendschutzgesetz[1], in welchem Alter Kinder und Jugendliche etwas dürfen oder können.

mit 13

- darf man in den Ferien arbeiten.
  aber: Die Eltern müssen es erlauben[2] und die Arbeit muss leicht sein.

mit 15

- kann man mit der Arbeit anfangen.
  aber: Man darf nur 8 Stunden am Tag und 5 Tage in der Woche arbeiten.
- darf man im Restaurant Bier oder Wein trinken.
  aber: Die Eltern müssen dabei sein[3].

mit 16

- darf man von zu Hause wegziehen[4].
  aber: Die Eltern müssen es erlauben.
- darf man heiraten[5].
  aber: Die Eltern müssen es erlauben.
  und: Der Partner muss über 18 Jahre alt sein.
- darf man bis 24.00 Uhr in die Disko gehen.

mit 18

- darf man den Führerschein[6] für ein Auto oder ein Motorrad machen.
- darf man ohne Erlaubnis heiraten.
- darf man wählen[7].
- darf man im Kino alle Filme sehen.
- darf man im Restaurant Alkohol trinken.
- darf man so lange in die Disko gehen, wie man will.
- darf man rauchen.

In Deutschland ist man mit 18 Jahren erwachsen[8].

Wie ist es in Ihrem Land? Machen Sie eine Tabelle.

Mit 13	Mit 15	Mit 16	Mit 18	Mit ...

heiraten	wählen	Alkohol trinken
in die Disko gehen	alle Filme sehen	Auto fahren
arbeiten	erwachsen sein	rauchen

[1] law for the protection of minors [2] permit [3] dabei ... be present [4] move away [5] marry [6] driver's license [7] vote [8] grown-up

KLI. In addition to providing cultural information, the KLI practices the modal verbs *dürfen, können, müssen.* Start by asking, e.g.: *Dürfen Kinder Auto fahren? Alkohol trinken? in den Ferien arbeiten? Wie alt muss man sein, damit man Auto fahren darf?* etc. Write the following items on the board: *in den Ferien arbeiten, im Restaurant Bier oder Wein trinken, von zu Hause wegziehen, heiraten, Auto fahren, wählen.* Explain or paraphrase new vocabulary. Then ask: *Was glauben Sie: Wie alt muss man in Deutschland sein, damit man diese Dinge machen kann?* Let sts. guess and write guessed age limits next to the items on the board. Then, sts. open their textbooks and verify how close they came by guessing. Let them work in pairs for a few minutes, then collect their responses. Ask them to work on the activity *Wie ist es in Ihrem Land?* in small groups. Rather than writing in this book, they may wish to create a table on a piece of paper with the relevant ages for their country/countries rather than the ages for Germany. Encourage them to go beyond the items mentioned in the box. If they don't know the correct age, let them guess. During the follow-up insist on complete sentences, e.g., *Mit sechzehn darf man Auto fahren.* **Note:** In some German states young adults can get a driver's license at 17, but until they reach 18, they can only drive with an accompanying adult.

Ach, wie nett!

Grammatik 3.3

Vocabulary Display
(1) Presentation: Tell (or ask sts. to tell) who and where the people are as you read what they are saying. *Maria und Michael zu Hause vor dem Fernseher; Frau Gretter und Frau Körner vor einem Schaufenster; Oma Schmitz und Helga auf dem Nachhauseweg; Jutta und Jens in einem Schauspiel, das im Mittelalter spielt; Silvias Freundin, die Silvia und Jürgen auf eine Party einlädt; zwei Tramperinnen, die mit Melanie und Josef nach Regensburg fahren wollen.* **(2) Recall:** Ask sts. to repeat the lines of the first drawing after you. Cover up the lines and ask sts. to write them down from memory. Uncover and ask sts. to check their answers. Do the same for the other drawings. **(3) Focus on form:** Ask sts. to work in small groups and to find all accusative pronouns, to write them on a piece of paper, and to write the nominative form next to each accusative one.

MARIA: Der Fernseher läuft ja den ganzen Tag.
MICHAEL: Soll ich ihn ausmachen?

FRAU KÖRNER: Ich finde den Mantel einfach toll!
FRAU GRETTER: Kaufen Sie ihn doch!

OMA SCHMITZ: Die Tasche ist so schwer.
HELGA: Komm, Oma, ich trage sie.

PRINZESSIN: Hier ist mein Taschentuch. Du darfst mich nie vergessen.
PRINZ: Nein, Geliebte, ich vergesse dich nie!

SILVIAS FREUNDIN: Samstag geben wir eine Party. Ich möchte euch gern einladen.

ZWEI TRAMPERINNEN: Hallo, wir wollen nach Regensburg. Nehmt ihr uns mit?

Situation 9 | Minidialoge

Sit. 9. Preparation: This is a problem-solving activity, so simply establish the context and describe the task. Point out to sts. that the gender of the pronoun will help them match the lines.
Activity: Have sts. work in groups of three.
Follow-up: Establish correct matches. Then ask sts. to create 2 more lines for each dialogue.

Was passt?

1. Es ist kalt und das Fenster ist offen!
2. Der Wein ist gut.
3. Du hast nächste Woche Geburtstag?
4. Der Koffer ist so schwer.
5. Die Suppe ist wirklich gut!
6. Wie findest du Paul Simon?
7. Das Haus ist schmutzig.

a. Komm, ich trage ihn.
b. Machen Sie es bitte zu.
c. Darf ich ihn probieren?
d. Ich mag sie aber nicht.
e. Ja, ich gebe eine Party und ich lade euch ein.
f. Ich mache es morgen sauber.
g. Ich mag ihn ganz gern.

 **Situation 10 | Dialog**

Sit. 10. (See the IM.) This dialogue provides a model for the role-play (*Sit. 11*). Use these steps while textbooks are closed: **(1)** Set the scene: *Heidi ist Studentin in Frau Schulz' Kurs. Sie hat Hunger und sucht einen Platz in der Mensa. Die Mensa ist ziemlich voll, aber ein Platz ist noch frei.* **(2)** Ask focus questions. First listening: *Wie heißt der Student? Woher kennen sich Heidi und der Student? Woher kommt der Student? Woher kommt Heidi?* Second listening: *Was ist Heidis Hauptfach? Was studiert Stefan? Wo möchte Stefan arbeiten?* **(3)** Play the dialogue. **(4)** Review sts.' answers. **(5)** Ask sts. to count the words in each sentence. **(6)** Divide sts. into 2 groups, assign one role to each group, and ask each group to repeat their lines. **(7)** Ask groups to repeat their lines from memory. **(8)** Ask 2 or 3 pairs of volunteers to present the dialogue in front of the class. Ask sts. to use their own names and their own personal information instead of that of the dialogue characters. **(9)** Sts. get up and work in pairs. While moving from one person to the next, they act out their own version of the dialogue several times.

Heidi sucht einen Platz in der Cafeteria.

HEIDI: Entschuldigung, <u>ist hier noch frei</u>?

STEFAN: Ja, sicher.

HEIDI: Danke.

STEFAN: <u>Kennen wir uns nicht</u>?

HEIDI: Ja, ich glaube schon. Bist du nicht auch in dem Deutschkurs um neun?

STEFAN: Na, klar. Jetzt <u>weiß</u> ich's wieder. Du <u>heißt</u> Stefanie, nicht wahr?

HEIDI: Nein, ich heiße Heidi.

STEFAN: Ach ja, richtig ... Heidi. Ich heiße Stefan.

HEIDI: <u>Woher</u> kommst du eigentlich, Stefan?

STEFAN: <u>Aus</u> Iowa City, und du?

HEIDI: Ich bin aus Berkeley.

STEFAN: Und was studierst du?

HEIDI: <u>Ich weiß noch nicht</u>. Vielleicht Sport, vielleicht Geschichte oder vielleicht Deutsch.

STEFAN: Ich studiere auch Deutsch, Deutsch und <u>Wirtschaft</u>. Ich möchte in Deutschland bei einer amerikanischen Firma arbeiten.

HEIDI: Toll! Da verdienst du sicherlich viel Geld.

STEFAN: <u>Hoffentlich</u>.

Situation 11 | Rollenspiel: In der Mensa

Sit. 11. Rollenspiel. (See the IM.) The role for s1 appears here, the role for s2 appears in Appendix B. **(1)** Set the scene as described in the role for s1. **(2)** Provide sts. with a model by working with the enactment of the role-play found in the workbook/lab manual. **(3)** Write the structure of the role-play on the board: *Begrüßen/Erkundigen (ob noch ein Platz frei ist); Fragen stellen; Verabschieden.* **(4)** Elicit sample greetings, questions, etc. and write on the board. Ask for appropriate responses and also write on the board. **(5)** Divide the class into two groups and assign one part of the role-play to each group. Ask sts. to practice the role-play in pairs. **(6)** Ask 2 or 3 pairs of sts. to perform their role-play in class. Provide feedback as to appropriateness and accuracy of language used after sts. have returned to their seats. **(7)** Ask sts. to find new partners and to practice the role-play in pairs again. **(8)** Optional homework assignment: Ask sts. to write up their version of the role-play.

Photo questions. *Essen Sie zu Hause oder an der Uni? Warum essen so viele Studenten in der Mensa? Möchten Sie in dieser Mensa essen? Sehen Sie nur Studenten im Bild? Sehen die Studenten aus wie amerikanische Studenten? Was trinken sie?*

Cultural note. Sharing tables is expected when restaurants are filling up. People do not usually engage in small talk, however. *Guten Tag, Guten Appetit,* and *Auf Wiedersehen* are the only exchanges necessary.

S1: Sie sind Student/Studentin an der Uni in Regensburg. Sie gehen in die Mensa und setzen sich zu jemand an den Tisch. Fragen Sie, wie er/sie heißt, woher er/sie kommt und was er/sie studiert.

Die Mensa der Universität Regensburg. Haben Sie Hunger?

Situation 12 | Ratespiel

Sit. 12. This activity is intended to give sts. more practice with third-person pronouns referring to things. Review items of clothing and accessories with the clothing transparency from *Kap. 2.* Explain any unfamiliar vocabulary in the numbered sentences. Model sentences and practice pronunciation. Tell sts. that the pronouns in the sentences provide them with clues as to what choices they have. Ask them which pronouns correspond to which articles. Ask them to complete the activity in pairs or small groups.
Follow-up: Ask sts. to come up with additional *Ratespiel* items to test one another's knowledge of clothing and of pronouns.

Was ist das?

1. __f__ Man trägt sie im Sommer an den Füßen.
2. __c__ Man trägt ihn nach dem Duschen.
3. __g__ Man trägt es im Bett.
4. __a__ Man trägt ihn im Winter um den Hals.
5. __b__ Man trägt sie im Ohr.
6. __d__ Man trägt sie unter der Kleidung.
7. __c__ Man trägt sie im Winter an den Händen.

a. der Schal
b. die Ohrringe
c. die Handschuhe
d. die Unterhose
e. der Bademantel
f. die Sandalen
g. das Nachthemd

Lektüre. This reading selection is a summary of the famous scholastic achievement study 2000-02 (PISA) that placed Germany in the last third of the participating countries and had a considerable impact on German self-esteem as far as the school system is concerned. The text's layout makes the brochure accessible to a high degree in spite of the vocabulary. Furthermore, cognates facilitate comprehension. **(1)** The task in *Vor dem Lesen* Part A involves recognizing this structure and thereby helps sts. to begin to understand the topic. ↓

Lektüre

Lesehilfe

Like most German newswriting, this text has many compound nouns and adjectives. They look daunting at first, but if you consider the meanings of the parts, it is easier to understand the whole. In this text the same parts are used over and over. Once you understand a few parts, you can understand many compounds.

Vor dem Lesen

For many years Germany's school system was held in high esteem, even internationally. In the following brochure on the PISA study, you will discover how dramatically things have changed.

A. Before reading the text, look at the section titles and write down the seven questions posed by the brochure.
B. Recognizing word parts. The PISA text is about scholastic achievement and contains a number of compound nouns and adjectives that refer to school and learning. Below is a list of several of those compounds. Read through the text and find them. Then use the **Nützliche Wörter** list to help you match each word with its English equivalent. Check your answers by looking them up in the glossary at the back of the book.

1. Schulleistungsstudie
2. leistungsfähig
3. Leistungsfähigkeit
4. leistungsstärkst
5. leistungsschwächst
6. Schulleistung
7. Grundwissen
8. Naturwissenschaft
9. Lesegewohnheit
10. Pflichtschulzeit
11. Grundschulniveau
12. Mindeststandard
13. Lehrkräfte
14. Vorschulalter
15. Ganztagsschule

a. ability to achieve
b. able to achieve
c. all-day school
d. basic knowledge
e. elementary school level
f. highest achieving
g. lowest achieving
h. minimum standard
i. natural science
j. preschool age
k. reading habit
l. required school time
m. scholastic achievement
n. study of scholastic achievement
o. teachers, faculty

NÜTZLICHE WÖRTER

fähig	*able*
Fähigkeit	*ability*
ganz	*whole*
Gewohnheit	*habit*
Grund	*basis*
Kraft	*power, force*
Leistung	*achievement*
mindestens	*at least*
Niveau	*level*
Pflicht	*requirement*
schwach	*weak*
stark	*strong*
vor	*before*
Wissen	*knowledge*
Wissenschaft	*science*
Zeit	*time*

Ask sts. to start individually by writing down the subtitles/questions. As an additional prereading activity and to "warm sts. up" to the text a little more, allow sts. to discover the many English cognate terms in the text. Have sts. make a list of all words and parts of words that look similar to English, i.e. *international, Kompetenz, mathematisch, testen, System, Studie, familiär, Strategie, Technologie, Karriere, finanziell, personell, Situation, Motivation, Element, Profil, enorm, akzeptabel, sozial, diskutieren, Standard, Qualifikation, realistisch.* **(2)** Then let sts. continue with *Vor dem Lesen* Part B in small groups. Part B can be done either as a prereading or a while-reading activity. Have sts. skim the text, looking for the compound nouns and adjectives, and not getting bogged down trying to understand every word. As noted in the *Lesehilfe* box, this →

Die PISA-Studie

Was heißt PISA? Die Abkürzung PISA steht für „Programme for International Student Assessment", eine internationale Schulleistungsstudie.

Was untersucht[1] PISA? PISA untersucht drei Bereiche[2]: Lesekompetenz, mathematisches Grundwissen und naturwissenschaftliches Grundwissen. PISA untersucht nicht nur, was die Schülerinnen und Schüler wissen, sondern auch ob[3] sie es anwenden[4] können.

Wer nimmt an der Studie teil[5]? Die Studie testet 15-jährige Schülerinnen und Schüler in ihren Schulen. 32 Länder nehmen teil. In jedem Land testet man zwischen 4.500 und 10.000 Schülerinnen und Schüler.

Welche Ziele[6] hat PISA? Die einzelnen Länder erfahren[7], wie gut ihre Schülerinnen und Schüler im internationalen Vergleich sind und wie leistungsfähig ihr Schulsystem ist.

Worum geht es bei PISA außerdem?[8] Außer der Leistungsfähigkeit der Schülerinnen und Schüler erfasst die Studie auch ihren familiären Hintergrund, ihre Einstellung zum Lernen, ihre Lernstrategien, ihre Lesegewohnheiten, ihren Umgang mit neuen Technologien und ihre schulische Karriere. Die Schulleiter beantworten Fragen zur Schule, zu ihrer finanziellen und personellen Situation, zur Klassengröße und zur Motivation von Eltern und Schülern. Aus diesen drei Elementen ergibt sich ein Profil der Schülerinnen und Schüler gegen Ende der Pflichtschulzeit.

Wie hat Deutschland abgeschnitten[9]? Bei der ersten PISA-Studie aus den Jahren 2000-02 liegt Deutschland im letzten Drittel[10] der teilnehmenden Länder. Fast jedes vierte Kind hat enorme Schwierigkeiten beim Lesen. Beim Rechnen und in den Naturwissenschaften erreicht ein Viertel[11] der Schüler höchstens Grundschulniveau. Außerdem ist Deutschland eines der Länder mit dem größten Abstand zwischen den leistungsstärksten und leistungsschwächsten Schülern. Im Gegensatz zu anderen Ländern schafft Deutschland es nicht, dass auch die schwachen Schüler ein akzeptables Leistungsniveau erreichen. Der Einfluss der sozialen Herkunft auf die Schulleistungen ist in Deutschland viel größer als in anderen Ländern. Das deutsche Schulsystem fördert nur die leistungsstärksten Schüler und selbst die nur im Mittelmaß.

Was kann man tun, damit deutsche Schüler künftig besser abschneiden[12]? Darüber wird in Deutschland heftig diskutiert. Folgende Maßnahmen[13] sind im Gespräch[14]:

- Man muss schwache Schüler mehr fördern[15].
- Man braucht Mindeststandards.
- Man muss Kinder früher einschulen.
- Man muss das Wiederholen von Klassen überdenken.
- Man braucht mehr Angebote für besonders gute Schüler.
- Man muss „schwache Leser" frühzeitig erkennen und fördern.
- Man muss die Qualifikation der Lehrkräfte verbessern[16].
- Man muss Kindern im Vorschulalter mehr Angebote zum Lernen machen.
- Man braucht in Deutschland mehr Ganztagsschulen.
- Man braucht realistische Lernziele.

Quelle: www.schulentwicklung-plus.de „Schulleistungsstudie PISA"

Arbeit mit dem Text

Beantworten Sie die folgenden Fragen zum Text.

1. Welche schulischen Bereiche untersucht PISA?
2. Welche beiden Aspekte dieser Bereiche untersucht PISA?
3. Wie alt sind die getesteten Schüler?
4. Wie viele Länder nehmen an der Studie teil?
5. Wie viele Schülerinnen und Schüler testet man in jedem Land?
6. Was erfahren die Länder aus der PISA-Studie?
7. Wie viel Prozent der deutschen Schüler haben große Probleme beim Lesen, und wie viele beim Rechnen und in den Naturwissenschaften?

brochure has a great number of long words that might intimidate some sts. You might want to remind sts. of the notion of compound parts introduced in the previous **Lektüre** in this chapter. Remind sts. also that they are not expected to understand every word of this text. The vocabulary covered in the exercises and the *Nützliche Wörter* list should be sufficient for the level of understanding that is required for the tasks associated with this reading. **(3)** The questions in *Arbeit mit dem Text* can be assigned as homework. **(4)** *Nach dem Lesen* focuses on measures to deal with the PISA shock. Working in small groups, sts. should go back to the text and make a list of the measures that are mentioned, evaluate them according to efficiency and cost, and then collectively decide on the five most important measures. **Note:** In response to the PISA study, several measures have been taken in recent years, including common *Bildungsstandards* for secondary education and more emphasis on continuing education for teachers. A *Schulinspektion*, a regular evaluation of all aspects of education, and a revised curriculum have also been introduced in several German states.

[1]*analyzes* [2]*areas* [3]*whether* [4]*use* [5]*nimmt teil participates* [6]*goals* [7]*discover* [8]*Worum … What else does PISA deal with?* [9]*fared* [10]*third* [11]*quarter* [12]*fare* [13]*measurers* [14]*im … being discussed* [15]*encourage* [16]*improve*

Nach dem Lesen

Der Text schlägt 10 Maßnahmen[1] als Reaktion auf den PISA-Schock vor[2]. Welche dieser Maßnahmen sind am wichtigsten? Welche kosten mehr Geld? Welche Maßnahmen soll Deutschland als erstes ergreifen[3]? Nennen Sie die fünf wichtigsten Maßnahmen und bringen Sie sie in eine Rangfolge[4] von 1 bis 5.

[1]*measures* [2]*vorschlagen to propose, suggest* [3]*here: take* [4]*order of importance*

Körperliche und geistige Verfassung

Vocabulary Display
Use pictures to teach adjectives that describe particular physical and mental states. Ask *Wie geht es der Frau / dem Mann / dem Hund usw.?* so sts. learn to recognize the question. Put the sketches on the overhead, cover the captions, and ask similar questions. (See the IM on using vocabulary displays.) You might want to ask sts. to identify the characters in each sketch.

Grammatik 3.4–3.5

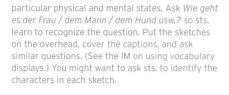

Er ist glücklich.

Sie sind traurig.

Er ist wütend.

Sie ist krank.

Sie sind in Eile.

Sie ist müde.

Sie haben Hunger.

Er hat Langeweile.

Er hat Durst.

Er hat Angst.

Situation 13 | Informationsspiel: Was machen sie, wenn ...?

Sit. 13. Have sts. work in pairs. The corresponding chart is in Appendix A. Remember to set a time limit for the activity. Sts. do not need to complete the entire chart. Make sure, however, that they ask each other all the questions that pertain to themselves (*Was machst du, wenn du traurig bist? müde bist? usw.*).

MODELL: s1: Was macht Renate, wenn sie müde ist?
s2: Sie trinkt Kaffee.
s1: Was machst du, wenn du müde bist?
s2: Ich gehe ins Bett.

	Renate	Ernst	mein(e) Partner(in)
1. *traurig ist/bist*	ruft ihre Freundin an	weint	
2. *müde ist/bist*	trinkt Kaffee	schläft	
3. *in Eile ist/bist*	nimmt ein Taxi	ist nie in Eile	
4. *wütend ist/bist*	wirft mit Tellern	schreit ganz laut	
5. *krank ist/bist*	geht zum Arzt	isst Hühnersuppe	
6. *glücklich ist/bist*	lädt Freunde ein	lacht ganz laut	
7. *Hunger hat/hast*	isst einen Apfel	schreit laut „Hunger!"	
8. *Langeweile hat/hast*	liest ein Buch	ärgert seine Schwester	
9. *Durst hat/hast*	trinkt Mineralwasser	trinkt Limo	
10. *Angst hat/hast*	schließt die Tür ab	läuft zu Mama	

Situation 14 | Interview: Wie fühlst du dich, wenn ...?

Sit. 14. Model pronunciation in the example given, and review the pronunciation of *ausgezeichnet*. Make sure sts. understand that adjectives are ordered from positive to negative (+ 0 −). Pronounce *mies* and explain that it is *Umgangssprache*, and pronounce the phrases in 1-10 (add *Wie fühlst du dich?*), having the sts. repeat after you. Then have sts. work in pairs. Afterward, you might choose to give them some additional (and preferably entertaining) situations to help them become familiar with word order when the *wenn*-clause is in the second half of the sentence: *Stellen Sie sich vor, Sie sind Präsident oder Präsidentin der USA. Wie fühlen Sie sich, wenn Sie mit einem Journalisten sprechen müssen? Sie sind in der Footballmannschaft von [your university]. Wie fühlen Sie sich, wenn Sie ein Spiel gegen [your rival university] gewinnen? verlieren? usw.*

MODELL: s1: Wie fühlst du dich, wenn du um fünf Uhr morgens aufstehst?
s2: Ausgezeichnet!

[+]	[0]	[−]
ausgezeichnet		nicht besonders gut
fantastisch		ziemlich schlecht
sehr gut	ganz gut	mies
gut		total mies

1. wenn du um fünf Uhr morgens aufstehst
2. wenn du die ganze Nacht nicht schlafen kannst
3. wenn du drei Filme hintereinander ansiehst
4. wenn deine Freunde dich auf eine Party einladen
5. wenn du eine Arbeit oder einen Test zurückbekommst
6. wenn du ein Referat schreiben musst
7. wenn das Semester zu Ende ist
8. wenn du einkaufen gehen willst, aber kein Geld hast
9. wenn alle deine T-Shirts schmutzig sind
10. wenn du eine gute Note bekommst

Situation 15 | Warum fährt Frau Ruf mit dem Bus?

Sit. 15. The goal of this *Sit.* is for sts. to become accustomed to placing the verb at the end of clauses that begin with the subordinating conjunction *weil*. Have sts. (in groups of 3) match the sentences in column A with those in column B. This exercise is divided into two sections to make the task more manageable. Sentences 1-5 go with a-e, 6-10 with f-j.

Kombinieren Sie!

MODELL: S1: Warum fährt Frau Ruf mit dem Bus?
S2: Weil ihr Auto kaputt ist.

1. Warum fährt Frau Ruf mit dem Bus?
2. Warum hat Hans Angst?
3. Warum geht Jutta nicht ins Kino?
4. Warum geht Jens nicht in die Schule?
5. Warum kauft Andrea Hans eine CD?

a. weil er Geburtstag hat
b. weil ihr Auto kaputt ist
c. weil er vielleicht nicht versetzt wird
d. weil sie für eine Klassenarbeit lernen muss
e. weil er blau macht (Klassenarbeit in Latein!)

6. Warum fährt Herr Wagner nach Leipzig?
7. Warum ist Ernst wütend?
8. Warum fährt Frau Gretter in die Berge?
9. Warum geht Herr Siebert um zehn Uhr ins Bett?
10. Warum ruft Maria ihre Freundin an?

f. weil er seinen Bruder besuchen will
g. weil sie wandern geht
h. weil er in Mathe so viele Hausaufgaben hat
i. weil sie sie ins Kino einladen will
j. weil er jeden Tag um sechs Uhr aufsteht

Situation 16 | Zum Schreiben: Auch in Ihnen steckt ein Dichter!

Sit. 16. Have students work in pairs and write their poems on transparencies to present to the class. (Remember to provide pens along with transparencies.) Students could also write on the board.

Schreiben Sie ein Gedicht!

MODELL:

Wasser	ein Nomen = Thema
kühl, nass	zwei Adjektive
schwimmen, segeln, tauchen	drei Verben
Sonne auf meiner Haut	vier Wörter, die ein Gefühl ausdrücken[1]
Sommer	ein Nomen = Zusammenfassung[2]

MÖGLICHE THEMEN

Hund
Oma
Wochenende
Uni
Deutsch ...

[1]*express* [2]*summary*

Schuljahr und Zeugnisse

Wie ist das in Ihrem Land?

1. Wann beginnt das Schuljahr? Wann endet es?
2. Welche Fächer hat man in der 9. Klasse?
3. Welche Fremdsprachen lernt man in der 9. Klasse?
4. Wie oft gibt es Zeugnisse[1]? Wann?
5. Muss jemand die Zeugnisse unterschreiben? Wer?
6. Was passiert, wenn ein Schüler in vielen Fächern sehr schlechte Noten[2] hat?

Sie hören einen Text über die deutschen Schulen. Hören Sie gut zu und beantworten Sie dann die Fragen.

- Das Schuljahr beginnt im _August_ oder _September_.
- Das Schuljahr ist im _Juni_, _Juli_ oder _August_ zu Ende.
- Wann gibt es Zeugnisse? In der _Mitte_ und am _Ende_ des Schuljahres.
- Schreiben Sie neben die Wörter die richtige Note (Zahl) und was es in Ihrem Land ist.

	IN DEUTSCHLAND	IN IHREM LAND
„sehr gut"	1	
„gut"	2	
„befriedigend"[3]	3	
„ausreichend"[4]	4	
„mangelhaft"[5]	5	
„ungenügend"[6]	6	

- Wann bleibt man sitzen[7]?

Miniwörterbuch

entscheiden	to decide
die **Klasse**, -n	grade, level
das **Resultat**, -e	result
die **Versetzung**	promotion into the next grade

ZEUGNIS

Schuljahr 20 **07/08**   1. Halbjahr   Klasse **9 b**

Jens Krüger
Vor- und Zuname des Schülers/der Schülerin

geboren am **22. 8. 93**   in   **München**

Pflichtunterricht

Deutsch	4	Mathematik (Fachleistungskurs____)	4
Rechtschreiben	4	Physik/Chemie	5
Englisch (Fachleistungskurs____)	5	Biologie	3
Latein	5	Musik	2
Welt- und Umweltkunde	3	Kunst	2
Religion	4	Werken	2
Werte und Normen	4	Textiles Gestalten	/
		Sport	1

Wahlpflichtunterricht und wahlfreier Unterricht

Italienisch 4

Bemerkungen

Jens ist bei seinen Mitschülern beliebt.

Goslar, den **1. Feb. 2008**
Datum der Ausstellung

Cramer   _K. Möller_
Klassenlehrer(in)   Schulleiter(in)

gesehen: _Arnd Krüger_
Unterschrift eines Erziehungsberechtigten

Cultural note. Austria uses the same grading system as Germany, whereas in Switzerland the opposite system is used: 6 is the best, 1 the worst.

---

[1]*report cards* [2]*grades* [3]*satisfactory* [4]*sufficient* [5]*poor* [6]*insufficient* [7]bleibt sitzen *flunks, is held back a grade*

KLI. (See the IM on how to present KLI notes.) Read the text or play the recording. *Das Schuljahr dauert von August oder September bis Juni, Juli oder August des nächsten Jahres. In jedem Fach schreiben die Schüler Klassenarbeiten und Tests. Die Resultate dieser Arbeiten und Tests ergeben die Noten im Zeugnis. Zweimal im Jahr – in der Mitte und am Ende – gibt es Zeugnisse. Das Zeugnis am Ende des Jahres entscheidet über die Versetzung, d.h. ob der Schüler oder die Schülerin in die nächste Klasse kommt oder nicht. Die Noten im Zeugnis gehen von 1 bis 6. Dabei ist 1 „sehr gut", 2 „gut", 3 „befriedigend", 4 „ausreichend", 5 „mangelhaft" und 6 „ungenügend". Bei zwei Fünfen oder einer Sechs müssen die Schüler eine Klasse noch einmal machen.*

Videoecke

Denis ist in Leipzig geboren. Er geht ans Gymnasium und macht gerade sein Abitur. Er spricht Englisch und Französisch.

Juliane ist in Bergen auf der Insel Rügen geboren. Sie studiert Spanisch und Biologie.

Aufgabe 1

Was können Juliane und Denis gut? ☺ Was müssen sie tun? 😐 Was können sie nicht gut und was mögen sie nicht? ☹ Kreuzen Sie an.

JULIANE ☺	😐	☹		DENIS ☺	😐	☹
☐	☐	☐	Porträts zeichnen	☐	☐	☐
☐	☐	☐	Grafiken zeichnen	☐	☐	☐
☐	☐	☐	Querflöte spielen	☐	☐	☐
☐	☐	☐	Fahrräder reparieren	☐	☐	☐
☐	☐	☐	bohren	☐	☐	☐
☐	☐	☐	Motorrad reparieren	☐	☐	☐
☐	☐	☐	Zimmer aufräumen	☐	☐	☐
☐	☐	☐	sauber machen	☐	☐	☐
☐	☐	☐	Müll runterbringen	☐	☐	☐
☐	☐	☐	Wäsche waschen	☐	☐	☐

Aufgabe 1

Was machen Juliane und Denis heute Abend? Schreiben Sie auf.

Wortschatz

Talente und Pläne — Talents and Plans

der Besuch, -e	visit
zu Besuch kommen	to visit
der Schlittschuh, -e	ice skate
Schlittschuh laufen, läuft	to go ice-skating
der Witz, -e	joke
Witze erzählen	to tell jokes
schneiden	to cut
Haare schneiden	to cut hair
stricken	to knit
tauchen	to dive
tippen	to type
zeichnen	to draw

Ähnliche Wörter

der Ski, -er; Ski fahren, fährt; der Walzer, -;
das Skateboard, -s; Skateboard fahren, fährt

Pflichten — Obligations

ab·räumen	to clear
den Tisch ab·räumen	to clear the table
decken	to set; to cover
den Tisch decken	to set the table
gerade stellen	to straighten
gießen	to water
die Blumen gießen	to water the flowers
putzen	to clean
sauber machen	to clean

Körperliche und geistige Verfassung — Physical and Mental States

die Angst, ⸚e	fear
Angst haben	to be afraid
die Eile	hurry
in Eile sein	to be in a hurry
die Langeweile	boredom
Langeweile haben	to be bored
das Glück	luck; happiness
viel Glück!	lots of luck! good luck!
das Heimweh	homesickness
Heimweh haben	to be homesick
ärgern	to annoy; to tease
schreien	to scream, yell
stören	to disturb
weinen	to cry
beschäftigt	busy
eifersüchtig	jealous
faul	lazy
krank	sick
müde	tired
wütend	angry

Ähnliche Wörter

der Durst; Durst haben; der Hunger; Hunger haben; das
Gefühl, -e; fühlen; wie fühlst du dich?; ich fühle mich …;
frustriert

Schule — School

die Nachhilfe	tutoring
die Sprechstunde, -n	office hour
der Satz, ⸚e	sentence
der Sommerkurs, -e	summer school
das Arbeitsbuch, ⸚er	workbook
das Beispiel, -e	example
zum Beispiel (z. B.)	for example
das Referat, -e	report
das Studium, Studien (R)	course of studies

Sonstige Substantive — Other Nouns

die Ärztin, -nen	female physician
die Blume, -n	flower
die Geige, -n	violin
die Geliebte, -n	beloved female friend, love
die Hauptstadt, ⸚e	capital city
die Haut	skin
die Kerze, -n	candle
die Kneipe, -n	bar, tavern
die Oma, -s	grandma
die Pflicht, -en	duty; requirement
der Arzt, ⸚e	male physician
der Papierkorb, ⸚e	wastebasket
der Punkt, -e	point
der Roman, -e	novel
das Gedicht, -e	poem
das Krankenhaus, ⸚er	hospital
das Lied, -er	song
das Mittagessen	midday meal, lunch
das Taschentuch, ⸚er	handkerchief
das Tier, -e	animal

Ähnliche Wörter

die CD, -s (R); die Disko, -s; die Firma, Firmen; die
Pflanze, -n; die Nacht, ⸚e; die Vase, -n; der DVD-Spieler, - (R);
der Mittag, -e; der Plan, ⸚e; der Platz, ⸚e; das Alphabet;
das Aspirin; das Licht, -er; das Talent, -e; das Taxi, -s;
das Tischtennis

Modalverben / Modal Verbs

dürfen, darf	to be permitted (to), may
können, kann	to be able (to), can; may
mögen, mag (R)	to like, care for
möchte	would like (to)
müssen, muss	to have to, must
sollen, soll	to be supposed to
wollen, will	to want; to intend, plan (to)

Sonstige Verben / Other Verbs

an·machen	to turn on, switch on
an·sehen, sieht ... an	to look at; to watch
an·ziehen	to put on (clothes)
an·zünden	to light
auf·machen	to open
auf·passen	to pay attention
aus·geben, gibt ... aus	to spend
aus·machen	to turn off
aus·leeren	to empty
aus·ziehen	to take off (clothes)
bekommen	to get, receive
belegen	to take (a course)
ein·steigen	to board
erzählen	to tell
mit·nehmen, nimmt ... mit	to take along
probieren	to try, taste
rauchen	to smoke
stellen	to put, place (upright)
verbringen	to spend (*time*)
verreisen	to go on a trip
vorbei·kommen	to come by, visit
werfen, wirft	to throw
zu·machen	to close

Ähnliche Wörter

baden, hängen, hoffen, kämmen, kombinieren, lachen, leben, mit·bringen; das Bild an die Wand hängen

Adjektive und Adverbien / Adjectives and Adverbs

ausgezeichnet	excellent
beliebt	popular
besonders	particularly
bestimmt	definitely, certainly
eigentlich	actually
fertig	ready; finished
die ganze Nacht	all night long
ganz schön viel	quite a bit
nass	wet
schnell	quick, fast
schwer	heavy; hard, difficult
wahr	true

Sonstige Wörter und Ausdrücke / Other Words and Expressions

bei dir	at your place
blau machen	to take the day off
dreimal	three times
einander	one another, each other
hintereinander	in a row
miteinander	with each other
Entschuldigung!	excuse me
gar nicht	not a bit
immer	always
jede	each, every
jede Woche	every week
jemand	someone, somebody
jetzt	now
kein bisschen	not at all
mit mir	with me
na	well
nach	after; to
neben	beside, in addition to
nur	only
pro	per
schade!	too bad
sicherlich	certainly
sofort	immediately
versetzt	promoted
von der Arbeit	from work
warum	why
weil	because
wieder	again
schon wieder	once again
wohin	where to
zu Fuß	on foot
zum Arzt	to the doctor
zum Mittagessen	for lunch

Strukturen und Übungen

3.1 The modal verbs *können, wollen, mögen*

Wissen Sie noch?

The **Satzklammer** forms a frame or a bracket consisting of a verb and either a separable prefix or an infinitive. This same structure is used with the modal verbs.

Review grammar 1.5 and 2.3.

Modal verbs, such as **können** (*can, to be able to, know how to*), **wollen** (*to want to*), and **mögen** (*to like to*) are auxiliary verbs that modify the meaning of the main verb. The main verb appears as an infinitive at the end of the clause.

The modal **können** usually indicates an ability or talent but may also be used to ask permission. The modal **wollen** expresses a desire or an intention to do something. The modal **mögen** expresses a liking; just as its English equivalent, *to like*, it is commonly used with an accusative object.

Kannst du kochen?	*Can you cook?*
Kann ich mitkommen?	*Can I come along?*
Sofie und Willi wollen tanzen gehen.	*Sofie and Willi want to go dancing.*
Ich mag aber nicht tanzen.	*I don't like to dance.*
Magst du Spaghetti?	*Do you like spaghetti?*

Modals do not have endings in the **ich-** and **er/sie/es-**forms. Note also that these modal verbs have one stem vowel in all plural forms and in the polite **Sie**-form, and a different stem vowel in the **ich-, du-,** and **er/sie/es-**forms.

3.1. *Modalverben: möchte* in Section 2.3 was a preview of modal auxiliary verbs. In this chapter, the forms and meanings of the 6 German modal verbs are introduced. If sts. can hear modal verbs repeatedly, the *Satzklammer* (which they have already encountered in Section 1.5 with separable-prefix verbs) will not cause much difficulty.

Point out the differences from the regular verb conjugation. Typical mistakes are using the vowel of the infinitive in the singular and adding endings to the *ich-* and *er/sie/es-*forms. Stress that the singular has a different vowel from the infinitive (except in *sollen*), whereas the vowel of the plural is always the same as the infinitive.

können = *can*
wollen = *to want to*
mögen = *to like (to)*

	können	**wollen**	**mögen**
ich	kann	will	mag
du	kannst	willst	magst
Sie	können	wollen	mögen
er/sie/es	kann	will	mag
wir	können	wollen	mögen
ihr	könnt	wollt	mögt
Sie	können	wollen	mögen
sie	können	wollen	mögen

Übung 1 | Talente

Üb. 1. This exercise is restricted to the forms of *können*. Assign for homework and have sts. read individual sentences in class.

A. Wer kann das?

MODELL: Ich kann Deutsch.
    oder Wir können Deutsch.

1. Deutsch	mein Freund / meine Freundin
2. Golf spielen	meine Eltern
3. Ski fahren	ich/wir
4. Klavier spielen	mein Bruder / meine Schwester
5. gut kochen	der Professor / die Professorin

B. **Kannst du das?**

MODELL: Gedichte schreiben → Kannst du Gedichte schreiben?
          oder   Könnt ihr Gedichte schreiben?

1. Gedichte schreiben   du
2. Auto fahren   ihr
3. tippen
4. stricken
5. zeichnen

Übung 2 | Pläne und Fähigkeiten

Üb. 2. Remind sts. that German *will* is not the equivalent of English "will." Give sts. many chances to hear this form of *wollen* used in a meaningful context

Was können oder wollen diese Personen (nicht) machen?

MODELL: am Samstag / ich / wollen →
          Am Samstag **will** ich **Schlittschuh laufen.**

Achtung!

German **will** is not the equivalent of English *will* but means rather "want(s)" or "intend(s) to."

Golf spielen
Haare schneiden
ins Kino gehen
nach Europa fliegen
schlafen
Ski fahren
Witze erzählen
zeichnen
_____ ?

1. heute Abend / ich / wollen
2. morgen / ich / nicht können
3. mein Freund (meine Freundin) / gut können
4. am Samstag / mein Freund (meine Freundin) / wollen
5. mein Freund (meine Freundin) und ich / wollen
6. im Winter / meine Eltern (meine Freunde) / wollen
7. meine Eltern (meine Freunde) / gut können

3.2   The modal verbs *müssen, sollen, dürfen*

3.2. The meaning of *sollen* as introduced here is "to be supposed to," primarily as a request by a person other than the speaker. Since the subjunctive is used more appropriately in German (*sollte* = "should") for making suggestions, this meaning is not introduced here.

Sts. may grasp the difference between *nicht dürfen* and *nicht müssen* and their relationship to *müssen* and *dürfen* better if it is explained in class.

The modal **müssen** stresses the necessity to do something. The modal **sollen** is less emphatic than **müssen** and may imply an obligation or a strong suggestion made by another person. The modal **dürfen,** used primarily to indicate permission, can also be used in polite requests.

Jens muss mehr lernen.	*Jens has to study more.*
Vati sagt, du sollst sofort nach Hause kommen.	*Dad says you're supposed to come home immediately.*
Frau Schulz sagt, du sollst morgen zu ihr kommen.	*Ms. Schulz says you should come to see her tomorrow.*
Darf ich die Kerzen anzünden?	*May I light the candles?*

	müssen	sollen	dürfen
ich	muss	soll	darf
du	musst	sollst	darfst
Sie	müssen	sollen	dürfen
er/sie/es	muss	soll	darf
wir	müssen	sollen	dürfen
ihr	müsst	sollt	dürft
Sie	müssen	sollen	dürfen
sie	müssen	sollen	dürfen

müssen = *must*
sollen = *to be supposed to*
dürfen = *may*

When negated, the English expressions *to have to* and *must* undergo a change in meaning. The expression *not have to* implies that there is no need to do something, while *must not* implies a strong warning. These two distinct meanings are expressed in German by **nicht müssen** and **nicht dürfen**, respectively.

nicht müssen = *not to have to, not to need to*
nicht dürfen = *mustn't*

Du musst das nicht tun.   *You don't have to do that.*
                          or: *You don't need to do that.*
Du darfst das nicht tun. *You mustn't do that.*

Übung 3 | Jutta hat eine Fünf in Englisch.

Üb. 3. Assign this exercise for *müssen* and *nicht dürfen* as homework and check it in class.

Was muss sie machen? Was darf sie nicht machen?

1. mit Jens zusammen lernen
2. viel fernsehen
3. in der Klasse aufpassen und mitschreiben
4. jeden Tag tanzen gehen
5. jeden Tag ihren Wortschatz lernen
6. amerikanische Filme im Original sehen
7. ihren Englischlehrer zum Abendessen einladen
8. für eine Woche nach London fahren
9. die englische Grammatik fleißig[1] lernen

Übung 4 | Minidialoge

Üb. 4. Assign for homework and have sts. perform the dialogues in class.

Ergänzen Sie **können, wollen, müssen, sollen, dürfen.**

Achtung!

Remember the two characteristics of modal verbs:

1. no ending in the **ich-** and **er/sie/es**-forms;
2. one stem vowel in the **ich-, du-,** and **er/sie/es**-forms and a different one in the plural, the formal **Sie,** and the infinitive. (Note, however, that **sollen** has the same stem vowel in all forms.)

1. ALBERT: Hallo, Nora. Peter und ich gehen ins Kino. _____[a] du nicht mitkommen?
   NORA: Ich _____[b] schon, aber leider _____[c] ich nicht mitkommen. Ich _____[d] arbeiten.
2. JENS: Vati, _____[a] ich mit Hans fischen gehen?
   HERR WAGNER: Nein! Du hast eine Fünf in Physik, eine Fünf in Latein und eine Fünf in Englisch. Du _____[b] zu Hause bleiben und deine Hausaufgaben machen.
   JENS: Aber, Vati! Meine Hausaufgaben _____[c] ich doch heute Abend machen.
   HERR WAGNER: Nein, aber du _____[d] zu Hans gehen und dann _____[e] ihr eure Hausaufgaben zusammen machen.
3. HEIDI: Hallo, Stefan. Frau Schulz sagt, du _____[a] morgen in ihre Sprechstunde kommen.
   STEFAN: Morgen _____[b] ich nicht, ich habe keine Zeit.
   HEIDI: Das _____[c] du Frau Schulz schon selbst sagen. Bis bald.

[1]*diligently*

3.3 Accusative case: personal pronouns

3.3. *Personalpronomen:* Akkusativ. This section continues the presentation of accusative forms that was begun in *Kapitel 2*.

Mich causes no problems because of the equivalent English form, but there will be confusion with *mir* when it is introduced in Section 5.5. The plural forms take longer to acquire, although giving sts. the chance to hear the forms used meaningfully will help.

As in English, certain German pronouns change depending on whether they are the subject or the object of a verb.

Ich bin heute Abend zu Hause. Rufst du **mich** an?	*I will be home tonight. Will you call me?*
Er kommt aus Wien. Kennst du **ihn?**	*He is from Vienna. Do you know him?*

A. First- and second-person pronouns: nominative and accusative forms

Nominative	Accusative	
ich	mich	*me*
du	dich	*you*
Sie	Sie	*you*
wir	uns	*us*
ihr	euch	*you*
Sie	Sie	*you*

Wissen Sie noch?

The accusative case is used to indicate direct objects of verbs.

Review grammar 2.1.

Wer bist **du?** Ich kenne **dich** nicht.	*Who are you? I don't know you.*
Wer seid **ihr?** Ich kenne **euch** nicht.	*Who are you (people)? I don't know you.*

B. Third-person pronouns: nominative and accusative forms

	Nominative	Accusative	
Masculine	er	ihn	*him, it*
Feminine	sie		*her, it*
Neuter	es		*it*
Plural	sie		*them*

der → er
den → ihn
das → es
die → sie

Recall that third-person pronouns reflect the grammatical gender of the noun they stand for: **der Film → er; die Gitarre → sie; das Foto → es.** This relationship also holds true for the accusative case: **den Film → ihn; die Gitarre → sie; das Foto → es.** Note that only the masculine singular pronoun has a different form in the accusative case.

Wo ist der Spiegel? Ich sehe **ihn** nicht.	*Where is the mirror? I don't see it.*
Das ist meine Schwester Jasmin. Du kennst **sie** noch nicht.	*This is my sister Jasmin. You don't know her yet.*
—Wann kaufst du die Bücher?	*—When will you buy the books?*
—Ich kaufe **sie** morgen.	*—I'll buy them tomorrow.*

Minidialoge

Ergänzen Sie **mich, dich, uns, euch, Sie.**

1. KATRIN: Holst du mich heute Abend ab, wenn wir ins Kino gehen?
   THOMAS: Natürlich hole ich _____ ab!
2. STEFAN: Hallooo! Hier bin ich, Albert! Siehst du _____^a denn nicht?
   ALBERT: Ach, *da* bist du. Ja, jetzt sehe ich _____^b.
3. SABINE: Guten Tag, Frau Schulz. Sie kennen _____ noch nicht. Wir sind neu in Ihrer Klasse. Das ist Rick, und ich bin Sabine.
   FRAU SCHULZ: Guten Tag, Rick. Guten Tag, Sabine.
4. MONIKA: Hallo, Albert. Hallo, Thomas. Katrin und ich besuchen _____ heute.
   ALBERT UND THOMAS: Toll! Bringt Kuchen mit!
5. STEFAN: Heidi, ich mag _____^a!
   HEIDI: Das ist schön, Stefan. Ich mag _____^b auch.
6. FRAU SCHULZ: Spreche ich laut genug? Verstehen Sie _____^a?
   KLASSE: Ja, wir verstehen _____^b sehr gut, Frau Schulz.
7. STEFAN UND ALBERT: Auf Wiedersehen, Frau Schulz! Schöne Ferien! Und vergessen Sie uns nicht!
   FRAU SCHULZ: Natürlich nicht! Wie kann ich _____ denn je vergessen?

Der Deutschkurs

MODELL: Machst du gern **das Arbeitsbuch für *Kontakte*?**
Ja, ich mache **es** gern. *Oder:* Nein, ich mache **es** nicht gern.

Tipp: das → es   den → ihn   die → sie

1. Machst du gern **das Arbeitsbuch für *Kontakte*?**
2. Kannst du **das deutsche Alphabet** aufsagen?
3. Kennst du **den beliebtesten deutschen Vornamen für Jungen?**
4. Liest du gern **die Grammatik?**
5. Lernst du gern **den Wortschatz?**
6. Kennst du **die Studenten und Studentinnen in der Klasse?**
7. Vergisst du oft **die Hausaufgaben?**
8. Magst du **deinen Lehrer oder deine Lehrerin?**

Was machen diese Personen?

Beantworten Sie die Fragen negativ.

MODELL: Kauft Michael das Buch? →
Nein, er kauft es nicht, er liest es.

Verwenden Sie diese Verben.

anrufen, ruft an
anziehen, zieht an
anzünden, zündet an
ausmachen, macht aus
essen, isst
kaufen
schreiben
trinken
verkaufen
waschen, wäscht

1. Liest Maria den Brief?　　2. Isst Michael die Suppe?　　3. Macht Maria den Fernseher an?

     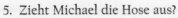

4. Kauft Michael das Auto?　　5. Zieht Michael die Hose aus?　　6. Trägt Maria den Rock?

7. Bestellt[1] Michael das Schnitzel?　　8. Besucht Michael seinen Freund?

9. Kämmt Maria ihr Haar?　　10. Bläst Michael die Kerzen aus[2]?

3.4　Word order: dependent clauses

3.4 *Wortstellung: Nebensätze.* Word order in dependent clauses in German is formally introduced here with the subordinating conjunctions *wenn* and *weil*. Though sts. can place the verb correctly in exercises, few will achieve this in spontaneous speech in the first year. Many will not even try to use dependent clauses. Verb-last position in dependent clauses is one of the last word-order rules acquired. Sts. will have fewer problems if they are given many chances to hear this word order in your speech before they are required to use it.

Sts. may be familiar with other terms. Point out that the terms "main clause" and "independent clause" can be used interchangeably, as can "dependent clause" and "subordinate clause."

Use a conjunction such as **wenn** (*when, if*) or **weil** (*because*) to add a modifying clause to a sentence.

Mehmet hört Musik, **wenn** er traurig ist.
Mehmet listens to music whenever he is sad.

Renate geht nach Hause, **weil** sie müde ist.
Renate is going home because she is tired.

In the preceding examples, the first clause is the main clause. The clause introduced by a conjunction is called a *dependent clause*. In German, the verb in a dependent clause occurs at the end of the clause.

[1]bestellen *to order* (*in a restaurant*)　　[2]Bläst ... aus? *Is* [*he*] *blowing out . . . ?*

MAIN CLAUSE	DEPENDENT CLAUSE
Ich bleibe im Bett,	wenn ich krank **bin.**
I stay in bed	*when I am sick.*

Point out that, in German, the first element in a statement can be a word, a phrase, or a clause. In each case, the conjugated verb is the second element. This rule is not acquired early.

When **wenn** or **weil** begins a clause, the conjugated verb appears at the end of the clause.

In sentences beginning with a dependent clause, the entire clause acts as the first element in the sentence. The verb of the main clause comes directly after the dependent clause, separated by a comma. As in all German statements, the verb is in second position. The subject of the main clause follows the verb.

	I	II	III
	DEPENDENT CLAUSE	VERB	SUBJECT
	Wenn ich krank bin,	bleibe	ich	im Bett.
	When I'm sick, I stay in bed.			
	Weil sie müde ist,	geht	Renate	nach Hause.
	Because she's tired, Renate is going home.			

Übung 8 | Warum denn?

Üb. 8. Tell sts. to pick phrases from the second column that make sense in response to the question in the first column. Tell them also to use *ich* or *wir* in response to questions with *du* or *ihr*. This shift also requires a change from *dein* to *mein* in sentences 2 and 6.

Beantworten Sie die Fragen.

MODELL: Warum gehst du nicht in die Schule? → Weil ich krank bin.

1. Warum gehst du nicht in die Schule?
2. Warum liegt dein Bruder im Bett?
3. Warum esst ihr denn schon wieder?
4. Warum kommt Nora nicht mit ins Kino?
5. Warum sieht Jutta schon wieder fern?
6. Warum sitzt du allein in deinem Zimmer?
7. Warum trinken sie Bier?
8. Warum machst du denn das Licht an?
9. Warum singt Jens den ganzen Tag?
10. Warum bleibst du zu Hause?

a. Durst haben
b. krank sein
c. traurig sein
d. Langeweile haben
e. Angst haben
f. glücklich sein
g. lernen müssen
h. müde sein
i. Hunger haben
j. keine Zeit haben

Übung 9 | Ist das immer so?

Üb. 9. Assign for homework. Sts. need to choose an action from the second column that makes sense when combined with the first column. Tell sts. that they can eliminate a number of choices by looking at the pronoun in the second column. Ask sts. to complete the exercise as in the model for the textbook characters *and* for themselves. Then, in the next class period, pair sts. up and ask them to interview each other.

Sagen Sie, wie das für andere Personen ist und wie das für Sie ist.

MODELL: s1: Was macht Albert, wenn er müde ist?
　　　s2: Wenn Albert müde ist, geht er nach Hause.
　　　s1: Und du?
　　　s2: Wenn ich müde bin, trinke ich einen Kaffee.

1. Albert ist müde.
2. Maria ist glücklich.
3. Herr Ruf hat Durst.
4. Frau Wagner ist in Eile.
5. Heidi hat Hunger.
6. Frau Schulz hat Ferien.
7. Hans hat Angst.
8. Stefan ist krank.

a. Sie trifft Michael.
b. Er geht nach Hause.
c. Sie fährt mit dem Taxi.
d. Sie kauft einen Hamburger.
e. Er trinkt eine Cola.
f. Er geht zum Arzt.
g. Er ruft: „Mama, Mama".
h. Sie fliegt nach Deutschland.

3.5 Dependent clauses and separable-prefix verbs

3.5. As was pointed out in section 3.4, most sts. cannot be expected to handle word order in dependent clauses correctly in spontaneous speech. Many will not even try to use dependent clauses. We introduce dependent word order here primarily for reading purposes so that sts. learn to look for the main verb of a clause in the right places.

As you know, the prefix of a separable-prefix verb occurs at the end of an independent clause.

Rolf **steht** immer früh **auf.**	*Rolf always gets up early.*

In a dependent clause, the prefix is attached to the verb form, which is placed at the end of the clause.

Rolf ist immer müde, wenn er früh **aufsteht.**	*Rolf is always tired when he gets up early.*
Helga, bitte **mach** das Fenster nicht **auf!** Es wird kalt, wenn du es **aufmachst.**	*Helga, please don't open the window. It gets cold when you open it.*

When there are two verbs in a dependent clause, such as a modal verb and an infinitive, the modal verb comes last, following the infinitive.

INDEPENDENT CLAUSE	Rolf **muss** früh **aufstehen.**	*Rolf has to get up early.*
DEPENDENT CLAUSE	Er ist müde, wenn er früh **aufstehen muss.**	*He is tired when he has to get up early.*
INDEPENDENT CLAUSE	Helga hat kein Geld. Sie **kann** nichts **machen.**	*Helga doesn't have any money. She can't do anything.*
DEPENDENT CLAUSE	Sie hat Langeweile, weil sie nichts **machen kann.**	*She's bored because she can't do anything.*

Übung 10 | Warum ist das so?

Üb. 10. Tell sts. that the choice of subject pronoun in column 2 helps them identify suitable responses for the questions in column 1 more quickly. Follow up next day in class by pairing sts. up to do the exercise orally.

MODELL: Jürgen ist wütend, weil er immer so früh aufstehen muss.

1. Jürgen ist wütend.
2. Silvia ist froh.
3. Claire ist in Eile.
4. Josef ist traurig.
5. Thomas geht nicht zu Fuß.
6. Willi hat selten Langeweile.
7. Marta hat Angst vor Wasser.
8. Mehmet fährt in die Türkei.

a. Sie muss noch einkaufen.
b. Er muss immer so früh aufstehen.
c. Seine Freundin nimmt ihn zur Uni mit.
d. Er sieht immer fern.
e. Sie kann nicht schwimmen.
f. Er will seine Eltern besuchen.
g. Melanie ruft ihn nicht an.
h. Sie muss heute nicht arbeiten.

Kiymet Benita Bock: *Kindheitserinnerungen* (1996)

Chapter opening artwork: The naive or childlike aura of this painting might be due to the fact that the artist is very likely not professionally trained and expressed her feelings and memories in a very original way. The artist called this picture *"Meine Pferde."*

Suggestion: Let students look at the picture. Use an *Assoziogramm* on the board to record their ideas. The following questions may help them get started. *Was sehen Sie auf dem Bild? Welches Tier ist das vielleicht? Wer hat das Bild gemalt? Wie alt ist der/die Maler/in? Wo hat er/sie das Bild gemalt? Welche Farben hat er/sie benutzt?*

KIYMET BENITA BOCK

Die Künstlerin Kiymet Benita Bock stellte dieses Werk im Rahmen[1] eines Projektes aus[2], in dem sich behinderte[3] Menschen zum bildnerischen Gestalten[4] treffen konnten. Aus dem Projekt entstand die Künstlergruppe „Die Schlumper", benannt[5] nach dem Standort des Ateliers im Hamburger Stadthaus „Schlump".

[1] *framework* [2] *stellte aus exhibited* [3] *handicapped* [4] *bildnerischen ... creative expression* [5] *named*

KAPITEL 4

Ereignisse und Erinnerungen

In **Kapitel 4**, you will begin to talk about things that happened in the past: your own experiences and those of others. You will also talk about different kinds of memories.

GOALS
The purpose of *Kapitel 4* is to give sts. chances to interact in situations dealing with past events. We formally introduce the perfect tense for this purpose. The simple past forms will be formally introduced in *Kapitel 7* and *9*.

PRE-TEXT ACTIVITIES
1. Use association techniques to introduce the forms of the perfect tense. In these activities, remember to follow the natural sequence of having sts. listen before they speak. **2.** Before each class period, spend about 5 minutes telling the sts. what you did the previous day. Clarify any new vocabulary. For additional listening practice, ask the sts. what they did the day before, but state the questions so they can answer with *ja* or *nein* or by raising their hands: *Wer hat gestern Hausaufgaben gemacht? Heben Sie bitte die Hand! Wer ist gestern in die Bibliothek gegangen? Wer hat gestern die Wäsche gewaschen? Wer hat gestern ferngesehen?* *usw.*

Themen
Der Alltag
Urlaub und Freizeit
Geburtstage und Jahrestage
Ereignisse

Kulturelles
Videoblick: Dresdner Bahnhof in neuem Glanz
Feiertage und Brauchtum
Universität und Studium
Videoecke: Feste und Feiern

Lektüren
Aufräumen (Martin Auer)
Film: *Das Wunder von Bern*

Strukturen
4.1 Talking about the past: the perfect tense
4.2 Strong and weak past participles
4.3 Dates and ordinal numbers
4.4 Prepositions of time: **um, am, im**
4.5 Past participles with and without **ge-**

Situationen

Der Alltag

Grammatik 4.1

Ich habe geduscht. | Ich habe gefrühstückt. | Ich bin in die Uni gegangen.

Ich bin in einem Kurs gewesen. | Ich habe mit meinen Freunden Kaffee getrunken. | Ich bin nach Hause gekommen.

Ich habe zu Mittag gegessen. | Ich bin nachmittags zu Hause geblieben. | Ich habe abends gelernt.

 **Situation 1** | Umfrage: Letzte Woche

MODELL: S1: Hast du Pizza zum Frühstück gegessen?
S2: Ja.
S1: Unterschreib bitte hier.

UNTERSCHRIFT

1. Hast du Pizza zum Frühstück gegessen? _____
2. Hast du kalten Kaffee getrunken? _____
3. Bist du mit dem Fahrrad zur Uni gefahren? _____
4. Bist du abends zu Hause geblieben? _____
5. Hast du im Bett Cola getrunken? _____

6. Hast du stundenlang telefoniert? _____
7. Hast du in der Bibliothek gearbeitet? _____
8. Hast du viele Hausaufgaben gemacht? _____
9. Bist du vor Mitternacht ins Bett gegangen? _____
10. Hast du deine Freunde zum Essen eingeladen? _____

Photo questions. *Kaufen Sie gern auf dem Markt ein? Was kann man auf dem Freiburger Markt kaufen? Was kauft wohl der junge Mann? Was hat er in seinem Rucksack? Ist er vielleicht Student? Was studiert er? Wie sieht er aus? Wie sieht die Frau aus?*

Gemüsemarkt in Freiburg. Sind Sie heute schon einkaufen gegangen?

 **Situation 2** | Dialog: Das Fest

Sit. 2. (See the IM.) Work with sts.' books either opened or closed. With sts.' books closed, ask the following focus questions. Questions for first listening: *Wie geht es Silvia? Wo war sie gestern Abend? Was hat sie da gemacht?* Questions for second listening: *Warum, glaubt Jürgen, ist Silvia müde? Wann ist sie nach Hause gekommen?*

Silvia und Jürgen sitzen in der Mensa und essen zu Mittag.

SILVIA: Ich bin furchtbar _müde_.
JÜRGEN: Bist du wieder so spät ins Bett _gegangen_?
SILVIA: Ja. Ich bin heute früh erst um vier Uhr nach Hause _gekommen_.
JÜRGEN: Wo _warst_ du denn so lange?
SILVIA: Auf einem Fest.
JÜRGEN: _Bis um vier Uhr früh_?
SILVIA: Ja, ich habe ein paar alte Freunde _getroffen_ und wir haben uns sehr gut unterhalten.
JÜRGEN: Kein Wunder, _dass du müde bist_!

MODELL: Wann hast du mit deiner Mutter gesprochen? →
Ich habe gestern mit meiner Mutter gesprochen.

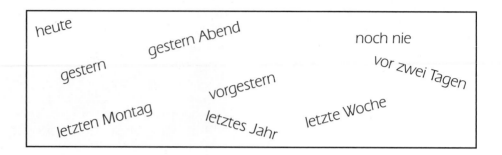

heute

gestern Abend

noch nie

gestern

vor zwei Tagen

vorgestern

letzten Montag

letztes Jahr

letzte Woche

1. Wann hast du dein Auto gewaschen?
2. Wann hast du geduscht?
3. Wann bist du ins Theater gegangen?
4. Wann hast du deine beste Freundin / deinen besten Freund getroffen?
5. Wann hast du einen Film gesehen?
6. Wann bist du in die Disko gegangen?
7. Wann hast du gelernt?
8. Wann bist du einkaufen gegangen?
9. Wann hast du eine Zeitung gelesen?
10. Wann hast du das Geschirr gespült?
11. Wann bist du spät ins Bett gegangen?
12. Wann bist du den ganzen Abend zu Hause geblieben?

 Situation 4 | Zum Schreiben: Ein Tagebuch

Schreiben Sie auch ein Tagebuch. Vielleicht haben Sie das früher schon einmal auf Englisch gemacht. Machen Sie sich zuerst ein paar Notizen. Was ist letzte Woche passiert? Was haben Sie gemacht? Was wollen Sie nicht vergessen?

MODELL: Letzte Woche habe/bin ich …

> 28. Juli 2008
>
> Habe einen total coolen Jungen kennengelernt! Er heißt Billy, eigentlich Paul, aber er sieht aus wie Billy Idol. Er ist total süß!! Habe gleich einen Brief an Geli geschrieben und ihr von Billy erzählt. Warte jetzt auf Gelis Antwort… Außerdem haben wir Zeugnisse bekommen. Das war nicht so gut…

Juttas Tagebuch

Lektüre 📖

Lektüre. This is a short story by Martin Auer from a book entitled *Was niemand wissen kann* (1986). **(1)** Use *Vor dem Lesen* to establish the context for this reading. Begin by asking: *Wann ist ein Kind erwachsen? Mit 10, mit 12, mit 16? Was für Arbeiten muss ein Kind zu Hause machen? Müll wegbringen, einkaufen, Rasen mähen, waschen? Macht ein Kind das gern? Warum?* Then ask sts. to work in small groups to complete the questions. Follow up with a discussion of sts.' answers. **(2)** Let sts. look at the title and illustration and try to predict what kind of chore this reading is about. Part A of *Arbeit mit dem Text* focuses on the many modal verbs that can be found in the text. Ask sts. to work in small groups to do this exercise. Set a time limit. Other words from the text that express feelings are *Spaß machen, sich freuen, traurig.* Sts. might also come up with other adjectives and related nouns from previous chapters. Follow up with a discussion of sts.' answers. **(3)** Assign *Arbeit mit dem Text* Part B as homework. **(4)** Ask sts. to do Part C in small groups and discuss afterwards. **(5)** *Nach dem Lesen* provides a starting point for sts. to write a simple role play with Kim and her mother as protagonists. It also asks sts. to go beyond the text and create a follow-up situation where the problem between the two is solved. Let sts. prepare the role play in small groups and act out the situation in class. To aid sts. in coming up with ideas and crafting the plot, present them with some questions: *Beginnt Kim mit dem Problem oder spricht sie erst über etwas anderes? Wie fühlt sich Kim? Wie drückt sie ihre Gefühle aus? Wie ein Kind oder eher wie ein Erwachsener? Wo spricht Kim mit ihrer Mutter? In ihrem Zimmer, in der Küche, oder noch woanders? Wie reagiert Kims Mutter auf Kims Problem? Nimmt sie sich Zeit für Kim? Denkt sie an ihre eigene Kindheit? Wie spricht Kims Mutter mit Kim? Wie mit einem Kind oder wie mit einem Erwachsenen? Nimmt sie sie in die Arme? Streichelt sie sie? Wie lösen Kim und ihre Mutter das Problem?*

Lesehilfe

The verb phrase **werden** + *infinitive,* as in **ich werde aufräumen,** is an example of the future tense. In German, this tense indicates a firm intention, a promise, or likelihood. In this story, the future tense serves both purposes: **ich werde aufräumen** (firm intention) and **sie wird schimpfen** (likelihood). You will learn more about the future tense in **Kapitel 8.**

Vor dem Lesen

Der folgende Text ist eine kurze Geschichte mit dem Titel „Aufräumen"[1]. Die Hauptfigur in dieser Geschichte ist das Kind „Kim". Wir wissen nicht, wie alt Kim ist. Wir wissen nur, dass sie heute eine Entscheidung trifft[2], die ihre Eltern normalerweise treffen. Denken Sie an Ihre Kindheit[3] und beantworten Sie die folgenden Fragen:

1. In welchem Alter glaubt man, dass man erwachsen[4] ist? Mit 10 Jahren schon? Mit 12 Jahren vielleicht? Mit 16 Jahren? Warum glaubt man, dass man erwachsen ist? Nennen Sie Beispiele.
2. Wie war es für Sie mit Hausarbeit als Kind? Welche Arbeiten haben Sie zu Hause gemacht? Haben Sie sie freiwillig[5] gemacht? Was ist passiert, wenn Sie sie nicht gemacht haben?

Miniwörterbuch	
auswandern	to emigrate
der **Ausweg**	way out
bis in alle Ewigkeit	for all eternity
einmal	for once
endlich	finally
keinen Spaß machen	to be no fun
merken	to notice, feel
schimpfen	to scold
schließlich	after all
sich freuen auf	to look forward to
sich umsehen	to look around

Aufräumen

von Martin Auer

H eute bin ich von der Schule nach Hause gekommen, bin in mein Zimmer gegangen, habe mich umgesehen und habe zu mir selber gesagt:
5 „Also, heute räume ich einmal mein Zimmer auf. So wie das aussieht, da macht es ja wirklich keinen Spaß mehr, hier zu wohnen. Nach dem Essen werde ich gleich mein Zimmer
10 aufräumen."
　　Und ich habe richtig gemerkt, wie ich mich gefreut habe auf mein aufgeräumtes Zimmer. Schließlich ist es ja mein

[1]*Cleaning Up* [2]eine Entscheidung ... *makes a decision* [3]*childhood* [4]*grown up* [5]*willingly*

Lesehilfe

In a negative context, the verb **brauchen** is like a modal verb. It means *to not have to* do something. Thus, **Niemand braucht es mir zu sagen** means *Nobody has to tell me.*

15 | Zimmer und ich muss drin wohnen, und ich habe zu mir selber gesagt: „Siehst du", habe ich zu mir gesagt, „ich bin alt genug, dass ich selber weiß, wann ich mein Zimmer aufräumen muss, und niemand braucht es mir zu sagen!" Und ich habe gemerkt, dass ich mich gefreut habe, dass ich ganz von selber mein Zimmer aufräumen werde, ohne dass es mir jemand gesagt hat.

Beim Mittagessen hat meine Mutter dann zu mir gesagt: „Kim", hat sie gesagt,
20 | „heute räumst du endlich einmal dein Zimmer auf!"

Da war ich ganz traurig.

Und jetzt sitze ich da und kann mein Zimmer nicht freiwillig aufräumen. Und unfreiwillig mag ich es nicht aufräumen. Und wenn ich es heute nicht aufräume, dann wird die Mutter mit mir schimpfen und wird morgen wieder sagen, ich soll mein Zimmer
25 | aufräumen und dann kann ich es morgen auch nicht freiwillig aufräumen. Und so weiter, bis in alle Ewigkeit.

Und in einem so unordentlichen Zimmer mag ich auch nicht wohnen. Ich sehe keinen Ausweg. Ich glaube, ich muss auswandern.

Arbeit mit dem Text

A. **Entscheidungen und Gefühle.** In diesem Text sehen wir viele Modalverben. Ergänzen Sie die Modalverben in den folgenden Sätzen. Sehen Sie dann im Text nach, ob sie auch im Text so stehen.

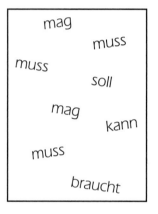

1. Schließlich ist es ja mein Zimmer und ich _____ drin wohnen.
2. Ich bin alt genug, dass ich selber weiß, wann ich mein Zimmer aufräumen _____.
3. Niemand _____ es mir zu sagen.
4. Und jetzt sitze ich da und _____ mein Zimmer nicht freiwillig aufräumen.
5. Dann wird die Mutter mit mir schimpfen und wird morgen sagen, ich _____ mein Zimmer aufräumen.
6. Und in einem so unordentlichen Zimmer _____ ich auch nicht wohnen.
7. Ich glaube, ich _____ auswandern.
8. Und unfreiwillig _____ ich es nicht aufräumen.

In dieser Geschichte drücken die Modalverben Gefühle aus[1]. Welche weiteren Wörter drücken Gefühle aus? Schreiben Sie sie auf!

B. Kim erzählt die Geschichte im Perfekt. Hier sind die Infinitive der Verben. Schreiben Sie die Perfektformen dazu, die Kim mit diesen Verben verwendet.

Infinitiv	Subjekt + Hilfsverb + Partizip
sich freuen	*ich habe mich gefreut*
gehen	
kommen	
merken	
sagen	

[1]ausdrücken *to express*

C. Wer, wo, wann, was? Arbeiten Sie in kleinen Gruppen und beantworten Sie die folgenden Fragen. Schreiben Sie die Antworten auf.

1. Wer sind die Personen der Geschichte?
2. Was wissen wir über sie?
3. Wo spielt die Geschichte? Welche Orte gibt es?
4. Welcher Ort ist wohl der wichtigste?
5. Wann spielt die Geschichte?
6. Wie lange dauern die Ereignisse?
7. Was passiert? Erzählen Sie die Geschichte in kurzen Sätzen wieder. („Kim kommt nach Hause …“)

Nach dem Lesen

Kim hat einen Entschluss gefasst[1]. Sie möchte mit ihrer Mutter über ihr Problem sprechen. Spielen Sie diese Szene.

[1]einen … *made a decision*

Urlaub und Freizeit

Vocabulary Display

In this section, sts. work with strong and weak past participles. The display provides examples of 3rd-person forms of the perfect tense. Present the new vocabulary in the usual way. As in the previous display, verbs that take *sein* are highlighted in red and verbs with *haben* in blue.

Grammatik 4.2

Jutta ist ins Schwimmbad gefahren.

Sie hat in der Sonne gelegen.

Sie ist geschwommen.

Sie hat Musik gehört.

Jens und Robert haben Postkarten geschrieben.

Sie sind in den Bergen gewandert.

Sie haben Tennis gespielt.

Sie haben viel gelesen.

Situation 6 | Dialog: Jens' und Juttas Wochenende

Es ist Montag. Jutta und Jens treffen sich auf dem Schulhof ihrer Schule und reden über ihr Wochenende.

> JENS: Hallo, Jutta!
> JUTTA: Grüß dich, Jens! Was hast du am Wochenende <u>gemacht</u>?
> JENS: Ach, nichts Besonders. Ich habe <u>ferngesehen</u> und Musik <u>gehört</u>. Es war langweilig. Und du?
> JUTTA: Ich bin mit meinen Eltern in die Berge <u>gefahren</u>. Wir sind viel <u>gewandert</u> und haben sogar ein Picknick gemacht. Das war ganz super.
> JENS: Das hört sich wirklich toll an!
> JUTTA: Ja, auf jeden Fall. Komm doch das nächste Mal mit.
> JENS: Au ja, gern.

Situation 7 | Am Wochenende

Schauen Sie auf die Bilder und finden Sie die passende Antwort auf jede Frage.

Sit. 7. Tell sts. that there are two strategies for completing the task: **1.** their knowledge of the characters' identities and **2.** the grammatical number of the subject pronoun and verb in the responses. Sts. will recognize most of the characters based on their appearance in activities in *Kontakte* thus far. Sts. can look at the pictures and find the proper responses based on what they see the characters doing. When students are not sure of a character's identity, they can look at the form of the pronoun and the verb. Point out that sentences 1-2 go with *sie* plus singular verb, sentences 3-4 with *sie* plus plural verb, and sentences 5-8 with *er* plus singular verb. The activities in this exercise are consistent with what sts. have discovered and will discover about these characters. For example, in Sit. 4 sts. read Jutta's diary entry in which she writes *Habe einen total coolen Jungen kennengelernt*. Mention other related facts as well, to make the contexts come alive. *Die Frischs wohnen in der Schweiz. Michael ist mit Maria verlobt. Jens ist faul; er sieht zu viel fern.*

1. __f__ Was hat Frau Ruf am Freitag gemacht?
2. __e__ Was hat Jutta am Samstag gemacht?
3. __a__ Was haben Jutta und Hans am Sonntag gemacht?
4. __c__ Was haben die Frischs am Sonntag gemacht?
5. __b__ Was hat Michael am Samstag gemacht?
6. __d__ Was hat Jens am Sonntag gemacht?
7. __g__ Was hat Herr Ruf am Freitag gemacht?
8. __h__ Was hat Richard am Samstag gemacht?

a. Sie haben den Hund gebadet.
b. Er hat mit Maria zu Abend gegessen.
c. Sie sind in den Bergen gewandert.
d. Er hat stundenlang ferngesehen.
e. Sie hat Billy kennengelernt.
f. Sie ist nach Augsburg gefahren.
g. Er hat für seine Familie die Wäsche gewaschen.
h. Er ist zum Strand gefahren.

Situation 8 | Umfrage: Hast du das gemacht?

Was hast du am Wochenende gemacht?

UNTERSCHRIFT

1. Hast du bis mittags geschlafen? _____
2. Bist du tanzen gegangen? _____
3. Hast du mit jemandem gefrühstückt? _____
4. Hast du Sport getrieben? _____
5. Hast du Hausaufgaben gemacht? _____
6. Hast du eine E-Mail geschrieben? _____
7. Bist du ins Kino gegangen? _____
8. Hast du ein Buch gelesen? _____
9. Hast du Wäsche gewaschen? _____
10. Hast du deine Wohnung geputzt? _____

Lektüre

Lektüre. (1) Use *Vor dem Lesen* 1–4 to establish the context. Most sts. will know little about Bern. Locate it on a map. For now, it is sufficient that sts. know it is in Switzerland. *Nach dem Lesen* allows opportunity for further inquiry into soccer. **(2)** Ask sts. to work in small groups to complete Part B of *Vor dem Lesen*. **(3)** Assign *Arbeit mit dem Text* to small groups or as homework. Follow up with discussion of correct answers. **(4)** *Nach dem Lesen.* Sts. can use the Internet or the library to research soccer and Wortmann. You may want to have sts. make presentations on their findings in class.

Vor dem Lesen

A. Beantworten Sie die folgenden Fragen.

1. Was sehen Sie auf dem Poster?
2. Wo liegt Bern?
3. Spielen Sie gern Fußball? Sehen Sie Fußballspiele im Fernsehen?
4. Ist Fußball in Ihrem Land ein beliebter Sport? Und in Deutschland?

B. Lesen Sie die Wörter im Miniwörterbuch auf der nächsten Seite. Suchen Sie sie im Text und unterstreichen Sie sie. Lesen Sie dann den Satz und versuchen Sie, ihn zu verstehen.

Film: *Das Wunder von Bern*

Es ist Sommer 1954. Richard Lubanski wird aus russischer Kriegsgefangenschaft entlassen und kommt nach Hause, nach Essen, zu seiner Frau und den drei Kindern. Durch die Jahre in Gefangenschaft ist Richard verschlossen und aggressiv geworden. Er kann sich in Deutschland nicht eingewöhnen. Seinem jüngsten Sohn Matthias
5   gehen die Probleme des Vaters besonders zu Herzen. Letztendlich ist es Matthias und seine Liebe zum Fußball, die Richards Willen zum Leben wieder aufleben lassen.

   Matthias' großes Idol ist der Fußballstar Helmut Rahn vom Verein Rot-Weiß Essen. Für ihn trägt Matthias die Sporttasche. Rahn ist ein Nationalspieler und soll bei der Fußballweltmeisterschaft in Bern für Deutschland spielen. Einmal hat Helmut Rahn
10   zu Matthias gesagt: „Ich kann nur gewinnen, wenn du zu den Spielen in die Schweiz kommst." Natürlich will Matthias dorthin, aber sein Vater hat kein Verständnis für den Traum seines Sohnes. Am Ende passiert jedoch ein Wunder: Matthias und sein Vater fahren gemeinsam nach Bern zum Endspiel–Deutschland gegen Ungarn. Und dann passiert ein zweites Wunder: Die Deutschen gewinnen die Weltmeisterschaft mit einem
15   3:2 gegen die Ungarn.

Arbeit mit dem Text

Was steht im Text, was nicht?

1. Richard Lubanski kommt 1945 nach Hause.
2. Richard hat Urlaub in Russland gemacht.
3. Familie Lubanski wohnt in einer Stadt namens Essen.
4. Matthias, der älteste Sohn, liebt Fußball.
5. Matthias will unbedingt[1] zur Fußballweltmeisterschaft nach Bern, aber er darf nicht.
6. Am Ende fährt die ganze Familie Lubanski nach Bern zum Endspiel.
7. Deutschland gewinnt die Fußballweltmeisterschaft gegen Ungarn.

Nach dem Lesen

Recherchieren Sie im Internet!

1. Was wissen Sie über die Fußballweltmeisterschaft? Wie oft findet sie statt?
2. Wie oft und in welchen Jahren hat Deutschland die Weltmeisterschaft gewonnen?
3. Warum ist der Sieg der Deutschen 1954 ein „Wunder"?
4. Welche Filme hat Sönke Wortmann noch gemacht?

[1]*absolutely*

Geburtstage und Jahrestage

Grammatik 4.3–4.4

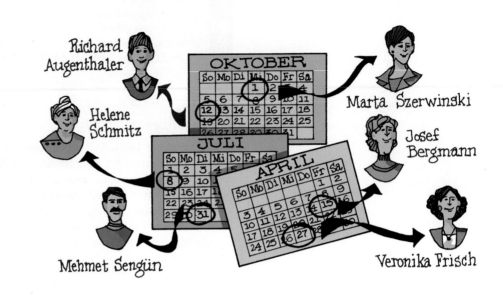

Marta hat am ersten Oktober Geburtstag.
Richard hat am zwölften Oktober Geburtstag.
Frau Schmitz hat am achten Juli Hochzeitstag.
Mehmet ist am einunddreißigsten Juli geboren.
Josef ist am fünfzehnten April geboren.
Veronika hat am siebenundzwanzigsten April Geburtstag.

 Situation 9 | Dialog: Welcher Tag ist heute?

Bringen Sie die Sätze in die richtige Reihenfolge.

Marta und Sofie sitzen im Café. Sofie fragt:

   3 Nein, welches Datum?

   2 Montag.

   6 Wirklich? Ich dachte, er hat im August Geburtstag.

   8 Hast du denn schon ein Geschenk?

   1 Welcher Tag ist heute?

   4 Ach so, der dreißigste.

   5 Der dreißigste? Mann, dann ist ja heute Willis Geburtstag!

   9 Das ist es ja! Ich hab' noch nicht einmal ein Geschenk.

   7 Nein, Christian hat im August Geburtstag, aber Willi im Mai.

   10 Na, dann viel Spaß beim Geschenke kaufen!

Situation 10 | Informationsspiel: Geburtstage

Sit. 10. The corresponding chart is in Appendix A.

MODELL: S1: Wann ist Sofie geboren?
S2: Am neunten November 1987.

Person	Geburtstag
Willi	30. Mai 1983
Sofie	9. November 1987
Claire	1. Dezember 1982
Melanie	3. April 1984
Nora	4. Juli 1990
Thomas	17. Januar 1990
Heidi	23. Juni 1987
mein(e) Partner(in)	
sein/ihr Vater	
seine/ihre Mutter	

Situation 11 | Erfindungen und Entdeckungen

Sit. 11. Review numbers by having sts. first read the years. Ask sts. to work in pairs, alternating asking and answering questions. The sts. asking the questions cover the captions and write the name and date spoken by their partner. Nationality: Cyril Demian (Austria), Friedrich Staedtler (Germany), Emil Berliner (Germany), Joseph Cayetti (USA), Melitta Bentz (Germany), Laszlo Biro (Hungary), Peter Mitterhofer (Germany), Marie Curie (originally from Poland, lived and worked in France), Friedrich Herschel (originally German but lived in England), Alexander Fleming (England), Leif Eriksson (Norway).

MODELL: S1: Wer hat den Bleistift erfunden?
S2: _____.
S1: Wann hat er ihn erfunden?
S2: _____.

Cyril Demian
1829

Friedrich Staedtler
1662

Emil Berliner
1887

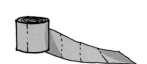
Joseph Cayetti
1857

Melitta Bentz
1908

Laszlo Biro
1938

Peter Mitterhofer
1864

das Toilettenpapier	der Kugelschreiber	die Schallplatte
der Bleistift	der Kaffeefilter	das Akkordeon
	die Schreibmaschine	

Situationen

151

MODELL: s1: Wer hat das Radium entdeckt?

s2: _____.

s1: Wann hat sie es entdeckt?

s2: _____.

Note. Before class, you might look up in the encyclopedia some additional information about these inventors and discoverers in case sts. have more questions.

| Marie Curie | Friedrich Herschel | Alexander Fleming | Leif Eriksson |
| 1898 | 1781 | 1928 | 1000 |

das Penizillin   Amerika   das Radium   der Uranus

Situation 12 | Interview

Sit. 12. Do the first half of the activity in one sitting and the second half in another. Or, select three lines of questions that are most pertinent to your class.

1. Wann bist du geboren (Tag, Monat, Jahr)? Wann ist dein Freund / deine Freundin geboren (Tag, Monat, Jahr)? Wann ist dein Vater / deine Mutter geboren (Tag, Monat, Jahr)?

2. Wann bist du in die Schule gekommen (Monat, Jahr)? Wann hast du angefangen zu studieren (Monat, Jahr)?

3. Was war der wichtigste Tag in deinem Leben? Was ist da passiert? In welchem Monat war das? In welchem Jahr?

4. In welchem Monat warst du zum ersten Mal verliebt? hast du zum ersten Mal Geld verdient? hast du einen Unfall gehabt?

5. An welchen Tagen in der Woche arbeitest du? hast du frei? gehst du ins Kino? besuchst du deine Eltern? hast du Geld? gehst du ins Sprachlabor?

6. Um wie viel Uhr stehst du auf? ist dein erster Kurs? gehst du nach Hause? gehst du ins Bett?

Videoblick

Dresdner Bahnhof in neuem Glanz[1]

Das jahrelange Chaos am Hauptbahnhof in Dresden hat nun ein Ende. Nach komplizierten Bauarbeiten wird die Eingangshalle[2] neu eröffnet.

- In welchem Bundesland[3] liegt Dresden?
- Wie alt ist der Dresdner Bahnhof?
- Wie lange haben die Bauarbeiten gedauert?
- Wie heißt der Architekt?
- Wie beschreibt man den Bahnhof jetzt?

[1]splendor [2]entrance hall [3]federal state

Der restaurierte Hauptbahnhof in Dresden

Feiertage und Brauchtum[1]

- Welches sind die Familienfeste in Ihrem Land?
- Was macht man an diesen Festen?
- Wer feiert[2] zusammen?
- Kennen Sie deutsche Feiertage und Bräuche[3]? Wenn ja, welche?

Photo questions. *Wie ist das Wetter? Was sehen Sie? Was machen die Leute? Wie sehen sie aus?*

Cultural note. This is a reproduction of a colored woodcut made in 1897 after a drawing by P. Bauer. **KLI.** (See the IM.) Bring in an *Adventskalender* and have sts. take turns opening windows/doors and describing what they see behind them. Sts. may not be familiar with these calendars and not know that the window for each day in December is opened until Christmas Eve arrives.

Auf dem Christkindlmarkt in München im Jahre 1897

Der Adventskalender: Ein deutscher Exportartikel in christlicher Tradition ist über 100 Jahre alt. Amerika ist das Importland Nummer 1.

- Weihnachten in Deutschland: An welchen Tagen feiert man?
- Welche deutschen Weihnachtstraditionen kennen Sie?
- Wie feiern die Deutschen am liebsten Weihnachten? Analysieren Sie die Umfrage.

TAG FÜR TAG: Adventskalender lassen die Erwartungen steigen

FOCUS-FRAGE

„Wo verbringen Sie Weihnachten?"

EIN FAMILIENFEST ZU HAUSE

von 1300 Befragten* antworteten

zu Hause	**73 %**
bei den Eltern/Kindern	**21 %**
bei Freunden	**3 %**
im Urlaub	**3 %**

83 Prozent der Deutschen verbringen Weihnachten im Kreis der Familie, 7 Prozent zusammen mit dem Partner, 6 Prozent mit Freunden, 4 Prozent feiern alleine.

* Repräsentative Umfrage des Sample-Instituts für FOCUS im Dezember

Cultural note. Apart from *Maifeiertag / Tag der Arbeit* (May 1) and the national holidays (Germany, October 3; Austria, October 26; Switzerland, August 1), most holidays are of religious origin. The most important ones are the following: *Neujahr* (January 1), *Karfreitag* (the Friday before Easter), *Ostern* (the first Sunday and Monday after the first full moon in spring, i.e., on or after March 21), *Christi Himmelfahrt* (the 6th Thursday after Easter), *Pfingsten* (the 7th Sunday and Monday after Easter), *Weihnachten* (December 25 and 26). Germany is 33% Catholic, 33% Protestant, 4% Muslim, and 0.1% Jewish. Austria is 75% Catholic, 5% Protestant, and 4% Muslim; Switzerland is 42% Catholic, 35% Protestant, and 4.5% Muslim.

[1]*tradition* [2]*celebrates* [3]*customs*

Ereignisse

Grammatik 4.5

Vocabulary Display

This section introduces the participles for separable-prefix verbs and reviews question forms. The first picture series shows Frau Schulz's day. Assume the role of Frau Schulz and have your sts. ask you the questions listed below to which you make up suitable responses in accordance with the pictures.

For the second picture series, ask the sts. to form pairs; one st. should assume the role of Albert. Tell sts. the setting is last Saturday. After completing the sequence, the questioner should make up one more question (Frame 7) to which "Albert" should respond.

1. Wann sind Sie aufgewacht?
2. Wann sind Sie aufgestanden?
3. Wann sind Sie von zu Hause weggegangen?
4. Wann hat Ihr Kurs angefangen?
5. Wann hat Ihr Kurs aufgehört?
6. Wann sind Sie nach Hause gekommen?
7. Wann haben Sie unsere Prüfungen korrigiert?

1. Wann hast du eingekauft?
2. Wann hast du das Geschirr gespült?
3. Wann hast du mit deiner Freundin telefoniert?
4. Wann hast du ferngesehen?
5. Wann hast du dein Fahrrad repariert?
6. Wann bist du abends ausgegangen?

Situation 13 | Michaels freier Tag

Sit. 13. Preteach new vocabulary: *tut mir leid* (as a set phrase), *denken an, zuerst, Keller, versuchen, dauern.* **Suggestion:** Photocopy the lines and cut them into strips. Then have sts. work in small groups to sequence them.

Michael telefoniert mit Maria. Sie reden über Michaels freien Tag. Bringen Sie die Sätze in die richtige Reihenfolge.

___10___ Tut mir leid, Maria, an dich habe ich leider nicht gedacht. Aber wenn du willst, können wir heute Abend etwas machen.

___2___ Hallo Maria. Hier ist Michael. Wie geht's?

___4___ Also, zuerst habe ich meinen kleinen Bruder besucht und sein Motorrad repariert.

___13___ Tschüss.

___8___ Dann habe ich meinen Keller aufgeräumt. Und am Abend bin ich ausgegangen, in die Kneipe, mit zwei Arbeitskollegen.

___6___ Nein, natürlich nicht. Mittags habe ich meinen neuen Nachbarn kennengelernt und wir haben zusammen Kaffee getrunken.

___7___ Und dann?

___1___ Schneider, guten Tag.

___9___ Und an mich hast du den ganzen Tag nicht gedacht, oder doch?

___11___ Also gut. Kannst du mich um acht Uhr abholen?

___3___ Ganz gut, danke. Du, sag mal, ich habe versucht, dich gestern anzurufen. Was hast du denn den ganzen Tag gemacht?

___12___ Ja gern. Bis dann um acht. Tschüss.

___5___ So, und das hat den ganzen Tag gedauert?

Situation 14 | Interview: Gestern

Sit. 14. Have sts. do this activity in pairs. This is the first occurrence of the simple past *war.* It should not hinder comprehension. Follow-up questions: *Wer hat Italienisch gegessen? Was hat Barbara getrunken? Wann ist Tom ins Bett gegangen?*

1. Wann bist du aufgestanden?
2. Was hast du gefrühstückt?
3. Wie bist du zur Uni gekommen?
4. Was war dein erster Kurs?
5. Was hast du zu Mittag gegessen?
6. Was hast du getrunken?
7. Wen hast du getroffen?
8. Was hast du nachmittags gemacht?
9. Wie war das Wetter?
10. Wo bist du um sechs Uhr abends gewesen?
11. Was hast du abends gemacht?
12. Wann bist du ins Bett gegangen?
13. Ist gestern etwas Interessantes passiert? Was?

Situation 15 | Informationsspiel: Zum ersten Mal

MODELL: S1: Wann hat Herr Thelen seinen ersten Kuss bekommen?
S2: Als er zwölf war.

	Herr Thelen	Frau Gretter	mein(e) Partner(in)
seinen/ihren/deinen ersten Kuss bekommen	als er 12 war	als sie 13 war	
zum ersten Mal ausgegangen	als er 14 war	als sie 15 war	
seinen/ihren/deinen Führerschein gemacht	mit 18	mit 25	
sein/ihr/dein erstes Bier getrunken	mit 16	mit 18	
seine/ihre/deine erste Zigarette geraucht	mit 21	noch nie	
zum ersten Mal nachts nicht nach Hause gekommen	noch nie	mit 21	

Sit. 15. The corresponding chart is in Appendix A. If your students do not respond well to the personal questions, you can ask them to adopt another persona (TV personality, pop star, politician, etc.) to answer the questions for the right column. Model pronunciation and and have sts. repeat key words: *zum ersten Mal, Kuss, Führerschein, Zigarette, noch nie.* Write sample answers on the board, e.g., *Als ich 15 war.* or *Mit 15.* Also write the phrase *Ich habe/bin noch nie _____.* for students who have never done some of these things.

Universität und Studium

- Wann haben Sie mit dem Studium am College oder an der Universität angefangen?
- Welche Voraussetzungen[1] (High-School-Abschluss, Prüfungen usw.) braucht man für ein Studium?
- An welchen Universitäten haben Sie sich beworben[2]?
- Studieren Sie an einer privaten oder staatlichen Hochschule[3]?
- Müssen Sie Studiengebühren[4] bezahlen?
- Wie lange dauert Ihr Studium voraussichtlich?
- Welchen Abschluss[5] haben Sie am Ende Ihres Studiums?
- Was für Kurse müssen Sie belegen?

Eine Demonstration gegen Studiengebühren in Hamburg

Die meisten Universitäten in Deutschland sind Institutionen der Bundesländer und damit öffentliche Universitäten. Es gibt nur wenige private Hochschulen. Bisher mussten Studenten für ihr erstes Studium keine Studiengebühren zahlen. Doch jetzt wird alles anders. Seit 2005 dürfen die Bundesländer Studierende zur Kasse bitten[6] und viele tun das auch. Bereits im Wintersemester 2006/2007 waren in Niedersachsen und Nordrhein-Westfalen Studiengebühren fällig, seit dem Sommersemester 2007 auch in Bayern und Baden-Württemberg und seit dem Wintersemester 2007/2008 in Hessen. Andere Bundesländer beraten[7] noch. Allerdings sind diese Studiengebühren im Vergleich zu anderen Ländern nicht besonders hoch. In den meisten Bundesländern bezahlt man 500 Euro pro Semester.

Viele Studenten arbeiten während des Semesters und in den Semesterferien. Nur ca. 20% der Studenten an deutschen Universitäten bekommen ein Stipendium oder eine finanzielle Hilfe vom Staat, das sogenannte BAföG (Bundesausbildungsförderungsgesetz)[8]. Der BAföG-Höchstsatz[9] beträgt zur Zeit knapp[10] 600 Euro im Monat.

Man braucht normalerweise das Abitur[11], um an einer Universität zu studieren. Beim Abitur nach 12 oder 13 Schuljahren sind die Studienanfänger 18 bis 20 Jahre alt. Für einige Fächer gibt es einen „Numerus clausus". Das heißt: Nur wer gute oder sehr gute Noten hat, darf studieren. Die Universitäten dürfen sich einen gewissen Prozentsatz ihrer Studenten selbst aussuchen und schauen nicht nur auf gute Schulnoten, sondern auch auf Ergebnisse von Eignungstests[12].

Die traditionellen Studienabschlüsse an der Universität sind das Diplom, das Staatsexamen und in den geisteswissenschaftlichen[13] Fächern der Magister. Doch diese Studiengänge sind bald Geschichte. Bis 2010 soll es überall in Deutschland und in Europa die neuen Bachelor- und Masterstudiengänge geben. Diese neuen Studiengänge werden eingeführt, um international vergleichbare[14] Studienabschlüsse zu haben. Ein Bachelorstudium dauert meist drei Jahre und ein Masterstudium zwei weitere Jahre.

7% der Studenten in Deutschland kommen aus dem Ausland[15], die meisten aus Osteuropa und Asien. Zum Vergleich: Der Anteil ausländischer Studenten in den USA beträgt knapp 4%. Allerdings studieren relativ wenig Deutsche im Ausland, nämlich nur knapp 3%, die meisten in Großbritannien und den USA. US-amerikanische Studenten gehen allerdings noch seltener für ein Semester oder mehr ins Ausland, nämlich nur knapp 1%.

- Vergleichen Sie das Studium in Deutschland und in Ihrem Land. Was ist anders? Was ist ähnlich?

KLI. (1) Set up the prereading questions as an interview. Practice changing the questions from *Sie* to *du*. Then ask sts. to interview each other while jotting down their partner's answers. Finally, put a summary on the board. Use three columns: an abbreviated question column, a column for your sts.' country to be filled in now, and a column for Germany to be filled in later. **(2)** Ask sts. to work in groups, to read the KLI note, and to find and jot down the differences between Germany and their country following the format on the board. Set a time limit of approximately 5 minutes. When the time is up, complete the chart on the board by filling in the column for Germany according to your sts.' answers. **(3)** Follow up by summarizing the major differences between the two systems.

---

[1]*prerequisites* [2]*sich ... applied* [3]*college, university* [4]*fees, tuition* [5]*degree; diploma* [6]*Studierende ... make students pay* [7]*are debating* [8]*federal law for the promotion of higher education* [9]*maximum amount* [10]*just under* [11]*roughly: high school diploma* [12]*aptitude tests* [13]*humanities* [14]*comparable* [15]*aus ... from abroad*

Situation 16 | Rollenspiel: Das Studentenleben

Sit. 16. (See the IM.) Role for s2 appears in Appendix B.

s1: Sie sind Reporter/Reporterin einer Unizeitung in Österreich und machen ein Interview zum Thema: Studentenleben in Ihrem Land. Fragen Sie, was Ihr Partner / Ihre Partnerin gestern alles gemacht hat: am Vormittag, am Mittag, am Nachmittag und am Abend.

Videoecke

- Wie hast du Pfingsten[1] verbracht?
- Was war das Interessanteste, das dir in den letzten Tagen passiert ist?
- Wann hast du Geburtstag?
- Wie feierst du deinen Geburtstag?
- Wie hast du deinen letzten Geburtstag gefeiert?
- Was war der schönste Tag in deinem Leben?

[1]Pentecost

Susann ist in Riesa in Sachsen geboren und als Kind mit ihrer deutschen Mutter und ihrem syrischen Vater nach Damaskus gezogen. Dort hat sie 18 Jahre gelebt, bevor sie wieder nach Deutschland gezogen ist, um in Leipzig Arabistik und Deutsch als Fremdsprache zu studieren.

Heike ist in Leipzig geboren. Sie ist mit einem Ukrainer verheiratet. Sie spricht Russisch, Weißrussisch, Ukrainisch und Polnisch und sie studiert Ostslawistik und Polonistik.

Aufgabe 1

Aufgabe 1. (1) Preview with photos: *Wie lange hat Susann in Damaskus gelebt? Warum ist sie jetzt wieder in Deutschland? Wo ist Heike geboren? Wen hat sie geheiratet? Was studiert sie? Welche Sprachen, glauben Sie, gehören zur Ostslawistik?* **(2)** Read the 4 questions referring to the interview with Susann. Play the video and ask sts. to put these questions in the right order. **(3)** Preview the answers. Ask sts. to knock or clap when they hear the answer to the first question. Stop the video, ask sts. for the answer, and play the answer again. Do the same for the remaining answers.

Susann. In welcher Reihenfolge stellt man die Fragen? Welche Antworten gehören zu den Fragen?

FRAGEN

1. _____ Was ist heute Morgen passiert?
2. _____ Was ist vor drei Wochen passiert?
3. _____ Wie hat sie letztes Jahr ihren Geburtstag gefeiert?
4. _____ Wie hat sie Pfingsten verbracht?

ANTWORTEN

a. Sie hat ihre Arabisch-Prüfung mit „sehr gut" bestanden.
b. Sie ist vom Lärm der Straße aufgewacht.
c. Sie war bei ihren Eltern und hat Geburtstag gefeiert.
d. Sie war mit ihrer Schwester in der Oper.

Heike. Welche Aussagen sind richtig, welche sind falsch? Verbessern Sie die falschen Aussagen.

	RICHTIG	FALSCH
1. Am Freitag hat sie verschlafen.	☐	☐
2. Am Sonntag und Montag war sie im Garten.	☐	☐
3. Sie hat den Rasen gemäht und Unkraut gejätet[1].	☐	☐
4. Dabei ist eine Maus draufgegangen[2].	☐	☐
5. Sie ist vom Sternzeichen[3] her ein Fisch.	☐	☐
6. Ihre Eltern wohnen in der Ukraine.	☐	☐
7. Sie feiert ihren Geburtstag immer in der Ukraine.	☐	☐

Aufgabe 3. Play the video once. Ask sts. to work on task in small groups. Play the video, pausing briefly after each of the missing words.

Student Interviews: (1) Ask sts. to jot down their own answers to the interview questions. **(2)** Pair sts. to interview each other. Ask them to jot down their partner's answers. **(3)** Follow up by sampling a few of the answers given in the interviews.

Die Mausgeschichte. Vervollständigen Sie den Text mit den folgenden Wörtern: erschreckt[4], Garten, gehoben[5], gejätet, gestrichen[6], Maus, Platte, verschlafen[7]

Am Sonnabend habe ich _____. Am Sonntag und Montag waren wir im _____. Wir haben Unkraut _____ und den Zaun[8] _____. Als wir im Garten waren, haben wir eine Gehwegplatte[9] hoch _____ und da kam eine _____ unten vor. Wir haben uns so _____, dass wir die _____ fallen lassen haben[10] und dabei ist die Maus draufgegangen.

[1]Unkraut ... *pulled weeds* [2]ist ... *got killed* (slang) [3]*(astrological) sign* [4]*got frightened* [5]*lifted* [6]*painted*
[7]*overslept* [8]*fence* [9]*stepping stone* [10]*fallen ... dropped*

Wortschatz

Unterwegs	On the Road
die **Fa**hrkarte, -n	ticket
der **Ba**hnhof, ⸚e	train station
der **Fü**hrerschein, -e	driver's license
der **Schla**fwagen, -	sleeping car
der **U**nfall, ⸚e	accident
der **U**rlaub, -e	vacation

Zeit und Reihenfolge	Time and Sequence
der **A**bend, -e (R)	evening
am **A**bend	in the evening
der **A**lltag	daily routine
der **Na**chmittag, -e	afternoon
der **Vo**rmittag, -e	late morning
das **Da**tum, **Da**ten	date
welches **Da**tum ist heute?	what is today's date?
das **Ma**l, -e	time
das **le**tzte Mal	the last time
zum **e**rsten Mal	for the first time
abends	evenings, in the evening

gestern	yesterday
gestern **A**bend	last night
letzt-	last
letzte **Wo**che	last week
letzten **Mo**ntag	last Monday
letzten **So**mmer	last summer
letztes **Wo**chenende	last weekend
nachmittags	afternoons, in the afternoon
nachts	nights, at night
vorgestern	the day before yesterday
an (R)	on; in
am **A**bend	in the evening
am **e**rsten Okt**o**ber	on the first of October
an welchem **Ta**g?	on what day?
bis (R)	until
bis um **vie**r Uhr	until four o'clock
einmal	once
warst du schon **ei**nmal ...?	were you ever . . . ?
erst	not until
erst um **vie**r Uhr	not until four o'clock
früh (R)	in the morning
bis um **vie**r Uhr **frü**h	until four in the morning

schon (R)	already
seit	since; for
seit zwei Jahren	for two years
über	over
übers Wochenende	over the weekend
vor	ago
vor zwei Tagen	two days ago

Schule und Universität	School and University
die Aufgabe, -n	assignment
die Grundschule, -n	elementary school
die Vorlesung, -en	lecture
der Kugelschreiber, -	ballpoint pen
das Gymnasium, Gymnasien	high school, college prep school
halten, hält, gehalten*	to hold
ein Referat halten	to give a paper / oral report

Feste und Feiertage	Holidays
der Feiertag, -e	holiday
der Nationalfeiertag, -e	national holiday
das Familienfest, -e	family celebration
(das) Weihnachten	Christmas

Ähnliche Wörter

die Tradition, -en; der Muttertag; der Valentinstag; das Picknick, -s

Ordinalzahlen	Ordinal Numbers
erst-	acht-
der erste Oktober	neunt-
zweit-	zehnt-
dritt-	elft-
viert-	zwölft-
fünft-	dreizehnt-
sechst-	zwanzigst-
siebt-	hundertst-

Sonstige Substantive	Other Nouns
die Erinnerung, -en	memory, remembrance
die Nachbarin, -nen	female neighbor
die Rechnung, -en	bill; check (in restaurant)
die Sandburg, -en	sandcastle
die Umfrage, -n	survey
die Unizeitung, -en	university newspaper

der Einwanderer, -	immigrant
der Keller, -	basement, cellar
der Kuss, ̈-e	kiss
der Liegestuhl, ̈-e	deck chair
der Nachbar, -n	male neighbor
der Ort, -e	place, town
der Strand, ̈-e	beach
das Erlebnis, -se	experience
das Ferienhaus, ̈-er	vacation house
das Geschirr	dishes
Geschirr spülen	to wash the dishes
das Jahrzehnt, -e	decade
das Sprachlabor, -s	language laboratory
das Tagebuch, ̈-er	diary

Ähnliche Wörter

die Computerfirma, Computerfirmen; die Information, -en; die Reporterin, -nen; die Rolle, -n; die Wäsche; die Zigarette, -n; der Garten, ̈-; der Kaffeefilter, -; der Reporter, -; der Tee; der Uranus; das Akkordeon, -s; das Café, -s; das Interview, -s; das Penizillin; das Prozent, -e; das Studentenleben; das Theater, -; das Thema, Themen; das Toilettenpapier; das Wunder, -; kein Wunder

Sonstige Verben	Other Verbs
ab·fahren, fährt ... ab, ist abgefahren	to depart
an·fangen, fängt ... an, angefangen	to begin
antworten†	to answer
auf·wachen, ist aufgewacht	to wake up
aus·wandern, ist ausgewandert	to emigrate
bezahlen	to pay (for)
dauern	to last
denken (an + *akk.*), gedacht	to think (of)
entdecken	to discover
erfinden, erfunden	to invent
ergänzen	to complete, fill in the blanks
los·fahren, fährt ... los, ist losgefahren	to drive off
passieren, ist passiert	to happen
spülen	to wash; to rinse
verdienen	to earn
verstehen, verstanden	to understand
versuchen	to try, attempt
war, warst, waren	was, were

*Strong and irregular verbs are listed in the **Wortschatz** with the third-person singular, if there is a stem-vowel change, and with the past participle. All verbs that use **sein** as the auxiliary in the present perfect tense are listed with **ist.**

†Regular weak verbs are listed only with their infinitive.

Ähnliche Wörter

diskutieren; essen, isst, gegessen (R); zu Abend essen; fotografieren; gewinnen, gewonnen; korrigieren; sitzen, gesessen; telefonieren; weg·gehen, ist weggegangen

Adjektive und Adverbien	Adjectives and Adverbs
furchtbar	terrible
geschlossen	closed
links	left
mit dem linken Fuß auf·stehen, ist aufgestanden	to get up on the wrong side of bed
pünktlich	punctual; on time
süß	sweet
verliebt	in love

Ähnliche Wörter

politisch, total

Sonstige Wörter und Ausdrücke	Other Words and Expressions
auf jeden Fall	by all means
das hört sich toll an	that sounds great
deshalb	therefore; that's why
diese, dieser, dieses (R)	this, that, these, those
doch!	yes (on the contrary)!
etwas (R)	something
etwas Interessantes/ Neues	something interesting/new
genug	enough
gleich	right away
in (R)	in; at
im Garten	in the garden
im Café	at the cafe
ja	indeed
das ist es ja!	that's just it!
stimmt!	that's right!
tut mir leid	I'm sorry
wem	whom (*dative*)
wen	whom (*accusative*)
zu	too
zu schwer	too heavy
zuerst	first

Strukturen und Übungen

4.1 Talking about the past: the perfect tense

4.1. *Perfekt: haben und sein.* In this section, we formally present for the first time the perfect tense. (The simple past tense of *haben* and *sein* are introduced in **Kapitel 7,** the simple past of other verbs in **Kapitel 9.**) The emphasis is on the use of the auxiliaries *haben* and *sein.* The formation of the participles will be explained in Section 4.2, and verbs with separable and inseparable prefixes are covered in Section 4.5. The perfect tense is another important instance of the sentence bracket. The word order itself causes sts. fewer →

In conversation, German speakers generally use the perfect tense to describe past events. The simple past tense, which you will study in **Kapitel 9,** is used more often in writing.

Ich **habe** gestern Abend ein Glas Wein **getrunken.**	*I drank a glass of wine last night.*
Nora **hat** gestern Basketball **gespielt.**	*Nora played basketball yesterday.*

German forms the perfect tense with an auxiliary (**haben** or **sein**) and a past participle (**gewaschen**). Participles usually begin with the prefix **ge-**.

	AUXILIARY		PARTICIPLE
Ich	**habe**	mein Auto	**gewaschen.**

The auxiliary is in first position in yes/no questions and in second position in statements and **w**-word questions. The past participle is at the end of the clause.

Hat Heidi gestern einen Film **gesehen?**	*Did Heidi see a movie last night?*
Ich **habe** gestern zu viel Kaffee **getrunken.**	*I drank too much coffee yesterday.*
Wann **bist** du ins Bett **gegangen?**	*When did you go to bed?*

Wissen Sie noch?

You've already seen how a **Satzklammer** forms a frame or a bracket consisting of a verb and either a separable prefix or an infinitive (grammar 1.5, 2.3, and 3.1). Note here how the **Satzklammer** is composed of **haben/sein** and the past participle.

Verbs with **sein** = no direct object; change of location or condition.

difficulties than the choice of auxiliary and the formation of the past participle. Use perfect forms in your speech as often as possible before asking sts. to use them.

Whereas most verbs form the present perfect tense with **haben,** several others use **sein.** To use **sein,** a verb must fulfill two conditions.

1. It cannot take a direct object.
2. It must indicate change of location or condition.

sein	**haben**
Ich **bin aufgestanden.**	Ich **habe gefrühstückt.**
I got out of bed.	*I ate breakfast.*
Stefan **ist** ins Kino **gegangen.**	Er **hat** einen Film **gesehen.**
Stefan went to the movies.	*He saw a film.*

Here is a list of common verbs that take **sein** as an auxiliary. For a more complete list, see Appendix F.

ankommen	*to arrive*	ich bin angekommen
aufstehen	*to get up*	ich bin aufgestanden
einsteigen	*to board*	ich bin eingestiegen
fahren	*to go, drive*	ich bin gefahren
gehen	*to go, walk*	ich bin gegangen
kommen	*to come*	ich bin gekommen
schwimmen	*to swim*	ich bin geschwommen
wandern	*to hike*	ich bin gewandert

In addition to these verbs, **sein** itself and the verb **bleiben** (*to stay*) take **sein** as an auxiliary.

Bist du schon in China **gewesen?**	*Have you ever been to China?*
Gestern **bin** ich zu Hause **geblieben.**	*Yesterday I stayed home.*

Übung 1 | Rosemaries erster Schultag

Üb. 1–2. These exercises ask the sts. to provide only the auxiliary verb. Point out the rule that, if the verb has a direct object, the auxiliary is always *haben*. Assign for homework and check in class. Ask sts. to write out the answers to the questions following both texts in complete sentences. As a follow-up in class, ask sts. to group the verbs according to their choice of auxiliary while writing them in two columns (*sein* and *haben*) on the board.

Ergänzen Sie **haben** oder **sein.** Beantworten Sie dann die Fragen.

Rosemarie _____ [a] bis sieben Uhr geschlafen. Dann _____ [b] sie aufgestanden und _____ [c] mit ihren Eltern und ihren Schwestern gefrühstückt. Sie _____ [d] ihre Tasche genommen und _____ [e] mit ihrer Mutter zur Schule gegangen. Ihre Mutter und sie _____ [f] ins Klassenzimmer gegangen und ihre Mutter _____ [g] noch ein bisschen dageblieben. Die Lehrerin, Frau Dehne, _____ [h] alle begrüßt. Dann _____ [i] Frau Dehne „Herzlich willkommen" an die Tafel geschrieben.

1. Wann ist Rosemarie aufgestanden?
2. Wohin sind Rosemarie und ihre Mutter gegangen?
3. Wer ist Frau Dehne?
4. Was hat Frau Dehne an die Tafel geschrieben?

Übung 2 | Eine Reise nach Istanbul

Ergänzen Sie **haben** oder **sein.** Beantworten Sie dann die Fragen.

JOSEF UND MELANIE:

Wir _____ [a] ein Taxi genommen. Mit dem Taxi _____ [b] wir zum Bahnhof gefahren. Dort _____ [c] wir uns Fahrkarten gekauft. Dann _____ [d] wir in den Orientexpress eingestiegen. Um 5.30 _____ [e] wir abgefahren. Wir _____ [f] im Speisewagen[1] gefrühstückt. Den ganzen Tag _____ [g] wir Karten gespielt. Nachts _____ [h] wir in den Schlafwagen gegangen. Wir _____ [i] schlecht geschlafen. Aber wir _____ [j] gut in Istanbul angekommen.

1. Wohin sind Josef und Melanie mit dem Taxi gefahren?
2. Wann sind sie mit dem Zug abgefahren?
3. Wo haben sie gefrühstückt?
4. Was haben sie nachts gemacht?

Übung 3 | Ein ganz normaler Tag

Üb. 3. Before assigning as homework, go through the list of verbs with your sts. determining which verbs use *sein* and which ones use *haben*.

Ergänzen Sie das Partizip.

aufgestanden	gefrühstückt	gehört
gearbeitet	gegangen	getroffen
geduscht	gegessen	getrunken

Heute bin ich um 7.00 Uhr _____ [a]. Ich habe _____ [b], _____ [c] und bin an die Uni _____ [d]. Ich habe einen Vortrag _____ [e]. Um 10 Uhr habe ich ein paar Mitstudenten _____ [f] und Kaffee _____ [g]. Dann habe ich bis 12.30 Uhr in der Bibliothek _____ [h] und habe in der Mensa zu Mittag _____ [i].

[1] *dining car*

4.2   Strong and weak past participles

weak verbs = **ge-** + verb stem + **-(e)t**

4.2. *Regelmäßige und unregelmäßige Partizipien.*
Point out that the forms of weak verbs are not
listed. Sts. may be interested to know that German
strong and weak participles and English participles
ending in *-en* (*eaten, written*) and *-ed* (*asked,
waited*) are related.

strong verbs = **ge-** + verb stem + **-en;** the verb
stem may have vowel or consonant changes.

German verbs that form the past participle with **-(e)t** are called *weak verbs.*

arbeiten	gearbeitet	*work*	*worked*
spielen	gespielt	*play*	*played*

To form the regular past participle, take the present tense **er/sie/es**-form and
precede it with **ge-**.

er	spielt	→	er	hat	gespielt
sie	arbeitet	→	sie	hat	gearbeitet
es	regnet	→	es	hat	geregnet

Verbs that form the past participle with **-en** are called *strong verbs.* Many verbs
have the same stem vowel in the infinitive and the past participle.

kommen	→	gekommen

Some verbs have a change in the stem vowel.

schwimmen	→	geschwommen

Some also have a change in consonants.

gehen	→	gegangen

Here is a reference list of common irregular past participles.

PARTICIPLES WITH **haben**

essen, gegessen	*to eat*
halten, gehalten	*to hold*
lesen, gelesen	*to read*
liegen, gelegen	*to lie, be situated*
nehmen, genommen	*to take*
schlafen, geschlafen	*to sleep*
schreiben, geschrieben	*to write*
sehen, gesehen	*to see*
sprechen, gesprochen	*to speak*
tragen, getragen	*to wear, carry*
treffen, getroffen	*to meet*
trinken, getrunken	*to drink*
waschen, gewaschen	*to wash*

PARTICIPLES WITH **sein**

ankommen, angekommen	*to arrive*
aufstehen, aufgestanden	*to get up*
bleiben, geblieben	*to stay, remain*
einsteigen, eingestiegen	*to board*
fahren, gefahren	*to go (using a vehicle), drive*
gehen, gegangen	*to go (walk)*
kommen, gekommen	*to come*
schwimmen, geschwommen	*to swim*
sein, gewesen	*to be*

Übung 4 | Das ungezogene[1] Kind

Üb. 4. Assign for homework. Have pairs of sts. play the roles in class.

Stellen Sie die Fragen!

> MODELL: SIE: Hast du schon geduscht?
> DAS KIND: Heute will ich nicht duschen.

1. Heute will ich nicht frühstücken.
2. Heute will ich nicht schwimmen.
3. Heute will ich keine Geschichte lesen.
4. Heute will ich nicht Klavier spielen.
5. Heute will ich nicht schlafen.
6. Heute will ich nicht essen.
7. Heute will ich nicht Geschirr spülen.
8. Heute will ich den Brief nicht schreiben.
9. Heute will ich nicht ins Bett gehen.

Übung 5 | Katrins Tagesablauf

Üb. 5. Assign as written homework. You might wish to add a creative section by asking students to describe an imaginary 11th picture.

Wie war Katrins Tag gestern? Schreiben Sie zu jedem Bild einen Satz. Verwenden Sie diese Ausdrücke.

> MODELL: Katrin hat bis 9 Uhr im Bett gelegen.

arbeiten
abends zu Hause bleiben
ein Referat halten
nach Hause kommen
bis neun im Bett liegen
regnen
mit Frau Schulz sprechen
einen Rock tragen
Freunde treffen
ihre Wäsche waschen

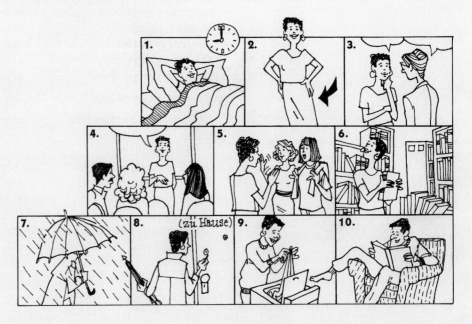

[1]naughty

4.3 Dates and ordinal numbers

To form ordinal numbers, add **-te** to the cardinal numbers 1 through 19 and **-ste** to the numbers 20 and above. Exceptions to this pattern are **erste** (*first*), **dritte** (*third*), **siebte** (*seventh*), and **achte** (*eighth*).

Ordinals 1–19 add **-te** to the cardinal number (but note: **erste, dritte, siebte, achte**).

4.3. *Datum und Ordnungszahlen.* We expect sts. to recognize the ordinal numbers and to state important dates in the 2 ways described, but we do not yet expect mastery of all the ordinal numbers.

eins	**erste**	*first*
zwei	zweite	*second*
drei	**dritte**	*third*
vier	vierte	*fourth*
fünf	fünfte	*fifth*
sechs	sechste	*sixth*
sieben	**siebte**	*seventh*
acht	**achte**	*eighth*
neun	neunte	*ninth*
. . .		
neunzehn	neunzehnte	*nineteenth*

Ordinals 20 and higher add **-ste** to the cardinal number.

zwanzig	zwanzigste	*twentieth*
einundzwanzig	einundzwanzigste	*twenty-first*
zweiundzwanzig	zweiundzwanzigste	*twenty-second*
. . .		
dreißig	dreißigste	*thirtieth*
vierzig	vierzigste	*fortieth*
. . .		
hundert	hundertste	*hundredth*
. . .		

Ordinal numbers usually end in **-e** or **-en.** Use the construction **der + -e** to answer the question **Welches Datum …?**

All dates are masculine:
der **zweite** Mai
am **zweiten** Mai

Welches Datum ist heute?	*What is today's date?*
Heute ist **der** achtzehnte Oktober.	*Today is October eighteenth.*

Use **am + -en** to answer the question **Wann …?**

Wann sind Sie geboren?	*When were you born?*
Am achtzehnten Juni 1983.	*On the eighteenth of June, 1983.*

Ordinal numbers in German can be written as words or figures.

am zweiten Februar	*on the second of February*
am 2. Februar	*on the 2nd of February*

Übung 6 | Wichtige Daten

Üb. 6. For oral pair-work in class.

Beantworten Sie die Fragen.

1. Welches Datum ist heute?
2. Welches Datum ist morgen?
3. Wann feiert man Weihnachten?
4. Wann feiert man den Nationalfeiertag in Ihrem Land?
5. Wann feiert man das neue Jahr?
6. Wann feiert man Valentinstag?
7. Wann ist dieses Jahr Muttertag?
8. Wann ist nächstes Jahr Ostern?
9. Wann beginnt der Frühling?
10. Wann beginnt der Sommer?

4.4 Prepositions of time: *um, am, im*

4.4. *Präpositionen der Zeit.* Here, as elsewhere, we introduce prepositions according to meaning rather than case. This section presents 3 prepositions that are used to answer the question *Wann?* The use of *an* and *in* to express location is described in Section 5.4. Point out to sts. that *am* and *im* are contractions of *an dem* and *in dem* but that *um* is just the basic preposition.

Use the question word **wann** to ask for a specific time. The preposition in the answer will vary depending on whether it refers to clock time, days and parts of days, months, or seasons.

um CLOCK TIME

—Wann beginnt der Unterricht?   *When does the class start?*
—Um neun Uhr.   *At nine o'clock.*

um

am DAYS AND PARTS OF DAYS*

—Wann ist das Konzert?   *When is the concert?*
—Am Montag.   *On Monday.*

—Wann arbeitest du?   *When do you work?*
—Am Abend.   *In the evening.*

am 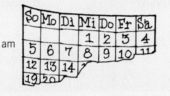   am

im SEASONS AND MONTHS

—Wann ist das Wetter schön?   *When is the weather nice?*
—Im Sommer und besonders im August.   *In the summer and especially in August.*

im

No preposition is used when stating the year in which something takes place.

—Wann bist du geboren?   *When were you born?*
—Ich bin 1990 geboren.   *I was born in 1990.*

*Note the exceptions: **in der Nacht** (*at night*) and **um Mitternacht** (*at midnight*).

Übung 7 | Melanies Geburtstag

Üb. 7. Assign for homework and check in class.

Ergänzen Sie **um, am, im** oder —.

Melanie hat _____ᵃ Frühling Geburtstag, _____ᵇ April. Sie ist _____ᶜ 1984 geboren, _____ᵈ 3. April 1984. _____ᵉ Dienstag kommen Claire und Josef _____ᶠ halb vier zum Kaffee. Melanies Mutter kommt _____ᵍ 16 Uhr. _____ʰ Abend gehen Melanie, Claire und Josef ins Kino. Josef hat auch _____ⁱ April Geburtstag, aber erst _____ʲ 15. April.

Übung 8 | Interview

Üb. 8. Set up as an in-class interview.

Beantworten Sie die Fragen.

1. Was machst du im Winter? im Sommer?
2. Wie ist das Wetter im Frühling? im Herbst?
3. Was machst du am Morgen? am Abend?
4. Was machst du am Freitag? am Samstag?
5. Was machst du heute um sechs Uhr abends? um zehn Uhr abends?
6. Was machst du am Sonntag um Mitternacht?

4.5 Past participles with and without *ge-*

Separable-prefix verbs form their past participles with **-ge-** before the verb stem.

WEAK VERBS

prefix + **-ge-** + stem + **-(e)t**

STRONG VERBS

prefix + **-ge-** + stem + **-en**

The verb stem may have vowel or consonant changes.

4.5. *Partizipien mit ge-*. This section deals with the participles of verbs with separable prefixes. Stress that the separable prefix and the participle constitute a single word. Point out that if sts. know the participle of the base verb, they can simply add the prefix to it.

A. Participles with **ge-**

German past participles usually begin with **ge-**. The past participles of separable-prefix verbs begin with the prefix; the ge- goes between the prefix and the verb.

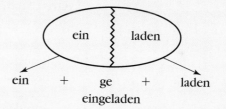

Frau Schulz **hat** Heidi und Nora zum Essen **eingeladen.**

Frau Schulz invited Heidi and Nora for dinner.

Here are the infinitives and past participles of some common separable-prefix verbs.

PAST PARTICIPLES WITH **haben**

anfangen	angefangen	*to start*
anrufen	angerufen	*to call up*
aufräumen	aufgeräumt	*to tidy up*
auspacken	ausgepackt	*to unpack*
fernsehen	ferngesehen	*to watch TV*

PAST PARTICIPLES WITH **sein**

ankommen	angekommen	*to arrive*
aufstehen	aufgestanden	*to get up*
ausgehen	ausgegangen	*to go out*
weggehen	weggegangen	*to go away, leave*

SEPARABLE PREFIXES

an
auf
aus
mit
weg
wieder
zusammen
and others

B. Participles without ge-

There are two types of verbs that do not add **ge-** to form the past participle: verbs that end in **-ieren** and verbs with inseparable prefixes.

Verbs ending in **-ieren** are weak: verb stem + **-t.**

1. Verbs ending in **-ieren** form the past participle with **-t: studieren →** **studiert.**

Paula hat Deutsch **studiert.**   *Paula studied German.*

Here is a list of common verbs that end in **-ieren.**

diskutieren	diskutiert	*to discuss*
fotografieren	fotografiert	*to take pictures*
korrigieren	korrigiert	*to correct*
probieren	probiert	*to try, taste*
reparieren	repariert	*to repair, fix*
studieren	studiert	*to study*
telefonieren	telefoniert	*to telephone*

4.5. *Partizipien ohne ge-.* For verbs ending in *-ieren,* emphasize that participles end in *-t* and do not add *ge-.*

Almost all verbs ending in **-ieren** form the perfect tense with **haben.** The verb **passieren** (*to happen*) requires **sein** as an auxiliary: **Was ist passiert?** (*What happened?*)

2. The past participles of inseparable-prefix verbs do not include **ge-:** **verstehen → verstanden.**

Stefan hat nicht **verstanden.**   *Stefan didn't understand.*

Verbs with inseparable prefixes may be weak or strong:

WEAK VERBS
verb stem + **-(e)t**

STRONG VERBS
verb stem + **-en**

The verb stem may have vowel or consonant changes.

INSEPARABLE PREFIXES

be-
ent-
er-
ge-
ver-
zer-

Separable prefixes can stand alone as whole words; inseparable prefixes are always un-stressed syllables.

Whereas separable prefixes are words that can stand alone (**auf, aus, wieder,** and so forth), inseparable prefixes are simply syllables: **be-, ent-, er-, ge-, ver-,** and **zer-.** The past participles of most inseparable-prefix verbs require **haben** as an auxiliary. Here is a list of common inseparable-prefix verbs and their past participles.

bekommen	bekommen	*to get*
besuchen	besucht	*to visit*
bezahlen	bezahlt	*to pay*
entdecken	entdeckt	*to discover*
erfinden	erfunden	*to invent*
erzählen	erzählt	*to tell*
verdienen	verdient	*to earn*
vergessen	vergessen	*to forget*
verlieren	verloren	*to lose*
verstehen	verstanden	*to understand*

Übung 9 | Ein schlechter Tag

Üb. 9. Assign as homework and check in class.

AA Ask sts. to form groups and describe a bad day in their own lives. They could report back orally or with texts written on transparencies.

Herr Thelen ist gestern mit dem linken Fuß aufgestanden. Zuerst hat er seinen Wecker nicht gehört und hat verschlafen. Dann ist er in die Küche gegangen und hat Kaffee gekocht. Nach dem Frühstück ist er mit seinem Auto in die Stadt zum Einkaufen gefahren. Er hat geparkt und ist erst nach zwei Stunden zurückgekommen. Herr Thelen hat einen Strafzettel[1] bekommen und 20 Euro bezahlt für falsches Parken. Er ist nach Hause gefahren, hat die Wäsche ge-waschen und hat aufgeräumt. Beim Aufräumen ist eine teure Vase auf den Boden gefallen und zerbrochen[2]. Als die Wäsche fertig war, war ein Pullover eingelaufen[3]. Herr Thelen ist dann schnell ins Bett gegangen. Fünf Minuten vor Mitternacht ist das Haus abgebrannt[4].

[1]*ticket* [2]*broken* [3]*shrunk* [4]*burned down*

A. Richtig (R) oder falsch (F)?

1. _____ Herr Thelen hat gestern verschlafen.
2. _____ Vor dem Frühstück ist er in die Stadt gefahren.
3. _____ Herr Thelen hat falsch geparkt.
4. _____ Er hat seine Wohnung aufgeräumt.
5. _____ Herr Thelen braucht ein neues Haus.

B. Suchen Sie die Partizipien heraus, bilden Sie die Infinitive und schreiben Sie sie auf.

PARTIZIPIEN MIT **ge-**   INFINITIVE

_____   _____

_____   _____

⋮   ⋮

PARTIZIPIEN OHNE **ge-**   INFINITIVE

_____   _____

_____   _____

⋮   ⋮

Übung 10 | In der Türkei

Üb. 10. For homework. Tell students that auxiliary verbs have separate blanks.

Mehmet ist in der Türkei. Was hat er gestern gemacht? Verwenden Sie die Verben am Rand[1].

gehen
ankommen
trinken
schlafen
begrüßen

Mehmet ist in der Türkei bei seinen Eltern. Gestern _____ er um 17 Uhr _____[a]. Er _____ seine Eltern und Geschwister _____[b] und einen Tee mit ihnen _____[c]. Dann _____ er in sein Zimmer _____[d] und _____ _____[e].

gehen
trinken
fragen
sprechen
gehen

Nach einer Stunde _____ er zum Abendessen in die Küche _____[f]. Seine Eltern _____ ihn viel über sein Leben in Deutschland _____[g] und Mehmet _____ über seine Arbeit und seine Freunde _____[h]. Sie _____ noch einen Tee _____[i] und _____ um 23 Uhr ins Bett _____[j].

Übung 11 | Interview

Üb. 11. Assign the questions for homework. Do the first 2 or 3 examples orally in class. As follow-up the next day in class, ask sts. to interview each other. Have them take notes, then ask them to tell the class something particularly amusing or interesting about their partners. If you tell them ahead of time that they will be relating information to the class, they are more likely to be creative in their interviews.

Fragen Sie Ihren Partner / Ihre Partnerin. Schreiben Sie die Antworten auf.

MODELL: mit deinen Eltern telefonieren (wie lange?) →

    s1: Hast du gestern mit deinen Eltern telefoniert?
    s2: Ja.
    s1: Wie lange?
    s2: Eine halbe Stunde.

1. früh aufstehen (wann?)
2. jemanden fotografieren (wen?)
3. jemanden besuchen (wen?)
4. ausgehen (wohin?)
5. etwas bezahlen (was?)

6. etwas reparieren (was?)
7. etwas Neues probieren (was?)
8. fernsehen (wie lange?)
9. etwas nicht verstehen (was?)
10. dein Zimmer aufräumen (wann?)

[1]*margin*

Adolph von Menzel: *Eisenwalzwerk*
(1872–75), Alte Nationalgalerie, Berlin

Chapter opening artwork: Industrial art never
really established itself in Western European
culture. In the Communist world, however, there
was a continuation of the early realistic beginnings
in the socialist realism of the former Soviet Union
and the GDR. Note: In 1898, Menzel became a
member of the *Hoher Orden vom Schwarzen Adler*
and acquired the *von* in his name.

Suggestion: Use the painting as a starting point to
talk about *Arbeit*. Let students look at the painting
and read the short text before answering the
following questions. *Was machen die Leute auf dem
Bild? Wo arbeiten sie? Wie ist die Temperatur dort?
In welchem Jahrhundert sah ein Eisenwalzwerk so
aus? Wie nennt man dieses Zeitalter? Wie ist die
Arbeit in diesem Werk? Wie finden Sie die
Atmosphäre des Bildes?*

ADOLPH VON MENZEL

Das *Eisenwalzwerk*[1] von Adolph von Menzel (1815–1905) ist ein Bild des
Realismus. Die Welt der Arbeit, besonders der Industriearbeit, als Thema der
Malerei war im 19. Jahrhundert neu. In Oberschlesien[2] (im heutigen[3] Polen) arbei-
tete von Menzel von 1872 bis 1875 an diesem Werk.

[1] *iron rolling mill*   [2] *Upper Silesia*   [3] *present-day*

Geld und Arbeit

In **Kapitel 5**, you will talk about shopping, jobs and the workplace, and daily life at home. You will expand your ability to express your likes and dislikes and learn to describe your career plans.

GOALS

In *Kapitel 5,* sts. talk about professions and work environments in addition to work performed in kitchens. (Other household chores are introduced in *Kapitel 6.*)

The grammar in this chapter focuses on the dative case, expressing change with *werden* and asking "who(m)." We do not expect sts. to master the dative forms in this lesson, simply to recognize them and use them in certain fixed expressions.

Themen
Geschenke und Gefälligkeiten
Berufe
Arbeitsplätze
In der Küche

Kulturelles
Ladenschluss in Deutschland
Videoblick: Azubibewerbung
Ausbildung und Beruf
Videoecke: Studium und Arbeit

Lektüren
Schüler arbeiten
Film: *Der Tunnel*

Strukturen
5.1 Dative case: articles and possessive adjectives
5.2 Question pronouns: **wer, wen, wem**
5.3 Expressing change: the verb **werden**
5.4 Location: **in, an, auf** + dative case
5.5 Dative case: personal pronouns

Situationen

Geschenke und Gefälligkeiten

Grammatik 5.1–5.2

Vocabulary Display
This vocabulary display focuses on verbs of giving and receiving and the dative vs. accusative case. Read the sentences and have sts. repeat. After pronouncing each sentence, do an association activity with sentences 4, 5, 7, and 8. (See the IM for suggestions). *Claire schreibt ihrer Mutter einen Brief. Wer von Ihnen schreibt manchmal Briefe? Wem schreiben Sie Briefe?* Associate one student with each activity and follow up with questions like *Wer schreibt seiner Freundin einen Brief?* or *Wem schreibt <name> einen Brief?* Then use the other sentences in the display by asking questions such as *Wem verkauft Heidi ein Wörterbuch? Was verkauft Heidi ihrem Mitstudenten Stefan?* Ask sts. to produce the sentences by asking: *Was macht Peter? usw.*

1. Peter kauft seinem Freund Albert eine Konzertkarte.

2. Ernst gibt seinem Vater die Tageszeitung.

3. Michael schenkt seiner Freundin Maria einen Ausflug an die Ostsee.

4. Hans leiht seiner Schwester einen MP3-Spieler.

5. Oma Schmitz kocht ihrem Enkel Rolf das Abendessen.

6. Heidi verkauft ihrem Mitstudenten Stefan ein Wörterbuch.

7. Melanie erzählt ihrer Freundin Claire ein Geheimnis.

8. Claire schreibt ihrer Mutter einen Brief.

Situation 1 | Ist das normal?

Sit. 1. Have sts. match each sentence with the picture it describes, then have them tell you how the two sentences differ in meaning. Although the spelling differences between the dative and accusative possessive articles are obvious to you, some sts. may not notice them unless you point them out.

AA. Bring pictures from the PF that show someone doing something for someone else: repairing a bicycle, selling flowers, etc. Describe the pictures: *A repariert B das Fahrrad. Und hier verkauft X Y Blumen.* Now ask: *Was verkauft X?* (Blumen.) *Wem verkauft X die Blumen?* (Y.) *Richtig, und wem repariert A das Fahrrad?* (B.) *Genau, A repariert B das Fahrrad.* Stress the question words *was* and *wer/wem* to make it clear that the former refers to things; the latter, to people. This will help students when they do *Sit. 2.* You can also write a list of verbs on the board and have sts. make up sentences of their own. Encourage them to make up humorous and therefore memorable examples. Verbs: *(ein)gießen, kaufen, kochen, renovieren, reparieren, geben usw.*

Welches Bild gehört zu welchem Satz?

1. a. _____ b.

_____ Jens gießt seiner Tante die Blumen.
_____ Jens gießt seine Tante.

2. a. _____ b.

_____ Jutta repariert ihren Bruder.
_____ Jutta repariert ihrem Bruder das Radio.

3. a. _____ b.

_____ Silvia kauft das Kind.
_____ Silvia kauft dem Kind die Schokolade.

4. a. _____ b.

_____ Herr Ruf kocht der Familie das Essen.
_____ Herr Ruf kocht die Familie.

Situation 2 | Sagen Sie *ja, nein* oder *vielleicht.*

Sit. 2. Demonstrate the activity by reading through the first example with a st. Read the question, emphasizing *wem*, then continue with the responses: *dem Professor? (Ja.) ihren Eltern? (Vielleicht.) usw.* As you pronounce the items in a–d, emphasize the dative form of the articles and the possessives. Quickly model pronunciation for the remaining questions and responses, having sts. repeat. Now have them work in pairs. It is acceptable to use *niemand* (as opposed to *niemandem*) as the negative answer to a dative question.

1. Wem geben die Studenten ihre Hausaufgaben?
   a. dem Professor
   b. ihren Eltern
   c. dem Hausmeister
   d. dem Taxifahrer

2. Wem schreibt Rolf einen Brief?
   a. seiner Katze
   b. dem Präsidenten
   c. seinem Friseur
   d. seinen Eltern

3. Wem kauft Andrea das Hundefutter?
   a. ihrer Mutter
   b. ihrem Freund Lukas
   c. ihrem Hund
   d. ihren Geschwistern

4. Wem repariert Herr Ruf das Fahrrad?
   a. seinem Hund
   b. seiner Mutter
   c. seinen Nachbarn
   d. seinem Sohn

Situation 3 | Interaktion: Was schenkst du deiner Mutter?

Sit. 3. Preteach vocabulary: *Roman, Mütze, Fahrradhelm, Badehose, Bikini, Regenschirm, Reiseführer, Kaffeemaschine, Parfüm.* Ask sts. to repeat after you as you read the words. Encourage sts. to use items above and beyond those in the display in their answers if they choose. Tell sts. the current exchange rate. (You may wish to ask sts. to check the financial pages of newspapers for current exchange rates.) Then model some responses, mentioning some humorous gifts to encourage creativity. You could have your examples written out on an overhead transparency with the dative and accusative endings underlined in different colors. Remind sts. of word order with indirect and direct objects. Expand on your responses to reinforce the use of *weil,* to recycle old vocabulary, and to give the sts. as much input as possible: *Ich kaufe meiner Mutter eine Reise nach Deutschland, weil sie deutsches Bier trinken möchte / weil sie ein Dirndl kaufen möchte. Ich kaufe meinem Vater einen Mercedes, weil er jetzt einen Golf fährt. Ich kaufe meinem Bruder einen Fahrradhelm, weil er gern Rad fährt. Ich habe keine Schwester.* Some sts. may need to say "stepfather," "-mother," etc.: *Stiefvater, -mutter usw.* Also, some may need to know *Mein/e _____ lebt nicht mehr.* Remind sts. that "I don't have a" is *Ich habe kein/ein ...* Afterward, have each st. tell the class the most unusual thing he or she bought.

Sie haben in der Lotterie 2 000 Euro gewonnen. Für 500 Euro wollen Sie Ihrer Familie und Ihren Freunden Geschenke kaufen. Was schenken Sie ihnen?

MODELL: S1: Was schenkst du deiner Mutter?
S2: Einen/Ein/Eine _____.
S1: Was schenkst du deinem Vater?
S2: Einen/Ein/Eine _____.

der Bikini
der Regenschirm
die Badehose
der Reiseführer
(Baedeker "Mallorca")
der Roman
(Thomas Mann
"Der Zauberberg")
die Mütze
das Parfüm
die Kaffeemaschine
der Fahrradhelm

	ich	mein(e) Partner(in)
deiner Mutter		
deinem Vater		
deiner Schwester		
deinem Bruder		
deinem Großvater		
deiner Großmutter		
deinem Freund / deiner Freundin		
deinem Professor / deiner Professorin		
deinem Mitbewohner / deiner Mitbewohnerin		

Ladenschluss in Deutschland

- Wann gehen Sie einkaufen?
- An welchen Tagen und zu welchen Zeiten können Sie in Ihrer Stadt einkaufen gehen?
- Gibt es Tage, an denen alles geschlossen ist?

Lesen Sie den Text und beantworten Sie die Fragen.

- Wann kann ein Berliner / eine Berlinerin wochentags einkaufen gehen?
- Kann man in Deutschland am Wochenende einkaufen? Wenn ja, wann?
- Wer regelt heute den Ladenschluss[1] in Deutschland?

Bis zum 1. September 2006 hat ein Gesetz[2], das Ladenschlussgesetz, sehr genau und streng geregelt, an welchen Tagen und wie lange Läden[3] überall in Deutschland geöffnet sein dürfen. Ein Ladenbesitzer[4] durfte seinen Laden von montags bis samstags von 6 bis 20 Uhr öffnen. An Sonn- und Feiertagen waren fast alle Läden geschlossen[5].

Ab September 2006 können die einzelnen Bundesländer[6] den Ladenschluss selbst regeln. Viele Länder haben schnell gehandelt und den Ladenschluss freigegeben[7] (montags bis samstags 0–24 Uhr). Zum Beispiel dürfen Läden in Berlin von Montag bis Samstag rund um die Uhr öffnen. Auch an den Adventssonntagen und bis zu sechs weiteren Sonntagen im Jahr können die Berliner von 13 bis 20 Uhr einkaufen. Bayern und das Saarland halten an der alten Regelung fest (montags bis samstags 6–20 Uhr). Sachsen und Rheinland-Pfalz erlauben 6 bis 22 Uhr. An Sonn- und Feiertagen ist bis auf[8] einige verkaufsoffene Sonntage, die individuell festgelegt[9] werden, geschlossen. Ausnahmen sind Tankstellen, Bäckereien, Bahnhofsgeschäfte und Apotheken stundenweise.

Die anderen Bundesländer, wie zum Beispiel Niedersachsen, sind noch nicht so weit, denn obwohl[10] die Geschäfte länger öffnen dürfen, heißt das nicht, dass sie das auch machen. Viele Läden machen morgens zwischen 8.30 und 9.30 Uhr, oder auch erst um 10 Uhr, auf oder schließen bereits um 18 oder 19 Uhr.

Sehen Sie sich die Tabelle an und vergleichen[11] Sie die Regelungen zum Ladenschluss in Deutschland vor und nach September 2006 mit anderen europäischen Ländern.

Ladenschluss in Europa

Land	Mo–Fr	Sa	Sonntage, Feiertage
Österreich	5–21	5–18	kein Verkauf bis auf Ausnahmen[12]
Italien	5–21	5–21	kein Verkauf bis auf Ausnahmen
Niederlande	6–22	6–22	kein Verkauf bis auf Ausnahmen
Dänemark	0–24	6–17	kein Verkauf bis auf Ausnahmen
Griechenland, Spanien	0–24	0–24	kein Verkauf bis auf Ausnahmen
Portugal	0–24	0–24	6–24
Schweden	0–24	0–24	5–24
Belgien	5–22	5–21	Öffnungsmöglichkeit nur für Selbstständige[13]
Frankreich	0–24	0–24	Öffnungsmöglichkeit nur für Selbstständige
Großritannien, Irland, Polen	0–24	0–24	0–24

Quelle: Bundeszentrale für politische Bildung (Stand: 2004)

Der Ladenschluss ist eine alte Geschichte. Ladenschlussregelungen gibt es in Deutschland seit dem 14. Jahrhundert. Das alte Ladenschlussgesetz hat es seit 1956 gegeben. Erst in den letzten 15 Jahren hat man es Schritt für Schritt[14] liberalisiert.

- Was meinen Sie: Warum war Ladenschluss bis 2006 so wichtig in Deutschland?
- Wer ist wahrscheinlich für (pro), wer gegen (contra) Ladenschlussregelungen?
- Warum diskutiert man besonders, ob Geschäfte auch am Sonntag öffnen dürfen?

[1]store hours [2]law [3]stores [4]store owner [5]closed [6]federal states [7]deregulated [8]bis ... except for
[9]determined [10]although [11]compare [12]exceptions [13]independent proprietors [14]Schritt für ... step by step

Situation 4 | Bildgeschichte: Josef kauft Weihnachtsgeschenke.

Es ist fast Weihnachten und Josef hat noch keine Geschenke.

Sit. 4. Sentences for narration series: **1.** *Josef macht sich eine Liste und geht einkaufen.* **2.** *Er kauft seinem Vater einen Roman.* **3.** *Er kauft seiner Mutter Parfüm.* **4.** *Er kauft seinem Bruder ein Videospiel.* **5.** *Er kauft seiner Schwester eine Halskette.* **6.** *Er kauft seinem Großvater eine Sonnenbrille.* **7.** *Er kauft seiner Großmutter einen Regenschirm.* **8.** *Er kauft seiner Freundin Melanie einen MP3-Spieler.* **9.** *Es ist sechs Uhr abends und Josef hat alles, was er braucht.* **Receptive recall:** *Welches Bild zeigt ...?* **Choral response. Productive recall:** *Was macht Josef im Bild ...?* **Personalization:** *Was kaufen Sie Ihren Verwandten und Freunden zu Weihnachten oder zum Geburtstag?*

Vocabulary Display

(See the IM.) Show sts. how to derive female professions from the male professions, using the *-in* suffix or *-frau.* Note that professions with *-mann* form their plural with *-leute* (e.g., *Geschäftsmann* → *Geschäftsleute*). After introducing several professions, use the verb *werden* in natural interactions. *Was studieren Sie? Was wollen Sie werden? Was möchten Sie werden? Jennifer studiert Jura. Sie wird Anwältin usw.*

Berufe

Grammatik 5.3

1. Der Arzt hilft kranken Menschen.

2. Der Verkäufer arbeitet in einem Laden.

3. Die Anwältin verteidigt den Angeklagten.

4. Der Pilot fliegt ein Flugzeug.

5. Der Richter arbeitet im Gericht.

6. Die Bauarbeiterin baut ein Parkhaus.

7. Die Architektin zeichnet ein Haus.

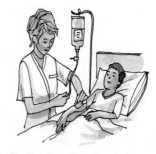

8. Die Krankenpflegerin arbeitet im Krankenhaus.

Situation 5 | Definitionen

Sit. 5. Point out that standard German generally has no article with professions, nationalities, and religions: *Er ist Pilot. Sie ist Ärztin.* Ask sts. to work in groups of 3. During the wrap-up, ask sts. if they can name other duties of these people—e.g., *Was muss ein/e Lehrer/in noch machen?*

AA. Show pictures of various people doing different jobs. Ask the question *Was macht er/sie?* Try to introduce verbs that describe what people do on the job, similar to what sts. have just learned in *Sit. 5,* and write these on an overhead transparency.

AA. Give sts. a list of professions and have them give simple definitions to encourage the use of verbs associated with each profession.
S₁: *Was macht ein Sekretär?*
S₂: *Er schreibt Briefe. Er tippt am Computer usw.*

Finden Sie den richtigen Beruf.

Anwältin	Verkäufer		Schriftsteller
Architekt(in)		Krankenpflegerin	
Ärztin	Lehrer		Pilot

1. Dieser Mann unterrichtet an einer Schule. Er ist _____.
2. Diese Frau untersucht Patienten im Krankenhaus. Sie ist _____.
3. Dieser Mann fliegt ein Flugzeug. Er ist _____.
4. Dieser Mann verkauft Computer in einem Laden. Er ist _____.
5. Diese Person zeichnet Pläne für Häuser. Sie ist _____.
6. Diese Frau arbeitet auf dem Gericht. Sie ist _____.
7. Diese Frau pflegt kranke Menschen. Sie ist _____.
8. Dieser Mann schreibt Romane. Er ist _____.

Situation 6 | Bildgeschichte: Was Michael Pusch schon alles gemacht hat

Sit. 6. Sentences for narration series:
1. *Als Michael 10 war, hat er seinen Nachbarn den Rasen gemäht.* **2.** *Als er 12 war, hat er Zeitungen ausgetragen.* **3.** *Als er 14 war, hat er dem Jungen von nebenan Nachhilfe in Mathematik gegeben.* **4.** *Als er mit der Schule fertig war, hat er Krankenpfleger gelernt.* **5.** *Als er bei der Bundeswehr war, hat er als Koch gearbeitet.* **6.** *Nach der Bundeswehr hat er als Taxifahrer gearbeitet.* **7.** *Als er 25 war, hat er Maria kennengelernt.* **8.** *Damals hat er in einem Schwimmbad als Bademeister gearbeitet.* **9.** *Später hat er Versicherungen verkauft.* Ask sts. if they remember what Michael now does professionally (*Werbeagent*).

Cultural note. In Germany, all men under 25 must serve 9 months in the military (*Wehrdienst*). Conscientious objectors have to complete 9 months of civil service (*Zivildienst*).

AA. Ask sts. what jobs they think Maria may have had, and, to personalize the activity, ask if they have held any of these jobs.

Sit. 7. Review the professions so that the vocabulary is fresh in sts.' minds. Have them work in pairs or groups of 3-4. After giving them 3-4 minutes to make their lists, have them close their books, keeping lists available. Then ask questions 1-8, but in a different order and without giving the number, so sts. must listen rather than simply read off their answers in the order they wrote them down. After hearing one group answer, ask the others if they agree or have other suggestions not yet mentioned: *Stimmt das? Haben Sie noch Vorschläge?*

Situation 7 | Berufe

Machen Sie Listen. Suchen Sie zu jeder Frage drei Berufe.

In welchen Berufen ...

1. verdient man sehr viel Geld?
2. verdient man nur wenig Geld?
3. gibt es mehr Männer als Frauen?
4. gibt es mehr Frauen als Männer?
5. muss man gut in Mathematik sein?
6. muss man gut in Sprachen sein?
7. muss man viel reisen?
8. muss man viel Kraft[1] haben?

Situation 8 | Interview

Sit. 8. This interview also recycles the perfect tense (4,5) and ways of expressing time. Be sure that sts. understand the difference between *lernen* and *studieren*. Model pronunciation and have sts. repeat. Then call on individuals to address questions to you so you can model responses as well. Now have sts. work in pairs. The st. asking the questions should take notes. Afterward, have 3-4 sts. report on their partner's responses.

1. Arbeitest du? Wo? Als was? Was machst du? An welchen Tagen arbeitest du? Wann fängst du an? Wann hörst du auf?
2. Was studierst du? Wie lange dauert das Studium?
3. Was möchtest du werden? Verdient man da viel Geld? Ist das ein Beruf mit viel Prestige?
4. Was ist dein Vater von Beruf? Was hat er gelernt (studiert)?
5. Was ist deine Mutter von Beruf? Was hat sie gelernt (studiert)?

[1]*strength*

Cultural note. *Grundsätzlich ist in Deutschland eine Erwerbstätigkeit von Kindern unter 16 Jahren verboten. Ausnahmen sind auf leichte Arbeiten (wie die Austragung von Werbebroschüren) beschränkt, wobei maximal 2 Std. pro Schultag gearbeitet werden darf und die Nachtarbeit (20-6 Uhr) verboten ist. Etwa 40% der Kinder im Alter von 13 bis 15 Jahren arbeiten in Deutschland, wovon sich circa die Hälfte nicht an die gesetzlichen Bestimmungen hält.*

Lektüre

Lektüre. (1) Establish the topic by asking sts. to complete *Vor dem Lesen 1-3* in small groups. Discuss afterward. **(2)** Introduction to the text. Ask sts. to complete *Vor dem Lesen 4-5* in small groups. Summarize the background information on Jens and Jutta and review sts.' answers to question 5. **(3)** Read the text out loud with sts. reading along, ask them to complete the *Arbeit mit dem Text* in small groups and discuss afterward, or assign as homework.

Vor dem Lesen

1. Haben Sie als Schüler/Schülerin gejobbt[1]? Was haben Sie gemacht?
2. Was haben Sie mit Ihrem Lohn[2] gemacht?
3. Ab welchem Alter[3] darf man in Ihrem Land arbeiten?
4. Was wissen Sie schon über Jens Krüger und Jutta Ruf? Lesen Sie im Vorwort[4] des Buches nach.
5. Lesen Sie den Titel, Untertitel und die Kurztexte zu den Fotos und tragen Sie die Informationen zu Marco und Kathrin in die Tabelle ein.

Name	Alter	Job	Stundenlohn	Geld für ...
Marco				
Kathrin				
Jens	16			
Jutta	16			

[1]*worked a part-time job* [2]*pay* [3]*Ab ... From what age* [4]*preface*

KAPITEL 5 Geld und Arbeit

DEUTSCHLAND

Marco, 16,
jobbt als Hilfsarbeiter auf dem
Bau. Verdienst: 7 Euro die Stunde.
Wunschtraum: ein Honda-Moped

Kathrin, 14,
Nachmittags Bürohilfskraft, abends
Babysitting. 2-3mal die Woche.
Ausgaben: CD's, USA-Urlaub

KINDERARBEIT

Schwitzen fürs Image

Mehr als 400 000 deutsche Schulkinder jobben, viele illegal. Ihr Antrieb fast immer: Designerklamotten, Statussymbole, mit anderen mithalten

Lesehilfe

Scanning a text is one way to find details without reading word for word. How many familiar words can you identify by scanning the text?

Schüler arbeiten

Zum Beispiel Jens Krüger aus München: Pünktlich morgens um sieben ist Jens im Supermarkt. Er räumt Regale ein und hilft hier und dort aus. Acht Stunden arbeitet er am Tag – für acht Euro pro Stunde. Samstags, während der Ferien und manchmal auch in der Woche.

5   Jens ist Gymnasiast in München, geht in die neunte Klasse. Im Supermarkt jobbt er seit seinem dreizehnten Lebensjahr.

    Jens ist einer von vielen. Die meisten seiner Klassenkameraden und -kameradinnen jobben. Von seinem Lohn kauft sich Jens teure Turnschuhe, Jacken für 225 Euro oder die schwarzen „Levi's" für 90 Euro. „Es gefällt mir, so viel Geld für Kla-

10 motten auszugeben und es sieht einfach cool aus", sagt er. Auch da ist er nicht der einzige. 90 Prozent aller arbeitenden Schüler jobben, um sich ihren Lifestyle zu erhalten. Denn das ist wichtig in der Clique. Die richtigen Rucksack-, Jeans-, oder Mountainbike-Marken sind genauso wichtig fürs Image wie das teure Cabrio für die Eltern.

15   Jens' Lehrer finden seine Freizeitaktivitäten nicht so toll, denn für Lernen und Hausaufgaben hat er natürlich wenig Zeit. Genauso wie Jutta Ruf. Sie jobbt als Babysitterin und in einer Boutique. Schlimm findet sie es nicht, wenn sie einmal ihre Hausaufgaben nicht machen kann. Zweimal die Woche hütet sie zwei Kleinkinder aus der Nachbarschaft. An zwei Nachmittagen und samstagvormittags jobbt sie jeweils

20 drei Stunden in einer Boutique – für fünf Euro die Stunde. Außerdem bekommt sie die Kleidung in der Boutique billiger. Sie braucht das Geld für Kino, Disko und CDs.

    Jens bekommt 50 Euro Taschengeld im Monat von seinen Eltern. Das reicht ihm nicht. Sein Vater hat nichts dagegen, dass Jens jobbt: „Solange er arbeitet, kommt er nicht auf dumme Gedanken", sagt er.

Arbeit mit dem Text

1. Tragen Sie in die Tabelle auf Seite 178 ein, wo Jens und Jutta jobben, wie viel sie verdienen und wofür sie das Geld ausgeben.
2. Warum ist die Kleidung so wichtig für die Jugendlichen?
3. Wofür haben Jutta und Jens wenig Zeit?
4. Ist das legal, was Jutta und Jens machen? Warum (nicht)?
5. Wann hat Jens angefangen, im Supermarkt zu arbeiten? War das legal?

Nach dem Lesen

1. Machen Sie eine Umfrage im Kurs. Stellen Sie die folgenden Fragen. Welche Jobs hattest du? Wie alt warst du, als du deinen ersten Job hattest? Wie viel hast du gearbeitet? Wie viel hast du verdient? Was hast du dir von deinem Geld gekauft?
2. Sammeln Sie die Antworten und machen Sie ein Plakat mit dem Titel: *Die Jobs unserer Kursteilnehmer.* Hängen Sie das Plakat aus.

Arbeitsplätze

Vocabulary Display

In this section, we introduce the concept of expressing a fixed location using the dative case while also introducing vocabulary for workplaces. **(1) Presentation:** *Was macht man an der Tankstelle? Wenn das Auto kein Benzin mehr hat, wenn es Benzin braucht, fährt man zur Tankstelle und tankt Benzin. usw.* **(2) Choral repetition. (3)** Based on the information you gave in step 1, ask short questions to elicit the locations in the display: *Wo tankt man? Wo schwimmt man? usw.*

Grammatik 5.4

Azubibewerbung

Wer in Deutschland nach der Schule einen Beruf lernen möchte, wird Azubi[1]. Man bewirbt sich[2] bei einer Firma oder in einem Betrieb[3] und lernt dort einen Beruf. Der Ausschnitt aus **Blickkontakte** zeigt, was bei einer Bewerbung[4] wichtig ist.

- Was bezahlt das Arbeitsamt?
- Was gehört in die Bewerbungsmappe[5]?
- Woraus besteht der Auswahltest?
- Was ist wichtig im Vorstellungsgespräch[6]?

[1]=Auszubildende(r): *apprentice* [2]*bewirbt ... applies* [3]*shop* [4]*application*
[5]*application package* [6]*job interview*

Rechtschreibtests bestehen meist aus Diktaten oder Aufsätzen; manchmal müssen Sie selbst falsche Wörter korrigieren.

Videoblick: The selection from the **Blickkontakte** video provides young Germans looking for an *Ausbildungsplatz* with advice on the various steps of the application process. The focus is on how to choose a job, how the *Arbeitsamt* supports *Azubis*, what kinds of things should be in the application package, and what kinds of questions are asked in tests and job interviews.

Situation 9 | Der Arbeitsplatz

Sit. 9. Before having sts. do this activity on their own, you can introduce the location phrases and reinforce the professions in the following way: Bring in pictures of the 10 locations mentioned; show them to the sts. as you model the pronunciation. As sts. repeat each phrase, tape the pictures at various locations around the room. To test sts.' recall, do two quick exercises.

First, say to sts. (books closed): *Ich bin Anwältin. Wo arbeite ich?* (*Auf dem Gericht.*) Walk to the picture of the courtroom, and, as you stand in front of it, continue: *Ja, ich bin Anwältin und eine Anwältin arbeitet auf dem Gericht.* Continue this, always standing in front of the appropriate picture. Or, mention TV characters representative of the various professions. Present the professions in a different order from that in the book.

Second, go to the various locations and say, for example, *Ich arbeite auf der Bank. Was bin ich von Beruf?* (*Sie sind Bankangestellte.*) *Ich arbeite in der Schule. Was bin ich von Beruf?* (*Sie sind Lehrerin.*) Now have sts. work in pairs to do the exercise. Partners can switch roles after S1 has asked 5 questions.

MODELL: S1: Wo arbeitet eine Anwältin?
S2: Auf dem Gericht.

im Krankenhaus

auf der Post

auf der Polizei

auf dem Gericht

im Schwimmbad

im Kaufhaus

auf der Bank

in der Kirche

auf der Universität

in der Schule

1. eine Anwältin
2. ein Arzt
3. eine Bademeisterin
4. ein Bankangestellter
5. ein Lehrer
6. eine Polizistin
7. ein Postbeamter
8. ein Priester
9. eine Professorin
10. eine Verkäuferin

Situation 10 | Minidialoge

Sit. 10. Model pronunciation of the locations. Give sts. a few minutes to do the activity. If you have pictures of each location in your PF, place them around the classroom. To model pronunciation, act out each minidialogue while standing in front of the appropriate picture. Have sts. repeat several times, with their books closed. After sts. have a good grasp of each minidialogue, have them choose partners. Send each pair to one of the pictures, where they should act out the appropriate exchange. Encourage them to be inventive; they need not simply repeat what they have heard. After performing for the class, one of the pair concludes, *Wo findet dieser Dialog statt?* to which the class must respond appropriately.

AA. Sts. could also create their own dialogues to present to the class. Classmates should then guess where they take place.

AA. Here is a guessing game about professions, similar to 20 Questions. It enables sts. to combine much of what they have learned in other situations. Say: *An welchen Beruf denke ich?* and have sts. ask you questions to determine the profession you have in mind. You could write sample questions down ahead of time to help sts. get from the more general, i.e., *Arbeitest du zu Hause? Arbeitest du im Büro? Arbeitest du im Krankenhaus? Arbeitest du im Freien? Verdienst du viel Geld? Musst du jeden Tag einen Anzug / ein Kostüm tragen? Musst du ein Diplom haben? usw.*, to the more specific job tasks learned in earlier activities: *Pflegst du kranke Menschen? Zeichnest du Pläne für Häuser? Untersuchst du Patienten? usw.*

Wo finden diese Dialoge statt?

auf der Post • im Hotel • an der Tankstelle • auf dem Bahnhof • in der Gaststätte • in der Bäckerei • an der Kinokasse • im Schwimmbad • auf der Bank

1. —Guten Tag, ich möchte ein Konto eröffnen.
   —Füllen Sie bitte dieses Formular aus und gehen Sie zum Schalter 3.
2. —Ich hätte gern eine Fahrkarte nach Bonn.
   —Hin und zurück oder einfach?
3. —Zwei Briefmarken für Postkarten in die USA, bitte.
   —Das sind zweimal einen Euro, zwei Euro zusammen.
4. —Guten Tag, einmal volltanken und kontrollieren Sie bitte das Öl.
   —Wird gemacht.
5. —Grüß Gott, geben Sie mir bitte ein Bauernbrot.
   —Bitte sehr! Sonst noch etwas?
6. —Guten Abend, ich hätte gern ein Doppelzimmer für eine Nacht.
   —Mit oder ohne Dusche?
7. —Könnten Sie mir sagen, wo die Umkleidekabinen sind?
   —Ja, die sind gleich hier um die Ecke.
8. —Zwei Eintrittskarten für *Das Leben der Anderen*, bitte.
   —Tut mir leid, der Film ist leider schon ausverkauft.
9. —Hallo! Zahlen bitte!
   —Gerne. Zusammen oder getrennt?

Situation 11 | Zum Schreiben: Vor der Berufsberatung

Sit. 11. This activity prepares sts. for the role-play in *Sit. 12*. Assign as homework. Ask sts. to write complete sentences and to provide as much detail as possible. **Note:** A *Berufsberater* helps high school and college students to find a profession or a field of study that fits their skills, interests, and personality. Every school and university offers consultations with a *Berufsberater*.

Morgen haben Sie einen Termin beim Berufsberater. Bereiten Sie sich auf das Gespräch vor. Machen Sie sich Notizen zu den Stichwörtern von der Liste.

- Schulbildung
- familiärer[1] Hintergrund (Beruf der Eltern usw.)
- Interessen, Hobbys
- Lieblingsfächer, besondere Fähigkeiten
- Qualifikationen (Fremdsprachen, Computerkenntnisse usw.)
- Erwartungen[2] an den zukünftigen[3] Beruf (Geld, Arbeitszeiten, Urlaub usw.)

Situation 12 | Rollenspiel: Bei der Berufsberatung

Sit. 12. (See the IM on how to present *Rollenspiele*.) Role for s2 appears in Appendix B. In preparation for this activity, have sts. do *Sit. 11*. You may wish to go over proper question formation with your sts. before doing the role-play.

Suggestion. This and other role-plays could also be recorded to help sts. focus on pronunciation and intonation.

S1: Sie arbeiten bei der Berufsberatung. Ein Student / Eine Studentin kommt in Ihre Sprechstunde. Stellen Sie ihm/ihr Fragen zu diesen Themen: Schulbildung, Interessen und Hobbys, besondere Kenntnisse, Lieblingsfächer.

[1]*family* [2]*expectations* [3]*future*

Ausbildung und Beruf

Wie ist es in Ihrem Land?

- Welchen Schulabschluss[1] braucht man für eine Berufsausbildung?
- Wie bekommt man eine Berufsausbildung?
- Wo lernt man die praktische Seite des Berufs? Wie lange dauert das?
- Wo lernt man die theoretische Seite? Wie lange dauert das?
- Macht man am Ende eine Prüfung? Was ist man dann?

Max hat keine Lust auf Schule und später Studium. Wenn er die zehnte Klasse erfolgreich[2] abschließt[3], hat er den Realschulabschluss. Er möchte am liebsten eine praktische Ausbildung machen, z. B. als Tischler oder Koch. Ein Facharbeiter[4] verdient mehr als ein ungelernter Arbeiter. Die Grafik zeigt, wie die Ausbildung für Max weitergeht.

Wie ist es in Deutschland?

- Wie lange dauert eine Ausbildung oder Lehre?
- Wo bekommt man die theoretische Ausbildung?
- Wo lernt man die praktische Seite des Berufs?
- Was bekommt man am Ende der Gesellenprüfung?
- Was ist man am Schluss[5]?

Photo questions. (*Praktische Ausbildung*) *Was lernt man in dieser Schule? Was lernen die Leute auf diesem Bild? Was tragen die jungen Männer auf dem Kopf? Warum? Wie alt sind sie? Wo werden Bäcker in Ihrer Stadt oder Ihrem Staat ausgebildet?*

(*Theoretische Ausbildung*) *Wie alt sind die Berufsschüler? Was sehen Sie auf den Tischen? Was lernt man in diesem Raum? Sehen Sie mehr Männer oder Frauen? Wer spricht auf diesem Bild? Schauen die Schüler den Lehrer an? Warum (nicht)?*

Auszubildende[6]

Ausbildungszeit
(3 Jahre)

Praktische Ausbildung

Theoretische Ausbildung

+

Betrieb[7]/Lehrwerkstatt[8]
(Gesellenprüfung[9])

=

Berufsschule
(8–10 Stunden pro Woche;
Berufsspezifische Fächer,
Wirtschaftskunde, Geschichte, Deutsch,
Englisch, u.a.)

Gesellenbrief[10]
Facharbeiter/Facharbeiterin

---

[1]*educational degree* [2]*successfully* [3]*completes* [4]*trade worker; skilled worker* [5]*am ... in the end*
[6]*those receiving a specialized education; apprentices* [7]*business* [8]*apprentice shop* [9]*trade workers' examination*
[10]*certificate of completed apprenticeship*

In der Küche

Grammatik 5.4–5.5

Vocabulary Display

This section exposes sts. to more dative prepositional phrases and introduces dative personal pronouns. **(1)** Ask sts. to repeat after you as you read the words of the display. **(2)** Ask sts. to write down which of these items they have in their possession. **(3)** Prepare the following interview by asking sts. to practice the sentence „*Hast du ein/e/n _____?*" with all the words in the display. **(4)** Ask sts. to interview each other about what items they have, jotting down what their partner owns.

die Tassen · der Topflappen · die Küchenwaage · das Besteck · das Geschirr · die Pfanne · die Salatschüssel · der Topf · die Küchenuhr · die Papiertücher

der Geschirrschrank · der Kühlschrank · der Wasserhahn · die Küchenlampe · das Spülbecken · der Küchentisch · der Herd · der Backofen · die Besteckschublade · die Geschirrspülmaschine

---

Situation 13	Wo ist …?

Sit. 13. This activity is based on the vocabulary display for this section. Have sts. work in pairs.

MODELL: S1: Wo ist der Küchentisch?
S2: Unter der Küchenlampe.

> am Fenster   unter dem Geschirrschrank   auf dem Herd   unter dem Herd
>
> im Geschirrschrank   in der Geschirrspülmaschine
>
> in der Besteckschublade   im Kühlschrank   unter dem Kühlschrank

1. Wo ist die Geschirrspülmaschine?
2. Wo ist die Küchenuhr?
3. Wo ist der Backofen?
4. Wo ist das Spülbecken?
5. Wo sind die Papiertücher?
6. Wo ist die Pfanne?
7. Wo ist das Geschirr?
8. Wo ist der Topf?
9. Wo sind die Gläser?
10. Wo ist das Besteck?

Situation 14 | Interaktion: Küchenarbeit

Sit. 14. Sts. who live in a dorm should be asked what they do (or did) when at home.

Cultural note. In Germany many bottles carry a deposit value, and so people are motivated to return them. For bottles without a deposit, there are recycling bins, one for each color of glass.

Wie oft spülst du das Geschirr?

mehrmals am Tag
jeden Tag
fast jeden Tag
zwei- bis dreimal in der Woche
einmal in der Woche
einmal im Monat
selten
nie

Wie oft ...?	ich	mein(e) Partner(in)
gehst du einkaufen		
kochst du		
deckst du den Tisch		
spülst du das Geschirr		
stellst du das Geschirr weg		
machst du den Herd sauber		
machst du den Tisch sauber		
machst du den Kühlschrank sauber		
fegst du den Boden		
bringst du die leeren Flaschen weg		

Situation 15 | Umfrage: Kochst du mir ein Abendessen?

Sit. 15. Encourage sts. to approach this activity playfully but also challenge those who claim to be able/willing to sing to demonstrate their skills.

MODELL: S1: Kochst du mir morgen ein Abendessen?
S2: Ja.
S1: Unterschreib bitte hier.

UNTERSCHRIFT

1. Kochst du mir morgen ein Abendessen? _____
2. Backst du mir einen Kuchen zum Geburtstag? _____
3. Kaufst du mir ein Eis? _____
4. Schenkst du mir deinen Kugelschreiber? _____
5. Hilfst du mir heute bei der Hausaufgabe? _____
6. Kannst du mir die Grammatik erklären? _____
7. Schreibst du mir in den Ferien eine Postkarte? _____
8. Kannst du mir ein Lied vorsingen? _____
9. Kannst du mir fünf Dollar leihen? _____

Situation 16 | Dialog: Chaos in der Küche

Sit. 16. (1) Have sts. close their books. (2) Preteach the vocabulary by writing only the German words on the board but saying the German word with its English equivalent. Here are the new words in the order of their appearance in the dialogue: *Chaos, sauer sein, Schweinestall, unglaublich, Kuchen, Lieblingsbeschäftigung.* (3) Establish the context by reminding sts. who Herr Ruf and Jutta are. (4) Set the scene for the dialogue. *Herr Ruf kommt nach Hause und in der Küche herrscht Chaos. Er ist sauer und schreit nach Jutta.* (5) Focus sts.' attention on the task by listing the questions you want them to answer. *Ich habe fünf Fragen. Erstens: Wie sieht es in der Küche aus? Zweitens: Was ist in der Besteckschublade? Drittens: Was ist auf dem Fußboden? Viertens: Was ist im Backofen? Und fünftens: Was ist im Spülbecken?* Write numbers 1 through 5 and the prepositional phrases on the board so sts. can remember what they are supposed to listen for. (6) Ask sts. to write the answers on a piece of paper while you read or play the dialogue. (7) Collect answers orally and write them on the board next to the prepositional phrases. Then, ask a second set of focus questions: *Warum ist Marmelade in der Besteckschublade? Warum ist die Kaffeemaschine auf dem Fußboden? Warum ist das Kochbuch im Backofen? Und warum ist der Kuchen im Spülbecken?* (8) Again, ask sts. to write the answers on a piece of paper while you read or play the dialogue. (9) Collect answers orally while writing key words on the board. (10) Read the lines of the dialogue individually, asking sts. to count the number of words per sentence. This helps their receptive pronunciation and it helps them to learn the lines of the dialogue. (11) Continue learning the lines of the dialogue with sts., e.g. by dividing the class in half and asking them to remember either Herr Ruf's or Jutta's lines with the help of the words and phrases on the board. (12) Erase the words on the board. Then ask sts. to open their books and fill in the blanks while you read or play the dialogue one more time.

In der Küche herrscht Chaos und Herr Ruf ist sauer.

HERR RUF: Jutta, komm mal her!

JUTTA: Ja, Papa. Warum schreist du denn so?

HERR RUF: Weil es hier aussieht wie im Schweinestall! Warum ist Marmelade in der Besteckschublade?

JUTTA: Ich habe mir ein Brot gemacht und das ist dann in die Schublade gefallen.

HERR RUF: Und warum ist die Kaffeemaschine auf dem Fußboden?

JUTTA: Hans brauchte Platz auf dem Küchentisch für seine Legos.

HERR RUF: Das Kochbuch liegt im Backofen! Unglaublich!

JUTTA: Weil es da warm ist. Es war leider nass.

HERR RUF: Und warum ist der Kuchen im Spülbecken?

JUTTA: Keine Ahnung!

HERR RUF: Ihr glaubt wohl, dass Aufräumen meine Lieblingsbeschäftigung ist!

JUTTA: Ach, Papa, das ist doch nicht so schlimm. Ich hole Hans und dann helfen wir dir.

Vor dem Lesen

A. Sehen Sie sich das Filmposter an.

1. Wie viele Leute sehen Sie?
2. Wie sehen sie aus?
3. Wie ist die Stimmung?
4. Sehen Sie Werkzeuge oder Materialien?
5. Warum bauen Menschen eigentlich Tunnel?

Der Tunnel

Regisseur: Roland Suso Richter

**Schauspieler in den Hauptrollen:
Nicolette Krebitz, Sebastian Koch,
Heino Ferch, Mehmet Kurtulus, Felix
Eitner, Alexandra Maria Lara**

Erscheinungsjahr: 2001

B. Lesen Sie die Wörter im Miniwörterbuch auf der nächsten Seite. Suchen Sie sie im Text und unterstreichen Sie sie.

abgrenzen	to fence off
sich anschließen (schließt sich an)	to join (joins)
beschließen	to decide
durchkreuzen	to thwart
fliehen	to flee
gefährlich	dangerous
der Geheimdienst	secret service
graben	to dig
das Grundwasser	groundwater
hinter jemandem her sein	to be after someone
kriegen	to get, to catch
der Oberst	colonel
die Stasi (Staatssicherheit)	East German secret service
der Verlobte	fiancé
versperrt sein	to be blocked
vertrauen	to trust
zusammenbrechen	to collapse

Miniwörterbuch

Film: *Der Tunnel*

13. August 1961: Die DDR-Regierung baut eine Mauer durch Berlin und grenzt den Osten der Stadt vom Westen ab. Schwimmstar Harry Melchior hat genug von der DDR und will weg. Noch im Herbst, kurz nach dem Bau der Berliner Mauer, flieht er mit seinem Freund Matthis Hiller in den Westteil Berlins. Die beiden beschließen, Harrys
5   Schwester Lotte und Matthis' Frau Carola in den Westen zu holen. Zusammen mit Fred von Klausnitz und dem Ex-GI Vittorio „Vic" Castanza wollen sie einen Tunnel von West nach Ost graben, weil alle anderen Fluchtwege versperrt sind. Im Keller einer alten Fabrik an der Bernauer Straße finden sie den idealen Ort für den Tunnel. Die junge, attraktive Friederike „Fritzi" schließt sich der Gruppe an. Sie will für ihren Verlobten
10   Heiner die Flucht in den Westen möglich machen.

Die Gruppe um Harry rekrutiert mehr Helfer, um die schwierige Aufgabe zu schaffen. Die Frage dabei ist immer: Wem kann man vertrauen? Einfach ist das Tunnelprojekt nicht. Einmal bricht der Tunnel beinah zusammen und ein anderes Mal läuft Grundwasser ein. Auch müssen die Fluchthelfer ihre Aktion finanzieren: Sie verkaufen die Rechte ihrer
15   Geschichte an die NBC und werden dafür bei ihrer Arbeit gefilmt. Und dann gibt es noch die Stasi, den Geheimdienst der DDR. Vor allem Stasi-Oberst Krüger ist hinter Harry und Matthis her. Er will ihren Plan durchkreuzen. Am Ende wird es gefährlich für Harry und seine Freunde, aber Krüger kriegt sie nicht!

Arbeit mit dem Text

Was gehört zusammen?

1. Harry hat genug von der DDR, …
2. Alle Fluchtwege sind versperrt, …
3. Harry und seine Freunde können den Tunnel nicht allein bauen, …
4. Harry und seine Leute haben nicht genug Geld, …
5. Kein DDR-Bürger darf das Land verlassen, …

a. deshalb helfen mehr Menschen beim Graben.
b. deshalb verfolgt Stasi-Oberst Krüger Fluchthelfer wie Harry und seine Freunde.
c. deshalb ist der Tunnel eine der letzten Möglichkeiten, die DDR zu verlassen.
d. deshalb verkaufen sie ihre Geschichte an das amerikanische Fernsehen.
e. deshalb will er weg.

Nach dem Lesen

Kreatives Schreiben. Oberst Krüger verfolgt Harry im Tunnel. Es kommt zu einem Gespräch zwischen den beiden. Was sagen sie? Schreiben Sie sich einen Dialog zwischen Harry und Oberst Krüger.

Videoecke

- Was studierst du?
- Was gefällt dir an deinem Studium?
- Was willst du damit mal machen?
- Wie sieht für dich ein typischer Studientag aus?
- Arbeitest du?
- Arbeitest du viel?
- Was machst du da genau?
- Wie viel Geld verdienst du?
- Gibt es etwas, worauf du sparst?

Marcus ist in Stolberg im Rheinland geboren. Er studiert Betriebswirtschaftslehre[1] und Politik. Seine Hobbys sind Sport, Lesen und Reisen.

Ayse ist in Köprübasi in der Türkei geboren. Sie studiert Kommunikations- und Medienwissenschaft, Soziologie und Politik. Ihre Hobbys sind Fotografieren und Volleyball.

Aufgabe 1

Aufgabe 1. (1) Preview with photos: *Wo ist Ayse geboren? Wo Marcus? Wer studiert Betriebswirtschaftslehre? Politik? Kommunikations- und Medienwissenschaft? Soziologie? Wer liest gern? Wer reist gern? Wer fotografiert gern? Wer spielt gern Volleyball?* **(2)** Read the statements and ask sts. to speculate to whom the statements might apply. **(3)** Play Ayse's interview once. **(4)** Ask sts. to discuss in small groups which statements are true of her. **(5)** Play Ayse's interview a second time and ask sts. to knock or clap when they hear her say any of the statements. If necessary, replay her response. **(6)** Do the same with Marcus's interview.

Ayse oder Marcus? Welche Aussagen treffen auf Ayse zu, welche auf Marcus? Schreiben Sie A (Ayse) oder M (Marcus) neben die folgenden Aussagen.

1. _____ Meine Nebenfächer[2] sind Soziologie und KMW.
2. _____ Ich studiere im 8. Semester.
3. _____ Mein Studium macht mir viel Spaß.
4. _____ Ich würde gern bei einer Zeitung arbeiten.
5. _____ Ich kann mir vorstellen[3], für die UNO zu arbeiten.
6. _____ Normalerweise stehe ich um acht oder neun Uhr auf.
7. _____ Ich gehe frühmorgens um neun zur Uni.
8. _____ Ich mache zur Zeit ein Praktikum.
9. _____ Ich spare auf[4] eine Reise[5] nach Lateinamerika.
10. _____ Ich würde mir gern einen Fotoapparat[6] kaufen.

---

[1]*business administration* [2]*minor subjects* [3]*mir ... imagine* [4]*spare ... am saving for* [5]*trip* [6]*camera*

Aufgabe 2. Read through the questions and statements and explain any unfamiliar vocabulary. Ask sts. to group the statements according to what questions they answer. Play both interview segments. Ask sts. to knock or clap when they hear an answer.

Student Interviews. (1) Ask sts. to jot down their own answers to the interview questions. **(2)** Pair sts. to interview each other. Ask them to jot down their partner's answers. **(3)** Follow up by sampling a few of the answers given in the interviews.

Studium und Beruf. Ordnen Sie jeder Frage eine passende Antwort zu.

1. Was gefällt Ayse/Marcus an ihrem/ seinem Studium?
2. Wo will Ayse/Marcus mal arbeiten?
3. Als was arbeitet Ayse/Marcus jetzt?

a. Ich arbeite als Promoter bei einem Fernsehsender.
b. Ich arbeite im Bereich Internet-Marketing und E-Commerce.
c. Ich kann mir alles sehr individuell gestalten.
d. Ich möchte für eine internationale Organisation arbeiten.
e. Ich möchte in einem großen internationalen Unternehmen arbeiten.
f. Ich würde gern im Auswärtigen Amt arbeiten.
g. Ich würde gern in der Politik arbeiten.
h. Mein Studium ist sehr vielfältig.
i. Mir gefällt die internationale Ausrichtung.

Wortschatz

Berufe	Professions
der Anwalt, ⸚e / die Anwältin, -nen	lawyer
der Arzt (R), ⸚e / die Ärztin, -nen	physician, doctor
der Bademeister, - / die Bademeisterin, -nen	swimming-pool attendant
der/die Bankangestellte, -n	bank employee
der Bauarbeiter, - / die Bauarbeiterin, -nen	construction worker
der Berufsberater, - / die Berufsberaterin, -nen	career counselor
der Dirigent, -en (*wk. masc.*) / die Dirigentin, -nen	(orchestra) conductor
der Friseur, -e / die Friseurin, -nen	hairdresser
der Hausmeister, - / die Hausmeisterin, -nen	custodian
der Krankenpfleger, - / die Krankenpflegerin, -nen	nurse
der/die Postangestellte, -n	postal employee
der Richter, - / die Richterin, -nen	judge
der Schriftsteller, - / die Schriftstellerin, -nen	writer
der Verkäufer, - / die Verkäuferin, -nen	salesperson
der Zahnarzt, ⸚e / die Zahnärztin, -nen	dentist

Ähnliche Wörter

der Arbeiter, - / die Arbeiterin, -nen; der Architekt, -en (*wk. masc.*) / die Architektin, -nen; der Bibliothekar, -e / die Bibliothekarin, -nen; der Fernsehreporter, - / die Fernsehreporterin, -nen; der Ingenieur, -e / die Ingenieurin, -nen; der Koch, ⸚e / die Köchin, -nen; der Pilot, -en (*wk. masc.*) / die Pilotin, -nen; der Polizist, -en (*wk. masc.*) / die Polizistin, -nen; der Präsident, -en (*wk. masc.*) / die Präsidentin, -nen; der Priester, - / die Priesterin, -nen; der Sekretär, -e / die Sekretärin, -nen; der Steward, -s / die Stewardess, -en; der Taxifahrer, - / die Taxifahrerin, -nen

Orte	Places
die Ecke, -n	corner
um die Ecke	around the corner
die Gaststätte, -n	restaurant
in der Gaststätte	at the restaurant
die Kasse, -n	ticket booth
an der Kasse	at the ticket booth
die Kirche, -n	church
in der Kirche	at church
die Polizei	police station
auf der Polizei	at the police station
die Post	post office
auf der Post	at the post office
die Tankstelle, -n	gas station
an der Tankstelle	at the gas station

der Bahnhof, ⸚e (R)	train station
auf dem Bahnhof	at the train station
der Schalter, -	ticket booth
am Schalter	at the ticket booth
das Büro, -s	office
im Büro	at the office
das Gericht, -e	courthouse
auf dem Gericht	at the courthouse
das Kaufhaus, ⸚er	department store
im Kaufhaus	at the department store
das Krankenhaus, ⸚er (R)	hospital
im Krankenhaus	in the hospital
das Schwimmbad, ⸚er (R)	swimming pool
im Schwimmbad	at the swimming pool

Ähnliche Wörter

die Bäckerei, -en; in der Bäckerei; die Bank, -en; auf der Bank; die Schule, -n (R); in der Schule; die Universität, -en (R); auf der Universität; der Supermarkt, ⸚e; im Supermarkt; das Hotel, -s (R); im Hotel

In der Küche	In the Kitchen
die Fensterbank, ⸚e	windowsill
die Flasche, -n	bottle
die Geschirrspül-maschine, -n	dishwasher
die Küche, -n	kitchen
die Küchenwaage, -n	kitchen scale
die Salatschüssel, -n	salad (mixing) bowl
die Schublade, -n	drawer
die Tasse, -n (R)	cup
der Backofen, ⸚	oven
der Herd, -e	stove
der Kühlschrank, ⸚e	refrigerator
der Topf, ⸚e	pot, pan
der Topflappen, -	potholder
der Wasserhahn, ⸚e	faucet
das Besteck	silverware, cutlery
das Geschirr (R)	dishes
das Papiertuch, ⸚er	paper towel
das Spülbecken, -	sink

Ähnliche Wörter

die Kaffeemaschine, -n; die Küchenarbeit, -en; die Küchenlampe, -n; die Küchenuhr, -en; die Pfanne, -n; der Küchentisch, -e; das Glas, ⸚er

Einkäufe und Geschenke	Purchases and Presents
die Badehose, -n	swim(ming) trunks
die Briefmarke, -n	stamp
die Halskette, -n (R)	necklace
die Mütze, -n	cap
der Badeanzug, ⸚e	bathing suit
der Regenschirm, -e	umbrella

der Reiseführer, -	travel guidebook
der Roman, -e (R)	novel
das Handtuch, ⸚er	hand towel
das Weihnachts-geschenk, -e	Christmas present

Ähnliche Wörter

die Konzertkarte, -n; die Tageszeitung, -en; der Bikini, -s; der Fahrradhelm, -e; der MP3-Spieler, -; das Parfüm, -e

Schule und Beruf	School and Career
die Ausbildung	specialized training
praktische Ausbildung	practical (career) training
die Bundeswehr	German army
bei der Bundeswehr	in the German army
die Schulbildung	education, schooling
das Abitur	college-prep-school degree

Sonstige Substantive	Other Nouns
die Dusche, -n	shower
die Eintrittskarte, -n	admissions ticket
die Enkelin, -nen	granddaughter
die Kundin, -nen	female customer
die Lehre, -n	apprenticeship
die Lieblingsbeschäfti-gung, -en	favorite activity
die Möglichkeit, -en	possibility
die Tätigkeit, -en	activity
die Umgebung, -en	surrounding area, environs
die Umkleidekabine, -n	dressing room
die Versicherung, -en	insurance
die Werkstatt, ⸚en	repair shop, garage
der Enkel, -	grandson
der Kuchen, -	cake
der Kunde, -n (wk. masc.)	male customer
der Rasen	lawn
der Rat, Ratschläge	advice
der Schweinestall, ⸚e	pigpen
der Termin, -e	appointment
der Urlaub, -e (R)	vacation
der Vorschlag, ⸚e	suggestion
das Bauernbrot, -e	(loaf of) farmer's bread
das Einzelzimmer, -	single room
das Geheimnis, -se	secret
das Hundefutter	dog food
das Interesse, -n	interest
Interesse haben an (+ dat.)	to be interested in
das Konto, Konten	bank account
ein Konto eröffnen	to open a bank account
das Lieblingsfach, ⸚er	favorite subject

das Öl	oil
das Öl kontrollieren	to check the oil
die Kenntnisse (*pl.*)	skills; knowledge about a field

Ähnliche Wörter

die Klasse, -n; erster Klasse; die Liste, -n; die Lotterie, -n; in der Lotterie gewinnen; die Patientin, -nen; die Politik; die Touristenklasse; der Patient, -en (*wk. masc.*); das Chaos; das Pfund, -e; das Prestige [presti:ʒ]

Verben	Verbs
aus·tragen, trägt ... aus, ausgetragen	to deliver
Zeitungen austragen	to deliver newspapers
ein·kaufen gehen, ist einkaufen gegangen (R)	to go shopping
entschuldigen	to excuse
entschuldigen Sie!	excuse me
erklären	to explain
erzählen (R)	to tell (a story, joke)
fegen	to sweep
feiern	to celebrate
heiraten	to marry
interessieren	to interest
sich interessieren für	to be interested in
leid·tun, leidgetan (+ *dat.*)	to be sorry
tut mir leid (R)	I'm sorry
leihen, geliehen	to lend
mähen	to mow
pflegen	to attend to; to nurse
raten, rät, geraten (+ *dat.*)	to advise (a person)
sagen (R)	to say, tell
schenken	to give (as a present)
statt·finden, stattgefunden	to take place
stellen (R)	to place, put
eine Frage stellen	to ask a question
unterrichten	to teach, instruct
untersuchen	to investigate; to examine
verkaufen (R)	to sell
voll·tanken	to fill up (with gas)
vor·schlagen, schlägt ... vor, vorgeschlagen	to suggest
weg·stellen	to put away

werden, wird, ist geworden	to become
zahlen	to pay
zeichnen (R)	to draw

Ähnliche Wörter

backen, gebacken; heilen; vor·singen, vorgesungen; weg·bringen, weggebracht; wieder·kommen, ist wiedergekommen

Adjektive und Adverbien	Adjectives and Adverbs
ausverkauft	sold out
getrennt	separately; separate checks
sauer	angry
unglaublich	incredible

Ähnliche Wörter

arbeitslos, flexibel, normal, praktisch, relativ

Sonstige Wörter und Ausdrücke	Other Words and Expressions
alles zusammen	all together; one check
als	as; when
als was?	as what?
als ich acht Jahre alt war	when I was eight years old
außerdem	besides
etwas (R)	something, anything
sonst noch etwas?	anything else?
fast	almost
gern (R)	gladly
ich hätte gern	I would like
hin und zurück	round-trip
irgendwelche, irgendwelcher, irgendwelches	any (+ *noun*)
jede, jeder, jedes (R)	each
mehrmals	several times
nebenan	next door
von nebenan	from next door
und so weiter	and so forth
unter	under, underneath
unter dem Fenster	under the window
zweimal	twice

Strukturen und Übungen

5.1 Dative case: articles and possessive adjectives

The dative case indicates the person to or for whom something is done.

A noun or pronoun in the dative case is used to designate the person to or for whom something is done.

Ernst schenkt **seiner Mutter** ein Buch.　　*Ernst gives his mother a book.*
Sofie gibt **ihrem Freund** einen Kuss.　　*Sofie gives her boyfriend a kiss.*

Note that the dative case frequently appears in sentences with three nouns: a person who does something, a person who receives something, and the object that is passed from the doer to the receiver. The doer, the subject of the sentence, is in the nominative case; the recipient, or beneficiary, of the action is in the dative case; and the object is in the accusative case.

Wissen Sie noch?

The nominative case designates the subject of a sentence. The accusative case designates the object of the action of the verb.

Review grammar 2.1.

5.1. *Dativ: Artikel und Possessiva.* This is the first formal presentation of the dative case. The forms of articles and possessive adjectives are introduced here; the dative forms of personal pronouns will be described in Section 5.5. Point out that here the dative is used to indicate the indirect object. Other important uses of the dative are presented later: two-way prepositions with the dative in Sections 5.4, 6.2, and 6.4; dative verbs in Section 6.1; *mit* and *bei* + dative in Section 6.6; and other prepositions with the dative in Section 10.1. The concept of case and the use of case forms are among the most difficult areas of German grammar for sts. Accuracy in speech is not expected at this stage. Not all sts. will achieve a good understanding of case in the first year. Even when monitoring in written work, some will have difficulty with the selection of correct forms. Give sts. as much input with case forms as possible to aid acquisition. Emphasize these markers for the dative. Another useful rule is that dative plural forms of all determiners and nouns (and, later, attributive adjectives) end in *-n* (except nouns with a plural in *-s*).

Doer		Recipient	Object
Nominative Case	*Verb*	*Dative Case*	*Accusative Case*
Maria	kauft	ihrem Freund	ein Hemd.

Maria is buying her boyfriend a shirt.

In German, the signal for the dative case is the ending **-m** in the masculine and neuter, **-r** in the feminine, and **-n** in the plural. Here are the dative forms of the definite, indefinite, and negative articles, and of the possessive adjectives.

	Masculine and Neuter	Feminine	Plural
Definite Article	dem	der	den
Indefinite	einem	einer	—
Negative Article	keinem	keiner	keinen
Possessive Adjective	meinem	meiner	meinen
	deinem	deiner	deinen
	seinem	seiner	seinen
	ihrem	ihrer	ihren
	unserem	unserer	unseren
	eurem	eurer	euren

Jutta schreibt **einem Freund** einen Brief.　　*Jutta is writing a letter to a friend.*

Jens erzählt **seinen Eltern** einen Witz.　　*Jens is telling his parents a joke.*

All plural nouns add an **-n** in the dative unless they already end in **-n** or in **-s.**

Claire erzählt **ihren Freunden**
von ihrer Reise nach Deutschland.

*Claire is telling her friends
about her trip to Germany.*

Here is a short list of verbs that often take an accusative object and a dative recipient.

erklären	*to explain something to someone*
erzählen	*to tell someone (a story)*
geben	*to give someone something*
leihen	*to lend someone something*
sagen	*to tell someone something*
schenken	*to give someone something as a gift*

Certain masculine nouns, in particular those denoting professions, add **-(e)n** in the dative and accusative singular as well as in the plural. They are often called weak masculine nouns.

	Singular	Plural
Nominative	der Student	die Studenten
Accusative	den Studenten	die Studenten
Dative	dem Studenten	den Studenten

Übung 1 | Was machen Sie für diese Leute?

Üb. 1–2. Assign these exercises for homework and have sts. read their answers in class.

Schreiben Sie mit jedem Verb einen Satz.

MODELL: Ich schenke meiner Mutter eine Kamera.

backen	Bruder/Schwester	ein Abendessen
erklären	Freund/Freundin	meine Bilder
erzählen	Großvater/Großmutter	einen Brief
geben	Mitbewohner/Mitbewohnerin	ein Buch
kaufen	Onkel/Tante	eine CD
kochen	Partner/Partnerin	mein Deutschbuch
leihen	Professor/Professorin	50 Dollar
schenken	Vater/Mutter	ein Geheimnis
schreiben	Vetter/Kusine	eine Geschichte
verkaufen		Kaffee
		eine Konzertkarte
		eine Krawatte
		einen Kuchen
		einen Kuss
		einen MP3-Spieler
		einen Witz

Übung 2 | Was machen diese Leute?

Bilden Sie Sätze.

MODELL: Heidi schreibt ihren Eltern eine Karte.

Bikini (*m.*) = der Bikini
Grammatik (*f.*) = die Grammatik
Zelt (*n.*) = das Zelt

Heidi	erklären	*ihren* Eltern		Armband (*n.*)
Peter	erzählen	Freund		Bikini (*m.*)
Thomas	geben	Freundin		Geheimnis (*n.*)
Katrin	kaufen	Mann		Grammatik (*f.*)
Stefan	kochen	Mutter	*eine* Karte (*f.*)
Albert	leihen	Professor		Regenschirm (*m.*)
Monika	schenken	Schwester		Rucksack (*m.*)
Frau Schulz	schreiben	Tante		Suppe (*f.*)
Nora	verkaufen	Vetter		Zelt (*n.*)

5.2 Question pronouns: *wer, wen, wem*

5.2. *Interrogativpronomen.* Point out that the endings are the same as those of the masculine definite article. These German forms correspond to the formal English *who, whom, to/for whom.*

wer (Who is it?) = nominative
wen (Whom do you know?) = accusative
wem (Whom did you give it to?) = dative

Use the pronouns **wer**, **wen**, and **wem** to ask questions about people: **wer** indicates the subject, the person who performs the action; **wen** indicates the accusative object; **wem** indicates the dative object.

Wer arbeitet heute Abend um acht?   *Who's working tonight at eight?*
Wen triffst du heute Abend?   *Whom are you meeting tonight?*
Wem leihst du das Zelt?   *To whom are you lending the tent?*

Übung 3 | Minidialoge

Ergänzen Sie **wer, wen** oder **wem.**

1. JÜRGEN: _____ hat meinen Regenschirm?
   SILVIA: Ich habe ihn.
2. MELANIE: _____ hast du in der Stadt gesehen?
   JOSEF: Claire.
3. SOFIE: _____ willst du die DVD schenken?
   WILLI: Marta. Sie wünscht sie sich schon lange.
4. FRAU AUGENTHALER: Na, erzähl doch mal. _____ hast du letztes Wochenende kennengelernt?
   RICHARD: Also, sie heißt Uschi und ...
5. MEHMET: _____ wollt ihr denn euren neuen Computer verkaufen?
   RENATE: Schülern und Studenten.
6. NATALIE: Weißt du, _____ heute Abend zu uns kommt?
   LYDIA: Nein, du?
   NATALIE: Tante Christa, natürlich.

5.3 Expressing change: the verb *werden*

Use a form of **werden** to talk about changing conditions.

Ich werde alt.   *I am getting old.*
Es wird dunkel.   *It is getting dark.*

werden: e → i
du wirst; er/sie/es wird

5.3. This section deals with the use of *werden* with predicate adjectives and predicate nouns. *Werden* with the future tense is described in Section 8.5. You may wish to point out to your sts. that indefinite articles are often not used when giving the profession or occupation of a person. There is, however, variation on this point, primarily in the spoken language. Remind sts. that *will* does not indicate the future tense in German.

werden			
ich	werde	*wir*	werden
du	wirst	*ihr*	werdet
Sie	werden	*Sie*	werden
er *sie* *es*	wird	*sie*	werden

In German, **werden** is also used to talk about what somebody wants to be.

Was willst du werden?   *What do you want to be (become)?*

Natalie will Ärztin werden.   *Natalie wants to be (become) a physician.*

Übung 4 | Was passiert?

Bilden Sie Fragen und suchen Sie dann eine logische Antwort darauf.

MODELL: Was passiert im Winter? —Es wird kalt.

1. am Abend
2. wenn man Bücher schreibt
3. wenn man krank wird
4. im Frühling
5. im Herbst
6. wenn Kinder älter werden
7. wenn man in der Lotterie gewinnt
8. wenn man Medizin studiert
9. am Morgen
10. im Sommer

a. Man wird Arzt.
b. Man wird bekannt[1].
c. Die Blätter werden bunt[2].
d. Es wird dunkel.
e. Sie werden größer.
f. Es wird wärmer.
g. Es wird hell[3].
h. Man bekommt Fieber.
i. Die Tage werden länger.
j. Man wird reich.

Übung 5 | Was werden sie vielleicht?

Üb. 5. This exercise uses only the 3rd-person singular form of *werden*. Assign for homework and check in class. Follow up with a discussion of what profession sts. will (or will not) choose.

Suchen Sie einen möglichen Beruf für jede Person.

MODELL: Jens hilft gern kranken Menschen. →
Vielleicht wird er Arzt.

[1]*well-known* [2]*colorful* [3]*bright; light*

1. Lydia kocht gern.
2. Sigrid interessiert sich für Medikamente.
3. Ernst fliegt gern.
4. Jürgen hat Interesse an Pädagogik.
5. Jutta zeichnet gern Pläne für Häuser.
6. Helga geht gern in die Bibliothek.
7. Hans möchte gern kranke Menschen heilen.
8. Andrea hört gern klassische Musik.

Apotheker/Apothekerin
Architekt/Architektin
Bibliothekar/Bibliothekarin
Dirigent/Dirigentin
Koch/Köchin
Krankenpfleger/Krankenpflegerin
Lehrer/Lehrerin
Pilot/Pilotin

5.4 Location: *in, an, auf* + dative case

When indicating where something is located, **in**, **an**, and **auf** take the dative case.

5.4. *Akkusativ-/Dativpräpositionen.* This is the first presentation of two-way prepositions. We limit it to the 3 most common prepositions and their use with the dative only, so that students acquire this complex set of forms through meaningful practice without having to focus simultaneously on all the prepositions and both cases. Two-way prepositions with the dative are dealt with as a group in Section 6.2. For their use with the accusative, see Sections 6.2, 6.4, and 10.3.

To express the location of someone or something, use the following prepositions with the dative case.

$$
\left.\begin{array}{l}
\textbf{in } (in, at) \\
\textbf{auf } (on, at) \\
\textbf{an } (on, at)
\end{array}\right\} \quad + \quad
\left\{\begin{array}{l}
\textbf{dem/einem} \ \underline{\quad} \ (m., n.) \\
\textbf{der/einer} \ \underline{\quad} \ (f.) \\
\textbf{den} \ \underline{\quad} \ (pl.)
\end{array}\right.
$$

Katrin wohnt **in der Stadt.**

Stefan und Albert sind **auf der Bank.**

Katrin lives in the city.

Stefan and Albert are at the bank.

A. Forms and Contractions

Remember the signals for dative case.

	Masculine and Neuter	Feminine	Plural
Dative	dem	der	den
	einem	einer	—

in + dem = im
an + dem = am

Note that the prepositions **in + dem** and **an + dem** are contracted to **im** and **am.**

Masculine and Neuter	Feminine	Plural
im Kino	**in der** Stadt	**in den** Wäldern
in einem Kino	**in einer** Stadt	**in** Wäldern
am See	**an der** Tankstelle	**an den** Wänden
an einem See	**an einer** Tankstelle	**an** Wänden
auf dem Berg	**auf der** Bank	**auf den** Bäumen
auf einem Berg	**auf einer** Bank	**auf** Bäumen

B. Uses

1. Use **in** when referring to enclosed spaces.

    im Supermarkt   *in the supermarket* (enclosed)

    in der Stadt   *in (within) the city*

2. **An,** in the sense of English *at,* denotes some kind of border or limiting area.

am Fenster	*at the window*
an der Tankstelle	*at the gas pump*
am See	*at the lake*

3. Use **auf,** in the sense of English *on,* when referring to surfaces.

auf dem Tisch	*on the table*
auf dem Herd	*on the stove*

4. **Auf** is also used to express location in public buildings such as the bank, the post office, or the police station.

auf der Bank	*at the bank*
auf der Post	*at the post office*
auf der Polizei	*at the police station*

Übung 6 | Was macht man dort?

Üb. 6. Assign for homework or use for pair work in class.

Stellen Sie einem Partner / einer Partnerin Fragen. Er/Sie soll eine Antwort darauf geben.

MODELL: S1: Was macht man am Strand?
S2: Man spielt Volleyball.

Benzin¹ tanken   ein Buch lesen   Geld wechseln³   tanzen

beten²   einen Film sehen   schwimmen   ?

Briefmarken kaufen   spazieren gehen   Volleyball spielen

1. im Kino
2. auf der Post
3. an der Tankstelle
4. in der Disko
5. in der Kirche
6. auf der Bank
7. im Meer
8. in der Bibliothek
9. im Park

¹*gasoline* ²*to pray* ³*to exchange*

Üb. 7. Have sts. also describe the location of objects and persons in the classroom and in pictures from your PF.

Übung 7 | **Wo?**

Wo sind die Leute? Wo sind das Poster, der Topf und der Wein?

MODELL: Stefan ist am Strand.

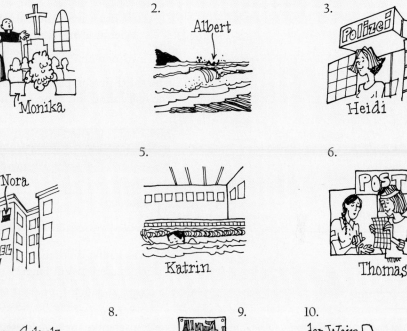

5.5 Dative case: personal pronouns

Wissen Sie noch?

The dative case designates the person to whom or for whom something is done.

Review grammar 5.1.

5.5. *Dativ: Personalpronomen.* This section continues the introduction of dative forms begun earlier in the chapter.

Mir and *mich, dir* and *dich* may be confused, because there is only one corresponding English form for both: *me* and *you.*

Personal pronouns in the dative case designate the person to or for whom something is done. (See also **Strukturen 5.1.**)

Kaufst du mir ein Buch?	*Are you buying me a book?*
Nein, ich schenke dir eine CD.	*No, I'm giving you a CD.*

A. First- and Second-person Pronouns

Here are the nominative and dative forms of the first- and second-person pronouns.

Singular		**Plural**	
Nominative	*Dative*	*Nominative*	*Dative*
ich	mir	wir	uns
du	dir	ihr	euch
Sie	Ihnen	Sie	Ihnen

Note that German speakers use three different pronouns to express the recipient or beneficiary in the second person (English *you*): **dir, euch,** and **Ihnen.**

> RICHARD: Leihst du mir dein Auto, Mutti? (*Will you lend me your car, Mom?*)
> FRAU AUGENTHALER: Ja, ich leihe **dir** mein Auto. (*Yes, I'll lend you my car.*)
>
> HERR THELEN: Viel Spaß in Wien! (*Have fun in Vienna!*)
> HERR WAGNER: Danke! Wir schreiben **Ihnen** eine Postkarte. (*Thank you! We'll write you a postcard.*)
>
> HANS: Ernst und Andrea! Kommt in mein Zimmer! Ich zeige **euch** meine Briefmarken. (*Ernst and Andrea! Come to my room! I'll show you my stamp collection.*)

B. Third-person Pronouns

The third-person pronouns have the same signals as the dative articles: **-m** in the masculine and neuter, **-r** in the feminine, and **-n** in the plural.

	Masculine and Neuter	Feminine	Plural
Article	dem	der	den
Pronoun	**ihm**	**ihr**	**ihnen**

Note the potential for confusion here, too. German *ihn* and *ihm* correspond to English *him*, German *sie* and *ihr* to English *her*.

de**m** → ih**m**
de**r** → ih**r**
de**n** → ih**nen**

Was kaufst du deinem Vater?	*What are you going to buy your dad?*
Ich kaufe **ihm** ein Buch.	*I'll buy him a book.*
Was schenkst du deiner Schwester?	*What are you going to give your sister?*
Ich schenke **ihr** eine Bluse.	*I'll give her a blouse.*
Was kochen Sie ihren Kindern heute?	*What are you going to cook for your kids today?*
Ich koche **ihnen** Spaghetti mit Ketchup.	*I'm making them spaghetti with ketchup.*

Note that the dative-case pronoun precedes the accusative-case noun.

Ich schreibe dir einen Brief.	*I'll write you a letter.*

Übung 8 | Minidialoge

Üb. 8. This exercise uses 1st- and 2nd-person pronouns.

Ergänzen Sie **mir, dir, uns, euch** oder **Ihnen.**

1. HANS: Mutti, kaufst du _____ Schokolade?
   FRAU RUF: Ja, aber du weißt, dass du vor dem Essen nichts Süßes essen sollst.
2. MARIA: Was hat denn Frau Körner gesagt?
   MICHAEL: Das erzähle ich _____ nicht.
3. ERNST: Mutti, kochst du Andrea und mir einen Pudding?
   FRAU WAGNER: Natürlich koche ich _____ einen Pudding.
4. HERR SIEBERT: Sie schulden[1] mir noch zehn Euro, Herr Pusch.
   HERR PUSCH: Was!? Wofür denn?
   HERR SIEBERT: Ich habe _____ doch für 100 Euro mein altes Motorrad verkauft, und Sie hatten nur 90 Euro dabei.
   HERR PUSCH: Ach, ja, richtig.
5. FRAU KÖRNER: Mein Mann und ich gehen heute Abend aus. Können Sie _____ vielleicht ein gutes Restaurant empfehlen, Herr Pusch?
   MICHAEL: Ja, gern …

[1]*owe*

Übung 9 | Wer? Wem? Was?

Üb. 9. For practice of 3rd-person pronouns. The exercise can be used for homework or for pair work in class. If sts. need additional practice, this activity could be expanded with personalizations. *Was haben Sie Ihrem Bruder gekauft?*

Beantworten Sie die Fragen mit Hilfe der Tabelle.

MODELL: Was hat Renate ihrem Freund geschenkt?
Sie hat ihm ein T-Shirt geschenkt.

	Renate	Mehmet
schenken	ein T-Shirt	einen Regenschirm
leihen	ihr Auto	500 Euro
erzählen	ein Geheimnis	eine Geschichte
verkaufen	ihre Sonnenbrille	seinen Fernseher
zeigen	ihr Büro	seine Wohnung
kaufen	eine neue Brille	einen Kinderwagen

1. Was hat Mehmet seiner Mutter geschenkt?
2. Was hat Renate ihrem Vater geliehen?
3. Was hat Mehmet seinem Bruder geliehen?
4. Was hat Renate ihrer Friseurin erzählt?
5. Was hat Mehmet seinen Nichten erzählt?
6. Was hat Renate ihrer Freundin verkauft?
7. Was hat Mehmet seinen Eltern verkauft?
8. Was hat Renate ihrem Schwager gezeigt?
9. Was hat Mehmet seinem Freund gezeigt?
10. Was hat Renate ihrer Großmutter gekauft?
11. Was hat Mehmet seiner Schwägerin gekauft?

Friedensreich Hundertwasser: *(630A) Mit der Liebe warten tut weh, wenn die Liebe woanders ist* (1971), Galerie Koller, Zürich

Chapter opening artwork: The artist adopted the name "Hundertwasser" in 1949. ("Sto" means "hundred" in several Slavic languages.) One of his favorite projects was *kreative Architektur*, in which nature and architecture harmoniously connect. He was buried on his land in New Zealand in the *Garten der glücklichen Toten* underneath a tulip tree. The "630A" in the title of the work actually appears on the piece itself, center left just outside the frame.

Suggestion: Use this colorful and extravagant presentation of architecture for an association activity. Students need to use their imagination to come up with possible answers to most of the following questions. *Was sehen Sie auf dem Bild? Welche Farben hat der Maler benutzt? Wo stehen diese Häuser? Wer könnte da wohnen? Wie sind die Menschen, die da wohnen? Wie wirken diese Häuser auf Sie? Was könnte der Titel „Mit der Liebe warten tut weh, wenn die Liebe woanders ist" bedeuten?*

FRIEDENSREICH HUNDERTWASSER

Friedensreich Hundertwasser wurde 1928 in Wien als Friedrich Stowasser geboren. Den Künstlernamen[1] legte er sich 1949 zu. 1943 wurden 69 Verwandte seiner jüdischen[2] Mutter deportiert und umgebracht[3]. Hundertwasser war Architekt, Maler, Grafiker und Zivilisationskritiker, er engagierte sich für Naturschutz[4] und Frieden[5]. Im Jahr 2000 ist er gestorben.

[1]*artistic name* [2]*Jewish* [3]*killed* [4]*environmental protection* [5]*peace*

KAPITEL 6

Wohnen

In **Kapitel 6**, you will learn vocabulary and expressions for describing where you live, for finding a place to live, and for talking about housework.

GOALS
In *Kapitel 6* sts. talk about living arrangements, how to look for an apartment, and about household chores. They also learn to specify location and direction, using both two-way prepositions and prepositions + fixed case (dative or accusative). In addition, they will learn more about separable-prefix verbs and about placement of adverbs and adverbial phrases of time and place. They are also introduced to the dative verbs.

Themen
- Haus und Wohnung
- Das Stadtviertel
- Auf Wohnungssuche
- Hausarbeit

Kulturelles
- Wohnen
- Auf Wohnungssuche
- Videoblick: Tausche Fahrrad reparieren gegen Bügeln
- Videoecke: Wohnen

Lektüren
- Regionale Baustile
- Film: *Good bye Lenin!*

Strukturen
- **6.1** Dative verbs
- **6.2** Location vs. destination: two-way prepositions with the dative or accusative case
- **6.3** Word order: time before place
- **6.4** Direction: **in/auf** vs. **zu/nach**
- **6.5** Separable-prefix verbs: the present tense and the perfect tense
- **6.6** The prepositions **mit** and **bei** + dative

Situationen

Haus und Wohnung

Grammatik 6.1–6.2

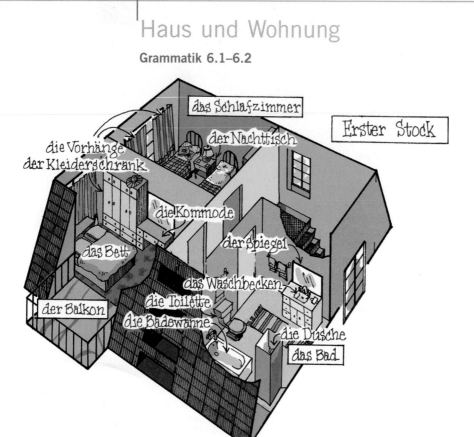

das Schlafzimmer

Erster Stock

der Nachttisch

die Vorhänge

der Kleiderschrank

die Kommode

der Spiegel

das Bett

das Waschbecken

der Balkon

die Toilette

die Badewanne

die Dusche

das Bad

Vocabulary Display

Use the transparency to teach the words for rooms in a house and common articles of furniture. For receptive recall ask: *Haben Sie ein/e/n _____ in Ihrer Wohnung?* Tell sts. to imagine they are moving into an apartment and need to buy furniture (money is no problem). Then begin the activity by saying: *Ich ziehe um und ich kaufe ein Bett.* You could show pictures of the items from your PF at the same time. Then call on a st.: *Chad, was kaufen Sie?* Chad must now list what you bought and add something he is buying. *Ich kaufe ein Bett und einen Stuhl.* Chad now asks someone else: *Matt, was kaufst du?* to which Matt responds, *Ich kaufe ein Bett und einen Stuhl und einen Spiegel* and so on. (Provide hints from your PF.)

Introduce the term *Einweihungsfeier* to the sts. and tell them that house/apartment-warming parties are popular among young Germans. Traditional gifts are a loaf of bread and salt. The bread symbolizes having plenty to eat, and salt represents prosperity.

Cultural note. Toilets are often in a separate room from bathrooms.

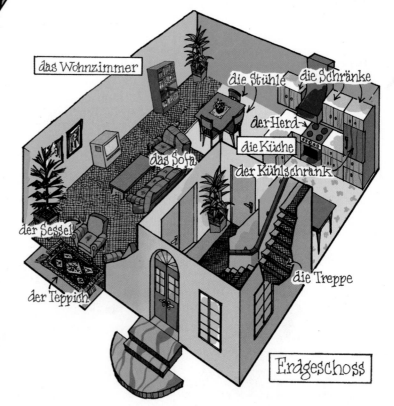

das Wohnzimmer

die Stühle

die Schränke

der Herd

die Küche

das Sofa

der Kühlschrank

der Sessel

die Treppe

der Teppich

Erdgeschoss

Cultural note. There are very few walk-in or built-in closets in German houses and apartments. Tenants have to provide their own freestanding closets.

Sit. 1. This introduces new words, recycles the display vocabulary, and familiarizes sts. with using *in* as a dative preposition: *im* _____, *in der* _____. Have sts. work in pairs, alternating who asks and who answers. Words for additional practice: *Das Bücherregal, der Fernseher, der Mikrowellenherd, die Stereoanlage, die Toilette, das Waschbecken.*

AA. Show sts. how to make new words (compounds) to expand their vocabulary. Say: *Ein Tisch zum Essen ist ein Esstisch.* (Stress the compound.) *Ein Tisch zum Arbeiten ist ein Arbeitstisch. Ein Tisch zum Schreiben ist ein* _____ *(Schreibtisch).* Then go to *Schrank: Ein Schrank für Kleider ist ein Kleiderschrank. Ein Schrank in der Küche ist ein* _____. *(Küchenschrank) usw.* Then *Lampe, Stuhl usw.* Compound three words: *Eine Lampe für den Schreibtisch ist eine Schreibtischlampe usw.* Point out that the last part of the compound always determines the gender.

MODELL: S1: Wo ist die Badewanne?
      S2: Im Bad.

die Badewanne	im Bad
das Bett	im Esszimmer
die Dusche	in der Küche
die Geschirrspülmaschine	im Schlafzimmer
der Herd	im Wohnzimmer
das Klavier	
die Kopfkissen	
der Kühlschrank	
der Nachttisch	
der Schrank	
das Sofa	
der Spiegel	
der Teppich	

Situation 2 | Das Zimmer

Sit. 2. Begin by reviewing the names and genders of the items in the picture. Write these on the board, perhaps grouped according to gender, to make sure that sts. ask about all 8 items. Then focus sts.' attention on form: **(1)** write the prepositions in a row on the board, **(2)** list the nouns used in the prepositional phrases, grouping them by gender (*der Tisch, der Schrank; die Wand; das Fenster*), and **(3)** be explicit about what happens to the article, depending on gender, with each preposition, e.g., **der** *Tisch: am Tisch, auf dem*

Wählen Sie ein Bild, aber sagen Sie die Nummer nicht. Ihr Partner oder Ihre Partnerin stellt Fragen und sagt, welches Bild Sie gewählt haben.

MODELL: S1: Ist die Katze auf dem Sofa?
      S2: Ja.
      S1: Ist es neun Uhr?
      S2: Ja.
      S1: Dann ist es Bild 1.
      S2: Richtig. Jetzt bist du dran.

Tisch, neben dem Tisch usw. Look at the whole picture on the overhead projector with the class. Describe the pictures in random order and ask sts. which picture you are describing, e.g.: „*Das Sofa steht an der Wand. Der Schrank steht neben dem Sofa. Der Tisch steht vor dem Schrank. Die Uhr hängt über dem Schrank. Die Katze ist auf →*

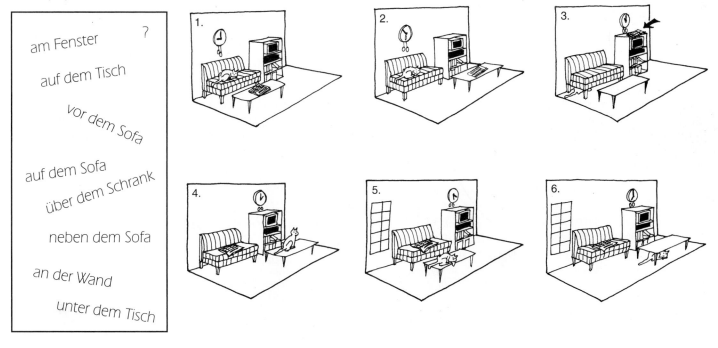

am Fenster ?

auf dem Tisch

vor dem Sofa

auf dem Sofa

über dem Schrank

neben dem Sofa

an der Wand

unter dem Tisch

dem Tisch. Die Zeitung liegt auf dem Sofa." (picture 4). Make sure sts. recognize all the things that are different in the pictures and have access to the phrases required to ask the right questions. Ask sts. to work in pairs. S2 selects one of the six pictures, but does not tell his or her partner which one it is. S1 then asks yes/no questions to determine which picture S2 has selected. You may want to write model questions on the board, e.g *Hängt die Uhr über dem Regal? Ist es neun Uhr? Gibt es ein Fenster?* To give the activity more structure, you may want to limit the number of questions to five or so.

Wohnen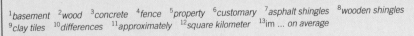

In Ihrem Land:

- Haben moderne Häuser in Ihrem Land einen Keller[1], eine Terrasse, einen Balkon?
- Haben sie einen Garten vor oder hinter dem Haus?
- Aus welchem Material sind die Häuser normalerweise? (aus Stein, aus Holz[2], aus Beton[3])
- Gibt es einen Zaun[4] um das ganze Grundstück[5] herum oder nur um den Garten hinter dem Haus?
- Wie viele Garagen sind üblich[6]? Wie groß sind die Garagen? (Platz für ein Auto, zwei Autos, drei Autos)
- Aus welchem Material ist das Dach? (aus Asphaltschindeln[7], aus Holzschindeln[8], aus Ziegeln[9])

Einfamilienhaus in München

Wohnblöcke im Ostteil Berlins

Mehrfamilienhaus in Wernigerode

In Deutschland:

- Schauen Sie sich die Fotos an. Welche Unterschiede[10] gibt es zu Häusern in Ihrem Land?

Hören Sie sich den Text an und beantworten Sie die folgenden Fragen.

- Wie viele Menschen leben in Deutschland?
- Wie groß ist Deutschland?
- In Deutschland leben ungefähr[11] 200 Menschen auf einem Quadratkilometer[12], das sind 563 auf einer Quadratmeile. In den USA z. B. sind es im Durchschnitt[13] 80. Wie viele sind es in Ihrem Bundesland?

KLI. *Play recording or read passage to sts: Ein modernes Einfamilienhaus in Deutschland hat einen Keller, eine Terrasse und oft auch einen Balkon. Es ist sehr massiv und aus Stein gebaut und von einem Zaun, einer Mauer oder Hecke umgeben. Das Dach ist meistens aus Ziegeln und hat einen Schornstein. Natürlich gibt es regionale Unterschiede. Ein typisches Haus in Süddeutschland sieht anders aus als ein Haus an der Nordseeküste. Weil Deutschland so dicht bevölkert ist – über 82 Millionen Menschen leben auf 357 000 Quadratkilometern – sind Häuser teuer. Nur 30% der Deutschen wohnen im eigenen Heim. Die anderen 70% wohnen zur Miete.* Ask sts. to discuss the questions relative to their countries. Collect sts.' answers and write on the board. Then, ask sts. to respond to the questions on Germany, again in small groups. Write sts.' answers on the board. Summarize the major differences between your country and Germany in simple German.

[1]basement [2]wood [3]concrete [4]fence [5]property [6]customary [7]asphalt shingles [8]wooden shingles [9]clay tiles [10]differences [11]approximately [12]square kilometer [13]im ... on average

Photo questions. *In welchem Bundesland stehen diese Häuser? Wo spielen die Kinder, die hier wohnen? Wann hat man diese Häuser gebaut? Können Sie viele Blumen und Bäume sehen? Können Sie viele Autos sehen? Wo kann man hier parken? Möchten Sie lieber in einem Zweifamilienhaus oder in einem Wohnblock wohnen?*

Situation 3 | Interview

Sit. 3. Model pronunciation and have sts. repeat. Have individual sts. ask you the questions and answer appropriately. Then have sts. work in pairs. Sts. asking the questions should also take notes. After each st. has asked all the questions, tell sts. to find a new partner. One st. could ask *Mit wem hast du gesprochen?* and then ask the interview questions regarding that person. This will give sts. practice using the possessive adjectives *sein/ihr* and their endings (*Kapitel 2*).

1. Wo wohnst du? (in einer Wohnung, in einem Studentenheim, in einem Haus, auf dem Land, in der Stadt, _____)
2. Wohnst du allein? (in einer Wohngemeinschaft, bei deinen Eltern, bei einer Familie, mit einem Mitbewohner, mit einer Mitbewohnerin, _____)
3. Wie lange brauchst du zur Uni? (zehn Minuten zu Fuß, fünf Minuten mit dem Fahrrad, eine halbe Stunde mit dem Auto oder mit dem Bus, _____)
4. Was kostet dein Zimmer / deine Wohnung pro Monat?
5. Was für Möbel hast du in deinem Zimmer / in deiner Wohnung?

Situation 4 | Interaktion: In der Wohnung

Beantworten Sie die Fragen für sich selbst und schreiben Sie Ihre Antworten auf. Stellen Sie dann die gleichen Fragen an Ihren Partner oder Ihre Partnerin.

	ich	mein(e) Partner(in)
Wie gefällt dir deine Wohnung oder dein Zimmer?		
Welches Möbelstück fehlt dir?		
Welches Möbelstück gehört dir nicht?		
Wie gefällt dir das Aufräumen und Putzen?		
Wer hilft dir beim Aufräumen und Putzen?		

Das Stadtviertel

Grammatik 6.3–6.4

Vocabulary Display

(See the IM.) Introduce nonguessable vocabulary by pointing to buildings and providing a simple definition using familiar words: *Im Rathaus arbeitet der Bürgermeister. In einer Metzgerei kann man Fleisch und Wurst kaufen. Ins Gefängnis kommt man, wenn man gestohlen oder getötet hat.* (You may need to act this out too.) Point out the difference between an *Apotheke* and a *Drogerie.* (*Metzgerei = Fleischerei* in northern Germany.)

Situation 5 | Wie weit weg?

MODELL: S1: Wie weit weg sollte die Apotheke von deiner Wohnung sein?
S2: _____

1. die Apotheke
2. die Universität
3. die Polizei
4. der Flughafen
5. das Kino
6. das Krankenhaus
7. das Gefängnis
8. der Kindergarten
9. der Supermarkt
10. die Kirche

gleich um die Ecke
gleich gegenüber
fünf Minuten zu Fuß
zwei Straßen weiter
eine halbe Stunde mit dem Auto
am anderen Ende der Stadt
so weit weg wie möglich
zehn Minuten mit dem Fahrrad
mir egal

Situation 6 | Umfrage

Sit. 6. This poll provides examples of the "time before place" rule. Model pronunciation before sts. work in pairs.

MODELL: S1: Wohnst du in der Nähe der Universität?
S2: Ja.
S1: Unterschreib bitte hier.

UNTERSCHRIFT

1. Wohnst du in der Nähe der Universität? _____
2. Übernachtest du manchmal in Hotels? _____
3. Gibt es in deiner Heimatstadt ein Schwimmbad? _____
4. Warst du letzte Woche auf der Post? _____
5. Warst du gestern im Supermarkt? _____
6. Gibt es in deiner Heimatstadt ein Rathaus? _____
7. Warst du letzten Freitag in der Disko? _____
8. Bist du oft in der Bibliothek? _____
9. Warst du letzten Sonntag in der Kirche? _____

Situation 7 | Wohin gehst du, wenn ...?

MODELL: S1: Wohin gehst du, wenn du ein Buch lesen willst?
S2: Wenn ich ein Buch lesen will? In die Bibliothek.

1. du schwimmen gehen willst?
2. du Briefmarken kaufen willst?
3. du Geld brauchst?
4. du Benzin brauchst?
5. du Brot brauchst?
6. du krank bist?
7. du verreisen willst?
8. du eine Zugfahrkarte kaufen willst?
9. _____?

zum Bahnhof
in die Bäckerei
zum Flughafen
zum Arzt
auf die Bank
zur Tankstelle
auf die Post
ins Schwimmbad
_____

Sit. 7. This activity works with word order in subordinate clauses. Model pronunciation. Then, have sts. work in pairs. Afterward, ask sts. individually, *Wohin gehst du, wenn du ...,* and then turn it around and ask as well, *Wann fährst du zur Tankstelle? usw.,* to which sts. must answer, *Wenn ich Benzin brauche.* This gives them additional practice with word order and conjugating verbs at the end of the clause. Sts. who complete the exercise quickly can redo it in this manner until the rest of the class has finished.

Wohin fahren Sie, wenn Sie Benzin brauchen?

Sit. 8. This is an information-gap activity that involves both scenes at once. Ask sts. to work in pairs. s1 works from the two scenes on this page, and s2 works from the corresponding pair of scenes in Appendix A. Eight locations are identified in the scenes, but each st. has complete information (*früher* and *heute*) for only four of them. As for the remaining four locations, each st. knows either the previous or the current identity, but not both. Remind sts. to negotiate meaning in German by using such phrases as *Wie bitte? Wie schreibt man das? Was ist das?* usw.

Situation 8 | Informationsspiel: Gestern und heute

Arbeiten Sie zu zweit und stellen Sie Fragen wie im Modell.

MODELL: S1: Früher war hier eine Reinigung. Was ist da heute?
S2: Heute ist hier ein Schreibwarengeschäft.

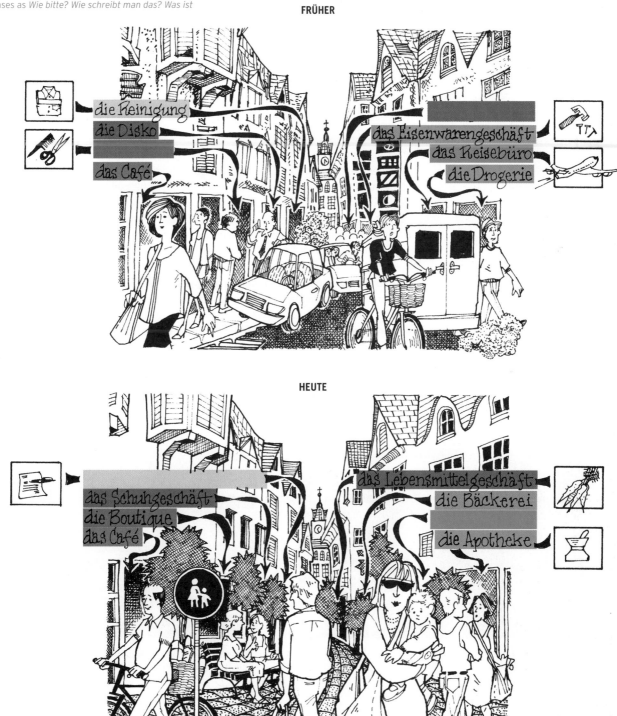

Situationen

209

Lektüre 📖

Vor dem Lesen

1. Gibt es regionale Baustile[1] in Ihrem Land? Wie heißen sie?
2. Sind die Wohnhäuser in einer Region anders als[2] die Häuser in einer anderen? Sind Häuser im Westen anders als Häuser im Osten? Sind Häuser auf dem Land anders als Häuser in der Stadt?
3. Gibt es öffentliche[3] Gebäude, die einen bestimmten Baustil haben?
4. Wie alt ist die Architektur? Welche historischen Baustile gibt es?
5. Kennen Sie Architekten aus Ihrem Land? Was haben sie gebaut[4]?
6. Kennen Sie Gebäude wie Kirchen oder Paläste in Europa, die einen bestimmten Baustil haben?

Regionale Baustile

der spitze Turm

der Zwiebelturm

In Deutschland und Österreich, wie in vielen anderen Ländern, gibt es unterschiedliche regionale Baustile. Traditionelle Wohnhäuser und Gebäude wie Rathäuser, Kirchen und Schlösser[5] unterscheiden sich[6] von einem Landesteil zu einem anderen. So haben zum Beispiel die Kirchen in Bayern häufig Zwiebeltürme und die Kirchen in Norddeutschland spitze Türme. In manchen Gegenden sind die Häuser von außen mit Holz verkleidet, an anderen sieht man Backstein[7] oder Putz[8].

Würzburg, Fulda, Dresden und Wien sind typische Beispiele für die Baukunst des Barock. Diesen Baustil gibt es seit dem 17. Jahrhundert. Man findet ihn vor allem im Süden von Deutschland und in Österreich. Viele Kirchen, Klöster und Schlösser sind im barocken Stil gebaut.

Wernigerode hat auch den Namen „Die bunte[9] Stadt am Harz", weil die Holzbalken[10] so bunt bemalt[11] sind. Diesen Baustil nennt man Fachwerk[12]. Man findet ihn in ganz Deutschland, aber ganz besonders in der Mitte des Landes, in Hessen, Sachsen-Anhalt und im südlichen Niedersachsen. Die ältesten Häuser im Fachwerkstil stammen aus dem 14. Jahrhundert.

Fachwerk: Alte Häuser in Wernigerode

Barock: Die Residenz in Würzburg

[1]*architectural styles* [2]anders ... *different from* [3]*public* [4]bauen: *to build* [5]*castles* [6]unterscheiden ... *differ*
[7]*brick* [8]*plaster* [9]*colorful* [10]*wooden beams* [11]*painted* [12]*half-timber*

Moderne: Das Bundeskanzleramt in Berlin

In Lübeck, Greifswald und Stralsund findet man viele Wohnhäuser, Kirchen, Rathäuser und selbst Stadttore aus rotem Backstein. Diesen Baustil nennt man Backsteingotik. Er ist vor allem in den Hansestädten[1] entlang der Nord- und Ostseeküste zu Hause.

Die Innenstädte vieler deutscher Städte und Großstädte wurden im zweiten Weltkrieg fast völlig zerstört. Man hat diese Städte meistens im modernen Stil geplant und wieder aufgebaut. Trotz einiger alter Gebäude hat man zum Beispiel in Hannover das Gefühl, eine neue und moderne Stadt zu besuchen. Viele Industrie- und Wirtschaftszentren in Deutschland, wie Leipzig mit seinem Messegelände und die Frankfurter City mit ihrer Bankenmetropole, wirken modern und international.

Arbeit mit dem Text

A. Beantworten Sie nun die folgenden Fragen.

1. Seit wann gibt es Gebäude im barocken Stil?
2. Warum nennt man Wernigerode „die bunte Stadt am Harz"?
3. Aus welcher Zeit sind die ältesten Häuser im Fachwerkstil?
4. Wo findet man viele Hansestädte?
5. Warum sehen die Innenstädte vieler deutscher Großstädte so modern aus?

Backsteingotik: Das Holstentor in Lübeck

[1] *Hanseatic cities*

B. Was erfahren Sie über die Baustile in den verschiedenen Regionen? Ergänzen Sie die Tabelle.

	im Süden und in Österreich	in der Mitte Deutschlands	im Norden Deutschlands
Baustil	Barock	Fachwerk	Backsteingotik
Baumaterial	Putz	Holz	Backstein
Kirchtürme	Zwiebeltürme		spitze Türme

Nach dem Lesen

Suchen Sie im Internet oder in der Bibliothek Informationen und Fotos über die genannten Städte, Länder und Baustile und stellen Sie sie in der Klasse vor.

Auf Wohnungssuche

das Reihenhaus

das Einfamilienhaus

die Villa

die Altbauwohnung

das Bauernhaus

die Skihütte

das Hochhaus

das Studentenheim

der Wohnwagen

Situation 9 | Wo möchtest du gern wohnen?

Sit. 9. Model pronunciation. Sts. work with a partner, first asking each other to rank the buildings in order of desirability and then working on attributes and locations for their top three choices. In your follow-up, ask sts. to give full information and possibly reasons for choices.

Fragen Sie fünf Personen und schreiben Sie die Antworten auf.

MODELL: s1: Wo möchtest du gern wohnen?
s2: In einem Bauernhaus mit alten Möbeln.
s1: Und wo soll es stehen?
s2: Auf dem Land.

in einem Bauernhaus	mit Weinkeller	in der Innenstadt
in einem Wohnwagen	mit schönem Ausblick	am Stadtrand
in einem Hochhaus	mit Terrasse	im Ausland
in einem Einfamilienhaus	mit Balkon	auf dem Land
in einem Reihenhaus	mit alten Möbeln	in den Bergen
in einer Skihütte	mit vielen Fenstern	an einem See
in einer Villa	mit einem Garten	in der Nähe der Stadt
im Studentenheim	mit Garage	in der Nähe der Uni

Situation 10 | Umfrage

MODELL: s1: Möchtest du gern in der Innenstadt leben?
s2: Ja.
s1: Unterschreib bitte hier.

UNTERSCHRIFT

1. Möchtest du gern in der Innenstadt leben? _____
2. Möchtest du gern am Stadtrand leben? _____
3. Kannst du dir ein Leben auf dem Land vorstellen? _____
4. Möchtest du gern im Ausland wohnen? _____
5. Möchtest du in einer Villa wohnen? _____
6. Möchtest du in einem Wohnwagen leben? _____
7. Kannst du dir ein Leben auf einem Hausboot vorstellen? _____
8. Möchtest du gern im Studentenheim wohnen? _____
9. Möchtest du gern eine Woche unter Wasser wohnen? _____
10. Möchtest du gern im Wald leben? _____

Auf Wohnungssuche

Wie haben Sie Ihr Zimmer / Ihre Wohnung gefunden? Kreuzen Sie an.

durch eine Anzeige[1] in der Zeitung ☐
mit Hilfe der Uni ☐
durch Freunde oder Bekannte ☐
durch eine Anzeige am schwarzen Brett ☐
durch die Gelben Seiten ☐
über das Internet ☐

Schauen Sie sich das Foto und die Anzeigen an.

- Welche der Anzeigen suchen nach einer Wohnung?
- Welche bieten eine Wohnung oder ein Zimmer an[2]?
- Unter welchen Umständen gibt es die Wohnung in St. Pauli billiger?
- Wann kann man in die Wohnung in Ottensen einziehen?

Schreiben Sie selbst eine Suchanzeige für eine Wohnung oder ein Zimmer in einer Wohngemeinschaft für ein Schwarzes Brett. Wohnungen sind sehr knapp. Machen Sie Ihre Anzeige so attraktiv wie möglich!

Photo questions. Was muss man machen, wenn man eine Wohnung finden möchte? Wo ist diese Studentin? Was hat sie in der Hand? Wo möchte sie lieber wohnen – in einer Wohngemeinschaft oder allein in einer Einzimmerwohnung? Sind die Anzeigen nur für Wohnungen?

Studentin sucht Wohnung

① **ER IST WIEDER DA ...**

ALIEN XIV

—DER NACHMIETER[3]—

. . . Ein halbes Jahr war er in Schweden. Aber plötzlich[4] ist er wieder in Hamburg. Manche nennen[5] ihn EL SYMPATICO. Doch die meisten Karsten. Er will nur eines: DEINE WOHNUNG! (1-2 Zi bis 250 Euro inkl.)

Wenn Du ihn anrufst, ruft er zurück . . .

Niemand hat es bis jetzt gewagt[6] . . .

| 04451 | 04451 | 04451 | 04451 | 04451 | 04451 | 04451 | 04451 | 04451 |
| -83591 | -83591 | -83591 | -83591 | -83591 | -83591 | -83591 | -83591 | -83591 |

② Vermiete im September[7]
2-Zimmer-Whg in St. Pauli (Hinterhof).
Miete 350 Euro + Heizung, Strom, Telefon.
wenn Katzenliebhaber/in[8] auch den Kater mitversorgt[9], gibt es die Wohnung billiger.

③ 2te Person für 3-Zimmer Wohnung in Ottensen (HH50) ab Juli gesucht.
Miete: EUR 250 + Kaution[10]
Tel. (040) 39 22 93

KLI. (See the IM.) These ads were found at the University of Hamburg. St. Pauli and Ottensen are parts or suburbs of Hamburg. *HH* (Hansestadt Hamburg) is the license plate code for the city. In Hamburg, with its severe housing shortage, the *Kaution* (security deposit) is usually very high—twice or even three times the monthly rent. The large ad is by far the most creative in style. The author is playing with several images or phrases from movies. Ask sts.: *An welche Filme denken Sie?* for the writing task, ask sts. to be creative and to compose a housing ad that is likely to get noticed on a crowded bulletin board in Hamburg. As a follow-up, bring a bulletin board to class and have sts. post their ads. Ask sts. to select the most creative ad, or ask each st. to pick an ad they like and role-play a "looking for a room" encounter based on the ad with the person who composed it.

[1]*ad* [2]*anbieten: to offer* [3]*subletter* [4]*suddenly* [5]*call* [6]*dared* [7]*renting out* [8]*cat lover* [9]*helps take care of* [10]*security deposit*

Situation 11 | Dialog: Auf Wohnungssuche

Silvia ist auf Wohnungssuche.

Sit. 11. (See the IM.) This dialogue provides a model for the role-play following it. You may wish to follow the steps for presenting the dialogue without the use of the textbook. Remind sts. they can listen to this dialogue in the laboratory. Questions for first listening: **1.** *Wie meldet man sich am Telefon?* **2.** *Was will Silvia wissen?* **3.** *Was ist die genaue Adresse?* Questions for second listening: **1.** *In welchem Stockwerk ist das Zimmer?* **2.** *Was kostet das Zimmer?* **3.** *Welche Möbel stehen darin?* **4.** *Wo kann Silvia baden?*

Cultural note. In Germany, the first floor (*1. Stock*) is equivalent to the second floor in the U.S. The first floor in the U.S. is the ground floor (*Erdgeschoss*) in Germany. (See also the following cultural note.)

Cultural note. Although renting a furnished room from a landlord/lady is not as widespread as it used to be among students, this is still a realistic dialogue. Arrangements to rent are made well in advance, often 2 or 3 months. Notice before moving out (*Kündigungsfrist*) is required.

FRAU SCHUSTER: <u>Schuster</u>!

SILVIA: Guten Tag. Hier Silvia Mertens. Ich rufe wegen des Zimmers an. Ist es noch <u>frei</u>?

FRAU SCHUSTER: Ja, das ist noch zu haben.

SILVIA: Prima, in welchem <u>Stadtteil</u> ist es denn?

FRAU SCHUSTER: Frankfurt-Süd, Waldschulstraße <u>22</u>.

SILVIA: Und in welchem <u>Stock</u> liegt das Zimmer?

FRAU SCHUSTER: Im fünften, gleich unter dem <u>Dach</u>.

SILVIA: Gibt es einen <u>Aufzug</u>?

FRAU SCHUSTER: Nein, leider nicht.

SILVIA: Schade. Was kostet denn das Zimmer?

FRAU SCHUSTER: Dreihundert Euro <u>möbliert</u>.

SILVIA: Möbliert? Was steht denn drin?

FRAU SCHUSTER: Also, ein Bett natürlich, ein Tisch mit zwei Stühlen und ein <u>Kleiderschrank</u>.

SILVIA: Ist auch ein Bad dabei?

FRAU SCHUSTER: Nein, aber baden können Sie <u>bei mir</u>. Und Sie haben natürlich Ihre <u>eigene</u> Toilette.

SILVIA: Wann könnte ich mir denn das Zimmer mal <u>anschauen</u>?

FRAU SCHUSTER: Wenn Sie wollen, können Sie gleich vorbeikommen.

SILVIA: Gut, dann komme ich gleich mal vorbei. Auf <u>Wiederhören</u>.

FRAU SCHUSTER: Auf <u>Wiederhören</u>.

 Situation 12 | Rollenspiel: Zimmer zu vermieten

Sit. 12. The role for s2 appears in Appendix B.

S1: Sie sind Student/Studentin und suchen ein schönes, großes Zimmer. Das Zimmer soll hell und ruhig sein. Sie haben nicht viel Geld und können nur bis zu 300 Euro Miete zahlen, inklusive Nebenkosten. Sie rauchen nicht und hören keine laute Musik. Fragen Sie den Vermieter / die Vermieterin, wie groß das Zimmer ist, was es kostet, ob es im Winter warm ist, ob Sie kochen dürfen und ob Ihre Freunde Sie besuchen dürfen. Sagen Sie dann, ob Sie das Zimmer mieten möchten.

Hausarbeit

Grammatik 6.5–6.6

Andrea putzt ihre Schuhe.

Paula wischt den Tisch ab.

Ernst mäht den Rasen.

der Besen

Jens fegt den Boden.

der Staubsauger

Josie saugt Staub.

das Bügeleisen

Uli bügelt sein Hemd.

Jochen macht die Toilette sauber.

Jutta wäscht die Wäsche.

Margret wischt den Boden auf.

Hans macht sein Bett.

216   KAPITEL 6   Wohnen

Situation 13 | Was macht man mit einem Besen?

MODELL: S1: Was macht man mit einem Besen?
S2: Mit einem Besen fegt man den Boden.

Staub saugen
Hemden oder Blusen bügeln
den Rasen sprengen
den Rasen mähen
die Blumen gießen
den Boden fegen
die Wäsche waschen
die Schuhe putzen
das Geschirr spülen
den Tisch abwischen

1. mit einem Staubsauger
2. mit einer Geschirrspülmaschine
3. mit einer Waschmaschine
4. mit einem Besen
5. mit einem Rasenmäher
6. mit einer Gießkanne
7. mit einem Bügeleisen
8. mit einem Putzlappen
9. mit einem Gartenschlauch

Situation 14 | Angenehm oder unangenehm?

Sit. 14. This activity recycles phrases from *Sit. 13* and introduces some new ones using familiar vocabulary. **Preparation:** Introduce new vocabulary: *Müll, (un)angenehm.* Pick two household chores, one which you like and one which you dislike. Ask sts. whether they like these chores. *Ich mache gar nicht gern das Bett. Das ist mir unangenehm. Machen Sie gern das Bett? Ist das angenehm? Ich putze sehr gern die Fenster. Putzen Sie gern die Fenster?* Explain the activity to sts. Ask sts. to work alone to rank the tasks. **Follow-up:** Ask how many chose each task as number 1, number 2, etc. Use this information to present on the board the class's most popular and least popular tasks. **Alternative:** Ask sts. to work in groups of 3 and come to a consensus within each group as to how to rank the tasks.

Welche Hausarbeit machen Sie gern, weniger gern oder gar nicht gern? Ordnen Sie die folgenden Tätigkeiten von sehr angenehm (1) zu sehr unangenehm (10).

_____ Hosen bügeln
_____ Regale abwischen
_____ eine Einkaufsliste schreiben
_____ die Toilette putzen
_____ den Müll wegbringen
_____ die Sessel absaugen
_____ die Vorhänge waschen
_____ Töpfe und Pfannen spülen
_____ das Bett machen
_____ Fenster putzen

Videoblick

Tausche[1] Fahrrad reparieren gegen[2] Bügeln

Das Netzwerk für die Generation 50plus bietet[3] nicht nur gemeinsame Freizeitaktivitäten, sondern auch eine Leistungstauschbörse[4]. Jeder bringt ein[5], was er kann.

- Was braucht Frau Steigleder?
- Wer macht das für sie?
- Wo hat sie das Angebot gefunden?
- Was bietet sie Herrn Merkelbach an?
- Welche anderen Leistungen findet man in der Leistungstauschbörse?

[1]*exchange* [2]*here: for* [3]*offers* [4]*task exchange* [5]*bringt ... contributes*
[6]*each other*

So hilft man sich[6], ganz ohne Geld.

Situation 15 | Bildgeschichte: Frühjahrsputz

Sit. 15. Sentences for the narration series:
1. *Gestern war bei Wagners der große Frühjahrsputz. Alle haben geholfen.* **2.** *Herr Wagner hat zuerst die Terrasse gefegt.* **3.** *Dann hat er den Keller aufgeräumt.* **4.** *Frau Wagner hat zuerst die Fenster geputzt.* **5.** *Dann hat sie im ganzen Haus Staub gesaugt.* **6.** *Jens hat zuerst die Flaschen weggebracht.* **7.** *Und Ernst hat zuerst sein Zimmer aufgeräumt.* **8.** *Dann hat Jens das Geschirr gespült.* **9.** *Und Ernst hat abgetrocknet.* **10.** *Und Andrea? Andrea war bei ihrer Freundin und hat ferngesehen.* Point out that spring cleaning is still an important tradition in much of the German-speaking world.

Sit. 16. (See the IM.) The corresponding chart is in Appendix A. **(1)** Establish the topic by asking such questions as: *Wer von Ihnen mäht gern den Rasen? hat heute sein Bett gemacht? usw.*
(2) Preteach vocabulary: *Staub wischen, nichts von alledem,* and practice model sentences both for Nora and Thomas (3rd person) and for a partner (2nd person). Ask sts. which time expressions in the chart signal present tense (the first 4), perfect tense (the following 2), and a sentence with the modal verb *muss* (the last 2). **(3)** Remind sts. to use phrases such as *Wie bitte?* and *Wie schreibt man das?* when comprehension problems arise and not to revert to English or look into each other's charts. Pair sts. up. Allow at least 5 minutes for completing the activity. **(4)** Follow up by asking questions about the *mein Partner / meine Partnerin* column and turn it into an association activity (see the IM) if time allows.

Situation 16 | Informationsspiel: Haus- und Gartenarbeit

MODELL: S1: Was macht Nora am liebsten?
S2: Sie geht am liebsten einkaufen.
S1: Was hat Thomas letztes Wochenende gemacht?
S2: Er hat das Geschirr gespült.
S1: Was muss Nora diese Woche noch machen?
S2: Sie muss den Boden aufwischen.

S1: Was machst du am liebsten?
S2: Ich _____ am liebsten _____.

	Thomas	Nora	mein(e) Partner(in)
am liebsten	den Rasen mähen	einkaufen gehen	
am wenigsten gern	das Bad putzen	die Fenster putzen	
jeden Tag	nichts von alledem	den Tisch abwischen	
einmal in der Woche	sein Bett machen	die Wäsche waschen	
letztes Wochenende	das Geschirr spülen	ihre Bluse bügeln	
gestern	die Blumen gießen	ihr Zimmer aufräumen	
diese Woche	seine Wäsche waschen	den Boden aufwischen	
bald mal wieder	die Flaschen wegbringen	Staub wischen	

 Lektüre

Vor dem Lesen. The photo in the background shows Erich Honecker, who was head of state from 1971 until 1989. Egon Krenz succeeded him for a very short time, from October 18 to December 13, 1989.

Vor dem Lesen

A. Sehen Sie sich das Foto aus dem Film an.

1. Welche Art[1] Fernsehsendung ist das?
2. Der Mann im Hintergrund war 1971 bis 1989 Staatschef[2] der DDR. Wie hieß er?
3. Was wissen Sie über die ehemalige[3] DDR und die Wiedervereinigung[4]? Sammeln Sie Informationen.

Good bye Lenin!

Regisseur: Wolfgang Becker

Schauspieler in den Hauptrollen: Daniel Brühl, Katrin Saß, Maria Simon

Erscheinungsjahr: 2003

B. Lesen Sie die Wörter im Miniwörterbuch auf der nächsten Seite. Suchen Sie sie im Text und unterstreichen Sie sie. Lesen Sie dann den Text.

[1]*type* [2]*head of state* [3]*former* [4]*reunification*

Situationen   219

die **Aufregung**	excitement
der **Bürger** / die **Bürgerin**	citizen
DDR (Deutsche Demokratische Republik)	GDR (German Democratic Republic)
entschlossen	determined
flüchten	to flee
gefälscht	fake
geht es nach Alex	if things go according to Alex
die **Gesundheit**	health
der **Herzinfarkt**	heart attack
der **Kosmonaut**	East German word for astronaut
schaden	to harm
der **Sperrmüll**	bulk refuse (heap)
der **Tod**	death
überzeugt	staunch
die **Veränderung**	change
verheimlichen	to conceal
vorspielen	to feign
wohlbekannt	well-known
der **Zusammenbruch**	collapse

Miniwörterbuch

Film: *Good bye Lenin!*

Christiane Kerner – eine engagierte DDR-Bürgerin und überzeugte Sozialistin – hat am 7. Oktober 1989 einen Herzinfarkt und fällt ins Koma. Während sie im Krankenhaus liegt und bewusstlos ist, fällt zwei Tage später die Berliner Mauer und die DDR wird ein Teil der Bundesrepublik Deutschland. Acht Monate später wacht sie auf und
5 die DDR existiert nicht mehr.

Jede Art von Aufregung schadet Christiane Kerners Gesundheit, deshalb beschließt ihr Sohn Alex die politischen Veränderungen vor seiner Mutter zu verheimlichen. Gemeinsam mit seiner Schwester Ariane will Alex seiner Mutter den ganz normalen DDR-Alltag vorspielen. Leichter gesagt als getan: Die alten DDR-Möbel der Familie sind
10 out und stehen im Keller oder liegen auf dem Sperrmüll; im Supermarkt gibt es jetzt westdeutsche Lebensmittel und keine aus DDR-Produktion; die wohlbekannten DDR-Fernsehsendungen laufen auch nicht mehr; West-Autos und Fast-Food-Restaurants überrollen den Osten; und am Haus gegenüber hängt ein großes Coca-Cola Werbeplakat. Dies alles ist für Alex und Ariane ein großes Problem. Aber Alex ist entschlossen und
15 kreativ. Selbst Freunde und Nachbarn spielen mit.

Am Ende, kurz vor ihrem Tod, erfährt Mutter Christiane aber doch vom Zusammenbruch der DDR. Sie sagt Alex nichts davon. Alex' DDR, die er mit gefälschten DDR-Nachrichtensendungen belebt, ist ganz anders als die alte DDR: Geht es nach Alex, ist die DDR das Wunschland aller Menschen; Westdeutsche flüchten in den Osten; und
20 Staatschef ist natürlich Alex' Idol, der DDR-Kosmonaut Sigmund Jähn.

Arbeit mit dem Text

Beantworten Sie die folgenden Fragen.

1. Warum sagt Alex seiner Mutter nicht, dass die DDR nicht mehr existiert?
2. In welchen alltäglichen Bereichen[1] ändert sich das Leben der Kerners nach dem Fall der Mauer?
3. Wie wünscht[2] sich Alex die DDR?

[1]*domains, spheres* [2]*wishes*

Nach dem Lesen

A. Recherchieren Sie im Internet über den Schauspieler Daniel Brühl, der im Film Alex Kerner spielt. Woher kommt er? Welche Filme hat er noch gemacht? Welche Preise hat er mit *Good bye Lenin!* gewonnen? Welche Projekte hat er gerade?

B. Die Resonanz[1] auf *Good bye Lenin!* war sehr groß in Ost- und Westdeutschland. Warum ist der Film in Deutschland so beliebt? Finden Sie Antworten (auch im Internet) und präsentieren Sie Ihre Gedanken und Lösungen auf einem Poster in der Klasse.

[1]*response*

Videoecke

- Wo wohnst du?
- Was gefällt dir an deinem Zimmer / an deiner Wohnung?
- Was gefällt dir nicht?
- Wie hast du deine Wohnung gefunden?
- Wie war der Umzug?
- Was musst du für deine Wohnung zahlen?
- Wohnst du allein? Gefällt dir das?

Niki ist in Graz, Österreich, geboren. Sie studiert Theologie und Gesang[1]. Ihre Mutter ist Lehrerin und ihr Vater ist Journalist.

Jan ist in Leipzig geboren. Er ist selbstständig im Baugewerbe[2] tätig[3]. Seine Hobbys sind Motorräder und Sport.

Aufgabe 1

Aufgaben 1 and 2. (1) Preview with photos: *Wo ist Niki geboren? Was studiert sie? Als was arbeitet Jan? Was sind seine Hobbys?* **(2)** Read the 3 questions in *Aufgabe 1* and ask sts. to speculate what Niki might say. **(3)** Ask sts. to write down the answers while you play Niki's interview once or twice. **(4)** Discuss the answers. **(5)** Read each of the paragraphs in *Aufgabe 2* out loud. Play the appropriate sections of the video several times until sts. find all errors.

Hören Sie dem Interview mit Niki zu und beantworten Sie folgende Fragen.

1. Wo wohnt Niki? Gefällt ihr das Zimmer?
2. Woher bekommt sie das Geld für die Miete?
3. Wohnt sie allein?

Aufgabe 2

Die folgenden Sätze kommen im Interview vor. Allerdings enthalten sie einige falsche Informationen. Korrigieren Sie die Sätze.

1. Das Zimmer ist schön. Es ist klein und gemütlich. Und ich habe auch viele Bilder an den Wänden.
2. Der Umzug war lustig. Ich bin zuerst nur mit einem Koffer nach Leipzig gekommen und erst sechs Wochen später sind meine Eltern mit dem Rest des Gepäcks gekommen.
3. Es ist schön, mit anderen Leuten zu wohnen. Man kann sich treffen und reden und Tee trinken. Aber manchmal ist es auch nicht so schön, weil keiner weiß, wer mit dem Kochen dran ist.

[1]*singing*   [2]*construction*   [3]*selbstständig tätig self-employed*

Was gefällt Jan an seiner Wohnung?

Sie liegt nahe am Park.

Sie ist in der Nähe der Universität.

Die Räume sind groß.

Sie liegt zentral.

Sie hat einen großen Garten.

Die Zimmer sind renoviert.

Sie hat eine Garage.

Beantworten Sie die folgenden Fragen.

1. Wie haben Jan und seine Freunde die Wohnung gefunden?
2. Mit wie vielen Leuten wohnt Jan zusammen?
3. Wohnt Jan gern mit Leuten zusammen?

Wortschatz

In der Stadt	In the City
die **Apotheke**, -n	pharmacy
die **Bushaltestelle**, -n	bus stop
die **Drogerie**, -n	drugstore
die **Fabrik**, -en	factory
die **Metzgerei**, -en	butcher shop
die **Reinigung**, -en	dry cleaner's
die **Stadt**, ̈-e (R)	town, city
die **Heimatstadt**, ̈-e	hometown
die **Innenstadt**, ̈-e	downtown
die **Straße**, -n	street, road
der **Buchladen**, ̈	bookstore
der **Flughafen**, ̈	airport
der **Stadtrand**, ̈-er	city limits
der **Stadtteil**, -e	district, neighborhood
das **Bürohaus**, ̈-er	office building
das **Eisenwarengeschäft**, -e	hardware store
das **Gebäude**, -	building
das **Gefängnis**, -se	prison, jail
das **Lebensmittel-geschäft**, -e	grocery store

das **Rathaus**, ̈-er (R)	town hall
das **Schreibwaren-geschäft**, -e	stationery store
das **Stadtviertel**, -	district, neighborhood

Ähnliche Wörter

die **Boutique**, -n; der **Kindergarten**, ̈; der **Marktplatz**, ̈-e; der **Parkplatz**, ̈-e; das **Reisebüro**, -s; das **Schuhgeschäft**, -e

Haus und Wohnung	House and Apartment
die **Badewanne**, -n	bathtub
die **Treppe**, -n	stairway
die **Waschküche**, -n	laundry room
die **Zentralheizung**	central heating
der **Aufzug**, ̈-e	elevator
der **Ausblick**, -e	view
der **Quadratmeter (qm)**, -	square meter (m^2)
der **Stock, Stockwerke**	floor, story
im **ersten Stock**[*]	on the second floor
das **Dach**, ̈-er	roof
das **Waschbecken**, -	(wash)basin

[*]The first floor is called **das Erdgeschoss.** All levels above the first floor are referred to as **Stockwerke.** Thus, **der erste Stock** refers to the second floor, and so on.

die Garage, -n [gara:ʒə]; die Terrasse, -n; die Toilette, -n;
der Balkon, -e; der Keller, - (R); der Weinkeller, -; das
Bad, -̈er; das Esszimmer, -; das Schlafzimmer, -; das
Wohnzimmer, -

Haus und Garten — House and Garden

die Bürste, -n	brush
die Gießkanne, -n	watering can
die Kommode, -n	dresser
die Seife, -n	soap
der Besen, -	broom
der Frühjahrsputz	spring cleaning
der Gartenschlauch, -̈e	garden hose
der Müll	trash, garbage
der Putzlappen, -	cloth, rag (for cleaning)
der Rasenmäher, -	lawn mower
der Schrank, -̈e (R)	closet; cupboard
der Kleiderschrank, -̈e	clothes closet, wardrobe
der Sessel, - (R)	armchair
der Spiegel, -	mirror
der Staubsauger, -	vacuum cleaner
der Vorhang, -̈e	drapery, curtain
das Bügeleisen, -	iron
das Kopfkissen, -	pillow
die Möbel (pl.)	furniture

Ähnliche Wörter

die Palme, -n; die Pflanze, -n (R); die Stereoanlage, -n;
die Waschmaschine, -n; der Nachttisch, -e; das Bett, -en
(R); das Möbelstück, -e; das Poster, -; das Sofa, -s

Wohnmöglichkeiten — Living Arrangements

die Skihütte, -n	ski lodge
die Villa, Villen	mansion
die Wohngemeinschaft, -en	shared housing
das Haus, -̈er (R)	house
das Bauernhaus, -̈er	farmhouse
das Baumhaus, -̈er	tree house
das Einfamilienhaus, -̈er	single-family home
das Hochhaus, -̈er	high-rise building
das Reihenhaus, -̈er	row house, town house

Ähnliche Wörter

das Hausboot, -e; das Iglu, -s; das Studentenheim, -e (R)

Auf Wohnungssuche — Looking for a Room or Apartment

die Anzeige, -n	ad
die Kaution, -en	security deposit
die Miete, -n	rent
die Mieterin, -nen	female renter
die Suchanzeige, -n	housing-wanted ad
die Vermieterin, -nen	landlady
der Mieter, -	male renter
der Vermieter, -	landlord
die Nebenkosten (pl.)	extra costs (e.g., utilities)

Sonstige Substantive — Other Nouns

die Bucht, -en	bay
die Nähe	vicinity
in der Nähe	in the vicinity
die Seite, -n	side; page
die Viertelstunde, -n	quarter hour
die Zugfahrkarte, -n	train ticket
das Ausland	foreign countries
im Ausland	abroad
das Benzin	gasoline
das Land, -̈er	country (rural)
auf dem Land	in the country
das Mitglied, -er	member

Verben — Verbs

ab·trocknen	to dry (dishes)
ab·wischen	to wipe clean
auf·wischen	to mop (up)
begegnen (+ dat.)	to meet
bügeln	to iron
fehlen (+ dat.)	to be missing
geben, gibt, gegeben	to give
es gibt ...	there is/are . . .
gibt es ...? (R)	is/are there . . . ?
gefallen, gefällt, gefallen (+ dat.)	to be to one's liking, to please
es gefällt mir	I like it
gehören (+ dat.)	to belong to
helfen, hilft, geholfen (+ dat.)	to help
mieten	to rent
passen (+ dat.)	to fit
putzen (R)	to clean
Rad fahren, fährt ... Rad, ist Rad gefahren	to bicycle
schaden (+ dat.)	to be harmful to
schmecken (+ dat.)	to taste good to
Staub saugen	to vacuum
stehen, gestanden (R)	to stand
stehen, gestanden (+ dat.)	to suit
tippen (R)	to type
übernachten	to stay overnight
vermieten	to rent out

vor·stellen	to introduce, present
sich etwas vorstellen	to imagine something
zu·hören (+ *dat.*)	to listen to

Ähnliche Wörter

kosten (R); wieder hören; auf Wiederhören!; zurück·kommen, ist zurückgekommen

Adjektive und Adverbien	Adjectives and Adverbs
angenehm	pleasant
dunkel	dark
eigen	own
hell	light
hoch	high
möbliert	furnished
nah	close
warm	heated, heat included
weit	far
wie weit weg?	how far away?

Ähnliche Wörter

attraktiv, dumm, leicht, liberal, modern

Sonstige Wörter und Ausdrücke	Other Words and Expressions
bei (R)	at; with
bei deinen Eltern	with/at your parents'
bei einer Bank	at a bank
ist ein/eine ... dabei?	does it come with a . . . ?
drin/darin	in it
egal	equal, same
das ist mir egal	it doesn't matter to me
gegenüber	opposite; across
gleich gegenüber	right across the way
gleich	right, directly
gleich um die Ecke	right around the corner
inklusive	included (utilities)
knapp	just, barely
möglichst (+ *adverb*)	as . . . as possible
ob	if, whether
prima!	great!
unter (R)	below, beneath; among
wegen	on account of; about

Strukturen und Übungen

6.1 Dative verbs

Dative verbs are verbs that require a dative object.

6.1 *Dativverben.* This section introduces another major use of the dative case. Verbs with dative and accusative objects were introduced in Section 5.1. Of all these dative verbs, *gefallen* is probably used most. Provide sts. with a lot of input containing the verb. Point out that the English equivalent is *to please* and that the thing *liked* is the subject of the verb. Sts. frequently equate *gefallen* with *to like*, and errors in its use may persist for a long time.

The dative object usually indicates the person to whom or for whom something is done. The dative case can be seen as the partner case. The "something" that is done (or given) is in the accusative case (it is the direct object).

Ich schenke **dir ein Bügeleisen.**	*I'll give you an iron. (I'll give an iron to you.)*
Ich kaufe **meinem Bruder ein Buch.**	*I'll buy my brother a book. (I'll buy a book for my brother.)*

Certain verbs, called "dative verbs," require only a subject and a dative object; there is no accusative object. These verbs fall into two groups.

In Group 1, both the subject and the dative object are persons.

antworten	*to answer*
begegnen	*to meet*
gratulieren	*to congratulate*
helfen	*to help*
zuhören	*to listen to*

Er antwortete mir nicht.	*He didn't answer me.*
Wir begegneten dem alten Vermieter.	*We met the old landlord.*
Ich gratuliere dir zum Geburtstag.	*Happy Birthday! (I congratulate you on your birthday.)*
Soll ich dir helfen?	*Do you want me to help you?*
Ich höre dir genau zu.	*I'm listening to you carefully.*

In Group 2, the subject is usually a thing; the dative object is the person who experiences or owns the thing.

gehören	*to belong to*
passen	*to fit*
schaden	*to be harmful to*
schmecken	*to taste good to*
stehen	*to suit*

Diese Poster gehören mir.	*These posters belong to me.*
Diese Hose passt mir nicht.	*These pants don't fit me.*
Rauchen schadet der Gesundheit.	*Smoking is bad for (damages) your health.*
Schmeckt Ihnen der Fisch?	*Does the fish taste good to you?*
Blau steht dir gut.	*Blue suits you well.*

Note that the following Group 2 verbs express ideas that are rendered very differently in English.

fehlen	*to be missing*
gefallen	*to be to one's liking, to please*

Mir fehlt ein Buch.	*I'm missing a book.*
Gefällt Ihnen dieser Schrank?	*Do you like this cupboard? (Does this cupboard please you?)*

Minidialoge

Ergänzen Sie das Verb. Nützliche Wörter:

antworten
begegnen
fehlen
gefallen
gehören
gratulieren
helfen
passen
schaden
schmecken
stehen
zuhören

1. MONIKA: Schau, ich habe mir einen neuen MP3-Spieler gekauft.
   KATRIN: Der ist aber toll! Der _____ mir!
2. MARTA: Hallo, Willi. Ich habe gehört, du hast endlich eine Wohnung gefunden. Ich _____ dir ganz herzlich.
   WILLI: Danke. Das ist aber lieb von dir.
3. FRAU RUF: Jochen, kannst du mir bitte _____? Ich kann die Vorhänge nicht allein tragen.
   HERR RUF: Ja, ich komme.
4. FRAU GRETTER: _____ Ihnen der Salat?
   HERR SIEBERT: Ja, sehr gut, die Soße ist ausgezeichnet.
5. FRAU KÖRNER: Dieser Rock _____ mir nicht. Ich brauche doch Größe 42.
   VERKÄUFER: Ich seh mal nach, ob wir Größe 42 haben.
6. JÜRGEN: Wem _____ denn dieser neue Staubsauger?
   SILVIA: Mir. Ich habe ihn gestern gekauft.
7. FRAU SCHULZ: Was suchst du, Albert? _____ dir etwas?
   ALBERT: Ja, ich kann mein Heft nicht finden.
8. FRAU KÖRNER: Wissen Sie, wer mir am Marktplatz _____ ist, Herr Siebert?
   HERR SIEBERT: Nein, wer denn?
   FRAU KÖRNER: Die Mutter von Maria. Und wissen Sie, was die mir erzählt hat?
   HERR SIEBERT: Nein, was denn?
   FRAU KÖRNER: Also, ...
9. ARZT: Also, Herr Ruf, Sie müssen jetzt wirklich mit dem Rauchen aufhören. Nikotin _____ Ihrer Gesundheit!
   HERR RUF: Aber, Herr Doktor, dann habe ich ja gar keine Freude mehr im Leben.
10. STEFAN: Entschuldigung, Frau Schulz, ich habe Ihnen nicht _____. Können Sie das noch mal wiederholen?
    FRAU SCHULZ: Na, gut.

Interview

1. Wem haben Sie neulich[1] gratuliert?
2. Wem sind Sie neulich begegnet?
3. Welches Essen schmeckt Ihnen am besten?
4. Wie steht Ihnen Ihr Lieblingshemd?
5. Wie gefällt Ihnen Ihre Wohnung oder Ihr Zimmer?
6. Welches Möbelstück fehlt Ihnen in der Wohnung oder im Zimmer?

[1]recently

6.2 Location vs. destination: two-way prepositions with the dative or accusative case

Wo asks about location. Questions about location are answered with a preposition + dative.

The prepositions **in** (*in*), **an** (*on, at*), **auf** (*on top of*), **vor** (*before*), **hinter** (*behind*), **über** (*above*), **unter** (*underneath*), **neben** (*next to*), and **zwischen** (*between*) are used with both the dative and accusative cases. When they refer to a fixed location, the dative case is required. In these instances, the prepositional phrase answers the question **wo** (*where [at]*).

Wissen Sie noch?

The prepositions **in, an,** and **auf** use the dative case when they indicate location.

Review grammar 5.4.

6.2. *Akkusativ-/Dativpräpositionen.* This section completes the introduction of the use of two-way prepositions with the dative which was begun in Section 5.4 with *in, an,* and *auf*.

To keep meaning (and a little humor) in this presentation and practice of preposition usage, you might want to ask sts. why things are where they are in the various illustrations—why the tennis shoes are in the bookcase, the cat under the sofa, etc.

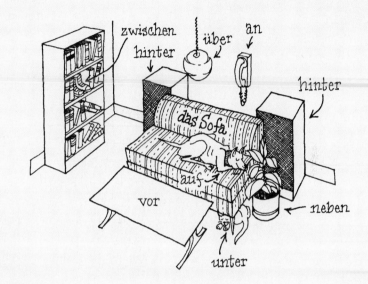

Im Wohnzimmer steht ein Sofa.
Hinter dem Sofa stehen zwei große Boxen.
An der Wand hängt ein Telefon.
Auf dem Sofa liegt ein Hund.
Unter dem Sofa liegt eine Katze.
Vor dem Sofa steht ein Tisch.
Über dem Sofa hängt eine Lampe.
Neben dem Sofa steht eine große Pflanze.
Zwischen den Büchern stehen Tennisschuhe.

Wohin asks about placement or destination. Questions about placement or destination are answered with a preposition + accusative.

When these prepositions describe movement toward a place or a destination, they are used with the accusative case. In these instances, the prepositional phrase answers the question **wohin** (*where [to]*).

Peter hat das Sofa **ins Wohnzimmer** gestellt.
Die Boxen hat er **hinter das Sofa** gestellt.
Das Telefon hat er **an die Wand** gehängt.
Der Hund hat sich gleich **auf das Sofa** gelegt.
Die Katze hat sich **unter das Sofa** gelegt.
Peter hat den Tisch **vor das Sofa** gestellt.
Die Lampe hat er **über das Sofa** gehängt.
Die große Pflanze hat er **neben das Sofa** gestellt.
Und seine Tennisschuhe hat er **zwischen die Bücher** gestellt.

	Wo?	Wohin?
	Location Dative	Placement/Destination Accusative
Masculine	Es ist auf **dem** Stuhl. *It is on the table.*	Leg es auf **den** Stuhl. *Put it on the table.*
Neuter	Es ist auf **dem** Bett. *It is on the bed.*	Leg es auf **das** Bett. *Put it on the bed.*
Feminine	Es ist auf **der** Kommode. *It is on the bureau.*	Leg es auf **die** Kommode. *Put it on the bureau.*
Plural	Es steht vor **den** Boxen. *It is in front of the speakers.*	Stell es vor **die** Boxen. *Put it in front of the speakers.*

Achtung!

in + dem = im
an + dem = am

in + das = ins
an + das = ans

Übung 3 | Alberts Zimmer

Üb. 3. For homework or class work. Use your PF and objects and people in the classroom for additional practice.

Schauen Sie sich Alberts Zimmer an.

1. Wo ist Albert?
2. Wo ist der Spiegel?
3. Wo ist der Kühlschrank?
4. Wo ist das Deutschbuch?
5. Wo ist die Lampe?
6. Wo ist der Computer?
7. Wo sind die Schuhe?
8. Wo ist die Hose?
9. Wo ist das Poster von Berlin?
10. Wo ist die Katze?

Übung 4 | Mein Zimmer

Üb. 4. Assign as written homework and check in class. Have one st. read his or her description out loud in class while the other sts. draw a picture of the room described. Then ask sts. to compare their drawings in groups of 3 and to ask questions in cases of disagreement.

Beschreiben Sie Ihr Zimmer möglichst genau. Schreiben Sie mindestens acht Sätze mit verschiedenen Präpositionen.

MODELL: Das Bett ist unter dem Fenster. Rechts neben dem Bett steht ein Nachttisch ...

6.3　Word order: time before place

In a German sentence, a time expression usually precedes a place expression. Note that this sequence is often reversed in English sentences.

Ich gehe heute Abend in die Bibliothek.

I'm going to the library tonight.

Übung 5 | Wo sind Sie wann?

Üb. 5. Assign for homework. Remind sts. to begin the sentences with *ich* and to create their own answers besides using those listed.

Bilden Sie Sätze aus den Satzteilen.

MODELL: heute Abend → Ich bin heute Abend im Kino.

1. heute Abend	in der Klasse
2. am Nachmittag	bei meinen Eltern
3. um 16 Uhr	im Bett
4. in der Nacht	auf einer Party
5. am frühen Morgen	im Urlaub
6. am Montag	am Frühstückstisch
7. am ersten August	in der Mensa
8. an Weihnachten	in der Bibliothek
9. im Winter	?
10. am Wochenende	

6.4. *Präpositionen: Antwort auf wohin?* This section presents sets of prepositions grouped according to their meaning rather than their form. Answers to the question *Wohin?* include both two-way and dative prepositions. This is a complex topic, and the correct choice of preposition and use of case are acquired only very gradually.

6.4　Direction: *in/auf* vs. *zu/nach*

Direction:
in/auf + accusative; **zu/nach** + dative

To refer to the place where you are going, use either **in** or **auf** + accusative, **zu** + dative, or **nach** + place name.

Albert geht **in die** Kirche.	*Albert goes to church.*
Katrin geht **auf die** Bank.	*Katrin goes to the bank.*
Heidi fährt **zum** Flughafen.	*Heidi drives to the airport.*
Rolf fliegt **nach** Deutschland.	*Rolf is flying to Germany.*

A. **in** + accusative

in for most buildings and enclosed spaces

In general, use **in** when you plan to enter a building or an enclosed space.

Heute Nachmittag gehe ich **in die Bibliothek.**	*This afternoon I'll go to (into) the library.*
Abends gehe ich **ins Kino.**	*In the evening I go to (into) the movies.*
Morgen fahre ich **in die Stadt.**	*Tomorrow I'll drive to (into) the city.*

in for countries with a definite article

Also use **in** with the names of countries that have a definite article, such as **die Schweiz, die Türkei,** and **die USA.**

Herr Frisch fliegt oft **in die** USA.	*Mr. Frisch often flies to the USA.*
Claire fährt **in die** Schweiz.	*Claire is going to Switzerland.*
Mehmet fährt alle zwei Jahre **in die** Türkei.	*Mehmet goes to Turkey every two years.*

B. auf + accusative

Use **auf** instead of **in** when the destination is a public building such as the post office, the bank, or the police station.

> Ich brauche Briefmarken. Ich
>   gehe **auf die** Post.
> *I need stamps. I'm going to the post office.*
>
> Ich brauche Geld. Ich gehe **auf
>   die** Bank.
> *I need money. I'm going to the bank.*

Zu and *nach* are the first dative prepositions presented. In this usage, *nach* is not followed by an article that indicates case. *Mit* and *bei* are introduced in Section 6.6; other dative prepositions are presented in Section 10.1.

zu for specifically named buildings, places in general, open spaces, and to people's places

C. zu + dative

Use **zu** to refer to destinations that are specific names of buildings, places or open spaces such as a playing field, or people.

> Ernst geht **zu** McDonald's.
> *Ernst is going to McDonald's.*
>
> Hans geht **zum** Sportplatz.
> *Hans goes to the playing field.*
>
> Andrea geht **zum** Arzt.
> *Andrea goes to the doctor.*

Note that **zu Hause** (*at home*) does not indicate destination but rather location.

zu Hause = *at home*

D. nach + place name

Use **nach** with names of countries and cities that have no article. Note that this applies to the vast majority of countries and cities.

> Renate fliegt **nach Paris.**
> *Renate is flying to Paris.*
>
> Melanie fährt **nach Österreich.**
> *Melanie is driving to Austria.*

nach Hause = *(going/coming) home*

Also use **nach** in the idiomatic construction **nach Hause** (*going/coming home*).

Übung 6 | ## Situationen

Heute ist Montag. Wohin gehen oder fahren die folgenden Personen?

MODELL: Katrin sucht ein Buch. → Sie geht in die Bibliothek.

> zum Arzt
> zum Flughafen
> zu ihrem Freund
> zum Fußballplatz
> ins Hotel
> auf die Post
> in den Supermarkt
> zur Tankstelle
> ins Theater
> in den Wald

Achtung!

in + das = ins
auf + das = aufs
zu + dem = zum
zu + der = zur

1. Albert ist krank.
2. Hans möchte Fußball spielen.
3. Frau Schulz ist auf Reisen in einer fremden[1] Stadt. Sie braucht einen Platz zum Schlafen.
4. Herr Ruf braucht Benzin.
5. Herr Thelen braucht Lebensmittel.
6. Herr Wagner muss Briefmarken kaufen.
7. Jürgen und Silvia gehen Pilze[2] suchen.
8. Jutta möchte mit ihrem Freund sprechen.
9. Mehmet möchte in die Türkei fliegen.
10. Renate möchte ein Musical sehen.

[1]foreign [2]mushrooms

KAPITEL 6   Wohnen

6.5 Separable-prefix verbs: the present tense and the perfect tense

Wissen Sie noch?

Separable-prefix verbs consist of a prefix plus an infinitive. In the present tense, the verb and the prefix form the **Satzklammer.**

Review grammar 1.5 and 3.5.

The infinitive of a separable-prefix verb consists of a prefix such as **auf, mit,** or **zu** followed by the base verb.

aufstehen	*to get up*
mitkommen	*to come along*
zuschauen	*to watch*

Most prefixes are derived from prepositions and adverbs.

abwaschen	*to do the dishes*
fernsehen	*to watch TV*

A. The Present Tense

Separable prefixes are placed at the end of the independent clause.

1. Independent clauses: In an independent clause in the present tense, the conjugated form of the base verb is in second position and the prefix is in last position.

Ich **stehe** jeden Morgen um sieben Uhr **auf.**	*I get up at seven every morning.*

Separable prefixes are "reconnected" to the base verb in dependent clauses.

2. Dependent clauses: In a dependent clause, the prefix and the base verb form a single verb. It appears at the end of the clause and is conjugated.

Rolf sagt, dass er jeden Morgen um sechs Uhr **aufsteht.**	*Rolf says that he gets up at six every morning.*
Hast du nicht gesagt, dass du heute **abwäschst?**	*Didn't you say that you would do the dishes today?*

Separable prefixes stay attached to the infinitive.

3. Modal verb constructions: In an independent clause with a modal verb (**wollen, müssen,** etc.), the infinitive of the separable-prefix verb is in last position. In a dependent clause with a modal verb, the separable-prefix verb is in the second-to-last position, and the modal verb is in the last position.

Jutta möchte ihren Freund **anrufen.**	*Jutta wants to call her boyfriend.*
Ernst hat schlechte Laune, wenn er nicht **fernsehen** darf.	*Ernst is in a bad mood when he's not allowed to watch TV.*

Wissen Sie noch?

The perfect tense is formed with **haben/sein** plus the past participle.

Review grammar 4.5.

B. The Perfect Tense

The past participle of a separable-prefix verb is a single word, consisting of the past participle of the base verb + the prefix.

Separable prefixes precede the **-ge-** marker in past participles.

Infinitive	Past Participle
auf**stehen**	auf**gestanden**
um**ziehen**	um**gezogen**
weg**bringen**	weg**gebracht**

6.5. *Zweiteilige Verben: Präsens und Perfekt.* This section consolidates descriptions of separable-prefix verbs given in Sections 1.5, 3.5, and 4.5. It summarizes the use of the present and present perfect tenses of these verbs in main and dependent clauses and with modals. For changes resulting from the spelling reform, see the IM.

Note that the prefix does not influence the formation of the past participle of the base verb; it is simply attached to it.

Herr Wagner **hat** gestern die Garage **aufgeräumt.** *Mr. Wagner cleaned up his garage yesterday.*

Ich **habe** vor einer Stunde **angerufen.** *I called an hour ago.*

Übung 7 | Minidialoge

Üb. 7. Point out that some blanks are to be filled with either a prefix or a verb form, but others represent the prefix and verb form in a single word.

Ergänzen Sie die Sätze.

ankommen
anrufen
aufräumen
aufstehen
ausmachen
einladen
fernsehen
mitkommen
mitnehmen
umziehen

1. HERR WAGNER: Ernst, aufwachen! Hast du nicht gestern gesagt, dass du heute um 7 Uhr _____?
   ERNST: Ich bin aber noch so müde!
2. FRAU WAGNER: Andrea, jetzt aber Schluss[1]! Ich _____ᵃ den Fernseher jetzt _____ᵇ. Du wirst noch dumm, wenn du den ganzen Tag nur _____ᶜ.
   ANDREA: Aber, Mami, nur noch das Ende. Der Film ist doch gleich vorbei!
3. SILVIA: Entschuldigen Sie bitte! Wann _____ᵃ der Zug aus Hamburg _____ᵇ?
   BAHNANGESTELLTER: Um 14 Uhr 56.
4. ANDREAS: Hallo, Jürgen. Ich habe gehört, dass ihr bald eine neue Wohnung habt. Wann _____ᵃ ihr denn _____ᵇ?
   JÜRGEN: Nächstes Wochenende.
5. MARTA: Hallo, Sofie. Ich habe morgen Geburtstag und ich möchte dich gern zu einer kleinen Feier _____.
   SOFIE: Das ist aber nett von dir. Ich komme gern.
6. CLAIRE: Hallo, Melanie. Wo ist Josef?
   MELANIE: Er ist zu Hause. Er _____ᵃ heute sein Zimmer _____ᵇ und das dauert bei ihm immer etwas länger.
7. JÜRGEN: Hallo, Silvia. Ich fahre heute mit dem Auto zur Uni. Willst du _____ᵃ?
   SILVIA: Ja, gern. Schön, dass du mich _____ᵇ.
8. KATRIN: Hier ist meine Telefonnummer. Warum _____ᵃ du mich nicht mal _____ᵇ!
   HEIDI: Gut, das mach' ich mal.

Übung 8 | Am Sonntag

Üb 8. Assign for homework and check in class.

Gestern war Sonntag. Was haben die folgenden Personen gestern gemacht?

Nützliche Wörter: abtrocknen, anrufen, anziehen, aufwachen, ausgehen, ausziehen, fernsehen, zurückkommen

[1]jetzt ... *finish up now*

Andrea

Kino →

Katrin und Peter

Heidi

Frau Schulz

Herr Ruf

Jürgen

Schlaf-zimmer

BAD

KÜCHE

Abendkleid

Jutta

aus Bulgarien

Maria

Herr Thelen

6.6 *Dativpräpositionen: mit und bei.* The introduction of dative prepositions continues here with *mit* and *bei*. Point out the difference between *mit* the preposition and *mit* the separable prefix, which occurred in *Üb. 7.* Sts. sometimes confuse prepositions and prefixes that have the same form (*an, auf, usw*).

6.6 The prepositions *mit* and *bei* + dative

The prepositions **mit** (*with, by*) and **bei** (*near, with*) are followed by the dative case.

Masculine	Neuter	Feminine	Plural
mit dem Staubsauger	mit dem Bügeleisen	mit der Bürste	mit den Eltern
beim Onkel	beim Fenster	bei der Tür	bei den Eltern

Strukturen und Übungen

233

Mit corresponds to the preposition *with* in English and is used in similar ways.

Herr Wagner fegt die Terrasse **mit** seinem neuen Besen.	*Mr. Wagner sweeps the patio with his new broom.*
Ich gehe **mit** meinen Freunden ins Kino.	*I'm going to the movies with my friends.*
Ich möchte ein Haus **mit** einem offenen Kamin.	*I want a house with a fireplace.*

Use **mit** with means of transportation.

The preposition **mit** also indicates the means of transportation; in this instance it corresponds to the English preposition *by*. Note the use of the definite article in German.

Rolf fährt **mit** dem Bus zur Uni.	*Rolf goes to the university by bus.*
Renate fährt **mit** dem Auto zur Arbeit.	*Renate drives to work (goes to work) by car.*

The preposition **bei** may refer to a place in the vicinity of another place; in this instance it corresponds to the English preposition *near*.

Bad Harzburg liegt **bei** Goslar.	*Bad Harzburg is near Goslar.*

The preposition **bei** also indicates placement with a person, a company, or an institution; in these instances it corresponds to the English prepositions *with*, *at*, or *for*.

Ich wohne **bei** meinen Eltern.	*I'm living (staying) with my parents / at my parents'.*
Hans arbeitet **bei** McDonald's.	*Hans works at (for) McDonald's.*

	German	English
Instrument	mit dem Hammer	*with the hammer*
Togetherness	mit Freunden	*with friends*
Means of transportation	mit dem Flugzeug	*by airplane*
Vicinity	bei München	*near Munich*
Somebody's place	bei den Eltern	*(staying) with parents*
Place of employment	bei McDonald's	*at McDonald's*

Übung 9 | Im Haus und im Garten

Üb 9. Assign as homework and check in class.

Womit machen Sie die folgenden Aktivitäten?

MODELL: s1: Womit mähst du den Rasen?
s2: Mit dem Rasenmäher.

1. Kaffee kochen	der Besen
2. Staub saugen	das Bügeleisen
3. die Zähne putzen	der Computer
4. den Boden fegen	der Gartenschlauch
5. bügeln	die Gießkanne
6. einen Brief tippen	die Kaffeemaschine
7. die Blumen im Garten gießen	der Putzlappen
8. den Boden wischen	der Staubsauger
9. die Blumen in der Wohnung gießen	die Zahnbürste

Übung 10 | Minidialoge

Ergänzen Sie die Sätze mit der Präposition **mit** oder **bei**.

1. FRAU KÖRNER: Fahren Sie _____^a dem Bus oder _____^b dem Fahrrad zur Arbeit?

   MICHAEL PUSCH: _____^c dem Bus. Ich arbeite jetzt _____^d Siemens. Das ist am anderen Ende von München.

2. PETER: Wohnst du in Krefeld _____^a deinen Eltern?

   ROLF: Ja, sie haben ein wunderschönes Haus _____^b einem riesigen Garten.

   PETER: Liegt Krefeld eigentlich _____^c Dortmund?

   ROLF: Nein, nach Dortmund fährt man über eine Stunde _____^d dem Auto.

3. JÜRGEN: Oh je, jetzt habe ich deinen Gummibaum[1] umgeworfen[2]! Soll ich die Erde[3] _____^a dem Staubsauger aufsaugen?

   SILVIA: Mach es lieber _____^b dem Besen. Er steht _____^c der Kellertür.

[1]*rubber plant* [2]*knocked over* [3]*dirt*

Albrecht Altdorfer: *Donaulandschaft mit Schloss Wörth* (1522), Alte Pinakothek, München

ALBRECHT ALTDORFER

Albrecht Altdorfer (1480–1538) war ein Maler und Kupferstecher[1] in Regensburg. Er ist ein Repräsentant der sogenannten[2] „Donauschule", einer süddeutschen Stilgruppe, die Landschaften bevorzugte[3], während ihre Zeitgenossen[4] lieber Menschen malten.

[1] *copperplate engraver* [2] *so-called* [3] *preferred* [4] *contemporaries*

Unterwegs

Kapitel 7 is about geography and transportation. You will learn more about the geography of the German-speaking world and about the kinds of transportation used by people who live there.

GOALS

The focus of this chapter is travel, with emphasis on sts.' own experiences. Relative pronouns are introduced, although we don't yet expect sts. to use them productively in speaking. Comparative and superlative are introduced as well.

Situationen

Geografie

Grammatik 7.1–7.2

Vocabulary Display
Model pronunciation of geographical terms and
have sts. repeat. Then ask questions related to the
topic: *Gibt es in (your state) Berge oder Hügel? Wo
gibt es Berge? Welche Staaten liegen am Meer? an
den großen Seen? Wie heißt die größte Insel der
Welt? (Grönland) Wo gibt es die schönsten Strände
der Welt? usw.*

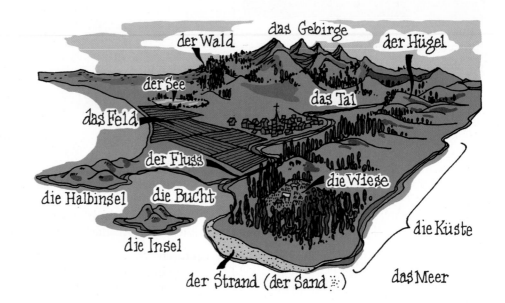

Situation 1 | Erdkunde: Wer weiß – gewinnt

Sit. 1. (See the IM for the use of content-based
activities.) This activity uses relative pronouns.
Stress that this is a guessing game, like "Trivial
Pursuit," not a research task. Sts. can figure out
the answers based on clues given. Have sts. work
in small groups. Afterward, restate definitions as
questions and have sts. answer: *Welcher Fluss fließt
durch Wien? In welchem Wald haben die Germanen
die Römer besiegt? usw.* **Answers:** 1. h, 2. d, 3. i,
4. b, 5. e, 6. a, 7. c, 8. f, 9. j, 10. g.

Cultural note. See the IM for detailed information
on the places and events mentioned here. Bring in
a large map to give sts. an idea where these places
are.

1. Fluss, der durch Wien fließt
2. Wald, in dem die Germanen[1] die Römer[2] besiegt haben
3. Insel in der Ostsee, auf der weiße Kreidefelsen[3] sind
4. Berg, auf dem sich die Hexen treffen
5. See, der zwischen Deutschland, Österreich und der Schweiz liegt
6. Meer, das Europa von Afrika trennt
7. Gebirge in Österreich, in dem man sehr gut Ski fahren kann
8. berühmte Wüste, die in Ostasien liegt
9. Inseln, die vor der Küste von Ostfriesland liegen
10. Fluss, an dem die Lorelei ihr Haar kämmt

a. das Mittelmeer
b. der Brocken im Harz (1 142 Meter hoch)
c. die Kitzbühler Alpen
d. der Teutoburger Wald
e. der Bodensee
f. die Wüste Gobi
g. der Rhein
h. die Donau
i. Rügen
j. die Ostfriesischen Inseln

---

[1]*Teutons*   [2]*Romans*   [3]*chalk cliffs*

Situation 2 | Ratespiel: Stadt, Land, Fluss

Sit. 2. This activity demonstrates the superlative form of adjectives. Sts. work in small groups with whole-class follow-up. Again, encourage them to approach the activity playfully. **Answers:** 1. c, 2. d, 3. f, 4. b, 5. h, 6. e, 7. i, 8. g, 9. a.

Suggestion. Invert columns and play "Jeopardy." Read the answers first, and have sts. respond with the corresponding question.

Cultural note. See the IM for detailed information on the geographic features mentioned here and for ideas for additional activities.

1. Wie heißt der tiefste See der Schweiz?
2. Wie heißt der höchste Berg Österreichs?
3. Wie heißt der längste Fluss Deutschlands?
4. Wie heißt das salzigste Meer der Welt?
5. Wie heißt der größte Gletscher der Alpen?
6. Was ist die heißeste Wüste der Welt?
7. Wie heißt die älteste Universitätsstadt Deutschlands?
8. Wie heißt das kleinste Land, in dem man Deutsch spricht?
9. Wie heißt die berühmteste Höhle in Österreich?

a. die Dachstein-Mammuthöhle
b. das Tote Meer
c. der Genfer See
d. der Großglockner
e. die Libysche Wüste
f. der Rhein
g. Liechtenstein
h. der Große Aletschgletscher
i. Heidelberg

Situation 3 | Informationsspiel: Deutschlandreise

Sit. 3. The corresponding chart is in Appendix A. s1 asks the location of cities labeled with a blank on the map; s2 consults the corresponding map in Appendix A, where missing cities are labeled. s2 tells s1 where to write in the name of each city, using the compass points. Then sts. switch roles: s2 asks about cities labeled with a blank on the map in the appendix; s1 gives location, using the map in the chapter.

Wo liegen die folgenden Städte? Schreiben Sie die Namen der Städte auf die Landkarte.

Aachen, Bayreuth, Dresden, Erfurt, Flensburg, Freiburg, Hannover, Heidelberg, Magdeburg, Wiesbaden

MODELL: S1: Wo liegt Hannover?
s2: Hannover liegt im Norden.
s1: Wo genau?
s2: Südlich von Hamburg.

AA. As a follow-up, photocopy the map onto a transparency and provide one or two *Bundesländer*. Introduce the *Länder* to sts. by saying, e.g., *Halle liegt in Sachsen-Anhalt. Sachsen-Anhalt liegt nördlich von Thüringen,* etc. Then ask sts. a few questions such as *Was liegt östlich von Sachsen-Anhalt? Welches Bundesland liegt im Norden? Welches im Süden? usw.*

Lektüre

Lektüre. (1) Set the scene by asking sts. to look at the picture and describe what is taking place. Ask if they know what river is depicted: *Wie heißt der Fluss, an dem die Lorelei ihr Haar kämmt?* **(2)** Ask sts. to work on *Vor dem Lesen* in small groups. Discuss afterwards. **(3)** Tell sts. that the language of the poem is archaic in some respects, and give them examples. Let sts. read the complete text. Play the audio recording in class. If you and your sts. enjoy singing, sing along after they've heard it once. Later in the semester/quarter, sts. could be challenged to sing the song without accompaniment. **(4)** Make sure sts. understand that they are to complete Part A of *Arbeit mit dem Text* without looking at the text again. Then compare their answers with the text. **(5)** Assign Part B of *Arbeit mit dem Text* for written homework. **(6)** Ask sts. to discuss *Nach dem Lesen* in small groups.

Vor dem Lesen

Schreiben Sie mögliche[1] Antworten auf die folgenden Fragen.

1. Ist das eine lustige oder eine traurige Geschichte? Woher wissen Sie das?
2. Was macht die Frau auf dem Bild? Warum macht sie das?
3. Neben ihr liegt eine Leier[2]. Warum liegt sie da?
4. Was macht der Mann im Boot? Was sollte er machen?
5. Was passiert mit dem Mann im Boot? Spekulieren Sie!

Die Loreley.

Die schönste Jungfrau sitzet
Dort oben wunderbar,
Ihr goldnes Geschmeide blitzet,
Sie kämmt ihr goldenes Haar.

Sie kämmt es mit goldenem Kamme
Und singt ein Lied dabei
Das hat eine wundersame,
Gewaltige Melodei.

Die Lorelei

von Heinrich Heine

Ich weiß nicht, was soll es bedeuten,
dass ich so traurig bin;
ein Märchen aus alten Zeiten,
das kommt mir nicht aus dem Sinn[3].

5 Die Luft ist kühl und es dunkelt[4],
und ruhig fließt der Rhein;
der Gipfel[5] des Berges funkelt[6]
im Abendsonnenschein.

Die schönste Jungfrau[7] sitzet
10 dort oben wunderbar;
ihr goldnes Geschmeide[8] blitzet,
sie kämmt ihr goldenes Haar.

Sie kämmt es mit goldenem Kamme[9]
und singt ein Lied dabei;
15 das hat eine wundersame,
gewaltige[10] Melodei.

Den Schiffer im kleinen Schiffe
ergreift[11] es mit wildem Weh[12];
er schaut nicht die Felsenriffe[13],
20 er schaut nur hinauf in die Höh'.

Ich glaube, die Wellen[14] verschlingen[15]
am Ende Schiffer und Kahn[16];
und das hat mit ihrem Singen
die Lore-Ley getan.

---

[1]*possible* [2]*lyre* [3]*das … I can't forget it* [4]*is growing dark* [5]*peak* [6]*is sparkling* [7]*virgin; young woman*
[8]*jewelry* [9]*comb* [10]*powerful* [11]*seizes* [12]*pain, longing* [13]*cliffs* [14]*waves* [15]*devour, swallow up* [16]*boat*

Arbeit mit dem Text

A. Ergänzen Sie die folgenden Sätze mit Wörtern aus dem Kasten, ohne den Text noch einmal zu lesen. Schauen Sie dann auf das Gedicht und korrigieren Sie Ihre Antworten.

1. Ein Lied _____ mir nicht aus dem Sinn.
2. Die Luft ist _____.
3. Der Fluss _____ ruhig.
4. Der Gipfel _____ im Abendsonnenschein.
5. Das goldene Geschmeide _____.
6. Sie _____ ihr goldenes Haar.
7. Sie _____ ein Lied.
8. Die Wellen _____ das Boot.

funkelt   kühl
kommt
fließt
blitzet
kämmt
singt
verschlingen

B. **Zeit, Ort, Personen und Handlung.** Beantworten Sie die folgenden Fragen und Aufgaben. Schreiben Sie dazu, in welcher Zeile[1] Sie die Antwort gefunden haben.

1. Wann spielt die Geschichte (vor wie vielen Jahren)? Zu welcher Jahreszeit oder Tageszeit spielt die Geschichte? Wie viel Zeit vergeht[2]?
2. Wo spielt die Geschichte (an welchem Fluss)? Beschreiben Sie den Ort!
3. Welche Personen treten auf[3]? Was wissen wir über sie? Was machen sie?
4. Handlung: Bringen Sie die Sätze in die richtige Reihenfolge.

   __4__ Unten auf dem Rhein hört ein Schiffer ihr Singen.
   __1__ Eine schöne Frau sitzt oben auf einem Berg am Rhein.
   __5__ Er schaut fasziniert nach oben zu der Frau.
   __2__ Ihr Schmuck funkelt in der Abendsonne.
   __7__ Sein Schiff sinkt und er ertrinkt[4].
   __3__ Sie kämmt sich und singt ein Lied dabei.
   __6__ Weil er nicht aufpasst, fährt er auf einen Felsen.

Nach dem Lesen

Welche Geschichten kennen Sie, in denen Frauen mit ihrer Schönheit oder mit ihrem Gesang Männer ins Unglück locken[5]? Erzählen Sie!

[1]*line* [2]*passes* [3]*treten ... appear* [4]*drowns* [5]*ins ... lure into misfortune*

Situation 4 | Interview: Landschaften

Sit. 4. In this situation, sts. use the perfect tense while discussing topics related to geography. Ask the class questions such as: *Wer von Ihnen ist schon mal auf einen Berg gestiegen/geklettert? Wo? Mit wem? Wer von Ihnen ist letzten Sommer an einen See gefahren? Sind Sie da windsurfen gegangen? usw.* Then, have sts. choose a partner and interview each other, taking notes.

1. Warst du schon mal im Gebirge? Wo? Was hast du da gemacht? Wie heißt der höchste Berg, den du gesehen (oder bestiegen) hast?
2. Warst du schon mal am Meer? Wo und wann war das? Hast du gebadet? Was hast du sonst noch gemacht?
3. Wohnst du in der Nähe von einem großen Fluss? Wie heißt er? Wie heißt der größte Fluss, an dem du schon warst? Was hast du da gemacht?
4. Wie heißt die interessanteste Stadt, in der du schon warst?
5. Warst du schon mal in der Wüste oder im Dschungel? Wie war das?

Transportmittel

Grammatik 7.1, 7.4

Vocabulary Display
Pronounce the vocabulary and have sts. repeat. Then cover up vocabulary and ask: *Was ist größer? ein Bus oder ein Auto? Was ist schneller? ein Fahrrad oder ein Motorrad? Gibt es in der Nähe von hier eine U-Bahn? Welches Transportmittel benutzen Sie, wenn Sie nach Europa wollen? nach New York City? nach Hause? usw.*

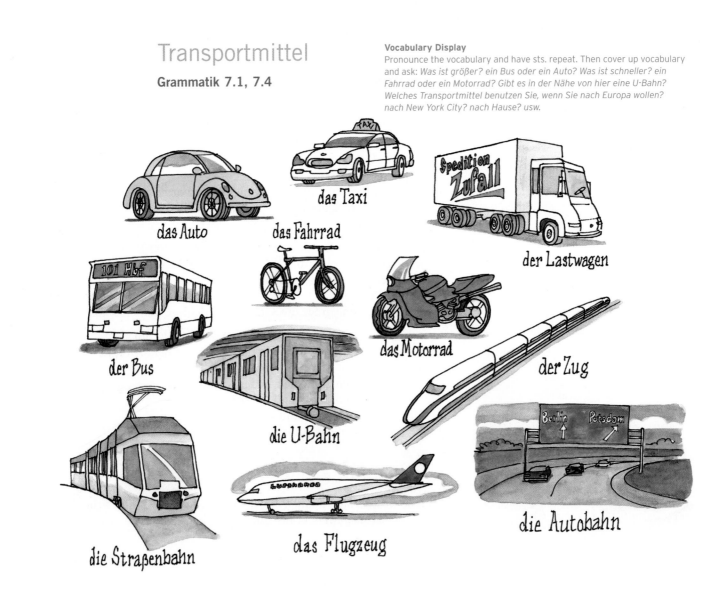

das Auto — das Taxi — das Fahrrad — der Lastwagen — der Bus — die U-Bahn — das Motorrad — der Zug — die Straßenbahn — das Flugzeug — die Autobahn

Masterplan Fahrrad

Wie kann man die Umwelt weniger verschmutzen[1]? Indem man weniger Auto fährt[2]. Wie bringt man Leute dazu, weniger Auto zu fahren? Indem man es leichter macht, mit dem Fahrrad zu fahren. Der Ausschnitt aus **Blickkontakte** stellt den Masterplan Fahrrad der deutschen Regierung[3] vor.

- Warum ist Fahrrad fahren besser als Auto fahren?
- Was ist das Ziel[4] des Masterplans Fahrrad?
- In welchen öffentlichen Verkehrsmitteln kann man das Fahrrad mitnehmen?
- Was sollen Verkehrsschilder zeigen?

Fahrräder machen keinen Lärm[5], verschmutzen nicht die Luft und sind leicht einzuparken.

[1]pollute [2]indem … fährt *by driving less* [3]government [4]goal [5]noise

Videoblick. The selection from the *Blickkontakte* video presents the German government's plans for encouraging people to use bicycles for transportation: more and more informative traffic signs; more bike paths; and more options for taking bikes along when using public transportation. Note: The announcer also refers viewers to a website for more information; this provides sts. a chance to hear how a German speaker reads the "dots" and "slashes" in an Internet address.

Situation 5 | Definitionen: Transportmittel

Sit. 5. Definitions and instructor's questions following the activity demonstrate use of relative pronouns. Have sts. work in small groups, and then ask: *Wie nennt man ein Transportmittel, das fliegt? Wie nennt man das Auto, das in Deutschland die Farbe beige hat und ein Schild auf dem Dach hat? usw.*

1. das Flugzeug
2. die Rakete
3. das Kamel
4. das Fahrrad
5. der Kinderwagen
6. der Zeppelin
7. der Zug
8. das Taxi

a. Transportmittel, das Waggons und eine Lokomotive hat
b. Transportmittel, das fliegt
c. Tier, das viele Beduinen als Transportmittel benutzen
d. Transportmittel, mit dem man zum Mond fliegen kann
e. Auto, das in Deutschland ein gelbes Schild auf dem Dach hat
f. Transportmittel in der Luft, das wie eine Zigarre aussieht
g. Transportmittel mit zwei Rädern, das ohne Benzin fährt
h. Wagen, in dem man Babys transportiert

Situation 6 | Interview

Sit. 6. You will notice that the interview activities are becoming increasingly more like discussions, involving follow-up questions that require sts. to explain their responses. Be sure to model possible answers–e.g., *Ich fahre selten mit dem Bus, weil die Verbindungen so schlecht sind und weil ich nicht gern warte. Ich fahre gern mit dem Zug, weil ich dabei lesen oder stricken kann.* Sts. should take notes on their partner's responses so that they can report them in the follow-up.

1. Welche Transportmittel hast du schon benutzt?
2. Fährst du oft mit der U-Bahn oder mit dem Bus? Warum (nicht)?
3. Fährst du gern mit dem Zug (oder möchtest du gern mal mit dem Zug fahren)? Welche Vorteile/Nachteile hat das Reisen mit dem Zug?
4. Fliegst du gern? Warum (nicht)? Welche Vorteile/Nachteile hat das Reisen mit dem Flugzeug?
5. Fährst du lieber mit dem Auto oder mit öffentlichen Verkehrsmitteln? Warum? Womit fährst du am liebsten?

Situation 7 | Dialog: Im Reisebüro in Berlin

Sit. 7. (See the IM.) This dialogue provides a model for the role-play following it. You may wish to follow the steps for presenting the dialogue without the use of the textbook. Questions for first listening: **1.** *Wohin möchte Renate fahren?* **2.** *Wann möchte sie fahren?* Questions for second listening: **1.** *Wann fährt der InterCity ab?* **2.** *Wann kommt er in Zürich an?* **3.** *Fährt Renate erster oder zweiter Klasse?*

RENATE: Guten Tag.

ANGESTELLTE: Guten Tag. <u>Bitte schön</u>?

RENATE: Ich möchte <u>mit dem Zug</u> nach Zürich fahren.

ANGESTELLTE: <u>Wann</u> möchten Sie denn fahren?

RENATE: Montagmorgen, <u>so</u> früh <u>wie</u> möglich.

ANGESTELLTE: Der erste InterCity geht <u>um sechs Uhr dreißig</u>. Ist das früh genug?

RENATE: Wann ist er denn in Zürich?

ANGESTELLTE: <u>Um vierzehn Uhr fünfundzwanzig</u>.

RENATE: Sehr gut. Reservieren Sie mir bitte einen Platz <u>in der zweiten Klasse</u>.

Situation 8 | Rollenspiel: Am Fahrkartenschalter

Sit. 8. The role for s2 appears in Appendix B.

S1: Sie stehen am Fahrkartenschalter im Bahnhof von Bremen und wollen eine Fahrkarte nach München kaufen. Sie wollen billig fahren, müssen aber vor 16.30 Uhr am Bahnhof in München ankommen. Fragen Sie, wann und wo der Zug abfährt und über welche Städte der Zug fährt.

Lektüre

Lesehilfe

In the following story, detective Julia Falk uses her well-honed skills to investigate a crime. As you read it, you become a detective, too. At right, under **Vor dem Lesen,** are some hints from her "Handbook for a Rookie Detective." They will help you to catch the important details as you read the story. As you might expect, taking notes is part of the investigation. When you take notes during the **Vor dem Lesen** activity, be sure to include: 1) important words to look up in the dictionary, three per paragraph at most; 2) words that seem key to the plot; and 3) interesting facts.

Vor dem Lesen

So lesen Sie wie ein Detektiv ...

1. Setzen Sie sich an einen ruhigen Ort, wo Sie sich konzentrieren können.
2. Legen Sie sich Papier und Schreibzeug bereit.
3. Lesen Sie den ganzen Text durch, um zu wissen, worum es geht.
4. Lesen Sie den Text jetzt absatzweise[1] etwas genauer und machen Sie sich dabei Notizen.
5. Vergleichen Sie Ihre Notizen mit Ihrem Partner oder mit Ihrer Partnerin.

Die Motorradtour

Hallo, Kollegin, wie war's in den Ferien?" Oberinspektor Eichhorn begrüßt Julia Falk mit einem freundschaftlichen Handschlag. „Hoffentlich ist es Ihnen nicht genauso ergangen wie der Familie Andres am Blumenweg 1. Als die von ihrer Reise zurückkehrte, fand sie ein gründlich ausgeraubtes Haus vor." Oberinspektor Eichhorn greift
5 nach einem Bündel Akten[2]. „Na ja, wenn Sie den Fall[3] gleich weiterverfolgen könnten ...? Die meisten Anwohner am Blumenweg haben wir bereits vernommen[4]. Zu befragen wären da noch ein Rentnerpaar, Familie Wächter im Haus Nummer 7, und deren junger Untermieter Heinz Hurtig."

Julia Falk drückt zum dritten Mal den Knopf[5] über dem Schildchen „Heinz Hurtig".
10 Eigenartig, dass er nicht aufmacht. Dabei hat sie doch gerade eben noch einen jungen Mann am Fenster oben stehen sehen. Julia schüttelt verwundert den Kopf. Sie dreht sich um und lässt ihren Blick[6] über den verlassenen[7] Hof und das funkelnagelneue Motorrad unter dem Garagenvordach schweifen.

Ein paar Minuten später klingelt Julia noch ein Mal. Ein Geräusch ist von drinnen zu
15 hören. Na endlich, das hat aber lange gedauert! Heinz Hurtig guckt durch den Türspalt.

---

[1]*one paragraph at a time* [2]*files* [3]*case* [4]*questioned* [5]*button* [6]*glance* [7]*deserted*

„Guten Tag, Herr Hurtig." Julia Falk zückt ihren Ausweis. „Darf ich einen Moment reinkommen? Ich ermittle[1] wegen des Einbruchs bei Familie Andres."

Erst im Flur bemerkt Julia, dass Hurtigs rechter Arm dick einbandagiert in einer Armschlinge liegt. „Hatten Sie einen Unfall[2]?" Heinz Hurtig nickt. „Ich habe letzte
20 Woche mit meinem Motorrad eine Kurve zu schnell genommen. Aber ich hatte noch Glück, ich habe mir bloß den Arm gebrochen."

Heinz Hurtig führt die Inspektorin in die Küche. Auf dem Küchentisch steht ein Teller mit Speck[3] und Rührei[4], daneben eine Tasse mit dampfend heißem Kaffee. „Darf ich Ihnen auch eine Tasse Kaffee anbieten? – Nein? Keinen Kaffee? Nun,
25 was den Einbruch betrifft[5], ich bin ja erst vorgestern von meiner Motorradtour heimgekommen, habe nichts gesehen und gehört. Und, sorry, falls ich ein Alibi brauche – mit meinem verletzten Arm hätte ich wirklich kein Haus ausrauben können, nicht wahr?"

„Leben Sie allein hier?", fragt die Inspektorin. „Nein, mit Schnurrli, meinem
30 Kater." Heinz Hurtig grinst und weist mit dem Kinn zum Fenstersims, wo sich eine prächtige rote Katze wohlig in der Sonne ausstreckt. „Tut mir leid, Herr Hurtig", meint Julia Falk sachlich. „Sie begleiten mich jetzt aufs Präsidium[6]. Mit Ihrem Alibi stimmt nämlich etwas ganz und gar nicht[7]."

Aus: *Aufgepasst, Julia Falk!* von Christine Egger

Arbeit mit dem Text

A. Locate each of the following words in the text, read the hint below, and write down what you think its English equivalent might be. Then check yourself by looking up the words in the glossary at the end of the book.

1. **Handschlag** (Zeile 2) HINT: You already know the word **Hand. Schlagen** means *to beat*, *strike*, or *hit*. How do people sometimes greet with their hands?
2. **ausgeraubt** (Zeile 4) HINT: This is the past participle of the verb **ausrauben.** What English word is similar to **raub** and is related to crime and houses?
3. **weiterverfolgen** (Zeile 5) HINT: **Weiter** is the comparative form of **weit.** The prefix **ver** adds a sense of continuation. The verb **folgen** means *to follow.*
4. **verwundert** (Zeile 11) HINT: The verb **verwundern** means *to surprise;* **verwundert** is the past participle.
5. **funkelnagelneu** (Zeile 12) HINT: The verb **funkeln** means *to sparkle* and **Nagel** means *nail.* In other words, something is so new the nails still sparkle.
6. **Einbruch** (Zeile 17) HINT: The prefix **ein** often means *in.* The word **Bruch** is a noun related to the verb **brechen,** which means *to break.*
7. **Armschlinge** (Zeile 19) HINT: You already know the word for the body part **Arm.** What English word is like **Schlinge** and has to do with an arm injury?
8. **heimgekommen** (Zeile 26) HINT: You know what **Heimweh** means. What English word is like **heim** and combines with *come* to indicate a destination?
9. **ausstrecken** (Zeile 31) HINT: German **-ck-** is occasionally equivalent to English *-tch-.* What might a cat do on a sunny **Fenstersims?**

[1] *am investigating* [2] *accident* [3] *bacon* [4] *scrambled eggs* [5] was ... betrifft *as far as ... is concerned*
[6] *police station* [7] stimmt ... *something isn't right at all*

B. Was ist passiert? Bringen Sie die folgenden Sätze in die richtige Reihenfolge.

   _3_ Als Frau Falk bei Heinz Hurtig klingelt, macht er zuerst nicht auf.

   _5_ Endlich macht Hurtig auf und lässt sie in seine Wohnung.

   _7_ Er erzählt der Kommissarin von seinem Motorradunfall in der vergangenen Woche.

   _6_ Julia bemerkt, dass Hurtig seinen rechten Arm einbandagiert hat.

   _4_ Julia Falk schaut sich inzwischen aufmerksam im Hof um.

  _10_ Julia Falk zweifelt stark an Heinz Hurtigs Alibi.

   _1_ Kommissarin Falk ist gerade aus dem Urlaub zurückgekommen.

   _9_ Sein Alibi ist sein verletzter Arm.

   _2_ Sie soll wegen des Einbruchs bei Familie Andres ermitteln.

   _8_ Weil er erst vor zwei Tagen von der Motorradtour zurückgekommen ist, hat er nichts gesehen und gehört.

Nach dem Lesen

Warum zweifelt Julia Falk am Alibi von Heinz Hurtig? Sammeln Sie alles, was nicht zusammenpasst.

Das Auto

Grammatik 7.3

Vocabulary Display Model pronunciation and have sts. repeat. Then ask: *Ist der Kofferraum vorn oder hinten? Was braucht man, wenn es regnet? Muss man in (your state) mit Sicherheitsgurt fahren? Woher kommt das Auto, dessen Nummernschild Sie sehen? (Neuss) Worauf tritt man, wenn man halten will? usw.* Have sts. guess where the following license plates are from: M (München); H (Hannover); B (Berlin); R (Regensburg); BN (Bonn); L (Leipzig); DD (Dresden); C (Chemnitz).

AA. You might want to ask your sts. to speculate further on the drawing: *Was legt der Mann in den Kofferraum? Warum ist der Mann, der eine Reifenpanne hat, so wütend? usw.*

1. Damit kann man hupen.
2. Daran sieht man, woher das Auto kommt.
3. Darin kann man seine Koffer verstauen.
4. Damit wischt man die Scheiben.

Situation 9 | Definitionen: Die Teile des Autos

Sit. 9. This activity demonstrates the use of *da*-compounds. Have sts. work in small groups to figure out the answers. As a wrap-up, ask: *Worauf setzt man sich? Was braucht man, wenn man bei Regen fährt? usw.*

1. die Bremsen
2. die Scheibenwischer
3. das Autoradio
4. das Lenkrad
5. die Hupe
6. das Nummernschild
7. die Sitze
8. das Benzin
9. der Tank

a. Man setzt sich darauf.
b. Man braucht sie, wenn man bei Regen fährt.
c. Damit lenkt man das Auto.
d. Damit warnt man andere Fahrer oder Fußgänger.
e. Daran sieht man, woher das Auto kommt.
f. Damit hört man Musik und Nachrichten.
g. Damit fährt das Auto.
h. Darin ist das Benzin.
i. Damit hält man den Wagen an.

Situation 10 | Rollenspiel: Ein Auto kaufen

Sit. 10. The role for s2 and the corresponding chart appear in Appendix B.

Cultural note. All cars in Germany must be inspected every two years by *TÜV (Technischer Überwachungsverein)*, the agency that checks brakes, steering, lights, tires, and even rust damage for safety hazards. Once a car has passed the TÜV test, the owner gets a sticker for the license plate that indicates when the next inspection is due.

Cultural note. Because of high gasoline prices in Europe, fuel efficiency is a major concern for many Europeans when selecting a car. It is figured differently from U.S. standards: how many liters per 100 km rather than miles per gallon.

s1: Sie wollen einen älteren Gebrauchtwagen kaufen und lesen deshalb die Anzeigen in der Zeitung. Die Anzeigen für einen Opel Corsa und einen Ford Fiesta sind interessant. Rufen Sie an und stellen Sie Fragen.

Sie haben auch eine Anzeige in die Zeitung gesetzt, weil Sie Ihren VW Golf und Ihren VW Beetle verkaufen wollen. Antworten Sie auf die Fragen der Leute über Ihre Autos.

MODELL: Guten Tag, ich rufe wegen des Opel Corsa an.
Wie alt ist der Wagen?
Welche Farbe hat er?
Wie ist der Kilometerstand?
Wie lange hat er noch TÜV?
Wie viel Benzin braucht er?
Was kostet der Wagen?

Modell	VW Golf	VW Beetle	Opel Corsa	Ford Fiesta
Baujahr	2006	2008	2002	2003
Farbe	rot	gelb	schwarz	blaugrün
Kilometerstand	65 000 km	5 000 km	84 500 km	52 000 km
TÜV	noch 1 Jahr	2 Jahre	6 Monate	fast 2 Jahre
Benzinverbrauch pro 100 km	5,5 Liter	7 Liter	6 Liter	6,5 Liter
Preis	12 500 Euro	17 200 Euro	5 000 Euro	4 000 Euro

Situation 11 | Interview: Das Auto

Sit. 11. In this interview, sts. use the superlative as an attributive adjective, as a predicate adjective, and as an adverb.

Cultural note. You must be 18 to get a driver's license in Germany. (At age 17 you can get a restricted one that requires an accompanying adult.) New drivers take a class at a driving school (*Fahrschule*) and also drive a certain number of hours with a professional instructor. A driver's license doesn't serve as an ID. It is valid for a lifetime. Regarding question 8: Germany is the only country in Europe with no general speed limit on the freeways.

1. Hast du einen Führerschein? Wann hast du ihn gemacht?
2. Was für ein Auto möchtest du am liebsten haben? Warum?
3. Welche Autos findest du am schönsten?
4. Welche Autos findest du am praktischsten (unpraktischsten)? Warum?
5. Wer von deinen Freunden hat das älteste Auto? Wie alt ist es ungefähr? Und wer hat das hässlichste (schnellste, interessanteste)?
6. Mit was für einem Auto möchtest du am liebsten in Urlaub fahren?
7. Was glaubst du: Was ist das teuerste Auto der Welt?
8. Was glaubst du: In welchem Land fährt man am schnellsten?
9. Was glaubst du: Was ist das kleinste Auto der Welt?

Situation 12 | Verkehrsschilder

Kennen Sie diese Verkehrsschilder? Was bedeuten sie?

1. Dieses Verkehrsschild bedeutet „Halt".
2. Hier darf man nicht halten.
3. Wer von rechts kommt, hat Vorfahrt.
4. Hier darf man nur in eine Richtung fahren.
5. Hier darf man nur mit dem Rad fahren.
6. Hier darf man auf dem Fußgängerweg parken.
7. Hier dürfen keine Autos fahren.
8. Achtung Radfahrer!
9. Dieser Weg ist nur für Fußgänger.
10. Hier dürfen keine Motorräder fahren.

Situation 13 | Zum Schreiben: Eine Anzeige

Sie wollen ein Fahrzeug (Auto, Boot, Motorrad, Fahrrad usw.) verkaufen. Schreiben Sie eine Anzeige. Machen Sie sie interessant!

Führerschein

Wie ist das in Ihrem Land?

- Wie alt muss man sein, bevor man den Führerschein machen kann?
- Wie lange dauert die Ausbildung und wo kann man sie machen?
- Was kostet der Führerschein?
- Welche Prüfungen muss man bestehen[1], um den Führerschein zu bekommen?
- Was braucht man sonst noch (z.B. einen Sehtest)?
- Braucht man einen besonderen Führerschein für LKWs[2] oder Motorräder?

KLI. Discuss the ad in class. Have sts. answer and talk about the following questions with a partner or in a group: *Was bietet die Fahrschule an? Welchen Punkt findest du am wichtigsten? Wie kann man die Fahrschule kontaktieren? Welche Kontaktmöglichkeit findest du am besten? Ist es wichtig für dich, einen Mann oder eine Frau als Fahrlehrer/in zu haben? Wenn ja, warum?*

Um in Deutschland einen Führerschein zu bekommen, muss man eine Fahrschule besuchen. Diese wird von einem geprüften[3] Fahrlehrer geleitet. Die Ausbildung teilt sich in einen theoretischen und in einen praktischen Teil. Die theoretische Ausbildung besteht aus mindestens 28 Stunden Unterricht. Außerdem braucht man einen Erste-Hilfe-Kurs und einen Sehtest. Wenn man anschließend die theoretische Prüfung ablegt, wird geprüft, ob man die Regeln und das Verhalten im Straßenverkehr theoretisch beherrscht.

Bei der praktischen Ausbildung lernt man zuerst in ungefähr 20 Stunden das Fahren und Teilnehmen am Straßenverkehr. Außerdem muss man noch mindestens 12 Stunden auf Landstraßen, auf der Autobahn und im Dunkeln fahren. Danach muss man eine praktische Prüfung ablegen, die ungefähr 45 Minuten dauert.

In Deutschland wie auch in der Schweiz und Österreich kann man mit 16 Jahren anfangen das Autofahren zu lernen. Mit 17 Jahren hat man dann eine eingeschränkte Fahrerlaubnis und eine Begleitperson muss bei jeder Fahrt dabei sein. Ab dem 18. Lebensjahr darf man dann auch allein fahren. Wenn man relativ schnell lernt und auch nicht durchfällt[4], dann kostet der Führerschein ungefähr 1 500,– Euro. In Österreich und der Schweiz ist es ähnlich, nur kann man hier Übungsfahrten auch mit einem Familienmitglied als Fahrlehrer machen.

Den Führerschein bekommt man in allen deutschsprachigen Ländern erst einmal zwei Jahre auf Probe. Während dieser Zeit darf man keine ernsten Verstöße[5] begehen, wie zu schnell oder alkoholisiert fahren, sonst wird einem der Führerschein wieder weggenommen. Für Motorräder, LKWs oder Busse braucht man jeweils einen eigenen Führerschein mit eigenen Fahrstunden und eigenen Prüfungen.

Wie ist das in Deutschland?

1. Wie alt muss man in Deutschland für den Führerschein sein?
2. Wo muss man in Deutschland die Ausbildung machen?
3. Was kostet die Ausbildung insgesamt?
4. Aus wie vielen Stunden besteht die theoretische Ausbildung?
5. Was darf man in der Probezeit[6] nicht tun?
6. Was braucht man zum Motorradfahren?

[1] *pass* [2] = Last̲kr̲aft̲wagen: *trucks* [3] *certified* [4] *fails* [5] *violations* [6] *probation period* [7] *classy*

Reiseerlebnisse

Grammatik 7.4–7.5

Vocabulary Display
This section introduces travel vocabulary and reviews the perfect tense.

AA. Show slides of one of your trips to a German-speaking country, or, if you are a native of a German-speaking country, show slides of your hometown. Describe each slide and have sts. take notes. Then, show the slides again, but this time have the sts. describe what is happening in each scene. Also, invite sts. in the class to bring in slides from a trip and talk about them.

Im letzten Urlaub waren Herr und Frau Frisch in Italien.

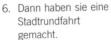

1. Am Morgen sind Herr und Frau Frisch am Strand spazieren gegangen.

2. Dann sind sie im Meer geschwommen.

3. Zu Mittag haben sie Spaghetti gegessen.

4. Später sind sie in die Stadt gefahren.

5. Zuerst hat Frau Frisch dort Souvenirs gekauft.

6. Dann haben sie eine Stadtrundfahrt gemacht.

7. Am Abend haben sie Wein getrunken.

Situation 14 | Umfrage: Warst du schon mal im Ausland?

> MODELL: S1: Warst du schon mal im Ausland?
> S2: Ja!
> S1: Unterschreib bitte hier.

UNTERSCHRIFT

1. Warst du schon mal im Ausland? _____
2. Bist du schon mal am Strand spazieren gegangen? _____
3. Hattest du schon mal einen Autounfall? _____
4. Warst du schon mal auf einem Oktoberfest? _____
5. Bist du schon mal Zug gefahren? _____
6. Hast du schon mal eine Stadtrundfahrt gemacht? _____
7. Hattest du schon mal eine Reifenpanne? _____
8. Warst du schon mal auf einer Insel? _____
9. Hast du schon mal deinen Pass verloren? _____
10. Bist du schon mal im Meer geschwommen? _____

Situation 15 | Bildgeschichte: Stefans Reise nach Österreich

Sit. 15. Sentences for narration series: **1.** *Stefan ist zuerst nach Frankfurt geflogen.* **2.** *Er hat sich auf dem Bahnhof eine Fahrkarte gekauft.* **3.** *Dann ist er mit dem Zug nach Österreich gefahren.* **4.** *Erst hat er eine Wanderung in den Alpen gemacht.* **5.** *Dann hat er Salzburg besichtigt.* **6.** *In einem Café hat er Christine, eine nette Österreicherin, kennengelernt.* **7.** *Sie sind in ein Konzert gegangen und haben in einer Disko getanzt.* **8.** *Schließlich sind sie auf dem Wolfgangsee Boot gefahren.* **9.** *Jetzt schreibt Stefan immer Briefe nach Salzburg.*

Suggestion. Have sts. form groups and create a 10th picture with commentary on transparencies to present to the class.

Sit. 16. Begin by relating to sts. a story about one of your own travel experiences. Before beginning the narration, ask sts. to listen for how you introduce people, how you talk about time and place, and what you do to make the story come alive. After telling your story, write four words on the board as column headers: *Personen, Ort, Zeit, Handlung.* Elicit responses from sts. as you recreate the structure of the story you just told in key words and phrases. *Wer war in meiner Geschichte dabei? Wo war es? Wann war es? Was ist zuerst passiert?* Write the key words and phrases in the four categories. Then, ask sts. to think about one of their own travel experiences and jot down notes following the same structure. Allow sts. to invent stories if they are so inclined. Move around the classroom and help sts. with vocabulary. Allow sts. to practice their stories twice, each time with a different partner. Then, ask two or three sts. to tell their stories to the class. Finally, ask sts. to write up their stories and turn them in as homework.

Situation 16 | Ein Reiseerlebnis erzählen

Hatten Sie schon mal ein interessantes Reiseerlebnis? Erzählen Sie darüber! Machen Sie sich zuerst Notizen und denken Sie an die folgenden Fragen.

1. Personen: Wer war dabei? Was muss man über diese Personen wissen, um Ihre Geschichte besser zu verstehen?
2. Ort: Wo hatten Sie das Erlebnis? Was war interessant an diesem Ort? Versuchen Sie den Ort zu visualisieren und beschreiben Sie ihn.
3. Zeit: Wann hatten Sie das Erlebnis? Vor wie vielen Jahren? Welche Tageszeit war es? War es ein besonderer Tag?
4. Handlung: Was ist zuerst passiert? Was haben Sie gefühlt und gedacht? Was ist dann passiert? Was war der Höhepunkt des Erlebnisses? Was war das Besondere?

Reisen und Urlaub

- Was ist für Ihre Landsleute im Urlaub besonders wichtig? Stellen Sie eine Rangliste auf.

    _____ Abenteuer[1] erleben
    _____ Land und Leute kennenlernen
    _____ ausschlafen[2]
    _____ gut essen
    _____ flirten
    _____ mit dem Partner / der Partnerin / der Familie zusammen sein
    _____ einkaufen
    _____ etwas für die Gesundheit tun
    _____ Sport treiben

- Was ist für Sie im Urlaub besonders wichtig? Nennen Sie drei Dinge.

Schauen Sie sich die Statistik an.

- Was ist für Deutsche im Urlaub besonders wichtig?
- Auf welchem Platz in dieser Statistik stehen Ihre Präferenzen?

[1]adventures [2]sleeping late

FOCUS-FRAGE

„Was ist für Sie im Urlaub besonders wichtig?"

FERIEN MIT DER FAMILIE

von 1300 Befragten antworteten

46%	mit dem Partner, der Familie zusammen sein
31%	ausschlafen
31%	Land und Leute kennenlernen
25%	etwas für die Gesundheit tun
20%	Abenteuer erleben
10%	flirten

KLI. Have sts. work in pairs or small groups and then compare their priorities with those of the rest of the class. Ask them to supply the information: *Für wie viele ist Ausschlafen besonders wichtig? Was steht bei Ihnen an erster Stelle?* You could also have some sts. focus on different groups–their parents' or grandparents' generations, for example–to provide a broader range of priorities.

Videoecke

- Woher kommst du?
- Wo liegt das? (Bundesland)
- Was ist dort besonders interessant?
- Was sind die schönsten Ausflugsziele in der Nähe?
- Wie bist du in Leipzig unterwegs?
- Hast du einen Führerschein?
- War's schwer, ihn zu bekommen?
- Gibt es ein Auto, das dir besonders gut gefällt?
- Was gefällt dir daran?

Birgit ist in Eisenach geboren. Sie studiert Indologie und Deutsch als Fremdsprache. Ihre Hobbys sind Lesen, Reisen und ins Kino gehen.

Judith ist in Horb am Neckar geboren. Sie studiert Sinologie und Deutsch als Fremdsprache. Ihre Hobbys sind chinesische Kultur, chinesisches Essen und Reisen.

Welche Städte, Orte oder Länder hören Sie in den beiden Interviews? Unterstreichen Sie sie.

Baden-Württemberg	Leipzig
Eisenach	Magdeburg
Erfurt	Rheinland-Pfalz
Frankfurt	Rostock
Halle	Sachsen-Anhalt
Hamburg	Stuttgart
Heidelberg	Thüringen
Horb	Tübingen
Hörschel	Weimar
Konstanz	

Aufgaben 1 and 2. (1) Focus sts.' attention on the photos by asking: *Wer ist in Eisenach geboren? Wer studiert Sinologie? Welche Sprache studiert sie dabei? Raten Sie! Was für Hobbys hat Judith? Wer geht gern ins Kino?* **(2)** Read through the list of cities and states and ask sts. to find the places mentioned on a map of Germany. Ignore Horb and Hörschel unless your map is detailed enough. **(3)** Play the first half of Birgit's interview once and ask sts. to underline the places mentioned. **(4)** Play it again and ask sts. to knock or clap when they hear any of the places mentioned. **(5)** Play it a third time and ask sts. to find out which of the items in *Aufgabe 2* go with the city of Horb. Do the same with the first half of Judith's interview. **(6)** For *Aufgabe 2*, let sts. focus on which items go with Hörschel and which ones with Eisenach.

Was erfahren Sie über Horb (HO), Hörschel (HÖ) und Eisenach (E)? Schreiben Sie die Buchstaben des Ortes vor die Aussagen, die sich auf diesen Ort beziehen.

1. _____ Es liegt in Baden-Württemberg.
2. _____ Es ist ein ganz kleines Dorf bei Eisenach.
3. _____ Es liegt in Thüringen.
4. _____ Es liegt in der Nähe von Stuttgart.
5. _____ Es ist eine schöne, alte, kleine Stadt.
6. _____ Es liegt in der Mitte von Deutschland.
7. _____ Es liegt sehr schön am Neckar.
8. _____ Es gibt eine große Stadtmauer und viele Türme.
9. _____ Dort gibt es das Bach-Haus und das Luther-Haus.
10. _____ Es ist eine ziemlich alte Stadt.
11. _____ Man ist schnell im Schwarzwald.
12. _____ Die Wartburg liegt in der Nähe.

Aufgabe 3. Read through the list of statements and ask sts. to guess whom the statements might be about. Play the second half of Birgit's interview and ask sts. to check the statements that refer to Birgit. Play it again and ask sts. to knock or clap when they hear a particular statement. Play the second half of Judith's interview and ask sts. to knock or snap their fingers when they hear the statements belonging to Judith.

Welche Aussagen treffen auf Birgit oder Judith zu? Schreiben Sie B (Birgit) oder J (Judith) neben die folgenden Aussagen.

1. _____ ist meistens mit der Straßenbahn oder zu Fuß unterwegs.
2. _____ fährt mit dem Fahrrad, wenn das Wetter schön ist.
3. _____ fährt mit der Straßenbahn, wenn es regnet.
4. _____ hat zwanzig Fahrstunden genommen.
5. _____ hat fünfzig Fahrstunden gebraucht.
6. _____ gefällt der VW Käfer, am besten ein Cabrio.
7. _____ gefällt der New Beetle, weil er so rund ist.

Student Interviews. (1) Ask students to jot down their own answers to the interview questions. **(2)** Pair students to interview each other. Ask them to jot down their partner's answers. **(3)** Follow up by sampling a few of the answers given in the interviews.

Wortschatz

Geografie	Geography
die Bucht, -en (R)	bay
die Insel, -n	island
die Halbinsel, -n	peninsula
die Richtung, -en	direction
die Wiese, -n	meadow, pasture
die Wüste, -n	desert
der Fluss, ⸚e	river
der Gipfel, -	mountaintop
der Gletscher, -	glacier
der Hügel, -	hill
der See, -n	lake
der Strand, ⸚e (R)	shore, beach
der Wald, ⸚er (R)	forest, woods
das Feld, -er	field
das Gebirge, -	(range of) mountains
das Meer, -e (R)	sea
das Tal, ⸚er	valley

Ähnliche Wörter

die Küste, -n; die Landkarte, -n; der Dschungel, -; die Alpen (*pl.*); nördlich (von); nordöstlich (von); nordwestlich (von); östlich (von); südlich (von); südöstlich (von); südwestlich (von); westlich (von)

Auto	Car
die Bremse, -n	brake
die Hupe, -n	horn
die Motorhaube, -n	hood
die Reifenpanne, -n	flat tire
der Gang, ⸚e	gear
der Gebrauchtwagen, -	used car
der Kilometerstand	mileage
der Kofferraum, ⸚e	trunk
der Reifen, -	tire
der Scheibenwischer, -	windshield wiper
der Sicherheitsgurt, -e	safety belt
der Sitz, -e	seat
der Tank, -s	(fuel) tank
das Autoradio, -s	car radio
das Lenkrad, ⸚er	steering wheel
das Nummernschild, -er	license plate
das Rad, ⸚er	wheel

Verkehr und Transportmittel	Traffic and Means of Transportation
die Bahn, -en	railroad
die Autobahn, -en	freeway
die Seilbahn, -en	cable railway
die Straßenbahn, -en	streetcar

die U-Bahn, -en (Untergrundbahn)	subway
die Einbahnstraße, -n	one-way street
die Kreuzung, -en	intersection
die Landstraße, -n	rural highway
die Parklücke, -n	parking space
die Radfahrerin, -nen	(female) bicyclist
die Rakete, -n	rocket
die Vorfahrt, -en	right-of-way
der Fahrkartenschalter, -	ticket window
der Flug, ⸚e	flight
der Fußgänger, -	pedestrian
der Fußgängerweg, -e	sidewalk
der Radfahrer, -	(male) bicyclist
der Radweg, -e	bicycle path
der Stau, -s	traffic jam
der Wagen, -	car
der Kinderwagen, -	baby carriage
der Lastwagen, -	truck
der Waggon [vagon], -s	train car
der Zug, ⸚e	train
der Personenzug, ⸚e	passenger train
das Fahrrad, ⸚er (R)	bicycle
das Flugzeug, -e	airplane
das Motorrad, ⸚er (R)	motorcycle
das Schild, -er	sign
das Verkehrsschild, -er	traffic sign
das Verbot, -e	prohibition
das Halteverbot, -e	no-stopping zone
die öffentlichen Verkehrsmittel (*pl.*)	public transportation

Ähnliche Wörter

die Fahrerin, -nen; die Lokomotive, -n; der Bus, -se (R); der Fahrer, -; der Zeppelin, -e; das Taxi, -s (R); parken; transportieren

Reiseerlebnisse	Travel Experiences
die Reise, -n	trip, journey
auf der Durchreise sein	to be traveling through
auf Reisen sein	to be on a trip
die Geschäftsreise, -n	business trip
die Stadtrundfahrt, -en	tour of the city
die Wanderung, -en	hike
die Welt, -en	world
der Höhepunkt, -e	highlight
der Reisescheck, -s	traveler's check
besichtigen	to visit, sightsee
besteigen, bestiegen	to climb

Ähnliche Wörter

der Pass, ⁼e; der Wein, -e; das Souvenir, -s; das Visum, Visa; die Spaghetti (pl.); buchen; packen; planen; reservieren

Sonstige Substantive	Other Nouns
die Achtung	attention
die Angestellte, -n	female clerk
die Fläche, -n	surface
die Hexe, -n	witch
die Luft	air
die Million, -en	million
die Scheibe, -n	windowpane
der Angestellte, -n	male clerk
der Regen	rain
bei Regen	in rainy weather
der Teil, -e	part
der Nachteil, -e	disadvantage
der Vorteil, -e	advantage
das Tier, -e (R)	animal
die Leute (pl.)	people
die Geschäftsleute (pl.)	businesspeople
die Nachrichten (pl.)	news

Ähnliche Wörter

die Mark, -; die Zigarre, -n; der Dollar, -s; zwei Dollar; der Euro, -; der Franken, -; der Liter, -; der Preis, -e; der Sand; der Schilling -e; zwei Schilling; das Baby [beːbi], -s; das Oktoberfest, -e; das Sauerkraut

Sonstige Verben	Other Verbs
an·halten, hält ... an, angehalten	to stop
benutzen	to use
besiegen	to conquer
ein·schlafen, schläft ... ein, ist eingeschlafen	to fall asleep
erlauben	to permit
fließen, ist geflossen	to flow

halten, hält, gehalten	to stop
hupen	to honk
nach·denken (über + akk.), nachgedacht	to think (about), consider
rennen, ist gerannt	to run
rufen, gerufen	to call, shout
schwimmen, ist geschwommen	to swim; to float
setzen	to put, place, set
sparen	to save (money)
trennen	to separate
vergleichen, verglichen	to compare
verlieren, verloren	to lose
versprechen, verspricht, versprochen	to promise
verstauen	to stow
warten	to wait
wischen	to wipe

Ähnliche Wörter

beantworten, warnen

Sonstige Wörter und Ausdrücke	Other Words and Expressions
berühmt	famous
bitte schön?	yes please?; may I help you?
dort	there
durch	through
lieb	dear
am liebsten	like (to do) best
rechts	to the right
schließlich	finally
ungefähr	approximately
zuerst (R)	first
zwischen	between

Ähnliche Wörter

exotisch, graugrün, interessant, mehr, salzig, seekrank, superschnell, tief

Strukturen und Übungen

7.1 Relative clauses

7.1. *Relativsätze und Relativpronomen.* We want to help sts. to understand the relative clauses they hear and see and to monitor the ones they write. First-year sts. rarely attempt to use relative clauses when speaking. Point out that relative clauses are another kind of dependent clause. (Unlike the adverbial *wenn-* and *weil-* clauses introduced in Section 3.4, they are adjectival clauses.)

The selection of the correct relative pronoun is often a difficult matter for sts. at this level. They can easily find the gender and case from the antecedent, but the determination of case from the relative clause can present a problem.

Relative clauses add information about a person, place, thing, or idea already mentioned in the sentence. The relative pronoun begins the relative clause, which usually follows the noun it describes. The relative pronoun corresponds to the English words *who, whom, that,* and *which.* The conjugated verb is in the end position.

RELATIVE CLAUSE

Der Atlantik ist das Meer, **das** Europa und Afrika von Amerika trennt.

VERB IN END POSITION

The Atlantic is the ocean that separates Europe and Africa from America.

Do not omit the relative pronoun in the German sentence.

While relative pronouns may sometimes be omitted in English, they cannot be omitted from German sentences.

Das ist der Mantel, **den** ich letzte Woche gekauft habe.
That is the coat (that) I bought last week.

Relative clauses are preceded by a comma.

Likewise, the comma is not always necessary in an English sentence, but it must precede a relative clause in German. If the relative clause comes in the middle of a German sentence, it is followed by a comma as well.

Der See, **der** zwischen Deutschland und der Schweiz liegt, heißt Bodensee.
The lake that lies between Germany and Switzerland is called Lake Constance.

Wissen Sie noch?

A relative clause is a type of dependent clause. As in other dependent clauses, the conjugated verb appears at the end of the clause.

Review grammar 3.4.

A. Relative Pronouns in the Nominative Case

In the nominative (subject) case, the forms of the relative pronoun are the same as the forms of the definite article **der, das, die.**

Der Fluss, **der** durch Wien fließt, heißt Donau.
Gobi heißt **die** Wüste, **die** in Innerasien liegt.

The relative pronoun and the noun it refers to have the same number and gender.

The relative pronoun has the same gender and number as the noun it refers to.

Masculine	der Mann, **der ...**	*the man who . . .*
Neuter	das Auto, **das ...**	*the car that . . .*
Feminine	die Frau, **die ...**	*the woman who . . .*
Plural	die Leute, **die ...**	*the people who . . .*

B. Relative Pronouns in the Accusative and Dative Cases

The case of a relative pronoun depends on its function within the relative clause.

When the relative pronoun functions as an accusative object or as a dative object within the relative clause, then the relative pronoun is in the accusative or dative case, respectively.

ACCUSATIVE

Nur wenige Menschen haben **den Mount Everest** bestiegen.
Only a few people have climbed Mount Everest.

Der Mount Everest ist ein Berg, **den** nur wenige Menschen bestiegen haben.
Mount Everest is a mountain that only a few people have climbed.

DATIVE

Ich habe **meinem Vater** nichts
davon erzählt.

*I haven't told my father
anything about it.*

Mein Vater ist der einzige
Mensch, **dem** ich nichts
davon erzählt habe.

*My father is the only person
whom I haven't told
anything about it.*

As in the nominative case, the accusative and dative relative pronouns have the same forms as the definite article, except for the dative plural, **denen.**

	Masculine	**Neuter**	**Feminine**	**Plural**
Accusative	den	das	die	die
Dative	dem	dem	der	denen

C. Relative Pronouns Following a Preposition

The case of the relative pronoun depends on the preposition that precedes it.

When a relative pronoun follows a preposition, the case is determined by that preposition. The gender and number of the pronoun are determined by the noun.

Point out that the German sequence of preposition and pronoun corresponds to formal English usage: *Who was the woman with whom I saw you yesterday?*

Ich spreche am liebsten **mit
meinem** Bruder.

*Most of all I like to talk with
my brother.*

Mein Bruder ist der Mensch, **mit
dem** ich am liebsten spreche.

*My brother is the person
(whom) I like to talk with
most of all.*

Auf der Insel Rügen sind weiße
Kreidefelsen.

*There are white chalk cliffs on the
island of Rügen.*

Rügen ist eine Insel in der
Ostsee, **auf der** weiße Kreidefelsen sind.

*Rügen is an island in the Baltic
Sea on which there are white
chalk cliffs.*

Preposition + relative pronoun = inseparable unit

The preposition and the pronoun stay together as a unit in German.

Wer war die Frau, **mit der** ich
dich gestern gesehen habe?

*Who was the woman (whom) I
saw you with yesterday?*

Übung 1 | Das mag ich, das mag ich nicht!

Üb. 1. The relative pronouns (all nominative) are already provided, and sts. get practice in forming relative clauses with the verb last. Assign for homework and have sts. state their preferences in class.

Bilden Sie Sätze!

MODELL: Ich mag Leute, die spät ins Bett gehen.

nett sein	interessant aussehen
laut lachen	exotisch sein
Spaß machen	langweilig sein
schnell fahren	gern verreisen
betrunken sein	viel sprechen
	?

1. Ich mag Leute, die ...
2. Ich mag keine Leute, die ...
3. Ich mag eine Stadt, die ...
4. Ich mag keine Stadt, die ...
5. Ich mag einen Mann, der ...
6. Ich mag keinen Mann, der ...
7. Ich mag eine Frau, die ...
8. Ich mag keine Frau, die ...
9. Ich mag einen Urlaub, der ...
10. Ich mag ein Auto, das ...

Risiko[1]

Üb. 2. Sts. convert the sentences in the righthand column into a question and match it with the correct answer from the left. You can help them by pointing out that the relative pronoun and the noun it stands for in the sentence will have the same case. Assign for homework and have sts. read out the question for the class to answer.

Hier sind die Antworten. Stellen Sie die Fragen!

MODELL: Diesen Kontinent hat Kolumbus entdeckt. →
Wie heißt der Kontinent, den Kolumbus entdeckt hat? (Amerika)

1. Europa
2. Mississippi
3. San Francisco
4. die Alpen
5. Washington
6. das Tal des Todes
7. Ellis
8. der Pazifik
9. die Sahara
10. der Große Salzsee

a. Auf diesem See in Utah kann man segeln.
b. Diese Insel sieht man von New York.
c. Diese Stadt liegt an einer Bucht.
d. Diese Wüste kennt man aus vielen Filmen.
e. Diesem Staat in den USA hat ein Präsident seinen Namen gegeben.
f. In diesem Tal ist es sehr heiß.
g. In diesen Bergen kann man sehr gut Ski fahren.
h. Dieser Kontinent ist eigentlich eine Halbinsel von Asien.
i. Über dieses Meer fliegt man nach Hawaii.
j. Von diesem Fluss erzählt Mark Twain.

7.2 Making comparisons: the comparative and superlative forms of adjectives and adverbs

7.2. *Komparativ und Superlativ.* This section deals with predicate adjectives and adverbs together, since their forms are the same. You might want to point out the distinction between adjectives and adverbs.

A. Comparisons of Equality: so ... wie

To say that two or more persons or things are alike or equal in some way, use the phrase **so ... wie** (*as ... as*) with an adjective or adverb.

so ... wie = *as ... as*

Deutschland ist ungefähr **so groß wie** Montana.	*Germany is about as big as Montana.*
Der Mount Whitney ist fast **so hoch wie** das Matterhorn.	*Mount Whitney is almost as high as the Matterhorn.*

Inequality can also be expressed with this formula and the addition of **nicht.**

Die Zugspitze ist **nicht so hoch wie** der Mount Everest.	*The Zugspitze is not as high as Mount Everest.*
Österreich ist **nicht ganz so groß wie** Maine.	*Austria is not quite as big as Maine.*

B. Comparisons of Superiority and Inferiority

All comparatives in German are formed with **-er.**

To compare two unequal persons or things, add **-er** to the adjective or adverb. Note that the comparative form of German adjectives and adverbs always ends in **-er,** whereas English sometimes uses the adjective with the word *more.*

als = *than*

Sts. generally have few problems with the comparative forms of adverbs and predicate adjectives presented here. Point out that the noun that occurs after *als* is in the nominative case.

Ein Fahrrad ist **billiger als** ein Motorrad.	*A bicycle is cheaper than a motorcycle.*
Lydia ist **intelligenter als** ihre Schwester.	*Lydia is more intelligent than her sister.*
Jens läuft **schneller als** Ernst.	*Jens runs faster than Ernst.*

[1]*Jeopardy*

Some adjectives that end in **-el** and **-er** drop the **-e-** in the comparative form.

teuer → teu¢rer
dunkel → dunk¢ler

Eine Wohnung in Regensburg ist teuer, aber eine Wohnung in München ist noch **teurer.**	*An apartment in Regensburg is expensive, but an apartment in Munich is even more expensive.*
Gestern war es dunkel, aber heute ist es **dunkler.**	*Yesterday it was dark, but today it is darker.*

C. The Superlative

To express the superlative in German, use the contraction **am** with a predicate adjective or adverb plus the ending **-sten.**

Ein Porsche ist schnell, ein Flugzeug ist schneller, und eine Rakete ist am schnellsten.	*A Porsche is fast, an airplane is faster, and a rocket is the fastest.*

Superlatives: **am** + **-sten**

Unlike the English superlative, which has two forms, all German adjectives and adverbs form the superlative in this way.

Hans ist **am jüngsten.**	*Hans is the youngest.*
Jens ist **am tolerantesten.**	*Jens is the most tolerant.*

When the adjective or adverb ends in **-d** or **-t,** or an s-sound such as **-s, -ß, -sch, -x,** or **-z,** an **-e-** is inserted between the stem and the ending.

frisch	→ am frisch**esten**
gesund	→ am gesünd**esten**
heiß	→ am heiß**esten**
intelligent	→ am intelligent**esten**

Um die Mittagszeit ist es oft am heißesten.	*The hottest (weather) is often around noontime.*

Groß is an exception to the rule: **am größten.**

Irregular comparatives and superlatives have an umlaut whenever possible.

D. Irregular Comparative and Superlative Forms

The following adjectives have an umlaut in the comparative and the superlative.

alt	älter	am ältesten
gesund	gesünder	am gesündesten
groß	größer	am größten
jung	jünger	am jüngsten
kalt	kälter	am kältesten
krank	kränker	am kränksten
kurz	kürzer	am kürzesten
lang	länger	am längsten
warm	wärmer	am wärmsten

Im März ist es oft **wärmer** als im Januar. Im August ist es **am wärmsten.**	*In March it's often warmer than in January. It's warmest in August.*

As in English, some superlative forms are very different from their base forms:

gern	lieber	am liebsten
gut	besser	am besten
hoch	höher	am höchsten
nah	näher	am nächsten
viel	mehr	am meisten

Ich spreche Deutsch, Englisch und Spanisch. Englisch spreche ich **am besten** und Deutsch spreche ich **am liebsten.**

I speak German, English, and Spanish. I speak English the best, and I like to speak German the most.

E. Superlative Forms Preceding Nouns

When the superlative form of an adjective is used with a definite article (**der, das, die**) directly *before* a noun, it has an **-(e)ste** ending in all forms of the nominative singular and an **-(e)sten** ending in the plural. You will get used to the **-e/-en** distribution as you have more experience listening to and reading German. (A more detailed description of adjectives that precede nouns will follow in **Kapitel 8.**)

Superlatives before nouns in the nominative:
der/das/die + **-(e)ste**
die (*pl.*) + **-(e)sten**

	Fluss (*m.*)	Tal (*n.*)	Wüste (*f.*)	Berge (*pl.*)
Nominative	der längst**e**	das tiefst**e**	die größt**e**	die höchst**en**

Only nominative case endings are introduced now. These are the forms most often used, and the two endings, -e for the singular and -en for the plural, can be handled relatively easily. This is the first formal introduction of attributive adjective endings. The main presentation of these endings is found in Sections 8.1, 8.2, and 8.4.

—Wie heißt der längste Fluss Europas?
—Wolga.

What is the name of the longest river in Europe?
The Volga.

—In welchem Land wohnen die meisten Menschen?
—In China.

What country has the most people?

China.

Übung 3 | Vergleiche

Üb. 3. Assign for homework and check in class. Remind sts. to think about the meaning of the comparison before forming the sentence.

Vergleichen Sie.

MODELL: Wien / Göttingen / klein → Göttingen ist kleiner als Wien.

1. Berlin / Zürich / groß
2. San Francisco / München / alt
3. Hamburg / Athen / warm
4. das Matterhorn / der Mount Everest / hoch
5. der Mississippi / der Rhein / lang
6. die Schweiz / Liechtenstein / klein
7. Leipzig / Kairo / kalt
8. ein Fernseher / eine Waschmaschine / billig
9. Schnaps / Bier / stark
10. ein Haus in der Stadt / ein Haus auf dem Land / schön
11. zehn Euro / zehn Cent / viel
12. eine Wohnung in einem Studentenheim / ein Appartement / teuer
13. ein Fahrrad / ein Motorrad / schnell
14. ein Sofa / ein Stuhl / schwer
15. Milch / Bier / gut

Übung 4 | Biografische Daten

Üb. 4. Assign the exercise for homework and check it in class. Make sure sts. understand the instructions. Where there are two names, they need to compare the two persons. Where there is a plus sign, they need to find out who is the oldest, biggest, etc.

Vergleichen Sie. [(+) = Superlativ]

MODELL: alt / Thomas / Stefan → Thomas ist **älter** als Stefan.
alt (+) → Heidi ist **am ältesten.**

	Thomas	Heidi	Stefan	Monika
Alter	19	22	18	21
Größe	1,89 m	1,75 m	1,82 m	1,69 m
Gewicht	75 kg	65 kg	75 kg	57 kg
Haarlänge	20 cm	15 cm	5 cm	25 cm
Note in Deutsch	B	A	C	B

1. schwer / Monika / Heidi
2. schwer (+)
3. gut in Deutsch / Thomas / Stefan
4. gut in Deutsch (+)
5. klein / Heidi / Stefan
6. klein (+)
7. jung / Thomas / Stefan
8. jung (+)
9. lang / Heidis Haare / Thomas' Haare
10. lang (+)
11. kurz / Monikas Haare / Heidis Haare
12. kurz (+)
13. schlecht in Deutsch / Heidi / Monika
14. schlecht in Deutsch (+)

Übung 5 | Geografie und Geschichte

MODELL: Das Tal des Todes (−86 m) liegt tiefer als das Kaspische Meer (−28 m). →
Das Tote Meer (−396 m) liegt am tiefsten.

1. In Rom (25,6°C) ist es im Sommer heißer als in München (17,2°C).
2. In Wien (−1,4°C) ist es im Winter kälter als in Paris (3,5°C).
3. Liechtenstein (157 km^2)* ist kleiner als Luxemburg (2 586 km^2).
4. Deutschland (911) ist älter als die Schweiz (1291).
5. Kanada (1840) ist jünger als die USA (1776).
6. Der Mississippi (6 021 km) ist länger als die Donau (2 850 km).
7. Philadelphia (40° nördliche Breite) liegt nördlicher als Kairo (30° nördliche Breite).
8. Der Mont Blanc (4 807 m) ist höher als der Mount Whitney (4 418 m).
9. Österreich (83 849 km^2) ist größer als die Schweiz (41 288 km^2).

a. Athen (27,6°C)
b. das Tote Meer (−396 m)
c. Deutschland (357 050 km^2)
d. Frankfurt (50° nördliche. Breite)
e. Frankreich (498)
f. Monaco (1,49 km^2)
g. Moskau (−9,9°C)
h. der Mount Everest (8 848 m)
i. der Nil (6 671 km)
j. Südafrika (1884)

*km^2 = Quadratkilometer

7.3 Referring to and asking about things and ideas: *da*-compounds and *wo*-compounds

7.3. *Pronominaladverbien.* Sts. may be interested to know that these German words with *da*- correspond to English words with *there-*, such as *therefore* and *thereafter.*

In both German and English, personal pronouns are used directly after prepositions when these pronouns refer to people or animals.

Ich werde bald **mit ihr** sprechen.	*I'll talk to her soon.*
—Bist du mit Josef gefahren?	*Did you go with Josef?*
—Ja, ich bin **mit ihm** gefahren.	*Yes, I went with him.*

da- or **dar-** + preposition

When the object of the preposition is a thing or concept, it is common in English to use the pronoun *it* or *them* with a preposition: *with it, for them,* and so on. In German, it is preferable to use compounds that begin with **da-** (or **dar-** if the preposition begins with a vowel).*

dadurch	*through it/them*
dafür	*for it/them*
dagegen	*against it/them*
dahinter	*behind it/them*
damit	*with it/them*
daneben	*next to it/them*
daran	*on it/them*
darauf	*on top of it/them*
daraus	*out of it/them*
darin	*in it/them*
darüber	*over it/them*
darunter	*underneath it/them*
davon	*from it/them*
davor	*in front of it/them*
dazu	*to it/them*
dazwischen	*between it/them*

—Was macht man mit einer Hupe?	*What do you do with a horn?*
—Man warnt andere Leute **damit.**	*You warn other people with it.*
—Hast du etwas gegen das Rauchen?	*Do you have something against smoking?*
—Nein, ich habe nichts **dagegen.**	*No, I don't have anything against it.*

Some **da**-compounds are idiomatic.

dabei	*on me/you …*
Hast du Geld **dabei?**	*Do you have any money on you?*
darum	*that's why*
Darum hast du auch kein Glück.	*That's why you don't have any luck.*

*Note that the following prepositions cannot be preceded by **da(r)-: ohne, außer, seit.**

Use a preposition + **wem** or **wen** to ask about people.

Questions about people begin with wer (*who*) or wen/wem (*whom*). If a preposition is involved, it precedes the question word.

—Mit **wem** gehst du ins Theater?

Who will you go to the theater with? (*With whom …?*)

—Mit Melanie.

With Melanie.

—In **wen** hast du dich diesmal verliebt?

Who did you fall in love with this time? (*With whom …?*)

Use **wo-** + a preposition to ask about things or ideas.

Questions about things and concepts begin with was (*what*). If a preposition is involved, German speakers use compound words that begin with wo- (or wor- if the preposition begins with a vowel).

—**Womit** fährst du nach Berlin?

How are you getting to Berlin?

—Mit dem Bus.

By bus.

—**Worüber** sprichst du?

What are you talking about?

—Ich spreche über den neuen Film von Doris Dörrie.

I'm talking about Doris Dörrie's new film.

People	Things and Concepts
mit wem	womit
von wem	wovon
zu wem	wozu
an wen	woran
für wen	wofür
über wen	worüber
auf wen	worauf
um wen	worum

—**Von wem** ist die Oper „Parsifal"?

Who is the opera Parzival by?

—Von Richard Wagner.

By Richard Wagner.

—**Wovon** handelt diese Oper?

What is the opera about?

—Von der Suche nach dem Gral.

About the search for the Holy Grail.

Übung 6 | Ein Interview mit Richard

Üb. 6. Assign as homework and have sts. play the roles in class.

Das folgende Interview ist nicht vollständig. Es fehlen die Fragen. Rekonstruieren Sie die Fragen aus den Antworten.

1. Ich gehe am liebsten **mit meiner Kusine** ins Theater.
2. Am meisten freue ich mich **auf die Ferien.**
3. Ich muss immer **auf meinen Freund** warten. Er kommt immer zu spät.
4. In letzter Zeit habe ich mich **über meinen Physiklehrer** geärgert.
5. Wenn ich „USA" höre, denke ich **an Hochhäuser und Gettos, an den Grand Canyon und die Rocky Mountains und natürlich an Iowa.**
6. Zur Schule fahre ich meistens **mit dem Fahrrad, manchmal auch mit dem Bus.**
7. Ich schreibe nicht gern **über Sachen,** die mich nicht interessieren, wie zum Beispiel die Vorteile und Nachteile des Kapitalismus.
8. Meinen letzten Brief habe ich **an einen alten Freund von mir** geschrieben. Der ist vor kurzem nach Graz gezogen, um dort Jura zu studieren.
9. Ich halte nicht viel **von meinen Lehrern.** Die tun nur immer so, als wüssten sie alles; in Wirklichkeit wissen die gar nichts.

Üb. 7. Assign as homework and check in class. These forms can also be illustrated with persons and objects in the classroom.

AA. You might want to have sts. speculate on why Hans is hiding behind the chair and where Jutta is, without her shoes.

Da-compounds:

dahinter
daneben
daran
darauf
darin
darüber
darunter
davor
dazwischen

Ergänzen Sie!

Links¹ ist eine Kommode. Eine Lampe steht *darauf*ª. Rechts ____ᵇ steht der Schreibtisch. ____ᶜ steht Juttas Tasche. An der Wand steht ein Schrank. ____ᵈ hängen Juttas Sachen. Links an der Wand steht Juttas Bett. ____ᵉ liegt die Katze auf dem Teppich. An der Wand ____ᶠ hängt ein Bild. Auf dem Bild ist eine Wiese mit einem Baum. ____ᵍ hängen Äpfel. Mitten im Zimmer steht ein Sessel. ____ʰ sieht man Juttas Schuhe und ____ⁱ hat sich Hans versteckt².

7.4 The perfect tense (review)

As you remember from **Kapitel 4**, it is preferable to use the perfect tense in oral communication when talking about past events.

Ich **habe** im Garten Äpfel **gepflückt.** | *I picked apples in the garden.*

To form the perfect tense, use **haben** or **sein** as an auxiliary with the past participle of the verb.

A. **haben** or **sein**

Haben is by far the more commonly used auxiliary. **Sein** is normally used only when both of the following conditions are met: (1) The verb cannot take an accusative object. (2) The verb implies a change of location or condition.

Bertolt Brecht **ist** 1956 in Berlin **gestorben.** | *Bertolt Brecht died in Berlin in 1956.*
Ernst **ist** mit seinem Hund **spazieren gegangen.** | *Ernst went for a walk with his dog.*

In spite of the fact that there is no change of location or condition, the following verbs also take **sein** as an auxiliary: **sein, bleiben,** and **passieren.**

Letztes Jahr **bin** ich in St. Moritz **gewesen.** | *Last year I was in St. Moritz.*
Was **ist passiert?** | *What happened?*

Wissen Sie noch?

The perfect tense consists of a form of the present tense of **haben** or **sein** + the past participle.

Review grammar 4.1.

Use **haben** with most verbs.
Use **sein** if the verb:
- cannot take an accusative object
- indicates change of location or condition.
See Appendix F (II) for a list of common verbs and their auxiliaries.

7.4. *Perfekt.* The perfect tense, introduced in *Kapitel 4,* is reviewed here to give students more practice in the oral narration of past events. Weak verbs with a stem change in the past participle (*denken, usw.*) are included here for the first time. Point out: *werden* implies a change of condition and is, therefore, used with the auxiliary *sein* in the perfect tense.

¹*To the left* ²*hat ... Hans has hidden himself*

B. Forming the Past Participle

There are basically two ways to form the past participle. Strong verbs add the prefix **ge-** and the ending **-en** to the stem. Weak verbs add the prefix **ge-** and the ending **-t** or **-et**.

Strong verbs end in **-en**; weak verbs end in **-t** or **-et**.

Suggestion. Have sts. identify which verbs in these lists are weak and which are strong.

rufen	hat **ge**ruf**en**	*to shout, call*
reisen	ist **ge**reis**t**	*to travel*
arbeiten	hat **ge**arbeit**et**	*to work*

In the past-participle form, most, but not all, strong verbs have a changed stem vowel or stem.

gehen	ist geg**a**ngen	*to walk*
werfen	hat gew**o**rfen	*to throw*
but: laufen	ist gelaufen	*to run*

Very few weak verbs have a change in the stem vowel. Here are some common weak verbs that do change.

dürfen	hat ge**du**rft	*to be allowed to*
können	hat ge**ko**nnt	*to be able to*
müssen	hat ge**mu**sst	*to have to*
bringen	hat ge**bra**cht	*to bring*
denken	hat ge**da**cht	*to think*
rennen	ist ge**ra**nnt	*to run*
wissen	hat ge**wu**sst	*to know (as a fact)*

C. Past Participles with and without ge-

no **ge-** with
• verbs ending in **-ieren**
• inseparable prefix verbs

Another group of verbs forms the past participle without **ge-**. You will recognize them because, unlike most verbs, they are not pronounced with an emphasis on the first syllable. These verbs fall into two major groups: those that end in **-ieren** and those that have inseparable prefixes.

Point out. *Verlieren* is not a verb ending in *-ieren*. Instead it is a strong verb with the stem *verlier-*, which changes to *verlor-* in the perfect tense.

passieren	ist passiert	*to happen*
studieren	hat studiert	*to study, go to college*
verlieren	hat verloren	*to lose*
erlauben	hat erlaubt	*to allow*

The most common inseparable prefixes are **be-, ent-, er-, ge-,** and **ver-**.

common inseparable prefixes
be-
ent-
er-
ge-
ver-

besuchen	hat besucht	*to visit*
entdecken	hat entdeckt	*to discover*
erzählen	hat erzählt	*to tell*
gewinnen	hat gewonnen	*to win*
versprechen	hat versprochen	*to promise*

The past participle of separable-prefix verbs is formed by adding the prefix to the past participle of the base verb.

anfangen	hat angefangen	*to begin*
aufstehen	ist aufgestanden	*to get up*
einschlafen	ist eingeschlafen	*to fall asleep*
nachdenken	hat nachgedacht	*to think over*

Übung 8 | Renate

Üb. 8. Remind sts. that a verb with a direct object always has *haben* as its auxiliary verb. Assign the exercise for homework and check it in class.

Ergänzen Sie **haben** oder **sein.**

1. In meiner Schulzeit _____ ich nie gern aufgestanden.
2. Meine Mutter _____ᵃ mich immer geweckt, denn ich _____ᵇ nie von allein aufgewacht.
3. Ich _____ᵃ ganz schnell etwas gegessen und _____ᵇ zur Schule gerannt.
4. Meistens hatte es schon zur Stunde geklingelt, wenn ich angekommen _____.
5. In der Schule war es oft langweilig; in Biologie _____ ich sogar einmal eingeschlafen.
6. Einmal in der Woche hatten wir nachmittags Sport. Am liebsten _____ᵃ ich Basketball gespielt und _____ᵇ geschwommen.
7. Auf dem Weg nach Hause _____ᵃ ich einmal einen Autounfall gesehen. Zum Glück _____ᵇ nichts passiert.
8. Aber viele Leute _____ᵃ herumgestanden, bis die Polizei gekommen _____ᵇ.
9. Sie _____ᵃ geblieben, bis eine Autowerkstatt die kaputten Autos abgeholt _____ᵇ.
10. Ich _____ nicht so lange gewartet, denn ich musste Hausaufgaben machen.

Übung 9 | Ernst

Üb. 9. Assign for homework and have pairs of sts. take the two roles in class.

Ernst war fleißig. Er hat schon alles gemacht. Übernehmen Sie seine Rolle.

MODELL: Steh bitte endlich auf! → Ich bin schon aufgestanden.

1. Mach bitte Frühstück!
2. Trink bitte deine Milch!
3. Mach bitte den Tisch sauber!
4. Lauf mal schnell zum Bäcker!
5. Bring bitte Brötchen mit!
6. Nimm bitte Geld mit!
7. Füttere bitte den Hund!
8. Mach bitte die Tür zu!

7.5 The simple past tense of *haben* and *sein*

7.5 Präteritum. This is the first formal presentation of the simple past tense. We begin with two of the verbs that generally use this tense for conversation: *haben* and *sein*. Sts. will have heard these forms in your speech. They became acquainted with verbs with identical *ich-* and *er/sie/es*-forms when they learned modal verbs in *Kapitel 3*. The use of the simple past tense of all other verbs is presented in *Kapitel 9*, where the focus is on fairy tales and narrative.

When talking about events that have already happened, people commonly use the verbs **haben** and **sein** in the simple past tense instead of the perfect tense. The conjugations appear below; notice that the **ich-** and the **er/sie/es**-forms are the same.

Warst du schon mal im Ausland?
Letzte Woche **hatte** ich einen Autounfall.

Have you ever been abroad?
Last week I had a car accident.

sein				haben			
ich	war	wir	waren	ich	hatte	wir	hatten
du	warst	ihr	wart	du	hattest	ihr	hattet
Sie	waren	Sie	waren	Sie	hatten	Sie	hatten
er sie es	war	sie	waren	er sie es	hatte	sie	hatten

Übung 10 | Minidialoge

Ergänzen Sie eine Form von **war** oder **hatte.**

1. FRAU GRETTER: Ihr Auto sieht ja so kaputt aus. _____^a Sie einen Unfall?
   HERR THELEN: Ja, leider _____^b ich wieder mal einen Unfall. Das ist schon der dritte in dieser Woche.

2. FRAU KÖRNER: Sie sind aber braun geworden. _____ Sie im Urlaub?
   MICHAEL PUSCH: Ja, ich war drei Wochen in der Türkei.

3. HANS: Warum _____^a ihr gestern nicht in der Schule?
   JENS UND JUTTA: Wir _____^b keine Zeit.

4. CLAIRE: _____^a du schon mal in Linz, Melanie?
   MELANIE: Ja, ich _____^b schon ein paar mal da. Aber nur auf der Durchreise.

5. MARIA SCHNEIDER: Wo warst du letzte Woche, Jens?
   JENS: Ich _____ Ferien und war bei meinen Großeltern auf dem Land.

6. JUTTA: Michael, sag mal, _____ du schon mal eine Reifenpanne?
   MICHAEL PUSCH: Nein, Gott sei Dank noch nie.

7. CLAIRE: Ich habe dich gestern im Kino gesehen. _____^a du allein?
   JOSEF: Ja, Melanie _____^b gestern zu Hause. Sie _____^c keine Lust, ins Kino zu gehen.

Georg Flegel: *Stillleben mit Obst und Krebsen*
(ca. 1630), Nationalgalerie, Warschau

GEORG FLEGEL

Georg Flegel (1563–1638) war der erste und vielleicht wichtigste Stilllebenmaler[1] in Deutschland. Seine Bilder sind ein perfektes Abbild der Gegenstände[2], aber im Sinne des Barock haben sie ein fast magisches Eigenleben[3]. Typisch für Flegels Werke ist, dass oft ein kleines Lebewesen[4] in Kontrast zu den leblosen Objekten des Stilllebens tritt.

Chapter opening artwork: Flegel placed not only mice, but also other living creatures such as stag beetles in some of his still lifes, of which there were many.

Suggestion: Use the painting as a starting point to talk about or expand on the topic of food. It also lends itself to an introduction of more detailed description (*Bildbeschreibung*). *Welche Lebensmittel sehen Sie auf diesem Bild? Welche Früchte fallen ins Auge? Welche Farben fallen auf? Wie sind die Lebensmittel arrangiert? Was ist in der Bildmitte? Was ist in den vier Bildecken? Was ist im Vordergrund? Wer sitzt vorn rechts und was macht sie?*

[1]*still life painter* [2]*Abbild … likeness of the objects* [3]*life of their own* [4]*living creature*

8

Essen und Einkaufen

In **Kapitel 8,** you will learn to talk about shopping for food and cooking and about the kinds of foods you like. You will also talk about household appliances and about dining out.

Themen
Essen und Trinken
Haushaltsgeräte
Einkaufen und Kochen
Im Restaurant

Kulturelles
Videoblick: Gesunde Ernährung
Essgewohnheiten
Stichwort „Restaurant"
Videoecke: Essen

Lektüren
Mord im Café König?
Film: *Jenseits der Stille*

Strukturen
8.1 Adjectives: an overview
8.2 Attributive adjectives in the nominative and accusative cases
8.3 Destination vs. location: **stellen/stehen, legen/liegen, setzen/sitzen, hängen/hängen**
8.4 Adjectives in the dative case
8.5 Talking about the future: the present and future tenses

Situationen

Essen und Trinken
Grammatik 8.1–8.2

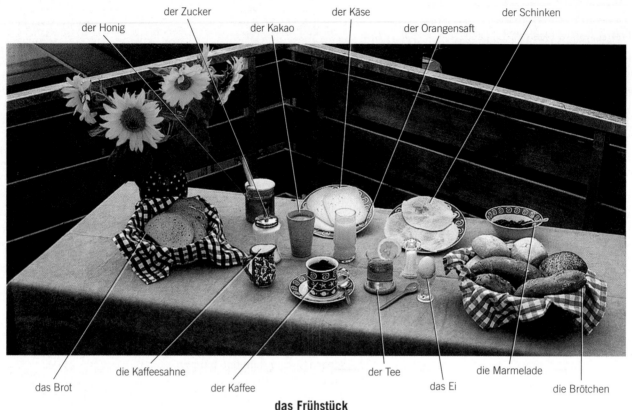

der Honig der Zucker der Kakao der Käse der Orangensaft der Schinken

das Brot die Kaffeesahne der Kaffee der Tee das Ei die Marmelade die Brötchen

das Frühstück

Meistens esse ich ein frisches Brötchen, ein gekochtes Ei und selbst gemachte
Marmelade zum Frühstück. Außerdem brauche ich einen starken Kaffee. Am
Wochenende esse ich auch Schinken und Käse und trinke einen frisch
gepressten Orangensaft. Als ich ein Kind war, habe ich meistens Milch mit
Honig getrunken, später auch Tee.

Zu Mittag esse ich am liebsten einen gemischten Salat, gebratenes Fleisch oder gegrillten Fisch mit gekochten Kartoffeln. Auch Hähnchen mag ich ganz gern und Karotten mit viel Salz und Pfeffer. Meistens trinke ich eine Apfelschorle. Das ist ein Gemisch aus Apfelsaft und Mineralwasser. Am Sonntag trinke ich vielleicht auch mal ein Glas Wein, am liebsten Rotwein.

die Cola — Hähnchen mit Karotten und Pommes — das Mineralwasser — der Apfelsaft — Buletten mit Kartoffelbrei — der Rotwein — Forelle blau — die Kartoffeln — das Salz — der Pfeffer — Hirschbraten mit Spätzle und Pfifferlingen

das Mittagessen

Am Abend esse ich gern rustikal: Brot, Butter, Schinken, Käse. Rohen Schinken esse ich gern mit Meerrettich. Manchmal mache ich mir auch ein paar warme Würstchen. Die esse ich dann mit Senf. Emmentaler esse ich gern mit sauren Essiggurken. Dazu trinke ich entweder ein Glas Milch oder Saft mit Mineralwasser.

das Mineralwasser — das Brot — der Camembert — der Meerrettich — der Emmentaler — das Bier — die Essiggurken — die Milch — die Butter — der Aufschnitt — der Schinken — die Würstchen — der Senf

das Abendessen

Situation 1 | Umfrage: Isst du gern fettige Hamburger?

Sit. 1. Preteach vocabulary: *gebratene Eier mit Speck, würzen, belegtes Brot,* and practice pronunciation.

MODELL: S1: Isst du gern fettige Hamburger?
S2: Ja!
S1: Unterschreib bitte hier!

UNTERSCHRIFT

1. Isst du gern fettige Hamburger? _____
2. Isst du oft Chinesisch? _____
3. Isst du oft frisches Obst? _____
4. Frühstückst du selten? _____
5. Isst du zum Frühstück gern gebratene Eier mit Speck? _____
6. Isst du meistens in der Mensa? _____
7. Isst du manchmal Pizza? _____
8. Würzt du dein Essen mit viel Pfeffer? _____
9. Isst du selten zu Hause? _____
10. Hast du für heute ein belegtes Brot dabei? _____

Situation 2 | Informationsspiel: Mahlzeiten und Getränke

MODELL: S1: Was isst Stefan zum Frühstück?
S2: _____

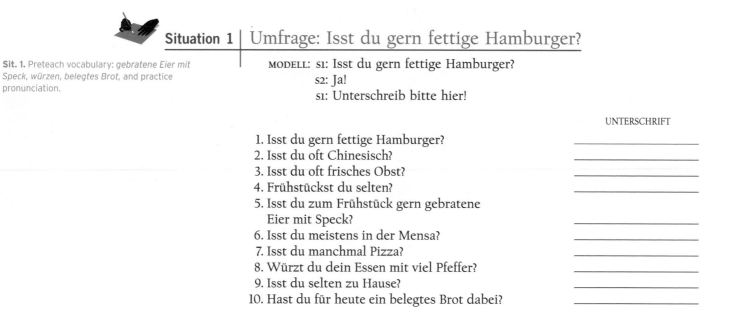

	Frau Gretter	Stefan	Andrea
zum Frühstück essen	frische Brötchen	frisches Müsli	Brot mit selbst gemachter Marmelade
zum Frühstück trinken	schwarzen Kaffee	kalten Orangensaft	heißen Kakao
zu Mittag essen	kalorienarmes Gemüse und Hähnchen	belegte Brote und Kartoffelchips	heiße Würstchen
zu Abend essen	nichts, sie will abnehmen	italienische Spaghetti	Brot mit Honig
nach dem Sport trinken	nichts, sie treibt keinen Sport	kalten Tee mit Zitrone	Apfelsaft
auf einem Fest trinken	deutschen Sekt	mexikanisches Bier	eiskalte Limonade
essen, wenn er/sie groß ausgeht	etwas für Kalorienbewusste	frischen Fisch mit französischer Soße	den schönsten Kinderteller

Sit. 2. Focus: adjective endings. The corresponding chart is in Appendix A. Before doing this activity, comment on the different names and functions of the 3 meals in Germany. **(1)** Preteach vocabulary and write on the board: *Müsli, Gemüse, Hähnchen, belegte Brote, Kartoffelchips, Zitrone, Apfelsaft, Sekt, Soße, Kinderteller, selbst gemacht, kalorienarm, kalorienbewusst, abnehmen.* **(2)** Remind sts. to use „*Wie bitte?*", „*Wie schreibt man das?*", „*Weißt du, was das heißt?*" usw. instead of using English or looking at each other's charts. Allow at least 5 minutes for completion of the charts. **(3)** Focus on form: Tell sts. that most adjectives are in the accusative case (except the 1 adjective that is preceded by the preposition *mit*), and ask them to come up with the rules for adjective endings for the 3 genders and the plural in the accusative.

Gesunde Ernährung¹

Wenn man gesund sein möchte, muss man sich gesund ernähren². Aber viele moderne Lebensmittel sind nicht gesund. Deshalb kaufen immer mehr Menschen Lebensmittel aus kontrolliertem ökologischen Anbau³, sogenannte Bioprodukte⁴. Der Ausschnitt aus **Blickkontakte** vergleicht Bioprodukte mit Produkten aus dem Supermarkt.

- Sind Biolebensmittel teurer als die Lebensmittel im Supermarkt?
- Wann spricht man von Bioeiern?
- Was unterscheidet Bioradieschen von Radieschen aus dem Supermarkt?
- Warum sind Biowürstchen so teuer?

¹nutrition ²sich ernähren: to eat, get nourishment ³cultivation
⁴organic products

Ein Bund Bioradieschen kostet einen Euro zwanzig, doppelt so viel wie im Supermarkt.

Videoblick. The selection from the **Blickkontakte** video focuses on organic products and why they are more expensive than nonorganic ones. It compares the price of eggs, radishes, and sausages bought in a supermarket with that of those bought at an organic farmers' market. The clip also explains why the organic eggs, radishes, and sausages are more expensive.

Situation 3 | Ratespiel: Regionale Spezialitäten

Sit. 3. (1) Present the new vocabulary: *deftig, Berliner Weiße* (relatively sour wheat beer, often drunk with raspberry juice), *Fleischchüechli (Frikadellen), Knödel (Kartoffelklöße), Semmeln (Brötchen), Rote Grütze (Mus aus roten Früchten).* **(2)** Introduce the concept of regional cuisine. Let sts. who have been to a German-speaking country talk about their eating experiences. **(3)** Then, ask sts. to work in groups and encourage them to guess when they don't know. **(4) Focus on form.** Ask sts. what gender or number the nouns have. Tell them that they can tell gender by looking at the adjective ending. Ask them to figure out what adjective ending goes with which gender or number. Answers may vary somewhat. Expected answers are: 1. *Berlin*, 2. *Schweiz*, 3. *USA*, 4. *Bayern*, 5. *Norddeutschland*, 6. *USA*, 7. *Bayern* or *Österreich*, 8. *USA*, 9. *Norddeutschland*, 10. *Sachsen*.

Was glauben Sie? Wo isst oder trinkt man diese regionalen Spezialitäten? Es gibt viele richtige Antworten.

1. Wo trinkt man Berliner Weiße?
2. Wo isst man selbst gemachte Fleischchüechli?
3. Wo isst man gebratene Eier und Speck?
4. Wo isst man deftige Knödel?
5. Wo isst man frischen Fisch aus der Nordsee?
6. Wo trinkt man frisch gepressten Orangensaft?
7. Wo isst man frische Semmeln?
8. Wo trinkt man eiskalten Eistee?
9. Wo isst man Rote Grütze?
10. Wo trinkt man sächsisches Schwarzbier?

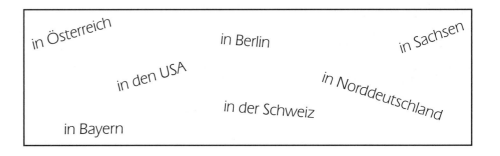

in Österreich   in Berlin   in Sachsen

in den USA   in Norddeutschland

in der Schweiz

in Bayern

Essgewohnheiten

- Was ist in Ihrem Land ein typisches Essen?
- Welche Art von ausländischem Essen ist in Ihrem Land besonders beliebt? Stellen Sie eine Rangliste von eins (am wenigsten beliebt) bis zehn (am meisten beliebt) auf.

_____	italienisch	_____	spanisch
_____	griechisch	_____	koreanisch
_____	französisch	_____	chinesisch
_____	mexikanisch	_____	japanisch
_____	deutsch	_____	indisch

- Welche Art von ausländischem Essen ist in Deutschland am beliebtesten? Raten Sie!

☐ chinesisch   ☐ griechisch
☐ türkisch   ☐ französisch
☐ italienisch

Lesen Sie den Text, und suchen Sie Antworten auf die Fragen.

ETHNIC FOOD

MULTI-KULTI-KÜCHE

Eine Studie über Essgewohnheiten zeigt: Am Kochtopf sind die Deutschen besonders ausländerfreundlich

Das morgendliche Croissant zum Cappuccino, die Pizza und die Frühlingsrolle animierten unlängst[1] das SZ-Magazin[2] zu der Frage: „Wie konnten wir früher satt werden,[3] ohne Mozzarella und Basilikum zu kennen?"

Der Deutsche, so belegt[4] ein Rundgang durch Supermärkte und Restaurants, serviert Grünkohl, Schweinebraten und Eisbein anscheinend[5] nur noch auf Volksfesten und für Touristenmenüs. Er aber wendet sich statt dessen[6] liebevoll griechischem Fetakäse, Curry und Couscous zu.[7] Und ohne Pasta kann er schon gar nicht mehr leben.

KLI. Have sts. do this in pairs and share their results with the class. Tally class results to arrive at a final order.

Cultural note. According to this same article, Italian food is the most popular food in Germany.

- Welche ausländischen Speisen und Getränke können Sie im Text identifizieren? Aus welchen Ländern kommen sie ursprünglich?
- Welche deutschen Speisen und Getränke können Sie identifizieren?
- Wo und für wen servieren die Deutschen anscheinend nur noch deutsches Essen?

Schauen Sie sich die Grafik genau an und beantworten Sie die Fragen.

- Wer isst zu Hause öfter ausländisch, Leute unter 35 oder über 55?
- Wie viel Prozent der Deutschen unter 35 gehen sehr häufig in ein ausländisches Restaurant?
- Wie viel Prozent der Deutschen über 55 gehen nie in ein ausländisches Restaurant?

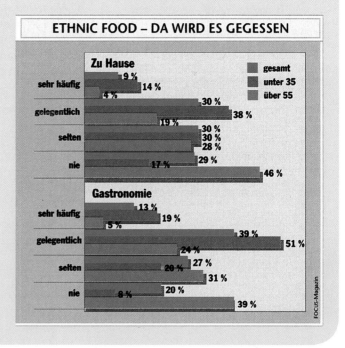

ETHNIC FOOD – DA WIRD ES GEGESSEN

[1]_not long ago, lately_   [2]_magazine supplement to the „Süddeutsche Zeitung"_   [3]_satt ... get sated, full_   [4]_verifies_   [5]_apparently_   [6]_statt ... instead (of that)_   [7]_wendet sich zu turns to_

Sit. 4. Sts. might want to add these questions. *Was ist dein Lieblingsessen/Lieblingsgetränk?*

AA. If some of your sts. have relatives from German-speaking countries, you might ask them to talk about special dishes or mealtime customs in their families. Similarly, many sts. may have German ancestors who have passed mealtime traditions down from generation to generation.

1. Was isst du normalerweise zum Frühstück? Was zu Mittag?
2. Isst du viel zu Abend? Was?
3. Isst du immer eine Nachspeise? Was isst du am liebsten als Nachspeise?
4. Trinkst du viel Kaffee?
5. Isst du zwischen den Mahlzeiten? Warum (nicht)?
6. Was isst du, wenn du mitten in der Nacht großen Hunger hast?
7. Was trinkst du, wenn du auf Feste gehst?
8. Was hast du heute Morgen gegessen und getrunken?
9. Was isst du heute zu Mittag?
10. Was isst du heute zu Abend?

Haushaltsgeräte

Vocabulary Display
This section provides examples of the verbs *stellen, stehen, legen, liegen, setzen, sitzen,* and *hängen.* Introduce vocabulary and the concept of 2-way prepositions and then reinforce them with TPR activities. For example, bring in plastic knives and forks, paper plates, glasses, and napkins, and tell each pair of sts. to pick up a set. Then demonstrate setting a table yourself with a commentary: *Ich stelle einen Teller auf den Tisch, dann lege ich eine Gabel links neben den Teller und ein Messer rechts. Ich stelle ein Glas rechts vor den Teller usw.* Then step back and describe the table setting: *Ein Teller steht auf dem Tisch. Neben dem Teller liegt eine Gabel, und vor dem Teller steht ein Glas.* In pairs, sts. should now follow your example except that one sets the table and narrates and the other describes the locations afterward. They then reverse roles.

Cultural note. *Wohngemeinschaften* are common in Germany. Young people–often sts.–prefer to share apartments not only for economic reasons but as an alternative way of living.

Grammatik 8.3

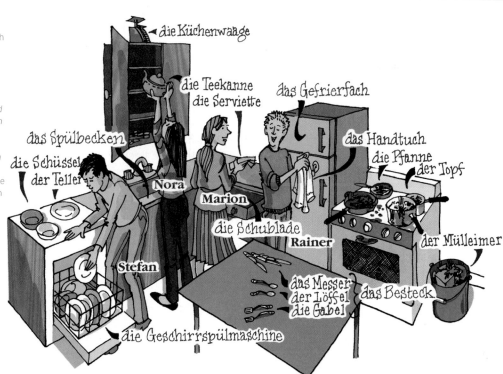

Stefan stellt die Schüsseln und Teller in die Geschirrspülmaschine.
Nora stellt die Teekanne in den Schrank.
Marion legt die Servietten in die Schublade.
Rainer hängt das Handtuch an den Haken.
Die schmutzigen Töpfe und Pfannen stehen auf dem Herd.
Messer, Gabeln und Löffel liegen auf dem Tisch.

Situation 5 | Was kosten diese Gegenstände?

Sit. 5. Sts. work together in small groups. Preteach vocabulary with pictures from your PF. For each item, ask how much it might cost. When students give you prices in dollars, simply use the same price and say euros. Explain the two tasks and ask sts. to work in groups of 3. Follow up by asking them to explain why they cannot do without certain items.

Listen Sie die Gegenstände in jeder Gruppe dem Preis nach. Beginnen Sie mit dem teuersten Gegenstand. Wählen Sie dann aus jeder Gruppe die vier Gegenstände aus, auf die Sie am wenigsten verzichten[1] könnten.

GRUPPE A	GRUPPE B
1. eine Kaffeemaschine	1. ein Mikrowellenherd
2. ein elektrischer Dosenöffner	2. ein Kühlschrank
3. eine Küchenmaschine	3. eine Geschirrspülmaschine
4. ein Korkenzieher	4. eine Waschmaschine
5. eine Kaffeemühle	5. ein Wäschetrockner
6. ein Bügeleisen	6. ein Grill
7. eine Küchenwaage	7. ein Staubsauger
8. ein Toaster	8. eine Gefriertruhe

Situation 6 | Was brauchen Sie dazu?

Sit. 6. Sts. read through the list of tasks and decide what items they need for each. If time permits, put sts. in small groups to think of other situations in which they would need these items. Afterward, they can read their lists to the class and have the class decide what would be useful in that situation. Encourage sts. to be imaginative, as well: *Ich habe ein Geburtstagsgeschenk bekommen und möchte die Schnur durchschneiden. Ich möchte für meine Freundin ein Wiener Schnitzel machen und muss das Fleisch zuschneiden usw.* In doing this, sts. reinforce not only the particular vocabulary items but many other phrases and grammatical structures as well.

1. Sie bekommen ein Paket, das mit einer Schnur zugebunden ist. Sie wollen die Schnur durchschneiden.
2. Sie wollen sich ein belegtes Brot machen und eine Scheibe Wurst abschneiden.
3. Sie wollen sich eine Dose Suppe heiß machen und müssen die Dose aufmachen.
4. Sie haben Gäste und wollen ein paar Flaschen Bier aufmachen.
5. Sie wollen eine Kerze anzünden.
6. Sie wollen Tee kochen und müssen Wasser heiß machen.
7. Sie haben eine Reifenpanne und müssen einen rostigen Nagel aus einem Autoreifen ziehen.
8. Sie wollen ein Bild aufhängen und müssen einen Nagel in die Wand schlagen.
9. Beim Gewitter ist der Strom ausgefallen. In Ihrem Zimmer ist es total dunkel.

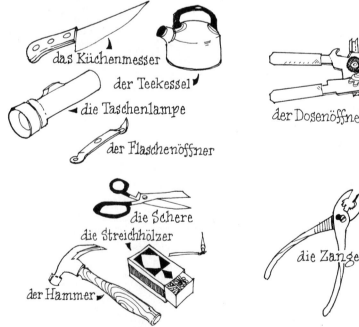

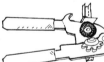

[1]*do without*

| Diskussion: Haushaltsgeräte

Sit. 7. Sts. work in groups of 3-4. Ask them to choose one person to be spokesperson for each question. After sts. have discussed the questions for a few minutes, each spokesperson then tells how the group answered.

1. Welche elektrischen Haushaltsgeräte haben Sie, Ihre Eltern oder Freunde? Welches Gerät finden Sie am wichtigsten?
2. Stellen Sie sich vor, Sie dürfen nur ein Gerät im Hause haben. Welches wählen Sie und warum?
3. Welche Werkzeuge sollte es in jedem Haushalt geben?
4. Sie wollen übers Wochenende zum Zelten. Machen Sie eine Liste, welche Geräte Sie zum Essen und Kochen brauchen.
5. Sie planen ein elegantes Picknick. Was packen Sie alles ein?

Lektüre

Lesehilfe

This reading is written in the present and past tenses. Note that the narration is in the present tense, while quotations are in the past tense. How does this mixing of tenses and the interspersing of narration with spoken text make the story more interesting?

Vor dem Lesen

Der Titel der Geschichte ist „Mord im Café König?". Welche Möglichkeiten gibt es bei einem typischen Mord? Füllen Sie die Tabelle aus, ohne den Text zu lesen.

Tat	*Mord*
Tatort	_____
Täter[1]	_____
Mordwaffe[2]	_____
Motiv	_____
Augenzeugen[3]	_____
Beweise[4]	_____

Lektüre. Ask sts. to complete the *Vor dem Lesen* in small groups. Encourage sts. to be creative and describe people (*Täter, Augenzeugen usw.*) by their occupations, ages, and appearance and to think of all sorts of murder weapons and motives. You may need to provide vocabulary such as *ein Dolch* (m.), *ein Gewehr* (n.), *eine Pistole, Eifersucht* (f.), *Erpressung usw.*

Assign the text to be read as homework along with Parts A and B of the *Arbeit mit dem Text.* In class, assign roles for each character mentioned in the story, take 2 newspapers to class, preferably the ones mentioned, and have sts. act out the story as you narrate/direct it. Sts. speak their lines as direct discourse and use mime elsewhere.

Nach dem Lesen Part A could be done in pairs or groups, and then sts. could compare answers. Encourage them to come up with their own ideas (option d). Assign Part B for written homework.

Miniwörterbuch		
aufschlagen		to open up
aussagen		to state
beachten		to notice
beobachten		to observe
betreten		to enter
bleich		pale
sich erinnern an (+ acc.)		to remember
hinunterbeugen		to bend over
der **Kiosk**		newsstand
sich kümmern um		to pay attention to
merken		to notice
nachher		afterward
quietschend		screeching
das **Steuer**		steering wheel
Streife gehen		to be on patrol
verlassen		to leave
verschütten		to spill
verschwinden		to disappear
wirken		to look

---

[1]*person(s) who did it, the perpetrator(s)* [2]*murder weapon* [3]*eyewitnesses* [4]*pieces of evidence*

Mord im Café König?

Ein Mann steigt auf der Königsallee in Düsseldorf aus einem Taxi, zahlt und geht zu einem Kiosk. Er wirkt nervös, sieht sich mehrmals um.

„Er hat mir über zwei Euro Trinkgeld gegeben", sagte der Taxifahrer nachher aus.

5 Am Kiosk kauft der Mann eine *Süddeutsche Zeitung* und eine *International Herald Tribune*. Wieder sieht er sich mehrere Male um und beobachtet die Straße.

„Ich glaube, er hörte nicht gut, er hat mich dreimal nach dem Preis gefragt", sagte der Kioskbesitzer aus.

Ein dunkelgrauer Mercedes 450 SL mit drei Männern und einer Frau am Steuer 10 parkt gegenüber. Die vier beobachten den Mann. Der sieht sie und geht schnell in die Köpassage, ein großes Einkaufszentrum mit vielen Geschäften, Restaurants und Cafés. Zwei der Männer steigen aus und folgen ihm.

„Sie trugen graue Regenmäntel", sagte ein Passant, als Inspektor Schilling ihm die Fotos der Männer zeigte.

15 Der Mann mit den beiden Zeitungen betritt das Café König, setzt sich in eine Ecke, schlägt sehr schnell eine der Zeitungen auf und versteckt sich dahinter.

„Er wirkte sehr nervös," sagte die Kellnerin.

Er bestellt einen Kaffee und einen Kognak und zahlt sofort.

„Er verschüttete die Milch, als er sie in den Kaffee goss, aber er gab mir ein sehr 20 gutes Trinkgeld", sagte die Kellnerin weiter aus.

Die beiden Männer in den Regenmänteln betreten das Café und sehen sich um. Als sie den Mann hinter der aufgeschlagenen *Herald Tribune* erkennen, gehen sie hinüber und setzen sich an den Nachbartisch.

„Sie waren sehr unfreundlich und bestellten beide Mineralwasser", meinte die 25 Kellnerin, die sie bediente.

Eine attraktive Frau, Mitte dreißig, betritt das Café, sieht sich um, lächelt, als sie den Mann mit der Zeitung sieht, wird bleich, als ihr Blick auf die beiden Männer fällt. Sie setzt sich in eine andere Ecke und beobachtet alles.

„Sie war sehr elegant gekleidet", sagte der Kellner, der an ihrem Tisch bediente.

30 Schließlich geht einer der Männer zu dem Mann mit der Zeitung hinüber, er beugt sich zu ihm hinunter und hinter die Zeitung. Plötzlich fällt der Mann mit der Zeitung mit dem Kopf auf den Tisch. Er bewegt sich nicht mehr. Der andere nimmt ihm die *Herald Tribune* aus der Hand, faltet sie schnell zusammen. Die ersten Leute werden unruhig, weil sie merken, dass etwas passiert ist. Die beiden Männer rennen aus dem 35 Café, über die Königsallee und springen in den parkenden Wagen.

„Sie sind mit quietschenden Reifen davongefahren", berichtete ein Polizist, der gerade Streife ging.

Die Gäste des Cafés laufen jetzt laut schreiend durcheinander. Keiner beachtet die Frau, die zu dem Toten hinübergeht und die *Süddeutsche Zeitung* nimmt, sie unter den 40 Arm steckt und schnell das Café verlässt.

„Ich erinnere mich so gut an sie, weil sie nicht bezahlt hat", sagte der Kellner.

Die Polizei ist sehr schnell da. Immer noch laufen alle Leute durcheinander, keiner kümmert sich um den Toten. Als die Polizei den Toten sehen will, ist der verschwunden.

Inspektor Schilling fragt: Was ist passiert?

Arbeit mit dem Text

A. Wer hat das gesagt? Suchen Sie die Namen bzw. Berufsbezeichnungen der Personen im Text.

> „Der Mann hat mir mehr als zwei Euro Trinkgeld gegeben."
> „Er hat bei mir zwei Zeitungen gekauft."
> „Die Männer trugen graue Regenmäntel."
> „Weil der Mann sehr nervös war, verschüttete er die Milch."
> „Sie bestellten Mineralwasser und waren sehr unfreundlich."
> „Die Frau war sehr elegant gekleidet."
> „Die Männer sind mit quietschenden Reifen weggefahren."
> „Die Frau hat nicht bezahlt, deshalb erinnere ich mich an sie."

B. Dieser Text hat zwei Teile: 1. Einen Bericht der Fakten im Präsens. 2. Zitate von Augenzeugen in der direkten Rede. Kennzeichnen Sie, was zum Bericht (B) oder zu den Zitaten (Z) gehört.

Nach dem Lesen

A. In dieser Geschichte bleiben viele Fragen offen. Welche von den drei möglichen Antworten finden Sie am logischsten? Oder haben Sie eine logischere Antwort?

1. Wer war der Mann mit den Zeitungen?
   a. Ein Spion.
   b. Ein Politiker.
   c. Ein Genforscher[1].
   d. Ein _____.
2. Warum war der Mann nervös?
   a. Weil er gefährliche[2] Feinde[3] hatte.
   b. Weil er an dem Tag eine Prüfung in Deutsch hatte.
   c. Weil er nur noch kurze Zeit zu leben hatte.
   d. Weil _____.
3. Warum hörte er nicht gut?
   a. Weil er erkältet war[4].
   b. Weil er sehr unkonzentriert war.
   c. Weil er ein Hörgerät im Ohr hatte.
   d. Weil _____.
4. Wer waren die Leute im Mercedes?
   a. Spione.
   b. Seine Leibwächter[5].
   c. Seine Freunde.
   d. _____.
5. Warum geht der Mann ins Café König?
   a. Weil er dort eine Verabredung[6] hat.
   b. Weil er noch einen Kaffee trinken will.
   c. Weil er sich verstecken will.
   d. Weil _____.
6. Wer ist die Frau?
   a. Seine Sekretärin.
   b. Seine Partnerin.
   c. Eine Spionin.
   d. _____.

B. Erklären Sie jetzt Inspektor Schilling, was passiert ist. Schreiben Sie ihm einen Brief.

[1]*geneticist* [2]*dangerous* [3]*enemies* [4]*erkältet ... had a cold* [5]*bodyguards* [6]*appointment*

Einkaufen und Kochen

Grammatik 8.4

Vocabulary Display

This section focuses on preparing meals (including shopping for food). It provides extended practice in describing and narrating in the present. After having practiced pronouncing the words in the display, ask sts. to interview each other about what foods in the display they like and don't like to eat. *„Fragen Sie, Was isst du gern in der Kategorie Fleisch und Fisch usw. und: Was isst du nicht gern, und schreiben Sie die Antworten auf!"* Follow up by asking: *„Wer von Ihnen isst gern Geflügel? Heben Sie bitte die Hand!" usw.*

Cultural note. Pork is much more common in Germany than in North America; it is also cheaper than beef. Bulk food (fruits, vegetables, sausage, cheese, meat, etc.) is priced by *Kilogramm (kg)* or by 100 *Gramm (g)*. Liquid measurements are *Liter (l)* and *Milliliter (ml)*. 1 *Pfund* (500 g) is used in spoken language but not found on most labels or price tags.

das Fleisch und der Fisch

das Gemüse

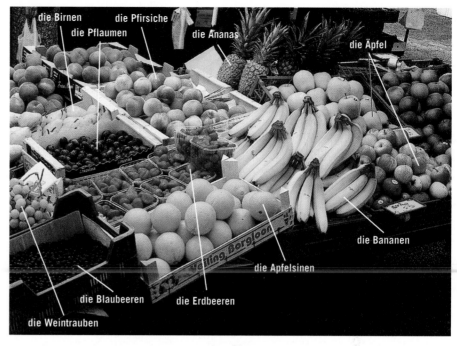

das Obst

| Bildgeschichte: Michaels bestes Gericht

Michael kocht heute wieder sein bestes Gericht: Omelett *à la haute cuisine* …

Sit. 8. Sentences for narration series: **1.** *Michael wäscht die Tomaten und Pilze mit kaltem Wasser.* **2.** *Dann schneidet er die Tomaten und Pilze in Scheiben.* **3.** *Dann schneidet er den Schinken in kleine Stücke.* **4.** *Dann schlägt Michael drei Eier in eine Schüssel.* **5.** *Er würzt die Eier mit Salz, Pfeffer und Paprika.* **6.** *Jetzt erhitzt er Öl in einer Pfanne.* **7.** *Michael gibt den Schinken in die Pfanne und bräunt ihn.* **8.** *Dann kommen die Tomaten und Pilze hinzu .***9.** *Zum Schluss gießt er die Eier darüber.* **10.** *Wenn das Omelett fast fertig ist, bestreut er es noch mit Käse.*

Deutsche Bioeier: Bioprodukte werden immer beliebter.

Situation 9 | Einkaufsliste

Sie wollen heute Abend kochen. Was wollen Sie kochen? Was brauchen Sie? (Sie finden Ideen im Wortkasten.) Machen Sie für jedes Gericht eine Einkaufsliste. Denken Sie auch an Salat, Gemüse und Gewürze, an Vorspeise und Nachspeise und an Getränke.

1. ein italienisches Gericht
2. ein amerikanisches Gericht
3. ein türkisches Gericht
4. ein deutsches Gericht
5. ein französisches Gericht

Fisch · Nudeln · Salz · Bohnen · Paprika · Oliven · Erbsen · Zwiebeln · Gurken · Schnitzel · Knoblauch · Kopfsalat · Pilze · Pfeffer · Schafskäse · Tomaten · Kartoffeln · Tomatensoße · Karotten · Essig und Öl · Hackfleisch

Situation 10 | Zum Schreiben: Ein Rezept

Ein Austauschstudent aus Deutschland möchte ein Rezept für ein typisches Gericht aus Ihrem Land. Geben Sie ihm/ihr Ihr persönliches Lieblingsrezept. Schreiben Sie zuerst auf, was man alles braucht und wie viel. Dann beschreiben Sie, wie man es zubereitet. Machen Sie auch kleine Zeichnungen dazu. (Keine Mikrowellenmahlzeit, bitte!)

ZUTATEN   ZUBEREITUNG

_____   _____

_____   _____

_____   _____

Situation 11 | Interview: Einkaufen und Kochen

1. Kannst du kochen? Was zum Beispiel?
2. Kochst du oft? Wer kocht in deiner Familie?
3. Was kochst du am liebsten? Welche Zutaten braucht man dazu?
4. Kaufst du jeden Tag ein? Wenn nicht, wie oft in der Woche? An welchen Tagen? Wo kaufst du meistens ein?

Sit. 9 Depending on whether or not your sts. like to cook, you might mention a few of the spices (*die Gewürze*): Basil = *Basilikum;* bay leaves = *Lorbeerblätter;* cinnamon = *Zimt;* cloves = *Gewürznelken;* ginger = *Ingwer;* nutmeg = *Muskatnuss;* oregano = *Oregano;* parsley = *Petersilie;* herbs = *Kräuter.*

Sit. 10. AA. Depending on the interests of the class, you might compile everyone's favorite recipes. Each st. could choose a favorite recipe and translate the directions into German. Don't convert ingredient quantities to the metric system; just use *Tasse, Esslöffel,* and *Teelöffel.* Give sts. examples of recipes to use as models for writing cooking directions.

Sit. 11. Model pronunciation. Sts. repeat. Sts. interview each other, then switch partners and report on the first partner's answers. Then, address questions to the whole class, and expand on some of them. If sts. are married or have partners, who does the cooking and the shopping? Always one or the other person, or do they share the responsibilities?

Lektüre

Lektüre. Vor dem Lesen. Before working with the photo and the accompanying questions, do an experiment in class by asking your sts. to communicate with each other without speaking. After that, collect sts.' communication strategies on the board. Did they communicate with their hands? Did they use some sort of sign language?

Vor dem Lesen

A. Beantworten Sie die folgenden Fragen.

1. Was assoziieren Sie mit Stille?
2. Schauen Sie sich das Filmposter an: Wie sehen die beiden jungen Leute auf dem Poster aus?
3. Welche Charaktereigenschaften haben sie vielleicht? Finden Sie Adjektive.
4. Was machen sie mit ihren Händen?

Jenseits der Stille

Regisseurin: Caroline Link

**Schauspieler in den Hauptrollen:
Sylvie Testud, Tatjana Trieb,
Howie Seago, Emmanuelle Laborit,
Sibylle Canonica**

Erscheinungsjahr: 1996

B. Lesen Sie die Wörter im Miniwörterbuch auf der nächsten Seite. Suchen Sie sie im Text und unterstreichen Sie sie.

Film: *Jenseits der Stille*

Die achtjährige Lara lebt mit ihren Eltern in Bayern. Sie ist die Einzige in der Familie, die sprechen und hören kann. Ihre Eltern sind beide gehörlos. Lara muss ihnen bei der Verständigung im Alltag oft helfen. Weil sie die Zeichensprache und die Sprache der Außenwelt beherrscht, übersetzt sie für ihre Eltern: bei jedem Telefonat, auf der Bank, in der Schule. Zu ihrem Vater hat Lara ein besonders gutes Verhältnis.

Eines Tages bekommt Lara eine Klarinette von ihrer Tante Clarissa. Lara lernt auf dem Instrument zu spielen und ist richtig gut. Sie hat Talent. Doch nicht nur das: Sie entdeckt eine große Welt außerhalb der häuslichen Stille, nämlich die Musik. Mit 18 will sie nach Berlin auf das Konservatorium und dort Musik studieren. Ihren Eltern sagt sie zunächst nichts davon. Als sie es dann doch erfahren, gibt es Ärger. Vor allem ihr Vater ist wütend und eifersüchtig. Er weiß, dass Lara dabei ist, sich von ihnen zu lösen und Welten zu entdecken, die ihnen verschlossen bleiben.

Lara geht trotzdem nach Berlin und bereitet sich auf die Aufnahmeprüfung vor. Auch als ihre Mutter plötzlich bei einem Verkehrsunfall ums Leben kommt, bessert sich das angespannte Verhältnis zwischen Vater und Tochter nicht. Aber in dem Moment, in dem Lara vor die Prüfungskommission des Konservatoriums tritt, sieht sie ihren Vater im Konzertsaal. Er will sie spielen sehen.

Arbeit mit dem Text

Welche Aussagen sind falsch? Verbessern Sie die falschen Aussagen.

1. Lara kann hören und sprechen, ihre Eltern aber nicht.
2. Lara hilft ihren Eltern im Alltag, weil sie gehörlos sind.
3. Lara hat ein besonders gutes Verhältnis zu ihrer Mutter.
4. Lara bekommt von ihrer Kusine Clarissa eine Klarinette.
5. Laras Eltern möchten, dass Lara nach Berlin auf das Konservatorium geht.
6. Das Verhältnis zwischen Lara und ihrem Vater wird nach dem Tod der Mutter auch nicht besser.
7. Laras Vater akzeptiert am Ende des Films Laras Wunsch, Musik zu studieren.

Nach dem Lesen

Nach dem Lesen. Have sts. develop the open-ended story into a creative writing activity. Hints: Is Lara accepted into the conservatory? How does the relationship with her father develop? How does she feel about the development of events?

Kreatives Schreiben. Wie geht die Geschichte weiter? Lara schreibt einen Brief an ihre beste Freundin oder ihren besten Freund und erzählt, wie es nach dem Vorspielen weitergegangen ist. Liebe … (Lieber …), wie geht es dir? Letzte Woche habe ich hier in Berlin am Konservatorium vorgespielt …

Im Restaurant

Vocabulary Display   **Grammatik 8.5**

This display features typical exchanges sts. might hear in a restaurant. Establish who says what when presenting the mini-dialogues, e.g., *Wer sagt: Ist hier noch frei? Die Frau, die steht, oder die Frau, die sitzt? Erkennen Sie die Frau, die steht? Richtig, das ist Frau Gretter. Und die Frau, die sitzt? Wir kennen sie nicht und Frau Gretter kennt sie auch nicht.* Similarly (going from left to right): Renate Röder (asking for the menu); Mehmet Sengün (asking for a mineral water); Herr and Frau Frisch (asking for the bill and leaving a tip); Herr Thelen and Frau Körner (discussing coffee). Ask sts. in which country the bill and tipping exchange takes place: *In welchem Land bezahlt man mit Franken?* (*In der Schweiz.*)

Cultural note. In the German-speaking countries, tax and a service charge (10-15%) are included in the final bill. Therefore, people commonly tip less than in North America. Often, they round up to the nearest currency unit, or, when bills get larger, to the nearest fifth unit or decimal.

a. —Ist hier noch frei?
    —Ja, bitte schön.

b. —Was darf ich Ihnen bringen?
    —Kann ich bitte die Speisekarte haben?
    —Ja, gern, einen Moment, bitte.

c. —Ein Wasser, bitte.
    —Ein Mineralwasser. Kommt sofort!

d. —Wir würden gern zahlen.
    —Gern. Das waren zwei Wiener Schnitzel, ein Glas Wein und eine Limo ...

e. —38,80 Franken, bitte schön.
    —Das stimmt so.
    —Vielen Dank.
    —Können Sie mir dafür eine Quittung geben?
    —Selbstverständlich.

f. —Darf ich Sie noch zu einem Kaffee einladen?
    —Das ist nett, aber leider muss ich mich jetzt beeilen.

Situation 12 | Was sagen Sie?

Sit. 12. Have sts. work in groups of 3.

Cultural note. Quite often, especially when a restaurant is full or someone is sitting alone, newly arriving customers will ask to share a table where there are empty seats.

Wählen Sie für jede Situation eine passende Aussage.

Nein, danke.

Ja, bitte sehr.

Das kann nicht stimmen. Ich habe doch einen Sauerbraten bestellt.

Morgen fliege ich in die USA.

Zahlen, bitte.

Das stimmt so.

Leider habe ich kein Geld.

Ich liebe Schweinebraten.

Herr Kellner, bitte, sehen Sie sich das mal an.

Die Speisekarte, bitte.

1. Sie sitzen an einem Tisch im Restaurant. Sie haben Hunger, aber noch keine Speisekarte. Sie sehen die Kellnerin und sagen: _____
2. Sie haben mit Ihren Freunden im Restaurant gegessen. Sie haben es eilig und möchten zahlen. Sie rufen den Kellner und sagen: _____
3. Sie gehen allein essen. Sie sitzen schon an einem Tisch. Das Restaurant ist voll. Es gibt keine freien Tische mehr. Plötzlich kommt jemand an Ihren Tisch, den Sie nicht kennen, und fragt, ob er sich zu Ihnen setzen kann. Sie sagen: _____
4. Ihr Essen und Trinken hat 19 Euro 20 gekostet. Sie haben der Kellnerin einen Zwanzigeuroschein gegeben. 80 Cent sind Trinkgeld. Sie sagen: _____
5. Sie essen mit Ihren Eltern in einem feinen Restaurant. Da stellen Sie fest, dass eine Fliege in der Suppe schwimmt. Sie rufen den Kellner und sagen: _____
6. Sie haben einen Sauerbraten mit Knödeln bestellt. Die Kellnerin bringt Ihnen einen Schweinebraten. Sie sagen: _____

 Situation 13 | Dialog: Melanie und Josef gehen aus.

Sit. 13. (See the IM.) This dialogue provides a model for the role-play following it. You may wish to follow the steps for presenting the dialogue without the use of the textbook. You may then want to have sts. complete the dialogue as homework. (Some main text dialogues are on the workbook/lab manual recordings. All are on the text recording.) Questions for listening comprehension: **1.** *Was möchten Melanie und Josef haben?* **2.** *Was möchte Melanie trinken? Und Josef?* **3.** *Was isst Melanie? Und Josef?*

Cultural note. In German-speaking countries, people usually drink sparkling mineral water instead of tap water (*Leitungswasser*). Water is not served in restaurants, and there are no drinking fountains in public places.

Melanie und Josef haben sich einen Tisch ausgesucht und sich hingesetzt. Der Kellner kommt an ihren Tisch.

KELLNER: Bitte schön?
MELANIE: Können wir die Speisekarte haben?
KELLNER: Natürlich. Möchten Sie etwas trinken?
MELANIE: Für mich ein Mineralwasser bitte.
JOSEF: Und für mich ein Bier.
KELLNER: Gern.
   [*etwas später*]
KELLNER: Wissen Sie schon, was Sie essen möchten?
MELANIE: Ich möchte das Rumpsteak mit Pilzen und Kroketten.
JOSEF: Und ich hätte gern die Forelle „blau" mit Kräuterbutter, grünem Salat und Salzkartoffeln. Dazu noch ein Bier bitte.
KELLNER: Gern. Darf ich Ihnen auch noch etwas zu trinken bringen?
MELANIE: Nein, danke, im Moment nicht.

286   KAPITEL 8   Essen und Einkaufen

Stichwort „Restaurant"

- Gehen Sie oft ins Restaurant?
- Haben Sie ein Lieblingsrestaurant?
- Was machen Sie, wenn alle Tische besetzt sind?
- Wie lange bleiben Sie normalerweise im Restaurant sitzen, nachdem Sie gegessen haben?

Wie ist es in deutschen Restaurants? Hören Sie zu.

KLI. Have students review the vocabulary in the *Miniwörterbuch* before playing the recording or reading the passage to sts. Read or play recording: *Wenn man in Deutschland ins Restaurant geht, sucht man sich selbst einen Platz. Wenn es voll ist und man keinen Tisch reserviert hat, geht man wieder. Kaum jemand kommt auf die Idee, auf einen freien Tisch zu warten. Das kann auch lange dauern, denn viele Leute bleiben nach dem Essen noch bei einem Bier, Wein oder einem alkoholfreien Getränk sitzen, um sich zu unterhalten. Beim Essengehen geht es auch um die Geselligkeit. Als Trinkgeld für die Bedienung rundet man die Rechnung auf oder gibt je nach Betrag ca. 5% bis 10% dazu. In Deutschland bekommen Kellner und Kellnerinnen in Restaurants und Lokalen einen festen Lohn, meist zwischen 10% und 15% des Umsatzes. Trinkgeld ist daher kein Muss, sondern eine Anerkennung für nette und aufmerksame Bewirtung.*

Miniwörterbuch	
die **Anerkennung**	acknowledgment
aufmerksam	attentive
die **Bewirtung**	service
die **Geselligkeit**	sociability, social life
je nach Betrag	depending on the amount
der **Umsatz**	sales, returns

In einem Restaurant in Berlin

Vergleichen Sie! Deutschland (D) oder Nordamerika (N)?

<u> D </u> Platz selbst aussuchen

<u> N </u> auf einen freien Tisch warten

<u> N </u> nach dem Essen bald gehen

<u> D </u> nach dem Essen noch eine Weile sitzen bleiben

<u> D </u> weniger Trinkgeld geben

<u> N </u> 15%–20% Trinkgeld geben

Photo questions. *Was kann man hier alles kaufen? Was macht man in der Metzgerei? Was ist hausgemacht? Was kann man gut grillen? Essen Sie oft Rouladen? Kennen Sie Weißwürste und Fleischsalat? Wie schmeckt Ihnen das?*

Eine Münchner Metzgerei. Nichts für Vegetarier.

Situation 14 | Rollenspiel: Im Restaurant

Sit. 14. The role for s2 appears in Appendix B. Bring a menu to class or have sts. refer to the vocabulary displays for ideas on what they might order.

s1: Sie sind im Restaurant und möchten etwas zu essen und zu trinken bestellen. Wenn Sie mit dem Essen fertig sind, bezahlen Sie und geben Sie der Bedienung ein Trinkgeld.

Situation 15 | Bildgeschichte: Abendessen mit Hindernissen

Sit. 15. Sentences for narration series: **1.** *Gestern sind Maria und Michael ins Restaurant Zum Löwen gegangen.* **2.** *Sie haben beim Kellner ihre Getränke und ihr Essen bestellt.* **3.** *Zuerst hat ihnen der Wein nicht geschmeckt.* **4.** *Dann hat Maria die falsche Suppe bekommen.* **5.** *Danach hat Michael eine Fliege in seiner Suppe gefunden.* **6.** *Zum Schluss hat der Kellner ihnen zu viel berechnet.* **7.** *Schließlich haben sich Maria und Michael beim Geschäftsführer beschwert.* **8.** *Sie haben bezahlt.* **9.** *Danach sind sie in ein Eiscafé gegangen und haben ein großes Eis als Nachspeise gegessen.*

Situation 16 | Interview

Sit. 16. Model pronunciation and have sts. repeat, then have them work in pairs. Ask everyone to switch partners, but for a change of pace, they should simply do the interview again, rather than having the second partner ask about the first partner's answers. Bring in any *Speisekarten* you might have saved from trips.

1. Gehst du oft essen? Wie oft in der Woche isst du nicht zu Hause? Wirst du heute Abend zu Hause essen?
2. Isst du oft im Studentenheim? Wirst du morgen im Studentenheim essen? Schmeckt dir das Essen da?
3. Gehst du oft in Fast-Food-Restaurants? Wirst du vielleicht noch diese Woche in so einem Restaurant essen?
4. Warst du schon mal in einem deutschen Restaurant? Wenn ja, was hast du gegessen? Wenn nein, was wirst du bestellen, wenn du mal in einem deutschen Restaurant bist?
5. In welchem Restaurant schmeckt es dir am besten? Gibt es ein Restaurant, in dem du oft isst? Wie heißt es? Was isst du da? Wirst du diese Woche noch einmal hingehen?
6. Was ist das feinste Restaurant in unserer Stadt? Wie viel muss man da für ein gutes Essen bezahlen?

Videoecke

- Was isst du zum Frühstück?
- Was isst du zu Mittag?
- Was ist dein Lieblingsessen?
- Was magst du gar nicht?
- Was kannst du besonders gut kochen?
- Wie machst du das?

Aufgabe 1. (1) Focus sts.' attention on the photos by asking: *Wer kommt aus der Schweiz? Woher kommt Sophie? Wer ist verheiratet? Was ist ihr Mann von Beruf? Wessen Vater ist Pfarrer? Wer arbeitet gern im Garten? Wer geht gern ins Kino?* **(2)** Go over items in vocabulary box and explain all new vocabulary. **(3)** Play both interviews several times to allow sts. to complete the task in pairs or in small groups.

Eveline Segner kommt aus der Schweiz. Sie ist in Wettingen in der Nähe von Zürich geboren. Von Beruf ist sie Fremdsprachensekretärin. Sie ist verheiratet. Ihr Mann ist Biologe. Ihre Hobbys sind Musik, Volkstanz und Gartenarbeit.

Sophie kommt aus Reutlingen in Baden-Württemberg. Ihre Mutter ist Lehrerin und ihr Vater Pfarrer. Sie liest gern, geht gern spazieren und sie geht gern ins Kino.

Aufgabe 1

Was erfahren Sie über Sophie und Frau Segner? Schreiben Sie die Informationen aus dem Wortkasten in die Tabelle.

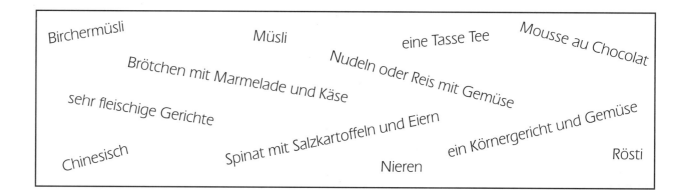

Birchermüsli   Müsli   eine Tasse Tee   Mousse au Chocolat
Brötchen mit Marmelade und Käse   Nudeln oder Reis mit Gemüse
sehr fleischige Gerichte
Chinesisch   Spinat mit Salzkartoffeln und Eiern   ein Körnergericht und Gemüse
Nieren   Rösti

	Frau Segner	Sophie
isst (trinkt) zum Frühstück		
isst zu Mittag		
Lieblingsessen		
mag überhaupt nicht		
kann besonders gut		

Aufgabe 2. A. Categorization.
(1) First ask sts. if they've heard of these two dishes before, and if so, where. Then ask sts. to guess which ingredients go with each of the two dishes. **(2)** Play the relevant segments from Frau Segner's and Sophie's interviews a couple of times so that sts. can check to make sure they have correctly categorized the ingredients. **B.** Sequencing. **(1)** Play the relevant segment from Frau Segner's interview several times, while sts. put the steps for preparing chocolate mousse in the proper sequence. **(2)** Ask if sts. know how to prepare chocolate mousse. If they do, ask if they do anything differently, and if so, what. **(3)** Finally, play the relevant segment from Sophie's interview several times and complete the same sequencing task for her recipe.

A. Rösti oder Mousse au Chocolat? Welche Zutaten gehören zu welchem Rezept?

	RÖSTI	MOUSSE AU CHOCOLAT
1. Kirsch	☐	☐
2. Schokolade	☐	☐
3. Kartoffeln	☐	☐
4. Käse	☐	☐
5. Tomaten	☐	☐
6. Salz	☐	☐
7. Pfeffer	☐	☐

B. Stellen Sie die Rezepte in der richtigen Reihenfolge zusammen.

RÖSTI

___4___ Man drückt das Wasser raus.
___2___ Man schält sie und reibt sie auf einer Reibe.
___5___ Man legt das in eine Pfanne und lässt es dort schmoren.
___3___ Man tut Salz und Pfeffer dazu.
___6___ Man tut noch Käse und Tomaten drauf.
___1___ Man nimmt rohe Kartoffeln.

MOUSSE AU CHOCOLAT

___3___ Man mischt sie zusammen mit der cremigen Schokolade.
___2___ Man verwendet Eischnee.
___1___ Man verwendet Schlagsahne.
___4___ Man gibt etwas Kirsch hinzu.

Wortschatz

Frühstück	Breakfast
die **Wurst**, -̈e	sausage
der **Käse**	cheese
der **Quark**	type of creamy cottage cheese
der **Schinken**	ham
der **Speck**	bacon
das **Brötchen**, -	roll
das **Ei**, -er	egg
gebratene **Eier**	fried eggs
gekochte **Eier**	boiled eggs
das **Hörnchen**, -	croissant
das **Würstchen**, -	frank(furter); hot dog

Ähnliche Wörter

die **Marmelade**, -n; der **Honig**; das **Omelett**, -s

Mittagessen und Abendessen	Lunch and Dinner
die **Forelle**, -n	trout
die **Krabbe**, -n	shrimp
die **Mahlzeit**, -en	meal
die **Nachspeise**, -n	dessert
die **Vorspeise**, -n	appetizer
der **Braten**, -	roast
der **Eisbecher**, -	dish of ice cream
der **Hummer**, -	lobster
der **Knödel**, -	dumpling
der **Pilz**, -e	mushroom
das **Brot**, -e	bread
das **belegte Brot**, die **belegten Brote**	open-face sandwich

das Fleisch	meat
das Hackfleisch	ground beef (or pork)
das Rindfleisch	beef
das Schweinefleisch	pork
das Geflügel	poultry
die Pommes (frites) [frit] or [frits] (*pl.*)	French fries

Ähnliche Wörter

die Krokette, -n; die Muschel, -n; die Nudel, -n; der Fisch, -e; der Reis; das Rumpsteak, -s; das Schnitzel, -

Obst und Nüsse	Fruit and Nuts
die Apfelsine, -n	orange
die Birne, -n	pear
die Erdbeere, -n	strawberry
die Kirsche, -n	cherry
die Weintraube, -n	grape
die Zitrone, -n	lemon
der Pfirsich, -e	peach

Ähnliche Wörter

die Banane, -n; die Nuss, ¨e; die Pflaume, -n

Gemüse	Vegetables
die Bohne, -n	bean
die Erbse, -n	pea
die Gurke, -n	cucumber
saure Gurken	pickles
die Kartoffel, -n	potato
die Salzkartoffeln	boiled potatoes
die Zwiebel, -n	onion
der Kohl	cabbage
der Blumenkohl	cauliflower
der Rosenkohl	Brussels sprouts

Ähnliche Wörter

die Karotte, -n; die Olive, -n; die Tomate, -n; der Salat, -e (R); der Heringssalat; der Kopfsalat; der Spinat

Getränke	Beverages
der Saft, ¨e	juice
der Apfelsaft	apple juice
der Orangensaft	orange juice

Ähnliche Wörter

die Milch; der Kakao [kakau]; das Mineralwasser

Zutaten	Ingredients
der Essig	vinegar
der Knoblauch	garlic
der Senf	mustard

das Gewürz, -e	spice; seasoning
die Kräuter (*pl.*)	herbs

Ähnliche Wörter

die Butter; die Kräuterbutter; die Mayonnaise; die Soße, -n; der Pfeffer; der Zucker; das Öl (R); das Salz

Küche und Zubereitung	Cooking and Preparation
auf·schneiden, aufgeschnitten	to chop
bestreuen	to sprinkle
braten, brät, gebraten	to fry
bräunen	to brown, fry
erhitzen	to heat
geben, gibt, gegeben (in + *akk.*)	to put (into)
gießen, gegossen	to pour
schlagen, schlägt, geschlagen	to beat
vermischen	to mix
würzen	to season

Im Restaurant	At the Restaurant
die Bedienung	service; waiter, waitress
die Fliege, -n	fly
die Geschäftsführerin, -nen	manager (female)
die Kellnerin, -nen	waitress
die Quittung, -en	receipt, check
die Speisekarte, -n	menu
die Suppe, -n	soup
der Geschäftsführer, -	manager (male)
der Kellner, -	waiter
der Schein, -e	bill, note (*of currency*)
der Zwanzigeuroschein, -e	twenty-euro note
der Teller, -	plate
das Gericht, -e	dish
das Stück, -e	slice; piece

Ähnliche Wörter

das Eiscafé, -s; das Trinkgeld, -er; die Öffnungszeiten (*pl.*)

Im Haushalt	In the Household
die Dose, -n	can
die Gabel, -n	fork
die Gefriertruhe, -n	freezer
die Küchenmaschine, -n	mixer
die Schere, -n	scissors
die Schnur, ¨e	string
die Schüssel, -n	bowl
die Serviette, -n	napkin
die Zange, -n	pliers, tongs

der Dosenöffner, -	can opener
der Haken, -	hook
der Löffel, -	spoon
der Mülleimer, -	garbage can
der Nagel, ¨	nail
der Strom	electricity, power
der Wäschetrockner, -	clothes dryer
das Gerät, -e	appliance
das Messer, -	knife
das Paket, -e	package
das Streichholz, ¨er	match
das Werkzeug, -e	tool

Ähnliche Wörter

die Kaffeemühle, -n; die Teekanne, -n; der
Flaschenöffner, -; der Grill, -s; der Hammer, ¨; der
Korkenzieher, -; der Teekessel, -; der Toaster, - [tosta]

Sonstige Verben	Other Verbs
ab·nehmen, nimmt ... ab, abgenommen	to lose weight
ab·schneiden, abgeschnitten	to cut off
aus·fallen, fällt ... aus, ist ausgefallen	to go out (power)
aus·rechnen	to figure, total (up)
aus·wählen	to select
sich beeilen	to hurry
berechnen (+ dat.)	to charge
sich beschweren (bei)	to complain (to)
bestellen	to order (food)
durch·schneiden	to cut through
stimmen	to be right
das stimmt so	that's right; keep the change

ziehen, gezogen	to pull
zu·bereiten	to prepare (food)

Adjektive und Adverbien	Adjectives and Adverbs
fettig	fat; greasy
frei	free, empty, available
ist hier noch frei?	is this seat available?
gebraten	roasted; broiled; fried
geräuchert	smoked
kalorienarm	low in calories
kalorienbewusst	calorie-conscious
leer	empty
verschieden	different, various
zart	tender
zugebunden	tied shut

Ähnliche Wörter

eiskalt, elegant, elektrisch, fein, frisch, gegrillt, gekocht,
gemischt, gesalzen, holländisch, japanisch, mexikanisch,
rostig, sauer, verboten

Sonstige Wörter und Ausdrücke	Other Words and Expressions
am wenigsten	the least
dazu	in addition
meistens	usually, mostly
nebeneinander	next to each other
normalerweise	normally
der Schluss, ¨e	end
zum Schluss	in the end, finally
selbst gemacht	homemade
selten	rare(ly), seldom
wofür	what for?

Strukturen und Übungen

8.1 Adjectives: an overview

Attributive adjectives precede nouns and have endings. Predicate adjectives follow the verb **sein** and have no endings.

8.1. *Adjektive.* Adjective endings are, of course, complex, and we do not expect first-year sts. to use most of them correctly in speaking. They can, however, use the description given here for focusing on endings when they read and for monitoring their own written work.

A. Attributive and predicate adjectives

Adjectives that precede nouns are called *attributive adjectives* and have endings similar to the forms of the definite article: **kalter, kaltes, kalte, kalten, kaltem.** Adjectives that follow the verb **sein** and a few other verbs are called *predicate adjectives* and do not have any endings.

VERKÄUFER: **Heiße** Würstchen! Ich verkaufe **heiße** Würstchen!	VENDOR: *Hot dogs! I'm selling hot dogs!*
KUNDE: Verzeihung, sind die Würstchen auch wirklich **heiß?**	CUSTOMER: *Excuse me, are the hot dogs really hot?*
VERKÄUFER: Natürlich, was denken Sie denn?!	VENDOR: *Of course, what do you think?!*

B. Attributive adjectives with and without preceding article

If *no* article or article-like word (**mein, dein, dieser,** or the like) precedes the adjective, then the adjective itself has the ending of the definite article **(der, das, die).** This means that the adjective provides the information about the gender, number, and case of the noun that follows.

Ich esse gern gegrill**ten** Fisch. *I like to eat grilled fish.*	**den** Fisch = masculine accusative
Stefan isst gern frisch**es** Müsli. *Stefan likes to eat fresh cereal.*	**das** Müsli = neuter accusative

If an article or article-like word precedes the adjective but does not have an ending, the adjective—again—has the ending of the definite article. **Ein**-words (the indefinite article **ein,** the negative article **kein,** and the possessive adjectives **mein, dein,** etc.) do *not* have an ending in the masculine nominative and in the neuter nominative and accusative. In these instances, as expected, the adjective gives the information about the gender, number, and case of the noun that follows.

Ein groß**er** Topf steht auf dem Herd. *There is a large pot on the stove.*	**der** Topf = masculine nominative
Ich esse ein frisch**es** Brötchen. *I am eating a fresh roll.*	**das** Brötchen = neuter accusative

If an article or article-like word with an ending precedes the adjective, the adjective ends in either **-e** or **-en.** (See Sections 8.2 and 8.4.)

Ich nehme das holländisch**e** Bier.	*I'll take the Dutch beer.*
Ich nehme die deutsch**en** Äpfel.	*I'll take the German apples.*

8.2 Attributive adjectives in the nominative and accusative cases

Rules of thumb:
1. In many instances, the adjective ending is the same as the ending of the definite article.
2. *But:* after **der** (nominative masculine) and **das,** the adjective ending is **-e.***
3. *But:* after **die** (plural), the adjective ending is **-en.**

As described in Section 8.1, adjective endings vary according to the gender, number, and case of the noun they describe and according to whether this information is already indicated by an article or article-like word. In essence, however, there are only a very limited number of possibilities. Study the following chart carefully and try to come up with some easy rules of thumb that will help you remember the adjective endings.

	Masculine	Neuter	Feminine	Plural
Nominative	der kalt**e** Tee	das kalt**e** Bier	die kalt**e** Milch	die kalt**en** Getränke
	ein kalt**er** Tee	ein kalt**es** Bier	eine kalt**e** Milch	
	kalt**er** Tee	kalt**es** Bier	kalt**e** Milch	kalt**e** Getränke
Accusative	den kalt**en** Tee	das kalt**e** Bier	die kalt**e** Milch	die kalt**en** Getränke
	einen kalt**en** Tee	ein kalt**es** Bier	eine kalt**e** Milch	
	kalt**en** Tee	kalt**es** Bier	kalt**e** Milch	kalt**e** Getränke

Üb. 1. All answers contain nominative inflections, which sts. may generate directly from the definite article. Stress the connection so that sts. will not think that the adjective endings are something different from endings on articles. Tell sts. to note that the gender of each noun is provided in parentheses.

NÜTZLICHE WÖRTER

amerikanisch
dänisch
deutsch
englisch
französisch
griechisch
holländisch
italienisch
japanisch
kolumbianisch
neuseeländisch
norwegisch
polnisch
russisch
ungarisch

Üb. 2. This exercise focuses on unpreceded accusative forms. Assign for homework and review in class.

Übung 1 | Spezialitäten!

Jedes Land hat eine Spezialität: ein Gericht oder ein Getränk, das aus diesem Land einfach am besten schmeckt. An welche Länder denken Sie bei den folgenden Gerichten oder Getränken?

MODELL: Salami → Italienische Salami!

1. Steak (*n.*)
2. Kaviar (*m.*)
3. Oliven (*pl.*)
4. Sushi (*n.*)
5. Champagner (*m.*)
6. Wurst (*f.*)
7. Käse (*m.*)
8. Spaghetti (*pl.*)
9. Paprika (*m.*)
10. Marmelade (*f.*)
11. Kaffee (*m.*)
12. Kiwis (*pl.*)

Übung 2 | Der Gourmet

Michael isst und trinkt nicht alles, sondern nur, was er für fein hält. Übernehmen Sie Michaels Rolle.

MODELL: Kognak (*m.*) / französisch →
Ich trinke nur französischen Kognak!

1. Brot (*n.*) / deutsch
2. Kaviar (*m.*) / russisch
3. Salami (*f.*) / italienisch
4. Kaffee (*m.*) / kolumbianisch
5. Kiwis (*pl.*) / neuseeländisch
6. Wein (*m.*) / französisch
7. Bier (*n.*) / belgisch
8. Muscheln (*pl.*) / spanisch
9. Marmelade (*f.*) / englisch
10. Thunfisch (*m.*) / japanisch

*Remember this rule as "**der** (nominative masculine)" because, as you will learn in Section 8.4, **der** may also refer to dative feminine, in which case the adjective ending will be **-en.**

Üb. 3. In this exercise, sts. are required to form the accusative forms (Michael's statement) and then both nominative forms and predicate adjectives in Maria's responses. Remind sts. that when there is an article, plural adjectives end in -en and that this distinguishes plural from feminine singular: *die gelbe Hose, die roten Socken.* Since it will take sts. time to think these endings through, assign as homework and review in class, with sts. playing the roles of Michael and Maria.

Übung 3 | Im Geschäft

Michael hat kein Geld, aber er möchte alles kaufen. Maria muss ihn immer bremsen.

> MODELL: der schicke Anzug / teuer →
> MICHAEL: Ich möchte den schicken Anzug da.
> MARIA: Nein, dieser schicke Anzug ist viel zu teuer.

1. der graue Wintermantel / schwer
2. die gelbe Hose / bunt
3. das schicke Hemd / teuer
4. die roten Socken / warm
5. der schwarze Schlafanzug / dünn
6. die grünen Schuhe / groß
7. der modische Hut / klein
8. die schwarzen Winterstiefel / leicht
9. die elegante Sonnenbrille / bunt
10. die roten Tennisschuhe / grell

Übung 4 | Minidialoge

Ergänzen Sie die Adjektivendungen.

1. HERR RUF: Na, wie ist denn Ihr neu_____[a] Auto?
   FRAU WAGNER: Ach, der alt_____[b] Mercedes war mir lieber.
   HERR RUF: Dann hätte ich mir aber keinen neu_____[c] Wagen gekauft!
2. KELLNER: Wie schmeckt Ihnen denn der italienisch_____[a] Wein?
   MICHAEL: Sehr gut. Ich bestelle gleich noch eine weiter_____[b] Flasche.
3. MICHAEL: Heute repariere ich mein kaputt_____[a] Fahrrad.
   MARIA: Prima! Dann kannst du meinen blöd_____[b] Computer auch reparieren. Er ist schon wieder kaputt.
   MICHAEL: Na gut, aber dann habe ich wieder kein frei_____[c] Wochenende.

8.3 Destination vs. location: *stellen/stehen, legen/liegen, setzen/sitzen, hängen/hängen*

Destination implies accusative case; location implies dative case.

Wissen Sie noch?

Prepositions of location are usually followed by the dative case, while prepositions of destination are usually followed by the accusative case.

Review grammar 6.2.

DESTINATION	LOCATION
Verbs of action and direction used with two-way prepositions followed by the accusative	Verbs of condition and location used with two-way prepositions followed by the dative

Maria stellt eine Flasche Wein **auf den** Tisch.

Die Flasche Wein steht **auf dem** Tisch.

stellen/stehen = vertical position

Stellen and **stehen** designate vertical placement or position. They are used with people and animals, as well as with objects that have a base and can "stand" without falling over.

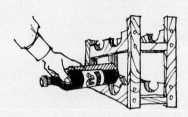

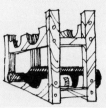

Michael legt eine Flasche Wein **ins** Weinregal.

Die Flasche Wein liegt **im** Weinregal.

legen/liegen = horizontal position

Legen and **liegen** designate horizontal placement or position. They are used with people and animals, as well as with objects that do not have a base and cannot "stand" without falling over.

Frau Wagner setzt Paula **in den** Hochstuhl.

Paula sitzt **im** Hochstuhl.

sitzen/setzen = sitting position (people and certain animals)

Setzen designates the act of being seated; **sitzen** the state of sitting. These verbs are used only with people and with animals that are capable of sitting.

Helga hängt das Handtuch **an den** Haken.   Das Handtuch hängt **am** Haken.

---

hängen/hängen = hanging position

Hängen (gehängt) designates the act of being hung; **hängen (gehangen)** the state of hanging.

The verbs **stellen, legen, setzen,** and **hängen** are weak verbs that require an accusative object. The two-way preposition is used with the accusative case.	The verbs **stehen, liegen, sitzen, hängen** are strong verbs that cannot take an accusative object. The two-way preposition is used with the dative case.
stellen hat gestellt	stehen hat gestanden
legen hat gelegt	liegen hat gelegen
setzen hat gesetzt	sitzen hat gesessen
hängen hat gehängt	hängen hat gehangen

Übung 5 | Minidialoge

Üb. 5. Use as homework and have sts. play the roles in class. Questions about the location and movement of people and objects in the classroom can provide further practice, but we do not expect sts. to acquire these forms quickly.

Ergänzen Sie die Artikel, die Präposition plus Artikel oder das Pronomen.

Genus der Wörter:

   die Bank
   das Bett
   die Gläser (*pl.*)
   der Herd
   das Regal
   der Schrank
   der Schreibtisch
   das Sofa
   die Tasche
   der Tisch

1. SILVIA: Wohin stellst du die Blumen?
   JÜRGEN: Auf _____ Tisch.
2. JOSEF: Warum setzt du dich nicht an _____[a] Tisch?
   MELANIE: Ich sitze hier auf _____[b] Sofa bequemer.
3. MARIA: Meine Bücher liegen auf _____[a] Tisch. Bitte stell sie auf _____[b] Regal.
   MICHAEL: Okay.
4. ALBERT: Ich kann Melanie nicht finden.
   STEFAN: Sie sitzt auf _____ Bank im Garten.
5. MONIKA: Hast du die Weinflaschen in _____[a] Schrank gestellt?
   HEIDI: Ja, sie stehen neben _____[b] Gläsern.

Strukturen und Übungen   297

6. SOFIE: (*am Telefon*) Was machst du heute?
   MARTA: Nichts! Ich lege mich (in) _____^a Bett.
   SOFIE: Liegst du schon (in) _____^b Bett?
   MARTA: Nein, jetzt sitze ich noch (an) _____^c Schreibtisch.
7. KATRIN: Darf ich mich neben _____^a (du) setzen?
   STEFAN: Ja, bitte setz _____^b (du).
8. FRAU RUF: Hast du die Suppe auf _____^a Herd gestellt?
   HERR RUF: Sie steht schon seit einer Stunde auf _____^b Herd.
9. HERR RUF: Wo ist der Stadtplan?
   FRAU RUF: Er liegt unter _____ Tasche.

Übung 6	Vor dem Abendessen

Üb. 6. Assign for homework and check in class.

Beschreiben Sie die Bilder. Nützliche Wörter:

legen/liegen	der Küchenschrank
setzen/sitzen	der Schrank
stehen/stellen	die Schublade
	die Serviette
	das Sofa
	der Teller
	der Tisch

MODELL: Die Schuhe → Die Schuhe liegen auf dem Boden.

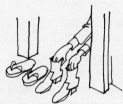

Peter → Peter stellt die Schuhe vor die Tür.

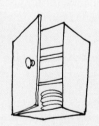

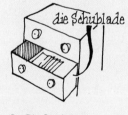

1. Die Teller _____. 2. Albert _____. 3. Die Servietten _____.

4. Monika _____. 5. Messer und Gabeln _____. 6. Stefan _____.

7. Die Kerze _____. 8. Heidi _____. 9. Thomas _____.

8.4 Adjectives in the dative case

8.4. *Adjektive im Dativ.* Unpreceded adjectives in the dative case are common only after prepositions and in the plural. In the singular, they are not very frequent, even with prepositions, and are exceedingly rare with datives referring to people. In the plural, the strong ending–that is, the unpreceded one–is also *-en.* Associating *-en* with dative will help sts. choose the correct pattern in the vast majority of cases and so will help them to learn the German case system a little more easily. The complete chart of adjective endings can be found in Appendix E.

In the dative case, nouns are usually preceded by an article (**dem, der, den; einem, einer**) or an article-like word (**diesem, dieser, diesen; meinem, meiner, meinen**). When adjectives occur before such nouns they end in **-en.***

Jutta geht mit ihrem neuen
    Freund spazieren.
Jens gießt seiner kranken Tante
    die Blumen.
Ich spreche nicht mehr mit diesen
    unhöflichen Menschen.

*Jutta is going for a walk with
    her new friend.*
*Jens is watering the flowers for
    his sick aunt.*
*I'm not talking with these
    impolite people any more.*

	Masculine	Neuter	Feminine	Plural
Dative	dies**em** lieb**en** Vater	dies**em** lieb**en** Kind	dies**er** lieb**en** Mutter	dies**en** lieb**en** Eltern
	mein**em** lieb**en** Vater	mein**em** lieb**en** Kind	mein**er** lieb**en** Mutter	mein**en** lieb**en** Eltern

Übung 7 | Was machen diese Leute?

Achtung!

All nouns have an **-n** in the dative plural unless their plural ends in **-s.**

Nominative: die Freunde

Dative: den Freunde**n** *but:* den Hobbys

Üb. 7. The focus is on dative forms. Assign for homework and check in class. When doing so, vary between asking *Was macht Jens?* and *Wem zeigt Ernst die Ratte?* so that sts. connect the interrogative *wem* with dative forms.

Schreiben Sie Sätze.

MODELL: Jens / seine alte Tante / einen Brief schreiben →
    Jens schreibt seiner alten Tante einen Brief.

1. Jutta / ihr neuer Freund / ihre Lieblings-CD leihen
2. Jens / der kleine Bruder von Jutta / eine Ratte verkaufen
3. Hans / nur seine besten Freunde / die Ratte zeigen
4. Jutta / ihre beste Freundin / ein Buch schenken
5. Jens / sein wütender Lehrer / eine Krawatte kaufen
6. Ernst / seine große Schwester / einen Witz erzählen
7. Jutta / die netten Leute von nebenan / Kaffee kochen
8. Ernst / das süße Baby von nebenan / einen Kuss geben

*Unpreceded adjectives in the dative case follow the same pattern as in the nominative and accusative case, that is, they have the ending of the definite article. For example, **mit frischem Honig** (*with fresh honey*), **mit kalter Milch** (*with cold milk*).

8.5 Talking about the future: the present and future tenses

You already know that **werden** is the equivalent of English *to become*.

Ich möchte Ärztin werden.	*I'd like to become a physician.*

future tense = **werden** + infinitive

You can also use a form of **werden** plus infinitive to talk about future events.

Wo wirst du morgen sein?	*Where will you be tomorrow?*
Morgen werde ich wahrscheinlich zu Hause sein.	*Tomorrow, I will probably be at home.*

8.5. *Präsens und Futur.* The future tense is the second use that German makes of *werden.* (It was introduced as a main verb in Section 5.3 and will be introduced as the passive auxiliary in Section 10.5.) Sts. find future construction relatively easy.

Point out to sts. that they have already often used the present tense in German to talk about the future.

When an adverb of time is present or when it is otherwise clear that future actions or events are indicated, German speakers normally use the present tense rather than the future tense to talk about what will happen in the future.

Nächstes Jahre **fahren** wir nach Schweden.	*Next year we're going to Sweden.*
Was **machst** du, wenn du in Schweden bist?	*What are you going to do when you're in Sweden?*

Use **wohl** with the future tense to express present or future probability.

The future tense with **werden** can express present or future probability. In such cases, the sentence often includes an adverb such as **wohl** (*probably*).

Mein Freund wird jetzt **wohl** zu Hause sein.	*My friend should be home now.*
Morgen Abend werden wir **wohl** zu Hause bleiben	*Tomorrow evening, we'll probably stay home.*

Don't forget to put **werden** at the end of the dependent clause.

Ich weiß nicht, ob ich einmal heiraten **werde.**	*I don't know if I'm ever going to get married.*

Übung 8 | Vorsätze

Sie wollen ein neues Leben beginnen? Schreiben Sie sechs Dinge auf, die Sie ab morgen machen werden oder nicht mehr machen werden.

MODELL: Ich werde nicht mehr so oft in Fast-Food-Restaurants gehen.
Ich werde mehr Obst und Gemüse essen.

---

weniger/mehr fernsehen

weniger/mehr arbeiten

früher/später ins Bett gehen

weniger/mehr Kurse belegen

weniger oft/öfter ins Kino gehen

weniger oft/öfter selbst kochen

weniger/mehr lernen

weniger gesund/gesünder essen

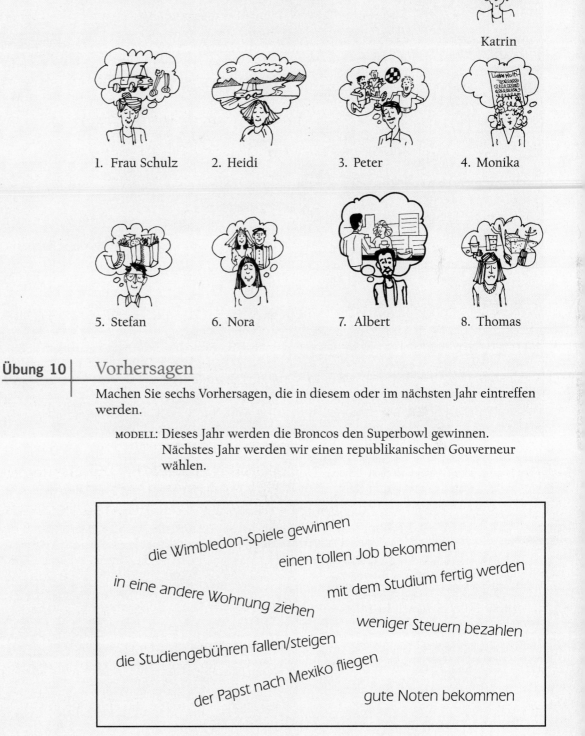

Übung 9 | ## Morgen ist Samstag

Üb. 9. Assign for homework. Check and compare sts.' answers in class.

Was machen Frau Schulz und ihre Studenten morgen?

MODELL: Katrin geht morgen ins Kino.

Katrin

1. Frau Schulz 2. Heidi 3. Peter 4. Monika

5. Stefan 6. Nora 7. Albert 8. Thomas

Übung 10 | ## Vorhersagen

Machen Sie sechs Vorhersagen, die in diesem oder im nächsten Jahr eintreffen werden.

MODELL: Dieses Jahr werden die Broncos den Superbowl gewinnen.
Nächstes Jahr werden wir einen republikanischen Gouverneur wählen.

die Wimbledon-Spiele gewinnen

einen tollen Job bekommen

in eine andere Wohnung ziehen

mit dem Studium fertig werden

weniger Steuern bezahlen

die Studiengebühren fallen/steigen

der Papst nach Mexiko fliegen

gute Noten bekommen

Strukturen und Übungen

301

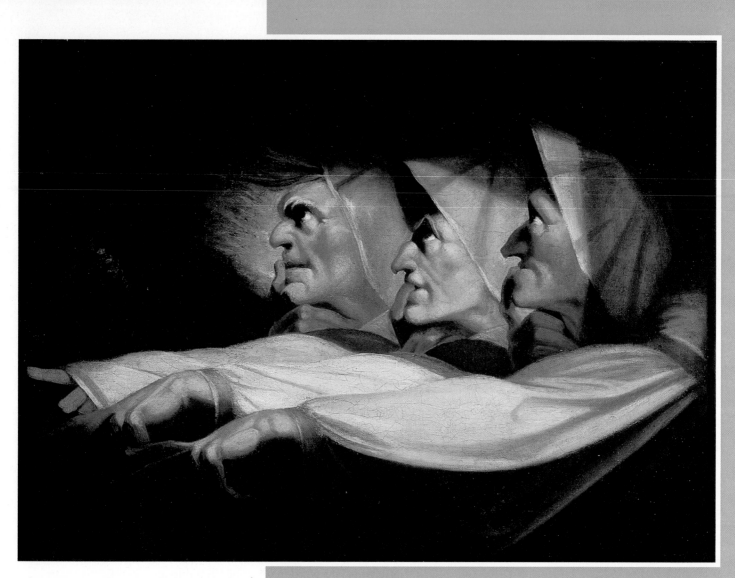

Johann Heinrich Füssli: *Die drei Hexen* (1783),
Royal Shakespeare Theater Collection, London

Chapter opening artwork: Famous for his Romantic
literary themes, Füssli became one of the best known
painters of his time.

Suggestion: You may wish to use this painting to
introduce the topic of fairy tales in general. You can
also use the following questions to deal with the
background that led to the creation of this painting,
which is an illustration for Shakespeare's Macbeth. *Wie
sehen diese drei Personen aus? Wie halten die drei ihre
Hände? Wohin schauen sie? Haben sie alle den gleichen
Gesichtsausdruck? Finden Sie die drei Personen
sympathisch? Welche Farben und Kontraste sind hier
wichtig? Welche Wirkung haben diese Farben? In
welchem Theaterstück spielen drei Hexen eine Rolle?*

JOHANN HEINRICH FÜSSLI

Johann Heinrich Füssli (1741–1825) wurde in Zürich geboren und studierte
dort zunächst[1] Theologie, später beschäftigte er sich[2] mit Literatur. 1763
ging er als Schriftsteller nach London. Dort fing er an, Shakespeare-Dramen zu
illustrieren. Er illustrierte neben Shakespeare auch die Dichtung[3] Miltons, sowie
Dante und Vergil.

[1]*initially* [2]*beschäftigte ... he occupied himself* [3]*literary works*

Kindheit und Jugend

Kapitel 9 deals with memories and past events. You will have the opportunity to talk about your childhood, and you will learn more about the tales that are an important part of childhood in the German-speaking world.

GOALS

In this chapter, sts. talk about childhood memories and learn to tell all kinds of stories using the perfect tense. They are introduced to the simple past and the past perfect by reading a variety of texts and retelling some of Grimm's fairy tales. We expect sts. to use the simple past of *haben, sein, werden, wissen,* and the modal verbs actively. All other simple past forms and the past perfect are presented here primarily for receptive mastery, i.e., for reading and listening comprehension.

Themen
Kindheit
Jugend
Geschichten
Märchen

Kulturelles
Jugend im 21. Jahrhundert
Die Jugend von heute – eine pragmatische Generation unter Druck
Videoblick: Die Sonne und die Frösche
Videoecke: Schule

Lektüren
Der standhafte Zinnsoldat (TEIL I)
Der standhafte Zinnsoldat (TEIL II)

Strukturen
9.1 The conjunction **als** with dependent-clause word order
9.2 The simple past tense of **werden,** the modal verbs, and **wissen**
9.3 Time: **als, wenn, wann**
9.4 The simple past tense of strong and weak verbs (receptive)
9.5 Sequence of events in past narration: the past perfect tense and the conjunction **nachdem** (receptive)

Situationen

Kindheit

Grammatik 9.1

Vocabulary Display
Before showing the vocabulary transparency, explain to sts. that you are going to talk about things you did when you were a child. Mix predictable statements with slightly shocking statements. You could then ask sts. to recall your statements. Do not expect perfect recall. Next show the transparency and ask about the characters. Do not let sts. see the captions at first, but encourage them to guess. Then uncover the text; model and have sts. repeat.

Jens hat seinem Onkel den Rasen gemäht.

Uli hat im Garten Äpfel gepflückt.

Richard hat mit seiner Mutter Kuchen gebacken.

Bernd hat Staub gesaugt und sauber gemacht.

Willi hat seiner Oma die Blumen gegossen.

Jochen hat seinem kleinen Bruder Geschichten vorgelesen.

Situation 1 | Melanies erstes Haustier

Sit. 1. In this activity, sts. continue to use the perfect tense they learned earlier. Introduce unfamiliar vocabulary: *Korb, füttern, Schleife, Knochen.* Model pronunciation and have sts. repeat the sentences. Then have them work in small groups to decide which activities would match which times. Several sequences are possible. You could also ask sts. to give reasons for their choices.

Als Melanie sechs Jahre alt war, hat sie einen Hund zum Geburtstag bekommen. Sie hat ihn Bruno genannt. Was hat sie wohl am nächsten Tag mit ihm gemacht? Ordnen Sie die Aktivitäten den Zeiten zu.

MODELL: Um sechs Uhr ist sie gemeinsam mit Bruno aufgestanden.

6.00 Uhr	10.15 Uhr	15.00 Uhr
6.30 Uhr	12.00 Uhr	16.00 Uhr
7.00 Uhr		
10.00 Uhr	14.30 Uhr	19.30 Uhr

1. Sie ist zusammen mit Bruno eingeschlafen.
2. Sie hat mit ihm gespielt.
3. Sie hat Brunos Korb[1] sauber gemacht.
4. Sie ist mit Bruno spazieren gegangen.
5. Sie ist gemeinsam mit Bruno aufgestanden.
6. Sie hat Bruno gefüttert.
7. Sie hat ihn ihren Freunden gezeigt.
8. Sie hat ihm eine Schleife[2] ins Haar gebunden.
9. Sie hat Bruno in der Badewanne gewaschen.
10. Sie hat ihm einen großen Knochen[3] gekauft.

 **Situation 2** | Umfrage

Sit. 2. First, ask the sts. the questions that they will ask each other afterward: *Wer von Ihnen hat als Kind Karten gespielt? Heben Sie bitte die Hand! Wer von Ihnen hat als Kind viel ferngesehen? usw.* Then have them ask you the questions: *Haben Sie ...*, and encourage them to ask you anything else they can think of. Finally, have them do the autograph activity.

MODELL: S1: Hast du als Kind Karten gespielt?
S2: Ja.
S1: Unterschreib bitte hier.

UNTERSCHRIFT

1. Karten gespielt _____
2. viel ferngesehen _____
3. dich mit den Geschwistern gestritten _____
4. manchmal die Nachbarn geärgert _____
5. einen Hund oder eine Katze gehabt _____
6. in einer Baseballmannschaft gespielt _____
7. Ballettunterricht genommen _____
8. Fensterscheiben kaputt gemacht _____

Situation 3 | Interaktion: Als ich 12 Jahre alt war ...

Sit. 3. Sts. first answer these questions for themselves and then ask their partners the same questions. Before they work in pairs, ask them to tell you how they will ask the questions, as there is no model supplied: *Sie sprechen jetzt mit Ihrem Partner / mit Ihrer Partnerin. Wie stellen Sie ihm/ihr die Fragen, z.B. Nummer 1? (Wie oft hast du dein Zimmer aufgeräumt?) und 2?* Tell sts. to watch for verbs that have the auxiliary *sein*.

Wie oft haben Sie das gemacht, als Sie 12 Jahre alt waren: **oft, manchmal, selten** oder **nie?**

1. mein Zimmer aufgeräumt
2. Kuchen gebacken
3. Liebesromane gelesen
4. Videos angeschaut
5. heimlich jemanden geliebt
6. spät aufgestanden
7. Freunde eingeladen
8. allein verreist
9. zu einem Fußballspiel gegangen
10. meine Hausaufgaben vergessen

[1]*basket* [2]*bow* [3]*bone*

Situationen

305

Jugend im 21. Jahrhundert

Welche verbotenen Dinge tun Sie manchmal? Wie sieht der ideale Freitagabend aus? Diese und viele andere Fragen haben 2 034 deutsche Jugendliche zwischen 14 und 29 Jahren für eine repräsentative Umfrage beantwortet. Die Antworten zeigen das Selbstporträt einer eigensinnigen[1], illusionslosen[2] Generation.

Beantworten Sie die folgenden Fragen zuerst für sich selbst. Vergleichen Sie dann Ihre Antworten mit den Antworten der anderen Studenten in Ihrem Deutschkurs und dann mit denen der deutschen Jugendlichen.

Timo Schacht, 22, Elektrotechniker.
Motto: Immer positiv denken.

Photo questions. Encourage students to speculate if answers are not apparent. *Wie finden Sie diesen jungen Mann / diese junge Frau? Was macht er/sie beruflich? Was für eine Familie hat er/sie? Was für Musik hört er/sie gern? Was sind seine/ihre Hobbys? Wie war er/sie als Kind?*

1. Wie haben Ihre Eltern Sie erzogen?

liebevoll	40 %
liberal	26 %
streng	19 %
antiautoritär	6 %
nachlässig[3]	5 %
mit Prügel[4] und Hausarrest	4 %
gar nicht	2 %

2. Wo sind Sie aufgewachsen?

bei beiden Elternteilen[5]	85 %
bei einem Elternteil	14 %
bei Verwandten	1 %

3. Wo wohnen Sie zur Zeit?

bei den Eltern	50 %
mit meinem Lebenspartner	24 %
allein	18 %
in einer Wohngemeinschaft	6 %
im Wohnheim	1 %

4. Wie viele Stunden sehen Sie jeden Tag fern?

gar nicht	3 %
unter 1 Stunde	21 %
1 bis 2 Stunden	42 %
2 bis 4 Stunden	28 %
4 bis 6 Stunden	5 %
mehr als 6 Stunden	1 %

Sandra Paul, 26, Modezeichnerin.
Motto: Sich immer wieder neu entdecken.

5. Wie viele Videos sehen Sie pro Woche?

keines	46 %
ein bis zwei	42 %
drei bis fünf	10 %
mehr als zehn	1 %

6. Wie häufig sehen Sie die Nachrichten im Fernsehen?

fast jeden Tag	39 %
oft	32 %
selten	23 %
nie	4 %

7. Wie oft lesen Sie eine Tageszeitung?

fast jeden Tag	42 %
oft	25 %
selten	26 %
nie	7 %

8. Wie viele Bücher haben Sie in den letzten drei Monaten gelesen?

keines	41 %
ein bis zwei	33 %
drei oder mehr	25 %

[1]*stubborn* [2]*without illusions* [3]*negligently* [4]*beatings* [5]*parents*

KLI. Ask questions from the introductory paragraph in class or let sts. poll one another. After sts. have checked answers to the 8 questions, have them compare their answers with those of the German youth. Provide one or two model responses. **AA:** Use the information for an interactive activity. Have sts. first check off their own answers for each question. Then in small groups have them guess about their classmates' answers. **Note:** Some categories do not total exactly 100%, because the percentages are rounded to the nearest whole number.

Situation 4 | Interview

Sit. 4. Sts. should work with a partner and interview each other alternately: s1: *Wo hast du gewohnt, als du acht Jahre alt warst?* s2: *In Pittsburgh. Und du? Wo hast du gewohnt?* s1: *In San Francisco. Hattest du Geschwister?* s2: *Ja. Zwei Brüder. Und du? Hattest du auch Geschwister? usw.* Sts. should take notes. Then have sts. change partners and describe the childhood of the first partner to the second partner. Finally, have sts. interview you.

Vocabulary Display
This display introduces simple past-tense forms of *haben, sein,* and the modals. Sts. will already be familiar with some of these forms, especially *sein.* Present by covering the captions and narrating the events. Then follow the regular method. (See the IM.) As a follow-up let students speculate what happened to Sybille after picture 8, and ask them to draw or describe a picture 9.

Als du acht Jahre alt warst ...

1. Wo hast du gewohnt? Hattest du Geschwister? Freunde? Wo hat dein Vater gearbeitet? deine Mutter? Was hast du am liebsten gegessen?
2. In welche Grundschule bist du gegangen? Wann hat die Schule angefangen? Wann hat sie aufgehört? Welchen Lehrer / Welche Lehrerin hattest du am liebsten? Welche Fächer hattest du am liebsten? Was hast du in den Pausen gespielt? Was hast du nach der Schule gemacht?
3. Hast du viel ferngesehen? Was hast du am liebsten gesehen? Hast du gern gelesen? Was? Hast du Sport getrieben? Was? Was hast du gar nicht gern gemacht?

Jugend

Grammatik 9.2–9.3

1. Sybille Gretter war sehr begabt. In der Schule wusste sie immer alles.

2. Sie brauchte für die Prüfungen nicht viel zu lernen.

3. Sie konnte auch sehr gut tanzen und wollte Ballerina werden.

4. Dreimal in der Woche musste sie zum Ballettunterricht.

5. Als sie in der letzten Klasse war, hatte sie einen Freund.

6. Ihr Vater durfte nichts davon wissen, denn er war sehr streng.

7. Eines Tages hat sie ihren Freund ihren Eltern vorgestellt.

8. Aber ihr Vater mochte ihn nicht und sie mussten sich trennen.

Die Jugend von heute – eine pragmatische Generation unter Druck

„Die Jugend von heute liebt den Luxus, hat schlechte Manieren und verachtet[1] die Autorität. Sie widerspricht[2] ihren Eltern, legt die Beine übereinander und tyrannisiert ihre Lehrer."

—Sokrates

- Sind Sie derselben Meinung? Warum?
- Wie beschreiben Sie sich als Jugendliche(r)? Finden Sie gute Adjektive.
- Welche Werte[3], Einstellungen[4] und Gewohnheiten[5] haben Jugendliche in Ihrem Land? Denken Sie an Bildung, Arbeit, Familie, Religion und Politik.

Im September 2006 hat der Mineralölkonzern[6] Shell in Zusammenarbeit mit der Universität Bielefeld die 15. Shell-Jugendstudie herausgebracht. Für die Studie wurden 2 500 deutsche Jugendliche zwischen 12 und 25 Jahren zu ihren Einstellungen und Werten unter anderem zu Bildung, Familie, Religion und Politik befragt.

Eine Studentin lernt in der Bibliothek.

Laut dieser Studie sehen immer mehr Jugendliche in einer guten Bildung den Grundstein[7] für ein glückliches Leben. Mädchen sind besonders strebsam[8] nach guten Noten und Abschlüssen[9]. Aber die Studie hat auch herausgefunden, dass mehr Jugendliche Angst vor Arbeitslosigkeit[10] und Armut[11] haben. Vor allem solche Jugendlichen denken so, die aus sozial schwachen Familien kommen. 57% der Gymnasiasten sehen positiv in die Zukunft, aber es sind nur 38% bei den Hauptschülern.

Die Sicht von Jugendlichen auf ihre Zukunft hat sich im Vergleich zur letzten Shell-Studie von 2002 leicht verdüstert[12]. Der Druck[13] auf junge Leute ist gestiegen. Doch die Forscher haben festgestellt, dass die Jugend sehr pragmatisch auf diese Situation reagiert. Sie ist leistungsfähiger[14] und zielorientierter[15] als früher. Bei dem großen Druck sucht sie Halt[16] in der Familie. Deshalb sind 72% der jungen Leute der Meinung, dass sie eine Familie brauchen, um glücklich zu sein.

- Was denken Sie: Hat es die Jugend im 21. Jahrhundert schwerer als ihre Vorgängergenerationen[17]? Warum?
- Gibt es in Ihrem Land auch repräsentative Studien, die die Einstellungen und Werte von Jugendlichen untersuchen? Recherchieren Sie im Internet. Wenn ja, wie schätzen die jungen Leute ihre allgemeine Situation ein[18]? Vergleichen Sie sie mit der Lage der jungen Deutschen.

[1]*disrespects* [2]*contradicts* [3]*values* [4]*attitudes, views* [5]*habits* [6]*oil company* [7]*basis, foundation* [8]*ambitious* [9]*degrees* [10]*unemployment* [11]*poverty* [12]*darkened* [13]*pressure* [14]*more capable* [15]*more goal-oriented* [16]*support, grounding* [17]*preceding generations* [18]einschätzen *to assess*

Situation 5 | Dialog: Jugendsünden

Sit. 5 (See the IM.) **(1)** Set the scene. **(2)** Preteach vocabulary: *sich erinnern an, damals, zufällig, der Ärger, der Direktor, stehlen.* **(3)** You may wish to have sts. keep their books closed while answering the following questions. Write them on the board. Questions for first listening: **1.** *Was macht Alexander heute?* **2.** *Was haben Michael, Alexander und ihre Mitschüler in Frau Müllers Klasse gemacht?* **3.** *Mit welcher Person haben die Schüler dann Ärger bekommen?* Questions for second listening: **1.** *Wie heißen die zwei anderen Lehrer, über die Michael und Alexander sprechen?* **2.** *Welche Fächer haben sie unterrichtet?* **3.** *Warum möchte Alexander nicht wieder Gymnasiast sein?* **(4)** Compare sts.' answers. Ask sts. to open their books. Play the dialogue for them once more while→

Michael Pusch geht zum zehnten Klassentreffen seiner Abiturklasse. Er trifft seinen alten Freund Alexander. Die beiden sprechen über ihre gemeinsame Schulzeit.

MICHAEL: Schön, dich mal wieder zu sehen, Alex. Was hast du eigentlich nach dem Abi <u>gemacht</u>?

ALEXANDER: Ich habe eine Tanzschule <u>eröffnet</u>.

MICHAEL: Nicht schlecht. Gern und gut <u>getanzt</u> hast du ja früher schon.

ALEXANDER: Stimmt. Erinnerst du dich an das Drama mit Frau Müller damals?

MICHAEL: Ach, als wir in ihrem Deutschunterricht laut Musik <u>gehört</u> und getanzt haben?

ALEXANDER: Genau. Sie war noch nicht in der Klasse, uns war langweilig und Hans hatte zufällig ein bisschen Musik dabei.

MICHAEL: Und als Frau Müller hereinkam, haben alle wild getanzt und gesungen. Das war ein Spaß.

ALEXANDER: Danach hat es nur leider viel Ärger mit dem Direktor gegeben.

MICHAEL: Richtig. Dabei hatten wir diese Sache noch nicht einmal geplant.

ALEXANDER: Und als wir Herrn Riedel die Geschichtsklausuren[1] gestohlen oder das Auto der Französischlehrerin Frau Häuser mit Toilettenpapier eingepackt haben ...

MICHAEL: Es war eigentlich eine schöne Zeit auf dem Gymnasium.

ALEXANDER: Na ja. Denk doch nur an die vielen Klassenarbeiten.

Situation 6 | Interview

Sit. 6. Sts. use the simple past-tense forms of the modals intensively in this situation, as well as *wenn*, *wann*, and *als*. Have sts. work in pairs and take notes on their partner's answers. At the end, have them report back to the class.

1. Musstest du früh aufstehen, als du zur Schule gegangen bist? Wann?
2. Wann musstest du von zu Hause weggehen?
3. Musstest du zur Schule, wenn du krank warst?
4. Durftest du abends lange fernsehen, wenn du morgens früh aufstehen musstest?
5. Konntest du zu Fuß zur Schule gehen?
6. Wolltest du manchmal lieber zu Hause bleiben? Warum?
7. Was wolltest du werden, als du ein Kind warst?
8. Durftest du abends ausgehen? Wann musstest du zu Hause sein?

Situation 7 | Geständnisse

Sit. 7. This activity reinforces the difference between *als* and *wenn*. Sts. work in small groups and write what they did in each situation. Encourage playfulness and provide a few models about yourself. Afterward, ask the class as a whole: *Was haben Sie gemacht, als Sie einmal mit einem Jungen / mit einem Mädchen im Kino waren?* and call on individuals.

Sagen Sie, was in diesen Situationen passiert ist, oder was Sie gemacht haben.

MODELL: Als ich zum ersten Mal allein verreist bin, habe ich meinen Teddy mitgenommen.

1. Als ich einmal mit einem Jungen / einem Mädchen im Kino war
2. Als ich zum ersten Mal Kaffee getrunken hatte
3. Wenn ich zu spät nach Hause gekommen bin
4. Als ich mein erstes F bekommen hatte
5. Wenn ich keine Hausaufgaben gemacht habe
6. Wenn ich total verliebt war
7. Als ich zum ersten Mal verliebt war
8. Als ich einmal meinen Hausschlüssel verloren hatte
9. Wenn ich eine schlechte Note bekommen habe
10. Wenn ich eine neue Hose kaputt gemacht habe

Situation 8 | Rollenspiel: Das Klassentreffen

Sit. 8. The role for S2 appears in Appendix B.

S1: Sie sind auf dem fünften Klassentreffen Ihrer alten High-School-Klasse. Sie unterhalten sich mit einem alten Schulfreund / einer alten Schulfreundin. Fragen Sie: was er/sie nach Abschluss der High School gemacht hat, was er/sie jetzt macht und was seine/ihre Pläne für die nächsten Jahre sind. Sprechen Sie auch über die gemeinsame Schulzeit.

[1] *history exams*

---

they fill in the blanks. **(5)** Write sts.' answers on the board, or ask them to write their answers on the board, while making any necessary corrections. **(6)** Ask sts. to work in groups to determine the infinitives of the participles. **(7)** Review sts.' answers.

Geschichten

Grammatik 9.4

Sentences for narration series: **1.** *Eines Abends war Willi allein zu Hause.* **2.** *Seine Eltern waren ins Theater gegangen.* **3.** *Willi lag im Bett und konnte nicht einschlafen.* **4.** *Plötzlich hörte er durch das Fenster ein Geräusch.* **5.** *Er schaute aus dem Fenster und sah einen Schatten.* **6.** *„Ein Einbrecher!", dachte Willi.* **7.** *Er hatte große Angst und rief die Großeltern an.* **8.** *Dann versteckte Willi sich mit einem Tennisschläger im Keller.* **9.** *Der Großvater fuhr sofort mit dem Fahrrad los.* **10.** *Unterwegs fing es an zu regnen und der Großvater wurde ganz nass.* **11.** *Großvater ging mit einer Taschenlampe in den Garten.* **12.** *Aber er fand keinen Einbrecher, nur Büsche und eine kleine Katze.*

After narrating the story and having sts. repeat, pass out a sheet of paper with the same drawings out of sequence. Reread the passage, and have sts. number the pictures correctly. To add a focus on form, ask sts. to work in small groups and to write down from memory all simple past forms they remember, to determine their infinitive forms, and to categorize them as weak or strong verbs.

Als Willi mal allein zu Hause war …

 Situation 9 | Informationsspiel: Was ist passiert?

Sit. 9. The corresponding chart is in Appendix A. This activity practices the past-tense forms that German speakers typically use in relating personal stories or events, i.e. the perfect tense for all verbs except *haben* and *sein* and the modal verbs, which are in the simple past. You may want to point out

MODELL: Was ist Sofie passiert? / Was ist dir passiert?
Wann ist es passiert?
Wo ist es passiert?
Warum ist es passiert?

	Sofie	Mehmet	Ernst	mein Partner / meine Partnerin
Was?	hat ihre Schlüssel verloren	hat sein Flugzeug verpasst	hat seine Hose zerrissen	
Wann?	als sie im Kino war	als er in die Türkei fliegen wollte	als er über den Zaun geklettert ist	
Wo?	in Leipzig	in Frankfurt	bei seiner Tante	
Warum?	weil ihre Jackentasche ein Loch hatte	weil der Flug aus Berlin Verspätung hatte	weil der Zaun zu hoch war	

that the simple past tense for other verb forms is commonly used in speaking only when retelling fairy tales or other tales referring to distant times or fictitious people. Preteach the new vocabulary (*Loch, Schlüssel, verpassen, Verspätung, Zaun, zerreißen*), e.g., by telling Sofie's, Mehmet's, and Ernst's misfortunes as if they had happened to you, acting out any new vocabulary items and writing them on the board. Ask sts. to think of something that happened to them before having them begin this activity with a partner.

Situation 10 | Und dann?

Suchen Sie für jede Situation eine logische Folge.

MODELL: Jutta konnte ihren Hausschlüssel nicht finden und kletterte durch das Fenster.

Sit. 10. This activity demonstrates use of the simple past in narration of past events. Have sts. work in small groups to match the events (1–9) with the outcomes (a–i). **Possible answers:** 1. e, 2. f, 3. a, 4. d, 5. b, 6. g, 7. c, 8. i, 9. h.

1. Ernst machte die Fensterscheibe kaputt
2. Jens reparierte sein Fahrrad
3. Richard sparte ein ganzes Jahr
4. Claire kam in Innsbruck an
5. Michael bekam ein neues Fahrrad
6. Rolf lernte sechs Jahre Englisch
7. Josef arbeitete drei Monate im Krankenhaus
8. Silvia wohnte zwei Semester allein
9. Melanie bekam ihren ersten Kuss

a. machte dann Urlaub in Spanien.
b. fuhr gleich gegen einen Baum.
c. kaufte sich ein Motorrad.
d. kaufte sich einen neuen Pulli.
e. lief weg.
f. machte eine Radtour.
g. flog dann nach Amerika.
h. sagte leise: „Ach du lieber Gott!“
i. zog dann in eine Wohngemeinschaft.
j. ?

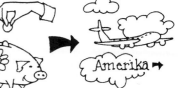

Situation 11 | Bildgeschichte: Beim Zirkus

Sit. 11. This narration series also demonstrates the simple past-tense forms of all types of verbs: weak, strong, *haben*, *sein*, and the modals. Sentences for narration series: **1.** *Als Michael Pusch fünfzehn Jahre alt war, kam eines Tages ein Zirkus in die Stadt.* **2.** *Am Abend ging Michael mit seinen Freunden in den Zirkus.* **3.** *Dort gab es Clowns und Artisten und die junge Seiltänzerin war sehr schön.* **4.** *Am nächsten Morgen musste Michael immer an die Seiltänzerin denken.* **5.** *Nach der Schule lief er sofort zurück zum Zirkus.* **6.** *Er wollte beim Zirkus bleiben, dort arbeiten und die schöne Seiltänzerin heiraten.* **7.** *Michael wurde Tierpfleger. Er fütterte die Pferde und die Elefanten.* **8.** *Aber nach ein paar Tagen kamen Michaels Eltern und er musste wieder nach Hause.* **9.** *Er ging wieder zur Schule und machte langweilige Hausaufgaben.* **10.** *Manchmal aber träumte er vom Zirkus und der schönen Seiltänzerin.*

To add a focus on form, ask sts. to work in small groups and to write down from memory all simple past forms they remember, to determine their infinitive forms, and to categorize them as weak or strong verbs. **AA.** You could also have sts. draw an 11th picture on a transparency and present it to the class with a commentary.

Die Sonne und die Frösche

Warum quaken die Frösche, wenn sie den Mond sehen? Der Videoclip beschreibt, wie es dazu kam.

- Was sollte mit dem Mond geschehen?
- Warum fürchteten sich die Frösche davor[1]?
- Auf welchen Plan verfielen[2] die Frösche?
- Was bewirkte[3] dieser Plan?

Videoblick. The video segment presents a short animated children's tale that explains why frogs croak when there is a full moon.

[1]fürchteten sich davor *were afraid of it* [2]*came up (with)* [3]*achieved*

Habt ihr denn nicht gehört? Die Sonne will Hochzeit machen!

Lektüre

Lektüre. This long fairy tale is divided into two parts (*Teil I* and *Teil II*). Each part is split up into sections to make it more accessible. The questions interspersed at intervals within the story are designed to aid extensive reading. **(1)** You or your sts. might know Donovan's pop version of the "Little Tin Soldier." If you have a recording of it, you can use it as an advance organizer to introduce or review the main points of the story. **(2)** Use Part A of *Vor dem Lesen* to establish the context. Let sts. work on it in small groups. **(3)** Before sts. begin working on Part B of *Vor dem Lesen,* direct their attention to the *Lesehilfe* box. Then ask sts. to read through the whole text once. At the end of each section they see three statements. Point out that more than one of the statements might accurately reflect various aspects of the story line; however, the sts.' task is to identify the one statement after each section that *best* summarizes the content of the segment just read. You may want to facilitate this task for the first few sections by assisting with the summarization before asking sts. to pick the best summary statement. **(4)** *Arbeit mit dem Text.* Part A asks sts. to read each section of the text intensively. Let sts. work in pairs or small groups to answer the questions. Then follow up with discussion. **(5)** Part B ("*Wörter erkennen*") relates to the information in *Lesehilfe* and asks sts. to deal with verbs in the past tense from the text. Assign this for homework. **(6)** *Nach dem Lesen* could be done as homework or group work in class. Discuss afterwards.

Vor dem Lesen

A. Kennen Sie das Märchen „Der standhafte Zinnsoldat[1]" von Hans Christian Andersen, dem bekannten dänischen Märchenerzähler? Sehen Sie sich die Zeichnung an. Wer sind die Hauptpersonen in diesem Märchen? Beschreiben Sie sie! Erfinden Sie eine Geschichte!

B. **Extensives Lesen.** Lesen Sie das Märchen „Der standhafte Zinnsoldat" (Teil I) einmal ganz durch. Nach jedem Abschnitt finden Sie drei Sätze. Kreuzen Sie den Satz an, der den Inhalt am besten wiedergibt und lesen Sie weiter.

[1]standhafte ... *steadfast tin soldier*

von Hans Christian Andersen

TEIL I

Es waren einmal fünfundzwanzig Zinnsoldaten, die alle Brüder waren, da man sie aus einem alten Zinnlöffel gegossen hatte. Das Gewehr hielten sie im Arm, das Gesicht nach vorne gerichtet. Rot und blau, schmuck und schön war ihre Uniform. Das erste Wort, das sie in dieser Welt hörten, nachdem der Deckel[1] der Schachtel abgenommen
5 wurde, war das Wort „Zinnsoldaten!". Das rief ein kleiner Junge und klatschte dabei vor Freude in die Hände, denn er hatte sie zum Geburtstag bekommen. Er stellte sie auf dem Tisch auf. Ein Soldat war genau wie der andere, nur einer war etwas verschieden[2]: Er hatte nur ein Bein, denn er war zuletzt gegossen worden und das Zinn reichte leider nicht mehr für ihn aus[3]. Doch er stand auf seinem einen Bein genauso fest wie seine
10 anderen Kameraden auf ihren beiden. Aber gerade er sollte noch ein besonderes Schicksal[4] erleiden.

☐ **a.** Ein kleiner Junge bekommt fünfundzwanzig Zinnsoldaten zum Geburtstag.
☐ **b.** Ein kleiner Junge stellt seinen Zinnsoldaten auf den Tisch.
☐ **c.** Ein kleiner Junge bekommt einen Zinnsoldaten mit nur einem Bein.

Auf dem Tisch, auf dem sie standen, war noch vieles andere Spielzeug[5]. Am meisten ins Auge aber fiel ein wunderschönes Schloss ganz aus Papier gebaut. Durch die kleinen Fenster konnte man in die Zimmer hineinsehen. Vor dem Schloss standen
15 kleine Bäume, die um ein Stückchen Spiegel gruppiert waren. Es stellte einen See dar. Schwäne aus Wachs glitten über seine Oberfläche[6] und spiegelten sich darin. Das war alles sehr niedlich[7], aber das niedlichste war doch ein kleines Mädchen, das in der offenen Schlosstür stand. Es war auch aus Papier, trug ein feines Seidenkleid und ein kleines blaues Band über den Schultern. Mitten darauf war eine glänzende Blume, so
20 groß wie ihr ganzes Gesicht. Das kleine Mädchen streckte beide Arme hoch, denn es war eine Tänzerin, und dann hob es das eine Bein so hoch, dass der Zinnsoldat es gar nicht mehr sehen konnte und glaubte, dass es, wie er, nur ein Bein hätte.

„Das wäre eine Frau für mich", dachte er, „aber sie ist etwas vornehm[8], sie wohnt in einem Schloss, und ich habe nur eine Schachtel mit vierundzwanzig anderen darin, das
25 ist kein Ort für sie. Doch ich möchte sie kennenlernen." Und dann legte er sich hinter eine Schnupftabakdose[9], die auf dem Tisch stand. Nun konnte er die kleine, feine Dame anschauen, die immer noch auf einem Bein stand, ohne umzufallen.

☐ **a.** Der Zinnsoldat sieht eine Tänzerin, die er kennenlernen möchte.
☐ **b.** Der Zinnsoldat denkt, dass die Tänzerin nur ein Bein hat, weil er das andere nicht sieht.
☐ **c.** Das Schloss und die Tänzerin sind ganz aus Papier, die Schwäne sind aus Wachs.

Als es Abend wurde, kamen die anderen Zinnsoldaten in ihre Schachtel, und die Leute im Haus gingen ins Bett. Nun begann das Spielzeug zu spielen, nämlich „Es
30 kommen Fremde", „Krieg[10] führen" und „Ball geben". Die Zinnsoldaten rasselten[11] in der Schachtel, denn sie wollten dabei sein, aber sie konnten den Deckel nicht aufheben[12]. Der Nussknacker machte Purzelbäume[13] und die Kreide malte fröhlich auf der Tafel. Es war ein Lärm[14], dass der Kanarienvogel aufwachte und anfing in Versen mitzusprechen. Die beiden einzigen, die sich nicht bewegten[15], waren der Zinnsoldat und die Tänzerin.
35 Sie stand auf der Zehenspitze und hatte beide Arme ausgestreckt. Er war genauso standhaft auf seinem einen Bein und schaute sie die ganze Zeit an.

Nun schlug die Uhr zwölf und der Deckel sprang von der Schnupftabakdose, aber da war kein Tabak drin, nein, sondern ein kleiner schwarzer Kobold[16].

---

[1]lid [2]different [3]reichte aus *was enough* [4]fate [5]toys [6]surface [7]cute [8]noble [9]snuffbox [10]war [11]rattled
[12]lift [13]somersaults [14]noise [15]moved [16]goblin

Lesehilfe

The fairy tale "Der standhafte Zinn-soldat" is one of many fairy tales that are well-known across cultures. Just as in English, a fairy tale in German typically contains certain formulaic expressions or phrases. English fairy tales often begin with the phrase *Once upon a time.* Look at the beginning of this fairy tale to see how German fairy tales typically begin.

Fairy tales in German are typically written and told in the simple past tense. As you read this one, you will encounter many such verb forms. Avoid the temptation to look them up upon the first reading; you will deal with them during the **Arbeit mit dem Text** activities at the end of the reading.

„Zinnsoldat!" sagte der Kobold. „Halte deine Augen im Zaum[1]!"
40 Aber der Zinnsoldat tat, als ob[2] er nicht hörte.
„Ja, warte nur bis morgen!" sagte der Kobold.

☐ **a.** Wenn die Menschen im Bett sind, spielt das Spielzeug. Der Kanarienvogel spricht mit.

☐ **b.** Das Spielzeug fängt nachts an zu spielen, nur der Zinnsoldat und die Tänzerin nicht. Sie schauen einander die ganze Zeit an.

☐ **c.** Um Mitternacht springt ein Kobold aus der Schnupftabakdose und warnt den Zinnsoldaten: „Halte deine Augen im Zaum!"

Als es nun Morgen wurde und die Kinder aufstanden, stellten sie den Zinnsoldaten ins Fenster – und war es nun der Kobold oder der Wind – auf einmal flog das Fenster auf[3], und der Soldat stürzte drei Stockwerke tief hinab[4]. Das war ein schrecklicher
45 Sturz. Er streckte sein Bein gerade in die Luft und blieb zwischen den Pflastersteinen[5] stecken.

Das Dienstmädchen[6] und der kleine Junge liefen sofort hinunter, um ihn zu suchen. Aber obwohl[7] sie fast auf ihn getreten[8] wären, fanden sie ihn nicht. Hätte der Zinnsoldat gerufen[9]: „Hier bin ich!" so hätten sie ihn sicher gefunden, aber er fand es
50 nicht passend[10], laut zu schreien, weil er Uniform trug.

Nun begann es zu regnen und die Tropfen fielen immer dichter[11]. Als der Regen vorbei war, kamen zwei Straßenjungen vorbei.

„Sieh", sagte der eine, „da liegt ein Zinnsoldat! Der soll segeln gehen!"

Sie machten aus Zeitungspapier ein Boot, setzten den Soldaten hinein und ließen
55 ihn den Rinnstein[12] hinuntersegeln. Beide Jungen liefen nebenher und klatschten in die Hände. Was für Wellen[13] waren da in dem Rinnstein! Das Papierboot schwankte[14] und drehte sich im Kreis[15]. Der Zinnsoldat aber blieb standhaft, verzog keine Miene[16], sah nach vorn und hielt das Gewehr im Arm.

☐ **a.** Der Zinnsoldat fällt aus dem Fenster. Zwei Jungen finden ihn und setzen ihn in ein Boot.

☐ **b.** Der Zinnsoldat will nicht laut schreien, weil er das in Uniform nicht passend findet.

☐ **c.** Zwei Jungen machen ein Boot aus Papier und laufen neben dem Rinnstein her.

Arbeit mit dem Text

A. **Intensives Lesen.** Lesen Sie jeden Abschnitt noch einmal und beantworten Sie die folgenden Fragen.

1. Was halten die Zinnsoldaten im Arm? Wie ist ihre Uniform?
2. Warum hat einer der Zinnsoldaten nur ein Bein? Ist das ein Problem?
3. Beschreiben Sie das Schloss! Was stellt der Spiegel dar?
4. Beschreiben Sie das Mädchen! Wie sieht es aus? Wie steht es da?
5. Was denkt der Zinnsoldat, als er sie sieht? Was macht er?
6. Was passiert, wenn die Leute im Haus ins Bett gehen?
7. Was machen der Zinnsoldat und die Tänzerin?
8. Was passiert um Mitternacht?
9. Warum fällt der Zinnsoldat auf die Straße?
10. Warum finden das Dienstmädchen und der kleine Junge ihn nicht?
11. Was machen die beiden Straßenjungen?

[1]Halte ... *Control your eyes* [2]tat ... *acted as if* [3]flog auf *flew open* [4]stürzte hinab *fell down* [5]cobblestones [6]maid [7]although [8]stepped [9]Hätte ... *If the tin soldier had called out* [10]proper [11]more heavily [12]gutter [13]waves [14]rocked [15]circle [16]verzog ... *did not bat an eyelid*

B. **Wörter erkennen.** Suchen Sie die folgenden Verben im Text und unterstreichen Sie sie. Schreiben Sie die Zeilennummer in die Tabelle. Schreiben Sie ebenfalls den Infinitiv und die englische Übersetzung in die Tabelle.

Präteritumsform	Zeilennummer	Infinitiv	Englisch
rief			
fiel			
glitten			
trug			
hob			
begann			
anfing			
schlug			
tat			
aufstanden			
flog ... auf			
liefen			
fand			
ließen			
blieb			
verzog			
sah			
hielt			

Nach dem Lesen

Erzählen Sie die Geschichte weiter. Was passiert mit dem Zinnsoldaten? Was passiert mit der Tänzerin? Sehen sie sich wieder?

Märchen

Vocabulary Display
These vocabulary words will help sts.
work with the fairy tales in the following activities.
Make sure sts. understand the importance of the
fairy tale tradition in the German-speaking world.
Although there is a lot of new vocabulary in this
section, much of it is guessable because sts. are
already familiar with the stories.

der König   die Königin

die böse Hexe

der Frosch →
(der verwunschene Prinz)

der Schatz

die gute Fee

das Schloss

der Jäger

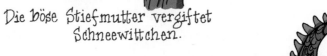

Die böse Stiefmutter vergiftet
Schneewittchen.

Der Prinz erlöst die
Prinzessin.

Der Prinz tötet den Drachen.

Bringen Sie die Sätze in die richtige Reihenfolge.

- 2 Die Königin starb bald darauf, und der König heiratete wieder.
- 12 Der Prinz und Schneewittchen heirateten, aber die böse Stiefmutter musste sterben.
- 4 Ein Jäger brachte Schneewittchen in den dunklen Wald.
- 10 Eines Tages kam ein Königssohn. Als er Schneewittchen sah, verliebte er sich in sie und wollte sie mit nach Hause nehmen.
- 3 Die böse Stiefmutter hasste Schneewittchen, weil sie so schön war.
- 6 Schneewittchen blieb bei den Zwergen und führte ihnen den Haushalt.
- 1 Es war einmal eine Königin, die bekam eine Tochter, die so weiß war wie Schnee, so rot wie Blut und so schwarzhaarig wie Ebenholz[1].
- 7 Die Stiefmutter hörte bald von ihrem Spiegel, dass Schneewittchen noch am Leben war.
- 5 Schneewittchen lief durch den Wald und kam zu den sieben Zwergen.
- 9 Die Zwerge weinten und legten sie in einen gläsernen Sarg.
- 11 Als seine Diener den Sarg wegtrugen, stolperte ein Diener. Das giftige Apfelstück rutschte aus Schneewittchens Hals und sie wachte auf.
- 8 Die Stiefmutter verkaufte Schneewittchen einen giftigen Apfel, Schneewittchen biss hinein und fiel tot um.

[1]ebony

Sit. 13. Use only for listening comprehension, i.e., read the fairy tale to your sts. and then do the receptive recall phase by reading the sentences out of order and asking: *Welches Bild zeigt: ...?* As follow-up, distribute 12 slips of paper, with one sentence from the tale written on each, to twelve sts. or groups of sts. Then, sts. line themselves up according to their sequence of sentences.

Sentences for narration series: **(1)** *Es waren einmal ein König und eine Königin, die wollten so gern ein Kind.* **(2)** *Als die Königin endlich eine Tochter bekam, war die Freude groß.* **(3)** *Sie veranstalteten ein Fest und luden zwölf Feen ein, vergaßen aber die dreizehnte.* **(4)** *Die dreizehnte Fee kam und verwünschte Dornröschen. Sie sollte sich an einer Spindel stechen und sterben.* **(5)** *Die zwölfte Fee änderte den bösen Wunsch. Dornröschen sollte nur hundert Jahre schlafen.* **(6)** *Als Dornröschen fünfzehn Jahre alt war, ging der böse Wunsch in Erfüllung. Sie stach sich an einer Spindel und fiel in einen tiefen Schlaf.* **(7)** *Mit ihr schlief das ganze Schloss ein, alle Menschen und alle Tiere.* **(8)** *Rund um das Schloss wuchs eine große Dornenhecke.* **(9)** *Als 100 Jahre vorbei waren, kam ein junger Prinz zur Hecke und die Dornen verwandelten sich in Blumen.* **(10)** *Er ging ins Schloss, fand Dornröschen und als er sie küsste, wachte sie auf.* **(11)** *Alle anderen Menschen und alle Tiere wachten auch auf.* **(12)** *Der Prinz und Dornröschen heirateten. Und wenn sie nicht gestorben sind, dann leben sie noch heute.*

Situation 13 | Bildgeschichte: Dornröschen

Situation 14 | Wer weiß – gewinnt

Aus welchem Märchen ist das?

Sit. 14. Have sts. work in groups to match the quotations with the correct fairy tale. **Answers:** 1. Hänsel und Gretel, 2. Schneewittchen, 3. Rotkäppchen, 4. Dornröschen, 5. Der Froschkönig, 6. Aschenputtel, 7. Rumpelstilzchen.

Dornröschen

Rumpelstilzchen

Aschenputtel

Der Froschkönig

Rotkäppchen

Hänsel und Gretel

Schneewittchen

1. „Knusper, knusper, knäuschen,
   wer knuspert an meinem Häuschen?"
   „Der Wind, der Wind, das himmlische Kind."
2. „Spieglein, Spieglein an der Wand, wer ist die Schönste im ganzen Land?"
   „Frau Königin, Ihr seid die Schönste hier, aber die junge Königin ist
   tausendmal schöner als Ihr."
3. „Ei, Großmutter, was hast du für große Ohren!"
   „Damit ich dich besser hören kann."
   „Ei, Großmutter, was hast du für große Augen!"
   „Damit ich dich besser sehen kann."
   „Ei, Großmutter, was hast du für ein großes Maul!"
   „Damit ich dich besser fressen kann."
4. „Die Königstochter soll an ihrem fünfzehnten Geburtstag in einen tiefen
   Schlaf fallen, der hundert Jahre dauert."
5. „Wenn ich am Tisch neben dir sitzen und von deinem Teller essen und
   aus deinem Becher trinken und in deinem Bett schlafen darf, dann will ich
   deinen goldenen Ball aus dem Brunnen heraufholen."
6. „Rucke di guh, rucke di guh,
   Blut ist im Schuh:
   Der Schuh ist zu klein,
   die rechte Braut sitzt noch daheim."
7. „Heute back ich, morgen brau ich,
   übermorgen hol' ich der Königin ihr Kind:
   ach, wie gut, dass niemand weiß,
   dass ich _____ heiß!"

Situation 15 | Was ist passiert?

Sit. 15. This activity provides examples of the past perfect tense with *nachdem*. **Answers:** 1. d, 2. g, 3. e, 4. h, 5. f, 6. a, 7. c, 8. b.

1. Nachdem Schneewittchen den giftigen Apfel gegessen hatte,
2. Nachdem Hänsel und Gretel durch den dunklen Wald gelaufen waren,
3. Nachdem die Prinzessin den Frosch geküsst hatte,
4. Nachdem die Müllerstochter keinen Schmuck mehr hatte,
5. Nachdem Aschenputtel alle Linsen[1] eingesammelt[2] hatte,
6. Nachdem der Wolf die Großmutter gefressen hatte,
7. Nachdem der Prinz Dornröschen geküsst hatte,
8. Nachdem Rumpelstilzchen seinen Namen gehört hatte,

a. legte er sich in ihr Bett.
b. wurde er sehr wütend.
c. wachte sie auf.
d. fiel sie tot um.
e. verwandelte er sich in einen Prinzen.
f. ging sie auf den Ball.
g. kamen sie zum Haus der Hexe.
h. versprach sie Rumpelstilzchen ihr erstes Kind.

[1]*lentils*   [2]*gathered*

Situation 16 | Zum Schreiben: Es war einmal …

Sit. 16. Do first in class as an oral group activity. Sts. can practice building simple story lines and working with known vocabulary and structures. Start them off with *Es war einmal* … Tell sts. something about the structure of fairy tales: Time and place are of no importance. There are good characters, bad characters, and a problem—often caused by evil forces—that has to be solved by the hero or heroine. Encourage sts. to be creative.

AA. You could also ask sts. to illustrate their stories and then present them to the class. This could be a group project.

Schreiben Sie ein Märchen. Wählen Sie aus den vier Kategorien etwas aus, oder erfinden Sie etwas.

DIE GUTEN

eine schöne Prinzessin
ein armer Student
eine tapfere Königin
ein treuer Diener
?

DIE AUSGANGSLAGE

frisst Menschen und Tiere
hat lange Zeit geschlafen
bekommt immer nur Fs
vergiftet das Wasser
?

DIE BÖSEN

eine böse Hexe
eine grausame Professorin
ein hungriger Drache
ein böser Stiefvater
?

DIE AUFGABE

drei Rätsel lösen
mit einem Riesen kämpfen
etwas Verlorenes wiederfinden
eine List erfinden
?

Lektüre

Lektüre. (1) Use *Vor dem Lesen* Part A to review the first part of the fairy tale. Let sts. work in small groups. An alternative is to write out each word or phrase from the box onto slips of paper and pass these out to pairs or groups of sts. Each pair or group is then responsible for formulating the 2 or 3 sentences that tell the corresponding segment of the story. Discuss afterwards. **(2)** Ask sts. to read the *Lesehilfe* and work on the questions in small groups before they do the extensive reading task in Part B of *Vor dem Lesen*. **(3)** *Vor dem Lesen* Part B. Let sts. read through the whole text once and check the sentence after each section that best summarizes the content. **(4)** Intensive reading is required for *Arbeit mit dem Text*. For Part A, ask sts. to work in pairs and discuss afterwards. **(5)** Assign Part B for homework. **(6)** *Nach dem Lesen* should be done as pair work where sts. take notes first and then tell the story to a partner. Set a time limit.

Vor dem Lesen

A. Hier ist der zweite Teil des Märchens „Der standhafte Zinnsoldat" von Hans Christian Andersen. Erinnern Sie sich an den ersten Teil? Erzählen Sie, was bisher[1] passiert ist. Die folgenden Ausdrücke helfen Ihnen dabei.

Geburtstag
fünfundzwanzig Zinnsoldaten
Schloss aus Papier
regnen
Kobold
Tänzerin
ein Bein
Boot
aus dem Fenster
Mitternacht
Rinnstein
nicht finden

[1]*thus far*

Lesehilfe

Knowing what fairy tales are like, you can anticipate language and events that you are likely to encounter. Like many fairy tales, this one contains an occasional comment directed to the readers or hearers of the tale. Before reading **Teil II,** scan the text and locate the phrase that is equivalent to English *Just imagine . . .* (Hint: The verb to look for is **sich vor·stellen.**) How many times does it appear? What effect does it have?

In many fairy tales, animals are imbued with the ability to speak a human language. Scan the text and determine what animal talks in this fairy tale. What other supernatural sorts of events might you expect to encounter in **Teil II?**

Der standhafte Zinnsoldat

von Hans Christian Andersen

TEIL II

Was bisher geschah: Ein kleiner Junge bekommt Zinnsoldaten zum Geburtstag geschenkt. Einer der Zinnsoldaten verliebt sich in eine kleine Tänzerin. Ein Kobold verwünscht den Zinnsoldaten. Der Zinnsoldat fällt aus dem Fenster. Zwei Jungen finden ihn und setzen ihn in ein Papierboot. Der Soldat segelt im Papierboot den Rinnstein hinunter.

Plötzlich trieb das Boot unter eine lange Rinnsteinbrücke[1]. Da wurde es so dunkel wie in seiner Schachtel.

„Wohin mag ich nur kommen?" dachte der Zinnsoldat. „Ja, ja, das ist die Schuld[2] des Kobolds! Ach, wäre doch das kleine Mädchen[3] hier im Boot, dann könnte es noch
5 so dunkel sein!"

Da kam plötzlich eine große Wasserratte, die unter der Rinnsteinbrücke wohnte. „Hast du einen Pass?" fragte die Ratte. „Her mit dem Pass!"

Aber der Zinnsoldat sagte nichts und hielt das Gewehr noch fester.

Das Boot fuhr davon und die Ratte lief hinterher. Sie rief: „Haltet ihn auf! Haltet
10 ihn auf. Er hat keinen Zoll[4] bezahlt, er hat den Pass nicht vorgezeigt!"

Aber die Strömung[5] wurde stärker und stärker! Und der Zinnsoldat konnte da, wo die Brücke aufhörte, schon das Tageslicht sehen, aber er hörte auch ein Brausen[6], das auch den tapfersten Mann erschrecken[7] konnte. Stellt euch vor, der Rinnstein stürzte, wo die Brücke endete, direkt in einen großen Kanal hinab.
15 Nun war er schon so nahe, dass er nicht mehr anhalten konnte. Das Boot fuhr hinaus, der arme Zinnsoldat hielt sich, so gut er konnte, aufrecht. Niemand sollte ihm nachsagen[8], dass er auch nur mit den Augen gezwinkert[9] hätte. Das Boot drehte sich drei-, viermal herum und füllte sich dabei bis zum Rand[10] mit Wasser, es musste sinken. Der Zinnsoldat stand bis zum Hals im Wasser, und tiefer und tiefer sank das Boot.
20 Das Papier löste sich auf[11], und nun ging das Wasser schon über den Kopf des Solda-ten. Da dachte er an die kleine niedliche Tänzerin, die er nie mehr sehen sollte und an das Lied:

„Fahre, fahre Kriegersmann[12]!
Den Tod sollst du erleiden[13]!"
25 Nun war das Papier aufgelöst, der Zinnsoldat stürzte hinab und wurde sofort von einem großen Fisch verschluckt[14].

☐ **a.** Der Zinnsoldat denkt, dass alles die Schuld des Kobolds aus der Schnupftabakdose ist.

☐ **b.** Eine große Wasserratte, die unter der Rinnsteinbrücke wohnt, will Zoll vom Zinnsoldaten.

☐ **c.** Das Boot geht unter und der Zinnsoldat stürzt in einen Kanal, wo ihn ein Fisch verschluckt.

Es war sehr dunkel, noch schlimmer als unter der Rinnsteinbrücke, und dann war es sehr eng. Aber der Zinnsoldat blieb standhaft und lag mit dem Gewehr im Arm.

---

[1]*gutter bridge* [2]*fault* [3]*wäre . . . if only the little girl were* [4]*customs duty* [5]*current* [6]*roaring* [7]*scare*
[8]*accuse* [9]*blinked* [10]*brim* [11]*löste . . . dissolved* [12]*warrior* [13]*suffer* [14]*swallowed*

Der Fisch schwamm umher und machte schreckliche Bewegungen[1]. Endlich[2] wurde
er ganz still. Dann wurde es plötzlich ganz hell und jemand rief laut: „Der Zinnsoldat!"
Der Fisch war gefangen, auf den Markt gebracht und verkauft worden. Dann hatte die
Köchin ihn in der Küche mit einem großen Messer aufgeschnitten und den Zinnsoldaten
gefunden. Sie nahm ihn und brachte ihn ins Wohnzimmer, wo alle den seltsamen[3] Mann
sehen wollten, der im Bauch eines Fisches herumgereist war. Und stellt euch vor, der
Zinnsoldat war in demselben Wohnzimmer, in dem er früher gewesen war. Er sah die-
selben Kinder und dasselbe Spielzeug stand auf dem Tisch: Das herrliche Schloss mit
der niedlichen kleinen Tänzerin, die noch immer auf einem Bein stand. Sie war auch
standhaft und das rührte[4] den Zinnsoldaten. Er war nahe daran, Zinn zu weinen, aber
das schickte sich nicht[5]. Er sah sie an, aber sie sagten gar nichts.

☐ **a.** Es ist sehr eng und dunkel im Bauch des Fisches, aber der Zinnsoldat bleibt
standhaft.

☐ **b.** Jemand fängt den Fisch, er kommt auf den Markt und zurück in die gleiche
Wohnung, wo der Zinnsoldat vorher war. Hier findet ihn die Köchin und bringt
ihn ins Wohnzimmer zurück.

☐ **c.** Das schöne Schloss ist immer noch da, und die Tänzerin steht standhaft auf ihrem
einen Bein.

Da nahm der eine der kleinen Jungen den Soldaten und warf ihn in den Ofen,
obwohl er gar keinen Grund[6] dafür hatte. Es war aber sicher der Kobold in der Dose[7],
der daran Schuld war.

Der Zinnsoldat stand da und fühlte eine Hitze, die schrecklich[8] war. Aber ob sie von
dem wirklichen Feuer oder von der Liebe kam, das wusste er nicht. Die Farben waren
ganz von ihm abgegangen. Ob das auf der Reise geschehen war oder ob der Kummer[9]
daran Schuld war, konnte niemand sagen. Er sah das kleine Mädchen an, sie blickte
ihn an, und er fühlte, dass er schmolz[10]. Aber noch immer stand er standhaft mit dem
Gewehr im Arm. Da ging eine Tür auf, der Wind ergriff[11] die Tänzerin, und sie flog direkt
in den Ofen zum Zinnsoldaten, loderte in Flammen auf und war sofort verschwunden[12].
Da schmolz der Zinnsoldat zu einem Klumpen[13], und als das Dienstmädchen am
nächsten Tag die Asche herausnahm, fand sie ihn als ein kleines Zinnherz. Von der
Tänzerin war nur noch die Blume da, und die war kohlschwarz gebrannt.

☐ **a.** Einer der kleinen Jungen wirft den Zinnsoldaten ohne Grund in den Ofen, wo er
anfängt zu schmelzen.

☐ **b.** Einer der kleinen Jungen wirft den Zinnsoldaten in den Ofen und der Wind bläst
die Tänzerin hinterher.

☐ **c.** Das Dienstmädchen findet am nächsten Tag ein kleines Zinnherz und eine
schwarze Blume.

Arbeit mit dem Text

A. **Intensives Lesen.** Lesen Sie jeden Abschnitt noch einmal und beantworten
Sie die folgenden Fragen.

1. Wem begegnet der Zinnsoldat unter der Rinnsteinbrücke? Was will sie von
ihm? Was passiert?
2. Was passiert, als der Zinnsoldat aus der Rinnsteinbrücke herauskommt?
3. Wie kommt der Zinnsoldat zurück in die Wohnung des kleinen Jungen?
4. Wen sieht der Zinnsoldat in der Wohnung? Wie fühlt er sich?
5. Was macht der Junge mit dem Zinnsoldaten? Warum macht er das?
6. Was passiert mit dem Zinnsoldaten?
7. Was passiert mit der Tänzerin?
8. Was findet das Dienstmädchen am nächsten Morgen?

[1]movements [2]Finally [3]strange [4]moved [5]schickte … wasn't proper [6]reason [7]box [8]horrible
[9]sorrow [10]was melting [11]caught [12]vanished [13]lump

B. **Kollokationen bilden.** Verbinden Sie das Objekt mit dem Verb. Suchen Sie dann die Kollokation im Text und unterstreichen Sie sie. Tipp: Die Objekte stehen im Text in der gleichen Reihenfolge. Übersetzen Sie dann die Kollokation ins Englische.

1.

OBJEKT	VERB	ENGLISCH
unter der Brücke	bezahlen	_____
Zoll	füllen	_____
den Pass	hören	_____
das Tageslicht	sehen	_____
ein Brausen	vorzeigen	_____
mit den Augen	wohnen	*to live under the bridge*
bis zum Rand	zwinkern	_____

2.

OBJEKT	VERB	ENGLISCH
den Fisch	auflodern	_____
auf den Markt	aufschneiden	_____
mit einem Messer	bringen	_____
auf einem Bein	fangen	_____
in den Ofen	schmelzen	_____
in Flammen	stehen	_____
zu einem Klumpen	werfen	_____

Nach dem Lesen

Erzählen Sie das Märchen. Machen Sie sich Notizen und erzählen Sie dann das Märchen einem Partner oder einer Partnerin.

Videoecke

- In welche Klasse gehst du?
- Was sind deine Lieblingsfächer?
- Was gefällt dir daran?
- Hast du gute Noten?
- Wann ist eure nächste Prüfung?
- Wie bereitest du dich darauf vor?
- Was gefällt dir an deiner Schule?
- Was gefällt dir nicht?
- Wie sieht dein Schulalltag aus?

Katharina geht in die 5. Klasse der Mittelschule. Ihr Hobby ist Fahrrad fahren.

Susann geht aufs Gymnasium, in die 8. Klasse. Ihre Hobbys sind Lesen, Fernsehen und Musik hören.

Aufgabe 1. (1) Focus sts.' attention on the photos by asking: *Wer ist älter, Susann oder Katharina? Wer geht aufs Gymnasium? Wer fährt gern Fahrrad? Wer sieht gern fern?* (2) Read through the statements and ask sts. which questions they answer. (3) Play the interview with Katharina and ask sts. to check the statements that apply to her. (4) Play the interview with Katharina again and ask sts. to find the remaining answers for the questions determined in step 2. (5) Do the same with Susann's interview.

Aufgabe 2. Play exact segments several times for sts. to figure out the sequence of events.

Cultural note. Some parts of Germany use a different tradition to refer to quarter past, half past, and quarter to when talking about time of day: *viertel sechs* = 5:15; *halb sechs* = 5:30; and *drei viertel sechs* = 5:45.

Student Interviews:
(1) Ask sts. to jot down their own answers to the interview questions. (2) Pair students to interview each other. Ask them to jot down their partner's answers. (3) Follow up by sampling a few of the answers given in the interviews.

Wer sagt das, Susann oder Katharina? Was sagt das andere Mädchen?

	KATHARINA	SUSANN
1. Ich geh' in die 8b.	☐	☐
2. Meine Lieblingsfächer sind Musik und Zeichnen.	☐	☐
3. Ich mag diese Fächer, weil ich damit meine Noten verbessern kann.	☐	☐
4. Wir schreiben morgen eine Mathearbeit.	☐	☐
5. Ich übe so lange, bis ich auch alles wirklich kann.	☐	☐
6. Mir gefällt nicht, dass die Jungs sich immer prügeln müssen.	☐	☐
7. Nach der Schule suche ich mir eine Lehre und fange einen Beruf an.	☐	☐

Aufgabe 2

Wie sieht der Schulalltag von Katharina aus? Bringen Sie die Sätze und Satzteile in die richtige Reihenfolge.

_____ Dann fahre ich mit der Straßenbahn zur Schule.
_____ Ich stehe morgens viertel sechs auf
_____ und füttere meine Katze.
_____ Nach sieben Stunden gehe ich dann nach Hause
_____ und mach' mich um sieben aus dem Staub.

Wortschatz

Kindheit und Jugend	Childhood and Youth
die **Ausbildung, -en** (R)	education
die **Klasse, -n**	grade (level)
die **Note, -n**	grade
die **Puppe, -n**	doll
der **Abschluss**	graduation
der **Ballettunterricht**	ballet class
das **Klassentreffen, -**	class reunion
das **Mädchen, -**	girl
das **Vorbild, -er**	role model, idol

Ähnliche Wörter

der **Clown, -s**; der **Spielplatz, ⸚e**; der **Teddy, -s**; der **Zirkus, -se**, das **Kostüm, -e**

Märchen	Fairy Tales
die **Braut, ⸚e**	bride
die **Fee, -n**	fairy
die **Hexe, -n** (R)	witch
die **Königin, -nen**	queen
die **List, -en**	deception, trick
der **Brunnen, -**	well; fountain
der **Diener, -**	servant

der **Drache, -n** (*wk. masc.*)	dragon
der **Jäger, -**	hunter
der **König, -e**	king
der **Riese, -n** (*wk. masc.*)	giant
der **Sarg, ⸚e**	coffin
der **Schatz, ⸚e**	treasure
der **Zwerg, -e**	dwarf
das **Märchen, -**	fairy tale
das **Rätsel, -**	puzzle, riddle
ein Rätsel lösen	to solve a puzzle/riddle
das **Schloss, ⸚er**	castle
erlösen	to rescue, free
kämpfen	to fight
klettern, ist geklettert	to climb
küssen	to kiss
sterben, stirbt, starb, ist gestorben	to die
töten	to kill
träumen	to dream
um·fallen, fällt ... um, fiel ... um, ist umgefallen	to fall over
vergiften	to poison
sich verwandeln in (+ *akk.*)	to change into

verwünschen	to curse, cast a spell on
böse	evil, mean
eklig	gross, loathsome
giftig	poisonous
gläsern	glass
grausam	cruel
heimlich	secret
tapfer	brave
tot	dead
treu	loyal, true
verwunschen	cursed; enchanted

Ähnliche Wörter

die **Prinzessin**, -nen; die **Stiefmutter**, ⸚; der **Prinz**, -en
(*wk. masc.*); der **Stiefvater**, ⸚; das **Blut**; das **Feuer**, -

Natur und Tiere	Nature and Animals
der **Baum**, ⸚e	tree
der **Frosch**, ⸚e	frog
der **Schnee**	snow
das **Maul**, ⸚er	mouth (of an animal)
das **Pferd**, -e (R)	horse
beißen, biss, gebissen	to bite
fressen, frisst, fraß, gefressen	to eat (*said of an animal*)
füttern	to feed
pflücken	to pick

Ähnliche Wörter

der **Busch**, ⸚e; der **Dorn**, -en; der **Elefant**, -en (*wk. masc.*);
der **Wind**, -e; der **Wolf**, ⸚e; das **Schwein**, -e

Sonstige Substantive	Other Nouns
die **Direktorin**, -nen	female (school) principal, director
die **Einbrecherin**, -nen	female burglar
die **Feier**, -n	celebration, party
die **Fensterscheibe**, -n	windowpane
die **Fremdsprache**, -n	foreign language
die **Freude**, -n	joy, pleasure
die **Mannschaft**, -en	team
die **Baseballmannschaft**, -en	baseball team
die **Naturwissenschaft**, -en	natural science
die **Radtour**, -en	bicycle tour
die **Regisseurin**, -nen	female (film/stage) director
die **Schauspielerin**, -nen	actress
die **Süßigkeit**, -en	sweet, candy
die **Taschenlampe**, -n	flashlight
die **Verspätung**, -en	delay
die **Wissenschaftlerin**, -nen	female scientist
der **Ärger**	trouble
der **Becher**, -	cup, mug
der **Direktor**, -en	(school) principal, director

der **Einbrecher**, -	male burglar
der **Hals**, ⸚e	neck; throat
der **Liebesroman**, -e	romance novel
der **Regisseur**, -e	male (film/stage) director
der **Schatten**, -	shadow, shade
der **Schauspieler**, -	actor
der **Schlüssel**, -	key
der **Hausschlüssel**, -	house key
der **Wissenschaftler**, -	male scientist
der **Zaun**, ⸚e	fence
das **Geräusch**, -e	sound, noise
das **Leben**, -	life
am **Leben** sein	to be alive
das **Loch**, ⸚er	hole

Ähnliche Wörter

die **Ballerina**, -s; die **Dramatikerin**, -nen; die
Fußballspielerin, -nen; die **Tennisspielerin**, -nen; der
Dramatiker, -; der **Fußballspieler**, -; der **Haushalt**, -e;
der **Schlaf**; der **Tennisspieler**, -; das **Glas**, ⸚er; das
Rockkonzert, -e; das **Video**, -s; das **Werk**, -e

Sonstige Verben	Other Verbs
ändern	to change
bitten (um + *akk.*), bat, gebeten	to ask (for)
sich **erinnern** (an + *akk.*)	to remember
eröffnen	to open
hassen	to hate
holen	to fetch, (go) get
los·fahren, fährt ... los, fuhr ... los, ist losgefahren (R)	to drive/ride off
rutschen, ist gerutscht	to slide, slip
schimpfen	to cuss; to scold
stehlen, stiehlt, stahl, gestohlen	to steal
stolpern, ist gestolpert	to trip
streiten, gestritten	to argue, quarrel
übersetzen	to translate
sich **unterhalten**, unterhält, unterhielt, unterhalten	to converse
sich **verlieben** (in + *akk.*)	to fall in love (with)
verpassen	to miss
sich **verstecken**	to hide
vor·lesen, liest ... vor, las ... vor, vorgelesen	to read aloud
wachsen, wächst, wuchs, ist gewachsen	to grow
zerreißen, zerriss, zerrissen	to tear

Ähnliche Wörter

fallen, fällt, fiel, ist gefallen; **wecken**; **weg·tragen**, trägt ...
weg, trug ... weg, weggetragen

Adjektive und Adverbien	Adjectives and Adverbs
arm	poor
bald	soon
bald darauf	soon thereafter
begabt	gifted
daheim	at home
damals	back then
endlich	finally
hinein	in(ward)
leise	quiet(ly)
mitten	in the middle
mitten in der Nacht	in the middle of the night
neulich	recently
plötzlich	suddenly
streng	strict
übermorgen	the day after tomorrow
unterwegs	on the road

vorbei	past, over
zufällig	accidental(ly)
zurück	back

Ähnliche Wörter

deutschsprachig, hungrig, schwarzhaarig, täglich

Sonstige Wörter und Ausdrücke	Other Words and Expressions
denn	for, because
gegen (+ *akk.*)	against
nachdem	after (*conj.*)
neben	next to
nichts	nothing
Sonstiges	other things
trotzdem	in spite of that

Strukturen und Übungen

9.1   The conjunction *als* with dependent-clause word order

9.1. *Als* was introduced as a lexical item in *Kapitel 5* (*Sit. 6*). It is presented here formally as a subordinating conjunction. Section 9.3 completes the introduction of *als* by contrasting it with *wenn* and *wann*.

> **Wissen Sie noch?**
>
> An **als**-clause is a type of dependent clause. As in other dependent clauses, the conjugated verb appears at the end of the clause.
>
> Review grammar 3.4 and 7.1.

The conjunction **als** (*when*) is commonly used to express that two events or circumstances happened at the same time. The **als**-clause establishes a point of reference in the past for an action or event described in the main clause.

Als ich zwölf Jahre alt war, bin ich zum ersten Mal allein verreist.	*When I was twelve years old, I traveled alone for the first time.*

When an **als**-clause introduces a sentence, it occupies the first position. Consequently, the conjugated verb in the main clause occupies the second position and the subject of the main clause the third position.

                         1   2   3

Als ich 12 Jahre alt **war, bin ich** zum ersten Mal allein verreist.

Note that the conjugated verb in the **als**-clause appears at the end of the clause.

Übung 1 | Meilensteine

Üb. 1. Assign for homework and discuss in class. It should be interesting to compare sts.' answers in class. Ask 4 or 5 sts. to read their 1st line, then their 2nd, and so forth.

Schreiben Sie 10–15 Sätze über Ihr Leben. Beginnen Sie jeden Satz mit **als**.

> MODELL: Als ich eins war, habe ich laufen gelernt.
> Als ich zwei war, habe ich sprechen gelernt.
> Als ich fünf war, bin ich in die Schule gekommen.
> Als ich ...

9.2   The simple past tense of *werden*, the modal verbs, and *wissen*

Use the simple past tense of **haben, sein, werden, wissen,** and the modal verbs in both writing and conversation.

9.2. *Präteritum.* The verbs *haben* and *sein* were introduced in 7.5. Here, we introduce additional verbs that generally use the simple past tense for conversation. Sts. will be familiar with some of these forms, having heard them in your speech. They became acquainted with verbs with identical *ich-* and *er-/sie-/es-*forms when they learned modal verbs in *Kapitel 3*. The use of the simple past tense of strong and weak verbs in written texts is presented in Section 9.4.

The simple past tense is preferred over the perfect tense with some frequently used verbs, even in conversational German. These verbs include **haben, sein, werden,** the modal verbs, and the verb **wissen.**

Frau Gretter **war** sehr begabt.	*Mrs. Gretter was very talented.*
In der Schule **wusste** sie immer alles.	*In school she always knew everything.*
Sie **hatte** viele Freundinnen und Freunde.	*She had many friends.*

The conjugations of **werden,** the modal verbs, and **wissen** appear on the following page. For **haben** and **sein,** refer back to **Strukturen 7.5.** Notice that the **ich-** and the **er/sie/es-**forms are the same.

A. The verb **werden**

Michael **wurde** Tierpfleger.   *Michael became an animal caretaker.*
Im August **wurde** er sehr krank.   *In August he became very sick.*

werden			
ich	wurde	*wir*	wurden
du	wurdest	*ihr*	wurdet
Sie	wurden	*Sie*	wurden
er *sie* *es*	wurde	*sie*	wurden

B. Modal Verbs

To form the simple past tense of modal verbs, use the stem, drop any umlauts, and add **-te-** plus the appropriate ending.

können → könn → konn → konnte → du konntest

Gestern **wollten** wir ins Kino gehen.

Mehmet **musste** jeden Tag um sechs aufstehen.

Helga und Sigrid **durften** mit sechs Jahren noch nicht fernsehen.

Yesterday, we wanted to go to the movies.

Mehmet had to get up at six every morning.

When they were six, Helga and Sigrid weren't yet allowed to watch TV.

Here are the simple past-tense forms of the modal verbs.

	können	**müssen**	**dürfen**	**sollen**	**wollen**	**mögen**
ich	konnte	musste	durfte	sollte	wollte	mochte
du	konntest	musstest	durftest	solltest	wolltest	mochtest
Sie	konnten	mussten	durften	sollten	wollten	mochten
er *sie* *es*	konnte	musste	durfte	sollte	wollte	mochte
wir	konnten	mussten	durften	sollten	wollten	mochten
ihr	konntet	musstet	durftet	solltet	wolltet	mochtet
Sie	konnten	mussten	durften	sollten	wollten	mochten
sie	konnten	mussten	durften	sollten	wollten	mochten

Note the consonant change in the past tense of **mögen**: mo***ch***te.

C. The verb **wissen**

The forms of the verb **wissen** are similar to those of the modal verbs.

Ich **wusste** nicht, dass du keine Erdbeeren magst.

I didn't know that you don't like strawberries.

Here are the simple past-tense forms.

wissen			
ich	wusste	wir	wussten
du	wusstest	ihr	wusstet
Sie	wussten	Sie	wussten
er sie es	wusste	sie	wussten

Übung 2 | Fragen und Antworten

Üb. 2. Assign this exercise and *Üb. 3* for homework and check in class by having sts. take the roles. *Üb. 2* requires only 1st-person singular forms.

Hier sind die Fragen. Was sind die Antworten?

MODELL: Lydia, warum bist du nicht mit ins Kino gegangen? (nicht können)
→ Ich konnte nicht.

1. Ernst, warum bist du nicht mit zum Schwimmen gekommen? (nicht dürfen)
2. Maria, warum bist du nicht gekommen? (nicht wollen)
3. Jens, gestern war Juttas Geburtstag! (das / nicht wissen)
4. Jutta, warum hast du eine neue Frisur? (eine/wollen)
5. Jochen, warum hast du das Essen nicht gekocht? (das / nicht sollen)

Übung 3 | Minidialoge

Setzen Sie Modalverben oder **wissen** ein.

1. SILVIA: Was hast du gemacht, wenn du nicht zur Schule gehen _____ᵃ, Jürgen?
   JÜRGEN: Ich habe gesagt: „Ich bin krank."
   SILVIA: Haben deine Eltern das geglaubt?
   JÜRGEN: Nein, meine Mutter _____ᵇ immer, was los war.
2. ERNST: Hans, warum bist du gestern nicht auf den Spielplatz gekommen?
   HANS: Ich _____ᵃ nicht. Ich habe eine Fünf in Mathe geschrieben und _____ᵇ zu Hause bleiben.
   ERNST: Schade. Wir _____ᶜ Fußball spielen, aber dann _____ᵈ wir nicht genug Spieler finden.
3. HERR RUF: Guten Tag, Frau Gretter. Tut mir leid, dass ich neulich nicht zu Ihrer kleinen Feier kommen _____ᵃ. Aber ich _____ᵇ meine alte Tante in Würzburg besuchen.
   FRAU GRETTER: Ja, wirklich schade. Ich _____ᶜ gar nicht, dass Sie eine Tante in Würzburg haben.
   HERR RUF: Sie zieht diese Woche nach Düsseldorf zu ihrer Tochter, und ich _____ᵈ sie noch einmal besuchen.

9.3   Time: *als, wenn, wann*

9.3. *Temporale Konjunktionen.* The choice of the correct conjunction is not easy for sts. at this stage. Except for direct questions with *wann*, they rarely attempt to use clauses of this type in speech. Some have difficulties even when they have time to monitor their work in writing. Point out that *als* and *wenn* introduce dependent clauses and that the rules of word order they learned for *wenn-* and *weil-*clauses (Section 3.4) apply here, too.

Als refers to a circumstance (time period) in the past or to a single event (point in time) in the past or present, but never in the future.

TIME PERIOD

Als ich 15 Jahre alt war, sind meine Eltern nach Texas gezogen.
When I was 15 years old, my parents moved to Texas.

POINT IN TIME

Als wir in Texas angekommen sind, war es sehr heiß.
When we arrived in Texas, it was very hot.

Als Veronika ins Zimmer kommt, klingelt das Telefon.
When (As) Veronika comes into the room, the phone rings.

Wenn has three distinct meanings: a conditional meaning and two temporal meanings. In conditional sentences, **wenn** means *if.* In the temporal sense, **wenn** may be used to describe events that happen or happened one or more times (*when[ever]*) or to describe events that will happen in the future (*when*).

CONDITION

Wenn man auf diesen Knopf drückt, öffnet sich die Tür.
If you press this button, the door will open.

REPEATED EVENTS

Wenn Herr Wagner nach Hause kam, freuten sich die Kinder.
When(ever) Mr. Wagner came home, the children were happy.

Wenn Herr Wagner nach Hause kommt, freuen sich die Kinder.
When(ever) Mr. Wagner comes home, the children are happy.

FUTURE EVENT

Wenn ich in Frankfurt ankomme, rufe ich dich an.
When I arrive in Frankfurt, I'll call you.

In the simple past, **wenn** refers to a habit or an action or event that happened repeatedly or customarily; **als** refers to a specific action or event that happened once, over a particular time period or at a particular point in time in the past.

Wenn ich nicht zur Schule gehen wollte, habe ich gesagt, dass ich krank bin.	*When(ever) I didn't want to go to school, I said that I was sick.*
Als ich mein erstes F bekommen habe, habe ich geweint.	*When I got my first F, I cried.*

Wann is an adverb of time meaning *at what time.* It is used in both direct and indirect questions.

Wann hast du deinen ersten Kuss bekommen?	*When did you get your first kiss?*
Ich weiß nicht, **wann** der Zug kommt.	*I don't know when the train is coming.*

Note that when **wann** is used in an indirect question, the conjugated verb comes at the end of the clause.

When	
Single event in past or present (*at one time*) Circumstance in the past	**als**
Condition (*if*) Repeated event in past, present, or future (*whenever*) Single event in the future (*when*)	**wenn**
Adverb of time (*at what time?*)	**wann**

Übung 4 | Minidialoge

Üb. 4. Sts. do not find it easy to recognize indirect questions. If *wann* is associated only with questions, there can be difficulties because indirect questions are often statements. A useful rule of thumb is that if *when* means "at what time," German uses *wann*. You can point out, too, that indirect questions are often introduced by a verb such as *wissen* or *fragen*.

Wann, wenn oder **als?**

1. ERNST: _____ᵃ darf ich fernsehen?
   FRAU WAGNER: _____ᵇ du deine Hausaufgaben gemacht hast.
2. ROLF: Oma, _____ᵃ hast du Opa kennengelernt?
   SOFIE: _____ᵇ ich siebzehn war.
3. STEFAN: Was habt ihr gemacht, _____ ihr in München wart?
   NORA: Wir haben sehr viele Filme gesehen.
4. MARTHA: _____ᵃ hast du Sofie getroffen?
   WILLI: Gestern, _____ᵇ ich an der Uni war.
5. ALBERT: _____ᵃ fliegst du nach Europa?
   PETER: _____ᵇ ich genug Geld habe.
6. MONIKA: Du spielst sehr gut Tennis. _____ᵃ hast du das gelernt?
   HEIDI: _____ᵇ ich noch klein war.

Übung 5 | Ein Brief

Üb. 5. Assign for homework and check in class. If sts. have noticed the similarity between Jutta's letter and the tale of *Rotkäppchen,* you could ask who the wolf is and how this modern version might have developed.

Wann, wenn oder **als?**

Liebe Tina,
gestern Nachmittag musste ich meiner Oma mal wieder Kuchen und Wein bringen. Immer _____ᵃ ich mich mit meinen Freunden verabrede[1], will mein Vater irgendetwas[2] von mir. Ich war ganz schön wütend. _____ᵇ ich den Korb[3] zusammengepackt habe, habe ich leise geschimpft. _____ᶜ ich meine Oma besuche, muss ich immer ein bisschen dableiben und mich mit ihr unterhalten. Das ist langweilig und anstrengend[4], denn die Oma hört nicht mehr so gut. Außerdem wohnt sie am anderen Ende der Stadt. Auch _____ᵈ ich mit dem Bus fahre, dauert es mindestens zwei Stunden.

_____ᵉ ich aus dem Haus gekommen bin, habe ich an der Ecke Billy auf seinem Moped gesehen. _____ᶠ ich ihn zum letzten Mal gesehen habe, haben wir uns prima unterhalten.

„_____ᵍ kommst du mal wieder ins Jugendzentrum?" hat Billy gerufen. „Vielleicht heute gegen Abend", habe ich geantwortet. _____ʰ ich mich auf den Weg gemacht habe, hat es auch noch angefangen zu regnen. Und natürlich ... wie immer ... _____ⁱ es regnet, habe ich keinen Regenschirm dabei. So viel für heute.

Tausend Grüße
deine Jutta

[1]*make a date* [2]*something* [3]*basket* [4]*strenuous*

9.4 The simple past tense of strong and weak verbs (receptive)

9.4. *Präteritum.* The strong and weak simple past-tense forms are presented here mainly so that sts. can learn to recognize them in written texts. The forms are relatively easy to associate with an infinitive, but for production they are acquired only gradually. It may be of interest that English also has strong and weak simple past-tense forms, with either a stem-vowel change or a (dental) suffix (*-ed*).

In written texts, the simple past tense is frequently used instead of the perfect to refer to past events.

Jutta **fuhr** allein in Urlaub.	*Jutta went on vacation alone.*
Ihr Vater **brachte** sie zum Bahnhof.	*Her father took her to the train station.*

In the simple past tense, just as in the present tense, separable-prefix verbs are separated in independent clauses but joined in dependent clauses.

Rolf **stand** um acht Uhr **auf.** Es war selten, dass er so früh **aufstand.**	*Rolf got up at eight. It was rare that he got up so early.*

A. Weak Verbs

weak verbs = **-(e)te-**

You can recognize the simple past of weak verbs by the **-(e)te-** that is inserted between the stem and the ending.

PRESENT	SIMPLE PAST	PRESENT	SIMPLE PAST
du sagst	: du sag**te**st	sie arbeitet	: sie arbei**te**te

Wir bad**ete**n, bau**te**n Sandburgen und spiel**te**n Volleyball.	*We went swimming, built sand castles, and played volleyball.*

Like modal verbs, simple past-tense forms do not have an ending in the **ich-** and the **er/sie/es-**forms: **ich sagte, er sagte.** Here are the simple past-tense forms of the verb **machen.**

machen			
ich	machte	*wir*	machten
du	machtest	*ihr*	machtet
Sie	machten	*Sie*	machten
er *sie* *es*	machte	*sie*	machten

irregular weak verbs = stem vowel change + **-te-**

For a few weak verbs, the stem of the simple past is the same as the one used to form the past participle.

PRESENT	SIMPLE PAST	PERFECT	
bringen	brachte	hat gebracht	*to bring*
denken	dachte	hat gedacht	*to think*
kennen	kannte	hat gekannt	*to know, be acquainted with*
wissen	wusste	hat gewusst	*to know (as a fact)*

B. Strong Verbs

All strong verbs have a different stem in the simple past: **schwimmen/ schwamm, singen/sang, essen/aß.** Since English also has a number of verbs with irregular stems in the past (*swim/swam, sing/sang, eat/ate*), you will usually have no trouble recognizing simple past stems. You will recognize the **ich-** and **er/sie/es-**forms of strong verbs easily, because they do not have an ending.

Through practice reading texts in the simple past, you will gradually become familiar with the various patterns of stem change that exist. Here are some common past-tense forms you are likely to encounter in your reading.* A more complete list of stem-changing verbs can be found in Appendix F.

bleiben	blieb	*to stay*
essen	aß	*to eat*
fahren	fuhr	*to drive*
fliegen	flog	*to fly*
geben	gab	*to give*
gehen	ging	*to go*
lesen	las	*to read*
nehmen	nahm	*to take*
rufen	rief	*to call*
schlafen	schlief	*to sleep*
schreiben	schrieb	*to write*
sehen	sah	*to see*
sprechen	sprach	*to speak*
stehen	stand	*to stand*
tragen	trug	*to carry*
waschen	wusch	*to wash*

Der Bus fuhr um sieben Uhr ab.	*The bus left at seven o'clock.*
Sechs Kinder schliefen in einem Zimmer.	*Six children were sleeping in one room.*
Jutta aß frische Krabben.	*Jutta ate fresh shrimp.*

Übung 6 | ## Die Radtour

Üb. 6. Have sts. do this exercise and *Üb.* 7 for homework, and check the answers in class.

Setzen Sie die Verben ein:

aßen	gingen	kamen	schwammen	standen
fuhren	hielten	schliefen	sprangen	

Willi und Sofie wollten eine Radtour machen, aber ihre Räder waren kaputt. Sie mussten sie reparieren, bevor sie losfahren konnten. Am Morgen der Tour _____ [a] sie um sechs Uhr auf, _____ [b] in die Garage, wo die Räder waren und machten sich an die Arbeit. Gegen acht waren sie fertig, sie frühstückten noch und dann _____ [c] sie ab. Gegen elf _____ [d] sie an einen kleinen See. Sie _____ [e] an und setzten sich ins Gras. Willis Mutter hatte ihnen Essen eingepackt. Sie waren hungrig und _____ [f] alles auf. Sie _____ [g] im See und legten sich dann in den Schatten und _____ [h]. Am späten Nachmittag _____ [i] sie noch mal ins Wasser und radelten dann zurück nach Hause. Die Rückfahrt dauerte eine Stunde länger als die Hinfahrt.

---

*It is fairly easy to make an educated guess about the form of the infinitive when encountering new simple past-tense forms. The following vowel correspondences are the most common.

SIMPLE PAST	INFINITIVE	EXAMPLES
a	e/i	gab - geben, fand - finden
i/ie	a/ei	ritt - reiten, hielt - halten, schrieb - schreiben

Übung 7 | Hänsel und Gretel

Ergänzen Sie die Verben.

brachten, fanden, gab, kamen, liefen, rannte, sahen, saß, schliefen, schloss, tötete, trug, wohnte

1. Vor einem großen Wald _____ eine arme Familie mit den beiden Kindern Hänsel und Gretel.

2. Als sie eines Tages nichts mehr zu essen hatten, _____ die Eltern die Kinder in den Wald.

3. Die Kinder _____ ein und als sie aufwachten, waren sie allein.

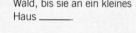

4. Dann _____ sie durch den Wald, bis sie an ein kleines Haus _____.

5. Durch das Fenster _____ sie eine alte Frau, die vor einem Kamin[1] _____ und strickte.

6. Als die Alte die Kinder bemerkte[2], holte sie sie herein und _____ ihnen etwas zu essen. Die Kinder _____ die Frau sehr freundlich.

7. Aber leider war sie eine böse Hexe. Sie packte[3] Hänsel, _____ ihn in einen Käfig und _____ die Tür. Er sollte dick werden, damit sie ihn essen konnte.

8. Gretel weinte und versuchte, Hänsel zu helfen. Sie _____ die Hexe und _____ mit Hänsel weg.

9.5 Sequence of events in past narration: the past perfect tense and the conjunction *nachdem* (receptive)

9.5. *Plusquamperfekt.* We focus here especially on the use of the past perfect with *nachdem* to make clear the relationship with the simple past tense. The sequence of tenses in past time is not an easy concept. This is a tense that sts. will need only to recognize. Remind them that the *nachdem*-clause counts as the first element in the sentence, so that the simple past-tense form will stand immediately after the comma.

A. Uses of the Past Perfect Tense

The past perfect tense is used to describe past actions and events that were completed before other past actions and events.

Nachdem Jochen zwei Stunden **ferngesehen hatte,** ging er ins Bett.	*After Jochen had watched TV for two hours, he went to bed.*
Nachdem Jutta mit ihrer Freundin **telefoniert hatte,** machte sie ihre Hausaufgaben.	*After Jutta had talked with her friend on the phone, she did her homework.*

[1]*hearth* [2]*noticed* [3]*grabbed*

The past perfect tense is often used in the clause with **nachdem.** The simple past tense is then used in the concluding (main) clause.

The past perfect tense often occurs in a dependent clause with the conjunction **nachdem** (*after*); the verb of the main clause is in the simple past or the perfect tense.

Nachdem Jens seine erste Zigarette **geraucht hatte, wurde** ihm schlecht.	*After Jens had smoked his first cigarette, he got sick.*

A dependent clause introduced by **nachdem** usually precedes the main clause. This results in the pattern "verb, verb."

DEPENDENT CLAUSE	MAIN CLAUSE
1	2

Nachdem ich die Schule **beendet hatte,** **machte** ich eine Lehre.
After I had finished school, I learned a trade.

The conjugated verb of the dependent clause is at the end of the dependent clause; the conjugated verb of the main clause is at the beginning of the main clause. Because the entire dependent clause holds the first position in the sentence, the verb-second rule applies here.

B. Formation of the Past Perfect Tense

past perfect tense = **hatte/war** + past participle

The past perfect tense of a verb consists of the simple past tense of the auxiliary **haben** or **sein** and the past participle of the verb.

Ich **hatte** schon **bezahlt** und wir konnten gehen.	*I had already paid, and we could go.*
Als wir ankamen, **waren** sie schon **weggegangen.**	*When we arrived, they had already left.*

Übung 8 | Was ist zuerst passiert?

Bilden Sie logische Sätze mit Satzteilen aus beiden Spalten.

MODELL: Nachdem Jutta den Schlüssel verloren hatte, kletterte sie durch das Fenster.

1. Nachdem Jutta den Schlüssel verloren hatte,
2. Nachdem Ernst die Fensterscheibe eingeworfen hatte,
3. Nachdem Claire angekommen war,
4. Nachdem Hans seine Hausaufgaben gemacht hatte,
5. Nachdem Jens sein Fahrrad repariert hatte,
6. Nachdem Michael die Seiltänzerin[1] gesehen hatte,
7. Nachdem Richard ein ganzes Jahr gespart hatte,
8. Nachdem Silvia zwei Semester allein gewohnt hatte,
9. Nachdem Willi ein Geräusch gehört hatte,

a. flog er nach Australien.
b. ging er ins Bett.
c. kletterte sie durch das Fenster.
d. lief er weg.
e. machte er eine Radtour.
f. rief er den Großvater an.
g. rief sie Melanie an.
h. war er ganz verliebt.
i. zog sie in eine Wohngemeinschaft.

[1]*tightrope walker*

Franz Marc: *Turm der blauen Pferde* (1913), verschollen

Chapter opening artwork: Franz Marc was born in Munich in 1880. He studied art at the *Münchner Kunstakademie* and traveled several times to Paris, the art center at the turn of the century. With Wassily Kandinsky he founded the artists' group *Der Blaue Reiter*. Marc is an important representative of Expressionism in Germany. His works often feature animals in bright colors. He liked animals and understood them as creatures that live in harmony with mother nature. His favorite motif is the horse. The painting *Turm der blauen Pferde* is considered one of the masterpieces of German Expressionism. The painting has been missing since World War II. The blue in this painting symbolizes spiritual integrity and harmony.

Suggestion: Use this colorful and unusual representation of horses—including the title—for an association activity. The painting also lends itself to introducing or reviewing animals. *Welche Tiere sehen Sie auf dem Bild? Welche Farbe haben sie? Welche Farben sind auf dem Gemälde noch wichtig? Was für Farben sind das? Sehen die Tiere realistisch aus? Warum (nicht)? Wie sind die Formen auf dem Gemälde? Warum heißt das Bild „Turm der blauen Pferde"? Was ist am linken Rand? Was ist im Hintergrund am Himmel?*

FRANZ MARC

Franz Marc (1880–1916) wurde in München geboren und fiel im Ersten Weltkrieg bei Verdun. Er war ein führender[1] Expressionist und gründete[2] 1911 mit Wassily Kandinsky die Künstlergruppe „Der Blaue Reiter". Das Original des berühmten Gemäldes „Turm der Blauen Pferde" ist im Zweiten Weltkrieg verschollen[3].

[1] *leading*   [2] *founded*   [3] *missing, lost*

10

Auf Reisen

Kapitel 10 focuses on travel. You will also learn to get around in the German-speaking world by following directions and reading maps.

Themen
Reisepläne
Nach dem Weg fragen
Urlaub am Strand
Tiere

Kulturelles
Reiseziele
Videoblick: Essen über den Wolken
Die deutschen Ostseebäder
Videoecke: Urlaub

Lektüren
Die Stadt (Theodor Storm)
Husum
Film: *Die fetten Jahre sind vorbei*

Strukturen
10.1 Prepositions to talk about places: **aus, bei, nach, von, zu**
10.2 Requests and instructions: the imperative (summary review)
10.3 Prepositions for giving directions: **an ... vorbei, bis zu, entlang, gegenüber von, über**
10.4 Being polite: the subjunctive form of modal verbs
10.5 Focusing on the action: the passive voice

GOALS

This chapter focuses on travel. Targeted skills: making travel plans and reservations, using maps, giving and asking for directions, going to hotels, youth hostels, etc. Sts. learn additional polite forms, and they are introduced to the passive voice.

Situationen

Reisepläne

Bring in a passport, ticket stubs, and foreign
currency and talk about a trip you made recently,
as a way of introducing new vocabulary items.
Encourage sts. to talk about their travels.

WILLI: Wo warst du in deinem
letzten Urlaub?
MARTA: Ich war in Schweden.

WILLI: Was hast du dort
gemacht?
MARTA: Ich bin Kanu gefahren
und viel gewandert.

WILLI: Bist du geflogen?
MARTA: Nein, ich bin mit dem
Auto gefahren und war die
ganzen zwei Wochen dort
auch mit dem Auto unterwegs.

WILLI: Wo hast du gewohnt?
MARTA: Ich habe auf
Campingplätzen gezeltet.

THOMAS: Ich will nächsten
Sommer nach Australien
fliegen.
PETER: Wie lange möchtest du
dort bleiben?

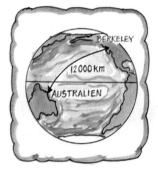

THOMAS: Vielleicht drei Wochen.
PETER: Warum willst du nach
Australien? Das ist doch so
weit weg und der Flug ist sehr
teuer.

THOMAS: Ich möchte die vielen interessanten Tiere sehen, zum Beispiel Kängurus. Und dann will ich meine Freundin in Sydney besuchen.

PETER: Da musst du dir bestimmt ein Auto mieten.

THOMAS: Nein, ich trampe. Und wohnen werde ich bei meiner Freundin und in Jugendherbergen. Dann wird alles ein bisschen billiger.

PETER: Gute Idee. Viel Spaß in Australien.

Situation 1 | Urlaub

Sit. 1. This could be done as a partner activity where one person has his/her book closed. As a follow-up the sentences can be used as a starting point to write a short connected paragraph about Marta's holiday in Sweden and Thomas' holiday plans.

Wer ist das, Marta (M) oder Thomas (T)?

_____ ist Kanu gefahren und viel gewandert.

_____ möchte Kängurus sehen.

_____ war in Schweden.

_____ hat auf Campingplätzen gezeltet.

_____ will in Jugendherbergen wohnen.

_____ war mit dem Auto unterwegs.

_____ möchte drei Wochen bleiben.

_____ will seine Freundin in Sydney besuchen.

Situation 2 | Informationsspiel: Reisen

Sit. 2. The corresponding chart is in Appendix A. Have sts. work with a partner. The model demonstrates asking for all the missing information referring to one character before moving on to the next person, but sts. might prefer to take turns asking all the *woher* questions, *wohin* questions, etc.

MODELL: S1: Woher kommt Sofie?   S2: Aus _____.

S1: Wohin fährt sie in den Ferien?   S2: Nach/In _____.

S1: Wo wohnt sie?   S2: Bei _____.

S2: Was macht sie da?   S1: Sie kauft Bücher und besucht Verwandte.

S1: Wann kommt sie zurück?   S2: In _____.

	Richard	Sofie	Mehmet	Peter	Jürgen	mein(e) Partner(in)
Woher?	aus Innsbruck	aus Dresden	aus Izmir	aus Berkeley	aus Bad Harzburg	
Wohin?	nach Frankreich	nach Düsseldorf	nach Italien	nach Hawaii	in die Alpen	
Wo?	bei einer Gastfamilie	bei ihrer Tante	bei alten Freunden	bei seiner Schwester	bei einem Freund	
Was?	Französisch lernen	Bücher kaufen; Verwandte besuchen	am Strand liegen; schwimmen	einen Vulkan besteigen	Ski fahren natürlich	
Wann?	in drei Monaten	in einer Woche	in zwei Wochen	nächstes Wochenende	in zwei Wochen	

Kultur ... Landeskunde ... Informationen

Reiseziele

Wenn einer eine Reise tut,
So kann er was erzählen;
Drum[1] nähm[2] ich meinen Stock und Hut
Und tät das Reisen wählen[3].

—Matthias Claudius (1740–1815)

Reiseziele der Deutschen 2006

Deutschland	29%
Spanien	14%
Italien	9%
Österreich	8%
Griechenland	6%
Türkei	5%
Frankreich	4%
Skandinavien	3%
USA	2%
Karibik	2%

- Welche Länder oder Städte sind für Sie beliebte Reiseziele? Warum?
- Was mögen Touristen an Ihrem Land besonders? Wohin fahren sie am liebsten?
- Welche Andenken (Souvenirs) bringen sie mit nach Hause? Spekulieren Sie!
- Welche Urlaubsländer sind bei Ihren Landsleuten beliebt?

Schauen Sie sich die Grafik an.

- Wo machen Deutsche am liebsten Urlaub?
- Was macht Spanien, Italien und Österreich attraktiv für deutsche Urlauber?
  - ☐ Man spricht dort Deutsch.
  - ☐ Der Urlaub ist relativ preisgünstig.
  - ☐ Man kann mit dem Auto hinfahren.
  - ☐ Es ist warm und die Sonne scheint.
  - ☐ Das Essen schmeckt sehr gut.
  - ☐ ?

[1] *Therefore*   [2] *would take*   [3] tät wählen *would choose*

KLI. Poem. You might want to use the poem as an introductory activity. In small groups have sts. answer the following questions: *Was will Claudius sagen? Warum kann man etwas erzählen, wenn man reist? Warum wollen Menschen außerdem noch reisen?* Sts. could also write a four-line poem about their travels or favorite destinations and present it in class. It is interesting to note that 29% of Germans stay in their own country for vacations (the favorite destinations are Schleswig-Holstein in the far north and Bavaria in the south). The top three foreign countries are favorite destinations for various reasons: Spain, primarily because of its climate; Austria, because it is a German-speaking country and just across the border; and Italy, the longtime favorite of Germans in search of the sun, because of its climate and its vicinity. For many Germans, price is certainly a factor when selecting vacation destinations (which may explain why so many stay in Germany), while food plays a minor role. As to "*deutschfreundlich,*" German tourists are probably considered a necessary evil, as most tourists are, particularly when they number in the millions. In the late nineties, German tourists traveled more and spent more money abroad than any other nationality. In 1998, for example, they spent about 40 billion euros (not including air travel) in foreign countries.

Suggestion. Have sts. write plans for a vacation in a place of their choice. *Was möchten Sie an diesem Ort / in diesem Land machen? Wann? Warum? usw.* Sts. could also present their plans in class and compare them.

Die Zugspitze

Photo questions. *Wie sind die Leute auf den Berg gekommen? Wo liegt die Zugspitze? Ist sie möglicherweise ein beliebtes Ausflugziel der Deutschen? Warum? Was können Urlauber in den Alpen machen?*

Situation 3 | Dialog: Am Fahrkartenschalter

Sit. 3. This dialogue contains a number of useful speech patterns. Preteach new vocabulary before working with the dialogue. You may wish to follow the steps for presenting the dialogue without the use of the textbook. Alternatively, use as a cloze dictation. When presenting without the book, ask the following focus questions. **(1)** Questions for first listening: 1. *Wohin möchte Silvia fahren?* 2. *Wann möchte sie dort sein?* 3. *Womit möchte sie bezahlen?* 4. *Wie viel kostet die Fahrkarte?* **(2)** Questions for second listening: 1. *Fährt sie einfach oder hin und zurück?* 2. *Fährt sie erster oder zweiter Klasse?* 3. *Wann genau fährt sie ab, wann genau kommt sie an?* 4. *Aus welchem Gleis fährt der Zug ab?*

Cultural note. Train travel is fast in Germany and a convenient alternative to flying or driving. The ICE train (Inter City Express) connects all major German cities on an hourly basis. It travels at speeds of up to 330 km per hour and covers, e.g., the 530 km (330 miles) between Göttingen and Munich in about 4 hours. Frequent travelers can travel cheaper with a BahnCard issued by the Deutsche Bahn. In 2007, a BahnCard for second-class travel cost between 50 and 200 euros and entitled the bearer to travel on all trains for one year while paying either 75% or even as little as 50% of the full ticket price.

Silvia steht am Fahrkartenschalter und möchte mit dem Zug von Göttingen nach München fahren.

BAHNANGESTELLTER: Bitte schön?

SILVIA: Eine <u>Fahrkarte</u> nach München, bitte.

BAHNANGESTELLTER: Einfach oder hin und zurück?

SILVIA: Hin und zurück bitte, mit BahnCard <u>zweiter</u> Klasse.

BAHNANGESTELLTER: Wann wollen Sie fahren?

SILVIA: Ich würde gern <u>so gegen Mittag</u> in München sein.

BAHNANGESTELLTER: Wenn Sie um 8.06 Uhr fahren, sind Sie um 12.11 Uhr in München.

SILVIA: Das ist gut. Wissen Sie, wo der Zug <u>abfährt</u>?

BAHNANGESTELLTER: Aus Gleis 10.

SILVIA: Ach ja, ich würde gern mit VISA bezahlen. <u>Geht das</u>?

BAHNANGESTELLTER: Selbstverständlich. Das macht dann 115 Euro 20.

SILVIA: Bitte sehr.

Göttingen → München Hbf

530 km

Ab	Zug		Umsteigen	An	Ab	Zug		An	Verkehrstage
5.56	ICE 997	¥¶	Fulda	6.49	7.00	ICE 987	¥¶	10.11	01
5.56	ICE 997	¥¶	Fulda	6.52	7.02	ICE 987	¥¶	10.11	02
7.03	ICE 581	¥¶						10.58	täglich
8.06	ICE 783	¥¶						12.11	täglich
9.03	ICE 583	¥¶						12.58	täglich
9.47	IC 1081	¥¶	Augsburg Hbf	14.04	14.10	SE 21139		14.54	täglich
10.03	ICE 91	¥¶	Nürnberg Hbf	12.26	12.30	IC 523	¥¶	14.17	täglich
10.30	IC 1087	☕	Nürnberg Hbf	13.23	13.34	IC 813	¥¶	15.17	03

Mit der Bahncard spart man.

Situation 4 | Interview

Sit. 4. Model pronunciation, have sts. repeat, and answer, based on your own experiences. Then have sts. work in pairs. Leave enough time for as many sts. as possible to tell about their trips, or arrange to do this during another class period.

1. Wo machst du gern Urlaub?
2. Fliegst du gern? Was gefällt dir daran? Stört dich etwas beim Fliegen? Was?
3. Wie suchst du dir deine Urlaubsziele aus? Wie besorgst du dir dein Ticket?
4. Wie packst du für eine Flugreise? Was nimmst du alles mit?
5. Erzähl von einer deiner letzten Reisen. Wo warst du? Wie bist du dahin gekommen? Warst du allein? Hast du jemanden kennengelernt? Was hast du am liebsten gemacht? Was war das Interessanteste, was dir passiert ist?

Nach dem Weg fragen

Grammatik 10.2–10.3

Vocabulary Display
Follow the usual steps (see the IM): presentation, receptive recall, choral repetition, and productive recall. After having done the productive recall orally (with the text covered up), ask sts. to write down the directions from memory in small groups. As follow-up, ask sts. to group the prepositions contained in these directions according to case.

Biegen Sie an der Ampel nach links ab.

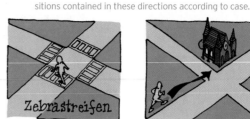

Gehen Sie über den Zebrastreifen.

Gehen Sie geradeaus, bis Sie eine Kirche sehen.

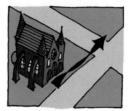

Gehen Sie an der Kirche vorbei, immer geradeaus.

Gehen Sie die Goetheallee entlang bis zur Bushaltestelle.

Gehen Sie über die Brücke. Auf der linken Seite ist dann das Rathaus.

Die U-Bahnhaltestelle ist gegenüber vom Markthotel.

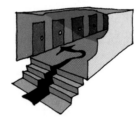

Gehen Sie die Treppe hinauf und dann ist es die zweite Tür links.

Situation 5 | Mit dem Stadtplan unterwegs in Regensburg

Sit. 5. Use as a listening comprehension exercise. Start sts. at the *Steinerne Brücke (Ausgangspunkt)*. Give them directions to several destinations without telling them what the destinations are. Then ask them where they ended up.

Suchen Sie sich ein Ziel in Regensburg aus dem Stadtplan auf der nächsten Seite aus. Beschreiben Sie Ihrem Partner / Ihrer Partnerin den Weg, ohne das Ziel zu verraten[1]. Wenn er/sie dort richtig ankommt, bekommen Sie einen Punkt und es wird gewechselt. Achtung: Ausgangspunkt[2] und Ziel dürfen nicht im selben Quadrat liegen!

MODELL: Also, wir sind jetzt an der Steinernen Brücke, auf dem Stadtplan oben in der Mitte. Siehst du die Steinerne Brücke? Gut. Von der Steinernen Brücke aus geh bitte nach links in die Goldene-Bären-Straße hinein und an der nächsten Straße gleich wieder rechts. Du kommst dann zum Krauterermarkt und zum Dom. Geh geradeaus über den Krauterermarkt hinüber und durch die Residenzstraße zum Neupfarrplatz. Dort gehst du bitte wieder links, die Schwarze-Bären-Straße ganz durch und über die Maximilianstraße hinüber. Noch ein paar Schritte weiter und du bist am _____.

[1]*give away* [2]*starting point*

NÜTZLICHE AUSDRÜCKE

links/rechts die (Goliath)straße entlang
links/rechts in die (Kram)gasse hinein
geradeaus über den (Krauterer)markt / über die (Kepler)straße hinüber
weiter bis zum/zur _____
an der (Steinernen Brücke) vorbei

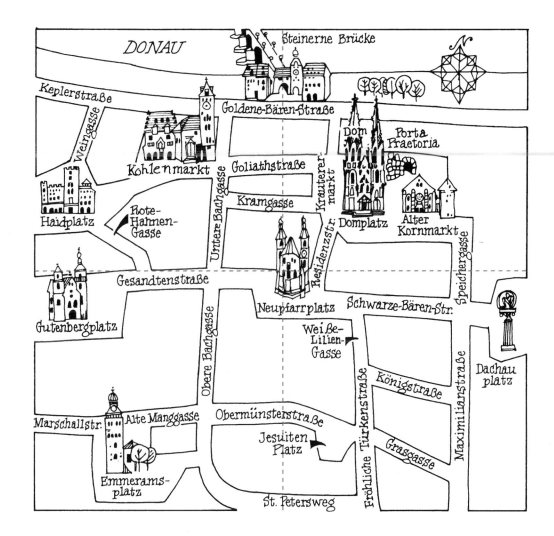

 Situation 6 | Dialoge

Sit. 6. Work with one dialogue at a time. **(1)** Set the scene by briefly reminding sts. who the characters are, where they are, where they want to go, and why. **(2)** Play (or read) each dialogue at least twice while sts. fill in the blanks. **(3)** Have sts. compare their answers with a partner. Ask sts. for their answers and write them on the board. **(4)** Ask sts. to work in small groups and to sketch a map according to the directions. **(5)** As grammatical follow-up, ask sts. to find all prepositional phrases and to group the prepositions according to case.

1. Jürgen ist bei Silvias Mutter zum Geburtstag eingeladen.

JÜRGEN: Wie komme ich denn zu eurem Haus?
SILVIA: Das ist ganz einfach. Wenn du <u>aus dem</u> Bahnhofsgebäude herauskommst, siehst du rechts <u>auf der</u> anderen Seite der Straße ein Lebensmittelgeschäft. Geh <u>über die</u> Straße, links <u>am</u> Lebensmittelgeschäft vorbei, und wenn du einfach geradeaus weitergehst, kommst du <u>auf die</u> Bismarckstraße. Die musst du nur ganz hinaufgehen, bis du <u>zu einem</u> Kreisverkehr kommst. Direkt <u>auf der</u> anderen Seite ist unser Haus.

Situationen   343

2. Claire und Melanie sind in Göttingen und suchen die Universitätsbibliothek.

MELANIE: Entschuldige, kannst du uns sagen, wo die Universitätsbibliothek ist?

STUDENT: Ach, da seid ihr aber ganz schön falsch. Also, geht erst die Straße mal wieder zurück <u>bis zu der</u> großen Kreuzung. <u>Über die</u> Kreuzung <u>hinüber</u> und <u>in die</u> Fußgängerzone <u>hinein</u>. Immer geradeaus <u>durch die</u> Fußgängerzone <u>bis zur</u> Prinzenstraße. Da rechts. <u>Auf der</u> rechten Seite seht ihr dann die Post. Direkt <u>gegenüber von der</u> Post ist die Bibliothek. Könnt ihr gar nicht verfehlen.

MELANIE
UND CLAIRE: Danke.

3. Frau Frisch findet ein Zimmer im Rathaus nicht.

FRAU FRISCH: Entschuldigen Sie, ich suche Zimmer 204.

SEKRETÄRIN: Das ist <u>im</u> dritten Stock. Gehen Sie den Korridor entlang <u>bis zum</u> Treppenhaus. Dann eine Treppe <u>hinauf</u> und oben links. Zimmer 204 ist die zweite Tür <u>auf der</u> rechten Seite.

FRAU FRISCH: Vielen Dank. Da hätte ich ja lange suchen können ...

Situation 7 | Wie komme ich ...?

Sit. 7. Have sts. use the classroom building as the starting point for their directions. First go over proper question formation with sts. After they have worked with their partners, ask for a volunteer to describe a route to a well-known destination and see if the others can guess where they will arrive.

Beschreiben Sie Ihrem Partner / Ihrer Partnerin,

1. wie man zu Ihrem Studentenheim oder zu Ihrer Wohnung kommt.
2. wo die nächste Post ist und wie man dahinkommt.
3. wo die beste Kneipe/Disko in der Stadt ist und wie man dahinkommt.
4. wie man zum Schwimmbad kommt.
5. wie man zur Bibliothek kommt.
6. wo der nächste billige Kopierladen ist und wie man dahinkommt.
7. wie man zum Büro von Ihrem Lehrer / Ihrer Lehrerin kommt.
8. wo der nächste Waschsalon ist und wie man dahinkommt.

Lektüre

Vor dem Lesen 1

Was assoziieren Sie mit den Jahreszeiten Frühling und Herbst? Schreiben Sie Gefühle, Farben, Geräusche, Gerüche, Tätigkeiten und Erinnerungen auf.

Lesehilfe

A short text like a poem usually requires intensive reading. Every single word is carefully chosen to convey the meaning and feelings one desires to express. One of the most famous poems of Theodor Storm, a well-known German poet and novelist, describes his hometown, Husum.

Vor dem Lesen 1. The prereading task asks sts. to free-associate feelings, colors, sounds, smells, activities, and memories with the two seasons spring and fall. Give them a minute to write down associations before writing them on the board. Read or play the poem. Then ask sts. to do *Arbeit mit dem Text 1* in small groups.

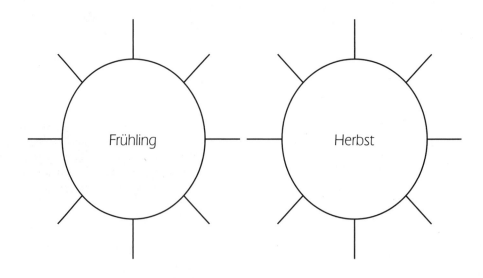

Miniwörterbuch		
brausen	to rage
eintönig	monotonously
für und für	forever
ohne Unterlass	incessantly
rauschen	to rustle
seitab	off to the side
wehen	to blow
der **Zauber**	charm

Die Stadt

Theodor Storm

Am grauen Strand, am grauen Meer
Und seitab liegt die Stadt;
Der Nebel drückt die Dächer schwer,
Und durch die Stille braust das Meer
5 Eintönig um die Stadt.

Es rauscht kein Wald, es schlägt im Mai
Kein Vogel ohn' Unterlaß;
Die Wandergans mit hartem Schrei
Nur fliegt in Herbstesnacht vorbei,
10 Am Strande weht das Gras.

Doch hängt mein ganzes Herz an dir,
Du graue Stadt am Meer;
Der Jugend Zauber für und für
Ruht lächelnd doch auf dir, auf dir,
15 Du graue Stadt am Meer.

Arbeit mit dem Text 1

A. Suchen Sie Beispiele aus dem Gedicht für die folgenden Kategorien: Landschaft, Wetter/Jahreszeit, Fauna und Flora, Geräusche. Schreiben Sie sie in die Tabelle.

Landschaft	Wetter/Jahreszeit	Fauna und Flora	Geräusche

Aktivität B. 1. *Frühling, grün, helle Farben* might come to mind in connection with woods, the month of May, and birds; migrating geese, autumn nights, the beach and grass might evoke *dunkle Erdfarben, Wind, Kälte, Dunkelheit*; typical words for contrast *kein, nur.* **2.** The negative associations the poet evokes in the first two stanzas are contrasted with his nevertheless positive feelings for his hometown in the third; the important word is *doch.*

B. Kontraste

1. Die ersten beiden Zeilen der zweiten Strophe und die drei weiteren bilden einen Kontrast. Welches Bild oder welche Farbe hat man bei Wald, Mai, Vögel vor Augen und woran denkt man bei Wandergans, Herbstesnacht, Strand und Gras? Welche Wörter (Negation und Adverb) sind typisch für einen Kontrast?
2. Die dritte Strophe steht im Kontrast zu den ersten beiden. Warum? Welches Wort ist hier sehr wichtig?

C. Wie ist die Stimmung in dem Gedicht? Fröhlich, melancholisch, dramatisch? Wie erreicht der Dichter das? Denken Sie an Rhythmus, Klang[1] und
Lautmalerei[2].

Nach dem Lesen 1

Nach dem Lesen 1. You may want to have sts. write their poems on poster board and hang them in the classroom. You could also have some sts. recite their poems in front of the class.

Sind Sie Dichter oder Dichterin? Schreiben Sie ein Gedicht über Ihre Heimatstadt,
über die Natur, über die Liebe oder über sich selbst. Das Gedicht muss sich
nicht reimen. Es kann auch ein modernes Gedicht sein.

Vor dem Lesen 2

Vor dem Lesen 2. Husum, a small North Sea town close to the border with Denmark in the north of Germany, is most famous for being the birthplace of Theodor Storm, who described it in one of his most famous poems as the "graue Stadt am grauen Meer." The text presented in this reading section is a tour guide description of Husum, which stresses its association with the poet. Begin by asking your sts. what the main attractions of your college town are, the kinds of things a travel guide might list. Then do the two prereading activities.

Give a time limit of 1–2 minutes for Activity B to encourage sts. to skim the text. After discussing the activity, read the text out loud while your sts. read along silently. Then go to the *Arbeit mit dem Text 2 B.* Ask sts. to complete Activity A in small groups. Read the instructions out loud and explain any difficult vocabulary. Ask sts. to solve the task by working in groups of 2 or 3.

A. Was für Informationen erwartet man in einem Reiseführer? Kreuzen Sie an.

☐ Museen   ☐ Unterkunft
☐ Restaurants und Kneipen   ☐ Stadtplan
☐ Wetter und Klima   ☐ Kultur und Feste
☐ Attraktionen   ☐ Zugfahrplan
☐ Rezepte   ☐ Nachtleben
☐ berühmte Personen   ☐ Wörterbuch

B. Überfliegen Sie den Text „Husum" und bestimmen Sie, in welcher Reihenfolge die folgenden Informationen gegeben werden.

_____ Anziehungspunkte in Husum
_____ Informationen zu Theodor Storm, der in Husum geboren wurde
_____ Kirchen und Museen
_____ Vorschläge für einen Stadtrundgang

Miniwörterbuch	
der **Amtsrichter**	district judge
der **Anziehungspunkt**	attraction
sich **befinden**	to be located
der **Bestandteil**	part
das **Freilichtmuseum**	open-air museum
gewidmet	dedicated
das **Herzogtum**	duchy
der **Rundgang**	(walking) tour
die **Sache**	cause
schaffen, schuf	to create
schildern	to portray
vertreten, vertrat	to plead for

Husum

Husum ist die Stadt Theodor Storms. Als „Graue Stadt am Meer" hat er sie liebevoll
in seinem ihr gewidmeten Gedicht angeredet. Storm wurde 1817 in Husum geboren
und schuf hier einen Teil seiner Gedichte und Novellen. Husum gehörte damals zu
den Herzogtümern Schleswig und Holstein und war Bestandteil des deutsch-dänischen
5 Gesamtstaates. Von 1852 bis 1864 konnte der Dichter, der im bürgerlichen Leben als
Anwalt, später als Amtsrichter tätig war, nicht in seiner Vaterstadt leben, weil er gegenüber

---

[1]*sound* [2]*onomatopoeia*

Lesehilfe

This selection is taken from a travel guide published by the German automobile association ADAC. Husum, a small town of 25,000, is best known for being the birthplace of Theodor Storm.

der dänischen Herrschaft die deutsche Sache vertrat. Er starb 1888 in Hademarschen, doch liegt er im Klosterfriedhof von Husum begraben.

10 Sie können in Husum Häuser anschauen, in denen Storm gelebt, und andere, die er in seinen Novellen geschildert hat. Weitere Anziehungspunkte sind der Hafen mit den Krabbenkuttern, das Schloss mit seinen Wiesen, auf denen im Frühling Millionen von Krokussen blühen, sowie die alten Kaufmannshäuser am Markt und in der Großstraße.

Ein Rundgang beginnt am Markt an der Großstraße, führt durch die Hohle Gasse und die Wasserreihe zum Hafen, durch das Westerende und die Nordhusumer Straße

15 zum „Ostenfelder Haus", einem Freilichtmuseum mit einem Niedersachsenhaus des 16./17. Jahrhunderts. Über den alten Friedhof und den Totengang geht man über die Neustadt zum Schloss (Sitz des Kreisarchivs) mit dem als „Cornils'sches Haus" bekannten Torhaus (1612) und durch den Schlossgang zum Markt zurück. Storms Grab auf dem Klosterkirchhof erreichen Sie vom Markt aus durch die Norderstraße.

20 Das Haus in der Wasserreihe 31, in dem der Dichter zwischen 1866 und 1880 wohnte, dient heute als Storm-Museum (täglich geöffnet von April bis Oktober). Im Nissenhaus befindet sich das Nordfriesische Museum zu den Themen Erd- und Vorgeschichte, Landschaftskunde und Kulturgeschichte (täglich geöffnet). Die Marktkirche Husums gilt als der bedeutendste klassizistische Kirchenbau Schleswig-Holsteins.

(aus: ADAC-Reiseführer Norddeutschland)

Arbeit mit dem Text 2

A. Ein Rundgang durch Husum. Zeichnen Sie den Weg, der im Reiseführer beschrieben wird, in den Stadtplan ein.

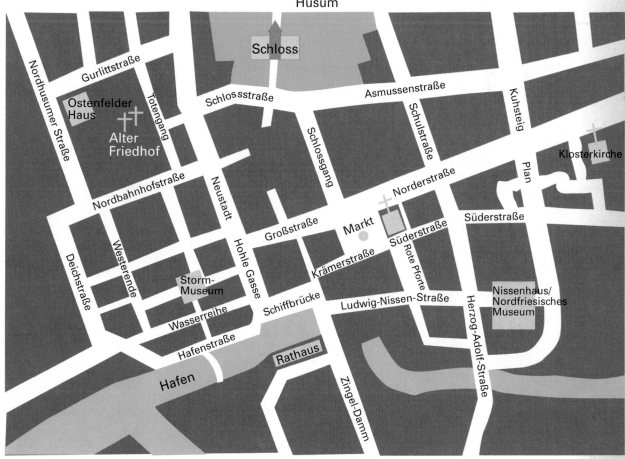

B. **Storms Leben.** Welche dieser Jahreszahlen und Ereignisse stehen im Text, welche nicht? Schreiben Sie die Zeilennummer dazu.

		ZEILE
1817	wird Theodor Storm in Husum geboren	_____
1843–1852	ist er Rechtsanwalt in Husum	_____
1846	erste Heirat mit Konstanze Esmarch	_____
1852–1856	ist er Assessor in Potsdam	_____
1852–1864	lebt er aus politischen Gründen nicht in Husum	_____
1856–1864	ist er Richter in Heiligenstadt	_____
1864–1867	ist er Landvogt[1] in Husum	_____
1866	zweite Heirat mit Dorothea Jensen	_____
1866–1880	wohnt er in der Wasserreihe 31	_____
1867	wird er Amtsrichter	_____
1888	stirbt er in Hademarschen und wird in Husum begraben	_____

Nach dem Lesen 2

Suchen Sie im Internet mehr Informationen über Husum und über Theodor Storm und stellen Sie sie in der Klasse vor.

[1]*governor*

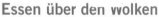

Videoblick

Essen über den Wolken

Hunderte von Menschen wollen im Flugzeug warm essen. Stewardessen zaubern[1] in kleinen Küchen Menüs[2]. Doch woher kommt das Essen über den Wolken?

- Wo liegt das Werk[3], das die Essen herstellt[4]?
- Wie viele Essen werden im Jahr gekocht?
- Wie wird das Hähnchen[5] zubereitet?
- Beschreiben Sie das Essen im Detail.
- Wohin kommen die Essen nach dem Kochen?

[1]*conjure up*   [2]*meals*   [3]*facility*   [4]*produces*   [5]*chicken*

Mit gerösteten Cashewkernen garniert ist das Hähnchen fertig.

Situation 8 | Umfrage: Urlaub am Strand

MODELL: S1: Hast du schon mal eine Sandburg gebaut?
S2: Ja.
S1: Unterschreib bitte hier.

UNTERSCHRIFT

1. Hast du schon einmal eine Sandburg gebaut? _____
2. Hast du eine Luftmatratze? _____
3. Bist du schon mal im Meer geschwommen? _____
4. Kannst du Wellen reiten? _____
5. Sammelst du gern Muscheln? _____
6. Warst du schon einmal windsurfen? _____
7. Liegst du gern im Liegestuhl? _____
8. Bist du schon mal Schlauchboot gefahren? _____
9. Bekommst du leicht einen Sonnenbrand? _____
10. Benutzt du oft Sonnenmilch? _____

Situation 9 | Informationsspiel: Wo wollen wir übernachten?

Sit. 9. The corresponding chart appears in Appendix A. Go over the questions with sts. before doing the activity to assure that they are using grammatically correct formulations with *im* and *in der*. Tell sts. that in most hotels and especially in *Pensionen*, breakfast is included in the price. Also mention that not all rooms in *Pensionen* have a private bath or shower. Preteach the following words: *Aufenthaltsraum, Herbergseltern, inbegriffen.*

MODELL: Wie viel kostet _____?

Haben die Zimmer im (in der) _____ eine eigene Dusche und Toilette?

Gibt es im (in der) _____ Einzelzimmer?

Gibt es im (in der, auf dem) _____ einen Fernseher?

Ist das Frühstück im (in der, auf dem) _____ inbegriffen?

Ist die Lage von dem (von der) _____ zentral/ruhig?

Gibt es im (in der, auf dem) _____ Telefon?

	Hotel Strandpromenade	das Gästehaus Ostseeblick	die Jugendherberge	der Campingplatz
Preis pro Person	78,- Euro	42,- Euro	12,50 Euro	11,- Euro
Dusche/Toilette	ja	nicht in allen Zimmern	nein	nein
Einzelzimmer	ja	ja	nein	natürlich nicht
Fernseher	in jedem Zimmer	im Fernsehzimmer	im Aufenthaltsraum	natürlich nicht
Frühstück	inbegriffen	inbegriffen	kostet extra	nein
zentrale Lage	ja	ja	im Wald	direkt am Strand
ruhige Lage	an der Strandpromenade	ja	ja	ja
Telefon	in jedem Zimmer	im Telefonzimmer	bei den Herbergseltern	Telefonzelle

Situation 10 | Dialog: Auf Zimmersuche

Sit. 10. (See the IM). This dialogue provides a model for the role-play following it. Follow the steps for presenting the dialogue without the use of the textbook and assign the dialogue for homework. (The dialogue is on the st. tape for the workbook/lab manual.) Questions for listening comprehension: 1. *Was für ein Zimmer möchten die Rufs?* 2. *Wie lange wollen sie bleiben?* 3. *Was kostet das Zimmer?* 4. *Wann und wo können sie frühstücken?*

Herr und Frau Ruf suchen ein Zimmer.

HERR RUF: Guten Tag, haben Sie noch ein Doppelzimmer mit Dusche frei?

WIRTIN: Wie lange möchten Sie denn bleiben?

HERR RUF: Drei Nächte.

WIRTIN: Ja, da habe ich ein Zimmer mit Dusche und Toilette.

FRAU RUF: Ist das Zimmer auch ruhig?

WIRTIN: Natürlich. Unsere Zimmer sind alle ruhig.

FRAU RUF: Was kostet das Zimmer denn?

WIRTIN: 54 Euro pro Nacht.

HERR RUF: Ist Frühstück dabei?

WIRTIN: Selbstverständlich ist Frühstück dabei.

FRAU RUF: Gut, wir nehmen das Zimmer.

HERR RUF: Und wann können wir frühstücken?

WIRTIN: Von acht bis zehn im Frühstückszimmer.

Situation 11 | Rollenspiel: Im Hotel

Sit. 11. The role for s2 appears in Appendix B.

S1: Sie sind im Hotel und möchten ein Zimmer mit Dusche und Toilette. Außerdem möchten Sie ein ruhiges Zimmer. Fragen Sie auch nach Preisen, Frühstück, Telefon und wann Sie morgens abreisen müssen.

Die deutschen Ostseebäder

- Gibt es in Ihrem Land bekannte Badeorte[1]?
- Wie alt sind diese Badeorte ungefähr?
- Wer macht dort Urlaub?
- Was kann man dort machen?
- Wie lange, glauben Sie, bleibt man im Durchschnitt?
- Warum fährt man in Ihrem Land ans Meer? Kreuzen Sie an:

□ weil man baden und in der Sonne liegen will.
□ weil man am Strand spazieren gehen will.
□ weil Seeluft gesund ist.
□ weil Meerwasser gut für die Haut ist.
□ weil man ausspannen will.
□ weil Kinder gern im Sand spielen.
□ weil man Wassersport treiben und fischen will.
□ weil man dort interessante Leute trifft.

Lesen Sie den Text und beantworten Sie die folgenden Fragen:

- Wo gab es die ersten Seebäder?
- Warum fuhren die Leute damals ans Meer?
- Wer konnte sich damals einen Badeurlaub leisten[2]?
- Wie kamen die Leute ins Wasser?
- Wo übernachteten die Urlauber in der DDR?
- Was machte man in den westdeutschen Ostseebädern?
- Wofür ist die Insel Rügen berühmt?

Die Kreidefelsen auf der Insel Rügen.

Die ersten Badeorte entstanden um 1750 an der englischen Kanalküste in Brighton und Margate, nachdem englische Ärzte das Meerwasser als Mittel[3] gegen Haut-[4] und Lungenkrankheiten entdeckt hatten.

An der deutschen Ostseeküste begann alles 1793 in Bad Doberan. Dort ließ ein norddeutscher Herzog[5] ein Kurhaus[6] bauen und bald war der Ort ein Sommertreffpunkt für den Adel[7]. Das Baden im Meer war für die Gesellschaft damals ein Problem, weil man sich nicht im Badeanzug zeigen[8] durfte. Man löste[9] es mit Hilfe der Badekarren. Am Ende des 19. Jahrhunderts boomten die Ostseebäder. Es kamen vor allem Gäste aus dem nahen Berlin.

Im Dritten Reich sollten die Menschen „Kraft durch Freude" an der Ostsee tanken[10] und auch in der DDR waren die „volkseigenen[11]" Seebäder populär. Die historischen Hotels baute man um und daneben gab es Bungalows und Zeltplätze für den bescheidenen[12] Urlaub im Sozialismus. In den westdeutschen Badeorten dagegen betonierte man die Küste ohne Bedenken[13] zu[14].

Die Wende 1989 war auch für den Ostseetourismus eine kleine Revolution. Vor allem die Insel Rügen mit ihren berühmten Kreidefelsen wurde wieder zu einer großen Attraktion. Jetzt besuchen jedes Jahr Touristen aus ganz Deutschland und aus der ganzen Welt die alten Ostseebäder. Viele historische Gebäude wurden restauriert oder wieder aufgebaut, damit man nicht nur die landschaftliche Schönheit[15], sondern auch die große kulturelle Tradition der deutschen Ostseebäder genießen[16] kann.

Ein historischer Badekarren.

Have sts. look up the different Ostseebäder on the Internet and gather more information about them: Welche Ostseebäder gibt es? Welche Unterkunftsmöglichkeiten gibt es für Urlauber? Wo kann man günstig wohnen? Was kann man in diesen Ostseebädern machen? In welchem möchten Sie am liebsten Urlaub machen? Warum?

[1]resorts [2]sich leisten *afford* [3]*medicine* [4]*skin* [5]*duke* [6]*spa house* [7]*nobility*
[8]sich zeigen *show oneself* [9]*solved* [10]*refuel on/with* [11]*state-owned* [12]*modest* [13]*second thoughts*
[14]betonierte zu *covered with concrete* [15]landschaftliche ... *scenic beauty* [16]*enjoy*

Tiere

Grammatik 10.5

Juttas Ratte wird gegen Tollwut geimpft.

Ernsts Meerschweinchen wird oft gebadet.

Schildkröten werden oft als Haustiere gehalten.

In der Wüste muss man aufpassen, dass man nicht von einer Schlange gebissen wird.

Gestern wurde Silvia von einer Biene gestochen.

Als Josef und Melanie gestern beim Baden waren, wurden sie von tausend Mücken gestochen.

Situation 12 | Ratespiel

die Klapperschlange

die Schildkröte

die Schnecke

der Kolibri

der Gepard

die Fledermaus

1. Das größte Landsäugetier: Es hat einen Rüssel und zwei Stoßzähne aus Elfenbein; wegen des Elfenbeins wird es oft illegal gejagt.
2. Die schnellste Katze der Welt: Sie läuft mindestens 80 Kilometer in der Stunde.
3. Das schwerste Tier: Es lebt im Wasser, aber es ist kein Fisch.
4. Das langsamste Tier: Es trägt oft ein Haus auf seinem Rücken und hat keine Beine.
5. Es sieht aus wie ein Hund, ist aber nicht so zahm.
6. Dieses Tier lebt länger als der Elefant.
7. Das ist die giftigste Schlange in Nordamerika.
8. Dieser Wasservogel hat eine Spannweite von mehr als drei Metern.
9. Dieses Tier hat die höchste Herzfrequenz, mit zirka 1 000 Schlägen pro Minute.
10. Dieses Tier hört besser als ein Delfin.

a. der Kolibri
b. der Elefant
c. die Riesenschildkröte
d. die Schnecke
e. die Fledermaus
f. der Blauwal
g. der Gepard
h. die Klapperschlange
i. der Albatros
j. der Wolf

der Blauwal

Situation 13 | Informationsspiel: Tiere

Sit. 12. Sts. read and complete the activity individually. Then ask for their answers. Find out how many other animals sts. know/remember. Focus by asking: *Welche Tiere findet man nur im Dschungel? Welche Tiere findet man in Australien? Welche Tiere findet man in der Wüste? Welche Tiere findet man in Nordamerika? in Südamerika? in Europa? in Asien?* As a warm-up exercise sometime, have sts. quickly draw pictures of various animals on the board. The first person to guess the animal correctly, wins and draws the next picture. **Answers:** 1. b, 2. g, 3. f, 4. d, 5. j, 6. c, 7. h, 8. i, 9. a, 10. e.

Sit. 13. The corresponding chart is in Appendix A. In the follow-up, focus on the choices made by the sts. and ask them to explain their responses.

MODELL: Welche Tiere findet _____ am tollsten?
Vor welchem Tier hat _____ am meisten Angst?
Welches Tier hätte _____ gern als Haustier?
Welches wilde Tier würde _____ gern in freier Natur sehen?
Wenn _____ an Afrika denkt, an welche Tiere denkt er/sie?
Wenn _____ an die Wüste denkt, an welches Tier denkt er/sie dann zuerst?
Welche Vögel findet _____ am schönsten?
Welchen Fisch findet _____ am gefährlichsten?
Welchem Tier möchte _____ nicht in Wald begegnen?

	Ernst	Maria	mein(e) Partner(in)
Lieblingstier	ein Krokodil	eine Katze	
Angst	vor dem Hund von nebenan	vor Mäusen	
Haustier	eine Schlange	einen Papagei	
wildes Tier	einen Elefanten	eine Giraffe	
Afrika	an Löwen	an Zebras	
Wüste	an einen Skorpion	an ein Kamel	
Vögel	Adler	Eulen	
Fisch	den weißen Hai	den Piranha	
Wald	einem Wolf	einem Wildschwein	

1. Was ist dein Lieblingstier? Warum?
2. Hast du oder hattest du ein Haustier? Was für eins? Wie heißt oder wie hieß es? Beschreib es. Erzähl eine Geschichte von ihm!
3. Vor welchen Tieren fürchtest du dich?
4. Welches Tier findest du am interessantesten?
5. Welches Tier findest du am hässlichsten?
6. Welches Tier wärst du am liebsten? Warum?
7. Findest du es wichtig, dass Kinder mit Tieren aufwachsen? Wenn ja, mit welchen? Warum?

Situation 15 | Bildgeschichte: Lydias Hamster

Sit. 15. Sentences for narration series: **1.** *Lydia Frisch bekam zum Geburtstag einen Hamster.* **2.** *Sie spielte jeden Tag mit ihrem Hamster.* **3.** *Eines Abends vergaß sie, die Käfigtür richtig zuzumachen.* **4.** *Als sie am nächsten Morgen aufstand, war der Hamster verschwunden.* **5.** *Lydia suchte den Hamster im ganzen Haus.* **6.** *Sie war sehr traurig, weil sie ihn nicht fand.* **7.** *Eine Woche später entdeckte sie ein komisches Loch in ihrer Jacke.* **8.** *Außerdem war die Pflanze in ihrer Fensterbank angefressen.* **9.** *Lydia suchte noch einmal überall. Mit ihrem Vater schaute sie sogar hinter den Kleiderschrank.* **10.** *Da fand sie schließlich den Hamster. Er hatte sich ein gemütliches Nest gebaut.*

Zwei ältere Menschen gehen mit Hunden Gassi.

Photo Questions. *Was macht dieses Paar? Wie nennt man diese Hunderasse? Wie oft gehen sie zusammen spazieren? Was sieht man sonst auf diesem Bild? Welche Jahreszeit ist es?*

In vielen Sprachen gibt es Sprichwörter, in denen Tiere vorkommen. Welche Sprichwörter fallen Ihnen auf Englisch ein? Ordnen Sie jeder Zeichnung das passende Sprichwort zu.

1. Wenn dem Esel zu wohl ist, geht er aufs Eis.
2. Einem geschenkten Gaul (= Pferd) sieht man nicht ins Maul.
3. Wenn die Katze nicht zu Hause ist, tanzen die Mäuse.
4. Den letzten beißen die Hunde.
5. In der Not[1] frisst der Teufel Fliegen.
6. Ein blindes Huhn findet auch mal ein Korn.

Answers: 1. f, 2. a, 3. c, 4. e, 5. b, 6. d.

Was bedeuten die Sprichwörter? Kombinieren Sie die Definitionen mit den Sprichwörtern.

a. Wenn man etwas geschenkt bekommt, sollte man nicht zu kritisch damit sein.
b. Wenn man etwas nötig braucht, muss man nehmen, was da ist.
c. Wenn der Chef nicht da ist, machen die Angestellten, was sie wollen.
d. Jemandem, der sonst wenig Erfolg hat, kann auch etwas gelingen.
e. Wenn man sich nicht beeilt, ergeht es einem schlecht.
f. Leute, die zu viel Erfolg oder Glück haben, werden übermütig[2].

[1]*emergency* [2]*cocky*

Vor dem Lesen

A. Schauen Sie sich das Foto an.

1. Welche Personen sehen Sie auf dem Foto?
2. Beschreiben Sie die junge Frau.
3. Welchen der beiden jungen Männer finden Sie am sympathischsten? Warum?

Die fetten Jahre sind vorbei

Regisseur: Hans Weingartner

Schauspieler in den Hauptrollen:
Daniel Brühl, Julia Jentsch, Stipe
Erceg, Burghart Klaußner

Erscheinungsjahr: 2004

B. Lesen Sie die Wörter im Miniwörterbuch. Suchen Sie sie im Text und unterstreichen Sie sie.

Miniwörterbuch			
verteilt	distributed	das **Vermögen**	fortune
einbrechen	to break in	beschädigen	to damage
verrücken	to move, to disarrange	entführen	to kidnap
verstecken	to hide	die **Berghütte**	mountain cabin
die **Nachricht**	message	aufbegehren	to revolt
unterzeichnen	to sign	verraten	to betray
die **Erziehungsberechtigten**	legal guardians	auf etwas verzichten	to go without something
im **Überschwang der Gefühle**	in exuberance		
schulden	to owe	aufbrechen	to take off

Film: *Die fetten Jahre sind vorbei*

Besitz und Geld sind auf der Welt ungerecht verteilt. Jan und Peter, zwei junge Berliner, wollen diese Situation ändern und haben eine eigene Methode dafür gefunden: Sie brechen nachts in Villen reicher Leute ein. Sie stehlen nichts, sondern verrücken Möbel, hängen Bilder um und verstecken wertvolle Gegenstände im Kühlschrank oder werfen sie
5 in den Swimmingpool. Die Nachrichten, die sie für die Hausbesitzer hinterlassen, lauten: „Die fetten Jahre sind vorbei" oder „Sie haben zu viel Geld", unterzeichnet mit „Die Erziehungsberechtigten". Ihr Ziel: Die Reichen sollen über ihren Luxus nachdenken.

Alles läuft immer nach Plan. Jan und Peter haben ihren Spaß und die Villenbewohner sind geschockt beim Anblick ihrer Häuser. Doch als sich dann Jan und Jule, Peters
10 Freundin, ineinander verlieben, brechen die beiden im Überschwang der Gefühle und ohne Peter in die Villa des Geschäftsmannes Justus Hardenberg ein. Dem schuldet Jule ein halbes Vermögen, weil sie bei einem Unfall sein teures Auto beschädigt hat. Ein harmloser Einbruch wie die anderen wird es nicht, denn sie werden vom Hausbesitzer überrascht. Jan und Jule schlagen Hardenberg nieder, entführen ihn und bringen
15 ihn mit Peters Hilfe in die Berghütte von Jules Onkel am Tiroler Achensee. In der Berghütte stellt sich heraus, dass Hardenberg in seinen jungen Jahren genauso gegen das etablierte Bürgertum aufbegehrte wie Jan, Peter und Jule jetzt. Seine Ideale von früher hat Hardenberg jedoch verraten.

Am Ende bringen die drei Entführer Hardenberg in seine Villa zurück. Er verzich-
20 tet auf das Geld, das ihm Jule wegen des Autounfalls schuldet. Als die Polizei wenig später die Wohnung der drei jungen Leute stürmt, sind sie schon verschwunden. Am Schluss brechen sie mit Hardenbergs Motorjacht zu neuen Taten auf.

Arbeit mit dem Text

Welche Aussagen sind falsch? Verbessern Sie die falschen Aussagen.

1. Peter und Jan brechen in Villen ein, weil sie Geld brauchen.
2. Jule ist Peters Freundin, verliebt sich aber in Jan.
3. Peter und Jan brechen in die Villa von Justus Hardenberg ein.
4. Hardenberg schuldet Jule sehr viel Geld.
5. Jan, Peter und Jule entführen Hardenberg, weil er sie beim Einbruch in seine Villa überrascht hat.
6. Die drei Entführer lassen Hardenberg in Tirol frei.
7. Jan, Peter und Jule melden sich[1] bei der Polizei.

Nach dem Lesen

Beantworten Sie die folgenden Fragen.

1. Glauben Sie, dass Jan, Peter und Jule mit ihren Aktionen Erfolg[2] haben? Rüttelt man mit so etwas die Gesellschaft wach[3]? Kann oder muss man die drei ernst[4] nehmen? Warum?
2. Justus Hardenberg gehörte zu den sogenannten „68ern". 1968 war ein aufregendes Jahr in der alten BRD. Forschen Sie im Internet nach, was in diesem Jahr in Westdeutschland passierte und welche Rolle die Studenten spielten.

[1]melden ... *turn themselves in*   [2]*success*   [3]rüttelt wach *shakes awake*   [4]*seriously*

Videoecke

- Wohin fährst du gern in Urlaub?
- Was machst du da?
- Was war dein schönster Urlaub?
- Was war daran besonders? (Erzähl mal.)
- Gab's mal einen Urlaub, in dem etwas schief ging?

Nicole ist in Leipzig geboren. Sie spricht Deutsch, Englisch und Russisch. Ihre Hobbys sind Tennis spielen und Musik hören.

Erwin ist in Regensburg geboren. Er spricht Deutsch, Englisch und Spanisch. Seine Hobbys sind Wandern und Gitarre spielen.

Aufgabe 1

Aufgabe 1. (1) Focus sts.' attention on the photos by asking: *Wer ist in Regensburg geboren? Wer spricht Russisch? Wer wandert gern? Was macht Nicole gern?* **(2)** Let sts. speculate who might say what. Then play the beginning of both interviews several times.

Wer sagt das, Nicole (N), Erwin (E) oder beide (B)?

1. _____ Ich fahr' eigentlich überall gern hin.
2. _____ Ich fahr' gern nach Amerika.
3. _____ Ich fahr' gern zu meinen Großeltern nach Odessa.

Aufgabe 2

Was machen Nicole und Erwin im Urlaub? Sind diese Aussagen richtig oder falsch? Korrigieren Sie die falschen Aussagen.

	RICHTIG	FALSCH
1. Nicole liegt selten die ganze Zeit am Strand.	☐	☐
2. Nicole fährt gern Fahrrad oder spielt Tennis.	☐	☐
3. Sie geht auch viel wandern.	☐	☐
4. Erwin hat noch kleine Kinder.	☐	☐

Aufgabe 3

Student Interviews. (1) Ask sts. to jot down their own answers to the interview questions. **(2)** Pair sts. to interview each other. Ask them to jot down their partner's answers. **(3)** Follow up by sampling a few of the answers given in the interviews.

Amerika oder Jerusalem? Ordnen Sie die folgenden Beschreibungen Amerika oder Jerusalem zu.

	AMERIKA	JERUSALEM
1. Erstens lieb ich das Land sowieso.	☐	☐
2. Die Leute sind sehr aufgeschlossen.	☐	☐
3. Es ist so eine alte Stadt.	☐	☐
4. Es ist viel zu sehen.	☐	☐
5. diese Häuser, diese weißen Wände	☐	☐
6. diese vielen unterschiedlichen Kulturen	☐	☐

Wortschatz

Reisen und Tourismus	Travel and Tourism
die **Bahnangestellte**, -n	female train agent
die **Fahrt**, -en	trip
die **einfache Fahrt**	one-way trip
die **Hin- und Rückfahrt**	round-trip
die **Führung**, -en	guided tour
die **Haltestelle**, -n	stop
die **Jugendherberge**, -n	youth hostel
die **Klasse**, -n (R)	class
erster Klasse fahren	to travel first class
die **Lage**, -n	place; position
die **Luftmatratze**, -n	air mattress
die **Möwe**, -n	seagull
die **Reisende**, -n	female traveler
die **Schiene**, -n	train track
die **Sonnenmilch**	suntan lotion
die **Unterkunft**, ⸚e	lodging
die **Welle**, -n	wave
der **Aufenthaltsraum**, ⸚e	lounge, recreation room
der **Ausweis**, -e	identification card
der **Bahnangestellte**, -n	male train agent
der **Hafen**, ⸚	harbor, port
der **Nichtraucher**, -	nonsmoker
der **Raucher**, -	smoker
der **Reisende**, -n	male traveler
(ein **Reisender**)	
der **Reisepass**, ⸚e	passport
der **Sonnenbrand**, ⸚e	sunburn
der **Sonnenschirm**, -e	sunshade
der **Spaziergang**, ⸚e	walk
der **Strandkorb**, ⸚e	beach chair
der **Wirt**, -e	host, innkeeper; barkeeper
der **Zug**, ⸚e (R)	train
das **Andenken**, -	souvenir
das **Fremdenverkehrs-amt**, ⸚er	tourist bureau
das **Gästehaus**, ⸚er	bed-and-breakfast (inn)
das **Gepäck**	luggage, baggage
das **Gleis**, -e	(set of) train tracks
das **Kanu**, -s	canoe
Kanu fahren	to go canoeing
das **Schlauchboot**, -e	inflatable dinghy
das **Ziel**, -e	destination

Ähnliche Wörter

die **Idee**, -n; die **Rezeption**, -en; der **Campingplatz**, ⸚e; das **Camping**; das **Doppelzimmer**, -; das **Fernsehzimmer**, -; das **Frühstückszimmer**

Den Weg beschreiben	Giving Directions
ab·biegen, bog ... **ab**, ist **abgebogen**	to turn

entlang·gehen	to go along
verfehlen	to miss, not notice
vorbei·gehen (an + *dat.*)	to go by
weiter·fahren	to keep on driving
weiter·gehen	to keep on walking
dorthin	there, to a specific place
entlang	along
gegenüber von (R)	across from
geradeaus	straight ahead
her(·kommen)	(to come) this way
heraus(·kommen)	(to come) out this way
herein(·kommen)	(to get/go) in this way
hin(·gehen)	(to go) that way
hinauf(·gehen)	(to go) up that way
hinüber(·gehen)	(to go) over that way
links (R)	left
oben	above
rechts (R)	right

In der Stadt	In the City
die **Brücke**, -n	bridge
die **Gasse**, -n	narrow street; alley
die **Gegend**, -en	area
der **Dom**, -e	cathedral
der **Kopierladen**, ⸚	copy shop
der **Kreisverkehr**	traffic roundabout
der **Waschsalon**, -s	laundromat
der **Zebrastreifen**, -	crosswalk

Ähnliche Wörter

die **Altstadt**, ⸚e; die **Fußgängerzone**, -n; die **Linie**, -n; der **Markt**, ⸚e; der **Stadtpark**, -s; der **Stadtplan**, ⸚e; der **Zoo**, -s; das **Einkaufszentrum**, **Einkaufszentren**; das **Fußball-stadion**, **Fußballstadien**

Tiere	Animals
die **Biene**, -n	bee
die **Fledermaus**, ⸚e	bat
die **Mücke**, -n	mosquito
die **Schildkröte**, -n	turtle
die **Schlange**, -n	snake
die **Klapperschlange**, -n	rattlesnake
die **Riesenschlange**, -n	boa constrictor; python
die **Schnecke**, -n	snail
der **Adler**, -	eagle
der **Gepard**, -e	cheetah
der **Hai**, -e	shark
der **Kolibri**, -s	hummingbird
der **Löwe**, -n (*wk. masc.*)	lion
der **Papagei**, -en	parrot
der **Rüssel**, -	trunk (*of an elephant*)

der Stoßzahn, ⸚e	tusk
der Vogel, ⸚	bird
der Wasservogel, ⸚	water fowl
das Meerschweinchen, -	guinea pig
das Tier, -e (R)	animal
das Haustier, -e	pet
das Landsäugetier, -e	land mammal

Ähnliche Wörter

die Giraffe, -n; die Maus, ⸚e; die Ratte, -n; der Albatros, -se; der Blauwal, -e; der Delfin, -e; der Hamster, -; der Piranha, -s; der Skorpion, -e; das Känguru, -s; das Krokodil, -e; das Wildschwein, -e; das Zebra, -s

Sonstige Substantive	Other Nouns
die Bürgerin, -nen	female citizen
die Tollwut	rabies
der Bürger, -	male citizen
der Geschäftsbrief, -e	business letter
der Gruß, ⸚e	greeting
mit freundlichen Grüßen	regards
der Käfig, -e	cage
der Vorfahre, -n (wk. masc.)	ancestor
das Elfenbein	ivory
das Familienmitglied, -er	family member
das Treppenhaus, ⸚er	stairwell

Ähnliche Wörter

die Hälfte, -n; der Staat, -en; das Nest, -er; in freier Natur

Sonstige Verben	Other Verbs
ab·reisen, ist abgereist	to depart
an·legen	to put on
ein·steigen (R), stieg ... ein, ist eingestiegen	to board
entscheiden, entschied, entschieden	to decide
sich erkundigen nach	to ask about, get information about
erleben	to experience
fest·stellen	to establish
sich fürchten vor (+ dat.)	to be afraid of
impfen gegen	to vaccinate against
sich informieren über (+ akk.)	to inform oneself about
mit·machen	to participate
nach·sehen, sieht ... nach, sah ... nach, nachgesehen	to look up
sammeln	to collect

sonnenbaden gehen	to go sunbathing
stechen, sticht, stach, gestochen	to sting; to bite (of insects)
trampen, ist getrampt	to hitchhike
vor·legen	to present, produce (documents)
sich (dat.) vor·stellen (R)	to imagine
wiederholen	to repeat

Ähnliche Wörter

antworten (+ dat.) (R)

Adjektive und Adverbien	Adjectives and Adverbs
auffällig	conspicuous
geehrt	honored; dear
sehr geehrter Herr	dear Mr.
sehr geehrte Frau	dear Ms.
gefährlich	dangerous
lieb	sweet; lovable
mehrere (pl.)	several
nützlich	useful
schriftlich	written
wunderschön	exceedingly beautiful
zahm	tame

Ähnliche Wörter

extra, voll, zentral

Sonstige Wörter und Ausdrücke	Other Words and Expressions
an ... vorbei	by
aus	of; from; out of
außerdem (R)	besides
bei (R)	at; with; near
bis zu	as far as; up to
danach	afterward
eilig	rushed
es eilig haben	to be in a hurry
hin und zurück (R)	there and back; round-trip
inbegriffen	included
nach (R)	to (a place)
nach Hause (R)	(to) home
ob (R)	whether
selbstverständlich	of course
vielen Dank	many thanks
von (R)	of; from
zu (R)	to (a place)
zu Hause (R)	at home
zuletzt	finally

Strukturen und Übungen

10.1 Prepositions to talk about places: *aus, bei, nach, von, zu*

10.1 *Präpositionen des Orts*. We have introduced the dative prepositions in different chapters according to their meanings, rather than as a single group of prepositions taking the dative. The idea of a dative preposition was introduced with *zu* in Section 6.4 and *mit* and *bei* in Section 6.6. In the present section, we describe the use of 5 dative prepositions that refer to place. *Aus* as a way of expressing origin appeared first in Section B.6. The use of *nach* and *zu* for indicating direction was introduced in Section 6.4. (See that section for other details.) In Section 10.3, *bis zu* and *gegenüber von*, which also take the dative, are introduced as a means of giving directions.

Point out that the preposition *in* with the accusative, not *nach*, is used with the names of countries that have a definite article.

Use the prepositions **aus** and **von** to indicate origin; **bei** to indicate a fixed location; and **nach** and **zu** to indicate destination. These five prepositions are always used with nouns and pronouns in the dative case.

Woher (kommt sie?)	Wo (ist sie?)	Wohin (geht/fährt sie?)
aus Spanien		nach Spanien
aus dem Zimmer		nach Hause
von rechts		nach links
von Erika	bei Erika	zu Erika
vom Strand		zum Strand

aus: enclosed spaces
countries
towns
buildings

A. The Prepositions **aus** and **von**

1. Use **aus** to indicate that someone or something comes from an enclosed or defined space, such as a country, a town, or a building.

Diese Fische kommen aus der Donau.	*These fish come from the Danube river.*
Jens kam aus seinem Zimmer.	*Jens came out of his room.*

Most country and city names are neuter; no article is used with these names.

Josef kommt **aus Deutschland.**
Silvia kommt **aus Göttingen.**

Wissen Sie noch?

The prepositions **aus** (*from*), **bei** (*near, with*), **mit** (*with*), **nach** (*to*), **von** (*from*), **zu** (*to*) are prepositions that take the dative case.

Review grammar B.6, 6.4, and 6.6.

However, the article is included when the country name is masculine, feminine, or plural.

Richards Freund Ali kommt **aus dem Iran.**
Mehmets Familie kommt **aus der Türkei.**
Ich komme **aus den USA.**

von: open spaces
directions
persons

2. Use **von** to indicate that someone or something comes not from an enclosed space but from an open space, from a particular direction, or from a person.

Melanie kommt gerade **vom Markt** zurück.	*Melanie's just returning from the market.*
Das rote Auto kam **von rechts.**	*The red car came from the right.*
Michael hat es mir gesagt. Ich weiß es **von ihm.**	*Michael told me. I know it through (from) him.*

B. The Preposition **bei**

Use **bei** before the name of the place where someone works or the place where someone lives or is staying.

Achtung!

von + dem = vom
bei + dem = beim
zu + dem = zum
zu + der = zur

Albert arbeitet **bei McDonald's.**	*Albert works at McDonald's.*
Rolf wohnt **bei einer Gastfamilie.**	*Rolf is staying with a host family.*
Treffen wir uns **bei Katrin.**	*Let's meet at Katrin's.*

bei: place of work
residence

C. The Prepositions nach and zu

Use **nach** with neuter names of cities and countries (no article), to indicate direction, and in the idiom **nach Hause** ([*going*] *home*).

Wir fahren morgen **nach Salzburg.**	*We'll go to Salzburg tomorrow.*
Biegen Sie an der Ampel **nach links ab.**	*Turn left at the light.*
Gehen Sie **nach Westen.**	*Go west.*
Ich muss jetzt **nach Hause.**	*I have to go home now.*

Use **zu** to indicate movement toward a place or a person, and in the idiom **zu Hause** (*at home*).

Wir fahren heute **zum Strand.**	*We'll go to the beach today.*
Wir gehen morgen **zu Tante Julia.**	*We'll go to Aunt Julia's tomorrow.*
Rolf ist nicht **zu Hause.**	*Rolf is not at home.*

Übung 1 | Die Familie Ruf

Kombinieren Sie Fragen und Antworten.

1. Hier kommt Herr Ruf. Er hat seine Hausschuhe an. Woher kommt er gerade?
2. Hans hat noch seine Schultasche auf dem Rücken. Woher kommt er?
3. Frau Ruf kommt mit zwei Taschen voll Obst und Gemüse herein. Woher kommt sie?
4. Jutta kommt herein. Sie hat eine neue Frisur[1]. Woher kommt sie?
5. Gestern Abend war Jutta nicht zu Hause. Wo war sie?
6. Ihre Mutter war auch nicht zu Hause. Wo war sie?
7. Morgen geht Herr Ruf aus. Wohin geht er?
8. Hans fährt am Wochenende weg. Wohin fährt er?
9. Frau Ruf ist am Wochenende geschäftlich unterwegs. Wohin fährt sie?
10. Jutta möchte mit ihrem Freund einen Skiurlaub machen. Wohin wollen sie?

a. Aus der Schule.
b. Aus seinem Zimmer.
c. Bei ihrem Freund.
d. Bei Frau Körner.
e. Nach Innsbruck.
f. Nach Berlin.
g. Vom Friseur.
h. Vom Markt.
i. Zu Herrn Thelen, Karten spielen.
j. Zu seiner Tante.

Übung 2 | Melanies Reise nach Dänemark

Beantworten Sie die Fragen. Verwenden Sie die Präpositionen **aus, bei, nach,** **von** oder **zu.**

MODELL: CLAIRE: Wohin bist du gefahren? (Dänemark) →
        MELANIE: Nach Dänemark.

1. Wohin genau? (Kopenhagen)
2. Wohin bist du am ersten Tag gegangen? (der Strand)
3. Und deine Freundin Fatima? Wohin ist sie gegangen? (ihre Tante Sule)
4. Woher kommt die Tante deiner Freundin? (die Türkei)

[1] *hairstyle*

5. Kommt deine Freundin auch aus der Türkei? (nein / der Iran)
6. Am Strand hast du Peter getroffen, nicht? Woher ist der plötzlich gekommen? (das Wasser)
7. Sein Freund war auch dabei, nicht? Woher ist der gekommen? (der Markt)
8. Weißt du, wo die beiden übernachten wollten? (ja/uns)
9. Und wo haben sie übernachtet? (Fatimas Tante)
10. Wohin seid ihr am nächsten Morgen gefahren? (Hause)

10.2 Requests and instructions: the imperative (summary review)

10.2. *Aufforderungen und Anweisungen: Der Imperativ.* This section reviews the *Sie*-imperative (introduced in Section A.1) and the *du*-imperative (introduced in Section 2.6) and describes for the first time the *ihr*-imperative and the imperative with *wir*. The rules for the formation of all forms except the *du*-imperative are straightforward and cause few difficulties.

> ### Wissen Sie noch?
>
> The imperative is used to form commands, sentences in which you tell others how to act.
>
> Review grammar 2.6.

As you have already learned, the imperative (command form) in German is used to make requests, to give instructions and directions, and to issue orders. To soften requests or to make them more polite, words such as **doch, mal,** and **bitte** are often included in imperative sentences.

Mach mal das Fenster **zu!**	*Close the window!*
Bringen Sie mir **bitte** noch einen Kaffee.	*Bring me another cup of coffee, please.*

The imperative has four forms: the familiar singular (**du**), the familiar plural (**ihr**), the polite (**Sie**), and the first-person plural (**wir**).

A. Sie and wir

In both the **Sie**- and **wir**-forms, the verb begins the sentence, and the pronoun follows.

Kontrollieren Sie bitte das Öl.	*Please check the oil.*
Gehen wir doch heute ins Kino!	*Let's go to the movies today.*

B. ihr

The familiar plural imperative consists of the present-tense **ihr**-form of the verb but does not include the pronoun **ihr.**

Lydia und Rosemarie, **kommt her** und **hört** mir **zu!**	*Lydia and Rosemarie, come here and listen to me.*
Sagt immer die Wahrheit!	*Always tell the truth.*

C. du

The familiar singular imperative consists of the present-tense **du**-form of the verb without the -(s)t ending and without the pronoun **du.**

du kommst	**Komm!**
du tanzt	**Tanz!**
du isst	**Iss!**

In written German, you will sometimes see a final **-e (komme, gehe),** but this **-e** is usually omitted in the spoken language for all verbs except those for which the present-tense **du**-form ends in **-est.**

du arbeitest	**Arbeite!**
du öffnest	**Öffne!**

Verbs that have a stem-vowel change from **-a-** to **-ä-** or **-au-** to **-äu-** do not have an umlaut in the **du**-imperative.

du fährst	**Fahr!**
du läufst	**Lauf!**
du hältst	**Halt!**

D. sein

The verb **sein** has irregular imperative forms.

du → **Sei** leise!			(*Paul!*)
ihr → **Seid** leise!	*Be quiet!*		(*You two!*)
Sie → **Seien Sie** leise!			(*Mrs. Smith!*)
wir → **Seien wir** leise!	*Let's be quiet!*		

Sei so gut und gib mir die
  Butter, Andrea.

*Be so kind and pass me the
  butter, Andrea.*

Seid keine Egoisten!

Don't be such egotists!

Übung 3 | Hans und sein Vater

Hans und sein Vater sind zu Hause. Hans fragt seinen Vater, was er tun darf oder tun muss. Spielen Sie die Rolle seines Vaters. Sie brauchen auch einen guten Grund!

MODELL: Darf ich den Fernseher einschalten? →
  Ja, schalte ihn ein. Es kommt ein guter Film.
  oder Nein, schalte ihn nicht ein. Ich möchte Musik hören.

1. Muss ich jetzt Klavier üben?
2. Darf ich Jens anrufen?
3. Darf ich die Schokolade essen?
4. Darf ich das Fenster aufmachen?
5. Muss ich dir einen Kuss geben?
6. Kann ich mit dir reden?
7. Muss ich das Geschirr spülen?
8. Darf ich in den Garten gehen?
9. Darf ich morgen mit dem Fahrrad in die Schule fahren?

Übung 4 | Aufforderungen!

Üb. 4. Remind sts. of the convention that *du*-forms are to be used with a single first name, *ihr*-forms with more than one first name, and *Sie*-forms with names preceded by *Herr* and/or *Frau*.

Sie sind die erste Person in jeder Zeile. Was sagen Sie?

MODELL: Frau Wagner: Jens und Ernst / Zimmer aufräumen →
  Jens und Ernst, räumt euer Zimmer auf!

1. Herr Wagner: Jens und Ernst / nicht so laut sein
2. Michael: Maria / bitte an der nächsten Ampel halten
3. Frau Wagner: Uli / an der nächsten Straße nach links abbiegen
4. Herr Ruf: Jutta / mehr Obst essen
5. Herr Siebert: Herr Pusch / nicht so schnell fahren
6. Jutta: Jens / an der Ecke auf mich warten
7. Frau Frisch: Natalie und Rosemarie / nicht ungeduldig sein
8. Herr Thelen: Andrea und Paula / Vater von mir grüßen
9. Frau Ruf: Hans / mal schnell zu Papa laufen
10. Oma Schmitz: Helga und Sigrid / jeden Tag die Zeitung lesen

Üb. 5. Assign for homework and have sts. read dialogues in pairs in class.

Verwenden Sie die folgenden Verben.

helfen
machen
sprechen
vergessen
warten

1. FRAU RUF: Ich sitze jetzt schon wieder seit sechs Stunden vor dem Computer.
   HERR RUF: Du arbeitest zu viel. _____ mal eine Pause.
2. HERR SIEBERT: _____ bitte lauter, ich verstehe Sie nicht.
   MARIA: Ja, wie laut soll ich denn sprechen? Wollen Sie, dass ich schreie?
3. MICHAEL: Na, was ist? Kommen Sie nun oder kommen Sie nicht?
   FRAU KÖRNER: Ich bin ja gleich fertig. Bitte _____ doch noch einen Moment.
4. HANS: Kann ich mit euch zum Schwimmen gehen?
   JENS: Ja, komm und _____ deine Badehose nicht.
5. OMA SCHMITZ: _____ mir bitte, ich kann die Koffer nicht allein tragen.
   HELGA UND SIGRID: Aber natürlich, Großmutter, wir helfen dir doch gern.

10.3. *Den Weg beschreiben.* Here we have brought together some prepositions of different types that are useful in giving directions.

ACCUSATIVE:

entlang (follows the noun)
über (precedes the noun)

10.3 Prepositions for giving directions: *an ... vorbei, bis zu, entlang, gegenüber von, über*

A. entlang (*along*) and **über** (*over*) + Accusative

Use the prepositions **entlang** and **über** with nouns in the accusative case. Note that **entlang** follows the noun.

Fahren Sie **den Fluß entlang.**	*Drive along the river.*
Gehen Sie **über den Zebra-streifen.**	*Walk across the crosswalk.*

The preposition **über** may also be used as the equivalent of English *via*.

Der Zug fährt **über** Frankfurt und Hannover nach Hamburg.	*The train goes to Hamburg via Frankfurt and Hanover.*

DATIVE:

an ... vorbei (encloses the noun)
bis zu (precedes the noun)
gegenüber von (precedes the noun)

B. an ... vorbei (*past*), **bis zu** (*up to, as far as*), **gegenüber von** (*across from*) + Dative

Use **an ... vorbei, bis zu,** and **gegenüber von** with the noun in the dative case. Note that **an ... vorbei** encloses the noun.

Gehen Sie **am Lebensmittelgeschäft vorbei.**	*Go past the grocery store.*
Fahren Sie **bis zur Fußgängerzone** und biegen Sie links ab.	*Drive to the pedestrian zone and turn left.*
Die U-Bahnhaltestelle ist **gegenüber vom Markthotel.**	*The subway station is across from the Markthotel.*

Üb. 6. Use for homework and/or class work. We expect sts. to be able to select the correct preposition, but the correct endings will be acquired only gradually, after a lot of input and practice.

Ein Ortsfremder[1] fragt Sie nach dem Weg. Antworten Sie! Nützliche Wörter:

entlang	an … vorbei	gegenüber von
über	bis zu	

1. Wie muss ich fahren?

2. Wie muss ich gehen?

3. Wie muss ich gehen?

4. Wie muss ich fahren?

5. Wo ist die Tankstelle?

6. Wie komme ich zum Zug?

7. Immer geradeaus?

8. Vor dem Rathaus links?

9. Das Hotel „Zum Patrizier"?

10. Wie komme ich nach Nürnberg?

[1]stranger

10.4. *Höflichkeitsformen: Konjunktiv der Modalverben.* The form we call subjunctive here is often referred to in other textbooks as the present subjunctive. In *Kontakte* we provide subjunctive forms only for certain frequently used verbs. The forms are presented according to their different uses. (We do not introduce the use of subjunctive forms in indirect speech.) Polite requests with the subjunctive of modal verbs are described in this section. Hypothetical statements with *würde, wäre,* and *hätte* will be introduced in Section 12.2. We do not introduce the subjunctive forms of any other verbs or the forms

The subjunctive is formed from the simple past-tense stem. Add an umlaut if there is an umlaut in the infinitive.

often called past subjunctive (*ich hätte gearbeitet, ich wäre gegangen*).

10.4 Being polite: the subjunctive form of modal verbs

Use the subjunctive form of modal verbs to be more polite.

Könnten Sie mir bitte dafür eine Quittung geben?	*Could you please give me a receipt for that?*
Ich **müsste** mal telefonieren.	*I have to make a phone call.*
Dürfte ich Ihr Telefon benutzen?	*Could I use your phone?*

To form the subjunctive of a modal verb, add an umlaut to the simple past form if there is also one in the infinitive. If the modal verb has no umlaut in the infinitive (**sollen** and **wollen**), the subjunctive form is the same as the simple past form.

Present	Past	Subjunctive
dürfen	ich durfte	ich d**ü**rfte
können	ich konnte	ich k**ö**nnte
mögen	ich mochte	ich m**ö**chte
müssen	ich musste	ich m**ü**sste
sollen	ich sollte	ich sollte
wollen	ich wollte	ich wollte

Here are the subjunctive forms of **können** and **wollen**.

können			
ich	könnte	*wir*	könnten
du	könntest	*ihr*	könntet
Sie	könnten	*Sie*	könnten
er *sie* *es*	könnte	*sie*	könnten

wollen			
ich	wollte	*wir*	wollten
du	wolltest	*ihr*	wolltet
Sie	wollten	*Sie*	wollten
er *sie* *es*	wollte	*sie*	wollten

In modern German, **möchte,** the subjunctive form of **mögen,** has become almost a synonym of **wollen.**

—Wohin wollen Sie fliegen?	*Where do you want to go (fly)?*
—Wir möchten nach Kanada fliegen.	*We want / would like to fly to Canada.*

Another polite form, **hätte gern,** is now used more and more, especially in conversational exchanges involving goods and services.

Ich hätte gern eine Cola, bitte.	*I'd like a Coke, please.*
Wir hätten gern die Speisekarte, bitte.	*We'd like the menu, please.*

Übung 7 | Überredungskünste

Üb. 7. The exercise can be done by pairs of sts. in class. The answers use the *du-* and *wir*-forms of the subjunctive of *können.*

Versuchen Sie, jemanden zu überreden[1], etwas anderes zu machen als das, was er/sie machen will.

> MODELL: S1: Ich fahre jetzt. (bleiben)
> S2: Ach, könntest du nicht bleiben?

1. Ich koche Kaffee. (Tee, Suppe, ?)
2. Ich lese jetzt. (später, morgen, ?)
3. Ich sehe jetzt fern. (etwas Klavier spielen, mit mir sprechen, ?)
4. Ich rufe meine Mutter an. (deinen Vater, deine Tante, ?)
5. Ich gehe nach Hause. (noch eine Stunde bleiben, bis morgen bleiben, ?)

> MODELL: S1: Wir fahren nach Spanien. (Italien)
> S2: Könnten wir nicht mal nach Italien fahren?

6. Wir übernachten im Zelt. (Hotel, Campingbus, ?)
7. Wir kochen selbst. (essen gehen, fasten, ?)
8. Wir gehen jeden Tag wandern. (schwimmen, ins Kino, ?)
9. Wir schreiben viele Briefe. (nur einen Brief, nur Postkarten, ?)
10. Wir sehen uns alle Museen an. (in der Sonne liegen, viel schlafen, ?)

Übung 8 | Eine Autofahrt

Üb. 8. Assign for homework and check in class. The subjunctive forms of all modal verbs except *mögen* are practiced here.

Sie wollen mit einem Freund ausgehen und fahren in seinem Auto mit. Stellen Sie Fragen. Versuchen Sie, besonders freundlich und höflich zu sein.

> MODELL: wir / jetzt nicht fahren können →
> Könnten wir jetzt nicht fahren?

1. du / nicht noch tanken müssen
2. wir / nicht Jens abholen sollen
3. zwei Freunde von mir / auch mitfahren können
4. wir / nicht zuerst in die Stadt fahren sollen
5. du / nicht zur Bank wollen
6. du / etwas langsamer fahren können
7. ich / das Autoradio anmachen dürfen
8. ich / das Fenster aufmachen dürfen

[1]*convince*

Focusing on the action: the passive voice

10.5. *Passiv.* Here we treat only the present- and simple past-tense forms of the passive, which are relatively easy for sts. to understand. We believe that the introduction of the other, more complex tenses can well be left until the second year. *Werden* as a main verb was introduced in Section 5.3. *Werden* as the future auxiliary verb was presented in Section 8.5. Stress that active and passive sentences are not necessarily interchangeable and that the use of the passive is appropriate when the doer of the action is not known or does not need to be specified.

Wissen Sie noch?

In addition to the passive auxiliary, **werden** can be used as a main verb meaning "to become" or as a future auxiliary with an infinitive to form the future tense.

Review grammar 5.3 and 8.5.

passive = **werden** + past participle

A. Uses of the Passive Voice

The passive voice is used in German to focus on the action of the sentence itself rather than on the person or thing performing the action.

ACTIVE VOICE

Der Arzt impft die Kinder.   *The physician inoculates the children.*

PASSIVE VOICE

Die Kinder **werden geimpft.**   *The children are (being) inoculated.*

Note that the accusative (direct) object of the active sentence, **die Kinder,** becomes the nominative subject of the passive sentence.

In passive sentences, the agent of the action is often unknown or unspecified. In the following sentences, there is no mention of who performs each action.

Schildkröten werden oft als   *Turtles are often kept as pets.*
   Haustiere gehalten.
1088 wurde die erste Universität   *The first university was*
   gegründet.   *founded in 1088.*

B. Forming the Passive Voice

The passive voice is formed with the auxiliary **werden** and the past participle of the verb. The present-tense and simple past-tense forms are the tenses you will encounter most frequently in the passive voice.

Passive Voice: fragen Present Tense			
ich	werde gefragt	*wir*	werden gefragt
du	wirst gefragt	*ihr*	werdet gefragt
Sie	werden gefragt	*Sie*	werden gefragt
er *sie* *es*	wird gefragt	*sie*	werden gefragt

Past Tense			
ich	wurde gefragt	*wir*	wurden gefragt
du	wurdest gefragt	*ihr*	wurdet gefragt
Sie	wurden gefragt	*Sie*	wurden gefragt
er *sie* *es*	wurde gefragt	*sie*	wurden gefragt

C. Expressing the Agent in the Passive Voice

Passive agents are indicated by **von** + noun.

In most passive sentences in German, the agent (the person or thing performing the action) is not mentioned. When the agent is expressed, the construction **von** + dative is used.

ACTIVE VOICE

Die Kinder füttern die Tiere.   *The children are feeding the animals.*

PASSIVE VOICE

AGENT: **von** + DATIVE

Die Tiere werden **von den Kindern** gefüttert.   *The animals are being fed by the children.*

Übung 9 | Geschichte

Hier sind die Antworten. Was sind die Fragen?

MODELL: 1492 → Wann wurde Amerika entdeckt?

1. vor 50.000 Jahren
2. um 2500 v. Chr.[1]
3. 44 v. Chr.
4. 800 n. Chr.[2]
5. 1088
6. 1789
7. 1885
8. 1945
9. 1963
10. 1990

a. Deutschland vereinigen
b. John F. Kennedy erschießen
c. die amerikanische Verfassung unterschreiben
d. die erste Universität (Bologna) gründen
e. die Atombomben auf Hiroshima und Nagasaki werfen
f. die ersten Pyramiden bauen
g. Cäsar ermorden
h. in Kanada die transkontinentale Eisenbahn vollenden
i. Karl den Großen zum Kaiser krönen
j. Australien von den Aborigines besiedeln

Übung 10 | Der Mensch und das Tier

MODELL: die Giraffe / langsam aus ihrem Lebensraum verdrängt →
Die Giraffe wird langsam aus ihrem Lebensraum verdrängt.

1. Mäuse
2. Meerschweinchen
3. Bienen
4. Mücken
5. die Fledermaus
6. Schnecken
7. der Gepard
8. die meisten Papageien
9. Delfine
10. viele Haie

[1]vor Christus [2]nach Christus

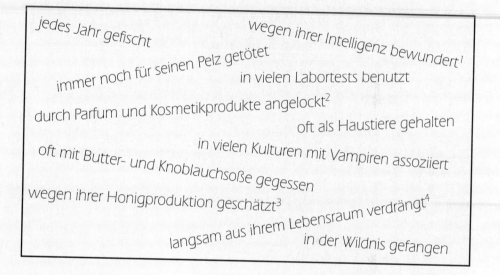

jedes Jahr gefischt

wegen ihrer Intelligenz bewundert[1]

immer noch für seinen Pelz getötet

in vielen Labortests benutzt

durch Parfum und Kosmetikprodukte angelockt[2]

oft als Haustiere gehalten

in vielen Kulturen mit Vampiren assoziiert

oft mit Butter- und Knoblauchsoße gegessen

wegen ihrer Honigproduktion geschätzt[3]

langsam aus ihrem Lebensraum verdrängt[4]

in der Wildnis gefangen

[1]*admired* [2]*attracted* [3]*valued* [4]*displaced*

Strukturen und Übungen

Johann Liss: *Beim Zahnausreißer* (ca. 1617),
Kunsthalle, Bremen

JOHANN LISS

Johann Liss wurde 1597 in Oldenburg (Holstein)
geboren und starb 1629 in Venedig, wo er zu den
führenden Malern seiner Zeit gehörte. Er malte
hochbarocke, religiöse, mythologische und Genre-
Bilder.

Gesundheit und Krankheit

Kapitel 11 focuses on health and fitness. You will talk about how to stay fit and about illness and accidents.

Themen

Krankheit

Körperteile und Körperpflege

Arzt, Apotheke, Krankenhaus

Unfälle

Kulturelles

Hausmittel

Videoblick: Charly hat Masern

Beim Arzt

Videoecke: Krankheiten

Lektüren

Juttas neue Frisur

Film: *Das Leben der Anderen*

Strukturen

11.1 Accusative reflexive pronouns

11.2 Dative reflexive pronouns

11.3 Word order of accusative and dative objects

11.4 Indirect questions: **Wissen Sie, wo ...?**

11.5 Word order in dependent and independent clauses (summary review)

Situationen

Krankheit

Grammatik 11.1

Vocabulary Display
This section introduces reflexive verbs with the reflexive pronoun in the accusative. Cover the captions and narrate the events, miming words sts. don't know. After sts. have grasped what is happening, ask them to find the reflexive verbs and tell you the tense. At the end of your presentation, hand out copies of each drawing. Each st. who has a drawing must act it out. Other sts. guess what is happening: *Was hat Kathy getan? Sie hat sich aufgeregt. usw.*

AA. Use TPR to introduce the following commands: *Atmen Sie ein/aus, zwinkern Sie, schnappen Sie nach Luft, schlucken Sie, husten Sie, niesen Sie, kauen Sie, entspannen Sie sich usw.* Distribute commands written out on slips of paper. Then have sts. demonstrate their commands and ask either/or questions: *Niest Thomas oder hustet er?* Then switch to questions in the perfect tense: *Was hat Shannon gemacht? geniest oder gehustet?*

Stefan hat sich erkältet.

Er fühlt sich nicht wohl.

Er hat Husten.

Er hat Schnupfen.

Er hat Kopfschmerzen.

Er hat Halsschmerzen.

Und er hat Fieber.

Er darf sich nicht aufregen.

Er muss sich ins Bett legen.

Er muss sich ausruhen.

Situation 1 | Hausmittel[1]

Sit. 1. Several of the questions and responses in this activity require sts. to use reflexive pronouns in the accusative case.

Give sts. a few minutes to read through the items and note what they do when they have a cold, headache, etc. Then have them work in pairs. Sts. alternate asking and answering in each situation: s1: *Was machst du, wenn du Fieber hast?* s2: *Ich nehme immer zwei Aspirin und lege mich ins Bett. Was machst du?* s1: *Normalerweise gehe ich zum Arzt. Was machst du, wenn du Husten hast? usw.* Encourage sts. to add ideas not listed in the book. Afterward, address the class: *Wer von Ihnen nimmt Aspirin, wenn Sie Fieber haben? Heben Sie die Hand! Wer von Ihnen trinkt Tee, wenn Sie sich erkältet haben? usw.* To continue to reinforce the word order used with *wenn*, spend a few minutes asking: *Wann bekommen Sie Kopfschmerzen? (Wenn ich nicht genug schlafe, wenn ich zu viel Hausaufgaben mache, wenn ich ohne meine Brille lese usw.)*

Was machst du immer, manchmal, nie?

1. Wenn ich Fieber habe,
   a. lege ich mich ins Bett.
   b. nehme ich zwei Aspirin.
   c. gehe ich zum Arzt.
   d. rege ich mich auf.

2. Wenn ich Husten habe,
   a. nehme ich Hustensaft.
   b. trinke ich heißen Tee mit Zitrone.
   c. rauche ich eine Zigarette.
   d. lutsche ich Hustenbonbons.

[1]Home remedies

3. Wenn ich mich erkältet habe,
   a. gehe ich schwimmen.
   b. ruhe ich mich aus.
   c. gehe ich in die Sauna.
   d. ärgere ich mich furchtbar.

4. Wenn ich Kopfschmerzen habe,
   a. gehe ich zum Friseur.
   b. nehme ich zwei Aspirin.
   c. bleibe ich im Bett.
   d. nehme ich ein heißes Bad.

5. Wenn ich Zahnschmerzen habe,
   a. trinke ich heißen Kaffee.
   b. gehe ich zum Zahnarzt.
   c. nehme ich Tabletten.
   d. setze ich mich aufs Sofa.

6. Wenn ich mich verletzt habe,
   a. desinfiziere ich die Wunde.
   b. falle ich in Ohnmacht.
   c. hole ich ein Pflaster.
   d. ziehe ich mich aus.

7. Wenn ich Muskelkater habe,
   a. lasse ich mich massieren.
   b. gehe ich zum Arzt.
   c. mache ich Muskeltraining.
   d. lege ich mich aufs Sofa.

8. Wenn ich mich in den Finger geschnitten habe,
   a. ärgere ich mich furchtbar.
   b. hole ich ein Pflaster.
   c. nehme ich Hustensaft.
   d. desinfiziere ich die Wunde.

9. Wenn ich einen Kater habe,
   a. gehe ich ins Krankenhaus.
   b. nehme ich zwei Aspirin.
   c. schlafe ich den ganzen Tag.
   d. gehe ich joggen.

10. Wenn ich Magenschmerzen habe,
   a. lege ich mich aufs Sofa.
   b. trinke ich Kamillentee.
   c. ziehe ich mich aus.
   d. esse ich viel Schokolade.

Hausmittel

- Welche von diesen Hausmitteln kennen Sie? Wogegen helfen sie?
  - ☐ Eisbeutel
  - ☐ grüner Tee
  - ☐ heißer Tee mit Zitrone
  - ☐ Hühnersuppe
  - ☐ Kamillentee
  - ☐ Knoblauch
  - ☐ Salzwasser
  - ☐ warme Umschläge[1]

- Benutzen Sie Hausmittel, wenn Sie sich nicht wohl fühlen? Wenn ja, welche?

Lesen Sie die drei Zeitungstexte. Kennen Sie diese Hausmittel? Glauben Sie, dass sie wirken? Warum?

> Bei Husten warmes Zuckerwasser mit Eidotter[2] vermischen. Das mildert den Hustenreiz[3]. Oder Hustenbier trinken: Einen halben Liter Bier erhitzen, mit fünf Löffeln flüssigem Honig verrühren[4] und abends trinken.

> Wenn die Augen müde sind, Hände reiben[5] bis sie warm sind, sie auf die geschlossenen Augen legen und an die Farbe Schwarz denken.

> Bei Fieber Zitronenscheiben auf die Schläfen[6] legen. Oder eine Kette aus Rettichscheiben[7] über Nacht um den Hals binden.

KLI. Natural remedies play an important role in Germany. Health insurance groups publish pamphlets about them, health food stores and pharmacies advertise homeopathic remedies, and great varieties of teas and herbs are available. People are sometimes reluctant to consume pills, especially antibiotics.

Hausmittel stehen oftmals der Pflanzenheilkunde[8] nahe[9]. Die Arnikapflanze ist nur ein Beispiel. Lesen Sie den Text und beantworten Sie die Fragen.

- Wo wächst die Arnika?
- Wofür wird Arnika verwendet?
- In welcher Form kann man heute Arnika bekommen?

Arnika ist eine beliebte Heilpflanze.

Die Arnika wächst in den Alpen. Seit jeher wird die Alpenpflanze von den Menschen in den Bergen bei Prellungen[10], Stauchungen[11] und schmerzenden Beinen verwendet. Man hat herausgefunden, dass die Arnika die Beine besonders gut durchblutet, Schmerzen lindert, Schwellungen[12] abbaut und entzündungshemmend[13] wirkt. Deshalb eignet sich Arnika bei Sportverletzungen sehr gut. Heute kann man Arnika-Salben, -Gels und -Beinsprays kaufen.

[1]compresses [2]egg yolk [3]irritation of the throat [4]stir [5]rub [6]temples [7]radish slices [8]herbal medicine [9]nahestehen to be similar to [10]bruises [11]sprains [12]swelling [13]as an anti-inflammatory

Situation 2 | Was tut dir weh?

Sit. 2. Have sts. work in groups of 3, then ask the class for responses. Point out that an alternative structure to the answer given in the model is *Die Ohren tun mir weh.*

MODELL: Du warst in einem Rockkonzert. →
Ich habe Ohrenschmerzen.

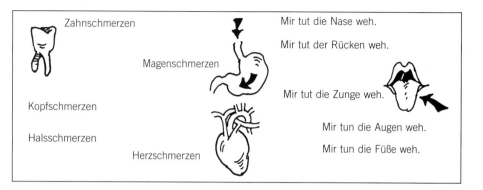

Zahnschmerzen

Magenschmerzen

Kopfschmerzen

Halsschmerzen

Herzschmerzen

Mir tut die Nase weh.

Mir tut der Rücken weh.

Mir tut die Zunge weh.

Mir tun die Augen weh.

Mir tun die Füße weh.

1. Du hast den ganzen Tag in der Bibliothek gesessen und Bücher gelesen.
2. Du hast zwei große Teller Chili gegessen.
3. Jemand hat dich auf die Nase geschlagen.
4. Du bist 20 Kilometer gewandert.
5. Du hast gestern Abend zu viel Kaffee getrunken.
6. Du warst bei einem Footballspiel und hast viel geschrien.
7. Du hast zu viele Bonbons gegessen.
8. Du hast furchtbaren Liebeskummer.
9. Du hast zwei Stunden Schnee geschaufelt.
10. Der Kaffee, den du getrunken hast, war zu heiß.

 ## Situation 3 | Umfrage

Sit. 3. In this autograph activity, sts. use reflexive verbs requiring the accusative case. Model pronunciation, have sts. repeat, and then have them collect signatures. Follow up with general questions: *Wer ist gegen Hunde allergisch? usw.*

MODELL: s1: Legst du dich ins Bett, wenn du dich erkältet hast?
s2: Ja.
s1: Unterschreib bitte hier.

UNTERSCHRIFT

1. Ruhst du dich aus, wenn du Kopfschmerzen hast? _____
2. Ärgerst du dich, wenn du in den Ferien krank wirst? _____
3. Legst du dich ins Bett, wenn du eine Grippe hast? _____
4. Bist du gegen Katzen allergisch? _____
5. Hast du einen niedrigen Blutdruck? _____
6. Freust du dich, wenn dein Lehrer / deine Lehrerin krank ist? _____
7. Regst du dich auf, wenn du dich verletzt hast? _____
8. Erkältest du dich oft? _____
9. Nimmst du Tabletten, wenn du dich nicht wohl fühlst? _____

Charly hat Masern[1]

Der arme Charly! Er hat die Masern. Der Zeichentrickfilm[2] erzählt, wie man aussieht und was passieren kann, wenn man die Masern hat.

- Wie fühlt sich Charly?
- Wie lange dauert seine Krankheit?
- Warum darf er nicht mehr in die Schule gehen?
- Warum dürfen seine Freunde ihn besuchen?

Videoblick. The video segment features an animated story about what happened to Charly when he caught the measles.

[1]*measles*   [2]*cartoon*   [3]*painted*

Oje, irgendjemand muss mich heute Nacht angemalt[3] haben.

Körperteile und Körperpflege

Vocabulary Display

This section introduces dative reflexive pronouns with body parts and contrasts them with accusative reflexive pronouns. The rule of thumb sts. should acquire is to use the dative when there is another object in the utterance and otherwise to use the accusative.

Grammatik 11.2–11.3

Ich wasche mich.

Ich wasche mir die Haare.

Ich trockne mich ab.

Ich trockne mir die Hände ab.

Ich kämme mir die Haare.

Ich schminke mich.

Ich rasiere mich.

Ich putze mir die Zähne.

Ich ziehe mich an.

Situation 4 | Körperteile

Sit. 4. Use TPR to introduce new verbs before beginning the activity. Then have sts. work in pairs.

MODELL: s1: Was macht man mit den Augen?
s2: Mit den Augen sieht man.

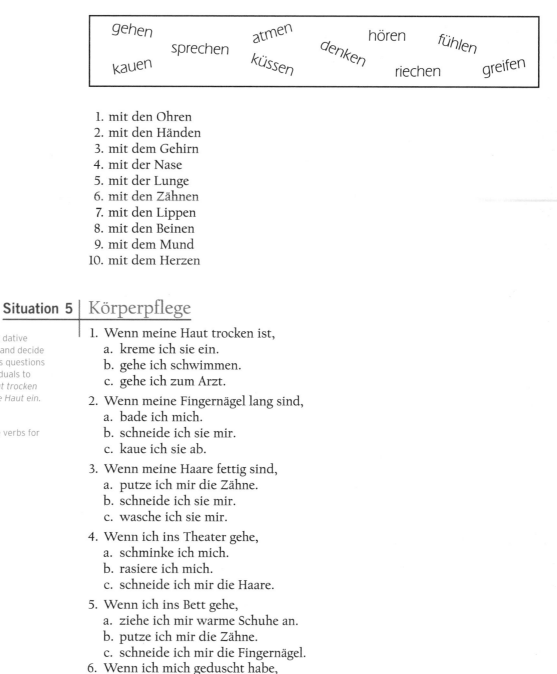

gehen   sprechen   atmen   küssen   denken   hören   riechen   fühlen   greifen   kauen

1. mit den Ohren
2. mit den Händen
3. mit dem Gehirn
4. mit der Nase
5. mit der Lunge
6. mit den Zähnen
7. mit den Lippen
8. mit den Beinen
9. mit dem Mund
10. mit dem Herzen

Situation 5 | Körperpflege

Sit. 5. Sts. use reflexive verbs requiring dative pronouns. Have sts. read the situations and decide what they do in each case. Then address questions to the class as a whole, calling on individuals to answer: *Was machen Sie, wenn Ihre Haut trocken ist? (Ich kreme sie ein.) Diane kremt ihre Haut ein. usw.*

AA. You could also have sts. act out the verbs for others to guess.

1. Wenn meine Haut trocken ist,
   a. kreme ich sie ein.
   b. gehe ich schwimmen.
   c. gehe ich zum Arzt.

2. Wenn meine Fingernägel lang sind,
   a. bade ich mich.
   b. schneide ich sie mir.
   c. kaue ich sie ab.

3. Wenn meine Haare fettig sind,
   a. putze ich mir die Zähne.
   b. schneide ich sie mir.
   c. wasche ich sie mir.

4. Wenn ich ins Theater gehe,
   a. schminke ich mich.
   b. rasiere ich mich.
   c. schneide ich mir die Haare.

5. Wenn ich ins Bett gehe,
   a. ziehe ich mir warme Schuhe an.
   b. putze ich mir die Zähne.
   c. schneide ich mir die Fingernägel.

6. Wenn ich mich geduscht habe,
   a. ziehe ich mich aus.
   b. trockne ich mich ab.
   c. föhne ich mir die Haare.

7. Wenn ich mich erholen will,
   a. gehe ich in die Sauna.
   b. rasiere ich mir die Beine.
   c. nehme ich Tabletten.

8. Wenn es draußen kalt ist,
   a. dusche ich mich heiß.
   b. ziehe ich mir eine warme Hose an.
   c. ziehe ich mich aus.

9. Wenn ich eine Verabredung habe,
   a. schminke ich mich.
   b. wasche ich mir die Haare.
   c. esse ich viel Knoblauch.

Situation 6 | Bildgeschichte: Maria hat eine Verabredung

Sit. 6. This narration series reviews the perfect tense and provides practice of the use of reflexive pronouns. Sentences for narration series: **1.** *Maria ist von der Arbeit nach Hause gekommen.* **2.** *Sie hat sich ausgezogen.* **3.** *Sie hat sich geduscht.* **4.** *Sie hat sich abgetrocknet.* **5.** *Dann hat sie sich die Zähne geputzt.* **6.** *Sie hat sich die Fingernägel geschnitten.* **7.** *Sie hat sich die Haare geföhnt.* **8.** *Sie hat sich die Beine eingekremt.* **9.** *Dann hat sie sich geschminkt.* **10.** *Schließlich hat sie sich ein schönes Kleid angezogen.*

AA. After narrating Maria's activities, you could discuss with sts. who her date is and what he does in preparation for their meeting–e.g., *Kremt er sich die Beine ein? Schminkt er sich?*

Situation 7 | Interview: Körperpflege

Sit 7. Additional vocabulary for makeup: *sich die Wimpern tuschen* = to apply mascara; *der Lippenstift* = lipstick; *Lippenstift auflegen* = to apply lipstick; *der Lidschatten* = eyeshadow; *Lidschatten auflegen* = to apply eyeshadow.

1. (für Frauen) Schminkst du dich jeden Tag? Was machst du?
2. (für Männer) Rasierst du dich jeden Tag? Hattest du schon mal einen Bart? Was für einen (Schnurrbart, Vollbart, Spitzbart, Backenbart)? Wie war das? Wenn du einen Bart hast: Seit wann hast du einen Bart?
3. Wäschst du dir jeden Tag die Haare? Föhnst du sie dir auch? Was für Haar hast du (trockenes, fettiges, normales Haar)?
4. Putzt du dir jeden Tag die Zähne? Gehst du oft zum Zahnarzt?
5. Wie oft gehst du zum Friseur? Hattest du mal eine Dauerwelle? Wie hast du ausgesehen?
6. Hast du trockene Haut? Kremst du dich oft ein?
7. Treibst du regelmäßig Sport? Was machst du? Wie oft? Gehst du manchmal in die Sauna oder ins Solarium?

Lektüre. Use cartoon as an advance organizer for reading. OH-transparency with speech bubbles covered. In groups, sts. fill in dialogue. Then they compare their own version with the original. Questions: *Was wissen Sie über Jutta Ruf (Alter, Interessen, Charakter)? Wie stellen Sie sich Juttas neue Frisur vor?* (Sts. can describe or draw the hairstyle.) *Was sagen ihre Eltern dazu?* Let sts. read first paragraph and start filling in chart (*Arbeit mit dem Text A*) in groups (Jutta's hairstyle is mentioned and depicted in a line drawing at the end of the reading).

Lektüre

Suggestion. You could also have your sts. tell you something about Billy Idol–his appearance, his music, etc.

Vor dem Lesen

A. Was wissen Sie über Jutta Ruf?
B. Lesen Sie den Cartoon auf der nächsten Seite. Welche „Haarmoden" (Frisuren) sind noch „kontrovers"? Zeichnen Sie eine „kontroverse" Haarmode oder bringen Sie Fotos mit in den Kurs.

Miniwörterbuch	allerdings	of course	die **Rasierklinge**	razor blade
	begeistert	thrilled	sprühen	to spray
	sich nicht hineintrauen	to be afraid to go inside	die Stirn	forehead
	kahl	bald	die **Strumpfhosen**	(pl.) tights
	kaum	hardly	tätowiert	tattooed
	die **Kette**	chain	der **Totenkopf**	skull
	der **Nacken**	neck	vor **Lachen**	from laughing (so hard)
	die **Narbe**	scar	zerrissen	torn

Lesehilfe

In this reading, Jutta Ruf takes on a new persona. Recall what you already know about Jutta and her boyfriend "Billy." Go back and read Jutta's diary entry in **Situation 4** of **Kapitel 4.** What kind of persona do you think Jutta will take on?

Juttas neue Frisur

Jutta Ruf hat einen neuen Freund, Billy. Eigentlich heißt er nicht Billy, sondern Paul, aber sein Vorbild ist Billy Idol und so nennt er sich nach ihm. Er hat sich auch die Haare ganz kurz geschnitten und hellblond gebleicht und trägt immer alte, kaputte Jeans, zerrissene T-Shirts und eine Lederjacke mit Ketten. Auf dem Oberarm hat er
5 einen Totenkopf tätowiert und auf seiner linken Hand steht „no future". Auf beiden Wangen hat er je drei parallele Narben. Die hat er sich auf einer Fete nach einem Billy-Idol-Konzert mit einer Rasierklinge geschnitten ... Jutta findet ihn toll! Sie trägt jetzt immer zerrissene schwarze Strumpfhosen, Turnschuhe, die sie silbern gesprüht hat, ein T-Shirt, auf dem „I love Billy" steht, und eine alte Jeansjacke.
10   Es ist Mittwochabend nach acht Uhr. Jutta steht vor der Tür und traut sich nicht hinein. Sie hat Angst, dass ihre Eltern ihre neue Frisur nicht so toll finden wie ihre Freunde, besonders Billy.
        Am Morgen ist sie nicht zur Schule gegangen, sondern hat sich mit Billy in einer Kneipe getroffen. Da haben sie noch eine Stunde über die neue Frisur gesprochen und
15 dann sind sie zum Friseur gegangen. Jutta hatte darauf gespart, denn so eine Frisur ist nicht billig. Nach drei Stunden war alles fertig und Billy war begeistert. Allerdings hat es dann auch 50,- Euro gekostet, wegen der neuen Farbe und so.
        Jutta hat jetzt einen ziemlich ungewöhnlichen Haarschnitt. In der Mitte steht ein zehn Zentimeter breiter Haarstreifen, der von der Stirn bis in den Nacken läuft. Die
20 Haare sind fünfzehn Zentimeter lang, stehen fest und gerade nach oben und sind violett und grün. Der Rest des Kopfes ist kahl. Billy wollte dann noch mit ihr zu einem Tätowierer gehen und ihr „Billy" auf die rechte Seite des Kopfes tätowieren lassen, aber sie

hatten kein Geld mehr. Alle Freunde fanden es toll ... aber jetzt steht sie allein vor der Tür. Sie will warten, bis ihre Eltern ins Bett gegangen sind.

25   Plötzlich hört sie jemanden.

    „Mensch, das bist ja du, Jutta!" Es ist ihr Bruder Hans, der aus dem Fenster schaut. „Wie siehst du denn aus?" Hans kann vor Lachen kaum sprechen. „Das sieht ja unmöglich aus!"

    „Ach, du hast doch keine Ahnung!"

30   „Mutti und Papi finden es sicher toll. Komm schnell herein!"

    „Nein, ich will noch warten, bis sie ins Bett gegangen sind."

    „Da kannst du lange warten, es ist doch erst acht Uhr! Komm, das will ich sehen, wie die reagieren!"

Arbeit mit dem Text

A. Wie sehen sie aus?

	Haarschnitt	Haarfarbe	Kleidung
Billy			
Jutta			

B. Mittwochmorgen oder Mittwochabend? Schreiben Sie ein M oder ein A vor die Sätze, und bringen Sie sie in die richtige Reihenfolge.

_____ Jutta steht vor der Tür und hat Angst.
_____ Hans will sehen, wie die Eltern reagieren.
_____ Jutta ist nicht in die Schule gegangen.
_____ Jutta hat Billy in einer Kneipe getroffen.
_____ Hans schaut aus dem Fenster.
_____ Jutta ist zum Friseur gegangen.
_____ Billy wollte mit Jutta zu einem Tätowierer gehen.

C. Fragen

1. Warum sind Jutta und Billy nicht mehr zum Tätowieren gegangen?
2. Wie findet Hans Juttas Frisur?
3. Was, glauben Sie, werden Juttas Eltern sagen?
4. Warum kleidet sich Jutta so wie im Text beschrieben? Warum bekommt sie eine solche außergewöhnliche Frisur und will sich sogar tätowieren lassen? Denken Sie an Juttas Alter.

Nach dem Lesen

Hatten Sie schon mal Schwierigkeiten mit Ihren Eltern, weil Sie einen anderen Geschmack hatten als sie? Im Aussehen? In der Wahl Ihrer Freunde? In der Wahl Ihrer Tätigkeiten? Erzählen Sie! Machen Sie sich zuerst Gedanken und schreiben Sie sich Stichwörter auf. Arbeiten Sie dann in Kleingruppen und erzählen Sie Ihre Geschichte. Die anderen Gruppenmitglieder helfen mit Fragen und kommentieren.

Vocabulary Display
This section focuses on more severe illnesses that need to be handled by physicians and in hospitals. It continues the grammatical focus on reflexive forms.

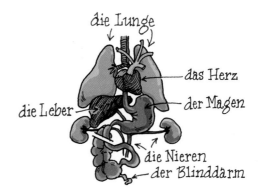

die Lunge

das Herz

der Magen

die Leber

die Nieren

der Blinddarm

Jürgen hat sich das Bein gebrochen. Jetzt muss er einen Gips tragen.

Silvia bekommt eine Spritze.

Josef bekommt einen Verband.

Der Zahnarzt zieht Melanie einen Zahn.

Die Ärztin gibt Claire ein Rezept.

Situation 8 | Medizinische Berufe

Wohin gehen Sie?

Sit. 8. This activity reviews prepositions. Have sts. work with a partner. s1 reads the description (1–8) and s2 answers, saying where he or she will go. (*Ich gehe in die Apotheke, ich gehe in die Drogerie usw.*) s2 should cover up the sentences as s1 reads. Then sts. switch roles.

Cultural note. Even nonprescription drugs can be bought only in pharmacies. All pain relievers, cold remedies, many ointments, etc., are marked *apothekenpflichtig* and won't be found in drugstores or supermarkets. Only "soft" drugs such as *Hustensaft* could be bought at a *Drogerie.* For new glasses, one needs a prescription from an eye specialist.

ins Krankenhaus   zum Hausarzt   zum Psychiater   in die Apotheke
in die Drogerie
zum Zahnarzt   zum Augenarzt   zum Tierarzt

1. Sie haben sich erkältet und brauchen Hustensaft.
2. Sie haben schon seit zwei Wochen eine schlimme Halsentzündung und wollen Antibiotika.
3. Ihr Freund / Ihre Freundin hat sich in den Finger geschnitten. Der Finger blutet stark.
4. Ihr Freund / Ihre Freundin hat Sie verlassen und Sie sind sehr deprimiert.
5. Ihr Goldfisch frisst schon seit mehreren Tagen nichts mehr.
6. Sie haben furchtbare Zahnschmerzen.
7. Sie können im Unterricht nicht lesen, was an der Tafel steht.
8. Ihr Arzt hat Ihnen ein Rezept ausgeschrieben und Sie wollen sich das Medikament abholen.

Sit. 9. Sts. use the *du*-form of the imperative.

Ein Mitstudent / Eine Mitstudentin ist krank. Was raten Sie ihm/ihr?

MODELL: S1: Ich habe Fieber.
S2: Leg dich ins Bett.

1. Ich habe Fieber.
2. Ich habe Kopfschmerzen.
3. Ich fühle mich nicht wohl.
4. Ich habe starken Husten.
5. Ich habe mich in den Finger geschnitten.
6. Ich habe mich erkältet.
7. Ich habe Zahnschmerzen.
8. Ich bin allergisch gegen Katzen.
9. Mir tun die Augen weh.
10. Ich habe Magenschmerzen.

a. Geh zum Arzt.
b. Nimm Hustensaft.
c. Leg dich ins Bett.
d. Geh nach Hause.
e. Kauf dir Kopfschmerztabletten.
f. Ruh dich aus.
g. Nimm ein warmes Bad.
h. Zieh dich warm an.
i. Verkauf deine Katze.
j. Geh zum Zahnarzt.
k. Kauf dir eine Brille.
l. ____?

Kultur … Landeskunde … Informationen

Beim Arzt

Lesen Sie das Gedicht von Ernst Jandl. Welche Situation beschreibt es?

fünfter sein

tür auf
einer raus
einer rein
vierter sein

tür auf
einer raus
einer rein
dritter sein

tür auf
einer raus
einer rein
zweiter sein

tür auf
einer raus
einer rein
nächster sein

tür auf
einer raus
selber rein
tagherrdoktor

—Ernst Jandl

Bevor man im Wartezimmer einer Arztpraxis Platz nehmen kann, muss man in Deutschland an der Anmeldung[1] seine Chipkarte abgeben. Jeder bekommt von seiner Krankenversicherung diese Karte. Auf ihr sind alle Informationen gespeichert[2]. Sie wird beim Arzt abgegeben und der Arzt rechnet nach der Behandlung[3] mit der Krankenversicherung ab[4]. In Deutschland ist eigentlich jeder krankenversichert.

KLI cultural note. There are two kinds of health insurance, public and private, depending on income. For people on welfare or unemployed, the insurance is paid for by the *Sozialamt* or *Arbeitsamt*. Although the system is not perfect, no one is without insurance for lack of money. *Soziale Sicherheit* is also assured by *Arbeitslosenversicherung, Rentenversicherung,* and *Unfallversicherung,* payment for which is mandatory and shared by employers and employees. The present insurance system (*Sozialversicherung*) has existed since Bismarck's era (1883-1889). AOK (*Allgemeine Ortskrankenkasse*) is the most common health insurance.

Rollenspiel: Beim Arzt. Bauen Sie alle Stationen ein: Anmeldung, Wartezimmer und das Gespräch mit dem Arzt.

[1]*reception* [2]*stored* [3]*treatment* [4]rechnet ab *settles*

Situation 10 | Informationsspiel: Krankheitsgeschichte

Sit. 10. The corresponding chart is in Appendix A. Model pronunciation and have sts. repeat. Ask sts. to choose partners, and set a time limit for the activity. Suggest that they fill in all the information for Claire and Herr Thelen, then take turns asking about each other.

Afterward, ask the class as a group: *Wer von Ihnen hat sich schon mal etwas gebrochen? Jim hat sich schon mal etwas gebrochen. Was haben Sie sich gebrochen? usw.* After asking several questions, review to see how well sts. remember: *Was hat Jim sich schon mal gebrochen? Warum ist Laura schon im Krankenhaus gewesen? usw.*

MODELL: Hat Claire sich (Hast du dir) schon mal etwas gebrochen? Was?
Ist Claire (Bist du) schon mal im Krankenhaus gewesen? Warum?
Hat Herr Thelen (Hast du) schon mal eine Spritze bekommen? Gegen was?
Erkältet sich Herr Thelen (Erkältest du dich) oft?
Ist Claire (Bist du) gegen etwas allergisch? Gegen was?
Hat man Claire (Hat man dir) schon mal einen Zahn gezogen?
Hatte Herr Thelen (Hattest du) schon mal hohes Fieber? Wie hoch?
Ist Claire (Bist du) schon mal in Ohnmacht gefallen?

	Claire	Herr Thelen	mein(e) Partner(in)
sich etwas brechen	den Arm	das Bein	
im Krankenhaus sein	Nierenentzündung	Lungenentzündung	
eine Spritze bekommen	Diphtherie	Tetanus	
sich oft erkälten	ja	nein	
gegen etwas allergisch sein	Sonne	Katzen	
einen Zahn gezogen haben	nein	ja	
hohes Fieber haben	104° F	41,2° C	
in Ohnmacht fallen	nein	nein	

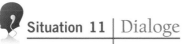 **Situation 11** | Dialoge

Sit. 11. (1) Set the scene. **(2)** Preteach vocabulary. *Termin; das passt gut; dagegen (here: for it); wirken.* **(3)** Ask sts. to open their books and play the dialogue for them at least twice while they fill in the blanks. **(4)** Write sts.' answers on the board, or ask them to write their answers on the board, while making any necessary corrections. **(5)** Ask sts. to practice the dialogues in pairs and ask a few pairs to act out the dialogues in front of the class.

1. Herr Thelen möchte einen Termin beim Arzt.

HERR THELEN: Guten Tag, ich hätte gern <u>einen Termin</u> für nächste Woche.
SPRECHSTUNDENHILFE: Gern, vormittags oder nachmittags?
HERR THELEN: Das ist mir eigentlich <u>egal</u>.
SPRECHSTUNDENHILFE: Mittwochmorgen um neun?
HERR THELEN: Ja, <u>das passt gut</u>. Vielen Dank.

2. Frau Körner geht in die Apotheke.

FRAU KÖRNER: Ich habe schon seit Tagen <u>Magenschmerzen</u>. Können Sie mir etwas <u>dagegen</u> geben?
APOTHEKERIN: Wir haben gerade etwas ganz Neues bekommen, Magenex.
FRAU KÖRNER: Hauptsache, <u>es hilft schnell</u>.
APOTHEKERIN: Es soll sehr gut <u>wirken</u>. Hier ist es.

3. Frau Frisch ist bei ihrem Hausarzt.

HAUSARZT: Guten Tag, Frau Frisch, wie geht es Ihnen?
FRAU FRISCH: Ich fühle mich gar nicht wohl. <u>Halsschmerzen, Fieber</u> ... alles tut mir weh.
HAUSARZT: Das klingt nach <u>Grippe</u>. Sagen Sie mal bitte „Ah".

 Situation 12 | Rollenspiel: Anruf beim Arzt

Sit. 12. The role for s2 appears in Appendix B. Assign roles and have sts. prepare schedules as homework without consulting with their partners; the doctor's secretary prepares an appointment schedule and the patient a class schedule. In class they try to come up with a time that suits both.

S1: Sie fühlen sich nicht wohl. Wahrscheinlich haben Sie Grippe. Rufen Sie beim Arzt an und lassen Sie sich einen Termin geben. Es ist dringend, aber Sie haben einen vollen Stundenplan.

Situation 13 | Interview

Sit. 13. Note the extensive use of the reflexive. This situation recycles many of the expressions used in *Sit. 10*.

1. Warst du schon mal schwer krank? Wann? Was hat dir gefehlt?
2. Warst du schon mal im Krankenhaus? Wann? Warum? Wie lange? Hat man dich untersucht? Hat man dir Blut abgenommen? Hast du eine Spritze bekommen?
3. Hast du dir schon mal etwas gebrochen? Was? Hattest du einen Gips? Wie lange?
4. Hat man dich schon mal geröntgt? Wann? Warum?
5. Erkältest du dich oft? Was machst du, wenn du eine Erkältung hast?
6. Bist du gegen etwas allergisch? Gegen was?

Unfälle

Vocabulary Display
This section focuses on accidents and injuries and what to do in such instances. It reviews the *als/wenn* contrast and gives additional practice in past narration.

Grammatik 11.4–11.5

Zwei Autos sind zusammengestoßen. Eine Frau ist schwer verletzt.

Situation 14 | Ein Autounfall

Sit. 14. Have sts. work in pairs to arrange the sentences in their logical order. Point out that, in this type of interview, the format will be a question followed by an answer. After the sts. have determined the correct sequence of events, have them prepare the situation as a role-play. Then have 3-4 pairs perform for the class.

Eine Polizistin spricht mit einem Zeugen über einen Unfall. Bringen Sie die Sätze in eine logische Reihenfolge.

    3   Können Sie mir sagen, wie spät es ungefähr war?
    2   Also, heute Morgen war ich auf dem Weg zur Uni.
    1   Bitte erzählen Sie genau, was passiert ist.
    6   Ein Auto ist aus einer Einfahrt gekommen.
   10   Ich glaube nicht, er hat jedenfalls nicht gebremst, bevor er auf die Straße gefahren ist.
    9   Wissen Sie, ob der Fahrer auf den Verkehr geachtet hat?
    8   Ja, ein anderes Auto kam von rechts und dann sind sie zusammengestoßen.
    4   So zwischen halb und Viertel vor neun.
    5   Was haben Sie da gesehen?
    7   Und dann?
   11   Vielen Dank für Ihre Hilfe.

Situation 15 | Unfälle

Sit. 15. Have sts. work in small groups to match the descriptions with the pictures. First team to finish, wins. For more listening practice, have sts. cover the text so they can only see the pictures (or use a transparency on an overhead projector) while you read through the descriptions at random, one at a time. After reading each sentence, ask sts. to identify the picture you described.

Sit. 15. AA. After sts. have matched the sentences to the pictures, you might ask them what happened next—e.g., *Hat Ernst sehr laut geschrien? Hat Maria oder ihr Freund dem Kind geholfen? Hat Herr Frisch schnell genug gebremst? Hat Jürgen weiter gelesen?*

Welcher Satz passt zu welchem Bild?

a.

b.

c.

d.

e.

f.

g.

h.

1. Michael und Maria waren beim Segeln, als das Boot umkippte.
2. Sofie schnitt gerade Tomaten, als plötzlich vor ihrem Haus ein Mann von einem Auto überfahren wurde.
3. Melanie und Josef waren auf dem Weg ins Konzert, als Melanie ausrutschte und hinfiel.
4. Jürgen saß gerade in der Bibliothek, als auf der Straße zwei Autos zusammenstießen.
5. Herr Frisch fuhr gerade zur Arbeit, als ihm ein Hund vors Auto lief.
6. Als Ernst mit seinen Freunden Fußball spielte, brach er sich das Bein.
7. Maria und ihr Freund liefen Schlittschuh, als ein Kind ins Eis einbrach.
8. Rolf wollte gerade nach Hawaii fliegen, als ein Flugzeug abstürzte.

Situation 16 | Notfälle

Sit. 16. Have sts. work in pairs. Then, question the class as a whole and have individuals respond. Ask if anyone might do something not mentioned in the text.

Was machst du, wenn ...

1. du einen Unfall siehst?
2. der Verletzte einen Schock hat?
3. der Fahrer von dem anderen Auto flüchtet?
4. du im Fahrstuhl stecken bleibst?
5. du ausrutschst und hinfällst?
6. du dir den Arm gebrochen hast?
7. du ins Wasser fällst?
8. es im Nachbarhaus brennt?
9. du dir die Zunge verbrannt hast?

a. den Krankenwagen rufen
b. die Feuerwehr rufen
c. die Autonummer aufschreiben
d. die Polizei rufen
e. eine Decke holen und den Verletzten zudecken
f. fluchen
g. liegen bleiben und warten, dass jemand kommt
h. schwimmen
i. um Hilfe rufen
j. _____?

Situation 17 | Bildgeschichte: Paulas Unfall

Sit. 17. Sentences for narration series. **1.** *Herr und Frau Wagner sind ausgegangen.* **2.** *Paula ist auf einen Stuhl geklettert und hat die Schranktür aufgemacht.* **3.** *Sie hat eine Tüte mit Bonbons aus dem Schrank geholt.* **4.** *Als sie herunterklettern wollte, ist sie ausgerutscht und auf den Boden gefallen.* **5.** *Ihr Arm hat sehr wehgetan, und sie hat angefangen zu weinen.* **6.** *Sie hat um Hilfe gerufen.* **7.** *Andrea ist gleich zur Nachbarin gelaufen.* **8.** *Die Nachbarin ist mit Andrea und Paula ins Krankenhaus gefahren.* **9.** *Eine Ärztin hat Paula untersucht.* **10.** *Dann hat Paula einen Gips bekommen, weil sie sich den Arm gebrochen hat.*

Sit. 17. AA. You might ask sts. to provide a moral to this narrative–e.g., *Eltern sollten hungrige Kinder nicht allein zu Hause lassen. Man sollte Bonbons nicht in einem hohen Schrank verstecken. Man sollte versteckte Bonbons nicht klauen. usw.*

AA. *Beschreiben Sie einen Unfall, den Sie einmal hatten, entweder einen Unfall im Haus oder einen Autounfall. Denken Sie an einen Unfall, bei dem etwas Seltsames passiert ist. Was ist passiert? Wie haben Sie reagiert? Was haben Sie gemacht? Was ist dann passiert?*

Lektüre

Vor dem Lesen

A. Beantworten Sie die folgenden Fragen.

1. Was macht der Mann auf dem Bild auf der nächsten Seite?
2. Warum macht er das?
3. Beschreiben Sie das Gesicht des Mannes. Was hört er?
4. Was wissen Sie über die DDR und die Rolle der Stasi[1]?

[1]Ministerium für Staatssicherheit

Das Leben der Anderen

Regisseur: Florian Henckel von Donnersmarck

Schauspieler in den Hauptrollen:
Ulrich Mühe, Sebastian Koch,
Martina Gedeck

Erscheinungsjahr: 2006

B. Lesen Sie die Wörter im Miniwörterbuch. Suchen Sie sie im Text und unterstreichen Sie sie.

Miniwörterbuch	
pflichtbewusst	conscientious
regimetreu	loyal to the regime
bespitzeln	to spy on
der **Spürsinn**	perceptiveness
die **Bewachung**	guarding
jemanden aus dem Weg schaffen	to get rid of someone
verwanzt	bugged
das **Abhörgerät**	bugging device
belastendes Material	incriminating evidence
das **Versteck**	hiding place
verschwinden lassen	to make disappear
das **Opfer**	victim
verraten	to reveal
widmen	to dedicate

Film: *Das Leben der Anderen*

Ost-Berlin 1984. Der pflichtbewusste Stasi-Mitarbeiter Gerd Wiesler soll den bekannten und angeblich regimetreuen Dramaturgen Georg Dreyman bespitzeln. Wiesler hat einen guten Spürsinn und glaubt, dass Dreyman nicht so treu ist, wie er tut. Kulturminister Hempf unterstützt die Bewachung des Theaterschriftstellers, weil er
5 ihn aus dem Weg schaffen will, um freie Bahn bei dessen Freundin, der Schauspielerin Christa-Maria Sieland, zu haben.

Dreymans Wohnung wird verwanzt, und auf dem Dachboden des Hauses installiert Wiesler Abhörgeräte. Wiesler, der allein in einer Neubauwohnung lebt und kein aufregendes Privatleben hat, erlebt durch die Bewachung Dreymans eine für ihn völlig neue
10 Welt: nämlich die der Kunst, der Literatur, des freien Geistes und der Liebe. Das Leben des Dramaturgen und der Schauspielerin beeindruckt den Stasi-Mann so sehr, dass er aufhört, belastendes Material über Dreyman zu sammeln. Wieslers Berichte über den Theaterschriftsteller sind trivial. Er unternimmt auch nichts, als Dreyman nach dem Selbstmord eines befreundeten Regisseurs anonym einen Essay über die hohe
15 Selbstmordrate in der DDR veröffentlicht. Wiesler schützt Dreyman sogar, indem er die Schreibmaschine, auf der Dreyman den Essay für den *Spiegel* geschrieben hat, aus ihrem Versteck nimmt und verschwinden lässt.

Ein Opfer gibt es dennoch: Die psychisch labile Schauspielerin Christa-Maria Sieland verrät der Stasi, dass Dreyman den Essay geschrieben hat und wo die Schreibma-
20 schine versteckt ist. Dann flüchtet sie, läuft vor ein Auto und stirbt. Als Dreyman nach der Wende Einsicht in seine Stasi-Akten bekommt, erfährt er, dass ein Stasi-Mitarbeiter ihn geschützt hat. Seine Erinnerungen schreibt Dreyman in einem Roman nieder. Sein Buch widmet er seinem Stasi-Spitzel Wiesler unter dessen Stasi-Deckcode-Namen HGW XX/7 – in Dankbarkeit.

Arbeit mit dem Text

Welche Aussagen sind falsch? Verbessern Sie die falschen Aussagen.

1. „Das Leben der Anderen" spielt vor dem Fall der Berliner Mauer.
2. Der Dramaturg Dreyman scheint ein Fan des DDR-Regimes zu sein.
3. Gerd Wiesler arbeitet für die Polizei und den Kulturminister.
4. Wiesler hat den Auftrag, den Dramaturgen Dreyman und dessen Freundin zu überwachen.
5. Dreyman unterschreibt den Essay im *Spiegel* mit seinem Namen.
6. Wiesler meldet seinem Chef, dass sich Dreyman nicht regimetreu verhält.
7. Christa-Maria Sieland schützt Dreyman und muss deshalb sterben.
8. Nach der Wiedervereinigung schreibt Dreyman ein Buch über seine Erinnerungen.

Nach dem Lesen

Georg Dreymans Tagebuch: Schreiben Sie zu einer der folgenden Situationen einen Eintrag aus Dreymans Perspektive.

a. nach der Veröffentlichung des Essays im *Spiegel*
b. nach dem Unfall von Christa-Maria Sieland
c. nach Einsicht in die eigenen Stasi-Akten nach der Wende

Videoecke

- Warst du letztes Jahr mal krank? Wie ist es dir gegangen?
- Woran merkst du, dass du eine Erkältung hast? Was tust du dagegen?
- Hattest du irgendwelche Kinderkrankheiten?
- Was findest du wichtig für die Körperpflege?
- Wie sieht deine tägliche Körperpflege aus?
- Schminkst du dich? Was machst du?
- Hattest du schon mal einen Unfall? Wie ist das passiert?
- Warst du schon mal im Krankenhaus? Wie war das?

Kristina ist in Hannover geboren. Sie studiert Jura. Sie treibt gern Sport, geht gern ins Kino und auf Reisen.

Brit ist in Leipzig geboren. Sie studiert Anglistik und Deutsch als Fremdsprache. Sie liest gern, fährt gern Rad und macht gern Stadtführungen durch Leipzig.

Aufgabe 1

Aufgaben 1–4. Start with Kristina's interview: Go over *Aufgaben 1–4* one by one, playing the interview at least once for each different task. Then do the same for Brit with *Aufgaben 1–3*.

Welche Krankheit hatten Kristina und Brit letztes Jahr?

Kristina: _____   Brit: _____

Aufgabe 2

Woran merken Kristina und Brit, dass sie eine Erkältung haben? Was tun sie dagegen? Wer hatte Windpocken, Röteln und Mumps?

	KRISTINA	BRIT
1. Ich bekomme Kopfschmerzen.	☐	☐
2. Mir tut der ganze Körper weh.	☐	☐
3. Meistens fängt es im Hals an.	☐	☐
4. Ich bin auch total schlapp.	☐	☐
5. Der Hals kratzt.	☐	☐
6. Man bekommt Kopfschmerzen.	☐	☐
7. Es tun einem die Glieder weh.	☐	☐
8. Ich trink' eine heiße Zitrone.	☐	☐
9. Ich nehme vielleicht eine Tablette.	☐	☐
10. Ich kaufe mir Vitamin C.	☐	☐

Aufgabe 3

Wer sagt das über die Körperpflege, Kristina (K) oder Brit (B)?

1. _____ Ich finde es wichtig, dass man gepflegt aussieht.
2. _____ Ich geh' früh nach dem Aufstehen duschen.
3. _____ Dreimal am Tag Zähne putzen.
4. _____ Wenn ich abends noch mal weggehe, dusch' ich meistens auch.
5. _____ Wenn ich mich erholen will, mach' ich ein heißes Bad.
6. _____ Ich wasch' mir die Haare und feil' mir die Fingernägel.
7. _____ Ich leg' ein bisschen Wimperntusche auf und auch Puder.
8. _____ Vielleicht mal Lippenstift oder so.

Was ist bei Kristinas Unfall passiert? Verbinden Sie die Satzteile.

1. Eine Freundin und ich
2. Und dann bin ich mit dem Fuß umgeknickt
3. Es war ziemlich schlimm,
4. Und das tat alles sehr weh

a. und ich musste operiert werden.
b. und dann war der Knöchel gebrochen.
c. sind Rollschuhlaufen gegangen.
d. weil ich war sehr weit weg von meinen Eltern.

Wortschatz

Krankheit und Gesundheit	Illness and Health
die **Entzündung**, -en	infection
die **Lungenentzündung**	pneumonia
die **Nierenentzündung**	kidney infection
die **Erkältung**, -en	(head) cold
die **Gesundheit**	health
die **Grippe**	influenza, flu
die **Krankheit**, -en	illness, sickness
die **Ohnmacht**	unconsciousness
in **Ohnmacht** fallen	to faint
der **Blutdruck**	blood pressure
niedrigen/hohen Blutdruck haben	to have low/high blood pressure
der **Husten**	cough
der **Hustensaft**, ⸚e	cough syrup
der **Kater**, -	hangover
der **Liebeskummer**	lovesickness
der **Muskelkater**, -	sore muscles
der **Schmerz**, -en	pain
die **Halsschmerzen**	sore throat
die **Herzschmerzen**	heartache
die **Kopfschmerzen**	headache
die **Magenschmerzen**	stomachache
die **Ohrenschmerzen**	earache
die **Zahnschmerzen**	toothache
der **Schnupfen**, -	cold (*with a runny nose*), sniffles
das **Bonbon**, -s	drop, lozenge
das **Halsbonbon**, -s	throat lozenge
das **Hustenbonbon**, -s	cough drop
sich **ärgern** (R)	to get angry
sich **auf·regen**	to get excited, get upset
sich **erkälten**	to catch a cold
fehlen (+ *dat.*) (R)	to be wrong with, be the matter with (*a person*)
weh·tun, tat … weh, wehgetan	to hurt

Ähnliche Wörter

das **Fieber**; das **Symptom**, -e; (sich) **fühlen**; sich **wohl fühlen**

Der Körper	The Body
die **Haut**, ⸚e (R)	skin
die **Niere**, -n	kidney
die **Zunge**, -n	tongue
der **Blinddarm**, ⸚e	appendix
der **Magen**, ⸚	stomach
der **Zahn**, ⸚e	tooth
das **Gehirn**, -e	brain
atmen	to breathe
greifen, griff, gegriffen	to grab, grasp
kauen	to chew
lutschen	to suck
riechen, roch, gerochen	to smell

Ähnliche Wörter

die **Leber**, -n; die **Lippe**, -n; die **Lunge**, -n; die **Nase**, -n; der **Finger**, -; der **Fingernagel**, ⸚; das **Haar**, -e (R); das **Herz**, -en

Apotheke und Krankenhaus	Pharmacy and Hospital
die **Apothekerin**, -nen	female pharmacist
die **Ärztin**, -nen (R)	female doctor, physician
die **Augenärztin**, -nen	eye doctor
die **Hausärztin**, -nen	family doctor
die **Arztpraxis**, Arztpraxen	doctor's office
die **Psychiaterin**, -nen	female psychiatrist
die **Spritze**, -n	shot, injection
die **Tierärztin**, -nen	female veterinarian
der **Apotheker**, -	male pharmacist
der **Arzt**, ⸚e (R)	male doctor, physician
der **Augenarzt**, ⸚e	eye doctor
der **Hausarzt**, ⸚e	family doctor

der Gips	cast (*plaster*)
der Psychiater, -	male psychiatrist
der Tierarzt, ⸚e	male veterinarian
der Verband, ⸚e	bandage
das Medikament, -e	medicine
ein Medikament gegen	medicine for
das Pflaster, -	adhesive bandage
das Rezept, -e	prescription
ab·nehmen, nimmt ... ab, nahm ... ab, abgenommen	to remove; to lose weight
Blut abnehmen	to take blood
röntgen	to X-ray
wirken	to work, take effect

Ähnliche Wörter

die Diphtherie; die Tablette, -n; die Kopfschmerztablette, -n; die Wunde, -n; der Schock; der Tetanus; das Aspirin (R); das Blut (R); die Antibiotika (*pl.*); bluten; desinfizieren

Unfälle	Accidents
die Feuerwehr	fire department
die Unfallstelle, -n	scene of the accident
die Verletzte, -n	injured female person
die Zeugin, -nen	female witness
der Schaden, ⸚	damage
der Unfallbericht, -e	accident report
der Verletzte, -n (ein Verletzter)	injured male person
der Zeuge, -n (*wk. masc.*)	male witness
ab·stürzen, ist abgestürzt	to crash
aus·rutschen, ist ausgerutscht	to slip
bremsen	to brake
brennen, brannte, gebrannt	to burn
hin·fallen, fällt ... hin, fiel ... hin, ist hingefallen	to fall down
schlagen, schlägt, schlug, geschlagen (R)	to hit
stecken bleiben, blieb ... stecken, ist stecken geblieben	to get stuck
überfahren, überfährt, überfuhr, überfahren	to run over
um·kippen	to knock over
verbrennen, verbrannte, verbrannt	to burn
sich (die Zunge) verbrennen	to burn (one's tongue)

sich verletzen	to injure oneself
zu·decken	to cover
zusammen·stoßen, stößt ... zusammen, stieß ... zusammen, ist zusammengestoßen	to crash

Ähnliche Wörter

der Krankenwagen, -; brechen, bricht, brach, gebrochen; sich (den Arm) brechen

Körperpflege	Personal Hygiene
die Dauerwelle, -n	perm
das Solarium, Solarien	tanning salon
sich ab·trocknen (R)	to dry oneself off
sich an·ziehen, zog ... an, angezogen (R)	to get dressed
sich aus·ruhen (R)	to rest
sich aus·ziehen, zog ... aus, ausgezogen (R)	to get undressed
(sich) duschen (R)	to shower (take a shower)
sich ein·kremen	to put lotion on
sich erholen	to recuperate
sich (die Haare) föhnen	to blow-dry (one's hair)
sich (die Zähne) putzen	to brush (one's teeth)
sich rasieren	to shave
sich schminken	to put makeup on
(sich) schneiden, schnitt, geschnitten (R)	to cut (oneself)
sich sonnen	to sunbathe

Ähnliche Wörter

die Sauna, -s; (sich) baden (R); sich (die Haare) kämmen (R); (sich) waschen, wäscht, wusch, gewaschen (R)

Sonstige Substantive	Other Nouns
die Anschrift, -en	address
die Decke, -n	blanket
die Einfahrt, -en	driveway
die Perücke, -n	wig
die Tüte, -n	(paper or plastic) bag
die Verabredung, -en	appointment; date
der Termin, -e (R)	appointment
der Terminkalender, -	appointment calendar
der Verkehr	traffic
das Fahrzeug, -e	vehicle

Ähnliche Wörter

die Autonummer, -n; der Chili; der Goldfisch, -e

Sonstige Verben	Other Verbs
achten auf (+ *akk.*)	to watch out for; to pay attention to

auf·schreiben, schrieb ... auf, aufgeschrieben	to write down
auf·stellen	to set up
beschreiben, beschrieb, beschrieben	to describe
ein·schalten	to turn on
fluchen	to curse, swear
flüchten, ist geflüchtet	to flee
sich freuen über (+ akk.)	to be happy about
sich gewöhnen an (+ akk.)	to get used to
grüßen	to greet, say hi to
herunter·klettern, ist heruntergeklettert	to climb down
sich hin·legen	to lie down
klingen (wie), klang, geklungen	to sound (like)
lassen, lässt, ließ, gelassen	to let
sich einen Termin geben lassen	to get an appointment
passen (R)	to fit
das passt gut	that fits well
rufen, rief, gerufen (R)	to call
schaufeln	to shovel
verlassen, verlässt, verließ, verlassen	to leave; to abandon

Ähnliche Wörter

markieren, sich setzen (R)

Adjektive und Adverbien	Adjectives and Adverbs
deprimiert	depressed
fettig (R)	greasy
gesund	healthy
regelmäßig	regularly
schlimm	bad
sichtbar	visible

stark	heavy, severe
trocken	dry
ungeduldig	impatient
verletzt	injured
schwer verletzt	critically injured

Ähnliche Wörter

allergisch, medizinisch

Sonstige Wörter und Ausdrücke	Other Words and Expressions
aber (R)	but
als (R)	when (conj.)
bevor	before (conj.)
bis (R)	until (prep., conj.)
dagegen	here: for it
haben Sie etwas dagegen?	do you have something for it (illness)?
damit	so that
dass	that (conj.)
denn (R)	for, because
draußen	outside
gemeinsam	together; common
herunter	down (toward the speaker)
Hilfe!	Help!
jedenfalls	in any case
mal	(word used to soften commands)
komm mal vorbei!	come on over!
nachdem (R)	after (conj.)
ob (R)	whether
obwohl	although
oder (R)	or
seit (R)	since, for (prep.)
seit mehreren Tagen	for several days
sondern (R)	on the contrary
und (R)	and
während	during
weil (R)	because
wenn (R)	if; whenever

Strukturen und Übungen

11.1. *Reflexivpronomen und reflexive Verben.* We introduce accusative reflexive pronouns first to reduce confusion between accusative and dative forms. The dative forms are covered in Section 11.2. Include plural forms in your input so sts. can begin to acquire these forms, too.

Sts. will probably realize that they have seen or heard some reflexive verbs before without a reflexive pronoun. Point out that some verbs are used only reflexively, and others can be either reflexive or nonreflexive.

Accusative reflexive pronouns

Reflexive pronouns are generally used to express the fact that someone is doing something to or for himself or herself.

Ich lege das Baby ins Bett.	*I'm putting the baby to bed.*
Ich lege mich ins Bett.	*I'm putting myself to bed (lying down).*

Some verbs are always used with a reflexive pronoun in German, whereas their English counterparts may not be.

Ich habe mich erkältet.	*I caught a cold.*
Warum regst du dich auf?	*Why are you getting excited?*

Here are some common reflexive verbs.

sich ärgern	*to get angry*
sich aufregen	*to get excited, get upset*
sich ausruhen	*to rest*
sich erkälten	*to catch a cold*
sich freuen	*to be happy*
sich (wohl) fühlen	*to feel (well)*
sich hinlegen	*to lie down*
sich verletzen	*to get hurt*

In most instances the forms of the reflexive pronoun are the same as those of the personal object pronouns. The only reflexive form that is distinct is **sich,** which corresponds to **er, sie** (*she*), **es, sie** (*they*), and **Sie*** (*you*).

Accusative Reflexive Pronouns		
ich → mich		*wir* → uns
du → dich		*ihr* → euch
Sie → sich		*Sie* → sich
er *sie* } → sich *es*		*sie* → sich

Ich fühle mich nicht wohl.	*I don't feel well.*
Michael hat sich verletzt.	*Michael hurt himself.*

Verbs with reflexive pronouns use the auxiliary **haben** in the perfect and past perfect tenses.

Heidi hat sich in den Finger geschnitten.	*Heidi cut her finger.*

*Even when it refers to **Sie,** the polite form of *you,* **sich** is not capitalized.

Üb. 1. Point out that the reflexive verbs in this exercise may have present- or perfect-tense forms, or they may be used with a modal verb.

Ergänzen Sie das Verb und das Reflexivpronomen.

sich ärgern (geärgert)
sich aufregen (aufgeregt)
sich ausruhen (ausgeruht)
sich erkälten (erkältet)
sich freuen (gefreut)
sich fühlen (gefühlt)
sich legen (gelegt)
sich schneiden (geschnitten)
sich verletzen (verletzt)

1. SILVIA: Ich _____ _____[a] gar nicht wohl.
   JÜRGEN: Warum denn?
   SILVIA: Ich glaube, ich habe _____ _____[b].
   JÜRGEN: Du Ärmste! Du musst _____ gleich ins Bett _____[c].
2. MICHAEL: Du, weißt du, dass Herr Thelen einen Herzinfarkt[1] hatte?
   MARIA: Kein Wunder, er hat _____ auch immer so furchtbar _____[a].
   MICHAEL: Na, jetzt muss er _____ erst mal ein paar Wochen _____[b].
3. FRAU RUF: Du blutest ja! Hast du _____ _____[a]?
   HERR RUF: Ja, ich habe _____ in den Finger _____[b].
4. HEIDI: Warum _____ du _____[a], Stefan?
   STEFAN: Ich habe in meiner Prüfung ein D bekommen.
   HEIDI: Du solltest _____ _____[b], dass du kein F bekommen hast.

11.2 Dative reflexive pronouns

11.2. *Reflexivpronomen und reflexive Verben.* A useful rule of thumb is if there is no other object, the reflexive pronoun will be accusative. If the sentence already has an accusative object, the reflexive pronoun will be dative. Sts. sometimes assume that adverbial phrases of time like *jeden Tag* and phrases beginning with a preposition are objects.

When a clause contains another object in addition to the reflexive pronoun, then the reflexive pronoun is in the dative case; the other object, usually a thing or a part of the body, is in the accusative case.

DAT.   ACC.
Ich ziehe mir den Mantel aus.   *I'm taking off my coat.*

Note that the accusative object (the piece of clothing or part of the body) is preceded by the definite article.

Wäschst du dir jeden Tag **die** Haare?   *Do you wash your hair every day?*
Natalie hat sich **den** Arm gebrochen.   *Natalie broke her arm.*

Only the reflexive pronouns that correspond to **ich** and **du** have different dative and accusative forms.

Reflexive Pronouns

	SINGULAR		PLURAL		
	Accusative	*Dative*	*Accusative*	*Dative*	
ich	**mich**	**mir**	**uns**		*wir*
du	**dich**	**dir**	**euch**		*ihr*
Sie	**sich**				*Sie*
er/sie/es					*sie*

[1]heart attack

Üb. 2. This exercise is limited to *ich*-forms and requires both accusative and dative reflexive pronouns. Sts. may begin adding a reflexive pronoun to a nonreflexive verb like *aufstehen* now that they have learned reflexive pronouns; watch out for this.

In welcher Reihenfolge machen Sie das?

MODELL: Erst stehe ich auf. Dann dusche ich mich. Dann ...

sich abtrocknen	sich die Fingernägel putzen
sich anziehen	sich das Gesicht waschen
aufstehen	sich die Haare föhnen
sich duschen	sich die Haare kämmen
frühstücken	sich die Haare waschen
sich rasieren	zur Uni gehen
sich schminken	sich die Zähne putzen

Übung 3 | Körperpflege

Üb. 3. 1st- and 3rd-person forms only. Use for homework and/or oral work in class.

Wer macht das? Sie, Ihre Freundin, Ihr Vater ...?

1. sich jeden Morgen rasieren	ich
2. sich zu sehr schminken	meine Freundin
3. sich nicht oft genug die Haare waschen	mein Freund
4. sich nach jeder Mahlzeit die Zähne putzen	mein Vater
5. sich immer verrückt anziehen	meine Mutter
6. sich jeden Tag duschen	meine Schwester
7. sich nie kämmen	meine Oma
8. sich nie die Haare föhnen	mein Onkel
9. sich nicht gern baden	_____?
10. sich immer elegant anziehen	

11.3 Word order of accusative and dative objects

11.3. *Wortstellung: Akkusativ- und Dativobjekt.* This rule states that the dative object usually precedes the accusative object, unless the accusative object is a pronoun. At this stage, sts. do not often attempt to use 2 object pronouns when speaking.

When the accusative object and the dative object are both *nouns*, then the dative object precedes the accusative object.

> DAT.   ACC.
> Ich schenke **meiner Mutter einen Ring.**   *I'm giving my mother a ring.*

When either the accusative object or the dative object is a *pronoun* and the other object is a *noun*, then the pronoun precedes the noun regardless of case.

> DAT.   ACC.
> Ich schenke **ihr einen Ring.**   *I'm giving her a ring.*

> ACC.   DAT.
> Ich schenke **ihn meiner Mutter.**   *I'm giving it to my mother.*

The dative object precedes the accusative object, unless the accusative object is a pronoun.

When the accusative object and the dative object are both *pronouns*, then the accusative object precedes the dative object.

> Ich schenke **ihn ihr.**   *I'm giving it to her.*

Note that English speakers use a similar word order. Remember that German speakers do *not* use a preposition to emphasize the dative object as English speakers often do (*to my mother, to her*).

Üb. 4. This exercise can be used for oral practice in class. Remind sts. that the choice of 3rd-person pronoun depends on the grammatical gender of the noun.

AA. To help sts. with vocabulary, you might bring in a collection of travel-size toilet articles (shampoo, soap, lotion, aftershave, etc.), so that the activity can be acted out.

Übung 4 | Im Hotel

Sie sind mit Ihrem Partner / Ihrer Partnerin in einem Hotel. Sie sind gerade aufgestanden und packen Ihre gemeinsame Toilettentasche aus.

MODELL: s1: Brauchst du den Lippenstift?
s2: Ja, kannst du ihn mir geben?
oder Nein, ich brauche ihn nicht.

1. Brauchst du das Shampoo?
2. Brauchst du den Spiegel?
3. Brauchst du den Rasierapparat?
4. Brauchst du die Seife?
5. Brauchst du das Handtuch?
6. Brauchst du den Föhn?
7. Brauchst du die Kreme?
8. Brauchst du das Rasierwasser?
9. Brauchst du den Kamm?

Übung 5 | Gute Ratschläge!

Üb. 5. This is a complex exercise, and preparation at home is advisable. Then have pairs of sts. give the statement and response in class.

Geben Sie Ihrem Partner / Ihrer Partnerin Rat.

NÜTZLICHE WÖRTER

| einkremen | putzen | waschen |
| föhnen | schneiden | |

MODELL: s1: Meine Hände sind schmutzig.
s2: Warum wäschst du sie dir nicht?

1. Mein Bart ist zu lang.
2. Meine Füße sind schmutzig.
3. Meine Fingernägel sind zu lang.
4. Meine Haut ist ganz trocken.
5. Meine Haare sind nass.
6. Mein Hals ist schmutzig.
7. Meine Nase läuft.
8. Meine Haare sind zu lang.
9. Mein Gesicht ist ganz trocken.
10. Meine Haare sind fettig.

11.4 Indirect questions: *Wissen Sie, wo ...?*

Indirect questions:
- dependent clause begins with a question word or **ob**
- conjugated verb in the dependent clause appears at the end of the clause

Indirect questions are dependent clauses that are commonly preceded by an introductory clause such as **Wissen Sie, ...** or **Ich weiß nicht, ...** Recall that the conjugated verb is in last position in a dependent clause.

| Wissen Sie, **wo** das Kind gefunden **wurde?** | *Do you know where the child was found?* |
| Können Sie mir sagen, **wann** die Polizei **ankommt?** | *Can you tell me when the police will arrive?* |

11.4. *Indirekte Fragen.* This section continues the discussion of subordinating conjunctions and dependent word order begun in Section 3.4 (*wenn, weil*) and carried on in Sections 7.1 (relative pronouns), 9.1 and 9.3 (*als, wenn, wann*), and 9.5 (*nachdem*). This discussion will be completed in 11.5 (summary review) and picked up again in 12.3 (*weil, damit*).

The question word of the direct question functions as a subordinating conjunction in an indirect question.

DIRECT QUESTION: **Wie** komme ich zur Apotheke?
INDIRECT QUESTION: Ich weiß nicht, **wie** ich zur Apotheke **komme.**

Use the conjunction **ob** (*whether, if*) when the corresponding direct question does not begin with a question word but with a verb.

DIRECT QUESTION: **Kommt** Michael heute Abend?
INDIRECT QUESTION: Ich weiß nicht, **ob** Michael heute Abend **kommt.**

Üb. 6. Assign for homework. You may want to remind sts. that there is no question word in 2, 5, or 6, and so they will need to use *ob*.

Übung 6 | Bitte etwas freundlicher!

Verwandeln Sie die folgenden direkten Fragen in etwas höflichere indirekte Fragen. Beginnen Sie mit **Wissen Sie, ...** oder **Können Sie mir sagen, ...**

MODELL: Wo war Herr Langen um sieben Uhr fünfzehn? →
Wissen Sie, wo Herr Langen um sieben Uhr fünfzehn war?
oder Können Sie mir sagen, wo Herr Langen um sieben Uhr fünfzehn war?

1. Was ist hier passiert?
2. Hat das Kind das Auto gesehen?
3. Wer war daran Schuld?
4. Warum hat Herr Langen das Kind nicht gesehen?
5. Hat Herr Langen gebremst?
6. Wann hat er gebremst?
7. Wie oft fährt Herr Langen diese Straße zur Arbeit?
8. Wie lange lag Lothar auf der Straße?
9. Wann hat die Polizei Lothars Mutter angerufen?

11.5 Word order in dependent and independent clauses (summary review)

11.5. *Wortstellung in Hauptsätzen und Nebensätzen.* This section provides a review of the coordination and subordination of clauses and lists the most common conjunctions used for each.

Stress that the coordinating conjunction does not count as the first element of the second clause. The subject is often the first element, but an adverbial phrase may also stand in first position.

Dependent clauses were introduced first in Section 3.4 (*wenn* and *weil*). Section 7.1 presented relative clauses, Sections 9.1 and 9.3 the conjunctions *als* and *wenn*, Section 9.5 *nachdem*, and Section 11.4 indirect questions. Section 12.2 will contrast the conjunctions *weil*, *damit*, and *um ... zu.*

To connect thoughts more effectively, two or more clauses may be combined in one sentence. There are essentially two kinds of combinations:

1. Coordination: both clauses are equally important and do not depend on each other structurally.
2. Subordination: one clause depends on the other one; it does not make sense when it stands alone.

COORDINATION

Heute ist ein kalter Tag und es schneit.	*Today is a cold day, and it is snowing.*

SUBORDINATION

Gestern war es wärmer, weil die Sonne schien.	*Yesterday was warmer because the sun was shining.*

A. Coordination

These are the five most common coordinating conjunctions.

und	*and*
oder	*or*
aber	*but*
sondern	*but, on the contrary*
denn	*because*

Wissen Sie noch?

Dependent clauses may be introduced by subordinating conjunctions, such as **als** (*when, as*), **wenn** (*when, whenever*), and **wann** (*when*); by relative pronouns such as **der, die,** and **das** (*who, whom, that, or which*); or by question words such as **was** (*what*), **wie** (*how*), and **warum** (*why*) in indirect questions. Main verbs in dependent clauses appear at the end of the clause.

Review grammar 3.4, 7.1, 9.1, 9.3, 9.5, and 11.4.

In clauses joined with these conjunctions, the conjugated verb is in second position in both statements.

CLAUSE 1	CONJ.	CLAUSE 2
I II		I II
Ich muss noch viel lernen,	denn	ich habe morgen eine Prüfung.

(*I have to study a lot, since I have a test tomorrow.*)

B. Subordination

Clauses joined by subordinating conjunctions follow one of two word order patterns.

1. When the sentence begins with the main clause, that clause has regular word order (verb second in statements) and the dependent clause introduced by the conjunction has dependent word order (verb last).

CLAUSE 1	CONJ.	CLAUSE 2
I II		I LAST
Ich muss noch viel lernen,	weil	ich morgen eine Prüfung habe.

(*I have to study a lot because I have a test tomorrow.*)

2. When a sentence begins with a dependent clause, the entire dependent clause is considered the first part of the main clause and occupies first position. The verb-second rule applies, then, moving the subject of the main clause after the verb.

CLAUSE 1	CLAUSE 2
I	II SUBJECT
Weil ich morgen eine Prüfung habe,	muss ich noch viel lernen.

(*Because I have a test tomorrow, I have to study a lot.*)

Here are the most commonly used subordinating conjunctions.

als	*when*
bevor	*before*
bis	*until*
damit	*so that*
dass	*that*
nachdem	*after*
ob	*whether, if*
obwohl	*although*
während	*while*
weil	*because, since*
wenn	*if, when*

Übung 7 | Opa Schmitz ist im Garten

Ergänzen Sie **dass, ob, weil, damit** oder **wenn.**

1. OMA SCHMITZ: Weißt du, _____ᵃ Opa schon den Rasen gemäht hat?
   HELGA: Ich weiß nur, _____ᵇ er schon seit zwei Stunden im Garten ist.
   OMA SCHMITZ: _____ᶜ Opa schon so lange im Garten ist, liegt er bestimmt in der Sonne.

2. HELGA: Du, Opi, was machst du denn im Gras?

   OPA SCHMITZ: Ich habe mich nur kurz hingelegt, _____[a] mich die Nachbarn nicht sehen.

   HELGA: Aber warum sollen die dich denn nicht sehen?

   OPA SCHMITZ: _____[b] ich mich heute noch nicht rasiert habe.

Übung 8 | Minidialoge

Ergänzen Sie **obwohl, als, nachdem, bevor** oder **während**.

1. HERR THELEN: Was hat denn deine Tochter gesagt, _____[a] du mit deiner neuen Frisur nach Hause gekommen bist?

   HERR SIEBERT: Zuerst gar nichts. Erst _____[b] sie ein paar Mal um mich herumgegangen war, hat sie angefangen zu lachen und gesagt: „Aber, Papi, erst fast eine Glatze und jetzt so viele Haare. Das sieht aber komisch aus!"

2. FRAU ROWOHLT: Guten Tag, Herr Frisch! Kommen Sie doch bitte erst zu mir, _____ Sie mit Ihrer Arbeit beginnen.

   HERR FRISCH: Aber natürlich, Frau Direktorin.

3. JOSEF: Ja, seid ihr denn immer noch nicht fertig? Was habt ihr eigentlich die ganze Zeit gemacht?

   MELANIE: _____ du dich stundenlang geduscht hast, haben wir die ganze Wohnung aufgeräumt.

4. MARIA: Aber, Herr Wachtmeister, könnten Sie nicht mal ein Auge zudrücken? Die Ampel war doch schon fast wieder grün.

   POLIZIST: Nein, leider nicht, _____ ich es gern tun würde, meine gnädige[1] Frau. Aber Sie wissen ja, Pflicht ist Pflicht.

[1] *dear*

Paula Modersohn-Becker: *Selbstbildnis vor grünem Hintergrund mit blauer Iris* (ca. 1905), Kunsthalle, Bremen

PAULA MODERSOHN-BECKER

Die Malerin Paula Modersohn-Becker (1876–1907) wurde in Dresden geboren. Sie starb nach der Geburt ihrer Tochter. Die Darstellung[1] des „schlichten[2]" Menschen ist ihr zentrales Anliegen[3], was in vielen Porträts zum Ausdruck kommt[4]. Die Nationalsozialisten diffamierten ihre Bilder als „entartete[5] Kunst".

[1] representation [2] plain [3] concern [4] zum ... is expressed [5] degenerate

Die moderne Gesellschaft

In **Kapitel 12**, you will discuss social relationships and some of the issues that arise in modern multicultural societies. In addition, you will learn to talk about money matters and about German art and literature.

GOALS

In this chapter, sts. learn to express their opinions about contemporary social issues, the economy, and German art and literature. Expressing causality and purpose and case are reviewed, while the genitive case and the subjunctive to express possibility are presented formally for the first time.

Themen
Familie, Ehe, Partnerschaft
Multikulturelle Gesellschaft
Das liebe Geld
Kunst und Literatur

Kulturelles
Gleichberechtigung im Haushalt und im Beruf
Videoblick: Frauentag
Wie bezahlt man in Europa?
Videoecke: Familie und Freunde

Lektüren
Deutsche Kastanien (Yüksel Pazarkaya)
afro-deutsch I (May Ayim)

Strukturen
12.1 The genitive case
12.2 Expressing possibility: **würde, hätte,** and **wäre**
12.3 Causality and purpose: **weil, damit, um ... zu**
12.4 Principles of case (summary review)

Situationen

Familie, Ehe, Partnerschaft

Grammatik 12.1–12.2

Vocabulary Display
This display provides examples of the genitive case. Sts. will probably not yet learn to use the genitive correctly in speaking, but they should learn to recognize its meaning when they read or hear it.

Die gute alte Zeit: der Herr im Haus

Eine Rolle des modernen Mannes

Kinder und Haushalt: eine mögliche Rolle der modernen Frau

Das Leben vieler Frauen: Erfolg im Beruf

Verliebt, verlobt, verheiratet

Er kümmert sich um die Kinder und sie kümmert sich um das Geld.

Situation 1 | Wer in der Klasse ...?

Sit. 1. This is a variation on the regular autograph activity. Practice forming the questions before asking sts. to do the activity. Follow up by turning sts.' findings into an optional association activity.

1. ist verheiratet
2. ist verlobt
3. hat einen Sohn oder eine Tochter
4. war noch nie verliebt
5. möchte einen Arzt / eine Ärztin heiraten
6. möchte keine Hausfrau / kein Hausmann sein
7. will mehr als drei Kinder haben
8. wird leicht eifersüchtig
9. findet gemeinsame Hobbys wichtig
10. ist gerade glücklich verliebt

Situation 2 | Informationsspiel: Der ideale Partner / Die ideale Partnerin

Sit. 2. The corresponding chart is in Appendix A.

MODELL: Wie soll Rolfs ideale Partnerin aussehen?
Was für einen Charakter soll sie haben?
Welchen Beruf soll Heidis idealer Partner haben?
Welche Interessen sollte er haben?
Wie alt sollte er sein?
Welche Konfession sollte er haben?
Welcher Nationalität sollte Rolfs Partnerin angehören?
Welche politische Einstellung sollte sie haben?

	Rolf	Heidi	mein(e) Partner(in)
Aussehen	schlank und sportlich	klein und dick	
Charakter	lustig und neugierig	fleißig und geduldig	
Beruf	egal	Rechtsanwalt	
Interessen	Kunst und Kultur	Sport und Reisen	
Alter	so alt wie er	ein paar Jahre jünger als sie	
Konfession	egal	kein Fanatiker	
Nationalität	deutsch	egal	
politische Einstellung	eher konservativ	liberal	

 **Situation 3** | Interview

Sit. 3. Sts. discuss these questions in small groups, then with the entire class. You could ask sts. to write their answers so you could take these home and construct a summary chart. For yes/no questions, note the percentage of people answering yes/no, and then break these percentages down by gender. For descriptive questions, list the most frequent responses, perhaps computing percentages here as well. Tally the results and distribute to sts. the next day for a follow-up discussion.

1. Willst du heiraten? (Bist du verheiratet?)
2. Wie sollte dein Partner / deine Partnerin sein? Welche Eigenschaften findest du an deinem Partner / deiner Partnerin wichtig?
3. Sind Aussehen und Beruf wichtig für dich? Was ist sonst noch wichtig?
4. Willst du Kinder haben? Wie viele? (Hast du Kinder? Wie viele?)
5. Würdest du zu Hause bleiben, wenn du Kinder hättest?
6. Was hältst du von einem Ehevertrag vor der Ehe?
7. Was würdest du tun, wenn du dich mit deinem Partner / mit deiner Partnerin nicht mehr verstehst?
8. Was wäre für dich ein Grund zur Scheidung?
9. Sollte sich vor allem die Mutter um die Kinder kümmern? Warum (nicht)?
10. Welche Eigenschaften hat ein guter Vater?

Junge Familie beim Frühstück.

Gleichberechtigung im Haushalt und im Beruf

„Es gibt zirka 2000 Berufe
für Mädchen nicht ganz so viele
also was willst du werden
Friseuse oder Verkäuferin?"

Charlotte Rauner

Haben sich Ihr Vater (V), Ihre Mutter (M) oder beide zusammen (b) um die folgenden Aufgaben im Alltag[1] gekümmert?

_____ Auto warten[2]
_____ einkaufen
_____ Geschirr spülen
_____ Kinder betreuen[3]
_____ kochen
_____ putzen
_____ Rasen mähen
_____ Rechnungen bezahlen
_____ Reparaturen im Haus
_____ waschen

Berufstätige Frauen arbeiten doppelt – am Arbeitsplatz und zu Hause, denn Hausarbeit ist immer noch meistens Frauensache[4]. Zwar[5] wollen 27% der Männer ihren Frauen grundsätzlich[6] helfen, aber Sache der Frauen ist es: zu waschen (90%), zu kochen (88%), zu putzen (80%), einzukaufen (75%) und zu spülen (71%).

Am Anfang des Zusammenlebens sind viele Männer noch bereit, ihrer Partnerin im Haushalt zu helfen. Doch nach der Geburt des ersten Kindes ziehen sich viele fast vollständig[7] von der Hausarbeit zurück[8]. Ebenso gibt es immer noch traditionelle Männeraufgaben: Reparaturen (80%) und das Auto (66%).

Die alte Rollenverteilung setzt sich im Berufsleben fort. Fast die Hälfte aller Frauen und Männer arbeiten in geschlechtertypischen[9] Berufen, in denen die Männer beziehungsweise die Frauen jeweils mit bis zu 80% aller Beschäftigten dominieren. Auch die Forderung: *gleicher Lohn*[10] *für gleiche Arbeit* ist immer noch eine Utopie. Frauen verdienen durchschnittlich ein Drittel weniger als ihre männlichen Kollegen und sind zu einem großen Teil in unteren Lohngruppen[11] oder in Wirtschaftsbereichen[12] mit geringeren Verdienstmöglichkeiten[13] beschäftigt. In der Wirtschaft oder Verwaltung sind Frauen in Führungspositionen[14] eher selten. Außerdem sind sie von Arbeitslosigkeit stärker betroffen[15] als Männer.

- Vergleichen Sie die Angaben im Text mit Ihren eigenen Erfahrungen. Hat Ihre Familie eine ähnliche Arbeitsteilung? Wo gibt es Unterschiede?
- Machen Sie eine Umfrage im Kurs und vergleichen Sie die Prozentzahlen.
- Arbeiten beide Eltern oder nur ein Elternteil? Wer verdient mehr, Ihr Vater oder Ihre Mutter?
- Gibt es bei Ihnen geschlechtertypische Berufe? Welche? Welche Gründe sprechen dafür, dass mehr Frauen oder Männer in diesen Berufen arbeiten?
- In welchen Berufen kann man mehr verdienen und besser Karriere machen: in den typischen Männerberufen oder in den Frauenberufen?

[1]im ... *day-to-day* [2]*doing maintenance on* [3]*taking care of* [4]*a woman's job* [5]*To be sure* [6]*in principle*
[7]*completely* [8]ziehen sich zurück *withdraw* [9]*gender-typical* [10]*wages, salary* [11]*wage brackets*
[12]*economic sectors* [13]*earning potential* [14]*leadership positions* [15]stärker ... *more strongly affected*

KLI. Discuss the cartoon first. Question: *Mit welchem Märchen assoziieren Sie den Text dieses Cartoons?* Then discuss the quote by the German author Charlotte Rauner. What does she mean by it? Does this quote make sense in the context of your country? Ask sts. to complete the prereading task in small groups and discuss. Then ask sts. to work with the text in small groups, writing down the information they consider important or interesting. After sts. have answered the questions after the text, tally the results and discuss. Throughout this section, you probably want to be sensitive about issues regarding nontraditional families. **Suggestion.** Have sts. write a personal ad in which they describe themselves and give an idea of the partner they are looking for. Sts. should also say what they expect their partner's role to be in terms of family and household. To make this activity more interactive, have sts. exchange their personal ads and then guess who wrote which ad.

Frauentag

Was ist ein Frauentag? Woran erinnert er[1] oder was wird gefeiert[2]? Der Ausschnitt aus **Blickkontakte** gibt Antwort auf diese und die folgenden Fragen.

- Wogegen protestieren Frauen in Deutschland?
- Wer macht in Deutschland mehr im Haushalt?
- Wie denken viele Männer in Deutschland über die Kindererziehung?
- Warum kommen Männer oft weiter im Beruf als Frauen?

[1]Woran ... *What does it commemorate* [2]*celebrated* [3]*Uns ... We've had enough.* [4]*Jetzt ... That's going too far.*

Uns reicht's.[3] Jetzt schlägt's dreizehn.[4]

Videoblick: The selection from the *Blickkontakte* video focuses on some continuing problems women face in German society. Its point of departure is the International Women's Day celebrated each year on March 8th. The clip uses off-the-wall remarks by boys and an old man to highlight and criticize various uneducated opinions about the role of women in society.

Multikulturelle Gesellschaft

Grammatik 12.3

Cultural note. In 2005, a total of 6.7 million foreign citizens lived in Germany. More than a quarter (26%) were of Turkish nationality, followed by Italians (8%), Poles and Greeks (5%), and immigrants from Serbia and Montenegro (4%). In 1999, the social-liberal government changed the citizenship law to give German citizenship to children born in Germany whose parents are legal residents of Germany. These children have dual citizenship until the age of 23. Then they must choose one of their citizenships.

CLAIRE: Ist Deutschland eigentlich ein multikulturelles Land?
JOSEF: Ja, natürlich. Ungefähr 7 Millionen Ausländer leben hier.

RENATE: Unsere ausländischen Mitbürger bereichern Deutschland mit ihrer Kultur und ihren Traditionen.

MEHMET: Deutschland braucht in bestimmten Branchen ausländische Arbeitskräfte, zum Beispiel im EDV-Bereich.

JÜRGEN: Wie in jedem anderen Land müssen Ausländer auch in Deutschland ihre Aufenthalts- und Arbeitserlaubnis beantragen. Dazu müssen sie viele Formulare ausfüllen.

Situation 4 | Definitionen

Sit. 4. After sts. have completed the activity, have them close books and do the following to test productive recall: *Was braucht man, damit man in Deutschland wohnen darf? usw.*

1. das Formular
2. die Aufenthaltserlaubnis
3. die Arbeitserlaubnis
4. der EDV-Bereich
5. das multikulturelle Land
6. etwas beantragen

a. Die braucht man, damit man in Deutschland wohnen darf.
b. Das muss man ausfüllen, um zum Beispiel eine Arbeitserlaubnis zu bekommen.
c. Die braucht man, damit man arbeiten kann.
d. Land, in dem Menschen aus verschiedenen Kulturen zusammen leben
e. Formulare ausfüllen und in einem Büro abgeben
f. So nennt man alles, was mit Computern zu tun hat.

Situation 5 | Interview

AA. If your area has a large immigrant population, you might ask recent immigrants to tell of their experiences – positive and negative.

1. Weißt du, wann deine Vorfahren eingewandert sind? Woher kamen sie? Welche Sprache haben sie gesprochen? Warum haben sie ihre Heimat verlassen?
2. Spricht man in deiner Familie mehr als eine Sprache? Welche? Welche Vorteile oder Nachteile hat das für dich?
3. Kennst du Einwanderer? Woher kommen sie? Sprechen sie Englisch? Warum sind sie eingewandert?
4. Weißt du, welche Formalitäten man erfüllen muss, um legal hier wohnen und arbeiten zu dürfen?
5. Welche Probleme können Einwanderer haben? Wie kann man diese Probleme lösen? (4–5 Probleme und Lösungsvorschläge bitte)

Situation 6 | Diskussion: Leben in einer fremden Kultur

Was ist an der Situation von Ausländern ein Problem? Was ist für die Integration von Ausländern wichtig? Arbeiten Sie in kleinen Gruppen. Schreiben Sie in jede Spalte fünf Dinge, die Sie für wichtig halten. Ordnen Sie die Dinge: das Wichtigste zuerst. Einige Ideen finden Sie im Wortkasten auf der nächsten Seite.

Probleme von Ausländern	für die Integration wichtig

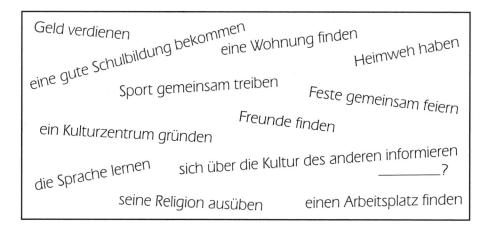

Geld verdienen

eine gute Schulbildung bekommen   eine Wohnung finden   Heimweh haben

Sport gemeinsam treiben   Feste gemeinsam feiern

ein Kulturzentrum gründen   Freunde finden

die Sprache lernen   sich über die Kultur des anderen informieren
_____?

seine Religion ausüben   einen Arbeitsplatz finden

Situation 7 | Diskussion: Rechtsextremismus

Sit. 7. Set the scene by briefly talking about and perhaps showing photos of right-wing radicalism, e.g., the federal building in Oklahoma City after the terrorist attack of 1995 or members of the Ku Klux Klan in "uniform." Then ask sts. to complete the activity in small groups and discuss afterward.

Cultural note: *2005 gab es in Deutschland 183 rechtsextremistische Organisationen. Die Zahl ihrer Mitglieder und anderer nicht organisierter Rechts- extremisten betrug 39 000. 27% von ihnen galten als gewaltbereit. 588 Gewaltdelikte wurden 2005 verzeichnet. Eigentlich ist die Zahl der Straftaten viel höher. Sie lag für 2005 bei 10 271. Dazu gehören Propagandadelikte wie das Tragen verfassungs- feindlicher Symbole und das Rufen verbotener Parolen. An der Spitze bei den Straftaten liegen die neuen Bundesländer. Die meisten Rechtsextremen sind junge Männer zwischen 15 und 24 Jahren mit niedrigem Bildungsniveau. Manchmal sind die Gewalttaten politisch motiviert, oft beruhen sie jedoch auf einem diffusen Gefühl einer generellen Bedrohung oder Benachteiligung der Deutschen durch Ausländer. Die Gewalttaten werden oft durch übermäßigen Alkoholkonsum, Musik und rechtsextremistische Hetze ausgelöst. Die Regierung versucht, dem Rechtsradikalismus u.a. durch ein Verbot rechtsradikaler politischer Gruppierungen und Verbot von gewaltverherrlichenden und rassistischen Schriften, Musiktexten und Symbolen Herr zu werden.*

1. Gibt es Rechtsextremisten in Ihrem Land? Wo? Was für Ziele haben sie? Was machen sie?
2. Was ist, Ihrer Meinung nach, ein typischer Rechtsextremist?

- ☐ Frau
- ☐ jung
- ☐ schlecht ausgebildet
- ☐ arm
- ☐ sympathisches Äußeres
- ☐ arbeitslos
- ☐ Einzelgänger

- ☐ Mann
- ☐ alt
- ☐ gut ausgebildet
- ☐ reich
- ☐ unsympathisches Äußeres
- ☐ mit gutem Arbeitsplatz
- ☐ nur in der Gruppe stark

3. Wodurch fallen Rechtsextreme auf?
4. Was kann man gegen Rechtsextremismus tun?

Lektüre

Vor dem Lesen

In den 1960er Jahren fehlten in Westdeutschland Arbeiter. Deshalb wurden Ausländer angeworben[1], um Lücken auf dem Arbeitsmarkt zu füllen. Sie wurden auch „Gastarbeiter" genannt. Die ausländischen Arbeiter waren wichtig: Der millionste „Gastarbeiter", der in Westdeutschland ankam, erhielt ein Motorrad als Geschenk. Bis zum Stopp der Anwerbung im Jahre 1973 sind insgesamt 2,3 Millionen „Gastarbeiter" nach Westdeutschland gekommen. Ungefähr 50% der ausländischen Arbeitskräfte leben seit über 10 Jahren in Deutschland und fast 30% von ihnen schon mehr als 30 Jahre. In einigen Großstädten liegt der Anteil der ausländischen Bevölkerung bei 20%. Die sozialdemokratische Regierung änderte 1999 das Staatsbürgerschaftsrecht[2]. Kinder von Ausländern mit rechtlich zulässiger Aufenthaltsgenehmigung[3] bekommen die deutsche Staatsbürgerschaft, wenn sie in Deutschland geboren wurden. Bis zu ihrem 23. Lebensjahr haben diese Kinder die doppelte Staatsbürgerschaft. Dann müssen sie sich für eine Staatsbürgerschaft entscheiden.

[1]*recruited* [2]*citizenship law* [3]*rechtlich ... legally valid residence permit*

1. Welche Gründe haben Menschen, ihr Heimatland zu verlassen?
2. Was für Probleme haben Fremde in Ihrem Land?
3. Was wissen Sie über ausländische Arbeitnehmer oder „Gastarbeiter" in der Bundesrepublik? Welche Probleme könnten sie haben?
4. Der Schriftsteller hat die folgende Kurzgeschichte in zwei Sprachen geschrieben, auf Deutsch und auf Türkisch. Warum?

Deutsche Kastanien

von Yüksel Pazarkaya

TEIL I

Miniwörterbuch

anfassen	to touch
jemandem Angst einjagen	to scare someone
sich aufrichten	to get back up
sich bücken	to bend over
erstarren	to stand paralyzed
das **Fangen**	tag (*children's game*)
fassen	to grab
fortrennen, rannte ... fort	to run away
sich halten für	to consider oneself
herausfordernd	challenging
hinzufügen	to add
das **Innere**	inside
die **Kastanie, -n**	chestnut
die **Mengenlehre**	set theory
die **Murmel, -n**	marble
sich nähern	to approach
die **Rechenart, -en**	arithmetical operation
schießen, schoss	to shoot
schweigen	to become silent
sich sträuben	to bristle
verdutzt	taken aback
verstummt	speechless
weshalb	why
wieso	why
zerbrechen, zerbrach	to break into pieces
sich etwas zuschulden kommen lassen	to do something wrong
zuwenden, zugewandt	to turn toward
zwar	to be sure

D u bist kein Deutscher!" sagte Stefan zu Ender in der Pause auf dem Schulhof. Weshalb nur wollte er heute mit Ender nicht Fangen spielen? Um eben einen Grund dafür zu nennen, sagte er einfach: „Du bist doch kein Deutscher." Ender war verdutzt und betroffen. Stefan war sein liebster Klassenkamerad, sein bester Spielfreund.

5 „Wieso?" konnte er nur fragen.

Stefan verstand ihn nicht. Was heißt da „wieso"? Oder hält sich Ender wohl für einen Deutschen? „Du bist eben kein Deutscher", sagte er. „Du bist kein Deutscher wie ich." Enders schöne dunkle Augen wurden traurig. Sein Inneres sträubte sich, als hätte er sich etwas zuschulden kommen lassen. In seinem Herzen zerbrach etwas. Er schwieg.

10 Er ließ den Kopf hängen. Er ging weg. An diesem Tag sprach er mit Stefan kein Wort mehr. Dem Unterricht konnte er nicht folgen. Dem Lehrer konnte er nicht zuhören. Sein Kopf wurde immer schwerer.

Auch im letzten Herbst war es ihm einmal so ergangen. In dem Wohnviertel gibt es einen hübschen kleinen Park, voll Blumen und Bäume. Im Herbst ist er am schönsten.

15 Dann ziehen die Kastanien alle Kinder in der Umgebung an. Die Kinder werfen die Kastanien mit Steinen herunter. Wer viel sammelt, verkauft sie an den Zoo als Futter für die Elefanten und Kamele. Andere bringen sie in die Schule mit. Man kann sie nämlich im Mathematikunterricht brauchen. Und die kleinen, die noch nicht zur Schule gehen, spielen mit den Kastanien wie mit Murmeln.

20 Der Lehrer sagte: „Jedes Kind bringt zehn Stück mit." Sie sind 34 Kinder in der Klasse. Wenn jedes Kind zehn Kastanien mitbringt, macht es genau 340 Stück. Und damit lassen sich ganz gut Mengenlehre und die vier Rechenarten üben.

Am Nachmittag ging Ender in den Park. Zwei Kinder warfen mit Steinen nach den Kastanien. Sie waren zwar keine Freunde von ihm, aber er kannte sie. Er sah sie öfters
25 in diesem Wohnviertel.

Ender näherte sich ihnen. Er bückte sich nach einer Kastanie, die auf dem Boden lag. Eines von den beiden Kindern sagte zu ihm: „Finger weg!" – „Ich will auch Kastanien sammeln", sagte Ender. Das zweite Kind rief: „Du darfst sie nicht sammeln, das sind deutsche Kastanien." Ender verstand nichts. Das erste Kind fügte hinzu: „Du bist
30 kein Deutscher." Dann sagte das andere: „Du bist Ausländer." Sie stellten sich herausfordernd vor Ender hin. Er verharrte gebückt und mit ausgestreckter Hand. Wenn er sich noch ein bißchen bückte, könnte er die Kastanie fassen. Doch er konnte sie nicht erreichen. Den Kopf nach oben, den Kindern zugewandt, erstarrte er eine Weile in gebückter Haltung. Dann richtete er sich auf. Natürlich ohne Kastanie. Verstummt.
35 Er wollte zwar sagen: „Der Park gehört allen, jeder kann Kastanien sammeln", doch er brachte kein Wort heraus. Dafür waren die anderen um so lauter: „Du bist Ausländer. Das sind deutsche Kastanien. Wenn du sie anfaßt, kannst du was erleben", wollten sie ihm Angst einjagen.

Ender war völlig durcheinander. „Soll ich mit denen kämpfen?" schoß es ihm
40 durch den Kopf. Dann sah er mal den einen, mal den anderen an. „Gegen zwei zu kämpfen ist unklug", dachte er. Er rannte fort, ohne die beiden noch einmal anzusehen.

TEIL II

<table>
<tr><td rowspan="21" style="writing-mode: vertical-rl;">Miniwörterbuch</td><td>ablenken</td><td>to get off the subject</td></tr>
<tr><td>annehmen, nahm ... an</td><td>to accept</td></tr>
<tr><td>sich ärgern</td><td>to get angry</td></tr>
<tr><td>jemanden auf den Arm nehmen</td><td>to tease someone</td></tr>
<tr><td>darauf eingehen, ging darauf ein</td><td>to get into something</td></tr>
<tr><td>entschlossen</td><td>determined</td></tr>
<tr><td>ersticken</td><td>to suffocate</td></tr>
<tr><td>hartnäckig</td><td>obstinate</td></tr>
<tr><td>herumschwirren</td><td>to buzz around</td></tr>
<tr><td>hoppla</td><td>oops, oh boy</td></tr>
<tr><td>im Grunde</td><td>in principle</td></tr>
<tr><td>einen Jux machen</td><td>to be joking</td></tr>
<tr><td>der Kummer</td><td>trouble</td></tr>
<tr><td>nützen</td><td>to do some good</td></tr>
<tr><td>quälen</td><td>to torment</td></tr>
<tr><td>der Ranzen</td><td>school bag</td></tr>
<tr><td>schleudern</td><td>to hurl</td></tr>
<tr><td>das Staunen</td><td>amazement</td></tr>
<tr><td>die Türschwelle</td><td>threshold</td></tr>
<tr><td>das Überlegen</td><td>consideration</td></tr>
<tr><td>der Unterschied</td><td>difference, distinction</td></tr>
<tr><td></td><td>zuschnüren</td><td>to constrict</td></tr>
</table>

Als er an jenem Tag nach Hause kam, stellte Ender seiner Mutter einige Fragen. Aber seine Mutter ging nicht darauf ein. Sie lenkte ab.

45 Nun war Ender entschlossen, nach dem, was heute zwischen Stefan und ihm passiert war, die Frage endlich zu lösen, die den ganzen Tag wieder in seinem Kopf herumschwirrte. Sobald er den Fuß über die Türschwelle setzte, schleuderte er der Mutter seine Frage ins Gesicht: „Mutti, was bin ich?"

Das war eine unerwartete Frage für seine Mutter. Ebenso unerwartet war ihre Antwort: „Du bist Ender."
50

„Ich weiß, ich heiße Ender. Das habe ich nicht gefragt. Aber was bin ich?" blieb Ender hartnäckig.

„Komm erstmal herein. Nimm deinen Ranzen ab, zieh die Schuhe aus", sagte seine Mutter.

55 „Gut", sagte Ender. „Aber sag du mir auch, was ich bin."

Daraufhin dachte Enders Mutter, daß er mit ihr einen Jux machte oder ihr vielleicht ein Rätsel aufgab. „Du bist ein Schüler", sagte sie.

Ender ärgerte sich. „Du nimmst mich auf den Arm", sagte er. „Ich frage dich, was ich bin. Bin ich nun Deutscher oder Türke, was bin ich?"

60 Hoppla! Solche Fragen gefielen Enders Mutter gar nicht. Denn die Antwort darauf fiel ihr schwer. Was sollte sie da sagen? Im Grunde war das keine schwere Frage. Sie kannte auch die genaue Antwort auf diese Frage. Aber würde Ender sie auch verstehen können? Würde er sie akzeptieren, akzeptieren können? Wenn er sie auch annahm, würde ihm das überhaupt nützen?

65 Seine Mutter und sein Vater sind Türken. In der Türkei sind sie geboren, aufgewachsen und in die Schule gegangen. Nach Deutschland sind sie nur gekommen, um zu arbeiten und Geld verdienen zu können. Sie können auch gar nicht gut Deutsch. Wenn sie Deutsch sprechen, muß Ender lachen. Denn sie sprechen oft falsch. Sie können nicht alles richtig sagen.

70 Bei Ender ist es aber ganz anders. Er ist in Deutschland geboren. Hier ist er in den Kindergarten gegangen. Jetzt geht er in die erste Klasse, in eine deutsche Schule. Deutsche Kinder sind seine Freunde. In seiner Klasse sind auch einige ausländische Kinder. Ender macht aber zwischen ihnen keinen Unterschied, er kann keinen machen, dieser Deutscher, dieser nicht oder so, denn außer einem sprechen sie alle sehr gut Deutsch.

75 Da gibt es nur einen, Alfonso. Alfonso tut Ender etwas leid. Alfonso kann nicht so gut Deutsch sprechen wie die anderen Kinder. Ender denkt, daß Alfonso noch gar nicht sprechen gelernt hat. Die kleinen Kinder können doch auch nicht sprechen: so wie ein großes Baby kommt ihm Alfonso vor.

Ender spricht auch Türkisch, aber nicht so gut wie Deutsch. Wenn er Türkisch
80 spricht, mischt er oft deutsche Wörter hinein. Wie eine Muttersprache hat er Deutsch gelernt. Nicht anders als die deutschen Kinder. Manchmal hat er das Gefühl, daß zwischen ihnen doch ein Unterschied ist, weil deutsche Kinder nicht Türkisch können. Doch wenn in der Klasse der Unterricht oder auf dem Schulhof das Spielen beginnt, vergeht dieses Gefühl wieder ganz schnell. Gerade wenn er mit Stefan spielt, ist es un-
85 möglich, daß ihm ein solches Gefühl kommt.

Deshalb war sein Staunen so groß über die Worte Stefans. Und wenn Stefan nie wieder mit ihm spielte? Dann wird er sehr allein sein. Er wird sich langweilen.

Am Abend kam Enders Vater von der Arbeit nach Hause. Noch bevor die Tür sich richtig öffnete, fragte Ender: „Vati, bin ich Türke oder Deutscher?"
90 Sein Vater war sprachlos.

„Warum fragst du?" sagte er nach kurzem Überlegen.

„Ich möchte es wissen", sagte Ender entschlossen.

„Was würdest du lieber sein, ein Türke oder ein Deutscher?" fragte sein Vater.

„Was ist besser?" gab Ender die Frage wieder zurück.
95 „Beides ist gut, mein Sohn", sagte sein Vater.

„Warum hat dann Stefan heute nicht mit mir gespielt?"

So kam Ender mit seinem Kummer heraus, der ihn den ganzen Tag gequält hatte.

Point out: *dieser Deutscher dieser nicht oder so* is elliptical for *dieser [ist] Deutscher, dieser [ist] nicht oder so.*

„Warum hat er nicht mit dir gespielt?" fragte sein Vater.

„‚Du bist kein Deutscher!' hat er gesagt. Was bin ich, Vati?"

100 „Du bist Türke, mein Sohn, aber du bist in Deutschland geboren", sagte darauf sein Vater hilflos.

„Aber die Namen der deutschen Kinder sind anders als mein Name."

Sein Vater begann zu stottern.

„Dein Name ist ein türkischer Name", sagte er. „Ist Ender kein schöner Name?"

105 Ender mochte seinen Namen. „Doch! Aber er ist nicht so wie die Namen anderer Kinder", sagte er.

„Macht nichts, Hauptsache, es ist ein schöner Name!" sagte sein Vater.

„Aber Stefan spielt nicht mehr mit mir."

Enders Vater schnürte es den Hals zu. Ihm war, als ob er ersticken müßte. „Sei

110 nicht traurig", sagte er nach längerem Schweigen zu Ender. „Ich werde morgen mit Stefan sprechen. Er wird wieder mit dir spielen. Er hat sicher Spaß gemacht."

Ender schwieg.

Arbeit mit dem Text

A. Deutsche oder Ausländer? Ordnen Sie die Personen in der Geschichte den zwei Kategorien zu.

B. Wer sagt das im Text?

Ender
Enders Vater
Enders Mutter
Enders Lehrer
Stefan
Kinder im Park

1. „Du bist kein Deutscher wie ich." _____
2. „Jedes Kind bringt zehn Stück mit." _____
3. „Ich will auch Kastanien sammeln." _____
4. „Das sind deutsche Kastanien." _____
5. „Du bist Ausländer." _____
6. „Du bist Ender." _____
7. „Du bist ein Schüler." _____
8. „Bin ich nun Deutscher oder Türke, was bin ich?" _____
9. „Was würdest du lieber sein, ein Türke oder ein Deutscher?" _____
10. „Dein Name ist ein türkischer Name." _____

C. Kombinieren Sie die Satzteile.

1. Stefan sagte, dass er nicht mit Ender spielen wollte,	aber er kannte sie.
2. Ender ging weg,	damit er wieder mit Ender spielt.
3. Alle Kinder sammeln im Herbst Kastanien,	denn man kann sie gut gebrauchen.
4. Die Kinder im Park waren keine Freunde von Ender,	denn sie wusste keine Antwort.
5. Ender sammelte keine Kastanien,	mischt er oft deutsche Wörter hinein.
6. Als Ender nach Hause kam,	nachdem er mit den Kindern gesprochen hatte.
7. Die Fragen gefielen der Mutter nicht,	stellte er seiner Mutter Fragen.
8. Wenn Ender Türkisch spricht,	weil er kein Deutscher war.
9. Deutsche Kinder sind anders,	weil er traurig war.
10. Der Vater will mit Stefan sprechen,	weil sie kein Türkisch können.

Nach dem Lesen

Wie geht es weiter? Spricht Enders Vater mit Stefan? Spricht er mit Stefans Vater? Bleiben Ender und Stefan Freunde? Welche Identität entwickelt Ender? Schreiben Sie eine Fortsetzung der Geschichte. Suchen Sie sich eine der folgenden Möglichkeiten aus oder erfinden Sie etwas Eigenes.

- der nächste Tag: Enders Vater spricht mit Stefans Vater
- Enders neuer Freund
- fünf Jahre später: Ender spricht über seine Identität
- Enders Kinder: Ender erzählt seinen Kindern eine Geschichte

Das liebe Geld

Grammatik 12.4

—Ich möchte gern ein Konto eröffnen.
—Ein Spar- oder ein Girokonto?

Für diesen Geldautomaten braucht man eine Euroscheckkarte.

Wenn man Geld auf einem Sparkonto hat, bekommt man Zinsen.

Wenn man Schulden hat, muss man Zinsen zahlen.

Wenn man Geld überweisen möchte, kann man das auch per Internet tun.

Der Börsenkrach vom September 2001 war einer der schlimmsten in der Geschichte.

414   KAPITEL 12   Die moderne Gesellschaft

Situation 8 | Wer weiß–gewinnt: Geld

Sit. 8. Read definitions and answers out loud and have sts. repeat before asking them to work in groups of 3 or 4. During the follow-up phase ask for or provide expansion on the terms and concepts relating German examples to comparable ones in the sts.' own country, e.g. *Wie steht der Wechselkurs heute? In welcher Stadt ist die Börse in Deutschland?* **Answers:** 1. e, 2. f, 3. h, 4. d, 5. c, 6. a, 7. g, 8. j, 9. b, 10. i.

1. der Ort, an dem mit Aktien gehandelt wird
2. die Karte, mit der man bargeldlos bezahlen kann
3. die zahlt man, wenn man seine Kreditkarte nicht abzahlen kann
4. der Kurs, zu dem man ausländische Währung kaufen oder verkaufen kann
5. Automat, aus dem man Bargeld holen kann
6. die Münzen und Geldscheine einer Währung
7. das offizielle Zahlungsmittel eines Landes
8. das macht man, wenn man Rechnungen bargeldlos bezahlt
9. das Konto für den täglichen Gebrauch
10. das macht man, wenn man bei einer Bank neu ist

a. das Bargeld
b. das Girokonto
c. der Geldautomat
d. der Wechselkurs
e. die Börse
f. die Kreditkarte
g. die Währung
h. die Zinsen
i. ein Konto eröffnen
j. Geld überweisen

Situation 9 | Dialog: Auf der Bank

PETER: Guten Tag, ich möchte ein Konto eröffnen.

BANKANGESTELLTE: Ein Spar- oder ein Girokonto?

PETER: Ein Girokonto.

BANKANGESTELLTE: Würden Sie dann bitte dieses Formular ausfüllen?

PETER: Bekomme ich bei dem Konto auch eine EC-Karte?

BANKANGESTELLTE: Die müssen Sie extra beantragen, aber das ist kein Problem, wenn regelmäßig auf das Konto eingezahlt wird.

PETER: Ich bekomme ein Stipendium. Das soll auf dieses Konto überwiesen werden.

BANKANGESTELLTE: Gut. Die EC-Karte und Ihre Geheimzahl bekommen Sie mit der Post.

PETER: Bekomme ich auf mein Guthaben auch Zinsen?

BANKANGESTELLTE: Nein, Zinsen gibt es nur auf Sparkonten.

PETER: Habe ich bei dem Girokonto einen Überziehungskredit?

BANKANGESTELLTE: Ja, die Höhe richtet sich nach Ihrem Einkommen.

PETER: Kann ich meine Überweisungen auch übers Internet ausführen?

BANKANGESTELLTE: Natürlich. Meine Kollegin, Frau Schröder, hilft Ihnen da weiter.

PETER: Vielen Dank. Auf Wiedersehen.

BANKANGESTELLTE: Auf Wiedersehen.

Situation 10 | Interview

Sit. 10. If sts. are uncomfortable sharing personal financial information, allow them to pretend to be someone else, such as a movie star or entertainer, and give answers based on that alter ego.

1. Hast du ein Konto bei der Bank? Welche Konten hast du? Benutzt du Internet-Banking?
2. Hast du eine Kreditkarte? Wie viel kannst du damit ausgeben? Wie viel Zinsen musst du bezahlen?
3. Wie viel sparst du im Monat? Worauf sparst du? Wenn du jetzt nicht sparen kannst: Worauf würdest du sparen, wenn du Geld hättest?
4. Womit zahlst du öfter: mit Schecks, mit Kreditkarte oder mit Bargeld?
5. Wie viel Geld hast du im Monat? Wie viel Geld gibst du aus? Wofür gibst du das meiste Geld aus?
6. Hast du schon einmal einen Kredit aufgenommen? Wie hast du das gemacht?

Wie bezahlt man in Europa?

Wie ist es bei Ihnen?

- Wie bezahlen Sie meistens, wenn Sie im Supermarkt einkaufen?
- Wie bezahlen Sie, wenn Sie Ihre Miete bezahlen?
- Wie bezahlen Sie Ihre Telefonrechnung?
- Wie bezahlen Sie, wenn Sie ein Kleidungsstück oder etwas Größeres wie ein Fahrrad, ein Auto oder einen Computer kaufen?
- Wie werden Sie bei Ihrem Job bezahlt, z.B. in Bargeld, mit Scheck oder Überweisung?
- In welcher Form bekommen Sie Geld von Ihren Eltern oder finanzielle Unterstützung für Ihr Studium?

In vielen Restaurants werden keine Kreditkarten akzeptiert.

Wie ist es in Europa? Lesen Sie den Text und beantworten Sie die Fragen.

1. Wie heißt die Karte, die in Deutschland am häufigsten zum Einkaufen benutzt wird?
2. Was muss man für diese Karte bei der Bank haben?
3. Wie heißt die „elektronische Geldbörse", die man in Österreich benutzt?
4. Wie wird in Österreich immer noch am häufigsten bezahlt?
5. Wie bezahlt man normalerweise in Deutschland Miete und Rechnungen?
6. Was ist ein Dauerauftrag?
7. Wie viel Prozent der Deutschen nehmen am Internet-Banking teil?

Man zahlt daher meistens bar.

Auch in vielen Ländern Europas bezahlt man inzwischen nicht mehr so häufig mit Bargeld wie noch vor einigen Jahren. Für bargeldlose[1] Transaktionen wird in Deutschland die EC-Karte am häufigsten benutzt. Man kann mit ihr im Supermarkt, beim Tanken und in den meisten Einzelhandelsgeschäften[2] bezahlen und Geld aus dem Geldautomaten bekommen. Für eine EC-Karte braucht man ein Konto bei einer Bank, das – anders als bei Kreditkarten – bei jeder Transaktion sofort belastet[3] wird. Manchmal muss man allerdings beim Einkauf außerdem noch seinen Personalausweis zeigen.

In Österreich ist die Quickcard eine beliebte Alternative zum Bargeld. Sie funktioniert wie eine elektronische Geldbörse[4]. Man muss sie „aufladen[5]" und kann dann z.B. an Parkautomaten, in Geschäften und an Tankstellen auch kleine Beträge[6] bezahlen. Die dominierende Zahlungsform in Österreich ist aber immer noch die Bargeldtransaktion. Die beliebteste Kreditkarte in Deutschland ist die Eurocard, die zu der Organisation von Mastercard (USA) gehört. Danach kommt die Visakarte.

Rechnungen für Telefon, Nebenkosten oder Miete bezahlt man bargeldlos mit Überweisungen vom Girokonto oder Bankeinzug[7] (der Betrag wird automatisch von der Bank des Empfängers[8] eingezogen). Damit man die monatlichen Zahlungen nicht vergisst, kann man sie per Dauerauftrag[9] überweisen lassen. Das heißt, man gibt seiner Bank einmal den Auftrag[10] und zu einem bestimmten Termin wird der Betrag automatisch überwiesen. Immer beliebter wird auch das Internet-Banking, das inzwischen von ungefähr 40% der Deutschen genutzt wird, vor allem für Überweisungen und Daueraufträge oder zum Überprüfen des Kontostandes.

[1]cash-free [2]retail shops [3]debited [4]wallet [5]charge, recharge [6]amounts [7]automatic withdrawal, i.e. electronic funds transfer [8]payee [9]standing order, i.e. recurring bill-pay [10]order

Situation 11 | Rollenspiel: Auf der Bank

Sit 11. The role for s2 appears in Appendix B.

S1: Sie haben ein Stipendium für ein Jahr an der Universität Leipzig. Sie wollen bei der Deutschen Bank ein Konto eröffnen. Fragen Sie auch nach den Zinsen, nach Onlinezugang und EC-Karte und ob Sie Ihr Konto überziehen dürfen.

die Mundharmonika

die Trompete

die Orgel

die Blockflöte

das Schlagzeug

die Querflöte

der Brennofen

die Töpferscheibe

die Figur aus Ton

die Ölfarben

der Pinsel

die Staffelei

der Meißel

der Stein

der Hammer

Situation 12 | Wer weiß–gewinnt: Kunst und Literatur

Sit. 12. Read questions and answers out loud and have sts. repeat before asking them to work in groups of 3 or 4. Sts. will know only some of these, but they can mark the ones they know and find others by process of elimination. During the follow-up phase ask for or give additional information on the people mentioned according to the interests of your particular class. **Answers:** 1. a, 2. c, 3. e, 4. g, 5. f, 6. d, 7. h, 8. b.

1. Welches Instrument gehört normalerweise nicht in ein Symphonieorchester?
2. Was braucht ein Bildhauer für seine Kunst?
3. Was war Theodor Storm von Beruf?
4. Von wem sind die Brandenburgischen Konzerte?
5. Was war Marlene Dietrich von Beruf?
6. Was brauchte Paul Klee für seine Kunst?
7. Wer schrieb die Tragödie „Faust"?
8. Welches Instrument spielt die Musikerin Anne-Sophie Mutter?

a. Blockflöte
b. Geige
c. Stein, Hammer und Meißel
d. Staffelei, Pinsel und Farben
e. Schriftsteller/in
f. Schauspieler/in
g. Johann Sebastian Bach
h. Johann Wolfgang von Goethe

Situation 13 | Interview

1. Hörst du gern Musik? Was für Musik? Hast du einen Lieblingskomponisten oder eine Lieblingskomponistin?
2. Spielst du ein Instrument oder singst du?
3. Liest du gern? Was liest du gern: Romane, Gedichte, Dramen, Comics? Welche Schriftsteller magst du besonders gern? Hast du etwas von deutschen Schriftstellern gelesen?
4. Hast du schon mal etwas geschrieben? Was?
5. Welche Maler, Bildhauer oder Grafiker magst du am liebsten?
6. Malst oder zeichnest du? Welche Motive magst du am liebsten? (Berge? das Meer? eine Blumenvase?) Arbeitest du mit anderen Materialien wie Holz, Ton oder Stein?
7. Gehst du gern ins Theater? Welche Stücke gefallen dir besonders gut?
8. Hast du schon mal Theater gespielt? Welche Rollen hast du gespielt? Wie war das?

Situation 14 | Faust: Die einfache Version

Eins der bekanntesten Werke der deutschen Literatur ist die Tragödie „Faust" von Goethe. Was in „Faust" geschieht, finden Sie in den folgenden Sätzen. Bringen Sie die Sätze in die richtige Reihenfolge.

TEIL 1

_2_ Als Faust an einem Osternachmittag spazieren geht, sieht er einen schwarzen Pudel, der ihm nach Hause folgt.

_5_ Nach ihrer Unterhaltung gehen Mephisto und Faust in eine Hexenküche. Dort zeigt ihm Mephisto einen magischen Spiegel.

_1_ Faust ist ein berühmter Wissenschaftler, der sehr unzufrieden ist, weil er nicht alles weiß.

_4_ Faust spricht lange mit Mephisto und verspricht ihm seine Seele für einen Augenblick vollkommenen Glücks.

_3_ In Fausts Studierzimmer verwandelt sich der Pudel in Mephisto.

_6_ Im Spiegel sieht Faust eine wunderschöne Frau.

_7_ Kurz danach lernt Faust Gretchen kennen und verliebt sich in sie.

___7___ Aber Gretchen will nicht vom Teufel gerettet werden und bittet Gott um Vergebung.

___8___ Als Gretchen stirbt, hört man eine Stimme von oben, die sagt: „Sie ist gerettet."

___3___ Als Gretchen vom Tod ihres Bruders hört, wird sie wahnsinnig, und als ihr Kind geboren wird, tötet sie es.

___6___ Auf dem Brocken hat Faust eine Vision von Gretchen, und er und Mephisto eilen ins Gefängnis, um sie zu retten.

___2___ Faust und Valentin kämpfen. Faust tötet Valentin und verlässt die Stadt.

___4___ Gretchen wird ins Gefängnis geworfen und zum Tode verurteilt.

___1___ Gretchen wird schwanger. Valentin, ihr Bruder, will deshalb Faust töten.

___5___ Während Gretchen im Gefängnis sitzt, steigen Faust und Mephisto in der Walpurgisnacht auf den Brocken und feiern mit den Hexen.

Situation 15 | Rollenspiel: An der Kinokasse

Sit. 14. Before sts. mark the statements, summarize the play with books closed, loosely following the description in the activity, e.g.: *Faust ist eine der berühmtesten Geschichten der deutschen Literatur. Faust selbst ist ein Wissenschaftler, der mit seinem Leben sehr unzufrieden ist, weil er nicht alles weiß. Er hat viele Fächer studiert, aber es gibt vieles, was er nicht weiß und das macht ihn sehr unzufrieden.*

s1: Sie wollen mit vier Freunden in die „Rocky Horror Picture Show". Das Kino ist schon ziemlich ausverkauft. Sie wollen aber unbedingt mit ihren Freunden zusammensitzen und Reis werfen. Fragen Sie, wann, zu welchem Preis und wo noch fünf Plätze übrig sind.

Lektüre

Vor dem Lesen

A. Beantworten Sie die folgenden Fragen.

1. Was bedeutet „afro-deutsch"? Was assoziieren Sie mit diesem Begriff?
2. Was meinen Sie, haben es Afro-Deutsche schwerer in der deutschen Gesellschaft als andere Deutsche? Warum?

Studentinnen in einer Vorlesung an einer Fachhochschule in Deutschland.

B. Lesen Sie die Wörter im Miniwörterbuch. Suchen Sie sie im Text und unterstreichen Sie sie.

afro-deutsch I

von May Ayim

Sie sind afro-deutsch?
… ah, ich verstehe: afrikanisch und deutsch. Ist ja 'ne interessante Mischung!
Wissen Sie, manche, die denken ja immer noch, die Mulatten, die würden's
nicht so weit bringen wie die Weißen.

5 Ich glaube das nicht. Ich meine, bei entsprechender Erziehung …
Sie haben ja echt Glück, dass Sie hier aufgewachsen sind. Bei deutschen
Eltern sogar. Schau an!

Wollen Sie denn mal zurück?
Wie, Sie waren noch nie in der Heimat vom Papa? Ist ja traurig … Also, wenn
10 Se mich fragen: So 'ne Herkunft, das prägt eben doch ganz schön. Ich z.B.,
ich bin aus Westfalen, und ich finde, da gehör' ich auch hin …

Ach Menschenskind! Dat ganze Elend in der Welt! Sei'n Se froh, dass Se nich
im Busch geblieben sind. Da wär'n Se heute nich so weit!

Ich meine, Sie sind ja wirklich ein intelligentes Mädchen. Wenn Se fleißig sind
15 mit Studieren, können Se ja Ihren Leuten in Afrika helfen: Dafür sind Sie doch
prädestiniert, auf Sie hör'n die doch bestimmt, während unsereins ist ja so 'n
Kulturgefälle …

Wie meinen Sie das? Hier was machen. Was woll'n Se denn hier schon
machen? Ok, ok, es ist nicht alles eitel Sonnenschein. Aber ich finde, jeder
20 sollte erstmal vor seiner eigenen Tür fegen!

Arbeit mit dem Text

1. Wer spricht hier (z.B. Herkunft, Geschlecht, Alter)? Ist es ein Monolog oder redet die Person mit jemandem? Wenn ja, mit wem?
2. Die Sprache des Gedichts scheint, als würde sie gesprochen. Woran sieht man das? Suchen Sie Beispiele im Text.
3. Suchen Sie Wörter, die im Gedicht Deutschland/Deutsche auf der einen und Afrika / Menschen afrikanischer Herkunft auf der anderen Seite beschreiben. Sind die Wörter positiv oder negativ?

4. Welche Meinung hat der Sprecher / die Sprecherin zu Afro-Deutschen? Suchen Sie Beispiele.
5. Charakterisieren Sie den Sprecher / die Sprecherin. Erarbeiten Sie ein Porträt der Person mit ihren Eigenschaften, Einstellungen und Meinungen. Ergänzen Sie gute Adjektive.
6. Was ist die Hauptaussage[1] des Gedichts?

Nach dem Lesen

Schreiben Sie aus der Perspektive des/der Afro-Deutschen in diesem Gedicht. Antworten auf die einzelnen Fragen.

> MODELL: A: Sie sind afro-deutsch?
> B: Ja, mein Vater ist aus Kenia und meine Mutter aus Berlin.
> A: … ah, ich verstehe: afrikanisch und deutsch. Ist ja 'ne interessante Mischung! …

[1] main message

Videoecke

- Hast du ausländische Bekannte?
- Wie fühlen die sich in Deutschland?
- Arbeiten deine Eltern?
- Wer macht was im Haushalt?
- Was ist für dich die ideale Rollenverteilung?
- Hast du ein Haustier? (Hattest du ein Haustier?)
- Wie hast du's bekommen?
- Was ist mit ihm passiert?

Ulrike ist in Langendorf geboren. Sie studiert Ethnologie und Deutsch als Fremdsprache. Sie spielt gern Klavier und geht gern ins Kino.

Anke ist in Leipzig geboren. Sie studiert Kommunikations- und Medienwissenschaft. Sie treibt gern Sport und sie geht gern auf Reisen.

Aufgabe 1

Ergänzen Sie den Text mit den passenden Wörtern.

türkische   koreanische
wohl   griechische

Ulrike hat eine _____ Freundin. Anke hat eine _____ Freundin und eine _____ Freundin. Alle drei fühlen sich in Deutschland _____.

Aufgabe 2

Welcher Beruf gehört zu wem? Verbinden Sie die Satzteile.

1. Ulrikes Mutter	ist Bauamtsleiter.
2. Ulrikes Vater	ist Diplomingenieur für Maschinenbau.
3. Ankes Mutter	ist Agraringenieur.
4. Ankes Vater	hat ein Modehaus.

Aufgabe 3

Welche Antwort gehört zu welcher Frage?

1. _____ Welches Haustier hatte Ulrikes Schwester?
2. _____ Was ist mit ihm passiert?
3. _____ Welches Haustier hat Anke?
4. _____ Warum hat sie es von ihrer Freundin bekommen?

a. Sie hat einen schwarzen Kater.
b. Sie hat eine Katzenallergie und konnte ihn nicht mehr behalten.
c. Sie hatte einen Wellensittich.
d. Er hat sich beim Fliegen verletzt und ist daran gestorben.

Wortschatz

Partner und Familie	Partners and Family
die Ehe, -n	marriage
die Konfession, -en	religious denomination, church
die Scheidung, -en	divorce
die Verantwortung, -en	responsibility
der Beschützer, -	protector
der Vertrag, ⸚e	contract
der Ehevertrag, ⸚e	prenuptial agreement
das Berufsleben	career, professional life
sich kümmern um	to take care of
mit·versorgen	to be equally responsible for taking care of
sorgen für	to take care of
übernehmen, übernimmt, übernahm, übernommen	to take on (responsibility)
sich verheiraten mit	to get married to
verheiratet sein	to be married
sich verlieben in (+ akk.) (R)	to fall in love with
verliebt sein	to be in love
sich verloben mit	to get engaged to
verlobt sein	to be engaged

Ähnliche Wörter

die Hausfrau, -en; die Partnerin, -nen; die Ehepartnerin, -nen; die Partnerschaft, -en; der Hausmann, ⸚er; der Partner, -; der Ehepartner, -

Multikulturelle Gesellschaft	Multicultural Society
die Arbeitserlaubnis, -se	work permit
die Arbeitskraft, ⸚e	labor; employee
die Aufenthaltserlaubnis, -se	residence permit
die Ausländerin, -nen	female foreigner
die Behörde, -n	public authority
die Branche, -n	sector
die EDV = elektronische Datenverarbeitung	electronic data processing
die Formalität, -en	formality
die Türkin, -nen	Turkish woman
der Ausländer, -	male foreigner
der Ausländerhass	hostility toward foreigners
der Bereich, -e	sector, area
der Einwanderer, - (R)	immigrant
der Einzelgänger, -	loner
der Flüchtling, -e	refugee
der Türke, -n (wk. masc.)	Turkish man
der Vorfahre, -n (wk. masc.) (R)	ancestor
das Einwohnermeldeamt, ⸚er	office to register town residents
das Vorurteil, -e	prejudice
die Personalien (pl.)	personal data
sich an·melden	to register
auf·fallen, fällt ... auf, fiel ... auf, ist aufgefallen	to be noticeable

aus·üben	to practice
aus·wandern, ist ausgewandert (R)	to emigrate
beantragen	to apply for
bereichern	to enrich
ein·wandern, ist eingewandert	to immigrate
sich registrieren lassen	to get registered
verfolgen	to persecute

Ähnliche Wörter

die Heimat, -en; die Integration; die Kultur, -en; die Tradition, -en (R); der Neonazi, -s; der Rechtsextremist, -en (*wk. masc.*); das Heimatland, ⸚er; das Visum, Visa (R); diskriminieren

Das liebe Geld	Beloved Money
die Aktie, -n	share, stock
die Börse, -n	stock exchange
die Euroscheckkarte, -n	Eurocheque Card
die Geheimzahl, -en	secret PIN (personal identification number)
die Höhe, -n	height; amount (*of money*)
die Schuld, -en	debt
die Überweisung, -en	transfer (*of money*)
die Währung, -en	currency
der Börsenkrach, ⸚e	stock market crash
der Gebrauch, ⸚e	use
der Geldautomat, -en (*wk. masc.*)	automatic teller machine (ATM)
der Überziehungskredit, -e	overdraft protection
der Zugang	access
das Bargeld	cash
das Einkommen	income
das Formular, -e	form
das Girokonto, Girokonten	checking account
das Guthaben	bank balance
das Sparkonto, Sparkonten	savings account
das Zahlungsmittel	means of payment
die Zinsen (*pl.*)	interest
ab·zahlen	to pay off
auf·nehmen, nimmt ... auf, nahm ... auf, aufgenommen	to take out (*a loan*)
aus·führen	to carry out, execute

Ähnliche Wörter

der Geldschein, -e

Kunst und Literatur	Art and Literature
die Bildhauerei	sculpture
die Bildhauerin, -nen	female sculptor

die Blockflöte, -n	recorder
die Kasse, -n (R)	cashier window
die Malerei	painting
die Ölfarbe, -n	oil color (*paint*)
die Orgel, -n	organ
die Querflöte, -n	(transverse) flute
die Seele, -n	soul
die Staffelei, -en	easel
die Stimme, -n	voice
die Töpferei	ceramic art
die Töpferscheibe, -n	potter's wheel
der Bildhauer, -	male sculptor
der Brennofen, ⸚	kiln
der Meißel, -	chisel
der Pinsel, -	paintbrush
der Stein, -e	stone
der Teufel, -	devil
der Tod, -e	death
der Ton	clay
das Gemälde, -	painting
das Holz, ⸚er	wood
das Motiv, -e	motif, theme
das Schauspiel, -e	play
das Schlagzeug, -e	drum
malen	to paint
vollkommen	flawless, perfect
wahnsinnig	crazy, insane

Ähnliche Wörter

die Figur, -en; die Mundharmonika, -s; die Skulptur, -en; die Tragödie, -n; die Trompete, -n; der Gott, ⸚er; der Pakt, -e; das Instrument, -e; das Material, -ien; klassisch; magisch

Sonstige Substantive	Other Nouns
die Einstellung, -en	attitude
die Gewalt	violence
der Stichpunkt, -e	main point
der Träger, -	recipient (*of a prize*)
der Unsinn	nonsense

Ähnliche Wörter

die Chance [ʃansə], -n; die Intelligenz; die Krise, -n; die Steinzeit; die Technik; der Charakter; der Chauvi [ʃovi], -s; der Fanatiker, -; der Fernsehfilm, -e; der Preis, -e; der Text, -e

Sonstige Verben	Other Verbs
an·gehören (+ *dat.*)	to belong to (*an organization*)
an·greifen, griff an, angegriffen	to attack

auf·wachsen, wächst ... auf,   to grow up
   wuchs ... auf, ist
   aufgewachsen
binden an (+ *akk.*)   to tie to
erreichen   to reach
erwarten   to expect
fördern   to promote
halten von, hält, hielt,   to think of
   gehalten
verschwinden,   to disappear
   verschwand,
   ist verschwunden

Ähnliche Wörter

auf·hängen, interviewen [intevjuan], protestieren

Adjektive und Adverbien	Adjectives and Adverbs
ausgebildet	educated
ausländisch	foreign
bargeldlos	cash-free
eng	tight; narrow; small
fleißig	industrious
geborgen	protected
geduldig	patient
handwerklich	handy

komisch   funny, strange
lustig   fun, funny
minderwertig   inferior
neugierig   curious
peinlich   embarrassing
rechtzeitig   timely, on time
selbstständig   independent
unbegabt   untalented

Ähnliche Wörter

afro-deutsch, dominant, gemütlich, ideal, illegal,
konkret, logisch, russisch

Sonstige Wörter und Ausdrücke	Other Words and Expressions
anstatt (+ *gen.*)	instead of
außerhalb (+ *gen.*)	outside of
eher	rather
einverstanden	in agreement
einverstanden sein mit	to be in agreement with
statt (+ *gen.*)	instead of
trotz (+ *gen.*)	in spite of
überall	everywhere
um ... zu	in order to
wohl	probably

Strukturen und Übungen

12.1 The genitive case

Spoken German: Possession may be indicated by **von**.

As you have learned, the preposition **von** followed by the dative case is commonly used in spoken German to express possession.

Das ist das Haus **von meinen Eltern.**	*This is my parents' house.*

Written German: Use the genitive case to indicate possession.

In writing, and sometimes in speech, this relationship between two noun phrases may also be expressed with the genitive case. The genitive case in German is equivalent to both the *of*-phrase and the possessive with 's in English.

Kennst du den Freund **meiner Schwester?**	*Do you know my sister's friend?*
Die Farbe **des Mantels** gefällt mir nicht.	*I don't like the color of the coat.*

Wissen Sie noch?

You can show possession using possessive adjectives, such as **mein** (*my*), **dein** (*your*), and **sein** (*his/its*), or by placing an **-s** after someone's name, for example **Julias Buch.**

Review grammar B.5 and 2.4.

The genitive is also required by certain prepositions. The most common ones are these:

(an)statt	*instead of*
trotz	*in spite of*
während	*during*
wegen	*because of*

Anstatt eines Fernsehers hätte ich mir ein neues Fahrrad gekauft.	*Instead of a TV, I would have bought myself a new bike.*
Trotz des vielen Regens ist noch nicht genügend Wasser in den Tanks.	*In spite of all the rain, there's still not enough water in the tanks.*
Während der letzten Tage bin ich nicht viel aus dem Haus gekommen.	*During the last few days I haven't gotten out of the house much.*
Wegen dieser dummen Situation kann ich jetzt nicht zur Hochzeit kommen.	*Because of this stupid situation, I can't come to the wedding now.*

12.1. *Genitiv.* We emphasize that the genitive case is used mostly in writing and that the construction *von* + dative usually indicates possession in speech. At this point, we do not expect sts. to be able to produce genitive endings with consistent accuracy when speaking.

Stress that, with the exception of names, word order in German with both the genitive and with *von* + dative corresponds to the word order of the English pattern with *of*.

When the attributive adjective is preceded by a determiner, sts. can use the following strategy: Look to see if the noun is dative, genitive, or plural. If it is, the adjective ending is always *-en*.

English tends to use the possessive 's with nouns denoting people (for example, *the girl's mother*). In German, -s (without the apostrophe) is added only to *proper names* of people and places.

Noras Vater	*Nora's father*
Englands Rettung	*England's salvation*

A. Nouns in the Genitive

Feminine nouns and plural nouns do not add any endings in the genitive case. In the singular genitive, masculine and neuter nouns of more than one syllable add -s and those of one syllable add -es: **die Farbe des Vogels, die Größe des Hauses.**

Masculine	Neuter	Feminine	Plural
des Vater**s**	des Kind**es**	der Mutter	der Eltern

B. Articles and Article-like Words in the Genitive

In the genitive case, all determiners (**der**-words and **ein**-words) end in -**es** in the masculine and neuter singular, and in -**er** in the feminine singular and all plural forms.

Masculine	Neuter	Feminine	Plural
d**es** Mannes	d**es** Kindes	d**er** Frau	d**er** Eltern
ein**es** Mannes	ein**es** Kindes	ein**er** Frau	
mein**es** Mannes	mein**es** Kindes	mein**er** Frau	mein**er** Eltern
dies**es** Mannes	dies**es** Kindes	dies**er** Frau	dies**er** Eltern

C. Adjectives in the Genitive

In the genitive, all adjectives end in -**en** when preceded by a determiner.*

Masculine and Neuter	Feminine and Plural
des arm**en** Mannes	der arm**en** Frau
des arm**en** Kindes	der arm**en** Leute

Eine mögliche Rolle des modernen Mannes ist es, zu Hause zu bleiben und auf die Kinder aufzupassen.

A possible role for a modern man is to stay home and take care of the children.

Übung 1 | Minidialoge

Üb. 1–3. The three exercises on the genitive can be given as homework and checked in class.

Ergänzen Sie die Wörter in Klammern.

1. KATRIN: Ist das dein Auto?
   ALBERT: Nein, das ist das Auto _____ Bruders. (mein)
2. BEAMTER: Was ist das Alter _____ Kinder? (Ihr)
   FRAU FRISCH: Natalie ist fünf, Rosemarie ist sechs und Lydia ist neun Jahre alt.
3. FRAU SCHULZ: Ist es wichtig, dass der Partner einen guten Beruf hat?
   THOMAS: Also, ich muss sagen, der Beruf _____ zukünftigen Partnerin ist mir ziemlich egal. (mein)
4. MONIKA: Möchtest du mit mir in die Berge fahren? Meine Eltern haben da ein Wochenendhaus.
   ROLF: Wo ist denn das Wochenendhaus _____ Eltern? (dein)
   MONIKA: In der Nähe von Lake Tahoe.
5. HEIDI: Kennst du den Film „M–Mörder unter uns"?
   ROLF: Ja.
   HEIDI: Wie heißt doch noch mal der Regisseur _____ Films? (dies-)
6. ROLF: Brauchst du denn kein neues Nummernschild?
   PETER: Ach, ich nehme einfach das Nummernschild meines _____ Autos. (alt)

---

*Unpreceded masculine and neuter adjectives also end in -**en;** unpreceded feminine and plural adjectives end in -**er.** Unpreceded adjectives, however, rarely occur in the genitive.

7. FRAU GRETTER: Wer ist denn das?

   FRAU KÖRNER: Das ist die zweite Frau meines _____ Mannes. (erst-)

8. FRAU AUGENTHALER: 24352 – was ist denn das für eine Telefonnummer?

   RICHARD: Das ist die Telefonnummer meiner _____ Freundin. (neu)

Übung 2 | Worüber sprechen sie?

Bilden Sie Sätze.

> MODELL: Albert sagt, dass sein Auto rot ist. →
> Albert spricht über die Farbe seines Autos.

das Alter
der Beruf
das Bild
die Kleidung
die Länge
die Qualität
die Situation
die Sprache

1. Monika sagt, dass ihre Schwester als Lehrerin arbeitet.
2. Thomas sagt, dass sein Vater einen Picasso besitzt.
3. Frau Schulz sagt, dass ihre Nichten fünf und acht Jahre alt sind.
4. Stefan sagt, dass sein Studium insgesamt fünf Jahre dauert.
5. Albert sagt, dass seine Großeltern nur Spanisch sprechen.
6. Nora sagt, dass ihr Freund gern Jeans und lange Pullover trägt.
7. Thomas sagt, dass das Leitungswasser in Berkeley sehr gut ist.
8. Katrin sagt, dass Frauen für die gleiche Arbeit immer noch weniger verdienen als Männer.

Übung 3 | Minidialoge

Ergänzen Sie **statt**, **trotz**, **während** oder **wegen**.

1. KATRIN: Bist du _____ des Regens spazieren gegangen?

   THOMAS: Ja, so ein bisschen Regen macht doch nichts.

2. MONIKA: Warst du gestern im Kino?

   HEIDI: Nein, _____ der Prüfung bin ich zu Hause geblieben.

3. ALBERT: Was machst du _____ der Ferien?

   PETER: Ich fliege nach Bali.

4. JÜRGEN: Ich muss _____ meiner Erkältung zur Uni.

   SILVIA: Du Ärmster, leg dich lieber ins Bett!

5. PETER: Fährst du nächste Woche weg?

   KATRIN: Ich kann doch _____ des Semesters nicht verreisen!

6. JOCHEN: Warum bist du mit dem Bus gefahren?

   JUTTA: _____ des schlechten Wetters.

7. MARIA: Hast du dir ein neues Auto gekauft?

   MICHAEL: Nein, _____ des Autos habe ich mir einen Computer gekauft.

8. KATRIN: In deinem Zimmer ist es _____ der Heizung kalt!

   STEFAN: Tut mir leid, sie funktioniert nicht richtig.

12.2 Expressing possibility: *würde, hätte, and ware*

würde = would

Use the construction **würde** + infinitive to talk about possibilities: things you would do, if you were in that particular situation.

Stell dir vor, du würdest nach Deutschland fliegen. Wo würdest du übernachten?	*Imagine you were flying to Germany. Where would you stay for the night?*

Here are the forms of **würde,** which are the subjunctive forms of the verb **werden.**

<table>
<tr><th colspan="4">werden</th></tr>
<tr><td>ich</td><td>würde</td><td>wir</td><td>würden</td></tr>
<tr><td>du</td><td>würdest</td><td>ihr</td><td>würdet</td></tr>
<tr><td>Sie</td><td>würden</td><td>Sie</td><td>würden</td></tr>
<tr><td>er
sie
es</td><td>würde</td><td>sie</td><td>würden</td></tr>
</table>

Wissen Sie noch?

Würde functions like a modal verb. In sentences with modal verbs, the infinitive appears at the end of the sentence.

Review grammar 3.1 and 3.2.

Instead of using **würde sein** and **würde haben,** German speakers prefer to say **ware** (*would be*) and **hätte** (*would have*).

Ich glaube, dass ich eine gute Mutter **ware.**	*I believe I would be a good mother.*
Ich **hätte** sicher viel Zeit für meine Kinder.	*I'm sure I would have plenty of time for my kids.*

Here are the forms of **ware** and **hätte,** which are the subjunctive forms of **sein** and **haben.**

<table>
<tr><th colspan="4">sein</th><th colspan="4">haben</th></tr>
<tr><td>ich</td><td>ware</td><td>wir</td><td>wären</td><td>ich</td><td>hätte</td><td>wir</td><td>hätten</td></tr>
<tr><td>du</td><td>wärst</td><td>ihr</td><td>wärt</td><td>du</td><td>hättest</td><td>ihr</td><td>hättet</td></tr>
<tr><td>Sie</td><td>wären</td><td>Sie</td><td>wären</td><td>Sie</td><td>hätten</td><td>Sie</td><td>hätten</td></tr>
<tr><td>er
sie
es</td><td>ware</td><td>sie</td><td>wären</td><td>er
sie
es</td><td>hätte</td><td>sie</td><td>hätten</td></tr>
</table>

Übung 4 | Kein Problem

Was würden Sie in diesen Situationen machen? Beantworten Sie die Fragen! Was würden Sie machen, ...

1. wenn Sie sich in Ihren Lehrer / Ihre Lehrerin verlieben würden?
2. wenn Sie sich um Ihre Eltern kümmern müssten?
3. wenn Ihr Partner / Ihre Partnerin eine andere Konfession hätte als Sie?
4. wenn Sie / Ihre Partnerin schwanger werden würden/würde?
5. wenn Sie sich mit Ihrem Partner / Ihrer Partnerin nicht mehr verstehen würden?

Was wäre, wenn ...

Schreiben Sie für jede Perspektive drei Sätze darüber, wie Ihr Leben aussehen würde. Verwenden Sie **hätte, wäre** und **würde** in Ihrer Antwort. Sie können nicht nur über sich selbst schreiben, sondern auch über andere (z.B. Kinder, Eltern, Partner und Freunde).

MODELL: Wenn ich Kinder hätte, würde ich nicht so oft ins Kino gehen. Ich hätte wahrscheinlich viel mehr Arbeit. Abends wäre ich bestimmt müder.

Was wäre, wenn ...

1. Sie (keine) Kinder hätten?
2. Sie (nicht) verheiratet wären?
3. Sie (kein) Geld hätten?
4. Sie in einem anderen Land leben würden?
5. Sie ein berühmter Schauspieler / eine berühmte Schauspielerin wären?

12.3. *Kausalsätze und Finalsätze.* We contrast here the use of *um ... zu* and *damit* for expressing a purpose. Point out that the word *damit* can be both a conjunction and a *da*-compound. This section also reviews *weil*-clauses, which were introduced in Section 3.4.

12.3 Causality and purpose: *weil, damit, um ... zu*

weil = reason for action
damit = goal of action
um ... zu = goal of action

Use **weil** + dependent clause to express the reason for a particular action. Use **damit** or **um ... zu** to express the goal of an action.

Viele Deutsche wanderten nach Australien aus, **weil ihnen Deutschland zu eng war.**	*Many Germans emigrated to Australia because Germany was too crowded for them.*
Sie wanderten nach Australien aus, **um dort eine bessere Arbeit zu finden.**	*They emigrated to Australia in order to find a better job there.*

Wissen Sie noch?

You can show reasons for action with the conjunctions **weil** and **denn.**

Review grammar 3.4 and 11.5.

Weil and **damit** introduce a dependent clause. Recall that the conjugated verb is in last position in a dependent clause.

Albert steht auf, damit Frau Schulz sich setzen **kann.**	*Albert gets up so that Frau Schulz can sit down.*

Damit and **um ... zu** both express the aim or goal of an action. But whereas **damit** introduces a dependent clause complete with subject and conjugated verb, **um ... zu** introduces a dependent infinitive without a subject and without a conjugated verb. Use **damit** when the subject of the main clause is different from the subject of the dependent clause.

Um ... zu clauses have no expressed subjects.

Heidi macht das Fenster zu, **damit** Stefan nicht friert.
Heidi closes the window so that Stefan won't be cold.

Use **um ... zu** when the understood subject of the dependent infinitive is the same as the subject of the main clause.

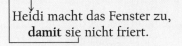

Heidi macht das Fenster zu, **damit** sie nicht friert.	→ Heidi macht das Fenster zu, **um** nicht **zu** frieren.
Heidi closes the window so that she won't be cold.	→ *Heidi closes the window so as not to be cold.*

Üb. 6. Point out that when the *um ... zu* clause is first, as it is here, it counts as the first sentence element, and the verb of the main clause follows the comma. Assign for homework and check in class.

Was muss man tun, um Erfolg an der Universität zu haben?

MODELL: Um gute Noten zu bekommen, muss man fleißig lernen.

1. morgens munter[1] sein
2. die Professoren kennenlernen
3. die Mitstudenten kennenlernen
4. am Wochenende nicht allein sein
5. die Kurse bekommen, die man will
6. in vier Jahren fertig werden
7. nicht verhungern
8. eine gute Note in Deutsch bekommen

a. früh ins Bett gehen
b. in die Sprechstunde gehen
c. jeden Tag zum Unterricht kommen
d. Leute einladen
e. regelmäßig essen
f. sich so früh wie möglich einschreiben
g. viel Gruppenarbeit machen
h. viel lernen and wenig Feste feiern

Übung 7 | Gute Gründe?

Verbinden Sie Sätze aus der ersten Gruppe mit Sätzen aus der zweiten Gruppe mit Hilfe der Konjunktionen **weil, damit, um ... zu.** Wenn Ihnen ein Grund nicht gefällt, suchen Sie einen besseren Grund.

MODELL: Ich möchte immer hier leben. Dieses Land ist das beste Land der Welt. →
Ich möchte immer hier leben, weil dieses Land das beste Land der Welt ist.

GRUPPE 1

Ich möchte immer hier leben.
Ich möchte für ein paar Jahre in Deutschland leben.
Ausländer haben oft Probleme.
Wenn ich Kinder habe, möchte ich hier leben.
Viele Ausländer kommen hierher.
Englisch sollte die einzige offizielle Sprache (der USA, Kanadas, Australiens, usw.) sein.

GRUPPE 2

Ausländer verstehen die Sprache und Kultur des Gastlandes nicht.
Ich möchte richtig gut Deutsch lernen.
Dieses Land ist das beste Land der Welt.
Hier kann man gut Geld verdienen.
Meine Kinder sollen als (Amerikaner, Kanadier, Australier, usw.) aufwachsen.
Aus der multikulturellen Bevölkerung soll eine homogene Gemeinschaft werden.

12.4 Principles of case (summary review)

Three main factors determine the choice of a particular case for a given noun: function, prepositions, and verbs.

A. Function

Function refers to the role a particular noun plays within a sentence: the subject, the direct object, the indirect object, or the possessive. The subject of a

---

[1]*wide awake*

sentence (who or what is doing something) is in the nominative case; the direct object (the thing or person to which or to whom the action is done) is in the accusative case; the indirect object (usually the person who benefits from the action) is in the dative case.

NOM   DAT   ACC

Maria schreibt ihrer Freundin einen Scheck.   *Maria is writing*
her friend a check.

Possessives express relationships of various kinds, such as belonging to or being part of someone or something. Possessives are in the genitive case.

Der Kurs **des Euro** ist leider   *The exchange rate of the euro*
    wieder gestiegen.   *has unfortunately risen again.*

B. Prepositions

Nouns or pronouns that follow prepositions are always in a case other than the nominative. You have encountered four groups of prepositions so far: those that take the accusative, those that take the dative, two-way prepositions that take either the accusative or the dative according to the meaning of the clause, and those that take the genitive.

Accusative	Dative	Accusative or Dative	Genitive
durch	aus	an	(an)statt
für	außer	auf	trotz
gegen	bei	hinter	während
ohne	mit	in	wegen
um	nach	neben	
	seit	über	
	von	unter	
	zu	vor	
		zwischen	

Bargeld können Sie **aus dem**   *You can get cash from the ATM.*
    Geldautomaten bekommen.
Wegen des Feiertags bleiben die   *Because of the holiday,*
    Banken geschlossen.   *the banks remain closed.*

Two-way prepositions require accusative objects when movement toward a *destination* is involved. They require dative objects when no such destination is expressed, when the focus is on the setting of the action or state (*location*).

Ich habe kein Geld **auf meinem**   *I don't have any money in my savings*
    Sparkonto.   *account.*
Ich muss Geld **auf mein Sparkonto**   *I have to transfer money to my savings*
    überweisen.   *account.*

C. Verbs

Certain verbs, just like prepositions, require a noun or pronoun to be in a particular case. The verbs **sein, werden, bleiben,** and **heißen** establish identity relationships between the subject and the predicate, and therefore require a predicate noun in the *nominative* case.

Thomas ist **ein fleißiger Student.**   *Thomas is a conscientious student.*

The following verbs are among those that require *dative* objects.

antworten	*to answer*
begegnen	*to meet*
fehlen	*to be missing*
gefallen	*to be to one's liking*
gehören	*to belong to*
gratulieren	*to congratulate*
helfen	*to help*
passen	*to fit*
schaden	*to be harmful (to)*
schmecken	*to taste good (to)*
stehen	*to suit, look good on* (e.g. clothing)
zuhören	*to listen to*

Die Aktien gehören **meiner Mutter.**	*The stocks belong to my mother.*
Eine schwache Wirtschaft schadet **den Aktienmärkten.**	*A weak economy hurts the stock markets.*

Most other verbs require the accusative, if they require an object at all.

Ich habe für mein Konto **keinen Überziehungskredit.**	*I don't have any overdraft protection for my account.*

Übung 8 | Der Umzug

Bestimmen Sie den Kasus (**Nom, Akk, Dat** oder **Gen**) der unterstrichenen Nominalphrasen und geben Sie an, ob dieser Kasus wegen der Funktion (**F**), wegen der Präposition (**P**) oder wegen des Verbs (**V**) benutzt wurde.

	KASUS	GRUND
1. <u>Meine Freundin</u> braucht einen neuen Schrank.	*Nom*	*F*
2. Sie möchte <u>Stewardess</u> werden.		
3. Die Möbel <u>meiner Freundin</u> sind ultramodern.		
4. Morgen kaufe ich <u>ihr</u> eine schöne Lampe.		
5. Diesen Teppich mag <u>sie</u> sicher nicht.		
6. Meine Tapeten gefallen <u>ihr</u> sicher auch nicht.		
7. Setzen wir uns doch an <u>diesen Tisch</u>.		
8. Ich habe nichts gegen <u>Vorhänge</u>.		
9. <u>Das Bett</u> tragen wir am besten zusammen.		
10. Der Wecker steht auf <u>dem Regal</u>.		
11. Diese Decke gehört <u>mir</u>.		
12. Der Umzug findet wegen <u>schlechten Wetters</u> nicht statt.		

Übung 9 | Jutta hat sich wieder verliebt!

Ergänzen Sie die richtigen Endungen. Unten finden Sie das Genus wichtiger Substantive.

die **Adresse**
die **Augen** (*pl.*)
der **Brief**
die **Disko**
die **Eltern** (*pl.*)
der **Fernseher**
das **Fest**
die **Hausaufgaben** (*pl.*)

die **Hose**
die **Jacke**
der **Mann**
der **Name**
der **Park**
die **Schule**
die **Stadt**
die **Tür**
der **Weg**

    Jutta hat sich total verliebt. Sie sah vor einem Monat auf ein_____[1] Klassenfest ein_____[2] jungen Mann, und jetzt denkt sie nur noch an ihn.

    Er trug an jenem Abend ein_____[3] Jeansjacke, unter sein_____[4] Jacke ein altes Unterhemd und ein_____[5] uralte Hose. Er stand die ganze Zeit neben d_____[6] Tür. Seine Kleidung und sein_____[7] blauen Augen gefielen ihr sehr. Er schaute oft zu ihr hin, aber sie sprach ihn nicht an, sie war zu schüchtern.

    Jetzt träumt sie von ihm. Sie möchte mit ihm durch d_____[8] Park gehen und in d_____[9] Stadt. Vielleicht könnten sie auch mal für ein paar Tage ohne d_____[10] Eltern wegfahren. Sie möchte ihm gern ein_____[11] Brief schreiben, aber sie weiß sein_____[12] Adresse nicht. Sie kennt nur sein_____[13] Vornamen, Florian. Dies_____[14] Namen wird sie nie mehr vergessen!

    Morgens in d_____[15] Schule denkt sie an ihn, mittags auf d_____[16] Weg nach Hause, nachmittags bei d_____[17] Hausaufgaben, abends vor d_____[18] Fernseher oder in d_____[19] Disko.

    Ach, wenn sie ihn doch nur noch einmal treffen könnte! Diesmal würde sie sicher zu ihm gehen und ihn ansprechen.

APPENDIX A
Informationsspiele: 2. Teil

Einführung A

Situation 6   10 Fragen

Stellen Sie zehn Fragen. Für jedes „Ja" gibt es einen Punkt.

MODELL S2: Trägt Frau Körner einen Hut?
S1: Nein. Trägt Nora einen Mantel?
S2: Nein.

	HERR SIEBERT		FRAU KÖRNER	
	JA	NEIN	JA	NEIN
einen Anzug	☐	☐	☐	☐
eine Bluse	☐	☐	☐	☐
eine Brille	☐	☐	☐	☐
ein Hemd	☐	☐	☐	☐
eine Hose	☐	☐	☐	☒
einen Hut	☐	☐	☐	☐
eine Jacke	☐	☐	☐	☐
eine Jeans	☐	☐	☐	☐
ein Kleid	☐	☐	☐	☐
eine Krawatte	☐	☐	☐	☐

	HERR SIEBERT		FRAU KÖRNER	
	JA	NEIN	JA	NEIN
einen Mantel	☐	☐	☐	☐
einen Pullover	☐	☐	☐	☐
einen Rock	☐	☐	☐	☐
ein Sakko	☐	☐	☐	☐
Schuhe	☐	☐	☐	☐
Socken	☐	☐	☐	☐
Sportschuhe	☐	☐	☐	☐
Stiefel	☐	☐	☐	☐
ein Stirnband	☐	☐	☐	☐
ein T-Shirt	☐	☐	☐	☐

Thomas   Nora

Herr   Frau
Siebert   Körner

Situation 12   Zahlenrätsel

Verbinden Sie die Punkte. Sagen Sie Ihrem Partner oder
Ihrer Partnerin, wie er oder sie die Punkte verbinden soll.
Dann sagt Ihr Partner oder Ihre Partnerin Ihnen, wie Sie die
Punkte verbinden sollen. Was zeigen Ihre Bilder?

s2: Start ist Nummer 1. Geh zu 17, zu 5, zu 60, zu 23, zu
14, zu 3, zu 19, zu 7, zu 21, zu 12, zu 6, zu 33, zu 8, zu
11, zu 40, zu 25, zu 13, zu 4, zu 15, zu 35, zu 50, zu 9,
und zum Schluss zu 16. Was zeigt dein Bild?

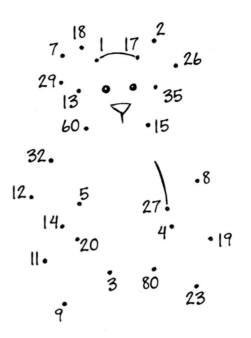

Einführung B

Situation 7   Familie

MODELL s2: Wie heißt Richards Vater?

 s1: Er heißt _____.

 s2: Wie schreibt man das?

 s1: _____. Wie alt ist er?

 s2: Er ist 39 Jahre alt. Wo wohnt er?

 s1: Er wohnt in _____. Wie heißt Richards Mutter?

 s2: Sie heißt Maria.

 s1: Wie schreibt man das?

 s2: M-A-R-I-A.

		Richard	Sofie	Mehmet
Vater	Name			Kenan
	Alter	39		
	Wohnort		Dresden	
Mutter	Name	Maria		
	Alter	38	47	54
	Wohnort			Izmir
Bruder	Name		Erwin	
	Alter			
	Wohnort	Innsbruck	Leipzig	Istanbul
Schwester	Name	Elisabeth	—	Fatima
	Alter	16	—	31
	Wohnort		—	

Situation 9   Temperaturen

MODELL s2: Wie viel Grad Fahrenheit sind 18 Grad Celsius?
s1: _____ Grad Fahrenheit.

°F	90		32		−5	
°C	32	18	0	−18	−21	−39

Kapitel 1

Situation 2   Freizeit

MODELL s2: Wie alt ist Richard?
s1: _____.
s2: Woher kommt Rolf?
s1: Aus _____.
s2: Was macht Jürgen gern?
s1: Er _____.
s2: Wie alt bist du?
s1: _____.
s2: Woher kommst du?
s1: _____.
s2: Was machst du gern?
s1: _____.

	Alter	Wohnort	Hobby
Richard		Innsbruck	geht gern in die Berge
Rolf	20		spielt gern Tennis
Jürgen		Göttingen	
Sofie			kocht gern
Jutta	16	München	
Melanie		Regensburg	
mein Partner / meine Partnerin			

Situation 7   Juttas Stundenplan

MODELL s2: Was hat Jutta am Montag um acht Uhr fünfzig?
s1: Sie hat Deutsch.

Uhr	Montag	Dienstag	Mittwoch	Donnerstag	Freitag
8.00–8.45	Latein			Biologie	
8.50–9.35		Englisch	Englisch		Physik
9.35–9.50	←		Pause		→
9.50–10.35			Mathematik		Religion
10.40–11.25	Geschichte	Französisch		Mathematik	
11.25–11.35	←		Pause		→
11.35–12.20		Musik		Sport	
12.25–13.10	Erdkunde		Kunst		frei

Situation 12   Diese Woche

MODELL s2: Was macht Mehmet am Montag?
    s1: Er geht um 7 Uhr zur Arbeit.
    s2: Was machst du am Montag?
    s1: Ich _____.

	Silvia Mertens	Mehmet Sengün	mein(e) Partner(in)
Montag	Sie steht um 6 Uhr auf.		
Dienstag		Er lernt eine neue Kollegin kennen.	
Mittwoch	Sie schreibt eine Prüfung.		
Donnerstag	Sie ruft ihre Eltern an.		
Freitag		Er hört um 15 Uhr mit der Arbeit auf.	
Samstag		Er räumt seine Wohnung auf.	
Sonntag		Er repariert sein Motorrad.	

Kapitel 2

Situation 3   Was machen sie morgen?

MODELL s2: Schreibt Jürgen morgen einen Brief?
    s1: Nein.
    s2: Schreibst du morgen einen Brief?
    s1: Ja. (Nein.)

	Jürgen	Silvia	mein(e) Partner(in)
1. schreibt/schreibst ... einen Brief		+	
2. kauft/kaufst ... ein Buch		+	
3. schaut/schaust ... einen Film an	–	–	
4. ruft/rufst ... eine Freundin an			
5. macht/machst ... Hausaufgaben		+	
6. isst/isst ... einen Hamburger	–	–	
7. besucht/besuchst ... einen Freund			
8. räumt/räumst ... das Zimmer auf		–	

Situation 15   Was machen sie gern?

MODELL s2: Was fährt Richard gern?
　　　　s1: Motorrad.
　　　　s2: Was fährst du gern?
　　　　s1: _____

	Richard	Josef und Melanie	mein(e) Partner(in)
fahren		Zug	
tragen	Pullis		
essen		Pizza	
sehen		Gruselfilme	
vergessen	seine Hausaufgaben		
waschen		ihr Auto	
treffen		ihre Lehrer	
einladen		ihre Eltern	
sprechen	Italienisch		

Kapitel 3

Situation 2   Kann Katrin kochen?

MODELL s2: Kann Katrin kochen?
　　　　s1: Ja, ganz gut.
　　　　s2: Kannst du kochen?
　　　　s1: Ja, aber nicht so gut.

[+]	[0]	[−]
ausgezeichnet	ganz gut	nicht so gut
fantastisch		nur ein bisschen
sehr gut		gar nicht
gut		kein bisschen

	Katrin	Peter	mein(e) Partner(in)
kochen		fantastisch	
zeichnen	sehr gut		
tippen		ganz gut	
Witze erzählen		ganz gut	
tanzen	fantastisch		
stricken	gar nicht		
Skateboard fahren		nicht so gut	
Geige spielen		nur ein bisschen	
schwimmen		nur ein bisschen	
ein Auto reparieren	nicht so gut		

Situation 13   Was machen sie, wenn ...?

MODELL s2: Was macht Renate, wenn sie traurig ist?
     s1: Sie ruft ihre Freundin an.
     s2: Was machst du, wenn du traurig bist?
     s1: Ich gehe ins Bett.

	Renate	Ernst	mein(e) Partner(in)
1. *traurig ist/bist*		weint	
2. *müde ist/bist*	trinkt Kaffee		
3. *in Eile ist/bist*	nimmt ein Taxi		
4. *wütend ist/bist*		schreit ganz laut	
5. *krank ist/bist*	geht zum Arzt		
6. *glücklich ist/bist*		lacht ganz laut	
7. *Hunger hat/hast*			
8. *Langeweile hat/hast*	liest ein Buch	ärgert seine Schwester	
9. *Durst hat/hast*		trinkt Limo	
10. *Angst hat/hast*	schließt die Tür ab		

Kapitel 4

Situation 10   Geburtstage

MODELL s2: Wann ist Willi geboren?
     s1: Am dreißigsten Mai 1983.

Person	Geburtstag
Willi	
Sofie	9. November 1987
Claire	
Melanie	3. April 1984
Nora	

Person	Geburtstag
Thomas	17. Januar 1990
Heidi	
mein(e) Partner(in)	
sein/ihr Vater	
seine/ihre Mutter	

Situation 15   Zum ersten Mal

MODELL s2: Wann hat Frau Gretter ihren ersten Kuss bekommen?
     s1: Als sie dreizehn war.

	Herr Thelen	Frau Gretter	mein(e) Partner(in)
seinen/ihren/deinen ersten Kuss bekommen	als er 12 war		
zum ersten Mal ausgegangen		als sie 15 war	
seinen/ihren/deinen Führerschein gemacht	mit 18		
sein/ihr/dein erstes Bier getrunken		mit 18	
seine/ihre/deine erste Zigarette geraucht	mit 21		
zum ersten Mal nachts nicht nach Hause gekommen	noch nie		

Kapitel 6

Situation 8 Gestern und heute

Arbeiten Sie zu zweit und stellen Sie Fragen wie im Modell.

MODELL S2: Heute ist hier ein Schuhgeschäft. Was war früher hier?
S1: Früher war hier eine Disko.

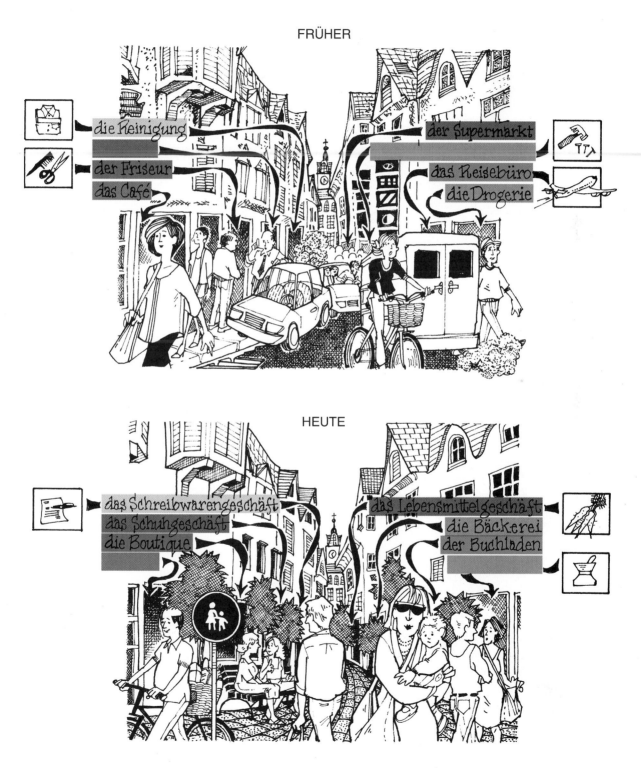

FRÜHER

die Reinigung
der Friseur
das Café
der Supermarkt
das Reisebüro
die Drogerie

HEUTE

das Schreibwarengeschäft
das Schuhgeschäft
die Boutique
das Lebensmittelgeschäft
die Bäckerei
der Buchladen

Situation 16   Haus- und Gartenarbeit

MODELL S2: Was macht Thomas am liebsten?
 S1: Er mäht am liebsten den Rasen.
 S2: Was hat Nora letztes Wochenende gemacht?
 S1: Sie hat ihre Bluse gebügelt.
 S2: Was muss Thomas diese Woche noch machen?
 S1: Er muss seine Wäsche waschen.
 S2: Was machst du am liebsten?
 S1: Ich _____ am liebsten _____.

	Thomas	Nora	mein(e) Partner(in)
am liebsten		einkaufen gehen	
am wenigsten gern	das Bad putzen		
jeden Tag	nichts von alledem		
einmal in der Woche		die Wäsche waschen	
letztes Wochenende	das Geschirr spülen		
gestern	die Blumen gießen		
diese Woche		den Boden aufwischen	
bald mal wieder		Staub wischen	

Kapitel 7

Situation 3   Deutschlandreise

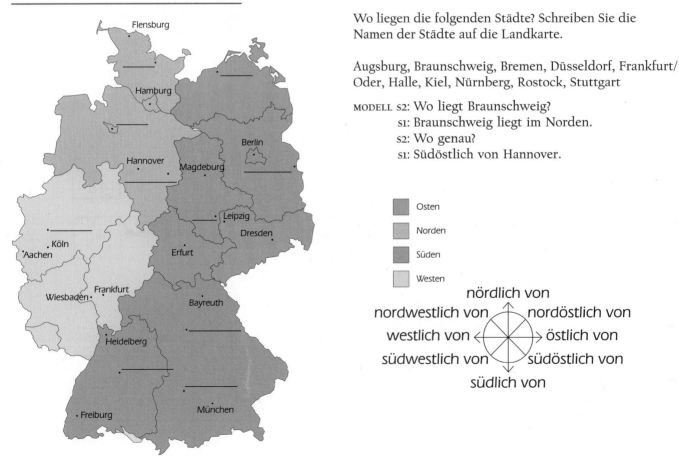

Wo liegen die folgenden Städte? Schreiben Sie die Namen der Städte auf die Landkarte.

Augsburg, Braunschweig, Bremen, Düsseldorf, Frankfurt/Oder, Halle, Kiel, Nürnberg, Rostock, Stuttgart

MODELL S2: Wo liegt Braunschweig?
 S1: Braunschweig liegt im Norden.
 S2: Wo genau?
 S1: Südöstlich von Hannover.

Kapitel 8

Situation 2   Mahlzeiten und Getränke

MODELL S2: Was isst Frau Gretter zum Frühstück?

S1: _____.

	Frau Gretter	Stefan	Andrea
zum Frühstück essen		frisches Müsli	Brot mit selbst gemachter Marmelade
zum Frühstück trinken		kalten Orangensaft	
zu Mittag essen	kalorienarmes Gemüse und Hähnchen		heiße Würstchen
zu Abend essen		italienische Spaghetti	
nach dem Sport trinken	nichts, sie treibt keinen Sport	kalten Tee mit Zitrone	
auf einem Fest trinken	deutschen Sekt		eiskalte Limonade
essen, wenn er/sie groß ausgeht		frischen Fisch mit französischer Soße	

Kapitel 9

Situation 9   Was ist passiert?

MODELL Was ist Mehmet passiert? / Was ist dir passiert?
Wann ist es passiert?
Wo ist es passiert?
Warum ist es passiert?

	Sofie	Mehmet	Ernst	mein Partner / meine Partnerin
Was?	hat ihre Schlüssel verloren		hat seine Hose zerrissen	
Wann?		als er in die Türkei fliegen wollte		
Wo?	in Leipzig		bei seiner Tante	
Warum?		weil der Flug aus Berlin Verspätung hatte		

Kapitel 10

Situation 2 Reisen

MODELL s2: Woher kommt Richard?
    s1: Aus _____.
    s2: Wohin fährt er in den Ferien?
    s1: Nach/In _____.
    s2: Wo wohnt er?
    s1: Bei _____. Was macht er da?
    s2: Er lernt Französisch. Wann kommt er zurück?
    s1: In _____.

	Richard	Sofie	Mehmet	Peter	Jürgen	mein(e) Partner(in)
Woher?		aus Dresden		aus Berkeley		
Wohin?		nach Düsseldorf		nach Hawaii		
Wo?		bei ihrer Tante	bei alten Freunden		bei einem Freund	
Was?	Französisch lernen		am Strand liegen; schwimmen		Ski fahren natürlich	
Wann?		in einer Woche	in zwei Wochen	nächstes Wochenende		

Situation 9 Wo wollen wir übernachten?

MODELL Wie viel kostet _____?
    Haben die Zimmer im (in der) _____ eine eigene Dusche und Toilette?
    Gibt es im (in der) _____ Einzelzimmer?
    Gibt es im (in der, auf dem) _____ einen Fernseher?
    Ist das Frühstück im (in der, auf dem) _____ inbegriffen?
    Ist die Lage von dem (von der) _____ zentral/ruhig?
    Gibt es im (in der, auf dem) _____ Telefon?

	Hotel Strandpromenade	das Gästehaus Ostseeblick	die Jugendherberge	der Campingplatz
Preis pro Person		42,- Euro		
Dusche/Toilette			nein	nein
Einzelzimmer				natürlich nicht
Fernseher	in jedem Zimmer	im Fernsehzimmer		natürlich nicht
Frühstück	inbegriffen		kostet extra	nein
zentrale Lage				
ruhige Lage				ja
Telefon	in jedem Zimmer	im Telefonzimmer	bei den Herbergseltern	Telefonzelle

Situation 13 Tiere

MODELL Welche Tiere findet ＿＿＿ am tollsten?
Vor welchem Tier hat ＿＿＿ am meisten Angst?
Welches Tier hätte ＿＿＿ gern als Haustier?
Welches wilde Tier würde ＿＿＿ gern in freier Natur sehen?
Wenn ＿＿＿ an Afrika denkt, an welche Tiere denkt er/sie?
Wenn ＿＿＿ an die Wüste denkt, an welches Tier denkt er/sie dann zuerst?
Welche Vögel findet ＿＿＿ am schönsten?
Welchen Fisch findet ＿＿＿ am gefährlichsten?
Welchem Tier möchte ＿＿＿ nicht im Wald begegnen?

	Ernst	Maria	mein(e) Partner(in)
Lieblingstier	ein Krokodil		
Angst		vor Mäusen	
Haustier		einen Papagei	
wildes Tier	einen Elefanten		
Afrika		an Zebras	
Wüste	an einen Skorpion		
Vögel	Adler		
Fisch		den Piranha	
Wald		einem Wildschwein	

Kapitel 11

Situation 10 Krankheitsgeschichte

MODELL Hat Herr Thelen sich (Hast du dir) schon mal etwas gebrochen? Was?
Ist Herr Thelen (Bist du) schon mal im Krankenhaus gewesen? Warum?
Hat Claire (Hast du) schon mal eine Spritze bekommen? Gegen was?
Erkältet sich Claire (Erkältest du dich) oft?
Ist Herr Thelen (Bist du) gegen etwas allergisch? Gegen was?
Hat man Herrn Thelen (Hat man dir) schon mal einen Zahn gezogen?
Hatte Claire (Hattest du) schon mal hohes Fieber? Wie hoch?
Ist Herr Thelen (Bist du) schon mal in Ohnmacht gefallen?

	Claire	Herr Thelen	mein(e) Partner(in)
sich etwas brechen	den Arm		
im Krankenhaus sein	Nierenentzündung		
eine Spritze bekommen		Tetanus	
sich oft erkälten		nein	
gegen etwas allergisch sein	Sonne		
einen Zahn gezogen haben	nein		
hohes Fieber haben		41,2° C	
in Ohnmacht fallen	nein		

Kapitel 12

Situation 2 Der ideale Partner / Die ideale Partnerin

MODELL Wie soll Heidis idealer Partner aussehen?
Was für einen Charakter soll er haben?
Welchen Beruf soll Rolfs ideale Partnerin haben?
Welche Interessen sollte sie haben?
Wie alt sollte sie sein?
Welche Konfession sollte sie haben?
Welcher Nationalität sollte Heidis Partner angehören?
Welche politische Einstellung sollte er haben?

	Rolf	Heidi	mein(e) Partner(in)
Aussehen	schlank und sportlich		
Charakter	lustig und neugierig		
Beruf		Rechtsanwalt	
Interessen		Sport und Reisen	
Alter		ein paar Jahre jünger als sie	
Konfession		kein Fanatiker	
Nationalität	deutsch		
politische Einstellung	eher konservativ		

Appendix B
Rollenspiele: 2. Teil

Einführung A
Situation 10   Begrüßen

s2: Begrüßen Sie einen Mitstudenten oder eine Mitstudentin. Schütteln Sie dem Mitstudenten oder der Mitstudentin die Hand. Sagen Sie Ihren Namen. Fragen Sie, wie alt er oder sie ist. Verabschieden Sie sich.

Einführung B
Situation 12   Herkunft

s2: Sie sind Student/Studentin an einer Universität in Deutschland. Sie lernen einen neuen Studenten/eine neue Studentin kennen. Fragen Sie, wie er/sie heißt, woher er/sie kommt, woher seine/ihre Familie kommt und welche Sprachen er/sie spricht.

Kapitel 1
Situation 15   Auf dem Auslandsamt

s2: Sie arbeiten auf dem Auslandsamt der Universität. Ein Student / Eine Studentin kommt zu Ihnen und möchte ein Stipendium für Österreich.

- Fragen Sie nach den persönlichen Daten und schreiben Sie sie auf: Name, Adresse, Telefon, Geburtstag, Studienfach.
- Sagen Sie „Auf Wiedersehen".

Kapitel 2
Situation 8   Am Telefon

s2: Das Telefon klingelt. Ein Freund / Eine Freundin ruft an. Er/Sie lädt Sie ein. Fragen Sie: **wo, wann, um wie viel Uhr, wer kommt mit.** Sagen Sie „ja" oder „nein", und sagen Sie „tschüss".

Kapitel 3
Situation 11   In der Mensa

s2: Sie sind Student/Studentin an der Uni in Regensburg und sind in der Mensa. Jemand möchte sich an Ihren Tisch setzen. Fragen Sie, wie er/sie heißt, woher er/sie kommt und was er/sie studiert.

Kapitel 4
Situation 16   Das Studentenleben

s2: Sie sind Student/Studentin an einer Uni in Ihrem Land. Ein Reporter / Eine Reporterin aus Österreich fragt Sie viel und Sie antworten gern. Sie wollen aber auch wissen, was der Reporter / die Reporterin gestern alles gemacht hat: am Vormittag, am Mittag, am Nachmittag und am Abend.

Kapitel 5

Situation 12   Bei der Berufsberatung

s2: Sie sind Student/Studentin und gehen zur Berufsberatung, weil Sie nicht wissen, was Sie nach dem Studium machen sollen. Beantworten Sie die Fragen des Berufsberaters / der Berufsberaterin.

Kapitel 6

Situation 12   Zimmer zu vermieten

s2: Sie möchten ein Zimmer in Ihrem Haus vermieten. Das Zimmer ist 25 Quadratmeter groß und hat Zentralheizung. Es kostet warm 310 Euro im Monat. Es hat große Fenster und ist sehr ruhig. Das Zimmer hat keine Küche und auch kein Bad, aber der Mieter / die Mieterin darf Ihre Küche und Ihr Bad benutzen. Der Mieter / Die Mieterin darf Freunde einladen, aber sie dürfen nicht zu lange bleiben. Sie haben kleine Kinder, die früh ins Bett müssen. Fragen Sie, was der Student / die Studentin studiert, ob er/sie raucht, ob er/sie oft laute Musik hört, ob er/sie Haustiere hat, ob er/sie Möbel hat.

Kapitel 7

Situation 8   Am Fahrkartenschalter

s2: Sie arbeiten am Fahrkartenschalter im Bahnhof von Bremen. Ein Fahrgast möchte eine Fahrkarte nach München kaufen. Hier ist der Fahrplan. Alle Züge fahren über Hannover und Würzburg.

	Abfahrt	Ankunft	2. Kl.	1. Kl.
IC	4.25	15.40	109,- Euro	169,- Euro
ICE	7.15	14.05	116,- Euro	182,- Euro
IC	7.30	20.45	109,- Euro	169,- Euro

Situation 10   Ein Auto kaufen

s2: Sie wollen einen neueren Gebrauchtwagen kaufen und lesen deshalb die Anzeigen in der Zeitung. Die Anzeigen für einen VW Golf und einen VW Beetle sind interessant. Rufen Sie an und stellen Sie Fragen.

Sie haben auch eine Anzeige in die Zeitung gesetzt, weil Sie Ihren Opel Corsa und Ihren Ford Fiesta verkaufen wollen. Antworten Sie auf die Fragen der Leute.

MODELL   Guten Tag, ich rufe wegen des VW Golf an.

Wie alt ist der Wagen?   Wie lange hat er noch TÜV?
Welche Farbe hat er?   Wie viel Benzin braucht er?
Wie ist der Kilometerstand?   Was kostet der Wagen?

Modell	VW Golf	VW Beetle	Opel Corsa	Ford Fiesta
Baujahr			2002	2003
Farbe			schwarz	blaugrün
Kilometerstand			84 500 km	52 000 km
TÜV			6 Monate	fast 2 Jahre
Benzinverbrauch pro 100 km			6 Liter	6,5 Liter
Preis			5 000 Euro	4 000 Euro

Kapitel 8

Situation 14   Im Restaurant

s2: Sie arbeiten als Kellner/Kellnerin in einem Restaurant. Ein Gast setzt sich an einen freien Tisch. Bedienen Sie ihn.

Kapitel 9

Situation 8   Das Klassentreffen

s2: Sie sind auf dem fünften Klassentreffen Ihrer alten High-School-Klasse. Sie unterhalten sich mit einem alten Schulfreund / einer alten Schulfreundin. Fragen Sie: was er/sie nach Abschluss der High School gemacht hat, was er/sie jetzt macht und was seine/ihre Pläne für die nächsten Jahre sind. Sprechen Sie auch über die gemeinsame Schulzeit.

Kapitel 10

Situation 11   Im Hotel

s2: Sie arbeiten an der Rezeption von einem Hotel. Alle Zimmer haben Dusche und Toilette. Manche haben auch Telefon. Frühstück ist inklusive. Das Hotel ist im Moment ziemlich voll. Ein Reisender / Eine Reisende kommt herein und erkundigt sich nach Zimmern. Denken Sie zuerst darüber nach: Was für Zimmer sind noch frei? Was kosten die Zimmer? Bis wann müssen die Gäste abreisen?

Kapitel 11

Situation 12   Anruf beim Arzt

s2: Sie arbeiten in einer Arztpraxis. Ein Patient / Eine Patientin ruft an und möchte einen Termin. Fragen Sie, was er/sie hat und wie dringend es ist. Der Terminkalender für diesen Tag ist schon sehr voll.

Kapitel 12

Situation 11   Auf der Bank

s2: Sie sind Bankangestellte(r) bei der Deutschen Bank und ein Kunde / eine Kundin möchte ein Konto eröffnen. Fragen Sie, ob der Kunde / die Kundin ein Girokonto oder ein Sparkonto eröffnen möchte. Zinsen gibt es nur auf Sparkonten. Eine EC-Karte bekommt man nur, wenn man ein festes Einkommen hat. Onlinezugang ist kostenlos. Man darf das Konto nicht überziehen.

Situation 15   An der Kinokasse

s2: Sie arbeiten an der Kinokasse und sind gestresst, weil Sie den ganzen Tag Karten verkauft haben. Sie haben vielleicht noch zehn Karten für die „Rocky Horror Picture Show" heute Abend, alles Einzelplätze. Auch die nächsten Tage sind schon völlig ausverkauft. Jetzt freuen Sie sich auf Ihren Feierabend, weil Sie dann mit Ihren Freunden selbst in die „Rocky Horror Picture Show" gehen wollen. Sie haben sich fünf ganz tolle Plätze besorgt, in der ersten Reihe. Da kommt noch ein Kunde.

Appendix C
Spelling Reform

A few years ago, there was a German spelling reform that changed the spelling of a handful of common words. The new rules also affected capitalization and compounding, and in some cases provided writers more than one correct option. Even today, you will often encounter words spelled according to the old rules when you read authentic texts. We provide here a brief summary of situations in which the current and the old rules differ from each other, with examples. The vocabulary lists at the end of each chapter and at the end of the student edition follow the new rules according to the recommendations of *Duden: Die deutsche Rechtschreibung* (24th ed.). (This is not a complete list of words affected by the spelling reform.)

- ß or ss? The new rule is simple: Write ss after a short vowel but ß after a long vowel or a diphthong. With the old rules, spelling didn't always follow this reasoning.

CURRENT	OLD
essen (isst), aß, gegessen	essen (ißt), aß, gegessen
lassen (lässt), ließ, gelassen	lassen (läßt), ließ, gelassen
müssen (muss), musste, gemusst	müssen (muß), mußte, gemußt
Schloss, Schlösser	Schloß, Schlösser

- Some words that are now divided were formerly written as compound words.

CURRENT	OLD
Rad fahren (fährt Rad), fuhr Rad, ist Rad gefahren	radfahren (fährt Rad), fuhr Rad, ist radgefahren
wie viel	wieviel

- When three of the same consonants occur together in a compound word, all are kept. This was formerly not necessarily the case.

CURRENT	OLD
Schifffahrt	Schiffahrt

- Some words that are now compounds used to be written separately.

CURRENT	OLD
leidtun	leid tun
irgendjemand	irgend jemand
Samstagmorgen	Samstag morgen

- Several common words that are capitalized under the new rules were formerly not capitalized.

CURRENT	OLD
heute Morgen	heute morgen
gestern Abend	gestern abend

- Many words formerly spelled with **ph** are now spelled with **f.**

CURRENT	OLD
Biografie, biografisch	Biographie, biographisch
Delfin	Delphin
Geografie, geografisch	Geographie, geographisch
Orthografie	Orthographie

Appendix D
Phonetics Summary Tables

I. Phoneme-Grapheme Relationships (Overview)

Note: The **Arbeitsbuch** presents the phoneme-grapheme relationship in reverse: The graphemes (letters of the alphabet) are the starting point for variations in pronunciation.

Vowels

Sound Group	Phonemes/Sounds	Graphemes	Examples
a-sounds	[aː]	a	Tafel
		ah	Zahl
		aa	Haar
	[a]	a	Hallo
i-sounds	[iː]	i	Ida
		ie	Liebe
		ih	ihr
		ieh	sich anziehen
	[ɪ]	i	Stift
e-sounds	[eː]	e	Peter
		eh	sehen
		ee	Tee
	[ɛ]	e	Herr
		ä	Ärger
	[ɛː]	ä	Cäsar
		äh	zählen
o-sounds	[oː]	o	Hose
		oh	Ohr
		oo	Boot
	[ɔ]	o	Kopf
u-sounds	[uː]	u	Fuß
		uh	Uhr
	[ʊ]	u	Mund
ö-sounds	[øː]	ö	hören
		öh	fröhlich
	[œ]	ö	öffnen
ü-sounds	[yː]	ü	Übung
		üh	früh
		y	Typ

(continued)

Sound Group	Phonemes/Sounds	Graphemes	Examples
	[ʏ]	ü	tschüss
		y	Ypsilon
reduced vowels	[ə]	e	beginnen
	[ɐ]	er	Vater
	[ɐ̯]	r	Ohr
dipthongs	[ae̯]	ei	Kleid
		ai	Mai
		ey/ay	Meyer, Bayern
	[ao̯]	au	Auge
	[ɔø̯]	eu	neun
		äu	Häuser

Rules

1. **Long vowels** may be represented in writing by doubled vowels and by <ie>—for example, T*ee*, B*oo*t, L*ie*be.
2. **Long vowels** may also be represented by a vowel followed by <h>, which is not pronounced but rather only indicates vowel length—for example, Z*ah*l, s*eh*en, fr*üh*.
3. **Single vowels** are often long when they appear in an open or potentially open syllable. Such syllables end in vowels—that is, they have no following end-consonant—for example, *Ü-bung, Ho-se, hörst* (from *hö-ren*), *gut* (from *gu-te*), *Fuß* (from *Fü-ße*). This rule applies above all to verbs, nouns, and adjectives.
4. **Diphthongs** consist of two closely associated short vowels within a syllable. Diphthongs are always long vowels—for example, *Auge, Kleid, neun*.
5. **Short vowels** generally precede double consonants—for example: *öffnen, Brille, doppelt*.
6. **Short vowels** may precede, though not always, a cluster of multiple consonants—for example, *Wurst, Gesicht, Herbst*.

Consonants

plosives	[p]	p	Paula
		pp	doppelt
		-b	gelb
	[b]	b	Brille
		bb	Krabbe
	[t]	t	Tür
		tt	bitte
		-d	Hemd
		th	Theorie
		dt	Stadt
	[d]	d	reden
		dd	Teddy
	[k]	k	Kleid
		ck	Rock
		-g	Tag
	[g]	g	Auge

(continued)

fricatives	[f]	**f**	**F**rau
		ff	ö**ff**nen
		v	**V**ater
	[v]	**w**	**W**ort
		v	**V**iktor
		(q)u	be**qu**em
	[s]	**s**	Hau**s**
		ss	Profe**ss**or
		ß	hei**ß**en
	[z]	**s**	Ho**s**e
	[ʃ]	**sch**	**Sch**ule
		s(t)	**S**tiefel
		s(p)	**S**prache
	[ʒ]	**j**	**J**ournalist
		g	Eta**ge**
(**ich**-sound)	[ç]	**ch**	Gesi**ch**t
		-ig	zwanzi**g**
	[j]	**j**	**j**a
(**ach**-sound)	[x]	**ch**	Bau**ch**
r-sounds	[r]	**r**	**r**ot
		rr	He**rr**
		rh	**Rh**ythmus
	[ʁ]	**r**	Tü**r**
	[ɐ]	**er**	Vat**er**
nasals	[m]	**m**	**M**antel
		mm	ko**mm**en
	[n]	**n**	**N**ame
		nn	Ma**nn**
	[ŋ]	**ng**	spri**ng**en
		n(k)	da**n**ke
liquids	[l]	**l**	**L**ehrer
		ll	Bri**ll**e
aspirants	[h]	**h**	**H**ose
glottal stops	[ʔ]		be·antworten
affricates	[pf]	**pf**	Ko**pf**
	[ts]	**z**	**z**ählen
		tz	se**tz**en
		ts	rech**ts**
		-t(ion)	Lek**ti**on
		zz	Pi**zz**a
	[ks]	**x**	Te**x**t
		ks	lin**ks**
		gs	du sa**gs**t
		chs	se**chs**

Rules

1. Double consonants are pronounced the same as single consonants; they merely indicate that the preceding vowel is short.
2. The letter pair <ch> is pronounced as:
   - a so-called "**ach**-sound" [x] after <u, o, a, au>, for example, *suchen, Tochter, Sprache, auch*;
   - a so-called "**ich**-sound" [ç] after all other vowels as well as after <l, n, r> and in *-chen*—for example, *nicht, Bücher, Töchter, Nächte, leicht, euch, Milch, durch, manchmal, Mädchen*;
   - [k] in the cluster <chs> as well as at the beginning of certain foreign words and German names—for example, *sechs, Charakter, Chemnitz*.
3. [ʃ] is represented:
   - by the letters <sch>: *schön, Tasche*; but not in *Häuschen* (*Häus-chen*);
   - by <s(t)>: *Straße*; <s(p)>: *Sprache*.
4. <r> can be clearly heard pronounced as a fricative, uvular, or trilled consonant [r]:
   - at the beginning of a word or syllable: *rot, hö-ren*;
   - after consonants and before vowels: *grün*;
   - after short vowels (when clearly enunciated): *Wort, Herr*.
5. <r> is pronounced as a vowel [ɐ]:
   - after long vowels: *Uhr*;
   - in the unstressed combinations *er-*, *ver-*, *zer-*, and *-er*: *erzählen, Verkäufer, zerstören, Lehrer, aber*.

II. German Vowels and Their Features (Overview)

There are 16 or 17 vowels (+ the vocalic pronunciation of <r>). They can be differentiated by:

- **quantity** (in their length)—they are either short or long;
- **quality** (in their tenseness)—they are either lax or tense.
  Quantity and quality are combined in German. The short vowels are lax; that is, in contrast to long vowels, they are formed with less muscular tension, less use of the lips, and less raising of the tongue. The **a**-vowels are only long and short. In addition, there is a long, open [ɛ:] as well as the reduced [ə] and [ɐ] (schwa).

The following minimal pairs illustrate these differences:

[a:] – [a]	Herr Mahler – Herr Maller
[e:] – [ɛ]	Herr Mehler – Herr Meller
[i:] – [ɪ]	Herr Mieler – Herr Miller
[o:] – [ɔ]	Herr Mohler – Herr Moller
[u:] – [ʊ]	Herr Muhler – Herr Muller
[ø:] – [œ]	Herr Möhler – Herr Möller
[y:] – [ʏ]	Herr Mühler – Herr Müller

Quality and quantity do not play a role with the reduced vowels [ə] as in *eine* and [ɐ] as in *einer*.

- the raising of the tongue—either the front, middle, or back of the tongue is raised. The following minimal pairs illustrate the differences in front vowels:

[eː] – [ɛ]	Herr Mehler – Herr Meller
[iː] – [ɪ]	Herr Mieler – Herr Miller
[ø] – [œ]	Herr Möhler – Herr Möller
[yː] – [ʏ]	Herr Mühler – Herr Müller

The following minimal pairs illustrate the differences in mid vowels:

[aː] – [a]	Herr Mahler – Herr Maller
[ə] – [ɐ]	eine – einer

The following minimal pairs illustrate the differences in back vowels:

[oː] – [ɔ]	Herr Mohler – Herr Moller
[uː] – [ʊ]	Herr Muhler – Herr Muller

- the rounding of the lips—there are rounded and unrounded vowels. The following minimal pairs illustrate the differences between rounded and unrounded vowels:

[øː] – [eː]	Herr Möhler – Herr Mehler
[œ] – [ɛ]	Herr Möller – Herr Meller
[yː] – [iː]	Herr Mühler – Herr Mieler
[ʏ] – [ɪ]	Herr Müller – Herr Miller

The German vowels can be systematized according to their features as follows:

	front		mid	back
long +	iː	yː	aː	uː
tense	eː ɛː	øː		oː
short +	ɪ	ʏ		ʊ
lax	ɛ	œ	a	ɔ
unstressed			ə ɐ	
		rounded		rounded

III. German Consonants and Their Features (Overview)

German consonants are differentiated according to:

- point of articulation: they are formed from the lips (in the front) to the velum (in the back) at different points in the mouth (see overview table on the next page);
- type of articulation:
  There are plosives/stops, in which the passage of air is interrupted:

  [p] as in Lippen, [b] as in lieben, [t] as in retten, [d] as in reden, [k] as in wecken, [g] as in wegen

  There are fricatives, in which the passage of air creates friction:

  [f] as in vier, [v] as in wir, [s] as in Haus, [z] as in Häuser, [ʃ] as in Tasche, [ʒ] as in Garage, [ç] as in Mädchen, [j] as in ja, [x] as in Tochter, [r] as in Torte

There are nasals, in which air passes through the nose:

[m] as in *Mai*, [n] as in *nie*, [ŋ] as in *la*ng*e*

There are isolated consonants—the liquid [l] as in *he*ll, the aspirant [h] as in *h*ier.

- tension—there are tense consonants that are always voiceless:

  [p] as in *Li*pp*en*, [t] as in *re*tt*en*, [k] as in *we*ck*en*, [f] as in *vier*, [s] as in *Hau*s, [ʃ] as in *Ta*sch*e*, [ç] as in *Mäd*ch*en*, [x] as in *To*ch*ter*

There are lax consonants that are voiced after vowels and voiced consonants:

  [b] as in *lie*b*en*, [d] as in *re*d*en*, [g] as in *we*g*en*, [v] as in *be*w*egen*, [z] as in *Häu*s*er*, [ʒ] as in *Ga*r*age*, [j] as in *Ka*j*ak*

After a pause in speech (for example at the beginning of a sentence after a pause) and after voiceless consonants, these consonants are also pronounced voiceless:

  [b̥] as in *mit*b*ringen*, [d̥] as in *bis* d*rei*, [g̊] as in *ins Haus* g*ehen*, [v̥] as in *auch* w*ir*, [z̥] as in *ab* s*ieben*, [ʒ̊] as in *das* J*ournal*, [j̥] as in *ach* j*a*

At the end of words and syllables, the following consonants are pronounced voiceless and tense—that is, as fortis consonants. This phenomenon is known as final devoicing:

  [b → p] as in *lie*b, [d → t] as in *un*d, [g → k] as in *we*g, [v → f] as in *explosi*v, [z → s] as in *Hau*s

The German consonants can be systematized according to their features as follows:

	front				→ back
PLOSIVE					
fortis	p		t		k
lenis	b		d		g
FRICATIVE					
fortis		f	s	ʃ	ç	x
lenis		v	z	ʒ	j	r
NASAL	m	n			ŋ
ISOLATED		l			h

IV. Rules for Melody and Accentuation

Melody
1. Melody falls at the end of a sentence (terminal) in:
   - statements—*Ich heiße Anna.* ↘
   - questions with question words—*Woher kommst du?* ↘
   - double questions—*Kommst du aus Bonn oder aus Berlin?* ↘
   - imperatives—*Setz dich!* ↘

2. Melody rises at the end of a sentence (interrogative) in:
   - yes-no questions—*Kommst du aus Bonn?* ↗
   - follow-up questions—*Woher kommst du?* ↘ *Aus Bonn?* ↗
   - questions posed in a friendly or curious tone of voice—*Wie heißt du?* ↗
     Was möchtest du trinken? ↗
   - imperatives and statements made in a friendly tone of voice—*Bleib noch*
     hier! ↗ *Die Blumen sind für dich.* ↗
3. Melody remains neutral (doesn't change) directly before pauses in
   incomplete sentences (progredient)—*Peter kommt aus Bonn,* → *Anna*
   kommt aus Berlin → *und Ute kommt aus Wien.* ↘

Sentence Stress

1. The most important word is stressed:
   Ich möchte ein Glas **Wein.** *(kein Bier)*
   Ich möchte ein **Glas** *Wein. (keine Flasche)*
   Ich möchte **ein** *Glas Wein. (nicht zwei)*

2. Longer sentences are divided by pauses into accent (rhythmic) groups, in
   which there is always a main accent:
   Ich möchte ein Glas **Wein,** / *ein Stück* **Brot,** / *etwas* **Käse** / *und viel* **Wasser.**

Word Stress

1. The stem is stressed:
   - in simple German words: *Mo*d*e,* **hö**ren;
   - in words with the prefixes **be-, ge-, er-, ver-, zer-:** be**halt**en;
   - in verbs with inseparable prefixes and in nouns ending in -*ung* that are
     derived from them—for example, *wieder***hol**en → *Wieder***hol**ung.
2. The beginning of a word (prefix) is stressed:
   - in verbs with separable prefixes and in nouns derived from them—
     aussprechen → die **Aus**sprache;
   - in compounds with *un-* and *ur-* — **Ur**laub, **un**genau.
3. The principally defining word is stressed:
   - in compound nouns and adjectives—**Schlaf**zimmer, **dunkel**grün.
4. The final syllable is stressed:
   - in German words with the suffix -*ei*—*Poli***zei**;
   - in abbreviations in which each letter is pronounced separately—*AB***C**;
   - in words that end in -*ion*—*Explo***sion.**

Appendix E
Grammar Summary Tables

I. Personal Pronouns

Nominative	Accusative	Accusative Reflexive	Dative	Dative Reflexive
ich	mich	mich	mir	mir
du	dich	dich	dir	dir
Sie	Sie	sich	Ihnen	sich
er	ihn	sich	ihm	sich
sie	sie	sich	ihr	sich
es	es	sich	ihm	sich
wir	uns	uns	uns	uns
ihr	euch	euch	euch	euch
Sie	Sie	sich	Ihnen	sich
sie	sie	sich	ihnen	sich

II. Definite Articles / Pronouns Declined Like Definite Articles

dieser/dieses/diese	*this*
mancher/manches/manche	*some, many a*
welcher/welches/welche	*which*
jeder/jedes/jede (*singular*)	*each, every*
alle (*plural*)	*all*

	Singular			Plural
	MASCULINE	NEUTER	FEMININE	
Nominative	der	das	die	die
	dieser	dieses	diese	diese
Accusative	den	das	die	die
	diesen	dieses	diese	diese
Dative	dem	dem	der	den
	diesem	diesem	dieser	diesen
Genitive	des	des	der	der
	dieses	dieses	dieser	dieser

III. Indefinite Articles / Negative Articles / Possessive Adjectives

mein/meine	*my*
dein/deine	*your (familiar singular)*
Ihr/Ihre	*your (polite singular)*
sein/seine	*his, its*
ihr/ihre	*her, its*
unser/unsere	*our*
euer/eure	*your (familiar plural)*
Ihr/Ihre	*your (polite plural)*
ihr/ihre	*their*

		Singular		Plural
	MASCULINE	NEUTER	FEMININE	
Nominative	ein	ein	eine	
	kein	kein	keine	keine
	mein	mein	meine	meine
Accusative	einen	ein	eine	
	keinen	kein	keine	keine
	meinen	mein	meine	meine
Dative	einem	einem	einer	
	keinem	keinem	keiner	keinen
	meinem	meinem	meiner	meinen
Genitive	eines	eines	einer	
	keines	keines	keiner	keiner
	meines	meines	meiner	meiner

IV. Relative Pronouns

	Singular			Plural
	MASCULINE	NEUTER	FEMININE	
Nominative	der	das	die	die
Accusative	den	das	die	die
Dative	dem	dem	der	denen
Genitive	dessen	dessen	deren	deren

V. Question Pronouns

	People	Things and Concepts
Nominative	wer	was
Accusative	wen	was
Dative	wem	
Genitive	wessen	

VI. Attributive Adjectives

		Masculine	Neuter	Feminine	Plural
Nominative	strong	guter	gutes	gute	gute
	weak	gute	gute	gute	guten
Accusative	strong	guten	gutes	gute	gute
	weak	guten	gute	gute	guten
Dative	strong	gutem	gutem	guter	guten
	weak	guten	guten	guten	guten
Genitive	strong	guten	guten	guter	guter
	weak	guten	guten	guten	guten

Nouns declined like adjectives: Angestellte, Deutsche, Geliebte, Reisende, Verletzte, Verwandte

VII. Comparative and Superlative of Adjectives and Adverbs

A. *Regular Patterns*

schnell	schneller	am schnellsten
intelligent	intelligenter	am intelligentesten
heiß	heißer	am heißesten
teuer	teurer	am teuersten
dunkel	dunkler	am dunkelsten

B. *Umlaut Patterns*

alt	älter	am ältesten
groß	größer	am größten
jung	jünger	am jüngsten

Similarly: arm, dumm, hart, kalt, krank, kurz, lang, oft, scharf, schwach, stark, warm

C. *Irregular Patterns*

gern	lieber	am liebsten
gut	besser	am besten
hoch	höher	am höchsten
nah	näher	am nächsten
viel	mehr	am meisten

VIII. Weak Masculine Nouns

These nouns add -**(e)n** in the accusative, dative, and genitive.

A. *International nouns ending in* -**t** *denoting male persons:* Dirigent, Komponist, Patient, Polizist, Präsident, Soldat, Student, Tourist
B. *Nouns ending in* -**e** *denoting male persons or animals:* Drache, Junge, Kunde, Löwe, Neffe, Riese, Vorfahre, Zeuge
C. *The following nouns:* Elefant, Herr, Mensch, Nachbar, Name[1]

	Singular	Plural
Nominative	der Student	die Studenten
	der Junge	die Jungen
Accusative	den Studenten	die Studenten
	den Jungen	die Jungen
Dative	dem Studenten	den Studenten
	dem Jungen	den Jungen
Genitive	des Studenten	der Studenten
	des Jungen	der Jungen

IX. Prepositions

Accusative	Dative	Accusative/Dative	Genitive
durch	aus	an	(an)statt
für	außer	auf	trotz
gegen	bei	hinter	während
ohne	mit	in	wegen
um	nach	neben	
	seit	über	
	von	unter	
	zu	vor	
		zwischen	

[1] *genitive:* des Namens

X. Dative Verbs

antworten	*to answer*
begegnen	*to meet*
danken	*to thank*
erlauben	*to allow*
fehlen	*to be missing*
folgen	*to follow*
gefallen	*to please, be pleasing to*
gehören	*to belong to*
glauben	*to believe*
gratulieren	*to congratulate*
helfen	*to help*
leidtun	*to be sorry; to feel sorry for*
passen	*to fit*
passieren	*to happen*
raten	*to advise*
schaden	*to be harmful*
schmecken	*to taste (good)*
stehen	*to suit*
wehtun	*to hurt*
zuhören	*to listen to*

XI. Reflexive Verbs

sich anziehen	*to get dressed*
sich ärgern	*to get angry*
sich aufregen	*to get excited*
sich ausruhen	*to rest*
sich ausziehen	*to get undressed*
sich beeilen	*to hurry*
sich erholen	*to relax, recover*
sich erkälten	*to catch a cold*
sich erkundigen	*to ask*
sich (die Haare) föhnen	*to blow-dry (one's hair)*
sich fragen (ob)	*to wonder (if)*
sich freuen	*to be happy*
sich (wohl) fühlen	*to feel (well)*
sich fürchten	*to be afraid*
sich gewöhnen an	*to get used to*
sich hinlegen	*to lie down*
sich infizieren	*to get infected*
sich informieren	*to get information*
sich interessieren für	*to be interested in*
sich kümmern um	*to take care of*
sich rasieren	*to shave*
sich schminken	*to put on makeup*
sich setzen	*to sit down*
sich umsehen	*to look around*
sich unterhalten	*to have a conversation*
sich verletzen	*to get hurt*
sich verloben	*to get engaged*
sich vorstellen	*to imagine*

XII. Verbs + Prepositions

ACCUSATIVE

bitten um	*to ask for*
denken an	*to think about*
glauben an	*to believe in*
nachdenken über	*to think about; to ponder*
schreiben an	*to write to*
schreiben/sprechen über	*to write/talk about*
sorgen für	*to care for*
verzichten auf	*to renounce, do without*
warten auf	*to wait for*

SICH + ACCUSATIVE

sich ärgern über	*to be angry at/about*
sich erinnern an	*to remember*
sich freuen über	*to be happy about*
sich gewöhnen an	*to get used to*
sich interessieren für	*to be interested in*
sich kümmern um	*to take care of*
sich verlieben in	*to fall in love with*

DATIVE

fahren/reisen mit	*to go/travel by*
halten von	*to think of; to value*
handeln von	*to deal with*
träumen von	*to dream of*

SICH + DATIVE

sich erkundigen nach	*to ask about*
sich fürchten vor	*to be afraid of*

XIII. Inseparable Prefixes of Verbs

A. *Common*

be-	bedeuten, bekommen, bestellen, besuchen, bezahlen
er-	erfinden, erkälten, erklären, erlauben, erreichen
ver-	verbrennen, verdienen, vergessen, verlassen, verletzen

B. *Less Common*

ent-	entdecken, entscheiden, entschuldigen
ge-	gefallen, gehören, gewinnen, gewöhnen
zer-	zerreißen, zerstören

Appendix F
Verbs

I. Conjugation Patterns

A. *Simple tenses and principal parts*

		Present	Simple Past	Subjunctive	Aux. + Past Participle
Strong	ich	komme	kam	käme	bin gekommen
	du	kommst	kamst	kämst	bist gekommen
	er/sie/es	kommt	kam	käme	ist gekommen
	wir	kommen	kamen	kämen	sind gekommen
	ihr	kommt	kamt	kämt	seid gekommen
	sie, Sie	kommen	kamen	kämen	sind gekommen
Weak	ich	glaube	glaubte	glaubte	habe geglaubt
	du	glaubst	glaubtest	glaubtest	hast geglaubt
	er/sie/es	glaubt	glaubte	glaubte	hat geglaubt
	wir	glauben	glaubten	glaubten	haben geglaubt
	ihr	glaubt	glaubtet	glaubtet	habt geglaubt
	sie, Sie	glauben	glaubten	glaubten	haben geglaubt
Irregular Weak	ich	weiß	wusste	wüsste	habe gewusst
	du	weißt	wusstest	wüsstest	hast gewusst
	er/sie/es	weiß	wusste	wüsste	hat gewusst
	wir	wissen	wussten	wüssten	haben gewusst
	ihr	wisst	wusstet	wüsstet	habt gewusst
	sie, Sie	wissen	wussten	wüssten	haben gewusst
Modal	ich	kann	konnte	könnte	habe gekonnt
	du	kannst	konntest	könntest	hast gekonnt
	er/sie/es	kann	konnte	könnte	hat gekonnt
	wir	können	konnten	könnten	haben gekonnt
	ihr	könnt	konntet	könntet	habt gekonnt
	sie, Sie	können	konnten	könnten	haben gekonnt
haben	ich	habe	hatte	hätte	habe gehabt
	du	hast	hattest	hättest	hast gehabt
	er/sie/es	hat	hatte	hätte	hat gehabt
	wir	haben	hatten	hätten	haben gehabt
	ihr	habt	hattet	hättet	habt gehabt
	sie, Sie	haben	hatten	hätten	haben gehabt
sein	ich	bin	war	wäre	bin gewesen
	du	bist	warst	wärst	bist gewesen
	er/sie/es	ist	war	wäre	ist gewesen
	wir	sind	waren	wären	sind gewesen
	ihr	seid	wart	wärt	seid gewesen
	sie, Sie	sind	waren	wären	sind gewesen
werden	ich	werde	wurde	würde	bin geworden
	du	wirst	wurdest	würdest	bist geworden
	er/sie/es	wird	wurde	würde	ist geworden
	wir	werden	wurden	würden	sind geworden
	ihr	werdet	wurdet	würdet	seid geworden
	sie, Sie	werden	wurden	würden	sind geworden

B. *Compound tenses*

1. *Active voice*

	Perfect	Past Perfect	Future	Subjunctive
Strong	ich habe genommen	hatte genommen	werde nehmen	würde nehmen
	ich bin gefahren	war gefahren	werde fahren	würde fahren
Weak	ich habe gekauft	hatte gekauft	werde kaufen	würde kaufen
	ich bin gesegelt	war gesegelt	werde segeln	würde segeln
Irregular Weak	ich habe gewusst	hatte gewusst	werde wissen	würde wissen
Modal	ich habe gekonnt	hatte gekonnt	werde können	würde können
haben	ich habe gehabt	hatte gehabt	werde haben	würde haben
sein	ich bin gewesen	war gewesen	werde sein	würde sein
werden	ich bin geworden	war geworden	werde werden	würde werden

2. *Passive voice*

	Present	Simple Past	Perfect
Strong	es wird genommen	wurde genommen	ist genommen worden
Weak	es wird gekauft	wurde gekauft	ist gekauft worden

II. Strong and Irregular Weak Verbs

backen (backt)	backte	hat gebacken	*to bake*
beginnen (beginnt)	begann	hat begonnen	*to begin*
beißen (beißt)	biss	hat gebissen	*to bite*
bekommen (bekommt)	bekam	hat bekommen	*to get, receive*
beschreiben (beschreibt)	beschrieb	hat beschrieben	*to describe*
besitzen (besitzt)	besaß	hat besessen	*to own, possess*
besteigen (besteigt)	bestieg	hat bestiegen	*to climb*
bitten (bittet)	bat	hat gebeten	*to ask*
bleiben (bleibt)	blieb	ist geblieben	*to stay*
braten (brät)	briet	hat gebraten	*to roast, fry*
brechen (bricht)	brach	hat gebrochen	*to break*
brennen (brennt)	brannte	hat gebrannt	*to burn*
bringen (bringt)	brachte	hat gebracht	*to bring*
denken (denkt)	dachte	hat gedacht	*to think*
dürfen (darf)	durfte	hat gedurft	*to be allowed to*
empfehlen (empfiehlt)	empfahl	hat empfohlen	*to recommend*
entscheiden (entscheidet)	entschied	hat entschieden	*to decide*
erfinden (erfindet)	erfand	hat erfunden	*to invent*
essen (isst)	aß	hat gegessen	*to eat*
fahren (fährt)	fuhr	ist gefahren	*to go, drive*
fallen (fällt)	fiel	ist gefallen	*to fall*
fangen (fängt)	fing	hat gefangen	*to catch*
finden (findet)	fand	hat gefunden	*to find*

fliegen (fliegt)	flog	ist geflogen	*to fly*
fliehen (flieht)	floh	ist geflohen	*to flee*
fließen (fließt)	floss	ist geflossen	*to flow*
fressen (frisst)	fraß	hat gefressen	*to eat*
geben (gibt)	gab	hat gegeben	*to give*
gefallen (gefällt)	gefiel	hat gefallen	*to please, be pleasing to*
gehen (geht)	ging	ist gegangen	*to go, walk*
gewinnen (gewinnt)	gewann	hat gewonnen	*to win*
gießen (gießt)	goss	hat gegossen	*to water*
haben (hat)	hatte	hat gehabt	*to have*
halten (hält)	hielt	hat gehalten	*to hold*
hängen (hängt)	hing	hat gehangen	*to hang, be suspended*
heben (hebt)	hob	hat gehoben	*to lift*
heißen (heißt)	hieß	hat geheißen	*to be called*
helfen (hilft)	half	hat geholfen	*to help*
kennen (kennt)	kannte	hat gekannt	*to know*
klingen (klingt)	klang	hat geklungen	*to sound*
kommen (kommt)	kam	ist gekommen	*to come*
können (kann)	konnte	hat gekonnt	*to be able to*
laden (lädt)	lud	hat geladen	*to load*
lassen (lässt)	ließ	hat gelassen	*to let, leave*
laufen (läuft)	lief	ist gelaufen	*to run*
leihen (leiht)	lieh	hat geliehen	*to lend, borrow*
lesen (liest)	las	hat gelesen	*to read*
liegen (liegt)	lag	hat gelegen	*to lie*
mögen (mag)	mochte	hat gemocht	*to like*
müssen (muss)	musste	hat gemusst	*to have to*
nehmen (nimmt)	nahm	hat genommen	*to take*
nennen (nennt)	nannte	hat genannt	*to name*
raten (rät)	riet	hat geraten	*to advise*
reiten (reitet)	ritt	ist geritten	*to ride*
riechen (riecht)	roch	hat gerochen	*to smell*
rufen (ruft)	rief	hat gerufen	*to call*
scheiden (scheidet)	schied	hat geschieden	*to leave, divorce*
schießen (schießt)	schoss	hat geschossen	*to shoot*
schlafen (schläft)	schlief	hat geschlafen	*to sleep*
schlagen (schlägt)	schlug	hat geschlagen	*to strike, beat*
schließen (schließt)	schloss	hat geschlossen	*to shut, close*
schneiden (schneidet)	schnitt	hat geschnitten	*to cut*
schreiben (schreibt)	schrieb	hat geschrieben	*to write*
schwimmen (schwimmt)	schwamm	ist geschwommen	*to swim*
sehen (sieht)	sah	hat gesehen	*to see*
sein (ist)	war	ist gewesen	*to be*
senden (sendet)	sandte	hat gesandt	*to send*
singen (singt)	sang	hat gesungen	*to sing*
sinken (sinkt)	sank	ist gesunken	*to sink*
sitzen (sitzt)	saß	hat gesessen	*to sit*
sprechen (spricht)	sprach	hat gesprochen	*to speak*
springen (springt)	sprang	ist gesprungen	*to spring, jump*
stehen (steht)	stand	hat gestanden	*to stand*

steigen (steigt)	stieg	ist gestiegen	*to climb*
sterben (stirbt)	starb	ist gestorben	*to die*
stoßen (stößt)	stieß	hat gestoßen	*to shove, push*
streiten (streitet)	stritt	hat gestritten	*to quarrel, fight*
tragen (trägt)	trug	hat getragen	*to wear, carry*
treffen (trifft)	traf	hat getroffen	*to meet, hit*
treiben (treibt)	trieb	hat getrieben	*to do sports*
trinken (trinkt)	trank	hat getrunken	*to drink*
tun (tut)	tat	hat getan	*to do*
verbrennen (verbrennt)	verbrannte	hat verbrannt	*to burn; to incinerate*
verbringen (verbringt)	verbrachte	hat verbracht	*to spend* (*time*)
vergessen (vergisst)	vergaß	hat vergessen	*to forget*
verlassen (verlässt)	verließ	hat verlassen	*to leave* (*a place*)
verlieren (verliert)	verlor	hat verloren	*to lose*
verschwinden (verschwindet)	verschwand	ist verschwunden	*to disappear*
versprechen (verspricht)	versprach	hat versprochen	*to promise*
wachsen (wächst)	wuchs	ist gewachsen	*to grow*
waschen (wäscht)	wusch	hat gewaschen	*to wash*
werden (wird)	wurde	ist geworden	*to become*
wissen (weiß)	wusste	hat gewusst	*to know*

Appendix G
Answers to Grammar Exercises

Einführung A

Übung 1: 1. Hören Sie zu! 2. Geben Sie mir die Hausaufgabe! 3. Öffnen Sie das Buch! 4. Schauen Sie an die Tafel! 5. Nehmen Sie einen Stift! 6. Sagen Sie „Guten Tag"! 7. Schließen Sie das Buch! 8. Schreiben Sie „Tschüss"! **Übung 2:** 1.a. heißt b. heiße c. heiße 2.a. heißen b. heiße 3.a. heiße b. heiße c. heißt **Übung 3:** 1. Sie 2. Es 3. Er 4. Sie 5. Es 6. Sie 7. Er 8. Sie 9. Sie 10. Er **Übung 4:** 1. Er ist orange. 2. Sie ist grün. 3. Es ist gelb. 4. Er ist schwarz und rot. 5. Sie sind rosa. 6. Sie sind braun. 7. Sie ist weiß. **Übung 5:** 1. du 2. Sie 3. du 4. ihr 5. Sie 6. Sie 7. Sie 8. ihr

Einführung B

Übung 1: 1.a. ein b. der c. rot 2.a. ein b. der c. grün 3.a. eine b. die c. grau 4.a. eine b. die c. braun 5.a. ein b. das c. orange 6.a. eine b. die c. schwarz **Übung 2:** 1. Nein, das ist eine Lampe. 2. Nein, das ist eine Tafel. 3. Nein, das ist ein Fenster. 4. Nein, das ist ein Kind. 5. Nein, das ist ein Heft. 6. Nein, das ist eine Uhr. 7. Nein, das ist ein Tisch. 8. Nein, das ist eine Tür. **Übung 3:** 1.a. bist b. bin c. sind 2.a. ist b. sind 3.a. seid b. bin c. ist. 4.a. bin b. bin **Übung 4:** 1.a. haben b. habe 2. hast 3.a. Habt b. hat c. haben d. habe **Übung 5:** Der Mensch hat zwei Arme, zwei Augen, zwei Beine, zehn Finger, zwei Füße, viele Haare, zwei Hände, eine Nase, zwei Ohren, zwei Schultern. **Übung 6:** (*Numbers will vary.*) In meinem Zimmer sind viele Bücher, ein Fenster, zwei Lampen, zwei Stühle, ein Tisch, eine Tür, eine Uhr, vier Wände. **Übung 7:** 1. Er ist schwarz. 2. Es ist weiß. 3. Sie ist blau. 4. Sie ist gelb. 5. Sie sind weiß. 6. Es ist rot. 7. Er ist lila. 8. Sie sind braun. 9. Sie ist grün. 10. Er ist rosa. **Übung 8:** 1.a. kommst b. komme 2.a. kommt b. aus c. Woher d. kommen e. ich f. aus 3.a. sie b. kommen 4.a. ihr b. wir **Übung 9:** 1. Ihre 2.a. dein b. mein 3.a. mein b. mein c. Dein 4.a. Ihre b. Meine c. mein **Übung 10:** (*Answers will vary.*) 1. Ich komme aus _____. 2. Meine Mutter kommt aus _____. 3. Mein Vater kommt aus _____. 4. Meine Großeltern kommen aus _____. / Mein Großvater kommt aus _____, und meine Großmutter kommt aus _____. 5. Mein Professor / Meine Professorin kommt aus _____. 6. Ein Student aus meinem Deutschkurs heißt _____, und er kommt aus _____. 7. Eine Studentin aus meinem Deutschkurs heißt _____, und sie kommt aus _____.

Kapitel 1

Übung 1: (*Answers may vary.*) 1. Ich besuche Freunde. 2. Ihr geht ins Kino. 3. Jutta und Jens lernen Spanisch. 4. Du spielst gut Tennis. 5. Melanie studiert in Regensburg. 6. Ich lese ein Buch. 7. Wir reisen nach Deutschland. 8. Richard hört gern Musik. 9. Jürgen und Silvia kochen Spaghetti. **Übung 2:** 1. sie 2. Sie 3.a. du b. Ich 4.a. ihr b. Wir 5.a. Ich b. ihr c. Wir **Übung 3:** 1.a. (tanz)t b. (tanz)e c. (tanz)t 2.a. (geh)t b. (mach)en c. (reis)t d. (arbeit)et 3.a. (koch)en b. (mach)t c. (besuch)en **Übung 4:** (*Answers may vary slightly.*) 1. Monika und Albert spielen gern Schach. 2. Heidi arbeitet gern. 3. Stefan besucht gern Freunde. 4. Nora geht gern ins Kino. 5. Peter hört gern Musik. 6. Katrin macht gern Fotos. 7. Monika zeltet gern. 8. Albert trinkt gern Tee. **Übung 5:** 1. Frau Ruf liegt gern in der Sonne. Jutta liegt auch gern in der Sonne, aber Herr Ruf liegt nicht gern in der Sonne. 2. Jens reitet gern. Ernst reitet auch gern, aber Jutta reitet nicht gern. 3. Jens kocht gern. Jutta kocht auch gern, aber Andrea kocht nicht gern. 4. Michael und Maria spielen gern Karten. Die Rufs spielen auch gern Karten, aber die Wagners spielen nicht gern Karten. **Übung 6:** 1. Es ist halb acht. 2. Es ist elf Uhr. 3. Es ist Viertel vor fünf. 4. Es ist halb eins. 5. Es ist zehn vor sieben. 6. Es ist Viertel nach zwei. 7. Es ist fünfundzwanzig nach fünf. 8. Es ist halb elf. **Übung 7:** 1. (Rolf) nach 2. (er) vor 3. (Seine Großmutter) nach 4. (Rolf) vor 5. (er) vor 6. (er) vor 7. (er) vor 8. (Er) nach **Übung 8:** (*Answers will vary.*) 1. Ich studiere

_____. 2. Im Moment wohne ich in _____. 3. Heute koche ich _____. 4. Manchmal trinke ich _____. 5. Ich spiele gern _____. 6. Mein Freund heißt _____. 7. Jetzt wohnt er in _____. 8. Manchmal spielen wir _____. **Übung 9:** 1. auf 2. auf 3. ein 4. an 5. aus 6. ab 7. ein 8. aus 9. auf **Übung 10:** 1. Rolf kommt in San Francisco an. 2. Thomas räumt das Zimmer auf. 3. Heidi ruft Thomas an. 4. Albert füllt das Formular aus. 5. Peter holt Monika ab. 6. Peter und Monika gehen aus. 7. Frau Schulz packt die Bücher ein. 8. Stefan steht um halb elf auf. 9. Katrin lernt Rolf kennen. **Übung 11:** 1. Wann bist du geboren? 2. Woher kommst du? 3. Wo wohnst du? 4. Welche Augenfarbe hast du? 5. Wie groß bist du? 6. Studierst du? 7. Welche Fächer studierst du? 8. Wie viele Stunden arbeitest du? 9. Was machst du gern? **Übung 12:** (*Answers may vary.*) 1. Wie heißt du? 2. Kommst du aus München? 3. Woher kommst du? 4. Was studierst du? 5. Wie heißt dein Freund? 6. Wo wohnt er? 7. Spielst du Tennis? 8. Tanzt du gern? 9. Trinkst du Bier? 10. Trinkt Willi gern Bier?

Kapitel 2

Übung 1: Ernst kauft die Tasche, die Stühle und den Schreibtisch. Melanie kauft die Tasche, das Regal und den Schreibtisch. Jutta kauft den Pullover, die Lampe und den DVD-Spieler. Ich kaufe … (*Answers will vary.*) **Übung 2:** (*Answers will vary.*) Ich habe ein Bett, Bilder, Bücher, einen Fernseher, eine Lampe, ein Telefon und einen Sessel. **Übung 3:** (*Sentences may vary.*) Heidi hat einen Computer, aber keinen Fernseher. Sie hat eine Gitarre, aber kein Fahrrad. Sie hat ein Telefon und einen Teppich, aber sie hat keine Bilder. Monika hat keinen Computer, keinen Fernseher und keine Gitarre. Aber sie hat ein Fahrrad, ein Telefon, Bilder und einen Teppich. Ich habe _____. **Übung 4:** (*Answers will vary.*) 1. Ich möchte ein Auto und eine Sonnenbrille. 2. Mein bester Freund möchte eine Katze. 3. Meine Eltern möchten einen Videorekorder. 4. Meine Mitbewohnerin und ich möchten einen Fernseher. 5. Mein Nachbar in der Klasse möchte ein Motorrad. 6. Meine Professorin möchte einen Koffer. 7. Mein Bruder möchte einen Hund. **Übung 5:** Seine Haare; Seine Augen; Seine Halskette; Seine Schuhe; Seine Gitarre; Sein Zimmer; Sein Fenster; Ihre Haare; Ihre Augen; Ihre Halskette ist kurz. Ihre Schuhe sind sauber. Ihre Gitarre ist neu. Ihr Zimmer ist klein. Ihr Fenster ist groß. **Übung 6:** 1. Ihren 2. Deine 3. eure 4. Deine 5. Ihr 6. deine 7. Euren **Übung 7:** (*Answers will vary.*) **Übung 8:** 1.a. ihr b. wir 2.a. Sie b. Ich 3.a. sie b. er 4.a. du b. Ich c. ihr d. Wir **Übung 9:** a. machen b. fährt c. sieht d. Isst e. isst f. isst g. macht h. lese i. schläft j. fahren **Übung 10:** (*Answers will vary.*) 1. Wir sprechen (nicht) gern Deutsch. Sprecht ihr auch (nicht) gern Deutsch? 2. Ich lade (nicht) gern Freunde ein. Lädst du auch (nicht) gern Freunde ein? 3. Ich laufe (nicht) gern im Wald. Läufst du auch (nicht) gern im Wald? 4. Ich trage (nicht) gern Pullis. Trägst du auch (nicht) gern Pullis? 5. Wir sehen (nicht) gern fern. Seht ihr auch (nicht) gern fern? 6. Ich fahre (nicht) gern Fahrrad. Fährst du auch (nicht) gern Fahrrad? 7. Wir vergessen (nicht) gern die Hausaufgabe. Vergesst ihr auch (nicht) gern die Hausaufgabe? 8. Ich schlafe (nicht) gern. Schläfst du auch (nicht) gern? **Übung 11:** 1. e. Schreib es dir auf! 2. c. Lies ein Buch! 3. d. Mach eine Pause! 4. a. Treib Sport! 5. b. Trink Cola! 6. g. Iss lieber Joghurt! 7. i. Kauf dir einen neuen Pullover! 8. j. Koch Chinesisch! 9. h. Lade deine Freunde ein! 10. f. Fahr Fahrrad! **Übung 12:** 1. Schlaf nicht den ganzen Tag! 2. Lieg nicht den ganzen Tag in der Sonne! 3. Vergiss deine Hausaufgaben nicht! 4. Lies deine Bücher! 5. Sieh nicht den ganzen Tag fern! 6. Trink nicht zu viel Cola! 7. Sprich nicht mit vollem Mund! 8. Trag deine Brille! 9. Geh spazieren! 10. Treib Sport! **Übung 13:** 1. Trag heute ein T-Shirt! 2. Spiel keine laute Musik! 3. Lern den Wortschatz! 4. Ruf deine Freunde an! 5. Lauf nicht allein im Park! 6. Lieg nicht zu lange in der Sonne! 7. Räum dein Zimmer auf! 8. Iss heute Abend in einem Restaurant! 9. Geh nicht zu spät ins Bett! 10. Steh früh auf!

Kapitel 3

Übung 1: (*Predicates and sequence will vary.*) A.1. Mein Freund / Meine Freundin kann _____. 2. Meine Eltern können _____. 3. Ich kann / Wir können _____. 4. Mein Bruder / Meine Schwester kann _____. 5. Der Professor / Die Professorin kann _____. B.1. Kannst du / Könnt ihr Gedichte schreiben? 2. Kannst du / Könnt ihr Auto fahren? 3. Kannst du / Könnt ihr tippen? 4. Kannst du / Könnt ihr stricken? 5. Kannst du / Könnt ihr zeichnen? **Übung 2:** (*Answers will vary.*) 1. Heute Abend will ich _____. 2. Morgen kann ich nicht _____. 3. Mein Freund / Meine Freundin kann gut _____. 4. Am Samstag will mein Freund / meine Freundin _____. 5. Mein Freund / Meine Freundin und ich wollen _____. 6. Im Winter wollen meine Eltern / meine Freunde _____. 7. Meine Eltern / Meine Freunde können gut _____. **Übung 3:** 1. Sie darf nicht mit Jens zusammen lernen. 2. Sie darf nicht viel fernsehen. 3. Sie muss in der Klasse aufpassen und mitschreiben. 4. Sie darf nicht jeden Tag tanzen gehen. 5. Sie muss jeden Tag ihren Wortschatz lernen. 6. Sie muss amerikanische Filme im Original sehen. 7. Sie muss ihren Englischlehrer zum Abendessen einladen. 8. Sie muss für eine Woche nach London fahren. 9. Sie muss die englische Grammatik fleißig lernen. **Übung 4:** 1.a. Willst b. will c. kann d. muss 2. a. darf b. musst c. kann d. darfst e. könnt 3.a. sollst b. kann c. musst **Übung 5:** 1. dich 2.a. mich b. dich 3. uns 4. euch 5.a. dich b. dich 6.a. mich b. Sie 7. Sie **Übung 6:** 1. Ja, ich mache es gern. / Nein, ich mache es nicht gern. 2. Ja, ich kann es aufsagen. / Nein, ich kann es nicht aufsagen. 3. Ja, ich kenne ihn. / Nein, ich kenne ihn nicht. 4. Ja, ich lese sie gern. / Nein, ich lese sie nicht gern. 5. Ja, ich lerne ihn gern. / Nein, ich lerne ihn nicht gern. 6. Ja, ich kenne sie. / Nein, ich kenne sie nicht. 7. Ja, ich vergesse sie oft. / Nein, ich vergesse sie nicht oft. 8. Ja, ich mag ihn/sie. / Nein, ich mag ihn/sie nicht. **Übung 7:** 1. Nein, sie liest ihn nicht, sie schreibt ihn. 2. Nein, er isst sie nicht, er trinkt sie. 3. Nein, sie macht ihn nicht an, sie macht ihn aus. 4. Nein, er kauft es nicht, er verkauft es. 5. Nein, er zieht sie nicht aus, er zieht sie an. 6. Nein, sie trägt ihn nicht, sie kauft ihn. 7. Nein, er bestellt es nicht, er isst es. 8. Nein, er besucht ihn nicht, er ruft ihn an. 9. Nein, sie kämmt es nicht, sie wäscht es. 10. Nein, er bläst sie nicht aus, er zündet sie an. **Übung 8:** 1. Weil ich krank bin. 2. Weil er müde ist. 3. Weil wir Hunger haben. 4. Weil sie keine Zeit hat. 5. Weil sie Langeweile hat. 6. Weil sie traurig ist. 7. Weil sie Durst haben. 8. Weil ich Angst habe. 9. Weil er glücklich ist. 10. Weil ich lernen muss. **Übung 9:** (*Answers will vary.*) 1. s1: Was macht Albert, wenn er müde ist? s2: Wenn Albert müde ist, geht er nach Hause. s1: Und du? s2: Wenn ich müde bin, _____. 2. s1: Was macht Maria, wenn sie glücklich ist? s2: Wenn Maria glücklich ist, trifft sie Michael. s1: Und du? s2: Wenn ich glücklich bin, _____. 3. s1: Was macht Herr Ruf, wenn er Durst hat? s2: Wenn Herr Ruf Durst hat, trinkt er eine Cola. s1: Und du? s2: Wenn ich Durst habe, _____. 4. s1: Was macht Frau Wagner, wenn sie in Eile ist? s2: Wenn Frau Wagner in Eile ist, fährt sie mit dem Taxi. s1: Und du? s2: Wenn ich in Eile bin, _____. 5. s1: Was macht Heidi, wenn sie Hunger hat? s2: Wenn Heidi Hunger hat, kauft sie einen Hamburger. s1: Und du? s2: Wenn ich Hunger habe, _____. 6. s1: Was macht Frau Schulz, wenn sie Ferien hat? s2: Wenn Frau Schulz Ferien hat, fliegt sie nach Deutschland. s1: Und du? s2: Wenn ich Ferien habe, _____. 7. s1: Was macht Hans, wenn er Angst hat? s2: Wenn Hans Angst hat, ruft er, "Mama, Mama". s1: Und du? s2: Wenn ich Angst habe, _____. 8. s1: Was macht Stefan, wenn er krank ist? s2: Wenn Stefan krank ist, geht er zum Arzt. s1: Und du? s2: Wenn ich krank bin, _____. **Übung 10:** 1. Jürgen ist wütend, weil er immer so früh aufstehen muss. 2. Silvia ist froh, weil sie heute nicht arbeiten muss. 3. Claire ist in Eile, weil sie noch einkaufen muss. 4. Josef ist traurig, weil Melanie ihn nicht anruft. 5. Thomas geht nicht zu Fuß, weil seine Freundin ihn zur Uni mitnimmt. 6. Willi hat selten Langeweile, weil er immer fernsieht. 7. Marta hat Angst vor Wasser, weil sie nicht schwimmen kann. 8. Mehmet fährt in die Türkei, weil er seine Eltern besuchen will.

Kapitel 4

Übung 1: a. hat b. ist c. hat d. hat e. ist f. sind g. ist h. hat i. hat **Fragen:** 1. Rosemarie ist um 7 Uhr aufgestanden. 2. Sie sind zur Schule gegangen. 3. Frau Dehne ist die Lehrerin. 4. Sie hat „Herzlich Willkommen" an die Tafel geschrieben. **Übung 2:** a. haben b. sind c. haben d. sind e. sind f. haben g. haben h. sind i. haben j. sind **Fragen:** 1. Josef und Melanie sind mit dem Taxi zum Bahnhof gefahren. 2. Sie sind um 5.30 mit dem Zug abgefahren. 3. Sie haben im Speisewagen gefrühstückt. 4. Nachts haben sie schlecht geschlafen. **Übung 3:** a. aufgestanden b. geduscht c. gefrühstückt d. gegangen e. gehört f. getroffen g. getrunken h. gearbeitet i. gegessen **Übung 4:** 1. Hast du schon gefrühstückt? 2. Bist du schon geschwommen? 3. Hast du schon eine Geschichte gelesen? 4. Hast du schon Klavier gespielt? 5. Hast du schon geschlafen? 6. Hast du schon gegessen? 7. Hast du schon Geschirr gespült? 8. Hast du den Brief schon geschrieben? 9. Bist du schon ins Bett gegangen? **Übung 5:** 1. Katrin hat bis 9 Uhr im Bett gelegen. 2. Sie hat einen Rock getragen. 3. Sie hat mit Frau Schulz gesprochen. 4. Sie hat ein Referat gehalten. 5. Sie hat Freunde getroffen. 6. Sie hat gearbeitet. 7. Es hat geregnet. 8. Sie ist nach Hause gekommen. 9. Sie hat ihre Wäsche gewaschen. 10. Sie ist abends zu Hause geblieben. **Übung 6:** 1. (*Answers will vary.*) 2. (*Answers will vary.*) 3. Am fünfundzwanzigsten Dezember. 4. (*Answers will vary according to country.*) 5. Am ersten Januar. 6. Am vierzehnten Februar. 7. (*Answers will vary.*) 8. (*Answers will vary.*) 9. (*Answers will vary according to country.*) 10. (*Answers will vary according to country.*) **Übung 7:** a. im b. im c. — d. am e. Am f. um g. um h. Am i. im j. am **Übung 8:** (*Answers will vary.*) **Übung 9:** A: 1. R 2. F 3. R 4. R 5. R
B: Partizipien mit **ge-:**

aufgestanden	aufstehen
gehört	hören
gegangen	gehen
gekocht	kochen
gefahren	fahren
geparkt	parken
zurückgekommen	zurückkommen
gewaschen	waschen
aufgeräumt	aufräumen
gefallen	fallen
eingelaufen	einlaufen
abgebrannt	abbrennen

Partizipien ohne **ge-:**

verschlafen	verschlafen
bekommen	bekommen
bezahlt	bezahlen
zerbrochen	zerbrechen

Übung 10: a. ist ... angekommen b. hat ... begrüßt c. getrunken d. ist ... gegangen e. hat ... geschlafen f. ist ... gegangen g. haben ... gefragt h. hat ... gesprochen i. haben ... getrunken j. sind ... gegangen **Übung 11:** (*Answers will vary.*) 1. —Bist du gestern früh aufgestanden? —Ja. —Wann? —Um 6 Uhr. 2. —Hast du gestern jemanden fotografiert? —Ja. —Wen? —Jane. 3. —Hast du gestern jemanden besucht? —Ja. —Wen? —Alan. 4. —Bist du gestern ausgegangen? —Ja. —Wohin? —Ins Kino. 5. —Hast du gestern etwas bezahlt? —Ja. —Was? —Die Rechnung. 6. —Hast du gestern etwas repariert? —Ja. —Was? —Mein Auto. 7. —Hast du gestern etwas Neues probiert? —Ja. —Was? —Segeln. 8. —Hast du gestern ferngesehen? —Ja. —Wie lange? —Eine Stunde. 9. —Hast du gestern etwas nicht verstanden? —Ja. —Was? —Sophies Referat. 10. —Hast du gestern dein Zimmer aufgeräumt? —Ja. —Wann? —Um 4 Uhr.

Kapitel 5

Übung 1: (*Answers will vary.*) Ich backe meiner Tante einen Kuchen. Ich erkläre meinem Partner einen Witz. Ich erzähle meiner Kusine ein Geheimnis. Ich gebe meinem Freund einen Kuss. Ich kaufe meinem Vater eine Krawatte. Ich koche meiner Mitbewohnerin Kaffee. Ich leihe meinem Bruder fünfzig Dollar. Ich schenke meiner Großmutter ein Buch. Ich schreibe meiner Mutter einen Brief. Ich verkaufe meinem Mitbewohner mein Deutschbuch. **Übung 2:** (*Answers will vary.*) Heidi erklärt ihrer

Freundin die Grammatik. Peter erzählt seinem Vetter ein Geheimnis. Thomas gibt seiner Mutter ein Armband. Katrin kauft ihrem Mann einen Rucksack. Stefan kocht seinem Freund eine Suppe. Albert leiht seinen Eltern einen Regenschirm. Monika schenkt ihrer Schwester einen Bikini. Frau Schulz schreibt ihrer Tante eine Karte. Nora verkauft ihrem Professor ein Zelt. **Übung 3:** 1. Wer 2. Wen 3. Wem 4. Wen 5. Wem 6. wer **Übung 4:** 1. Was passiert am Abend? d. Es wird dunkel. 2. Was passiert, wenn man Bücher schreibt? b. Man wird bekannt. 3. Was passiert, wenn man krank wird? h. Man bekommt Fieber. 4. Was passiert im Frühling? i. Die Tage werden länger. 5. Was passiert im Herbst? c. Die Blätter werden bunt. 6. Was passiert, wenn Kinder älter werden? e. Sie werden größer. 7. Was passiert, wenn man in der Lotterie gewinnt? j. Man wird reich. 8. Was passiert, wenn man Medizin studiert? a. Man wird Arzt. 9. Was passiert am Morgen? g. Es wird hell. 10. Was passiert im Sommer? f. Es wird wärmer. **Übung 5:** 1. Vielleicht wird sie Köchin. 2. Vielleicht wird sie Apothekerin. 3. Vielleicht wird er Pilot. 4. Vielleicht wird er Lehrer. 5. Vielleicht wird sie Architektin. 6. Vielleicht wird sie Bibliothekarin. 7. Vielleicht wird er Krankenpfleger. 8. Vielleicht wird sie Dirigentin. **Übung 6:** 1. Was macht man im Kino? Man sieht einen Film 2. Was macht man auf der Post? Man kauft Briefmarken. 3. Was macht man an der Tankstelle? Man tankt Benzin. 4. Was macht man in der Disko? Man tanzt. 5. Was macht man in der Kirche? Man betet. 6. Was macht man auf der Bank? Man wechselt Geld. 7. Was macht man im Meer? Man schwimmt. 8. Was macht man in der Bibliothek? Man liest ein Buch. 9. Was macht man im Park? Man geht spazieren. **Übung 7:** 1. Monika ist in der Kirche. 2. Albert ist im Meer. 3. Heidi ist auf der Polizei. 4. Nora ist in einem Hotel. 5. Katrin ist im Schwimmbad. 6. Thomas ist auf der Post. 7. Frau Schulz ist in der Küche. 8. Das Poster ist an der Wand. 9. Der Topf ist auf dem Herd. 10. Der Wein ist im Kühlschrank. **Übung 8:** 1. mir 2. dir 3. euch 4. Ihnen 5. uns **Übung 9:** 1. Er hat ihr einen Regenschirm geschenkt. 2. Sie hat ihm ihr Auto geliehen. 3. Er hat ihm 500 Euro geliehen. 4. Sie hat ihr ein Geheimnis erzählt. 5. Er hat ihnen eine Geschichte erzählt. 6. Sie hat ihr ihre Sonnenbrille verkauft. 7. Er hat ihnen seinen Fernseher verkauft. 8. Sie hat ihm ihr Büro gezeigt. 9. Er hat ihm seine Wohnung gezeigt. 10. Sie hat ihr eine neue Brille gekauft. 11. Er hat ihr einen Kinderwagen gekauft.

Kapitel 6

Übung 1: 1. gefällt 2. gratuliere 3. helfen 4. Schmeckt 5. passt 6. gehört 7. Fehlt 8. begegnet 9. schadet 10. zugehört **Übung 2:** (*Answers will vary.*) **Übung 3:** (*Answers may vary.*) 1. Albert ist unter der Dusche. 2. Der Spiegel hängt an der Wand. 3. Der Kühlschrank steht neben dem Fernseher. 4. Das Deutschbuch liegt im Kühlschrank. 5. Die Lampe hängt über dem Tisch. 6. Der Computer steht auf dem Schreibtisch. 7. Die Schuhe liegen auf dem Bett. 8. Die Hose liegt auf dem Tisch. 9. Das Poster von Berlin hängt über dem Fernseher. 10. Die Katze liegt unter dem Bett. **Übung 4:** (*Answers will vary.*) **Übung 5:** (*Answers may vary*). 1. Ich bin heute Abend in der Bibliothek. 2. Ich bin am Nachmittag in der Mensa. 3. Ich bin um 16 Uhr bei Freunden. 4. Ich bin in der Nacht im Bett. 5. Ich bin am frühen Morgen am Frühstückstisch. 6. Ich bin am Montag in der Klasse. 7. Ich bin am 1. August im Urlaub. 8. Ich bin an Weihnachten auf einer Party. 9. Ich bin im Winter bei meinen Eltern. 10. Ich bin am Wochenende auf einer Party. **Übung 6:** 1. Er geht zum Arzt. 2. Er geht zum Fußballplatz. 3. Sie geht ins Hotel. 4. Er fährt zur Tankstelle. 5. Er geht in den Supermarkt. 6. Er geht auf die Post. 7. Sie gehen in den Wald. 8. Sie geht zu ihrem Freund. 9. Er fährt zum Flughafen. 10. Sie geht ins Theater. **Übung 7:** 1. aufstehst 2.a. mache b. aus c. fernsiehst 3.a. kommt b. an 4.a. zieht b. um 5. einladen 6.a. räumt b. auf 7.a. mitkommen b. mitnimmst 8.a. rufst b. an **Übung 8:** Andrea hat ferngesehen. Katrin und Peter sind ausgegangen. Heidi hat Frau Schulz angerufen. Herr Ruf hat das Geschirr abgetrocknet. Jürgen ist ausgezogen. Jutta hat ihr Abendkleid angezogen. Maria ist aus Bulgarien zurückgekommen. Herr Thelen ist aufgewacht. **Übung 9:** 1. Womit kochst du den Kaffee? Mit der Kaffeemaschine. 2. Womit saugst du den Staub? Mit dem Staubsauger. 3. Womit putzt du dir die Zähne? Mit der Zahnbürste. 4. Womit fegst du den Boden? Mit dem Besen. 5. Womit bügelst du? Mit dem Bügeleisen. 6. Womit tippst du einen Brief? Mit dem Computer. 7. Womit gießt du die

Blumen im Garten? Mit dem Gartenschlauch. 8. Womit wischst du den Boden? Mit dem Putzlappen. 9. Womit gießt du die Blumen in der Wohnung? Mit der Gießkanne. **Übung 10:** 1.a. mit b. mit c. Mit d. bei 2.a. bei b. mit c. bei d. mit 3.a. mit b. mit c. bei.

Kapitel 7

Übung 1: (*Answers will vary.*) 1. Ich mag Leute, die laut lachen. 2. Ich mag keine Leute, die viel sprechen. 3. Ich mag eine Stadt, die Spaß macht. 4. Ich mag keine Stadt, die langweilig ist. 5. Ich mag einen Mann, der gern verreist. 6. Ich mag keinen Mann, der interessant aussieht. 7. Ich mag eine Frau, die nett ist. 8. Ich mag keine Frau, die betrunken ist. 9. Ich mag einen Urlaub, der exotisch ist. 10. Ich mag ein Auto, das schnell fährt. **Übung 2:** 1. Europa → Wie heißt der Kontinent, der eigentlich eine Halbinsel von Asien ist? 2. Mississippi → Wie heißt der Fluss, von dem Mark Twain erzählt? 3. San Francisco → Wie heißt die Stadt, die an einer Bucht liegt? 4. die Alpen → Wie heißen die Berge, in denen man sehr gut Ski fahren kann? 5. Washington → Wie heißt der Staat in den USA, dem ein Präsident seinen Namen gegeben hat? 6. das Tal des Todes → Wie heißt das Tal, in dem es sehr heiß ist? 7. Ellis → Wie heißt die Insel, die man von New York sieht? 8. der Pazifik → Wie heißt das Meer, über das man nach Hawaii fliegt? 9. die Sahara → Wie heißt die Wüste, die man aus vielen Filmen kennt? 10. der Große Salzsee → Wie heißt der See in Utah, auf dem man segeln kann? **Übung 3:** 1. Berlin ist größer als Zürich. 2. München ist älter als San Francisco. 3. Athen ist wärmer als Hamburg. 4. Der Mount Everest ist höher als das Matterhorn. 5. Der Mississippi ist länger als der Rhein. 6. Liechtenstein ist kleiner als die Schweiz. 7. Leipzig ist kälter als Kairo. 8. Ein Fernseher ist billiger als eine Waschmaschine. 9. Schnaps ist stärker als Bier. 10. Ein Haus auf dem Land ist schöner als ein Haus in der Stadt. (*oder* Ein Haus in der Stadt ist schöner als ein Haus auf dem Land.) 11. Zehn Euro ist mehr als zehn Cent. 12. Ein Appartement ist teurer als eine Wohnung in einem Studentenheim. 13. Ein Motorrad ist schneller als ein Fahrrad. 14. Ein Sofa ist schwerer als ein Stuhl. 15. Bier ist besser als Milch. (*oder* Milch ist besser als Bier.) **Übung 4:** 1. Heidi ist schwerer als Monika. 2. Thomas und Stefan sind am schwersten. 3. Thomas ist besser in Deutsch als Stefan. 4. Heidi ist in Deutsch am besten. 5. Heidi ist kleiner als Stefan. 6. Monika ist am kleinsten. 7. Stefan ist jünger als Thomas. 8. Stefan ist am jüngsten. 9. Thomas' Haare sind länger als Heidis. 10. Monikas Haare sind am längsten. 11. Heidis Haare sind kürzer als Monikas. 12. Stefans Haare sind am kürzesten. 13. Monika ist schlechter in Deutsch als Heidi. 14. Stefan ist in Deutsch am schlechtesten. **Übung 5:** 1. In Athen ist es am heißesten. 2. In Moskau ist es am kältesten. 3. Monaco ist am kleinsten. 4. Frankreich ist am ältesten. 5. Südafrika ist am jüngsten. 6. Der Nil ist am längsten. 7. Frankfurt liegt am nördlichsten. 8. Der Mount Everest ist am höchsten. 9. Deutschland ist am größten. **Übung 6:** 1. Mit wem gehen Sie am liebsten ins Theater? 2. Worauf freuen Sie sich am meisten? 3. Auf wen müssen Sie immer warten? 4. Über wen haben Sie sich in letzter Zeit geärgert? 5. Woran denken Sie, wenn Sie „USA" hören? 6. Womit fahren Sie zur Schule? 7. Worüber schreiben Sie nicht gern? 8. An wen haben Sie Ihren letzten Brief geschrieben? 9. Von wem halten Sie nicht viel? **Übung 7:** a. darauf b. daneben c. Dazwischen d. Darin e. Davor/daneben f. darüber g. Daran h. Darunter i. dahinter **Übung 8:** 1. bin 2.a. hat b. bin 3.a. habe b. bin 4. bin 5. bin 6.a. habe b. bin 7.a. habe b. ist 8.a. haben b. ist 9.a. ist/sind b. hat 10. habe **Übung 9:** 1. Ich habe schon Frühstück gemacht. 2. Ich habe meine Milch schon getrunken. 3. Ich habe den Tisch schon sauber gemacht. 4. Ich bin schon zum Bäcker gelaufen. 5. Ich habe schon Brötchen mitgebracht. 6. Ich habe schon Geld mitgenommen. 7. Ich habe den Hund schon gefüttert. 8. Ich habe die Tür schon zugemacht. **Übung 10:** 1.a. Hatten b. hatte 2. Waren 3.a. wart b. hatten 4.a. Warst b. war 5. hatte 6. hattest 7.a. Warst b. war c. hatte.

Kapitel 8

Übung 1: (*Answers will vary.*) 1. Amerikanisches Steak! 2. Russischer Kaviar! 3. Griechische Oliven! 4. Japanisches Sushi! 5. Französischer Champagner! 6. Deutsche Wurst! 7. Dänischer Käse! 8. Italienische Spaghetti! 9. Ungarischer Paprika! 10. Englische Marmelade! 11. Kolumbianischer

APPENDIX G Answers to Grammar Exercises

Kaffee! 12. Neuseeländische Kiwis! **Übung 2:** 1. Ich esse nur deutsches Brot. 2. Ich esse nur russischen Kaviar. 3. Ich esse nur italienische Salami. 4. Ich trinke nur kolumbianischen Kaffee. 5. Ich esse nur neuseeländische Kiwis. 6. Ich trinke nur französischen Wein. 7. Ich trinke nur belgisches Bier. 8. Ich esse nur spanische Muscheln. 9. Ich esse nur englische Marmelade. 10. Ich esse nur japanischen Thunfisch. **Übung 3:** 1. Michael: Ich möchte den grauen Wintermantel da. Maria: Nein, der graue Wintermantel ist viel zu schwer. 2. Michael: Ich möchte die gelbe Hose da. Maria: Nein, die gelbe Hose ist viel zu bunt. 3. Michael: Ich möchte das schicke Hemd da. Maria: Nein, das schicke Hemd ist viel zu teuer. 4. Michael: Ich möchte die roten Socken da. Maria: Nein, die roten Socken sind viel zu warm. 5. Michael: Ich möchte den schwarzen Schlafanzug da. Maria: Nein, der schwarze Schlafanzug ist viel zu dünn. 6. Michael: Ich möchte die grünen Schuhe da. Maria: Nein, die grünen Schuhe sind viel zu groß. 7. Michael: Ich möchte den modischen Hut da. Maria: Nein, der modische Hut ist viel zu klein. 8. Michael: Ich möchte die schwarzen Winterstiefel da. Maria: Nein, die schwarzen Winterstiefel sind viel zu leicht. 9. Michael: Ich möchte die elegante Sonnenbrille da. Maria: Nein, die elegante Sonnenbrille ist viel zu bunt. 10. Michael: Ich möchte die roten Tennisschuhe da. Maria: Nein, die roten Tennis-schuhe sind viel zu grell. **Übung 4:** 1.a. Ihr neues Auto b. der alte Mercedes c. keinen neuen Wagen 2.a. der italienische Wein b. eine weitere Flasche 3.a. mein kaputtes Fahrrad b. meinen blöden Computer c. kein freies Wochenende **Übung 5:** 1. den 2.a. den b. dem 3.a. dem b. das 4. der 5.a. den b. den 6.a. ins b. im c. am 7.a. dich b. dich 8.a. den b. dem 9. der **Übung 6:** 1. Die Teller stehen im Küchenschrank. 2. Albert stellt die Teller auf den Tisch. 3. Die Servietten liegen in der Schublade. 4. Monika legt die Servietten auf den Tisch. 5. Messer und Gabeln liegen in der Schublade. 6. Stefan legt Messer und Gabeln auf den Tisch. 7. Die Kerze steht auf dem Schrank. 8. Heidi stellt die Kerze auf den Tisch. 9. Thomas sitzt auf dem Sofa. **Übung 7:** 1. Jutta leiht ihrem neuen Freund ihre Lieblings-CD. 2. Jens verkauft dem kleinen Bruder von Jutta eine Ratte. 3. Hans zeigt die Ratte nur seinen besten Freunden. 4. Jutta schenkt ihrer besten Freundin ein Buch. 5. Jens kauft seinem wütenden Lehrer eine Krawatte. 6. Ernst erzählt seiner großen Schwester einen Witz. 7. Jutta kocht den netten Leuten von nebenan Kaffee. 8. Ernst gibt dem süßen Baby von nebenan einen Kuss. **Übung 8:** (*Answers and sequence will vary.*) 1. Ich werde weniger fernsehen. 2. Ich werde mehr lernen. 3. Ich werde weniger oft ins Kino gehen. 4. Ich werde früher ins Bett gehen. 5. Ich werde mehr arbeiten. 6. Ich werde öfter selbst kochen. **Übung 9:** (*Answers may vary.*) 1. Frau Schulz repariert morgen das Auto. 2. Heidi fährt morgen aufs Land. 3. Peter spielt morgen Fußball. 4. Monika schreibt morgen einen Brief. 5. Stefan geht morgen einkaufen. 6. Nora heiratet morgen. 7. Albert geht morgen in den Supermarkt. 8. Thomas räumt morgen sein Zimmer auf. **Übung 10:** (*Answers will vary.*)

Kapitel 9

Übung 1: (*Answers will vary.*) **Übung 2:** 1. Ich durfte nicht. 2. Ich wollte nicht. 3. Das wusste ich nicht. 4. Ich wollte eine. 5. Ich sollte das nicht. **Übung 3:** 1.a. wolltest b. wusste 2.a. durfte b. musste c. wollten d. konnten 3.a. konnte b. musste c. wusste d. wollte **Übung 4:** 1.a. Wann b. Wenn 2.a. wann b. Als 3. als 4.a. Wann b. als 5.a. Wann b. Wenn 6.a. Wann b. Als **Übung 5:** a. wenn b. Als c. Wenn d. wenn e. Als f. Als g. Wann h. Als i. wenn **Übung 6:** a. standen b. gingen c. fuhren d. kamen e. hielten f. aßen g. schwammen h. schliefen i. sprangen **Übung 7:** 1. wohnte 2. brachten 3. schliefen 4. liefen, kamen 5. sahen, saß 6. gab, fanden 7. trug, schloss 8. tötete, rannte **Übung 8:** 1. Nachdem Jutta den Schlüssel verloren hatte, kletterte sie durch das Fenster. 2. Nachdem Ernst die Fensterscheibe eingeworfen hatte, lief er weg. 3. Nachdem Claire angekommen war, rief sie Melanie an. 4. Nachdem Hans seine Hausaufgaben gemacht hatte, ging er ins Bett. 5. Nachdem Jens sein Fahrrad repariert hatte, machte er eine Radtour. 6. Nachdem Michael die Seiltänzerin gesehen hatte, war er ganz verliebt. 7. Nachdem Richard ein ganzes Jahr gespart hatte, flog er nach Australien. 8. Nachdem Silvia zwei Semester allein gewohnt hatte, zog

sie in eine Wohngemeinschaft. 9. Nachdem Willi ein Geräusch gehört hatte, rief er den Großvater an.

Kapitel 10

Übung 1: 1. b. 2. a. 3. h. 4. g. 5. c. 6. d. 7. i. 8. j. 9. f. 10. e. **Übung 2:** 1. Nach Kopenhagen. 2. Zum Strand. 3. Zu ihrer Tante Sule. 4. Aus der Türkei. 5. Nein, sie kommt aus dem Iran. 6. Aus dem Wasser. 7. Vom Markt. 8. Ja, bei uns. 9. Bei Fatimas Tante. 10. Nach Hause. **Übung 3:** (*Answers will vary.*) 1. Ja, üb jetzt Klavier. Du hast morgen Klavierstunde. (*oder* Nein, üb jetzt nicht Klavier. Wir gehen gleich aus.) 2. Ja, ruf ihn an. Er wollte mit dir sprechen. (*oder* Nein, ruf ihn nicht an. Du musst deine Hausaufgaben machen.) 3. Ja, iss sie mal. Du hast heute noch keine Süßigkeiten gegessen. (*oder* Nein, iss sie nicht. Wir essen gleich zu Abend.) 4. Ja, mach es auf. Die Luft ist hier schlecht. (*oder* Nein, mach es nicht auf. Es ist draußen zu kalt.) 5. Ja, gib mir einen Kuss. Ich fahre weg. (*oder* Nein, gib mir keinen Kuss. Du hast gerade Schokolade auf den Lippen.) 6. Ja, rede doch mal mit mir. Du hast wohl etwas zu erklären. (*oder* Nein, rede im Moment nicht mit mir. Ich bin beschäftigt.) 7. Ja, spül bitte das Geschirr. Ich bin nicht dazu gekommen. (*oder* Nein, spül das Geschirr nicht. Ich mache es nachher.) 8. Ja, geh mal in den Garten. Du brauchst die frische Luft. (*oder* Nein, geh nicht in den Garten. Es regnet.) 9. Ja, fahr mal morgen mit dem Fahrrad in die Schule. Ich kann dich mit dem Auto nicht hinbringen. (*oder* Nein, fahr morgen nicht mit dem Fahrrad in die Schule. Ich bringe dich mit dem Auto hin.) **Übung 4:** 1. Jens und Ernst, seid nicht so laut! 2. Maria, halte bitte an der nächsten Ampel! 3. Uli, bieg an der nächsten Straße nach links ab! 4. Jutta, iss mehr Obst! 5. Herr Pusch, fahren Sie nicht so schnell! 6. Jens, warte an der Ecke auf mich! 7. Natalie und Rosemarie, seid nicht ungeduldig! 8. Andrea und Paula, grüßt euren Vater von mir! 9. Hans, lauf mal schnell zu Papa! 10. Helga und Sigrid, lest jeden Tag die Zeitung! **Übung 5:** 1. Mach 2. Sprechen Sie 3. warten Sie 4. vergiss 5. Helft **Übung 6:** (*Answers may vary.*) 1. Fahren Sie den Fluss entlang. 2. Gehen Sie über die Brücke. 3. Gehen Sie an der Kirche vorbei. 4. Fahren Sie vor dem Bahnhof links. 5. Die Tankstelle ist gegenüber von der Post. 6. Gehen Sie über die Schienen. 7. Ja, und dann biegen Sie in die Bismarckstraße rechts ein. 8. Nein, gehen Sie an dem Rathaus vorbei und dann links. 9. Das Hotel „Zum Patrizier" ist gegenüber von dem Rathaus. 10. Fahren Sie 10 km die Straße entlang. **Übung 7:** (*Answers will vary.*) **Übung 8:** 1. Müsstest du nicht noch tanken? 2. Sollten wir nicht Jens abholen? 3. Könnten zwei Freunde von mir auch mitfahren? 4. Sollten wir nicht zuerst in die Stadt fahren? 5. Wolltest du nicht zur Bank? 6. Könntest du etwas langsamer fahren? 7. Dürfte ich das Autoradio anmachen? 8. Dürfte ich das Fenster aufmachen? **Übung 9:** 1. vor 50 000 Jahren → Wann wurde Australien von den Aborigines besiedelt? 2. um 2500 v. Chr. → Wann wurden die ersten Pyramiden gebaut? 3. 44 v. Chr. → Wann wurde Cäsar ermordet? 4. 800 n. Chr. → Wann wurde Karl der Große zum Kaiser gekrönt? 5. 1088 → Wann wurde die erste Universität (Bologna) gegründet? 6. 1789 → Wann wurde die amerikanische Verfassung unterschrieben? 7. 1885 → Wann wurde in Kanada die transkontinentale Eisenbahn vollendet? 8. 1945 → Wann wurden die Atombomben auf Hiroshima und Nagasaki geworfen? 9. 1963 → Wann wurde John F. Kennedy erschossen? 10. 1990 → Wann wurde Deutschland vereinigt? **Übung 10:** 1. Mäuse werden in vielen Labortests benutzt. 2. Meerschweinchen werden oft als Haustiere gehalten. 3. Bienen werden wegen ihrer Honigproduktion geschätzt. 4. Mücken werden durch Parfum und Kosmetikprodukte angelockt. 5. Die Fledermaus wird in vielen Kulturen mit Vampiren assoziiert. 6. Schnecken werden oft mit Butter- und Knoblauchsoße gegessen. 7. Der Gepard wird immer noch für seinen Pelz getötet. 8. Die meisten Papageien werden in der Wildnis gefangen. 9. Delfine werden wegen ihrer Intelligenz bewundert. 10. Viele Haie werden jedes Jahr gefischt.

Kapitel 11

Übung 1: 1.a. fühle mich b. mich erkältet c. dich ... legen 2.a. sich ... aufgeregt b. sich ... ausruhen 3.a. dich verletzt b. mich ... geschnitten 4.a. ärgerst ... dich b. dich freuen **Übung 2:** (*Answers will vary.*) Erst stehe ich auf. Dann dusche ich mich. Dann wasche ich mir das Gesicht. Dann wasche ich mir die Haare. Dann trockne ich mich ab. Dann putze ich mir die Fingernägel. Dann rasiere ich mich. Dann kämme ich mir die Haare. Dann ziehe ich mich an. Dann frühstücke ich. Dann putze ich mir die Zähne und gehe zur Uni.   **Übung 3:** (*Answers will vary.*) 1. Ich rasiere mich jeden Morgen. 2. Meine Oma schminkt sich zu sehr. 3. Mein Freund wäscht sich nicht oft genug die Haare. 4. Mein Vater putzt sich nach jeder Mahlzeit die Zähne. 5. Mein Onkel zieht sich immer verrückt an. 6. Meine Schwester duscht sich jeden Tag. 7. Meine Freundin kämmt sich nie. 8. Mein Bruder föhnt sich nie die Haare. 9. Meine Kusine badet sich nicht gern. 10. Meine Mutter zieht sich immer elegant an.   **Übung 4:** 1. Ja, kannst du es mir geben? / Nein, ich brauche es nicht. 2. Ja, kannst du ihn mir geben? / Nein, ich brauche ihn nicht. 3. Ja, kannst du ihn mir geben? / Nein, ich brauche ihn nicht. 4. Ja, kannst du sie mir geben? / Nein, ich brauche sie nicht. 5. Ja, kannst du es mir geben? / Nein, ich brauche es nicht. 6. Ja, kannst du ihn mir geben? / Nein, ich brauche ihn nicht. 7. Ja, kannst du sie mir geben? / Nein, ich brauche sie nicht. 8. Ja, kannst du es mir geben? / Nein, ich brauche es nicht. 9. Ja, kannst du ihn mir geben? / Nein, ich brauche ihn nicht.   **Übung 5:** 1. Warum schneidest du ihn dir nicht? 2. Warum wäschst du sie dir nicht? 3. Warum schneidest du sie dir nicht? 4. Warum kremst du sie dir nicht ein? 5. Warum föhnst du sie dir nicht? 6. Warum wäschst du ihn dir nicht? 7. Warum putzt du sie dir nicht? 8. Warum lässt du sie dir nicht schneiden? 9. Warum kremst du es dir nicht ein? 10. Warum wäschst du sie dir nicht?   **Übung 6:** (*Some answers will vary.*) 1. Wissen Sie, was hier passiert ist? (*oder* Können Sie mir sagen, was hier passiert ist?) 2. Wissen Sie, ob das Kind das Auto gesehen hat? (*oder* Können Sie mir sagen, ob das Kind das Auto gesehen hat?) 3. Wissen Sie, wer daran Schuld war? (*oder* Können Sie mir sagen, wer daran Schuld war?) 4. Wissen Sie, warum Herr Langen das Kind nicht gesehen hat? (*oder* Können Sie mir sagen, warum Herr Langen das Kind nicht gesehen hat?) 5. Wissen Sie, ob Herr Langen gebremst hat? (*oder* Können Sie mir sagen, ob Herr Langen gebremst hat?) 6. Wissen Sie, wann er gebremst hat? (*oder* Können Sie mir sagen, wann er gebremst hat?) 7. Wissen Sie, wie oft Herr Langen diese Straße zur Arbeit fährt? (*oder* Können Sie mir sagen, wie oft Herr Langen diese Straße zur Arbeit fährt?) 8. Wissen Sie, wie lange Lothar auf der Straße lag? (*oder* Können Sie mir sagen, wie lange Lothar auf der Straße lag?) 9. Wissen Sie, wann die Polizei Lothars Mutter angerufen hat? (*oder* Können Sie mir sagen, wann die Polizei Lothars Mutter angerufen hat?)   **Übung 7:** 1.a. ob b. dass c. Wenn 2.a. damit b. Weil   **Übung 8:** 1.a. als b. nachdem 2. bevor 3. Während 4. obwohl

Kapitel 12

Übung 1: 1. meines 2. Ihrer 3. meiner 4. deiner 5. dieses 6. alten 7. ersten 8. neuen   **Übung 2:** 1. Monika spricht über den Beruf ihrer Schwester. 2. Thomas spricht über das Bild seines Vaters. 3. Frau Schulz spricht über das Alter ihrer Nichten. 4. Stefan spricht über die Länge seines Studiums. 5. Albert spricht über die Sprache seiner Großeltern. 6. Nora spricht über die Kleidung ihres Freundes. 7. Thomas spricht über die Qualität des Leitungswassers in Berkeley. 8. Katrin spricht über die Situation der Frauen.   **Übung 3:** 1. trotz 2. wegen 3. während 4. trotz 5. während 6. Wegen 7. statt 8. trotz   **Übung 4:** (*Answers will vary.*)   **Übung 5:** (*Answers will vary.*)   **Übung 6:** 1. Um morgens munter zu sein, muss man früh ins Bett gehen. 2. Um die Professoren kennenzulernen, muss man in die Sprechstunde gehen. 3. Um die Mitstudenten kennenzulernen, muss man viel Gruppenarbeit machen. 4. Um am Wochenende nicht allein zu sein, muss man Leute einladen. 5. Um die Kurse zu bekommen, die man will, muss man sich so früh wie möglich einschreiben. 6. Um in vier Jahren fertig zu werden, muss man viel lernen und wenig Feste feiern. 7. Um nicht zu verhungern, muss man regelmäßig essen. 8. Um eine gute Note in Deutsch zu bekommen, muss man jeden Tag zum Unterricht kommen.   **Übung 7:** (*Answers may vary.*) 1. Ich möchte immer hier leben, weil dieses Land das beste Land der Welt ist. 2. Ich möchte für ein paar Jahre in Deutschland leben, um richtig gut Deutsch zu lernen. 3. Ausländer haben oft Probleme, weil sie die Sprache und Kultur des Gastlandes nicht verstehen. 4. Wenn ich Kinder habe, möchte ich hier leben, damit meine Kinder als (Amerikaner, Kanadier, Australier usw.) aufwachsen. 5. Viele Ausländer kommen hierher, weil man hier gut Geld verdienen kann. 6. Englisch sollte die einzige offizielle Sprache (der USA, Kanadas, Australiens usw.) sein, damit eine homogene Gemeinschaft aus der multikulturellen Bevölkerung wird.   **Übung 8:** 1. Nom, F 2. Nom, V 3. Gen, F 4. Dat, F 5. Nom, F 6. Dat, V 7. Akk, P 8. Akk, P 9. Akk, F 10. Dat, P 11. Dat, V 12. Gen, P   **Übung 9:** 1. em 2. en 3. e 4. er 5. e 6. er 7. e 8. en 9. ie 10. ie 11. en 12. e 13. en 14. en 15. er 16. em 17. en 18. em 19. er

Vokabeln

Deutsch-Englisch

Note to Students: The definitions in this vocabulary are based on the words as used in this text. For additional meanings, please refer to a dictionary.

Proper nouns are given only if the name is feminine or masculine or if the spelling is different from that in English. Compound words that do not appear in the chapter vocabulary lists have generally been omitted if they are easily analyzable and their constituent parts appear elsewhere in the vocabulary.

The letters or numbers in parentheses following the entries refer to the chapters in which the words occur in the chapter vocabulary lists.

Abbreviations

acc.	accusative	*n.*	noun
adj.	adjective	*neut.*	neuter
adv.	adverb	*nom.*	nominative
coll.	colloquial	*o.s.*	oneself
coord. conj.	coordinating conjunction	*pl.*	plural
dat.	dative	*p.p.*	past participle
def. art.	definite article	*prep.*	preposition
dem. pron.	demonstrative pronoun	*pron.*	pronoun
dial.	dialectal form	*rel. pron.*	relative pronoun
fem.	feminine	*sg.*	singular
for.	formal	*s.o.*	someone
gen.	genitive	*s.th.*	something
inf.	infinitive	*subord. conj.*	subordinating conjunction
infor.	informal	*v.*	verb
interj.	interjection	*wk.*	weak masculine noun
masc.	masculine		

ab (+ *dat.*) from; as of, effective

ab·bauen, abgebaut to reduce

ab·biegen (biegt … ab), bog … ab, ist abgebogen to turn (10)

das **Abbild, -er** copy, likeness

ab·brennen (brennt … ab), brannte … ab, ist abgebrannt to be burned down

der **Abend, -e** evening (1, 4); **am Abend** in the evening, at night (4); **gestern Abend** last night (4); **guten Abend!** good evening (A); der **Heilige Abend** Christmas Eve; **heute Abend** this evening (2); **morgen Abend** tomorrow evening; **zu Abend essen** to dine, have dinner (4)

das **Abendessen, -** dinner, supper, evening meal (1, 8); **zum Abendessen** for dinner

abends evenings, in the evening (4)

das **Abenteuer, -** adventure; **Abenteuer erleben** to have adventures

aber (*coord. conj.*) but (A, 11)

ab·fahren (fährt … ab), fuhr … ab, ist abgefahren to leave, depart (4)

die **Abfahrt, -en** departure

ab·geben (gibt … ab), gab … ab, abgegeben to hand over (to); to deliver (to)

ab·gehen (geht … ab), ging … ab, ist abgegangen to go away, leave; to come off

ab·grenzen, abgegrenzt to separate

ab·holen, abgeholt to pick (*s.o./s.th.*) up (from a place); to fetch (1)

das **Abhörgerät, -e** listening device, bug

das **Abi** = das **Abitur**

das **Abitur** college-prep-school degree, high school diploma (5)

ab·kauen, abgekaut to chew off

die **Abkürzung, -en** abbreviation

ab·legen, abgelegt to take (*a test*)

ab·lenken, abgelenkt to divert; to change/get off the subject

ab·nehmen (nimmt … ab), nahm … ab, abgenommen to take off/away; to remove; to lose weight (8, 11); **Blut abnehmen** to take blood (11)

die **Aborigines** (*pl.*) aborigines (*native people of Australia*)

ab·räumen, abgeräumt to clear; to remove (3); **den Tisch abräumen** to clear the table (3)

ab·rechnen, abgerechnet to tally up; to settle an account

ab·reisen, ist abgereist to depart (10)

ab·reißen (reißt … ab), riss … ab, abgerissen to tear off; to pluck

der **Absatz, ⸚e** paragraph

absatzweise one paragraph at a time

ab·saugen, abgesaugt to vacuum

der **Abschiedsgruß, ⸚e** goodbye, farewell

ab·schließen (schließt … ab), schloss … ab, abgeschlossen to lock (up); to finish; to graduate

der **Abschluss, ⸚e** completion; final examination; graduation; degree; diploma (9)

ab·schneiden (schneidet … ab), schnitt … ab, abgeschnitten to cut off (8); to do (well/badly)

der **Abschnitt, -e** segment, section

ab·schreiben (schreibt … ab), schrieb … ab, abgeschrieben to copy (from another person)

der **Abstand,** ⸚e distance

ab·stürzen, ist abgestürzt to crash (11)

ab·trocknen, abgetrocknet to dry (*dishes*) (6); **sich abtrocknen** to dry (*o.s.*) off (11)

ab·waschen (wäscht ... ab), wusch ... ab, abgewaschen to wash (dishes)

ab·wischen, abgewischt to wipe off; to wipe clean (6)

ab·zahlen, abgezahlt to pay off (12)

ach oh; **ach so** I see

acht eight (A)

acht- eighth (4)

achten (auf + acc.), geachtet to watch out (for); to pay attention (to) (11)

achtjährig eight years old

achtundzwanzig twenty-eight (A)

die **Achtung** attention (7)

achtzehn eighteen (A)

achtzehnt- eighteenth

achtzig eighty (A)

ächzen, geächzt to creak

die **Action** action

der **ADAC = Allgemeiner Deutscher Automobilclub** *German automobile club*

addieren, addiert to add

der **Adel** nobility

die **Ader, -n** vein

das **Adjektiv, -e** adjective

der **Adler, -** eagle (10)

die **Adresse, -n** address (1)

der **Adventskalender, -** calendar counting the days of Advent

der **Adventssonntag, -e** Sunday in Advent

das **Adverb, -ien** adverb

(das) **Afrika** Africa (B)

afrikanisch African (*adj.*)

afro-deutsch Afro-German (*adj.*) (12)

aggressiv aggressive(ly)

der **Agraringenieur, -e** / die **Agraringenieurin, -nen** agricultural engineer

(das) **Ägypten** Egypt (B)

der **Ägypter, -** / die **Ägypterin, -nen** Egyptian (*person*)

ähnlich similar(ly) (A)

die **Ahnung, -en** idea, suspicion; **keine Ahnung** (I have) no idea

das **Akkordeon, -s** accordion (4)

der **Akkusativ, -e** accusative

die **Akte, -n** file; record

die **Aktie, -n** share, stock (12)

der **Aktienmarkt,** ⸚e stock market

die **Aktion, -en** action, campaign

die **Aktivität, -en** activity

aktuell current; present-day

der **Akzent, -e** accent

die **Akzentuierung, -en** accentuation

akzeptabel acceptable

akzeptieren, akzeptiert to accept; to agree to

(das) **Albanien** Albania (B)

der **Albatros, -se** albatross (10)

der **Aletschgletscher: der Große Aletschgletscher** *glacier in the Swiss Alps*

(das) **Algerien** Algeria (B)

das **Alibi, -s** alibi

der **Alkohol** alcohol

alkoholisiert inebriated

der **Alkoholkonsum** alcohol consumption

all all; **alle** (*pl.*) everybody; **nichts von alledem** none of this; **vor allem** above all

allein(e) alone; by oneself; **von allein** on one's own; by oneself

allerdings however; of course

allergisch (gegen + acc.) allergic (to) (11)

alles everything (2); **alles Mögliche** everything possible (2); **alles zusammen** all together; one check (*restaurant*) (5); **dies alles** all of this; **was man alles braucht** everything one needs

allgemein general(ly)

der **Alltag, -e** daily routine (4)

alltäglich everyday, daily

die **Alpen** (*pl.*) the Alps (7)

das **Alphabet, -e** alphabet (3)

alpin alpine

als (*after comparative*) than; (*subord. conj.*) when; as (5, 11); **als ich acht Jahre alt war** when I was eight years old (5); **als ob** as if; as though; **als was?** as what? (5); **anders als** different from

also so; thus; well (2)

alt old (A)

das **Alter, -** age (1)

die **Altbauwohnung, -en** *apartment in a building built before June 20, 1948*

die **Alternative, -n** alternative

die **Altstadt,** ⸚e old part of town (10)

am = an dem at/on the

(das) **Amerika** America; the United States (B)

der **Amerikaner, -** / die **Amerikanerin, -nen** American (*person*) (B)

amerikanisch American (*adj.*)

die **Ampel, -n** traffic light

das **Amt,** ⸚er public office

der **Amtsrichter, -** / die **Amtsrichterin, -nen** local or district court judge

an (+ acc./dat.) at; on; to; in (2, 4); **am Abend** in the evening (4); **am ersten Oktober** on the first of October (4); **am Leben sein** to be alive (9); **am liebsten** like (*to do s.th.*) best (7); **am Samstag** on Saturday (2); **am Schalter** at the ticket booth (5); **am Telefon** on the telephone (2); **am wenigsten** the least (8); **am Wochenende** over the weekend (1); **an der Kasse** at the ticket booth (5); **an der Tankstelle** at the gas station (5); **an der Uni** at the university; **ans Meer** to the sea (2); **an ... vorbei** past, by (10); **an welchem Tag?** on what day? (4); **das Bild an die Wand hängen** to hang the picture on the wall (3)

analysieren, analysiert to analyze

die **Ananas, -** *or* **-se** pineapple

der **Anbau** cultivation

an·bieten (bietet ... an), bot ... an, angeboten to offer

der **Anblick, -e** sight

an·blicken, angeblickt to look at

das **Andenken, -** souvenir (10)

ander- other; different; **anders** different; **etwas anderes** something else; **unter anderem** among other things

(sich) **ändern, geändert** to change (9)

die **Anerkennung, -en** acknowledgment, appreciation

der **Anfang,** ⸚e beginning

an·fangen (fängt ... an), fing ... an, angefangen to begin, start (4)

an·fassen, angefasst to touch

die **Angabe, -n** information

an·geben (gibt ... an), gab ... an, angegeben to give; to state, declare

angeblich supposed(ly); alleged(ly)

das **Angebot, -e** offer

an·gehören, angehört to belong to (*an organization*) (12)

der/die **Angeklagte, -n (ein Angeklagter)** accused; defendant

angeln, geangelt to fish

angenehm pleasant (6)

angespannt tense(ly)

der/die **Angestellte, -n (ein Angestellter)** employee; clerk (7)

die **Anglistik** English language and literature

an·greifen (greift ... an), griff ... an, angegriffen to attack (12)

die **Angst,** ⸚e fear (3); **Angst einjagen** (+ *dat.*) to scare; **Angst haben (vor** + *dat.*) to be afraid (of) (3)

an·haben (hat ... an), hatte ... an, angehabt to have on (*clothes*)

an·halten (hält ... an), hielt ... an, hat/ist angehalten to stop (7)

an·heben (hebt ... an), hob ... an, angehoben to lift

(sich) **an·hören, angehört** to listen to; **sich anhören** to sound; **das hört sich toll an** that sounds great (4)

animieren, animiert to encourage

an·kommen (kommt ... an), kam ... an, ist angekommen to arrive (1)

an·kreuzen, angekreuzt to mark with a cross, mark with an x

die **Ankunft,** ⸚e arrival

der **Anlass,** ⸚e cause; reason

an·legen, angelegt to lay down; to put on (10); **den Sicherheitsgurt anlegen** to put on one's seatbelt

das **Anliegen** matter

an·locken, angelockt to attract

an·machen, angemacht to turn on, switch on (3)

an·malen, angemalt to paint

(sich) **an·melden, angemeldet** to register (12)

die **Anmeldung, -en** registration; reception (desk)

an·nehmen (nimmt ... an), nahm ... an, angenommen to accept; to take; to adopt anonym anonymous(ly)

die Anrede, -n salutation

an·reden, angeredet to speak to; to address

der Anruf, -e phone call

an·rufen (ruft ... an), rief ... an, angerufen to call up (*on the telephone*) (1)

ans = an das to/on the

(sich) an·schauen, angeschaut to look at; to watch (2)

anscheinend apparently

sich an·schließen (+ *dat.*) (schließt ... an), schloss ... an, angeschlossen to join

anschließend subsequent(ly)

der Anschluss, -̈e connection

die Anschrift, -en address (11)

(sich) an·sehen (sieht ... an), sah ... an, angesehen to look at; to watch (3)

an·sprechen (spricht ... an), sprach ... an, angesprochen to speak to (*s.o.*)

anstatt (+ *gen.*) instead of (12)

an·stehen (steht ... an), stand ... an, angestanden to line up; to stand in line

anstrengend strenuous; tiring

der Anteil, -e share

antiautoritär antiauthoritarian

der Antrag, -̈e application

der Antragsteller, - / die Antragstellerin, -nen applicant

der Antrieb, -e motivation

die Antwort, -en answer (A)

antworten (+ *dat.*), geantwortet to answer (*s.o.*) (4, 10); auf eine Frage antworten to answer a question

der Anwalt, -̈e / die Anwältin, -nen lawyer (5)

an·wenden (wendet ... an), wandte ... an, angewandt to use

an·werben (wirbt ... an), warb ... an, angeworben to recruit, enlist

die Anwerbung, -en recruitment

der Anwohner, - / die Anwohnerin, -nen resident

die Anzeige, -n ad (6)

an·ziehen (zieht ... an), zog ... an, angezogen to attract; to put on (*clothes*) (3); sich anziehen to get dressed (11)

der Anziehungspunkt, -e attraction

der Anzug, -̈e suit (A)

an·zünden, angezündet to light; to set on fire (3)

die AOK = Allgemeine Ortskrankenkasse *insurance company*

der Apfel, -̈ apple

der Apfelsaft, -̈e apple juice (8)

die Apfelschorle, -n apple juice with mineral water

die Apfelsine, -n orange (8)

die Apotheke, -n pharmacy (6, 11)

der Apotheker, - / die Apothekerin, -nen pharmacist (11)

der Apparat, -e telephone; apparatus

das Appartement, -s apartment

der April April (B)

das Aquarell, -e watercolor painting

arabisch Arabian (*adj.*)

(das) Arabisch Arabic (*language*) (B)

(die) Arabistik study of Arabic language and literature

die Arbeit, -en work (1); von der Arbeit from work (3); zur Arbeit gehen to go to work (1)

arbeiten, gearbeitet to work (1); arbeiten Sie mit einem Partner work with a partner (A)

der/die Arbeitende, -n (ein Arbeitender) working person

der Arbeiter, - / die Arbeiterin, -nen worker (5)

der Arbeitnehmer, - / die Arbeitnehmerin, -nen employee

das Arbeitsamt, -̈er employment office

das Arbeitsbuch, -̈er workbook (3)

die Arbeitserlaubnis, -se work permit (12)

die Arbeitskraft, -̈e labor; employee (12)

arbeitslos unemployed (5)

die Arbeitslosigkeit unemployment

die Arbeitsteilung, -en division of labor

der Architekt, -en (*wk.*) / die Architektin, -nen architect (5)

die Architektur, -en architecture

der Ärger trouble (9)

ärgern, geärgert to annoy; to tease; to bother (3); sich ärgern (über + *acc.*) to get angry (about) (11)

arm poor (9)

der Arm, -e arm (B); jemanden auf den Arm nehmen to tease someone; to pull someone's leg; sich den Arm brechen to break one's arm (11)

das Armband, -̈er bracelet (2)

die Armbanduhr, -en watch, wristwatch (A)

die Armschlinge, -n sling

die Armut poverty

die Arnika, -s arnica

die Art, -en kind, type (2)

der Artikel, - article

der Arzt, -̈e / die Ärztin, -nen doctor; physician (3, 5, 11); zum Arzt to the doctor (3)

die Arztpraxis, Arztpraxen doctor's office (11)

die Asche, -n ash(es)

(das) Aschenputtel Cinderella

(das) Asien Asia (B)

der Aspekt, -e aspect

die Asphaltschindel, -n asphalt shingle

das Aspirin aspirin (3, 11)

der Assessor, -en / die Assessorin, -nen assistant judge

assoziieren (mit + *dat.*), assoziiert to associate (with)

das Atelier, -s studio

(das) Athen Athens

(der) Atlantik Atlantic Ocean

atmen, geatmet to breathe (11)

die Atombombe, -n atomic bomb

die Attraktion, -en attraction

attraktiv attractive (6)

au: au ja oh yes

auch also; too; as well (A)

auf (+ *dat./acc.*) on; upon; on top of; onto; to; at; (*adv.*) up; open; auf dem Bahnhof at the train station (5); auf dem Gericht at the courthouse (5); auf dem Land in the country (6); auf dem Rathaus at the town hall (1); auf der Bank at the bank (5); auf der Durchreise sein to be traveling through (7); auf der Polizei at the police station (5); auf der Post at the post office (5); auf der Uni(versität) sein to be at the university (1, 5); auf Deutsch in German; auf die Bank gehen to go to the bank; auf eine Party gehen to go to a party (1); auf einmal at once; auf jeden Fall by all means (4); auf Reisen sein to be on a trip (7); auf Wohnungssuche looking for a room or apartment; bis auf down to; jemanden auf den Arm nehmen to tease someone; to pull someone's leg

auf Wiederhören! good-bye! (*on the telephone*) (6)

auf Wiedersehen! good-bye! (A)

auf·bauen, aufgebaut to build

auf·begehren, aufbegehrt to rebel

auf·bleiben (bleibt ... auf), blieb ... auf, ist aufgeblieben to stay open

auf·brechen (bricht ... auf), brach ... auf, ist aufgebrochen to set off; to start out

die Aufenthaltserlaubnis, -se residence permit (12)

die Aufenthaltsgenehmigung, -en residence permit

der Aufenthaltsraum, -̈e lounge, recreation room (10)

auf·essen (isst ... auf), aß ... auf, aufgegessen to eat up

auf·fallen (fällt ... auf), fiel ... auf, ist aufgefallen to be noticeable (12)

auffällig conspicuous (10)

auf·fliegen (fliegt ... auf), flog ... auf, ist aufgeflogen to fly open

die Aufforderung, -en request; instruction (A)

die Aufgabe, -n assignment; task; homework; job (4)

auf·geben (gibt ... auf), gab ... auf, aufgegeben to give up; to check (luggage); to assign

auf·gehen (geht ... auf), ging ... auf, ist aufgegangen to open

aufgeregt excited(ly)

aufgeschlossen open; approachable

auf·greifen (greift ... auf), griff ... auf, aufgegriffen to take up

auf·halten (hält ... auf), hielt ... auf, aufgehalten to halt; to hold up

auf·hängen, aufgehängt to hang up (12)

auf·heben (hebt ... auf), hob ... auf, aufgehoben to lift

auf·hören (mit + *dat.*), aufgehört to stop (*doing s.th.*) (1); to be over

auf·klappen, aufgeklappt to open up

auf·kriegen, aufgekriegt to get (*s.th.*) open

auf·laden (lädt ... auf), lud ... auf, aufgeladen to charge, recharge (*a battery*) auf·leben, ist aufgelebt to come to life

auf·legen, aufgelegt to put on

auf·lodern, aufgelodert to blaze

(sich) auf·lösen, aufgelöst to dissolve

auf·machen, aufgemacht to open (3); to open the door

aufmerksam attentive(ly)

die Aufnahmeprüfung, -en entrance examination

auf·nehmen (nimmt ... auf), nahm ... auf, aufgenommen to pick up; to take (a photo); Kredit aufnehmen to take out a loan (12)

auf·passen (auf + acc.), aufgepasst to pay attention (to); to watch out (for) (3)

auf·räumen, aufgeräumt to clean (up); to tidy up (1)

aufrecht upright

sich auf·regen, aufgeregt to get excited; to get upset (11)

aufregend exciting

die Aufregung, -en excitement

sich auf·richten, aufgerichtet to stand up; to get back up

aufs = auf das on/onto/to the

auf·sagen, aufgesagt to recite

der Aufsatz, ⸗e essay

auf·saugen, aufgesaugt to vacuum

auf·schlagen (schlägt ... auf), schlug ... auf, aufgeschlagen to open up

auf·schneiden (schneidet ... auf), schnitt ... auf, aufgeschnitten to chop (8)

der Aufschnitt cold cuts

auf·schreiben (schreibt ... auf), schrieb ... auf, aufgeschrieben to write down (11)

auf·springen (springt ... auf), sprang ... auf, ist aufgesprungen to jump up; to pop up

auf·stehen (steht ... auf), stand ... auf, ist aufgestanden to get up; to rise; to stand up (1); mit dem linken Fuß aufstehen to get up on the wrong side of bed (4); stehen Sie auf get up, stand up (A)

auf·stellen, aufgestellt to set up (11)

der Auftrag, ⸗e instruction; task; order

auf·treten (tritt ... auf), trat ... auf, ist aufgetreten to appear; to happen, take place

auf·wachen, ist aufgewacht to wake up (4)

auf·wachsen (wächst ... auf), wuchs ... auf, ist aufgewachsen to grow up (12)

auf·wischen, aufgewischt to mop (up) (6)

der Aufzug, ⸗e elevator (6)

das Auge, -n eye (B); blaue Augen (pl.) blue eyes (B)

der Augenarzt, ⸗e / die Augenärztin, -nen eye doctor (11)

der Augenblick, -e moment

die Augenfarbe, -n color of eyes (1)

der August August (B)

aus (+ dat.) out of; from; of (10); made of; due to; aus Stein made (out) of stone; von ... aus from

die Ausbildung, -en education (9); (specialized) training (5); praktische Ausbildung practical (career) training (5)

aus·blasen (bläst ... aus), blies ... aus, ausgeblasen to blow out

der Ausblick, -e view (6)

der Ausdruck, ⸗e expression

ausdrücken, ausgedrückt to express

aus·fallen (fällt ... aus), fiel ... aus, ist ausgefallen to fall out; to fail; to go out (power) (8)

der Ausflug, ⸗e excursion

aus·führen, ausgeführt to carry out; to execute (12)

aus·füllen, ausgefüllt to fill out (1)

die Ausgabe, -n expenditure

die Ausgangslage, -n starting position; initial situation

der Ausgangspunkt, -e starting point

aus·geben (gibt ... aus), gab ... aus, ausgegeben to spend (money) (3)

ausgebildet educated (12)

aus·gehen (geht ... aus), ging ... aus, ist ausgegangen to go out (1)

ausgezeichnet excellent (3)

aus·hängen, ausgehängt to put up

das Aushängeschild, -er sign

aus·helfen (hilft ... aus), half ... aus, ausgeholfen to help out

das Ausland foreign countries (6); im Ausland abroad (6)

der Ausländer, - / die Ausländerin, -nen foreigner (12)

ausländerfreundlich friendly/open to foreigners

der Ausländerhass hostility toward foreigners (12)

ausländisch foreign (12)

das Auslandsamt, ⸗er center for study abroad (1)

aus·leeren, ausgeleert to empty (3); den Papierkorb ausleeren to empty the wastebasket

aus·leihen (leiht ... aus), lieh ... aus, ausgeliehen to borrow; to lend

aus·machen, ausgemacht to turn off (3)

die Ausnahme, -n exception

aus·packen, ausgepackt to unpack

aus·rauben, ausgeraubt to rob (of everything)

aus·rechnen, ausgerechnet to figure; to total (up) (8)

aus·reichen, ausgereicht to be enough

ausreichend sufficient

die Ausrichtung, -en orientation; organization

sich aus·ruhen, ausgeruht to rest (11)

aus·rutschen, ist ausgerutscht to slip (11)

die Aussage, -n statement

aus·sagen, ausgesagt to testify; to state

aus·schlafen (schläft ... aus), schlief ... aus, ausgeschlafen to sleep late; to sleep in

der Ausschnitt, -e excerpt

aus·schreiben (schreibt ... aus), schrieb ... aus, ausgeschrieben to write out

aus·sehen (sieht ... aus), sah ... aus, ausgesehen to look; to appear (2); es sieht gut aus it looks good

das Aussehen appearance

außen (adv.) outside

die Außenwelt outside world

außer (+ dat.) except, besides

außerdem besides (5, 10)

das Äußere (ein Äußeres) outward appearance

außergewöhnlich extraordinary

außerhalb (+ gen.) outside of (12)

aus·spannen, ausgespannt to take a break; to relax

die Aussprache pronunciation

aus·sprechen (spricht ... aus), sprach ... aus, ausgesprochen to pronounce

aus·spucken, ausgespuckt to spit out

aus·steigen (steigt ... aus), stieg ... aus, ist ausgestiegen to get out/off

aus·stellen, ausgestellt to display; to exhibit

die Ausstellung, -en exhibition

aus·strecken, ausgestreckt to stretch out

aus·suchen, ausgesucht to choose; to pick out

der Austauschstudent, -en (wk.) / die Austauschstudentin, -nen exchange student

aus·tragen (trägt ... aus), trug ... aus, ausgetragen to deliver (5); Zeitungen austragen to deliver newspapers (5)

(das) Australien Australia (B)

der Australier, - / die Australierin, -nen Australian (person) (B)

aus·trinken (trinkt ... aus), trank ... aus, ausgetrunken to drink up

aus·üben, ausgeübt to practice (12)

ausverkauft sold out (5)

aus·wählen, ausgewählt to select (8)

der Auswahltest, -s selection test

aus·wandern, ist ausgewandert to emigrate (4, 12)

auswärtig foreign

der Ausweg, -e way out

der Ausweis, -e identification card (10)

aus·ziehen (zieht ... aus), zog ... aus, ausgezogen to take off (clothes) (3); sich ausziehen to get undressed (11)

der/die Auszubildende, -n (ein Auszubildender) apprentice; trainee

das Auto, -s car (A, 7); Auto fahren to drive (a car)

die Autobahn, -en interstate highway; freeway (7)

der Autodidakt, -en (wk.) / die Autodidaktin, -nen self-taught person

das Autofahren driving

der Autofahrer, - / die Autofahrerin, -nen driver

der Automat, -en (wk.) vending machine

automatisch automatic(ally)

die Autonummer, -n license plate number (11)

das Autoradio, -s car radio (7)

die Autorität, -en authority

das Autotelefon, -e car phone (2)

der/die Azubi -s (coll.) = der/die Auszubildende apprentice; trainee

das Baby, -s baby (7)

der Babysitter, - / die Babysitterin, -nen babysitter

das Babysitting babysitting

der Bachelor, -s bachelor's degree

backen (bäckt), backte, gebacken to bake (5)

der Backenbart, ⸗e sideburns

der Bäcker, - / die Bäckerin, -nen baker

die **Bäckerei, -en** bakery (5); **in der Bäckerei** at the bakery (5)

der **Backofen, ÷** oven (5)

der **Backstein, -e** brick

die **Backsteingotik** Gothic architecture in brick

das **Bad, ÷er** bathroom; bath (6)

der **Badeanzug, ÷e** bathing suit (5)

die **Badehose, -n** swimming trunks (5)

der **Badekarren, -** bathing cart

der **Bademantel, ÷** bathrobe (2)

der **Bademeister, -** / die **Bademeisterin, -nen** swimming pool attendant (5)

baden, gebadet to bathe; to swim (3); **sich baden** to bathe (*o.s.*) (11)

der **Badeort, -e** bathing resort

die **Badewanne, -n** bathtub (6)

das **BAföG** = das **Bundesausbildungsförderungsgesetz** *financial aid for students from the German government*

die **Bahn, -en** railroad (7); **freie Bahn** clear path

der/die **Bahnangestellte, -n (ein Bahnangestellter)** train agent; railway employee (10)

die **Bahncard, -s** *discount card for rail travel in Germany*

der **Bahnhof, ÷e** train station (building) (4, 5); **auf dem Bahnhof** at the train station (5)

bald soon (9); **bald darauf** soon thereafter (9); **bis bald!** so long, see you soon! (A)

der **Balkon, -e** balcony (6)

der **Ball, ÷e** ball (A, 1)

die **Ballerina, -s** ballerina (9)

der **Ballettunterricht** ballet class (9)

die **Banane, -n** banana (8)

das **Band, ÷er** ribbon; strap

die **Band, -s** band, music group

die **Bank, ÷e** bench

die **Bank, -en** bank (5); **auf der Bank** at the bank (5); **bei einer Bank** at a bank (6)

der/die **Bankangestellte, -n (ein Bankangestellter)** bank employee (5)

der **Bankeinzug, ÷e** automatic withdrawal; electronic transfer of funds

die **Bankenmetropole, -n** banking metropolis

der **Bankräuber, -** / die **Bankräuberin, -nen** bank robber

der **Bär, -en** (*wk.*) bear

das **Bargeld** cash (12)

bargeldlos cash-free (12)

barock baroque

das/der **Barock** baroque

der **Bart, ÷e** beard (B)

die **Baseballmannschaft, -en** baseball team (9)

(das) **Basel** Basel

das **Basilikum** basil

der **Basketball, ÷e** basketball (2)

basteln, gebastelt to build things; to tinker; to do handicrafts

der **Bau** construction

der **Bauamtsleiter, -** / die **Bauamtsleiterin, -nen** head of department of planning and building inspection

der **Bauarbeiter, -** / die **Bauarbeiterin, -nen** construction worker (5)

der **Bauch, ÷e** belly, stomach (B)

der **Bauchnabel, -** belly button, navel

bauen, gebaut to build

der **Bauer, -n** / die **Bäuerin, -nen** farmer

das **Bauernbrot, -e** (loaf of) farmer's bread (5)

das **Bauernhaus, ÷er** farmhouse (6)

das **Baugewerbe** construction; building trade

die **Baukunst** architecture

der **Baum, ÷e** tree (9)

das **Baumhaus, ÷er** tree house (6)

der **Baustil, -e** architectural style

(das) **Bayern** Bavaria

beachten, beachtet to notice; to pay attention to

der **Beamte, -n (ein Beamter)** / die **Beamtin, -nen** civil servant

beantragen, beantragt to apply for (12)

beantworten, beantwortet to answer (7)

der **Becher, -** cup; mug; glass (9)

das **Bedenken** concern; reflection

bedeuten, bedeutet to mean

bedeutend important

bedienen, bedient to serve

die **Bedienung, -en** service; waiter, waitress (8)

die **Bedingung, -en** condition

die **Bedrohung, -en** threat

der **Beduine, -n** (*wk.*) / die **Beduinin, -nen** Bedouin

sich beeilen, beeilt to hurry (8)

beeindrucken, beeindruckt to impress

beenden, beendet to end

sich befinden (befindet), befand, befunden to be located; to be situated

befragen, befragt to interview; to interrogate

befreundet (*adj.*): **ein befreundeter Regisseur** a director who is a friend

befriedigend satisfactory

begabt gifted (9)

begegnen (+ *dat.*), **ist begegnet** to meet, encounter (6)

begehen (begeht), beging, begangen to commit

begeistert (*p.p. of* **begeistern**) thrilled; enthusiastic

beginnen (beginnt), begann, begonnen to begin, start (1)

begleiten, begleitet to accompany

die **Begleitperson, -en** accompanying person

begraben (begräbt), begrub, begraben to bury

der **Begriff, -e** concept

begrüßen, begrüßt to greet

das **Begrüßen** greeting (A)

behalten (behält), behielt, behalten to keep

die **Behandlung, -en** treatment

beherrschen, beherrscht to master

behindert handicapped

die **Behörde, -n** public authority (12)

bei (+ *dat.*) at; with; near (2, 6, 10); during; upon; among; **bei deinen Eltern** with your parents, at your parents' place (6); **bei der Bundeswehr** in the German army (5); **bei dir** at your place (3); **bei einer Bank** at a bank (6); **bei Monika** at Monika's (place) (2); **bei Regen** in rainy weather (7)

bei.bringen (bringt ... bei), brachte ... bei, beigebracht to teach

beide both

bei·liegen (+ *dat.*) **(liegt ... bei), lag ... bei, beigelegen** to be contained in

beim = **bei dem** at/with/near the

das **Bein, -e** leg (B)

beinah almost; nearly

der/das **Beinspray, -s** leg spray

das **Beispiel, -e** example (3); **zum Beispiel** for example (3)

beißen (beißt), biss, gebissen to bite (9)

bei·treten (+ *dat.*) **(tritt ... bei), trat ... bei, ist beigetreten** to join

bekannt well-known

der/die **Bekannte, -n (ein Bekannter)** acquaintance

bekommen (bekommt), bekam, bekommen to get; to receive (3)

belasten, belastet to load; to debit

belastend incriminating

beleben, belebt to liven up

belegen, belegt to cover; to take (*a course*) (3)

belegtes Brot (open-faced) sandwich (8)

(das) **Belgien** Belgium (B)

belgisch Belgian (*adj.*)

(das) **Belgrad** Belgrade

beliebt popular (3)

der/die **Beliebte, -n (ein Beliebter)** beloved friend

bemalen, bemalt to paint; to decorate

bemerken, bemerkt to notice

die **Bemerkung, -en** remark; comment

die **Benachteiligung, -en** discrimination

benennen (benennt), benannte, benannt to name

benutzen, benutzt to use (7)

das **Benzin** gasoline (6)

der **Benzinverbrauch** gasoline consumption

beobachten, beobachtet to observe

bequem comfortable (2)

beraten (berät), beriet, beraten to advise

berechnen (+ *dat.*), **berechnet** to change (8)

der **Bereich, -e** sector, area (12)

bereichern, bereichert to enrich (12)

bereit ready; prepared

bereit·legen, bereitgelegt to lay out, have ready

bereits already; just

der **Berg, -e** mountain (1); **in den Bergen wandern** to hike in the mountains (1); **in die Berge gehen** to go to the mountains (1)

die **Berghütte, -n** mountain hut

der **Bericht, -e** report

berichten, berichtet to report

Berliner (*adj.*) (of) Berlin; **die Berliner Mauer** the Berlin Wall; **die Berliner Weiße** *light, fizzy beer mixed with raspberry syrup*

der **Berliner, -** / die **Berlinerin, -nen** person from Berlin (das) **Bern** Bern(e)

der **Beruf**, -e profession; career (1, 5); **was sind Sie von Beruf?** what's your profession? (1)

beruflich professional(ly)

der **Berufsberater**, - / die **Berufsberaterin**, -nen career counselor (5)

die **Berufsberatung**, -en job counseling

das **Berufsleben** career, professional life (12)

die **Berufsschule**, -n vocational school

berufsspezifisch job-specific

berufstätig working; employed

beruhen (auf + *dat.***), beruht** to be based (on)

beruhigen, beruhigt to calm

berühmt famous (7)

beschädigen, beschädigt to damage

beschäftigt busy (3)

der **Bescheid**, -e information; **Bescheid wissen** to know; to have an idea

bescheiden modest

beschließen (beschließt), beschloss, beschlossen to decide

beschreiben (beschreibt), beschrieb, beschrieben to describe (11); **den Weg beschreiben** to give directions

die **Beschreibung**, -en description (B)

der **Beschützer**, - / die **Beschützerin**, -nen protector (12)

sich **beschweren (bei** + *dat.***), beschwert** to complain (to) (8)

der **Besen**, - broom (6)

besetzt (*p.p. of* **besetzen**) occupied, taken

besichtigen, besichtigt to see, visit (*a landmark*); to sightsee (7)

besiedeln, besiedelt to settle

besiegen, besiegt to conquer (7)

der **Besitz** possessions

besitzen (besitzt), besaß, besessen to possess

besonder- special, particular

besonders particularly (3)

besorgen, besorgt to get

bespitzeln, bespitzelt to spy on

besser better (2)

(sich) **bessern, gebessert** to improve

best- best

der **Bestandteil**, -e part, component

das **Besteck** silverware, cutlery (5)

bestehen (besteht), bestand, bestanden to exist; to last; to pass (*a test*); (**aus** + *dat.***)** to consist (of)

besteigen (besteigt), bestieg, bestiegen to climb (7)

bestellen, bestellt to order (*food*) (8)

bestimmen, bestimmt to determine

bestimmt definite(ly); certain(ly) (3)

bestreuen, bestreut to sprinkle (8)

der **Besuch**, -e visit (3); **zu Besuch kommen** to visit (3)

besuchen, besucht to visit (1)

beten, gebetet to pray

der **Beton** concrete

betonieren, betoniert to cover with concrete

der **Betrag**, ̈-e amount (*of money*)

betragen (beträgt), betrug, betragen to amount to

betreffen (betrifft), betraf, betroffen to concern; to affect

betreten (betritt), betrat, betreten to enter

betreuen, betreut to take care of; to look after

der **Betrieb**, -e business; firm; shop

die **Betriebswirtschaftslehre (BWL)** business administration

betroffen upset; affected

betrunken drunk

das **Bett**, -en bed (1, 6); **ins Bett gehen** to go to bed (1)

sich **beugen, gebeugt** to bend down

die **Bevölkerung**, -en population

bevor (*subord. conj.*) before (11)

bevorzugen, bevorzugt to prefer

die **Bewachung**, -en guarding

bewaffnet (*p.p. of* **bewaffnen**) armed

(sich) **bewegen, bewegt** to move

die **Bewegung**, -en movement

der **Beweis**, -e (piece of) evidence

sich **bewerben (um** + *acc.***) (bewirbt), bewarb, beworben** to apply (for)

die **Bewerbung**, -en application

die **Bewerbungsmappe**, -n application package

bewirken, bewirkt to cause; to bring about

die **Bewirtung**, -en service

bewundern, bewundert to admire

bewusstlos unconscious

bezahlen, bezahlt to pay (for) (4)

sich **beziehen (auf** + *acc.***) (bezieht), bezog, bezogen** to relate (to); to refer (to)

beziehungsweise (bzw.) or; and . . . respectively

die **Bibliothek**, -en library (2)

der **Bibliothekar**, -e / die **Bibliothekarin**, -nen librarian (5)

die **Biene**, -n bee (10)

das **Bier**, -e beer (2)

der **Bikini**, -s bikini (5)

das **Bild**, -er picture (2); **das Bild an die Wand hängen** to hang the picture on the wall (3); **was zeigen Ihre Bilder?** what do your pictures show? (A)

bilden, gebildet to form

der **Bildhauer**, - / die **Bildhauerin**, -nen sculptor (12)

die **Bildhauerei** sculpture (12)

bildnerisch artistic(ally)

die **Bildung**, -en education

der **Bildungsstandard**, -s educational standard

billig cheap(ly), inexpensive(ly) (2)

binden (an + *acc.***) (bindet), band, gebunden** to tie (to) (12)

das **Bioei**, -er organic egg

biografisch biographical(ly)

das **Biolebensmittel**, - organic food

der **Biologe**, -n (*wk.*) / die **Biologin**, -nen biologist

die **Biologie** biology (1)

das **Bioprodukt**, -e organic product

das **Bioradieschen**, - organic radish

das **Biowürstchen**, - organic sausage

das **Birchermüsli** *breakfast cereal with fruit*

die **Birne**, -n pear (8)

bis (*prep.* + *acc.; subord. conj.*) until (2, 4, 11); **bis acht Uhr** until eight o'clock (2); **bis auf** down to; **bis bald!** so long; see you soon! (A); **bis um vier Uhr** until four o'clock (4); **bis zu** as far as; up to (10)

bisher thus far; up to now

bisschen: ein bisschen a little (bit); some (B); **kein bisschen** not at all (3)

bitte please (A); **bitte schön** help yourself; there you go; **bitte schön?** yes please? may I help you? (7); **bitte sehr** there you go; **wie bitte?** excuse me?; could you repeat that?

bitten (um + *acc.***) (bittet), bat, gebeten** to ask (for) (9)

blass pale

das **Blatt**, ̈-er leaf; sheet (*of paper*)

blau blue (A); **blau machen** to take the day off (3); **blaue Augen** (*pl.*) blue eyes (B)

die **Blaubeere**, -n blueberry

der **Blauwal**, -e blue whale (10)

bleiben (bleibt), blieb, ist geblieben to stay, remain (1); **liegen bleiben** to stay in bed; to remain in a prone position; **stecken bleiben** to get stuck (11)

bleich pale

bleichen, gebleicht to bleach

der **Bleistift**, -e pencil (A, B)

der **Blick**, -e look; glance; view

der **Blickkontakt**, -e eye contact

blind blind

der **Blinddarm**, ̈-e appendix (11)

blitzen, geblitzt to be a flash of lightning; to flash

die **Blockflöte**, -n recorder (12)

blöd(e) stupid

blond blond (B); **blondes Haar** blond hair (B)

bloß mere(ly); only

blühen, geblüht to bloom

die **Blume**, -n flower (3); **die Blumen gießen** to water the flowers (3)

der **Blumenkohl** cauliflower (8)

die **Bluse**, -n blouse (A)

das **Blut** blood (9, 11); **Blut abnehmen** to take blood (11)

der **Blutdruck** blood pressure (11); **niedrigen/ hohen Blutdruck haben** to have low/high blood pressure (11)

bluten, geblutet to bleed (11)

das **Blütenblatt**, ̈-er petal

die **Blutkonserve**, -n blood bag

der **Boden**, ̈- floor (B); ground

der **Bodensee** Lake Constance

der **Bogen**, - curve; arc; bow

die **Bohne**, -n bean (8)

bohren, gebohrt to drill

das **Bonbon**, -s drop, lozenge (11)

boomen, geboomt (*coll.*) to boom

das **Boot, -e** boat (2)
die **Börse, -n** stock exchange; stock market (12)
der **Börsenkrach, ⸚e** stock market crash (12)
böse evil; mean (9); angry, angrily
(das) **Bosnien** Bosnia (B)
die **Boutique, -n** boutique (6)
die **Box, -en** stereo speaker
boxen, geboxt to box (1)
die **Branche, -n** sector (12)
das **Brandenburger Tor** the Brandenburg Gate
die **Brandenburgischen Konzerte** (*pl.*) the
    Brandenburg Concertos
(das) **Brasilien** Brazil (B)
braten (brät), briet, gebraten to fry (8)
der **Braten, -** roast (8)
die **Bratwurst, ⸚e** (fried) sausage
brauchen, gebraucht to need; to use (1)
das **Brauchtum, ⸚er** tradition; custom(s)
brauen, gebraut to brew
braun brown (A)
bräunen, gebräunt to brown, fry (8)
(das) **Braunschweig** Braunschweig, Brunswick
brausen, gebraust to roar; to rage
das **Brausen** roar
die **Braut, ⸚e** bride (9)
die **BRD** = die **Bundesrepublik Deutschland**
    Federal Republic of Germany
brechen (bricht), brach, gebrochen to break (11);
    sich den Arm brechen to break one's arm (11)
breit broad, wide
die **Breite, -n** (*geographical*) latitude
die **Bremse, -n** brake (7)
bremsen, gebremst to brake (11)
brennen (brennt), brannte, gebrannt to burn (11)
der **Brennofen, ⸚** kiln (12)
das **Brett, -er** board; **das schwarze Brett** bulletin
    board
das **Brettspiel, -e** board game
der **Brief, -e** letter, epistle (1)
die **Briefmarke, -n** (postage) stamp (5)
die **Brille, -n** (eye)glasses (A)
bringen (bringt), brachte, gebracht to bring (2);
    es weit bringen to do very well
der **Brocken** highest mountain in the Harz range
die **Brosche, -n** brooch
das **Brot, -e** (loaf of) bread (8); **belegtes Brot**
    (open-faced) sandwich (8); **ein Stück Brot** a
    piece of bread
das **Brötchen, -** (bread) roll (8)
die **Brücke, -n** bridge (10)
der **Bruder, ⸚** brother (B)
der **Brunnen, -** well; fountain (9)
das **Buch, ⸚er** book (A, B, 2)
buchen, gebucht to book, reserve (7)
der **Bücherwurm, ⸚er** bookworm
der **Buchladen, ⸚** bookstore (6)
der **Buchstabe, -n** (*wk.*) letter (*of the alphabet*)
buchstabieren, buchstabiert to spell
die **Bucht, -en** bay (6, 7)
sich bücken (nach + *dat.*)**, gebückt** to bend
    down (toward)

das **Bügeleisen, -** iron (6)
bügeln, gebügelt to iron (6)
die **Bulette, -n** rissole, meatball, hamburger patty
(das) **Bulgarien** Bulgaria (B)
bummeln, ist gebummelt to stroll
das **Bund, -e** bunch
das **Bündel, -** bundle
das **Bundesausbildungsförderungsgesetz** *financial
    aid for students from the German government*
das **Bundeskanzleramt** Federal Chancellery
das **Bundesland, ⸚er** German state
die **Bundesrepublik** federal republic; **die
    Bundesrepublik Deutschland** Federal Repub-
    lic of Germany
die **Bundeswehr** German army (5); **bei der
    Bundeswehr** in the German army (5)
die **Bundeszentrale, -n** federal headquarters
der **Bungalow, -s** bungalow
bunt colorful
der **Bürger, - / die Bürgerin, -nen** citizen (10)
bürgerlich bourgeois, middle-class
das **Bürgertum** middle class; bourgeoisie
das **Büro, -s** office (5); **im Büro** at the office (5)
das **Bürohaus, ⸚er** office building (6)
die **Bürohilfskraft, ⸚e** clerical assistant
die **Bürste, -n** brush (6)
der **Bus, -se** bus (2, 7)
der **Busch, ⸚e** bush (9)
die **Bushaltestelle, -n** bus stop (6)
die **Butter** butter (8)

ca. = **circa/zirka** circa
das **Cabrio, -s** convertible
das **Café, -s** café (4); **im Café** at the café (4)
die **Cafeteria, -s** cafeteria
der **Camembert** Camembert (cheese)
das **Camping** camping (10)
der **Campingplatz, ⸚e** campsite (10)
der **Cappuccino** cappuccino
der **Cartoon, -s** cartoon
(der) **Cäsar** Caesar
die **CD, -s** CD, compact disc (A, 3)
der **CD-Spieler, -** CD player (2)
Celsius Celsius, centigrade (B); **18 Grad Celsius**
    18 degrees Celsius (B)
der **Cent**, cent (*one hundredth of a euro*); **die
    10-Cent-Münze** 10-cent coin
der **Champagner, -** champagne
die **Chance, -n** chance; opportunity (12)
das **Chaos** chaos (5)
der **Charakter, -e** character; personality (12)
charakterisieren, charakterisiert to characterize
der **Chauvi, -s** (*coll.*) chauvinist (12)
der **Chef, -s / die Chefin, -nen** boss; director
die **Chemie** chemistry (1)
der **Chili, -s** chili (11)
(das) **China** China (B)
chinesisch Chinese (*adj.*)
(das) **Chinesisch** Chinese (*language*) (B)
die **Chipkarte, -n** *plastic card that stores data on a
    computer chip*

der **Chor, ⸚e** choir (1) chorus
Chr. = (der) **Christus** Christ; **n. Chr.** = **nach
    Christus/Christo** A.D.; **v. Chr.** = **vor
    Christus/Christo** B.C.
das **Christkindl** Christ child, baby Jesus
der **Christkindlmarkt, ⸚e** Christmas market
christlich Christian
die **City, -s** *business district in large cities*
der **Clip, -s** (video) clip
die **Clique, -n** clique
der **Clown, -s** clown (9)
cm = der **Zentimeter, -** centimeter
die **Cola, -s** cola
das **College, -s** college
der **Comic, -s** comic strip; comic book
der **Computer, -** computer (2)
die **Computerfirma, -firmen** computer company
    (4)
cool cool; fabulous; decent
der/das **Couscous** couscous
cremig creamy
das **Croissant, -s** croissant
das **Curry, -s** curry

da (*adv.*) there (2); then; (*subord. conj.*) as, since
dabei in that connection; while doing so; (along)
    with it (6); **dabei sein** to be present; **ist ein/
    eine ... dabei?** does it come with a . . . ? (6)
**dabei·haben (hat ... dabei), hatte ... dabei,
    dabeigehabt** to have (*s.th.*) with/on (*oneself*)
**da·bleiben (bleibt ... da), blieb ... da, ist
    dageblieben** to stay, remain (there)
das **Dach, ⸚er** roof (6)
der **Dachauplatz** Dachau Square
der **Dachboden, ⸚** attic; loft
die **Dachsteinmammuthöhle** *long cave in Austria*
dadurch through it/them
dafür for it/them; for that reason; on behalf of it
dagegen against it/them (11); **haben Sie etwas
    dagegen?** do you have something for it
    (*illness*)? (11)
daheim at home (9)
daher from there; from that; therefore
dahin there, thither; to that (*place*)
dahinter behind it/them
damals (*adv.*) back then, at that time (9)
(das) **Damaskus** Damascus
die **Dame, -n** lady
damit (*adv.*) with it/them; (*subord. conj.*) so that (11)
dampfen, ist gedampft to steam
danach after it/them; afterward (10)
daneben next to it/them; in addition to that
(das) **Dänemark** Denmark (B)
dänisch Danish (*adj.*)
der **Dank** thanks; **Gott sei Dank!** thank God!
    vielen Dank many thanks (10)
die **Dankbarkeit** gratitude
danke thank you (A)
danken (+ *dat.*)**, gedankt** to thank
dann then (A)
daran at/on/to it/them

darauf after/for/on it/them; afterward, then; **bald darauf** soon thereafter (9); **darauf eingehen** to get into something

daraufhin following that, thereupon

daraus out of it/them

darin in it/them (6)

dar·stellen, dargestellt to represent, depict

die **Darstellung, -en** portrayal; representation

darüber over/above/about it/them

darum around/about it/them; therefore, for that reason, that's why

darunter underneath/below it/them

das (*def. art., neut. nom./acc.*) the; (*dem. pron., neut. nom./acc.*) this/that; (*rel. pron., neut. nom./acc.*) which, who(m); **das ist** this/that is (B); **das ist es ja!** that's just it! (4); **das sind** these/those are (B)

dass (*subord. conj.*) that (11)

dat (*dial.*) = **das** the

die **Daten** (*pl.*) data; **persönliche Daten** biographical information (1)

die **Datenverarbeitung** data processing (12)

der **Dativ, -e** dative

das **Datum, Daten** date (4); **welches Datum ist heute?** what is today's date? (4)

der **Dauerauftrag, ⁼e** standing order

dauern, gedauert to last (4)

die **Dauerwelle, -n** perm, permanent wave (11)

der **Daumen, -** thumb

davon of/from/about it/them

davon·fahren (**fährt ... davon**), **fuhr ... davon, ist davongefahren** to drive away

davor in front of it/them

dazu to it/them; for it/them; in addition (8)

dazu·schreiben (**schreibt ... dazu**), **schrieb ... dazu, dazugeschrieben** to add (in writing)

dazwischen between/among them; in between

die **DDR** = **Deutsche Demokratische Republik** German Democratic Republic (former East Germany)

der **Deckcode-Name, -n** (*wk.*) code name

die **Decke, -n** ceiling (B); blanket, covers (11)

der **Deckel, -** cover, lid

decken, gedeckt to cover; to set (3); **den Tisch decken** to set the table (3)

die **Deckung, -en** covering; **in Deckung gehen** to take cover

die **Definition, -en** definition

deftig good and solid

dein(e) your (*infor. sg.*) (B, 2)

der **Delfin, -e** dolphin (10)

dem (*def. art., masc./neut. dat.*) the; (*dem. pron., masc./neut. dat.*) this/that; (*rel. pron., masc./neut. dat.*) which, whom

demokratisch democratic(ally)

den (*def. art., masc. acc., pl. dat.*) the; (*dem. pron., masc. acc.*) this/that; (*rel. pron., masc. acc.*) which, whom

denen (*dem. pron., pl. dat.*) these/those; (*rel. pron., pl. dat.*) which, whom

denken (**denkt**), **dachte, gedacht** to think; **denken an** (+ *acc.*) to think of (4); **denken über** (+ *acc.*) to think about

denn (*coord. conj.*) for, because (9, 11); *particle used in questions:* **wo willst du denn hin?** where are you going? (A)

dennoch nevertheless

deportieren, deportiert to deport

deprimiert depressed (11)

der (*def. art., masc. nom., fem. dat./gen., pl. gen.*) the; (*dem. pron., masc. nom., fem. dat.*) this/that; (*rel. pron., masc. nom., fem. dat.*) which, who(m)

deren (*dem. pron., fem. gen., pl. gen.*) of this/that/these/those; (*rel. pron., fem. gen., pl. gen.*) of which, whose

derselbe, dasselbe, dieselbe(n) the same

des (*def. art. masc./neut. gen.*) (of) the

deshalb therefore; that's why (4)

die **Designerklamotten** (*coll., pl.*) designer clothes

desinfizieren, desinfiziert to disinfect (11)

dessen (*dem. pron., masc./neut. gen.*) of this/that; (*rel. pron., masc./neut. gen.*) of which, whose

der **Detektiv, -e** / die **Detektivin, -nen** detective

deutlich clear(ly); distinct(ly)

deutsch German (*adj.*)

(das) **Deutsch** German (*language*) (B); **auf Deutsch** in German

der/die **Deutsche, -n** (**ein Deutscher**) German (*person*) (B); **ich bin Deutscher** / **ich bin Deutsche** I am German (B)

die **Deutsche Demokratische Republik (DDR)** German Democratic Republic (former East Germany)

der **Deutschkurs, -e** German (*language*) course; German class (A)

(das) **Deutschland** Germany (B); **die Bundesrepublik Deutschland** Federal Republic of Germany

die **Deutschlandreise, -n** trip to Germany; tour of Germany

der **Deutschlehrer, -** / die **Deutschlehrerin, -nen** German (*language*) teacher

deutschsprachig German-speaking (9)

der **Dezember** December (B)

der **Dialog, -e** dialogue

dich (*infor. sg. acc.*) you (2)

der **Dichter, -** / die **Dichterin, -nen** poet

die **Dichtung, -en** poetry; literary work

dick fat; large (B); thick(ly)

die (*def. art., fem. nom./acc., pl. nom./acc.*) the; (*dem. pron., fem. nom./acc., pl. nom./acc.*) this/that/these/those; (*rel. pron., fem. nom./acc., pl. nom./acc.*) which, who(m)

die **Diele, -n** front entryway

dienen, gedient (**als**) to serve (as)

der **Diener, -** / die **Dienerin, -nen** servant (9)

der **Dienstag, -e** Tuesday (1)

das **Dienstmädchen, -** maid

dieser, dies(es), diese this, that, these, those (2, 4)

diesmal this time

diffamieren, diffamiert to defame

diffus vague

das **Diktat, -e** dictation

das **Ding, -e** thing (2)

die **Diphtherie** diphtheria (11)

das **Diplom, -e** degree; diploma

der **Diplomingenieur, -e** / die **Diplomingenieurin, -nen** certified engineer

dir (*infor. sg. dat.*) you

direkt direct(ly)

der **Direktor, -en** / die **Direktorin, -nen** director, manager; (school) principal (9)

der **Dirigent, -en** (*wk.*) / die **Dirigentin, -nen** (orchestra) conductor (5)

die **Disko, -s** disco(theque) (3)

die **Diskothek, -en** discotheque

diskriminieren, diskriminiert to discriminate (12)

die **Diskussion, -en** discussion

diskutieren, diskutiert to discuss (4)

die **DM** = **D-Mark (Deutsche Mark)** German mark (*former monetary unit*)

doch however; nevertheless; yet

doch! yes (on the contrary)! (4)

der **Doktor, -en** / die **Doktorin, -nen** doctor

der **Dollar, -s** dollar (7); **der 20-Dollar-Schein** 20-dollar bill; **zwei Dollar** two dollars (7)

dolmetschen, gedolmetscht to act as interpreter

der **Dom, -e** cathedral (10)

dominant dominant (12)

dominieren, dominiert to dominate

der **Domplatz, ⁼e** cathedral square

die **Donau** Danube (River)

der **Donnerstag, -e** Thursday (1)

doof (*coll.*) stupid, dumb

doppelt double; twofold; **doppelt so viel** twice as much

das **Doppelzimmer, -** double room, accommodations for two people (10)

das **Dorf, ⁼er** village

der **Dorn, -en** thorn (9)

(das) **Dornröschen** Sleeping Beauty, Briar Rose

dort there (7)

dorthin there, thither, to a specific place (10)

die **Dose, -n** can (8); box

der **Dosenöffner, -** can opener (8)

Dr. = **Doktor** Dr.

der **Drache, -n** (*wk.*) dragon (9)

das **Drama, Dramen** drama

der **Dramatiker, -** / die **Dramatikerin, -nen** playwright (9)

dramatisch dramatic(ally)

der **Dramaturg, -en** / die **Dramaturgin, -nen** artistic director (*in a theater*)

dran = **daran** at/on/to it/them; **du bist dran** (*coll.*) it's your turn

drauf = **darauf** after/for/on it/them

drauf·gehen (**geht ... drauf**), **ging ... drauf, ist draufgegangen** (*coll.*) to die; to get killed

draußen outside (11)

(sich) **drehen, gedreht** to turn; to twist

drei three (A)

dreihundert three hundred

dreimal three times (3)

dreißig thirty (A)

dreißigst- thirtieth

dreiundzwanzig twenty-three (A)

dreizehn thirteen (A)

dreizehnt- thirteenth (4)

drin = darin in it/them (6)

dringend urgent(ly) (2)

drinnen inside, indoors

dritt- third (4); **das Dritte Reich** the Third Reich (Nazi Germany)

das Drittel, - third

die Drogerie, -n drugstore (6)

der Druck, ⸚e pressure

drücken, gedrückt to press

drum = darum around/about it/them; therefore, for that reason, that's why

der Dschungel, - jungle (7)

du (*infor. sg. nom.*) you (A)

dumm stupid, dumb (6)

dunkel dark (6)

das Dunkel darkness; **im Dunkeln** in the dark

dunkeln, gedunkelt to grow dark

dünn thin(ly)

durch (+ *acc.*) through (7); by means of

durchbluten, durchblutet to supply with blood

durcheinander in confusion

durch·fallen (fällt ... durch), fiel ... durch, ist durchgefallen to fall through; to fail, flunk

die Durchfallversicherung insurance against failure

durchkreuzen, durchkreuzt to thwart; to foil

durch·lesen (liest ... durch), las ... durch, durchgelesen to read (all the way) through

die Durchreise, -n journey through; **auf der Durchreise sein** to be traveling through (7)

durchs = durch das through the

durch·schneiden (schneidet ... durch), schnitt ... durch, durchgeschnitten to cut through (8)

der Durchschnitt average; **im Durchschnitt** on average

durchschnittlich (on) average

dürfen (darf), durfte, gedurft to be permitted (to), may (3); **nicht dürfen** must not

der Durst thirst (3); **Durst haben** to be thirsty

die Dusche, -n shower (5)

(sich) duschen, geduscht to (take a) shower (1, 11)

die DVD, -s DVD

der DVD-Spieler, - DVD player (2, 3)

eben simply, just; just now

ebenfalls also, likewise

das Ebenholz ebony

ebenso likewise; just as

echt real(ly) (2)

die EC-Karte, -n = die Eurocheque-Karte, -n Eurocheque card (*debit card*)

die Ecke, -n corner (5); **(gleich) um die Ecke** (right) around the corner (5, 6)

der Eckzahn, ⸚e canine tooth

das E-Commerce e-commerce, electronic commerce

die EDV = elektronische Datenverarbeitung electronic data processing (12)

egal equal(ly), same (6); **das ist mir egal** it doesn't matter to me (6)

der Egoist, -en (*wk.*) / **die Egoistin, -nen** egotist

egoistisch egotistic(ally)

die Ehe, -n marriage (12)

die Eheleute (*pl.*) married couple

ehemalig former

der Ehepartner, - / die Ehepartnerin, -nen spouse (12)

eher rather (12); more

der Ehering, -e wedding ring

der Ehevertrag, ⸚e prenuptial agreement (12)

ehrgeizig ambitious(ly)

ei! oh! hey!

das Ei, -er egg (8); **gebratene Eier** (*pl.*) fried eggs (8); **gekochte Eier** (*pl.*) boiled eggs (8)

der/das Eidotter egg yolk

eifersüchtig jealous (3)

eigen own (6)

eigenartig strange, peculiar

das Eigenleben life of one's own

die Eigenschaft, -en trait, characteristic

eigensinnig stubborn

eigentlich actual(ly) (3)

sich eignen, geeignet to be suitable

der Eignungstest, -s aptitude test

die Eile hurry (3); **in Eile sein** to be in a hurry (3)

eilen, geeilt to hurry

eilig rushed (10); **es eilig haben** to be in a hurry (10)

ein(e) a(n); one

ein bisschen a little (bit); some (B)

ein paar a few (2)

einander one another, each other (3)

die Einbahnstraße, -n one-way street (7)

ein·bandagieren, einbandagiert to wrap in bandages

ein·bauen, eingebaut to build in; to install

ein·biegen (biegt ... ein), bog ... ein, ist eingebogen to turn

ein·brechen (in + acc.) (bricht ... ein), brach ... ein, ist eingebrochen to break in; to break through; **ins Eis einbrechen** to go through the ice

der Einbrecher, - / die Einbrecherin, -nen burglar (9)

der Einbruch, ⸚e burglary; break-in

einfach simple, simply (2); **die einfache Fahrt** one-way trip (10)

die Einfahrt, -en driveway (11)

ein·fallen (+ dat.) (fällt ... ein), fiel ... ein, ist eingefallen to come to mind; to occur (*to s.o.*)

das Einfamilienhaus, ⸚er single-family home (6)

der Einfluss, ⸚e influence

ein·führen, eingeführt to introduce

die Einführung, -en introduction (A)

ein·gehen (geht ... ein), ging ... ein, ist eingegangen to arrive; **darauf eingehen** to get into something

sich ein·gewöhnen (in + acc.), eingewöhnt to get accustomed (to)

ein·gravieren, eingraviert to engrave

einige some; several; a few

ein·jagen, eingejagt: jemandem Angst einjagen to scare someone

der Einkauf, ⸚e purchase

ein·kaufen, eingekauft to shop (1); **einkaufen gehen** to go shopping (1, 5)

das Einkaufszentrum, -zentren shopping center (10)

das Einkommen, - income (12)

(sich) ein·kremen, eingekremt to put cream/lotion on (11)

ein·laden (lädt ... ein), lud ... ein, eingeladen to invite (2)

die Einladung, -en invitation (2)

ein·laufen (läuft ... ein), lief ... ein, ist eingelaufen to run in; to come in; to shrink

einmal once (4); for once; **auf einmal** at once; suddenly; **es war einmal ...** once upon a time there was . . . ; **noch einmal** once more; again; **warst du schon einmal ... ?** were you ever . . . ? (4)

ein·packen, eingepackt to pack up (1)

ein·parken, eingeparkt to park

ein·räumen, eingeräumt to clear; to put away; to stock

ein·reisen, ist eingereist to enter

eins one (A)

die Eins (the numeral) one

ein·sammeln, eingesammelt to gather, collect

ein·schalten, eingeschaltet to turn on (11)

ein·schätzen, eingeschätzt to assess

ein·schenken, eingeschenkt to pour

ein·schlafen (schläft ... ein), schlief ... ein, ist eingeschlafen to fall asleep (7)

ein·schränken, eingeschränkt to restrict; to limit

sich ein·schreiben (schreibt ... ein), schrieb ... ein, eingeschrieben to register, enroll

ein·schulen, eingeschult to put into school

ein·setzen, eingesetzt to insert

die Einsicht, -en view

ein·steigen (steigt ... ein), stieg ... ein, ist eingestiegen to board; to get in/on (3, 10)

die Einstellung, -en attitude (12)

eintönig monotonous(ly)

der Eintrag, ⸚e entry (*in a list or ledger*)

ein·tragen (trägt ... ein), trug ... ein, eingetragen to enter (*into a list or ledger*)

ein·treffen (trifft ... ein), traf ... ein, ist eingetroffen to arrive

die Eintrittskarte, -n admission ticket (5)

einundzwanzig twenty-one (A)

einverstanden in agreement (12); **einverstanden sein (mit + dat.)** to be in agreement (with) (12)

der Einwanderer, - / die Einwanderin, -nen immigrant (4, 12)

ein·wandern, ist eingewandert to immigrate (12)

ein·werfen (wirft ... ein), warf ... ein, eingeworfen to break, smash (*a window*) der **Einwohner, -** / die **Einwohnerin, -nen** inhabitant, resident

das **Einwohnermeldeamt, ⁻er** *office to register town residents* (12)

ein·zeichnen, eingezeichnet to draw in

der **Einzelgänger, -** / die **Einzelgängerin, -nen** loner, solitary person (12)

das **Einzelhandelsgeschäft, -e** retail shop, retail store

einzeln individual

der **Einzelplatz, ⁻e** individual seat

das **Einzelzimmer, -** single room (5)

ein·ziehen (zieht ... ein), zog ... ein, hat eingezogen to collect; to withdraw

ein·ziehen (zieht ... ein), zog ... ein, ist eingezogen to move in

einzig only; single; sole

das **Eis** ice; ice cream (2); **ins Eis einbrechen** to go through the ice

der **Eisbecher, -** dish of ice cream (8)

das **Eisbein** knuckle of pork

der **Eisbeutel, -** ice pack

das **Eiscafé, -s** ice cream parlor (8)

der **Eischnee** stiffly beaten egg whites

die **Eisenbahn, -en** railroad

das **Eisenwalzwerk, -e** iron-rolling mill

das **Eisenwarengeschäft, -e** hardware store (6)

eiskalt ice-cold (8)

der **Eistee** iced tea

eitel empty; pure; **etwas ist eitel Sonnenschein** something is positive/happy

eklig gross, loathsome (9)

der **Elefant, -en** (*wk.*) elephant (9)

elegant elegant(ly) (8)

elektrisch electric(ally) (8)

elektronisch electronic(ally); **die elektronische Datenverarbeitung (EDV)** electronic data processing (12)

der **Elektrotechniker, -** / die **Elektrotechnikerin, -nen** electrician; electronic engineer

das **Element, -e** element

das **Elend** misery

elf eleven (A)

das **Elfenbein** ivory (10)

elft- eleventh (4)

die **Eltern** (*pl.*) parents (B)

der **Elternteil, -e** parent

die **E-Mail, -s** e-mail

emanzipiert emancipated, liberated

der **Emmentaler** Emmenthaler (cheese)

der **Empfänger, -** / die **Empfängerin, -nen** recipient; payee

empfehlen (empfiehlt), empfahl, empfohlen to recommend

das **Ende, -n** end

enden, geendet to end

endlich finally (9)

das **Endspiel, -e** final game

die **Endung, -en** ending; suffix

eng tight, narrow, small; closely (12)

sich **engagieren (für + *acc.*), engagiert** to commit oneself (to)

engagiert committed; (politically) involved

(das) **England** England (B)

der **Engländer, -** / die **Engländerin, -nen** English (*person*) (B)

englisch English (*adj.*)

(das) **Englisch** English (*language*) (B); **auf Englisch** in English

der **Enkel, -** / die **Enkelin, -nen** grandson/granddaughter (5)

enorm enormous(ly)

entartet (*adj.*) degenerate

entdecken, entdeckt to discover (4)

die **Entdeckung, -en** discovery

entführen, entführt to kidnap; to abduct

der **Entführer, -** / die **Entführerin, -nen** kidnapper

enthalten (enthält), enthielt, enthalten to contain; to include

entlang along (10)

entlang·fahren (fährt ... entlang), fuhr ... entlang, ist entlanggefahren to drive along

entlang·gehen (geht ... entlang), ging ... entlang, ist entlanggegangen to go along (10)

entlassen (entlässt), entließ, entlassen to release

(sich) **entscheiden (entscheidet), entschied, entschieden** to decide (10)

die **Entscheidung, -en** decision; **eine Entscheidung treffen** to make a decision

entschlossen determined

der **Entschluss, ⁻e** decision; **einen Entschluss fassen** to make a decision

entschuldigen, entschuldigt to excuse (5); **entschuldigen Sie!** excuse me! (5)

die **Entschuldigung, -en** excuse; **Entschuldigung!** excuse me! (3)

(sich) **entspannen, entspannt** to relax

entsprechend corresponding

entstehen (entsteht), entstand, ist entstanden to emerge, arise; to be created; to be built

entweder ... oder either . . . or

entwickeln, entwickelt to develop

die **Entzündung, -en** infection; inflammation (11)

entzündungshemmend anti-inflammatory

die **Epoche, -n** epoch, era, period

er (*pron., masc. nom.*) he, it

erarbeiten, erarbeitet to work on; to work out

die **Erbse, -n** pea (8)

die **Erdbeere, -n** strawberry (8)

die **Erde, -n** earth; ground; soil, dirt

die **Erdgeschichte** history of the earth

das **Erdgeschoss, -e** first floor, ground floor

die **Erdkunde** earth science; geography (1)

das **Ereignis, -se** event

erfahren (erfährt), erfuhr, erfahren to find out, learn; to experience; to discover

die **Erfahrung, -en** experience

erfassen, erfasst to grasp

erfinden (erfindet), erfand, erfunden to invent (4)

die **Erfindung, -en** invention

der **Erfolg, -e** success; **Erfolg haben** to be successful

erfolgreich successful(ly)

die **Erfolgsgeschichte, -n** success story

erfüllen, erfüllt to fulfil

ergänzen, ergänzt to complete, fill in the blanks (4)

ergeben (ergibt), ergab, ergeben to result in; to produce; **sich ergeben** to arise

das **Ergebnis, -se** result

ergehen (+ *dat.*) (ergeht), erging, ist ergangen to go (*for s.o.*)

ergreifen (ergreift), ergriff, ergriffen to grab; to take; to catch

erhalten (erhält), erhielt, erhalten to receive; to maintain

erhitzen, erhitzt to heat (8)

erhöhen, erhöht to increase

sich **erholen, erholt** to recuperate (11)

erinnern (an + *acc.*), erinnert to remind (*of s.o./s.th.*); to commemorate (*s.o./s.th.*)

sich **erinnern (an + *acc.*) erinnert** to remember (*s.o./s.th.*) (9)

die **Erinnerung, -en** memory, remembrance (4)

sich **erkälten, erkältet** to catch a cold (11)

die **Erkältung, -en** (head) cold (11)

erkennen (erkennt), erkannte, erkannt to recognize; to see

erklären, erklärt to explain (5)

sich **erkundigen (nach + *dat.*), erkundigt** to ask (about), get information (about) (10)

erlauben, erlaubt to permit, allow (7)

die **Erlaubnis, -se** permission

erleben, erlebt to experience (10)

das **Erlebnis, -se** experience (4)

erledigen, erledigt to take care of; to handle; to settle

erleiden (erleidet), erlitt, erlitten to suffer

erlösen, erlöst to rescue, free (9)

ermitteln, ermittelt to investigate

ermorden, ermordet to murder

sich **ernähren, ernährt** to eat, get nourishment

die **Ernährung** nutrition; diet

ernst serious(ly); **ernst nehmen** to take seriously

ernsthaft serious(ly) (B)

eröffnen, eröffnet to open (9); **ein Konto eröffnen** to open a bank account (5)

erreichen, erreicht to reach; to achieve (12)

das **Erscheinungsjahr, -e** year of publication/release

erschießen (erschießt), erschoss, erschossen to shoot dead

erschrecken, erschreckt to scare, frighten

erst first; not until (4); **am ersten Oktober** on the first of October (4); **der erste Oktober** the first of October (4); **erst mal** for now; **erst um vier Uhr** not until four o'clock (4); **erste Hilfe** first aid; **erster Klasse fahren** to travel first class (5, 10); **im ersten Stock** on the second floor (6); **zum ersten Mal** for the first time (4)

erstarren, ist erstarrt to stand paralyzed
erstaunen, erstaunt to astonish
erstens firstly
ersticken, ist erstickt to suffocate
ertrinken (ertrinkt), ertrank, ist ertrunken to drown
erwachsen grown-up
erwarten, erwartet to expect (12)
die Erwartung, -en expectation
erzählen, erzählt to tell (3, 5); Witze erzählen to tell jokes (3)
erziehen (erzieht), erzog, erzogen to raise, bring up; to educate
die Erziehung upbringing; education
der/die Erziehungsberechtigte, -n (ein Erzie-hungsberechtigter) parent or legal guardian
die Erziehungswissenschaft, -en education (academic subject)
es (pron., neut. nom./acc.) it
der Esel, - donkey
der Essay, -s essay
essen (isst), aß, gegessen to eat (2, 4); essen gehen to go to a restaurant; zu Abend essen to dine, have dinner (4); zu Mittag essen to eat lunch (3)
das Essen food
die Essgewohnheit, -en eating habit
der Essig vinegar (8)
die Essiggurke, -n pickle
das Esszimmer, - dining room (6)
(das) Estland Estonia
etablieren, etabliert to establish
die Etage, -n floor; story
etc. = et cetera etc.
die Ethnologie ethnology
etwas something, anything (2, 4, 5); somewhat; etwas Interessantes/Neues something interest-ing/new (4); haben Sie etwas dagegen? do you have something for it? (illness) (11); sonst noch etwas? anything else? (5)
die EU = Europäische Union European Union
euch (infor. pl. pron., dat./acc.) you; yourselves
euer, eu(e)re (infor. pl.) your (2)
die Eule, -n owl
der Euro, - euro (European monetary unit) (7)
die Eurocard European credit card
das Eurogebiet countries of the European Union in which the euro is the unit of currency
(das) Europa Europe (B)
europäisch European (adj.)
die Europäische Union (EU) European Union
die Euroscheckkarte, -n Eurocheque Card (debit card) (12)
die Eurozone = das Eurogebiet
e.V. = eingetragener Verein registered organization
ewig eternal(ly)
die Ewigkeit eternity; in alle Ewigkeit for all eternity
Ex- ex-
existieren, existiert to exist
exotisch exotic(ally) (7)

die Explosion, -en explosion
explosiv explosive(ly)
der Exportartikel, - export article
der Expressionist, -en (wk.) / die Expressionistin, -nen expressionist
extensiv extensive(ly)
extra extra; additional; separate(ly); in addition (10)

die Fabrik, -en factory (6)
das Fach, ¨er academic subject (1)
der Facharbeiter, - / die Facharbeiterin, -nen trade/skilled worker
der Fachleistungskurs, -e extension course
das Fachwerk half-timbered construction
fähig able, capable
die Fähigkeit, -en ability, capability
fahren (fährt), fuhr, ist/hat gefahren to drive; to ride (2); Auto fahren to drive a car; erster Klasse fahren to travel first class (10); Fahrrad/Rad fahren to ride a bicycle (6); Kanu fahren to go canoeing (10); Motorrad fahren to ride a motorcycle (1); Ski fahren to ski (3)
Fahrenheit Fahrenheit (B); 18 Grad Fahrenheit 18 degrees Fahrenheit (B)
der Fahrer, - / die Fahrerin, -nen driver (7)
der Fahrgast, ¨e passenger
die Fahrkarte, -n ticket (4)
der Fahrkartenschalter, - ticket window; ticket counter (7)
der Fahrlehrer, - / die Fahrlehrerin, -nen driving instructor
der Fahrplan, ¨e schedule (train, bus, etc.)
das Fahrrad, ¨er bicycle (2, 7); Fahrrad fahren to ride a bicycle
der Fahrradhelm, -e bicycle helmet (5)
das Fahrschulauto, -s driving school car
die Fahrschule, -n driving school
der Fahrstuhl, ¨e elevator, lift
die Fahrstunde, -n driving lesson
die Fahrt, -en trip (10); die einfache Fahrt one-way trip (10)
das Fahrzeug, -e vehicle (11)
der/das Fakt, -en fact
der Fall, ¨e fall; case; auf jeden Fall by all means (4);
fallen (fällt), fiel, ist gefallen to fall (9); fallen lassen to drop; in Ohnmacht fallen to faint (11); ins Auge fallen to catch the eye, be noticeable; schwer fallen (+ dat.) to seem/feel difficult (to s.o.)
fällig due
falls (subord. conj.) if; in case
falsch wrong(ly); false(ly) (2)
familiär family (adj.); familiar, informal
die Familie, -n family (B)
das Familienfest, -e family celebration (4)
das Familienmitglied, -er family member (10)
der Familienname, -n (wk.) family name (A, 1)
der Familienstand marital status (1)
der Fan, -s fan; enthusiast

der Fanatiker, - / die Fanatikerin, -nen fanatic (12)
fangen (fängt), fing, gefangen to catch
das Fangen tag (children's game)
die Fantasie, -n fantasy
fantastisch fantastic(ally)
die Farbe, -n color (A, 1); welche Farbe hat ...? what color is . . . ? (A)
fassen, gefasst to grab, grasp; einen Entschluss fassen to make a decision
fast almost (5)
fasten, gefastet to fast
das Fast Food fast food
fasziniert fascinated
faul lazy, lazily (3)
faulenzen, gefaulenzt to take it easy, be lazy
die Fauna fauna; animal life
das Fax, -e fax (2)
das Faxgerät, -e fax machine
der Februar February (B)
die Fee, -n fairy (9)
fegen, gefegt to sweep (5)
fehlen (+ dat.), gefehlt to lack; to be missing (6); to be wrong with, be the matter with (a person) (11)
die Feier, -n celebration, party (9)
der Feierabend, -e evening after work
feiern, gefeiert to celebrate (5)
der Feiertag, -e holiday (4)
fein fine(ly) (8)
der Feind, -e / die Feindin, -nen enemy
das Feld, -er field (7)
der Felsen, - rock; cliff
das Felsenriff, -e (rocky) cliff
das Fenster, - window (B); unter dem Fenster under the window (5)
die Fensterbank, ¨e windowsill (5)
die Fensterscheibe, -n windowpane (9)
der/das Fenstersims, -e windowsill
die Ferien (pl.) vacation (1)
das Ferienhaus, ¨er vacation house (4)
fern·sehen (sieht ... fern), sah ... fern, ferngesehen to watch TV (1)
das Fernsehen television
der Fernseher, - TV set (2)
der Fernsehfilm, -e TV movie (12)
der Fernsehreporter, - / die Fernsehreporterin, -nen TV reporter (5)
der Fernsehsender, - TV broadcaster; TV station
die Fernsehsendung, -en TV program; TV broadcast
das Fernsehzimmer, - TV room (10)
fertig ready; finished (3)
fest stiff(ly); steady; fixed
das Fest, -e party; festival (4)
fest·halten (hält ... fest), hielt ... fest, festge-halten to hold on to
fest·legen, festgelegt to arrange; to establish
fest·schnallen, festgeschnallt to fasten
fest·stehen (steht ... fest), stand ... fest, festge-standen to stand fast

fest·stellen, festgestellt to establish (10); to detect; to realize

der Fetakäse feta cheese

die Fete, -n (*coll.*) party

fett fatty, fat; **fette Jahre** good times; years of plenty

fettig fat(ty), greasy (8, 11)

feucht damp; humid (B)

das Feuer, - fire (9)

die Feuerwehr fire department (11)

das Fieber fever (11)

die Figur, -en figure; character (12)

der Film, -e film (2)

filmen, gefilmt to film

finanziell financial(ly)

finanzieren, finanziert to finance; to pay for

finden (findet), fand, gefunden to find (2); **wie findest du das?** how do you like that?

der Finger, - finger (11)

der Fingernagel, ⁻ fingernail (11)

(das) Finnland Finland (B)

die Firma, Firmen company, firm (3)

der Fisch, -e fish (8)

fischen, gefischt to fish

das Fischfilet, -s fish fillet

die Fläche, -n surface; area (7)

die Flamme, -n flame

die Flasche, -n bottle (5)

der Flaschenöffner, - bottle opener (8)

die Fledermaus, ⁻e bat (10)

das Fleisch meat (8)

das Fleischchuechli rissole, meatball, hamburger patty

fleischig meaty

fleißig industrious(ly); diligent(ly) (12)

flexibel flexible, flexibly (5)

die Fliege, -n fly (8)

fliegen (fliegt), flog, ist/hat geflogen to fly (1)

fliehen (flieht), floh, ist geflohen to flee

fließen (fließt), floss, ist geflossen to flow (7)

flippig (*coll.*) perky

flirten, geflirtet to flirt

der Floh, ⁻e flea

der Flohmarkt, ⁻e flea market (2)

die Flora flora; plant life

fluchen, geflucht to curse, swear (11)

die Flucht flight; escape

flüchten (vor + *dat.*), ist geflüchtet to flee (from) (11)

der Flüchtling, -e refugee (12)

der Flug, ⁻e flight (7)

der Flugbegleiter, - / die Flugbegleiterin, -nen flight attendant

der Flughafen, ⁻ airport (6)

der Flugsteig, -e gate (*at an airport*)

das Flugzeug, -e airplane (7)

der Flur, -e hallway

der Fluss, ⁻e river (7)

flüssig (*adj.*) liquid; flowing

flüstern, geflüstert to whisper

die Focus-Frage, -n focus question

der Föhn, -e föhn (*warm, dry alpine wind*); blow-dryer, hair-dryer

föhnen, geföhnt to blow-dry; **sich (die Haare) föhnen** to blow-dry (one's hair) (11)

die Folge, -n consequence, result; sequence

folgen (+ *dat.*), ist gefolgt to follow

folgend following

das Footballspiel, -e football game

fördern, gefördert to promote (12)

die Forderung, -en demand

die Forelle, -n trout (8)

die Form, -en form

die Formalität, -en formality (12)

das Formular, -e form (12)

der Forscher, - / die Forscherin, -nen researcher

fort·rennen (rennt ... fort), rannte ... fort, ist fortgerannt to run away

fort·setzen, fortgesetzt to continue

die Fortsetzung, -en continuation

das Foto, -s photo (1)

der Fotoapparat, -e camera

die Fotografie photography

fotografieren, fotografiert to take pictures (4)

die Frage, -n question (A); **eine Frage stellen** to ask a question (A, 5)

fragen, gefragt to ask; **fragen nach (+ *dat.*)** to inquire about; **nach dem Weg fragen** to ask for directions; **sich fragen (ob)** to wonder (whether)

der Franken, - (Swiss) franc (7)

Frankfurter (*adj.*) (of) Frankfurt

(das) Frankreich France (B)

der Franzose, -n (*wk.*) / **die Französin, -nen** French (*person*) (B)

französisch French (*adj.*)

(das) Französisch French (*language*) (B)

(das) Französisch-Guayana French Guiana

die Frau, -en woman; Mrs., Ms. (A); wife (B)

die Frauensache, -n woman's job, woman's concern

frei free(ly); empty, available (3); **in freier Natur** out in the open (country) (10); **ist hier noch frei?** is this seat available? (8)

frei·geben (gibt ... frei), gab ... frei, freigegeben to release; to pass

frei·haben (hat ... frei), hatte ... frei, freigehabt to have free; to have time off

frei·lassen (lässt ... frei), ließ ... frei, freigelassen to set free; to let go

das Freilichtmuseum, -museen open-air museum

der Freitag, -e Friday (1)

freiwillig voluntary; optional; voluntarily, willingly

die Freizeit leisure time (1)

die Freizeitbeschäftigung, -en leisure activity

fremd foreign

der/die Fremde, -n (ein Fremder) stranger; foreigner

das Fremdenverkehrsamt, ⁻er tourist bureau (10)

die Fremdsprache, -n foreign language (9)

fressen (frisst), fraß, gefressen to eat (*said of animals*) (9)

die Freude, -n joy; pleasure (9)

sich freuen, gefreut (über + *acc.*) to be happy (about) (11); **(auf + *acc.*)** to look forward (to)

der Freund, -e / die Freundin, -nen friend; boyfriend/girlfriend (A)

freundlich friendly (B); **mit freundlichen Grüßen** regards (10)

freundschaftlich friendly

freundschaftsbezogen inclined towards friendship

der Frieden, - peace

der Friedhof, ⁻e cemetery

frieren (friert), fror, gefroren to freeze

das Frisbee, -s Frisbee

frisch fresh(ly) (8)

der Friseur, -e / die Friseurin, -nen hairdresser (5); **zum Friseur gehen** to go to the hair salon

die Friseuse, -n (female) hairdresser

die Frisur, -en hairstyle

froh happy; cheerful

fröhlich happy, happily; cheerful(ly)

der Frosch, ⁻e frog (9)

„Der Froschkönig" "The Frog Prince" (*fairy tale*)

früh early (1); in the morning (4); **bis um vier Uhr früh** until four in the morning (4)

das Frühjahr, -e spring

der Frühjahrsputz spring cleaning (6)

der Frühling, -e spring (B); **im Frühling** in the spring (B)

die Frühlingsrolle, -n spring roll

frühmorgens early in the morning

das Frühstück, -e breakfast (2, 8)

frühstücken, gefrühstückt to eat breakfast (1)

das Frühstückszimmer, - breakfast room (10)

frühzeitig early

frustriert frustrated (3)

(sich) fühlen, gefühlt to feel; to touch (3, 11); **ich fühle mich wohl** I feel well (3, 11); **wie fühlst du dich?** how do you feel? (3)

führen, geführt to lead; **Krieg führen** to wage war

führend leading; prominent

der Führer, - leader

der Führerschein, -e driver's license (4)

die Führung, -en guided tour (10)

die Führungsposition, -en leadership position

füllen, gefüllt to fill

fünf five (A)

die Fünf: eine Fünf poor (*school grade*)

fünft- fifth (4)

fünfundzwanzig twenty-five (A)

fünfzehn fifteen (A)

fünfzehnt- fifteenth

fünfzig fifty (A)

funkeln, gefunkelt to sparkle; to glitter

funkelnagelneu (*coll.*) brand-new

die Funktion, -en function

funktionieren, funktioniert to work, function

funktionstüchtig in (good) working order

für (+ *acc.*) for (2); **Tag für Tag** day after day; **was für …?** what kind of . . . ?; **was für eins?** what kind?

furchtbar terrible, terribly (4)

sich **fürchten (vor** + *dat.***), gefürchtet** to be afraid (of) (10)

fürs = für das for the

der Fuß, ̈-e foot (B); **mit dem linken Fuß aufstehen** to get up on the wrong side of bed (4); **zu Fuß** on foot (3)

der Fußball, ̈-e soccer ball; soccer (A, 1)

der Fußballplatz, ̈-e soccer field

der Fußballspieler, - / die Fußballspielerin, -nen soccer player (9)

das Fußballstadion, -stadien soccer stadium (10)

das Fußballtraining soccer training

der Fußboden, ̈- floor

der Fußgänger, - / die Fußgängerin, -nen pedestrian (7)

der Fußgängerweg, -e sidewalk (7)

die Fußgängerzone, -n pedestrian mall (10)

das Futter feed; fodder

füttern, gefüttert to feed (9)

die Gabel, -n fork (8)

der Gang, ̈-e gear (7)

ganz whole; entire(ly); quite; rather (2); **den ganzen Tag** all day long, the whole day (1); **die ganze Nacht** all night long (3); **ganz gut** quite good; **ganz in der Nähe** very near; **ganz schön viel** quite a bit (3); **ganz und gar nicht** absolutely not, not at all

die Ganztagsschule, -n all-day school

gar: **gar nicht** not at all, not a bit (3); **ganz und gar nicht** absolutely not, not at all; **gar kein(e)** no . . . at all; **gar nichts** nothing at all

die Garage, -n garage (6)

das Garagenvordach, ̈-er garage canopy

der Garten, ̈- garden; yard (4, 6); **im Garten** in the garden (4)

der Gartenschlauch, ̈-e garden hose (6)

die Gärtnerei, -en nursery (gardening business)

die Gasse, -n narrow street; alley (10)

Gassi: **Gassi gehen** (*coll.*) to walk the dog

der Gast, ̈-e guest; patron, customer

der Gastarbeiter, - / die Gastarbeiterin, -nen foreign worker

das Gästehaus, ̈-er bed-and-breakfast (inn) (10)

die Gastfamilie, -n host family

das Gastland, ̈-er host country

die Gastronomie restaurant trade; gastronomy

die Gaststätte, -n restaurant (5); **in der Gast-stätte** at the restaurant (5)

der Gaul, ̈-e horse

das Gebäude, - building (6)

geben (gibt), gab, gegeben to give (6); (in + *acc.*) to put (into) (8); **es gibt …** there is/are . . . (6); **geben Sie mir …** give me . . . (A); **gibt es …?** is/are there . . . ? (A, 6); **Nachhilfe geben** to tutor (3); **sich einen Termin geben lassen** to get an appointment (11)

das Gebiet, -e region; area

das Gebirge, - (range of) mountains (7)

geboren (*p.p. of* gebären) born (1); **wann sind Sie geboren?** when were you born? (1)

geborgen protected (12)

gebraten (*p.p. of* braten) roasted; broiled; fried (8); **gebratene Eier** (*pl.*) fried eggs (8)

der Gebrauch, ̈-e use (12)

gebrauchen, gebraucht to use

der Gebrauchtwagen, - used car (7)

gebückt (*p.p. of* bücken) bent over; **in gebückter Haltung** bending over, bending forward

die Geburt, -en birth

der Geburtstag, -e birthday (1, 2); **zum Geburtstag** for someone's birthday (2)

die Geburtstagskarte, -n birthday card (2)

der Gedanke, -n (*wk.*) thought

das Gedicht, -e poem (3)

geduldig patient(ly) (12)

geehrt (*p.p. of* ehren) honored; dear (10); **sehr geehrte Frau** dear Ms. (10); **sehr geehrter Herr** dear Mr. (10)

gefährlich dangerous (10)

gefallen (+ *dat.*) (gefällt), gefiel, gefallen to be to one's liking; to please (6); **es gefällt mir** I like it; it pleases me (6)

die Gefälligkeit, -en favor

gefälscht (*p.p. of* fälschen) fake; forged

die Gefangenschaft imprisonment, captivity

das Gefängnis, -se prison; jail (6)

das Geflügel poultry (8)

das Gefrierfach, ̈-er freezer compartment

die Gefriertruhe, -n freezer (8)

das Gefühl, -e feeling (3)

gegen (+ *acc.*) against (9)

die Gegend, -en area (10)

der Gegensatz, ̈-e opposite; contrast

der Gegenstand, ̈-e object

gegenüber opposite; across (6); **(von** + *dat.*) across from (10); **gleich gegenüber** right across the way (6)

gegrillt (*p.p. of* grillen) broiled; barbecued (8)

der Geheimdienst secret service

das Geheimnis, -se secret (5)

die Geheimzahl, -en secret PIN (personal identification number) (12)

gehen (geht), ging, ist gegangen to go; to walk (A); **einkaufen gehen** to go shopping (1, 5); **geht das?** is that okay?; **ich gehe lieber …** I'd rather go . . . (2); **in die Berge gehen** to go to the mountains (1); **ins Bett gehen** to go to bed (1); **ins Museum gehen** to go to the museum (1); **nach Hause gehen** to go home (1); **spazieren gehen** to go for a walk (1); **wie geht es dir?** (*infor.*) / **wie geht es Ihnen?** (*for.*) how are you?

das Gehirn, -e brain (11)

gehören (+ *dat.*), gehört to belong to (*s.o.*) (6)

gehörlos deaf

die Gehwegplatte, -n stepping stone; paving stone

die Geige, -n violin (3)

der Geist, -er spirit; mind

geisteswissenschaftlich pertaining to the arts/humanities

geistig mental; intellectual; **geistige Verfassung** mental state

gekocht (*p.p. of* kochen) boiled (8); **gekochte Eier** (*pl.*) boiled eggs (8)

das Gel, -s gel

gelb yellow (A)

das Geld money (2)

der Geldautomat, -en (*wk.*) automatic teller machine (ATM) (12)

die Geldbörse, -n purse; wallet

der Geldschein, -e note, bill (*of currency*) (12)

die Gelegenheit, -en opportunity; occasion

gelegentlich occasional(ly)

der/die Geliebte, -n (ein Geliebter) lover, beloved (*person*) (3)

gelingen (gelingt), gelang, ist gelungen to succeed

gelten (gilt), galt, gegolten to be valid; to be regarded

das Gemälde, - painting (12)

gemäßigt moderate

die Gemeinde, -n community

gemeinsam together; common (11)

die Gemeinschaft, -en community; coexistence

das Gemisch, -e mixture

gemischt (*p.p. of* mischen) mixed (8)

das Gemüse, - vegetable (8)

gemütlich comfortable, cozy (12)

genau exact(ly) (B)

genauso just as

die Generation, -en generation

generell general(ly)

Genfer (*adj.*) (of) Geneva; **der Genfer See** Lake Geneva

der Genforscher, - / die Genforscherin, -nen geneticist

genießen (genießt), genoss, genossen to enjoy

der Genitiv, -e genitive

genug enough (4)

genügend sufficient(ly)

das Genus, Genera gender

die Geografie geography (7)

das Gepäck luggage, baggage (10)

der Gepard, -e cheetah (10)

gepflegt well-groomed

gerade right now; just (at the moment); straight; upright; **gerade stellen** to straighten (3); **die Bücher gerade stellen** to straighten the books

geradeaus straight ahead (10)

das Gerät, -e appliance (8)

geräuchert (*p.p. of* räuchern) smoked (8)

das Geräusch, -e sound, noise (9)

das Gericht, -e dish (8); court(house) (5); **auf dem Gericht** at the courthouse (5)

gering low; minor

der Germane, -n (*wk.*) / die Germanin, -nen Teuton, ancient German gern(e) gladly; willingly; with pleasure; (with verb) to like to (1, 5); **ich habe ... gern** I like (s.o./s.th.); **ich hätte gern** I would like to (have) (s.th.) (5); **wir singen gern** we like to sing (1)

der Geruch, ⸚e smell, odor

gesalzen salted (8)

gesamt whole; entire

der Gesamtstaat, -en combined state, combined nation

der Gesang singing

das Geschäft, -e store; shop (2)

geschäftlich (relating to) business; **geschäftlich unterwegs sein** to be away on business

der Geschäftsbrief, -e business letter (10)

der Geschäftsführer, - / die Geschäftsführerin, -nen manager (8)

die Geschäftsleute (pl.) businesspeople (7)

die Geschäftsreise, -n business trip (7)

geschehen (geschieht), geschah, ist geschehen to happen; to occur

das Geschenk, -e present, gift (2)

die Geschichte, -n history (1); story

die Geschichtsklausur, -en history exam

das Geschirr (sg.) dishes (4, 5); **Geschirr spülen** to wash the dishes (4)

der Geschirrschrank, ⸚e cupboard

die Geschirrspülmaschine, -n dishwasher (5)

geschlechtertypisch gender-typical, typical for a particular sex

geschlossen (p.p. of schließen) closed (4)

der Geschmack, ⸚e taste

das Geschmeide, - jewelry

die Geschwister (pl.) brother(s) and sister(s), siblings (B)

der Gesellenbrief, -e journeyman's diploma, certificate of completed apprenticeship

die Gesellenprüfung, -en examination for an apprentice to become a journeyman

die Geselligkeit sociability; conviviality

die Gesellschaft, -en society; company; association (12)

das Gesetz, -e law

gesetzlich legal(ly); **gesetzliches Zahlungsmittel** legal tender

das Gesicht, -er face (B)

das Gespräch, -e conversation

die Gestalt, -en form; shape

gestalten, gestaltet to form, fashion

das Geständnis, -se confession

gestern yesterday (4); **gestern Abend** last night (4)

gestresst (p.p. of stressen) under stress; stressed out

gesund healthy (11)

die Gesundheit health (11)

die Gesundheitskasse, -n health insurance company

das Getränk, -e beverage (8)

getrennt (p.p. of trennen) separate(ly); on separate checks (in a restaurant) (5)

das Getto, -s ghetto

die Gewalt violence; force (12)

gewaltbereit ready for violence

das Gewaltdelikt, -e violent offense

gewaltig powerful

die Gewalttat, -en act of violence

die Gewaltverherrlichung, -en glorification of violence

das Gewehr, -e rifle

das Gewicht, -e weight

gewinnen (gewinnt), gewann, gewonnen to win; to gain (4)

gewiss certain(ly)

das Gewitter, - storm; thunderstorm

sich gewöhnen (an + acc.), gewöhnt to get used to, get accustomed to (11)

die Gewohnheit, -en habit

das Gewürz, -e spice; seasoning (8)

gierig greedy, greedily

gießen (gießt), goss, gegossen to pour; to water (3, 8); **die Blumen gießen** to water the flowers (3)

die Gießkanne, -n watering can (6)

giftig poisonous (9)

der Gipfel, - peak, mountaintop (7)

der Gips cast; plaster (11)

die Giraffe, -n giraffe (10)

das Girokonto, -konten checking account (12)

die Gitarre, -n guitar (1)

glänzend shining

das Glas, ⸚er glass (5, 9)

gläsern (adj.) (made of) glass (9)

die Glatze, -n bald head

glauben (an + acc.), geglaubt to believe (in) (2)

gleich (adj.) same, equal; (adv.) right away, immediately; directly; just (4, 6); **gleich gegenüber** right across the way (6); **gleich um die Ecke** right around the corner (6)

die Gleichberechtigung equal rights

das Gleis, -e (set of) train tracks (10)

gleiten (gleitet), glitt, ist geglitten to glide

der Gletscher, - glacier (7)

das Glied, -er limb

die Glotze, -n (coll.) TV

das Glück luck; happiness (3); **Glück haben** to have luck, be lucky; **viel Glück!** lots of luck! good luck! (3)

glücklich happy, happily (B)

die Glückszahl, -en lucky number

gnädig gracious, kind, dear; **gnädige Frau** very formal way of addressing a woman

golden gold(en)

der Goldfisch, -e goldfish (11)

das Golf golf (1)

der Golf VW car model

der Gott, ⸚er god (12); **Gott sei Dank!** thank God! **grüß Gott!** hello! (for.; southern Germany, Austria)

der Gourmet, -s gourmet

der Gouverneur, -e governor

das Grab, ⸚er grave, tomb

graben (gräbt), grub, gegraben to dig

der Grad, -e degree (B); **18 Grad Celsius/ Fahrenheit** 18 degrees Celsius/Fahrenheit (B)

die Grafik, -en drawing; graphic(s)

der Grafiker, - / die Grafikerin, -nen graphic designer

der Gral the (Holy) Grail

die Grammatik, -en grammar (A)

das Gras, ⸚er grass

gratulieren (+ dat.), gratuliert to congratulate (2)

grau gray (A)

graugrün grayish green (7)

grausam cruel(ly) (9)

greifen (greift), griff, gegriffen to grab, grasp (11); **(nach + dat.)** to reach for

grell gaudy, shrill; cool, neat (2)

die Grenze, -n border

grenzen (an + acc.), gegrenzt to border (on)

der Grieche, -n (wk.) / die Griechin, -nen Greek (person)

(das) Griechenland Greece (B)

griechisch Greek (adj.)

(das) Griechisch Greek (language)

der Grill, -s grill, barbecue (8)

grillen, gegrillt to grill; to barbecue

grinsen, gegrinst to grin

die Grippe, -n influenza, flu (11)

groß large, big; tall (B); **ziemlich groß** pretty big (2)

großartig magnificent(ly)

(das) Großbritannien Great Britain (B)

die Größe, -n size; height (1)

die Großeltern (pl.) grandparents (B)

der Großglockner mountain peak in Austria

die Großmutter, ⸚ grandmother (B)

der Großvater, ⸚ grandfather (B)

grüezi! hi! (Switzerland) (A)

grün green (A)

der Grund, ⸚e reason; basis; **im Grunde** in principle; basically

gründen, gegründet to found

gründlich thorough(ly)

grundsätzlich in principle; fundamental(ly)

die Grundschule, -n elementary school (4)

das Grundschulniveau, -s elementary school level

der Grundstein, -e foundation stone

das Grundstück, -e property, lot (land)

das Grundwasser groundwater

das Grundwissen basic knowledge

der Grünkohl kale

die Gruppe, -n group

gruppieren, gruppiert to arrange

die Gruppierung, -en grouping; faction

der Gruselfilm, -e horror film (2)

der Gruß, ⸚e greeting (10); **mit freundlichen Grüßen** regards (10)

grüßen, gegrüßt to greet; to say hello to (11); **grüß dich!** hi! (infor; southern Germany, Austria); **grüß Gott!** hello! (for.; southern Germany, Austria) (A) die **Grütze, -n** groats; **rote Grütze** *red fruit pudding*

gucken, geguckt (*coll.*) to look (at)

der **Gummibaum, ¨e** rubber tree

günstig reasonable, reasonably

die **Gurke, -n** cucumber (8); **saure Gurken** (*pl.*) pickles (8)

der **Gürtel, -** belt (2)

gut good; well; **das passt gut** that fits well (11); **das steht dir gut** that looks good on you (2); **es sieht gut aus** it looks good (2); **ganz gut** very good; quite well; **guten Abend!** good evening! (A); **guten Morgen!** good morning! (A); **guten Tag!** good afternoon! hello! (*for.*) (A); **mach's gut!** so long! take care (A)

das **Guthaben, -** bank balance (12)

der **Gymnasiast, -en** (*wk.*) / die **Gymnasiastin, -nen** pupil at a Gymnasium

das **Gymnasium, Gymnasien** high school, college prep school (4)

das **Haar, -e** hair (B, 11); **blondes Haar** blond hair (B); **Haare schneiden** to cut hair (3); **kurzes Haar** short hair (B); **mit dem kurzen/langen Haar** with the short/long hair (A); **sich die Haare föhnen** to blow-dry one's hair (11); **sich die Haare kämmen** to comb one's hair (11)

die **Haarfarbe, -n** hair color (1)

die **Haarlänge, -n** hair length

die **Haarmode, -n** hairstyle

der **Haarschnitt, -e** haircut, hairstyle (2)

der **Haarstreifen, -** strip of hair

haben (hat), hatte, gehabt to have (A); **das ist noch zu haben** that is still available; **er/sie hat ...** he/she has . . . (A); **es eilig haben** to be in a hurry (10); **haben Sie etwas dagegen?** do you have something for it? (*illness*) (11); **hast du ...?** do you have . . . ? (A); **hast du Lust?** do you feel like it? (2); **Heimweh haben** to be homesick; **Hunger haben** to be hungry; **ich habe ... gern** I like (*s.o./s.th.*); **ich hätte gern** I would like (to have) (*s.th.*) (5); **recht haben** to be right

das **Hackfleisch** ground beef (or pork) (8)

der **Hafen, ¨** harbor, port (10)

der **Hahn, ¨e** rooster

das **Hähnchen, -** (grilled) chicken

der **Hai, -e** shark (10)

der **Haken, -** hook (8)

halb half; **um halb drei** at two thirty (1)

die **Halbinsel, -n** peninsula (7)

die **Hälfte, -n** half (10)

hallo! hi! (*infor.*) (A)

der **Hals, ¨e** neck; throat (9)

das **Halsbonbon, -s** throat lozenge (11)

die **Halskette, -n** necklace (2, 5)

die **Halsschmerzen** (*pl.*) sore throat (11)

das **Halstuch, ¨er** scarf; bandanna (1)

halt (*particle*) simply, just

halten (hält), hielt, gehalten to hold (4); to keep; to stop (7); **ein Referat halten** to give a paper or oral report (4); **halten an** (+ *dat.*) to hold onto; **halten für** (+ *acc.*) to consider, think of as; **halten von** (+ *dat.*) to think of (12)

die **Haltestelle, -n** stop (10)

das **Halteverbot, -e** no-stopping zone (7)

die **Haltung, -en** posture

Hamburger (*adj.*) (of) Hamburg

der **Hamburger, -** hamburger

der **Hammer, ¨** hammer (8)

der **Hamster, -** hamster (10)

die **Hand, ¨e** hand (A, B); **die Hand schütteln** to shake hands (A)

handeln, gehandelt (mit + *dat.*) to deal (with/in); **(von** + *dat.*) to be about

das **Handgepäck** carry-on luggage

die **Handlung, -en** action; plot

der **Handschlag, ¨e** handshake

der **Handschuh, -e** glove (2)

das **Handtuch, ¨er** hand towel (5)

handwerklich handy (12)

das **Handy, -s** cellular phone (2)

hängen (hängt), hing, gehangen to hang, be in a hanging position (3)

hängen, gehängt to hang (up), put in a hanging position (3); **das Bild an die Wand hängen** to hang the picture on the wall (3)

(das) **Hannover** Hanover

die **Hansestadt, ¨e** *city that once belonged to the Hanseatic League*

harmlos harmless(ly)

hart hard

die **Hartfaserplatte, -n** hardboard

hartnäckig obstinate(ly), stubborn(ly)

der **Harz** *mountain range in central Germany*

hassen, gehasst to hate (9)

hässlich ugly (2)

häufig often, frequent(ly); common(ly)

die **Hauptaussage, -n** main statement

der **Hauptbestandteil, -e** main component

das **Hauptfach, ¨er** major; main subject

die **Hauptfigur, -en** main character

die **Hauptperson, -en** central figure

die **Hauptrolle, -n** leading role

die **Hauptsache, -n** main thing

der **Hauptschüler, -** / die **Hauptschülerin, -nen** secondary school student

die **Hauptstadt, ¨e** capital city (3)

das **Haus, ¨er** house (1, 2, 6); **nach Hause gehen** to go home (1, 10); **zu Hause sein** to be at home (A, 1, 10)

die **Hausarbeit, -en** housework; homework

der **Hausarrest, -e** house arrest

der **Hausarzt, ¨e** / die **Hausärztin, -nen** family doctor (11)

die **Hausaufgabe, -n** homework assignment (A)

der **Hausbesitzer, -** / die **Hausbesitzerin, -nen** homeowner

das **Hausboot, -e** houseboat (6)

das **Häuschen, -** small house, cottage

die **Hausfrau, -en** housewife, (*female*) homemaker (12)

hausgemacht homemade

der **Haushalt, -e** household (8, 9); **im Haushalt** in the household (8)

häuslich domestic(ally)

der **Hausmann, ¨er** (*male*) homemaker (12)

der **Hausmeister, -** / die **Hausmeisterin, -nen** custodian (5)

das **Hausmittel, -** home remedy

die **Hausnummer, -n** house number (1)

der **Hausschlüssel, -** house key (9)

der **Hausschuh, -e** slipper

das **Haustier, -e** pet (10)

die **Haut, ¨e** skin (3, 11)

Hbf. = der **Hauptbahnhof, ¨e** main train station

heben (hebt), hob, gehoben to raise; to lift

(das) **Hebräisch** Hebrew

das **Heft, -e** notebook (B)

heftig violent(ly); heated(ly)

heilen, geheilt to cure; to heal (5)

heilig holy; **der Heilige Abend** Christmas Eve

das **Heim, -e** home

die **Heimat, -en** home, hometown, homeland (12)

das **Heimatland, ¨er** homeland (12)

die **Heimatstadt, ¨e** hometown (6)

heim·kommen (kommt ... heim), kam ... heim, ist heimgekommen to come home

heimlich secret(ly) (9)

das **Heimweh** homesickness (3); **Heimweh haben** to be homesick (3)

die **Heirat, -en** marriage

heiraten, geheiratet to marry (5)

heiser hoarse(ly)

heiß hot (B)

heißen (heißt), hieß, geheißen to be called, to be named (A); **ich heiße ...** my name is . . . (A); **wie heißen Sie?** (*for.*) / **wie heißt du?** (*infor.*) what's your name? (A)

die **Heizung, -en** heating

helfen (+ *dat.*) **(hilft), half, geholfen** to help (6)

der **Helfer, -** / die **Helferin, -nen** helper

hell light; bright (6)

hellwach wide awake

das **Hemd, -en** shirt (A)

her *direction toward*; (to) here, hither (10)

herauf up (*toward the speaker*)

herauf·holen, heraufgeholt to bring up, retrieve

heraus (**aus** + *dat.*) out (of) (10)

heraus·bringen (bringt ... heraus), brachte ... heraus, herausgebracht to bring out; to utter, say

heraus·finden (findet ... heraus), fand ... heraus, herausgefunden to find out

herausfordernd challenging(ly); provocative(ly)

heraus·kommen (kommt ... heraus), kam ... heraus, ist herausgekommen to come out (this way) (10)

heraus·nehmen (nimmt ... heraus), nahm ... heraus, herausgenommen to take out, remove

sich heraus·stellen, herausgestellt to turn out

heraus·suchen, herausgesucht to pick out

die **Herbergseltern** (*pl.*) wardens of a youth hostel

der **Herbst, -e** fall, autumn (B)

der **Herd**, **-e** stove (5)

herein in; inside (10)

herein·holen, **hereingeholt** to bring in

herein·kommen (**kommt … herein**), **kam … herein**, **ist hereingekommen** to come in (this way) (10)

der **Heringssalat**, **-e** herring salad (8)

her·kommen (**kommt … her**), **kam … her**, **ist hergekommen** to come here, come this way (10)

die **Herkunft**, **⸗e** origin; nationality (B)

her·laufen (**läuft … her**), **lief … her**, **ist hergelaufen** to run here

der **Herr**, **-en** (*wk.*) Mr.; gentleman (A)

herrlich marvelous(ly), magnificent(ly)

die **Herrschaft**, **-en** rule; dominion

herrschen, **geherrscht** to reign, rule

herum around, round about; **um** (*+ acc.*) … **herum** around

sich **herum·drehen**, **herumgedreht** to turn (*o.s.*) around

herum·gehen (**um** + *acc.*) (**geht … herum**), **ging … herum**, **ist herumgegangen** to go around (*s.th.*)

herum·reisen, **ist herumgereist** to travel around

herum·schwirren, **ist herumgeschwirrt** to buzz around

herum·stehen (**steht … herum**), **stand … herum**, **herumgestanden** to stand around, loiter

herunter down (*toward the speaker*) (11); off

herunter·klettern, **ist heruntergeklettert** to climb down (11)

herunter·kommen (**kommt … herunter**), **kam … herunter**, **ist heruntergekommen** to come down

herunter·werfen (**wirft … herunter**), **warf … herunter**, **heruntergeworfen** to throw down

das **Herz**, **-en** heart (11)

(das) **Herzegowina** Herzegovina (B)

die **Herzfrequenz**, **-en** heart rate

der **Herzinfarkt**, **-e** heart attack

herzlich hearty, heartily

der **Herzog**, **⸗e** duke

das **Herzogtum**, **⸗er** duchy

die **Herzschmerzen** (*pl.*) heartache (11)

(das) **Hessen** Hessen

die **Hetze** hate campaign

heute today (B, 1); **heute Abend** this evening (2); **heute Morgen** this morning; **welcher Tag ist heute?** what day is today? (1); **welches Datum ist heute?** what is today's date? (4)

heutig (*adj.*) today's; present-day

die **Hexe**, **-n** witch (7, 9)

hier here (A); **ist hier noch frei?** is this seat available? (8)

hierher (to) here, hither

die **Hilfe**, **-n** help (11); **erste Hilfe** first aid

hilflos helpless(ly)

der **Hilfsarbeiter**, **-** / die **Hilfsarbeiterin**, **-nen** (unskilled) worker

das **Hilfsverb**, **-en** auxiliary verb

der **Himmel**, **-** sky; heaven

himmlisch heavenly

hin *direction away from*; (to) there, thither (10); **hin und zurück** there and back; round-trip (5, 10); **wo willst du denn hin?** where are you going? (A)

die **Hin- und Rückfahrt**, **-en** round-trip (10)

hinab·stürzen, **ist hinabgestürzt** to fall down; to plummet

hinauf up that way (10)

hinauf·gehen (**geht … hinauf**), **ging … hinauf**, **ist hinaufgegangen** to go up (that way) (10)

hinauf·schauen, **hinaufgeschaut** to look up

hinaus·fahren (**fährt … hinaus**), **fuhr … hinaus**, **ist hinausgefahren** to go/drive out

hinaus·schauen, **hinausgeschaut** to look out

hin·bringen (**bringt … hin**), **brachte … hin**, **hingebracht** to take (there)

das **Hindernis**, **-se** obstacle

hinein in(ward) (9); (**in** + *acc.*) into

hinein·beißen (**beißt … hinein**), **biss … hinein**, **hineingebissen** to bite in

hinein·gehen (**geht … hinein**), **ging … hinein**, **ist hineingegangen** to go/walk in

hinein·mischen, **hineingemischt** to mix in

hinein·sehen (**sieht … hinein**), **sah … hinein**, **hineingesehen** to look in

hinein·setzen, **hineingesetzt** to put (*s.th.*) in

sich **hinein·trauen**, **hineingetraut** to dare to go inside

hin·fahren (**fährt … hin**), **fuhr … hin**, **ist hingefahren** to go/drive (that way)

die **Hinfahrt**, **-en** journey there; outbound journey

hin·fallen (**fällt … hin**), **fiel … hin**, **ist hingefallen** to fall down (11)

hin·gehen (**geht … hin**), **ging … hin**, **ist hingegangen** to go/walk (that way) (10)

hin·gehören, **hingehört** to belong

sich **hin·legen**, **hingelegt** to lie down (11)

hin·schauen, **hingeschaut** to look

sich **hin·setzen**, **hingesetzt** to sit down

hin·stellen, **hingestellt** to put, put down; **sich hinstellen** to stand; to position oneself

hinter (+ *dat./acc.*) behind

hintereinander in a row (3)

der **Hintergrund**, **⸗e** background

hinterher·blasen (**bläst … hinterher**), **blies … hinterher**, **hinterhergeblasen** to blow behind

hinterher·laufen (**läuft … hinterher**), **lief … hinterher**, **ist hinterhergelaufen** to run behind

hinterher·schleichen (**schleicht … hinterher**), **schlich … hinterher**, **ist hinterhergeschlichen** to creep behind

der **Hinterhof**, **⸗e** courtyard

hinterlassen (**hinterlässt**), **hinterließ**, **hinterlassen** to leave (behind)

hinüber over that way (10)

hinüber·gehen (**geht … hinüber**), **ging … hinüber**, **ist hinübergegangen** to go over (that way) (10)

sich **hinunter·beugen**, **hinuntergebeugt** to bend over

hinunter·laufen (**läuft … hinunter**), **lief … hinunter**, **ist hinuntergelaufen** to run down

hinunter·segeln, **ist hinuntergesegelt** to sail down

hinzu·fügen, **hinzugefügt** to add

hinzu·geben (**gibt … hinzu**), **gab … hinzu**, **hinzugegeben** to add

der **Hip-Hop** hip-hop

der **Hirschbraten**, **-** roast venison

historisch historical(ly)

die **Hitze** heat

das **Hobby**, **-s** hobby (1)

hoch high (6); **hohen Blutdruck haben** to have high blood pressure (11)

das **Hochhaus**, **⸗er** high-rise building (6)

hoch·heben (**hebt … hoch**), **hob … hoch**, **hochgehoben** to lift up; to raise

hoch·klappen, **hochgeklappt** to fold up

die **Hochschule**, **-n** college, university

der **Höchstsatz**, **⸗e** maximum amount

die **Hochzeit**, **-en** wedding

der **Hof**, **⸗e** court; courtyard; yard

hoffen, **gehofft** to hope (3)

hoffentlich hopefully

die **Hoffnung**, **-en** hope

höflich polite(ly)

die **Höhe**, **-n** height; amount (*of money*) (12)

der **Höhepunkt**, **-e** high point, highlight (7)

hohl hollow(ly); empty, emptily

die **Höhle**, **-n** cave

holen, **geholt** to fetch, (go) get (9)

(das) **Holland** Holland (B)

holländisch Dutch (*adj.*) (8)

das **Holz**, **⸗er** wood (12)

der **Holzbalken**, **-** wooden beam

die **Holzschindel**, **-n** wooden shingle

homogen homogeneous(ly)

der **Honda** *make of car*

der **Honig** honey (8)

hoppla! oops! oh boy!

hören, **gehört** to hear; to listen (1); (**auf** + *acc.*) to listen to; **wieder hören** to hear again (6)

das **Hörgerät**, **-e** hearing aid

das **Hörnchen**, **-** croissant (8)

der **Horrorfilm**, **-e** horror film

die **Hose**, **-n** pants, trousers (A)

das **Hotel**, **-s** hotel (2, 5); **im Hotel** at the hotel (5)

die **H. T.** = die **Herald Tribune**

hübsch pretty (A, 2)

der **Hügel**, **-** hill (7)

das **Huhn**, **⸗er** chicken

die **Hühnersuppe**, **-n** chicken soup

die **Humanmedizin** human medicine

der **Hummer**, **-** lobster (8)

humorvoll humorous(ly)

der **Hund**, **-e** dog (2)

das **Hundefutter** dog food (5)

die **Hunderasse**, **-n** breed of dog

hundert hundred (A)

hundertst- hundredth (4)

der **Hunger** hunger (3); **Hunger haben** to be hungry (3)

hungrig hungry (9)
die **Hupe, -n** horn (7)
hupen, gehupt to honk (7)
der **Husten, -** cough (11)
das **Hustenbonbon, -s** cough drop (11)
der **Hustenreiz** need to cough
der **Hustensaft, ⁻e** cough syrup (11)
der **Hut, ⁻e** hat (A)
hüten, gehütet to look after; to watch

der **ICE = der Intercityexpresszug, ⁻e** intercity
   express train
ich I
ideal ideal(ly) (12)
die **Idee, -n** idea (10)
identifizieren, identifiziert to identify
die **Identität, -en** identity
das **Idol, -e** idol
das **Iglu, -s** igloo (6)
ihm him, it (*dat.*)
ihn him, it (*acc.*) (2)
ihnen them (*dat.*)
Ihnen you (*for. dat.*)
ihr you (*infor. nom. pl.*); her, it (*dat.*)
ihr(e) her, its; their (1, 2)
Ihr(e) your (*for.*) (B, 2)
illegal illegal(ly) (12)
illusionslos without illusions
illustrieren, illustriert to illustrate
im = in dem in the
das **Image, -s** image
immer always (3); **immer mehr** more and more;
   immer noch still
impfen (gegen + acc.), geimpft to vaccinate
   (against) (10)
das **Importland, ⁻er** importer, country that
   imports
in (+ *dat./acc.*) in; into; at (A, 4); **im Café** at the café
   (4); **im ersten Stock** on the second floor (6); **im
   Garten** in the garden (4); **in den Bergen wandern** to hike in the
   mountains (1); **in der Woche** during the week
   (1); **in die Berge gehen** to go to the mountains
   (1); **ins Kino gehen** to go to the movies (1)
inbegriffen included (10)
indem (*subord. conj.*) while; as
indirekt indirect(ly)
indisch Indian (*adj.*)
individuell individual(ly)
die **Indologie** *study of languages and culture of India*
die **Industrie, -n** industry
ineinander: sich ineinander verlieben to fall in
   love with each other
der **Infinitiv, -e** infinitive
sich **infizieren, infiziert** to get infected
die **Informatik** computer science (1)
die **Information, -en** (piece of) information (4)
(sich) **informieren (über + acc.), informiert** to
   inform (*o.s.*) (about) (10)
der **Ingenieur, -e** / die **Ingenieurin, -nen**
   engineer (5)

der **Inhalt, -e** contents
inkl. = inklusive included (*utilities*) (6)
das **Inline-Skaten** inline skating
der **Inliner, -** inline skate
die **Innenstadt, ⁻e** downtown (6)
(das) **Innerasien** Central Asia
das **Innere (ein Inneres)** inside
ins = in das in(to) the
die **Insel, -n** island (7)
insgesamt altogether
der **Inspektor, -en** / die **Inspektorin, -nen**
   inspector
installieren, installiert to install
das **Institut, -e** institute
die **Institution, -en** institution
das **Instrument, -e** instrument (12)
die **Integration, -en** integration (12)
intelligent intelligent (B)
die **Intelligenz, -en** intelligence (12)
intensiv intensive(ly)
die **Interaktion, -en** interaction
der **Intercity(zug)** intercity train
interessant interesting (7)
das **Interesse, -n** interest (5); **Interesse haben
   (an + dat.)** to be interested (in) (5)
interessieren, interessiert to interest (5); **sich
   interessieren (für + acc.)** to be interested (in)
   (5)
das **Internat, -e** boarding school
international international(ly)
das **Internet** internet
das **Internet-Banking** internet banking
das **Internet-Marketing** internet marketing
das **Interview, -s** interview (4)
interviewen, interviewt to interview (12)
inzwischen in the meantime, meanwhile
der **Iran** Iran
irgendetwas something; anything
irgendjemand someone; anyone
irgendwas something; anything
irgendwelch- some; any (5)
(das) **Irland** Ireland (B)
ironisch ironic(ally)
(das) **Israel** Israel (B)
(das) **Italien** Italy (B)
italienisch Italian (*adj.*)
(das) **Italienisch** Italian (*language*) (B)

ja yes; indeed (4); **das ist es ja!** that's just it! (4);
   na ja oh well; **wenn ja** if so
die **Jacke, -n** jacket (A)
die **Jackentasche, -n** jacket pocket
jagen, gejagt to hunt
der **Jäger, -** / die **Jägerin, -nen** hunter (9)
das **Jahr, -e** year (2); **als ich acht Jahre alt war**
   when I was eight years old (5); **im Jahr(e) ...** in
   the year . . . ; **mit fünf Jahren** at the age of
   five; **seit zwei Jahren** for two years (4); **vor
   zwei Jahren** two years ago
der **Jahrestag, -e** anniversary
die **Jahreszahl, -en** date (year)
die **Jahreszeit, -en** season

das **Jahrhundert, -e** century
-jährig -year-old; **ein dreijähriges Kind** a three-
   year-old child
das **Jahrzehnt, -e** decade (4)
der **Januar** January (B); **im Januar** in January (B)
(das) **Japan** Japan (B)
der **Japaner, -** / die **Japanerin, -nen** Japanese
   (person)
japanisch Japanese (*adj.*) (8)
(das) **Japanisch** Japanese (*language*) (B)
jäten, gejätet to pull weeds
je ever; each; **je nach Betrag** depending on the
   amount
je: oh je! oh dear! oh no!
die **Jeans** (*pl.*) jeans (2)
die **Jeansjacke, -n** denim jacket
jedenfalls in any case (11)
jeder, jedes, jede each; every (3, 5); **auf jeden Fall**
   by all means (4); **jede Woche** every week (3)
jedoch however
jeher: seit jeher always: from time immemorial
jemand someone, somebody (3)
jener, jenes, jene (*dem. pron.*) that, those
jenseits (+ *gen.*) on the other side of
der **Jesuit, -en** (*wk.*) Jesuit
jetzt now (3)
jeweils each time; each; every
der **Job, -s** job
jobben, gejobbt to work a part-time job
joggen, ist gejoggt to jog
der **Joghurt** yogurt
das **Journal, -e** journal; (daily) newspaper
der **Journalist, -en** (*wk.*) / die **Journalistin, -nen**
   journalist
die **Journalistik** journalism
jubeln, gejubelt to cheer
jüdisch Jewish
die **Jugend** youth; young people (9)
das **Jugendarbeitsschutzgesetz, -e** *law governing
   working conditions for adolescents*
die **Jugendherberge, -n** youth hostel (10)
der/die **Jugendliche, -n (ein Jugendlicher)** young
   person
der **Jugendschutz** protection of young people
der **Jugendstil** art nouveau
(das) **Jugoslawien** Yugoslavia (B)
der **Juli** July (B)
jung young (B)
der **Junge, -n** (*wk.*); **Jungs** (*coll. pl.*) boy
die **Jungfrau, -en** virgin
der **Juni** June (B)
(die) **Jura** (*pl.*) law (*as field of study*)
der **Jux, -e** joke; **einen Jux machen** to be joking;
   to play a prank

der **Kachelofen,** tile stove, hearth
der **Käfer, -** beetle; VW bug
der **Kaffee** coffee (1)
der **Kaffeefilter, -** coffee filter (4)
die **Kaffeemaschine, -n** coffeemaker (5)
die **Kaffeemühle, -n** coffee grinder (8)
die **Kaffeesahne** coffee cream

der Käfig, -e cage (10)

kahl bald

der Kahn, ⸚e boat

(das) Kairo Cairo

der Kaiser, - / die Kaiserin, -nen emperor/
empress

der Kakao cocoa; hot chocolate (8)

der Kalbsbraten, - roast veal

(das) Kalifornien California

kalorienarm low in calories (8)

kalorienbewusst calorie-conscious (8)

kalt cold (B)

das Kamel, -e camel

die Kamera, -s camera (2)

der Kamerad, -en (wk.) / die Kameradin, -nen
companion; friend; comrade

der Kamillentee chamomile tea

der Kamin, -e hearth, fireplace

der Kamm, ⸚e comb

kämmen, gekämmt to comb (3); sich (die Haare)
kämmen to comb one's hair (11)

kämpfen, gekämpft to fight (9)

(das) Kanada Canada (B)

der Kanadier, - / die Kanadierin, -nen Canadian
(person) (B)

der Kanal, ⸚e canal; channel

der Kanarienvogel, ⸚ canary

das Känguru, -s kangaroo (10)

das Kanu, -s canoe (10); Kanu fahren to go
canoeing (10)

der Kapitalismus capitalism

das Kapitel, - chapter (A)

kaputt broken (A)

kaputt·machen, kaputtgemacht to break; to ruin

die Karibik the Caribbean

Karl der Große Charlemagne

die Karotte, -n carrot (8)

die Karriere, -n career

die Karte, -n card; ticket; map (1, 2)

die Kartoffel, -n potato (8)

der Kartoffelbrei mashed potatoes

der Kartoffelchip, -s potato chip

der Käse, - cheese (8)

(das) Kaspische Meer the Caspian Sea

die Kasse, -n ticket booth (5); cashier window
(12); an der Kasse at the ticket booth (5)

die Kassette, -n cassette

die Kastanie, -n chestnut

der Kasus, - (grammatical) case

die Kategorie, -n category

der Kater, - tomcat; hangover (11)

die Katze, -n cat (2)

die Katzenallergie, -n allergy to cats

der Katzenliebhaber, - / die Katzenliebhaberin,
-nen cat lover

kauen, gekaut to chew (11)

kaufen, gekauft to buy (1)

der Käufer, - / die Käuferin, -nen buyer; customer

das Kaufhaus, ⸚er department store (5); im
Kaufhaus at the department store (5)

(das) Kaufland department store chain

das Kaufmannshaus, ⸚er merchant's house

kaum hardly

die Kaution, -en security deposit (6)

der Kaviar, -e caviar

kein(e) no; none (2); kein bisschen not at all (3);
kein … mehr not another; kein Wunder no
wonder; keine Ahnung (I have) no idea

der Keller, - basement, cellar (4, 6)

der Kellner, - / die Kellnerin, -nen waiter/
waitress (8)

(das) Kenia Kenya

kennen (kennt), kannte, gekannt to know, be
acquainted with (B)

kennen·lernen, kennengelernt to meet, get
acquainted with (1)

die Kenntnisse (pl.) skills; knowledge about a
field (5)

das Kennzeichen, - sign, mark; feature

kennzeichnen, gekennzeichnet to label; to
characterize

die Kerze, -n candle (3)

kerzengerade bolt upright

der/das Ketchup, -s ketchup

die Kette, -n chain

kg = das Kilogramm, -e kilogram

der Kilometer, - kilometer (2)

der Kilometerstand, ⸚e mileage (7)

das Kind, -er child (B)

der Kindergarten, ⸚ kindergarten (6)

der Kinderreim, -e nursery rhyme

der Kinderwagen, - baby carriage (7)

die Kindheit childhood (9)

das Kinn, -e chin

das Kino, -s movie theater, cinema (1); ins Kino
gehen to go to the movies (1)

die Kinokarte, -n movie ticket (2)

die Kinokasse, -n movie theater ticket booth; an
der Kinokasse at the movie theater ticket
booth

der Kiosk, -e kiosk, newsstand

der Kioskbesitzer, - / die Kioskbesitzerin, -nen
newsstand owner

die Kirche, -n church (5); in der Kirche at
church (5)

der Kirchenbau, -ten church building

der Kirchturm, ⸚e church tower; steeple

der Kirsch, - kirsch (distilled spirit made from cherries)

die Kirsche, -n cherry (8)

der Kirschsaft, ⸚e cherry juice

das Kissen, - cushion, pillow

die Kitzbühler Alpen (pl.) the Kitzbühel Alps

die Kiwi, -s kiwi (fruit)

Kl. = die Klasse, -n class

die Klammer, -n parenthesis

die Klamotten (pl., coll.) clothes

der Klang, ⸚e sound; tone

die Klapperschlange, -n rattlesnake (10)

klar clear; of course (2)

die Klarinette, -n clarinet

klasse (coll.) great; awesome

die Klasse, -n class (5, 10); grade, level (9); erster
Klasse fahren to travel first class (5, 10)

die Klassenarbeit, -en (written) class test

der Klassenkamerad, -en (wk.) / die
Klassenkameradin, -nen classmate

der Klassenlehrer, - / die Klassenlehrerin, -nen
homeroom teacher

das Klassentreffen, - class reunion (9)

das Klassenzimmer, - classroom

klassisch classical(ly) (12)

klassizistisch classical(ly)

klatschen, geklatscht to clap

das Klavier, -e piano (2); Klavier spielen to play
the piano

die Klavierstunde, -n piano lesson

kleben, geklebt to stick; to paste

das Kleid, -er dress (A); (pl.) clothes

kleiden, gekleidet to clothe; sich kleiden to
dress (oneself)

der Kleiderschrank, ⸚e clothes closet,
wardrobe (6)

die Kleidung clothes (A, 2)

klein small, little; short (B)

klemmen, geklemmt to stick

klettern, ist geklettert to climb (9)

das Klima, -s climate

klingeln, geklingelt to ring (2)

klingen (wie) (klingt), klang, geklungen to sound
(like) (11); klingen nach (+ dat.) to sound like

klopfen, geklopft to knock

das Kloster, - monastery; convent

der Klosterkirchhof, ⸚e cloister churchyard

der Klumpen, - lump

km = der Kilometer, - kilometer

KMW = die Kommunikations- und Medienwissenschaft communication and media science

der Knabe, -n (wk.) boy

knapp meager; scarce(ly); just, barely (6)

knarren, geknarrt to creak

die Kneipe, -n bar, tavern (3)

der Knoblauch garlic (8)

der Knöchel, - ankle; knuckle

der Knochen, - bone

der Knödel, - dumpling (8)

der Knopf, ⸚e button

knuspern (an + dat.), geknuspert to nibble (at)

der Kobold, -e goblin

der Koch, ⸚e / die Köchin, -nen cook, chef (5)

kochen, gekocht to cook; to boil (1)

der Koffer, - suitcase

der Kofferraum, ⸚e trunk (in car) (7)

der Kognak, -s cognac

der Kohl cabbage (8)

kohlschwarz coal-black

der Kolibri, -s hummingbird (10)

der Kollege, -n (wk.) / die Kollegin, -nen
colleague, co-worker

die Kollokation, -en collocation

(das) Köln Cologne

kolumbianisch Colombian (adj.)

(der) Kolumbus Columbus

das **Koma, -s** coma
kombinieren, kombiniert to combine (3)
komisch funny, strange (12)
kommen (kommt), kam, ist gekommen to come; (**aus** + *dat.*) to come from (*a place*) (B); **sich etwas zuschulden kommen lassen** to do something wrong; **ums Leben kommen** to lose one's life; **zu Besuch kommen** to visit
kommentieren, kommentiert to comment on
der **Kommissar, -e** / die **Kommissarin, -nen** detective superintendent; commissioner
die **Kommode, -n** dresser, chest of drawers (6)
die **Kommunikations- und Medienwissenschaft** communication and media science
die **Komödie, -n** comedy
der **Komponist, -en** (*wk.*) / die **Komponistin, -nen** composer
die **Konfession, -en** religious denomination, church (12)
der **König, -e** / die **Königin, -nen** king/queen (9)
der **Königssohn, -̈e** prince
die **Königstochter, -̈** princess
konjugieren, konjugiert to conjugate
die **Konjunktion, -en** conjunction
konkret concrete (12)
können (kann), konnte, gekonnt to be able (to), can (3)
konservativ conservative(ly) (B)
das **Konservatorium, Konservatorien** conservatory
die **Konserve, -n** can
der **Kontakt, -e** contact
kontaktieren, kontaktiert to contact
der **Kontinent, -e** continent
kontinental continental
das **Konto, Konten** bank account (5); **ein Konto eröffnen** to open a bank account (5)
der **Kontostand, -̈e** balance; account status
der **Kontrast, -e** contrast
kontrollieren, kontrolliert to check; to control; **das Öl kontrollieren** to check the oil (5)
kontrovers controversial
sich **konzentrieren, konzentriert** to concentrate
das **Konzert, -e** concert (1); concerto; **die Brandenburgischen Konzerte** (*pl.*) the Brandenburg Concertos; **ins Konzert gehen** to go to a concert (1)
die **Konzertkarte, -n** concert ticket (5)
der **Konzertsaal, Konzertsäle** concert hall
die **Kopassage** *a shopping center*
(das) **Kopenhagen** Copenhagen
der **Kopf, -̈e** head (B)
der **Kopfhörer, -** headphones
das **Kopfkissen, -** pillow (6)
der **Kopfsalat** lettuce (8)
die **Kopfschmerzen** (*pl.*) headache (11)
die **Kopfschmerztablette, -n** headache tablet (11)
der **Kopierladen, -̈** copy shop (10)
der **Korb, -̈e** basket
koreanisch Korean (*adj.*)
der **Korkenzieher, -** corkscrew (8)

das **Korn, -̈er** grain; corn
das **Körnergericht, -e** dish made from grain
der **Körper, -** body (B, 11)
körperlich physical
die **Körperpflege** personal hygiene (11)
der **Korridor, -e** corridor, hall
korrigieren, korrigiert to correct (4)
das **Kosmetikprodukt, -e** cosmetics product
der **Kosmonaut, -en** (*wk.*) / die **Kosmonautin, -nen** cosmonaut (*East German word for astronaut*)
kosten, gekostet to cost (2, 6)
kostenlos free of charge
das **Kostüm, -e** costume (9)
die **Krabbe, -n** shrimp (8)
der **Krabbenkutter, -** shrimp boat
krächzen, gekrächzt to squawk
die **Kraft, -̈e** power; strength
krank sick (3)
das **Krankenhaus, -̈er** hospital (3, 5, 11); **im Krankenhaus** in the hospital (5)
der **Krankenpfleger, -** / die **Krankenpflegerin, -nen** nurse (5)
die **Krankenversicherung, -en** health insurance
der **Krankenwagen, -** ambulance (11)
die **Krankheit, -en** illness, sickness (11)
die **Krankheitsgeschichte, -n** medical history
kratzen, gekratzt to scratch
das **Kraut, -̈er** herb (8)
die **Kräuterbutter** herb butter (8)
der **Kräutermarkt, -̈e** herb market
die **Krawatte, -n** tie, necktie (A)
kreativ creative(ly)
der **Krebs, -e** crab
der **Kredit, -e** credit; loan; **Kredit aufnehmen** to take out a loan
die **Kreide, -n** chalk (B)
der **Kreis, -e** circle; (administrative) district
das **Kreisarchiv, -e** district archives
kreischen, gekreischt to screech
der **Kreisverkehr, -e** traffic roundabout (10)
die **Kreme, -s** cosmetic cream
die **Kreuzung, -en** intersection (7)
der **Krieg, -e** war; **Krieg führen** to wage war
kriegen, gekriegt (*coll.*) to get
der **Kriegersmann, -̈er** warrior
der **Krimi, -s** detective story or film
die **Krise, -n** crisis (12)
kritisch critical(ly)
(das) **Kroatien** Croatia (B)
die **Krokette, -n** croquette (8)
das **Krokodil, -e** crocodile (10)
der **Krokus, -se** crocus
krönen, gekrönt to crown
(das) **Kuba** Cuba (B)
die **Küche, -n** kitchen (5); cooking, cuisine; **in der Küche** in the kitchen (5)
der **Kuchen, -** cake (5)
die **Küchenarbeit, -en** kitchen work (5)
die **Küchenbank, -̈e** kitchen bench seat
die **Küchenlampe, -n** kitchen lamp (5)
die **Küchenmaschine, -n** mixer (8)

der **Küchentisch, -e** kitchen table (5)
die **Küchenuhr, -en** kitchen clock (5)
die **Küchenwaage, -n** kitchen scale (5)
der **Kugelschreiber, -** ballpoint pen (4)
kühl cool(ly) (B)
der **Kühlschrank, -̈e** refrigerator (5)
der **Kuhsteig, -e** cow path
die **Kultur, -en** culture (12)
kulturell cultural(ly)
das **Kulturgefälle, -** cultural difference
der **Kulturminister, -** / die **Kulturministerin, -nen** minister for culture
der **Kummer** sorrow; grief; trouble
sich **kümmern (um** + *acc.*)**, gekümmert** to take care (of); to pay attention (to) (12)
der **Kunde, -n** (*wk.*) / die **Kundin, -nen** customer (5)
künftig (*adj.*) coming; future
die **Kunst, -̈e** art (1, 12)
die **Kunstakademie, -n** art college
die **Kunstgeschichte** art history (1)
der **Künstler, -** / die **Künstlerin, -nen** artist
künstlerisch artistic(ally)
die **Kunstsammlung, -en** art collection
der **Kupferstecher, -** / die **Kupferstecherin, -nen** copperplate engraver
das **Kurhaus, -̈er** spa house, resort
der **Kurs, -e** (*academic*) course, class (A, 1); exchange rate
der **Kursteilnehmer, -** / die **Kursteilnehmerin, -nen** course participant
die **Kurve, -n** curve; bend
kurz short; **kurzes Haar** short hair (B); **mit dem kurzen/langen Haar** with the short/long hair (A); **vor kurzem** a short time ago
die **Kusine, -n** (female) cousin (B)
der **Kuss, -̈e** kiss (4)
küssen, geküsst to kiss (9)
die **Küste, -n** coast (7)

labil frail; unstable
der **Labortest, -s** lab test
lächeln, gelächelt to smile
lachen, gelacht to laugh (3); **vor Lachen** from laughing (so hard)
der **Lachs, -e** salmon
der **Laden, -̈** store, shop
der **Ladenbesitzer, -** / die **Ladenbesitzerin, -nen** store owner
der **Ladenschluss** store closing time
die **Lage, -n** place; position; location (10)
die **Lampe, -n** lamp (B)
das **Land, -̈er** land, country (B, 6); **auf dem Land** in the country (*rural*) (6)
die **Landeskunde** *study of a country's geography and history*
der **Landesteil, -e** part of a country
die **Landkarte, -n** map (7)
das **Landsäugetier, -e** land mammal (10)
die **Landschaft, -en** landscape; scenery; region
landschaftlich scenic

die **Landschaftskunde** study of the landscape
die **Landsleute** (*pl.*) compatriots
die **Landstraße, -n** rural highway (7)
der **Landvogt, ⸚e** governor (*of an imperial province*)
lang long (B); **lange Zeit** for a long time; **mit dem langen Haar** with the long hair (A)
lange (*adv.*) a long time; **wie lange** how long
die **Langeweile/Langweile** boredom (3); **Langeweile/Langweile haben** to be bored (3)
langsam slow(ly)
sich **langweilen, gelangweilt** to be bored
langweilig boring (2)
der **Lärm, -e** noise
lassen (lässt), ließ, gelassen to let; to leave; to have something done (11); **fallen lassen** to drop; to let fall; **sich einen Termin geben lassen** to get an appointment (11); **sich etwas zuschulden kommen lassen** to do something wrong; **sich registrieren lassen** to get registered (12)
der **Lastwagen, -** truck (7)
(das) **Latein** Latin (*language*) (1)
(das) **Lateinamerika** Latin America
laufen (läuft), lief, ist gelaufen to run (A, 2); **im Wald laufen** to run in the woods (2); **Schlittschuh laufen** to go ice-skating (3)
die **Laune, -n** mood
laut loud(ly); (+ *gen./dat.*) according to
lauten, gelautet to read, go, run
die **Lautmalerei, -en** onomatopoeia
leben, gelebt to live (3)
das **Leben, -** life (9); **am Leben sein** to be alive (9); **ums Leben kommen** to lose one's life
das **Lebensgefühl, -e** awareness of life
die **Lebenshaltungskosten** (*pl.*) cost of living
das **Lebensmittel, -** food; groceries
das **Lebensmittelgeschäft, -e** grocery store (6)
der **Lebensraum, ⸚e** living space; habitat
die **Leber, -n** liver (11)
der **Leberkäse** *loaf made of minced liver, eggs, and spices*
das **Lebewesen, -** living creature
leblos lifeless(ly)
der **Ledergürtel, -** leather belt
die **Lederjacke, -n** leather jacket
ledig unmarried, single (1)
leer empty (8)
legal legal(ly)
legen, gelegt to lay, put, place (*in a horizontal position*); **sich legen** to lie down
die **Lehre, -n** apprenticeship (5)
der **Lehrer, -** / die **Lehrerin, -nen** teacher, instructor (A, 1)
die **Lehrkraft, ⸚e** teacher(s); **Lehrkräfte** (*pl.*) faculty
die **Lehrwerkstatt, ⸚en** apprentice shop
der **Leibwächter, -** bodyguard
leicht easy, easily; light (6)
das **Leid** suffering; harm; **Leid tun: Alfonso tut ihm Leid** he feels sorry for Alfonso
leider unfortunately (B)
leid·tun (+ *dat.*) **(tut ... leid), tat ... leid, leidgetan** to be sorry (5); **tut mir leid** I'm sorry (4, 5)

die **Leier, -n** lyre
leihen (leiht), lieh, geliehen to lend (5)
leise quiet(ly); soft(ly) (9)
sich **leisten, geleistet** to afford
die **Leistung, -en** achievement, accomplishment
leistungsfähig able to achieve
die **Leistungsfähigkeit, -en** ability to achieve
leistungsschwächst- lowest-achieving
leistungsstärkst- highest-achieving
leiten, geleitet to lead
das **Leitungswasser** tap water
die **Lektion, -en** lesson
die **Lektüre, -n** reading material
lenken, gelenkt to steer
das **Lenkrad, ⸚er** steering wheel (7)
lernen, gelernt to learn; to study (1)
die **Lernstrategie, -n** learning strategy
das **Lernziel, -e** educational goal
die **Lesegewohnheit, -en** reading habit
die **Lesehilfe, -n** reading aid
die **Lesekompetenz, -en** reading competency
lesen (liest), las, gelesen to read (A, 1); **Zeitung lesen** to read the newspaper (1); **zwischen den Zeilen lesen** to read between the lines
der **Leser, -** / die **Leserin, -nen** reader
(das) **Lettland** Latvia
letzt- last (4); **das letzte Mal** the last time (4); **letzte Woche** last week (4); **letzten Montag** last Monday (4); **letzten Sommer** last summer (4); **letztes Wochenende** last weekend (4)
letztendlich in the end
die **Leute** (*pl.*) people (7)
die **Levi's** Levi's (jeans)
liberal liberal (6)
liberalisieren, liberalisiert to liberalize; to relax
libysch Libyan (*adj.*)
das **Licht, -er** light (3)
lieb dear, beloved (7); sweet, lovable (10); **am liebsten** like (*to do s.th.*) best (7)
die **Liebe, -n** love
lieben, geliebt to love (2)
lieber rather (2); **ich gehe lieber ...** I'd rather go . . . (2)
der **Liebesfilm, -e** romantic film
der **Liebeskummer** lovesickness (11)
der **Liebesroman, -e** romance novel (9)
liebevoll loving(ly)
Lieblings- favorite (A)
die **Lieblingsbeschäftigung, -en** favorite activity (5)
das **Lieblingsfach, ⸚er** favorite subject (*in school*) (5)
die **Lieblingsfarbe, -n** favorite color (A)
der **Lieblingsname, -n** (*wk.*) favorite name (A)
(das) **Liechtenstein** Liechtenstein (B)
das **Lied, -er** song (3)
liegen (liegt), lag, gelegen to lie, be (in a horizontal position) (1); to recline; to be situated; **in der Sonne liegen** to lie in the sun (1); **lie-**

gen bleiben (bleibt ... liegen), blieb ... liegen, ist liegen geblieben to stay in bed; to remain in a prone position
der **Liegestuhl, ⸚e** deck chair (4)
der **Lifestyle, -s** lifestyle
lila purple (A)
die **Lilie, -n** lily
die **Limo, -s** = **Limonade** soft drink; lemonade
die **Limonade, -n** soft drink; lemonade
lindern, gelindert to relieve
die **Linguistik** linguistics (1)
die **Linie, -n** line (10)
link- (*adj.*), **links** (*adv.*) left; on the left (4, 10); **mit dem linken Fuß aufstehen** to get up on the wrong side of bed (4); **nach links** (to the) left
die **Linse, -n** lentil
die **Lippe, -n** lip (11)
der **Lippenstift, -e** lipstick
die **List, -en** deception, trick (9)
die **Liste, -n** list (5)
listen, gelistet to list
(das) **Litauen** Lithuania
der **Liter, -** liter (7)
die **Literatur, -en** literature (1, 12)
der **LKW, -s** = der **Lastkraftwagen, -** truck
das **Loch, ⸚er** hole (9)
locken, gelockt to entice, lure
der **Löffel, -** spoon (8)
logisch logical(ly) (12)
der **Lohn, ⸚e** pay; wages, salary; reward
die **Lokomotive, -n** locomotive (7)
die **Lorelei** Loreley
los loose; away; **was ist los?** what's happening? what's the matter
lösen, gelöst to solve; **ein Rätsel lösen** to solve a puzzle/riddle (9); **sich lösen** to break away
los·fahren (fährt ... los), fuhr ... los, ist losgefahren to drive/ride off (4, 9)
die **Lösung, -en** solution
die **Lotterie, -n** lottery (5); **in der Lotterie gewinnen** to win the lottery (5)
der **Löwe, -n** (*wk.*) lion (10)
die **Lücke, -n** gap; vacancy
die **Luft, ⸚e** air (7)
die **Luftmatratze, -n** air mattress (10)
die **Lunge, -n** lung (11)
die **Lungenentzündung** pneumonia (11)
die **Lust, ⸚e** desire (2); **hast du Lust?** do you feel like it? (2)
lustig fun, funny (12); cheerful, jolly
lutschen, gelutscht to suck (11)
(das) **Luxemburg** Luxembourg
der **Luxus** luxury
(das) **Luzern** Lucerne

m = der **Meter, -** meter
machen, gemacht to make; to do; **blau machen** to take the day off (3); **(es) macht nichts** it doesn't matter; **mach's gut!** (*infor.*) take care! (A); **sauber machen** to clean (3); **selbst gemacht** homemade (8)

das **Mädchen**, - girl (9)

das **Magazin**, -e magazine; supplement

der **Magen**, ˗ stomach (11)

die **Magenschmerzen** (*pl.*) stomachache (11)

magisch magical(ly) (12)

der **Magister**, - master's degree

mähen, **gemäht** to mow (5)

die **Mahlzeit**, -en meal (8)

der **Mai** May (B)

mal once; (*word used to soften commands*) (11); **komm mal vorbei!** come on over! (11)

das **Mal**, -e time (4); **das letzte Mal** the last time (4); **zum ersten Mal** for the first time (4)

malen, **gemalt** to paint (12)

der **Maler**, - / die **Malerin**, -nen painter

die **Malerei**, -en painting (12)

die **Mama**, -s mama, mom

die **Mami**, -s mommy

man one; people, they

manch- some

manchmal sometimes (B)

mangelhaft poor, deficient, unsatisfactory

die **Manier**, -en manner

der **Mann**, ˗er man; husband (B)

männlich masculine; male

die **Mannschaft**, -en team (9)

der **Mantel**, ˗ coat; overcoat (A)

das **Märchen**, - fairy tale (9)

der **Märchenerzähler**, - / die **Märchenerzählerin**, -nen teller of fairy tales

die **Mark**, - mark (*former German monetary unit*) (7)

die **Marke**, -n brand

markieren, **markiert** to mark (11)

der **Markt**, ˗e market (10)

die **Marktkirche**, -n church on the market square

der **Marktplatz**, ˗e marketplace; market square (6)

die **Marmelade**, -n jam; marmelade (8)

(das) **Marokko** Morocco (B)

marschieren, **ist marschiert** to march

der **März** March (B)

der **Maschinenbau** mechanical engineering (1)

die **Masern** (*pl.*) measles

massieren, **massiert** to massage

die **Maßnahme**, -n measure

die **Mastercard** *type of credit card*

der **Masterplan**, ˗e master plan

der **Masterstudiengang**, ˗e / das **Masterstudium**, -studien course of study for a master's degree

das **Material**, -ien material, substance (12)

die **Mathe** math

die **Mathearbeit**, -en math test

die **Mathematik** mathematics (1)

mathematisch mathematical(ly)

das **Matterhorn** *mountain in Switzerland*

die **Mauer**, -n wall; **die Berliner Mauer** the Berlin Wall

das **Maul**, ˗er mouth (of an animal) (9)

die **Maus**, ˗e mouse (10)

maximal maximum; at the most

die **Mayonnaise** mayonnaise (8)

(das) **Mazedonien** Macedonia

die **Medienwissenschaft** media science

das **Medikament**, -e medicine (11); **ein Medikament gegen** (+ *acc.*) medicine for (11)

die **Medizin** medicine

medizinisch medical(ly) (11)

das **Meer**, -e sea (1, 7); **ans Meer** to the sea (2); **im Meer schwimmen** to swim in the sea (1)

der **Meerrettich** horseradish

das **Meerschweinchen**, - guinea pig (10)

mehr more (7)

mehrere (*pl.*) several (10); **seit mehreren Tagen** for several days (11)

die **Mehrfachnennung**, -en multiple naming

das **Mehrfamilienhaus**, ˗er house with several apartments

mehrmals several times (5)

der **Meilenstein**, -e milestone

mein(e) my (A, 2)

meinen, **gemeint** to mean; to think

die **Meinung**, -en opinion; **der Meinung sein, dass ...** to be of the opinion that . . . ; **Ihrer Meinung nach** (*for.*) in your opinion

der **Meißel**, - chisel (12)

meist most(ly); **am meisten** mostly; the most; **die meisten** most (of)

meistens usually; mostly (8)

melancholisch melancholy

melden, **gemeldet** to report; **sich melden** to report; to answer the phone

die **Melodei**, -en (*poetic and archaic*) melody

die **Mengenlehre** set theory

die **Mensa**, **Mensen** student cafeteria (2)

der **Mensch**, -en (*wk.*) person; human being (2); **Mensch!** (*coll.*) man! oh boy! (2)

Menschenskind! man alive! wow!

der **Mercedes** *make of car*

merken, **gemerkt** to notice

das **Messegelände**, - site of trade fair

das **Messer**, - knife (8)

der **Meter**, - meter

die **Methode**, -n method

die **Metzgerei**, -en butcher shop (6)

der **Mexikaner**, - / die **Mexikanerin**, -nen Mexican (*person*) (B)

mexikanisch Mexican (*adj.*) (8)

(das) **Mexiko** Mexico (B)

mich me (*acc.*)

die **Miene**, -n facial expression; **keine Miene verziehen** not to bat an eyelid

mies (*coll.*) crummy

die **Miete**, -n rent (6)

mieten, **gemietet** to rent (6)

der **Mieter**, - / die **Mieterin**, -nen renter (6)

der **Mikrowellenherd**, -e microwave oven

die **Mikrowellenmahlzeit**, -en microwave meal

die **Milch** milk (8)

mild mild(ly)

mildern, **gemildert** to soothe

die **Million**, -en million (7)

minderwertig inferior (12)

mindestens at least

der **Mindeststandard**, -s minimum standard

der **Mineralölkonzern**, -e group of petroleum companies

das **Mineralwasser** mineral water (8)

der **Minidialog**, -e mini-dialogue

das **Ministerium**, **Ministerien** ministry

das **Miniwörterbuch**, ˗er mini-dictionary

minus minus

die **Minute**, -n minute

mir me (*dat.*)

mischen, **gemischt** to mix

die **Mischung**, -en mixture

der **Mississippi** Mississippi (River)

der **Mist** dung, manure

mit (+ *dat.*) with (A); **mit dem kurzen/langen Haar** with the short/long hair (A); **mit mir** with me (3)

der **Mitarbeiter**, - / die **Mitarbeiterin**, -nen co-worker; collaborator

der **Mitbewohner**, - / die **Mitbewohnerin**, -nen roommate, housemate (2)

mit·bringen (**bringt ... mit**), **brachte ... mit**, **mitgebracht** to bring along (3)

der **Mitbürger**, - / die **Mitbürgerin**, -nen fellow citizen

miteinander with each other (3)

mit·fahren (**fährt ... mit**), **fuhr ... mit**, **ist mitgefahren** to ride/travel along

das **Mitglied**, -er member (6)

mit·halten (**mit** + *dat.*) (**hält ... mit**), **hielt ... mit**, **mitgehalten** to keep up (with)

mit·kommen (**kommt ... mit**), **kam ... mit**, **ist mitgekommen** to come along

mit·machen, **mitgemacht** to participate; to join in (10)

mit·nehmen (**nimmt ... mit**), **nahm ... mit**, **mitgenommen** to take along (3)

mit·schreiben (**schreibt ... mit**), **schrieb ... mit**, **mitgeschrieben** to write along (at the same time)

der **Mitschüler**, - / die **Mitschülerin**, -nen schoolmate, fellow pupil

mit·spielen, **mitgespielt** to play along

mit·sprechen (**spricht ... mit**), **sprach ... mit**, **mitgesprochen** to join in saying

der **Mitstudent**, -en (*wk.*) / die **Mitstudentin**, -nen fellow student (A)

der **Mittag**, -e midday, noon (3); **zu Mittag essen** to eat lunch

das **Mittagessen**, - midday meal, lunch (3, 8); **zum Mittagessen** for lunch (3)

mittags at noon (2)

die **Mitte** middle, center; in the middle of; **Mitte dreißig sein** to be in one's mid-thirties

mittel- mid-; medium

das **Mittel**, - means; method; medicine

der **Mittelfinger**, - middle finger

das **Mittelmaß** average

das **Mittelmeer** Mediterranean Sea (B)

die **Mittelschule, -n** middle school; secondary school

mitten in the middle (9); **mitten in der Nacht** in the middle of the night (9)

die **Mitternacht** midnight; **um Mitternacht** at midnight

der **Mittwoch, -e** Wednesday (1)

mit·versorgen, mitversorgt to be equally responsible for taking care of (12)

die **Möbel** (*pl.*) furniture (6)

das **Möbelstück, -e** piece of furniture (6)

das **Mobil.** = das **Mobiltelefon, -e** cellular phone

möbliert furnished (6)

das **Modalverb, -en** modal verb

die **Mode, -n** fashion

das **Modell, -e** model, example

modern modern, in a modern fashion (6)

der **Mode-Schnick-Schnack** fashionable frills

der **Modezeichner, -** / die **Modezeichnerin, -nen** fashion designer

modisch fashionable, fashionably

mögen (mag), mochte, gemocht to like (to), care for (1, 3); **möchte** would like (to) (2, 3)

möglich possible; **alles Mögliche** everything possible (2)

möglicherweise possibly

die **Möglichkeit, -en** possibility (5)

möglichst (+ *adv.*) as . . . as possible (6)

(das) **Moldawien** Moldavia, Moldova (B)

der **Moment, -e** moment (1); **im Moment** at the moment; right now (1)

momentan at the moment

der **Monat, -e** month

monatlich monthly

der **Mond, -e** moon

der **Monolog, -e** monologue

das **Monster, -** monster

der **Montag, -e** Monday (1); **letzten Montag** last Monday (4)

montags on Monday(s)

das **Moped, -s** moped

der **Mord, -e** murder

der **Mörder, -** / die **Mörderin, -nen** murderer

die **Mordwaffe, -n** murder weapon

morgen tomorrow (2); **morgen Abend** tomorrow evening

der **Morgen, -** morning; **am Morgen** in the morning; **guten Morgen!** good morning! (A); **heute Morgen** this morning

morgendlich morning (*adj.*)

das **Morgengebet, -e** morning prayer

morgens in the morning(s)

die **Morgentoilette** morning grooming routine

(das) **Moskau** Moscow

das **Motiv, -e** motive; motif, theme; design (12)

die **Motivation, -en** motivation

motivieren, motiviert to motivate

die **Motorhaube, -n** hood (*of a car*) (7)

die **Motorjacht, -en** motor yacht

das **Motorrad, ̈ -er** motorcycle (1, 7); **Motorrad fahren** to ride a motorcycle (1)

das **Motto, -s** motto

der **Mount Everest** Mount Everest

der **Mount Whitney** Mount Whitney

das **Mountainbike, -s** mountain bike

die **Mousse, -s** mousse (*dessert*)

die **Möwe, -n** seagull (10)

der **Mozzarella** mozzarella cheese

der **MP3-Spieler, -** MP3 player (5)

die **Mücke, -n** mosquito (10)

müde tired (3)

der **Mulatte, -n** (*wk.*) / die **Mulattin, -nen** mulatto

der **Müll** trash; garbage (6)

der **Mülleimer, -** garbage can (8)

die **Müllerstochter, ̈** miller's daughter

die **Multikultiküche** multicultural cuisine

multikulturell multicultural(ly) (12)

multiplizieren, multipliziert to multiply

der **Mumps** mumps

(das) **München** Munich

Münchner (*adj.*) (of) Munich

der **Mund, ̈ -er** mouth (B)

die **Mundharmonika, -s** harmonica (12)

munter cheerful(ly); lively; wide awake

die **Münze, -n** coin; **die 10-Cent-Münze** 10-cent coin

die **Murmel, -n** marble

die **Muschel, -n** mussel; shell (8)

das **Museum, Museen** museum (1); **ins Museum gehen** to go to the museum (1)

die **Musik, -en** music (1)

der **Musiker, -** / die **Musikerin, -nen** musician

der **Muskelkater, -** sore muscles (11)

das **Muskeltraining** muscle exercise

das **Müsli, -s** granola

müssen (muss), musste, gemusst to have to, must (3); **nicht müssen** not to have to, not to need to

die **Mutter, ̈** mother (A, B)

die **Muttersprache, -n** mother tongue, native language

der **Muttertag** Mother's Day (4)

die **Mutti, -s** mom, mommy

die **Mütze, -n** cap (5)

na (*interj.*) well, so (3); **na gut** well, okay; **na ja** oh well; **na klar** of course

nach (+ *dat.*) after; past; according to; toward; to (*a place*) (3, 10); **je nach Betrag** depending on the amount; **nach dem Weg fragen** to ask for directions; **nach draußen** outside; **nach Hause gehen** to go home (1, 10); **nach links** to the left; **nach oben** upwards; **nach vorn(e)** to the front, forwards; **nach Westen** to the west, westwards; **um zwanzig nach fünf** at twenty after/past five (1); (*postposition* + *dat.*) according to; **Ihrer Meinung nach** in your opinion

der **Nachbar, -n** (*wk.*) / die **Nachbarin, -nen** neighbor (4)

die **Nachbarschaft, -en** neighborhood

nachdem (*subord. conj.*) after; (*adv.*) afterward (9, 11)

nach·denken (über + *acc.*) **(denkt ... nach), dachte ... nach, nachgedacht** to think (about); to consider (7)

nacheinander one after the other

nach·forschen, nachgeforscht to investigate

nachher afterward

die **Nachhilfe** tutoring (3); **Nachhilfe nehmen** to be tutored

nachlässig lax; careless(ly)

nach·lesen (liest ... nach), las ... nach, nachgelesen to look up, check

der **Nachmieter, -** / die **Nachmieterin, -nen** subletter

der **Nachmittag, -e** afternoon (4); **am Nachmittag** in the afternoon; **heute Nachmittag** this afternoon

nachmittags in the afternoon(s) (4)

die **Nachricht, -en** report; message; (*pl.*) news (7)

die **Nachrichtensendung, -en** news program

nach·sagen, nachgesagt to repeat; to accuse

nach·sehen (sieht ... nach), sah ... nach, nachgesehen to look up; to check (10)

die **Nachspeise, -n** dessert (8)

nächst- next; **in den nächsten Tagen** in the next few days

die **Nacht, ̈ e** night (3); **die ganze Nacht** all night long (3); **heute Nacht** tonight; **in der Nacht** at night; **mitten in der Nacht** in the middle of the night (9)

der **Nachteil, -e** disadvantage (7)

das **Nachthemd, -en** nightshirt (2)

nachts nights, at night (4)

der **Nachttisch, -e** nightstand, bedside table (6)

der **Nacken, -** neck

der **Nagel, ̈** nail (8)

nah(e) near, close (6); **nahe am Park** near the park

die **Nähe** closeness, proximity; vicinity (6); **in der Nähe** in the vicinity (6)

sich nähern, genähert to approach

nahe·stehen (+ *dat.*) **(steht ... nahe), stand ... nahe, hat nahegestanden** to be close to

der **Name, -n** (*wk.*) name (A, 1)

namens by the name of; named

nämlich namely; actually

die **Narbe, -n** scar (1)

die **Nase, -n** nose (11)

nass wet (3)

der **Nationalfeiertag, -e** national holiday (4)

die **Nationalgalerie, -n** national gallery

die **Nationalität, -en** nationality

der **Nationalsozialist, -en** (*wk.*) / die **Nationalsozialistin, -nen** National Socialist, Nazi

der **Nationalspieler, -** / die **Nationalspielerin, -nen** national player

die **Natur, -en** nature (9); disposition, temperament; **in freier Natur** out in the open (country) (10)

natürlich natural(ly); of course (2)

der **Naturschutz** nature conservation

die **Naturwissenschaft, -en** natural science (9)

naturwissenschaftlich pertaining to natural science

der **Nebel**, - fog, mist

neben (+ *dat./acc.*) next to, beside; alongside; in addition to (3, 9)

nebenan next door (5); **von nebenan** from next door (5)

nebeneinander next to each other (8)

das **Nebenfach**, ̈-er minor subject

nebenher·laufen (läuft ... nebenher), lief ... nebenher, ist nebenhergelaufen to run alongside

die **Nebenkosten** (*pl.*) extra costs (*e.g., utilities*) (6)

der **Neckar** Neckar (River)

der **Neffe**, -n (*wk.*) nephew (B)

die **Negation**, -en negation

negativ negative(ly)

nehmen (nimmt), nahm, genommen to take (A); **jemanden auf den Arm nehmen** to tease someone; to pull someone's leg; **Nachhilfe nehmen** to be tutored; **Platz nehmen** to take a seat

der **Neid** envy, jealousy

nein no (A)

nennen (nennt), nannte, genannt to name; to call

der **Neonazi**, -s neo-Nazi (12)

nervös nervous(ly) (B)

der **Nest**, -er nest (10)

nett nice(ly) (B)

neu new(ly) (A); **etwas Neues** something new

der **Neubau**, -ten *building completed after Dec. 1, 1949*

der/die **Neugeborene**, -n (**ein Neugeborener**) newborn (baby)

neugierig curious(ly); nosy, nosily (12)

neulich recently (9)

neun nine (A)

neunt- ninth (4)

neunundzwanzig twenty-nine (A)

neunzehn nineteen (A)

neunzehnt- nineteenth

neunzig ninety (A)

(das) **Neuseeland** New Zealand (B)

neuseeländisch of/from New Zealand

die **Neustadt**, ̈-e new part of town

der **New Beetle** *VW car model*

nicht not (A); **gar nicht** not at all, not a bit (3, 9); **nicht mehr** no longer; **nicht (wahr)?** isn't that right?; **noch nicht** not yet

die **Nichte**, -n niece (B)

der **Nichtraucher**, - / die **Nichtraucherin**, -nen nonsmoker (10)

nichts nothing (9); **gar nichts** nothing at all; **nichts von alledem** none of this

nicken, genickt to nod

nie never (2); **nie mehr** never again; **noch nie** never (before)

die **Niederlande** (*pl.*) the Netherlands (B)

(das) **Niedersachsen** Lower Saxony

der **Niederschlag**, ̈-e precipitation

nieder·schlagen (schlägt ... nieder), schlug ... nieder, niedergeschlagen to knock down

nieder·schreiben (schreibt ... nieder), schrieb ... nieder, niedergeschrieben to write down

niedlich cute(ly)

niedrig low; **niedrigen Blutdruck haben** to have low blood pressure (11)

niemand nobody, no one (2)

die **Niere**, -n kidney (11)

die **Nierenentzündung** kidney infection (11)

das **Nikotin** nicotine

der **Nil** Nile (River)

das **Niveau**, -s level

noch even, still; yet; else; in addition (B); **auch noch** on top of it all; **immer noch** still; **ist hier noch frei?** is this seat available? (8); **noch ein(e)** another, an additional (one); **noch (ein)mal** once more, again; **noch etwas** anything/something else; **noch nicht** not yet; **noch nie** never (before); **noch zu haben** still available; **nur noch** only; **sonst noch** otherwise; in addition; else; **sonst noch etwas?** anything/something else? (5)

nochmals again

das **Nomen**, - noun

die **Nominalphrase**, -n noun phrase

der **Nominativ**, -e nominative

(das) **Nordamerika** North America

norddeutsch Northern German (*adj.*)

(das) **Norddeutschland** Northern Germany

der **Norden** north

nordfriesisch North Frisian (*adj.*)

(das) **Nordirland** Northern Ireland (B)

nördlich (**von** + *dat.*) north (of) (7)

nordöstlich (**von** + *dat.*) northeast (of) (7)

(das) **Nordrhein-Westfalen** North Rhine-Westphalia

die **Nordsee** North Sea (B)

der **Nordwesten** northwest

nordwestlich (**von** + *dat.*) northwest (of) (7)

die **Norm**, -en norm

normal normal (5)

normalerweise normally (8)

(das) **Norwegen** Norway (B)

die **Not**, ̈-e need; hardship; trouble

die **Note**, -n grade, mark (*in school*) (3, 9)

der **Notfall**, ̈-e emergency

nötig necessary; **nötig brauchen** to need urgently

die **Notiz**, -en note

notwendig ncessary, necessarily

die **Novelle**, -n novella

der **November** November (B)

die **Nudel**, -n noodle (8)

null zero

der **Numerus clausus**, - *limited number of students allowed to study a particular subject at a university*

die **Nummer**, -n number (1)

das **Nummernschild**, -er license plate (7)

nun now; well

nur only (3)

(das) **Nürnberg** Nuremberg

Nürnberger (*adj.*) (of) Nuremberg

die **Nuss**, ̈-e nut (8)

der **Nussknacker**, - nutcracker

nützen, genützt to do some good; to be of use

nützlich useful(ly) (10)

ob (*subord. conj.*) whether, if (6, 10, 11)

oben above (10); on top; upstairs; **nach oben** upwards; **von oben** from above

ober- upper

der **Oberarm**, -e upper arm

(das) **Oberbayern** Upper Bavaria

die **Oberfläche**, -n surface

der **Oberinspektor**, -en / die **Oberinspektorin**, -nen chief inspector

(das) **Oberschlesien** Upper Silesia

der **Oberst**, -en (*wk.*) colonel

das **Objekt**, -e object

das **Obst** fruit

obwohl (*subord. conj.*) although (11)

oder (*coord. conj.*) or (A, 11)

die **Odyssee**, -n odyssey

der **Ofen**, ̈ oven; stove

offen open(ly)

öffentlich public(ly); **die öffentlichen Verkehrsmittel** (*pl.*) public transportation (7)

offiziell official(ly)

öffnen, geöffnet to open (A)

die **Öffnungsmöglichkeit**, -en possibility of a (job) opening

die **Öffnungszeiten** (*pl.*) business hours (8)

oft often (A)

öfter(s) now and then, once in a while

oftmals often

oh oh; **oh je** oh dear; oh no

ohne (+ *acc.*) without; **ohne den Text zu lesen** without reading the text

die **Ohnmacht**, -en unconsciousness (11); **in Ohnmacht fallen** to faint (11)

das **Ohr**, -en ear (B)

die **Ohrenschmerzen** (*pl.*) earache (11)

der **Ohrring**, -e earring (A, 2)

oje oh dear

okay (*coll.*) okay

ökologisch ecological(ly)

der **Oktober** October (B); **am ersten Oktober** on the first of October (4); **der erste Oktober** the first of October (4)

das **Oktoberfest**, -e *festival held yearly (in Munich) during late September and early October* (7)

das **Öl** oil (5, 8); **das Öl kontrollieren** to check the oil (5)

der **Oldie**, -s oldie (*classic pop song*)

die **Ölfarbe**, -n oil paint (12)

die **Olive**, -n olive (8)

die **Oma**, -s grandma (3)

das **Omelett**, -s omelet (8)

der **Onkel**, - uncle (B)

der **Onlinezugang**, ̈-e online access

der **Opa**, -s grandpa

der **Opel** *make of car*

die **Oper**, -n opera

operieren, operiert to operate on

das **Opfer**, - sacrifice; victim
der **Opi**, -s (*coll.*) grandpa
optimistisch optimistic(ally) (B)
orange orange (*color*) (A)
der **Orangensaft** orange juice (8)
die **Ordinalzahl**, -en ordinal number
ordnen, **geordnet** to arrange, put in order
die **Organisation**, -en organization
organisieren, **organisiert** to organize
die **Orgel**, -n organ (*musical instrument*) (12)
der **Orientexpress** Orient Express (*train*)
das **Original**, -e original
der **Ort**, -e place; town (1, 4)
der/die **Ortsfremde**, -n (ein Ortsfremder)
   stranger, nonresident
Ost east
der **Osten** east
das **Ostern**, - Easter
der **Osternachmittag**, -e Easter afternoon
(das) **Österreich** Austria (B)
der **Österreicher**, - / die **Österreicherin**, -nen
   Austrian (*person*) (B)
österreichisch Austrian (*adj.*)
ostfriesisch East Frisian (*adj.*)
(das) **Ostfriesland** East Frisia (*northwest part of*
   Germany)
östlich (**von** + *dat.*) east (of) (7)
die **Ostsee** Baltic Sea (B)
das **Ostseebad**, ⁻er *bathing resort on the Baltic coast*
(die) **Ostslawistik** *study of eastern Slavic languages*
   and literatures
ozeanisch oceanic

paar: **ein paar** a few; a couple of (2)
das **Paar**, -e couple; pair (of)
packen, **gepackt** to pack (7)
die **Pädagogik** pedagogy
das **Paket**, -e package (8)
der **Pakt**, -e pact (12)
der **Palast**, ⁻e palace
(das) **Palästina** Palestine (B)
die **Palme**, -n palm tree (6)
der **Papa**, -s daddy, dad
der **Papagei**, -en parrot (10)
der **Papi**, -s (*coll.*) daddy
das **Papier**, -e paper (B)
der **Papierkorb**, ⁻e wastebasket (3); **den**
   Papierkorb ausleeren to empty the wastebasket
das **Papiertuch**, ⁻er paper towel (5)
der **Paprika** paprika
die **Paprika**, -s bell pepper
der **Papst**, ⁻e pope
parallel parallel
das **Parfüm**, -e perfume (5)
der **Park**, -s park (1); **im Park spazieren gehen** to
   walk in the park (1)
der **Parkautomat**, -en (*wk.*) parking machine
parken, **geparkt** to park (7)
das **Parkhaus**, ⁻er multistory parking structure
die **Parklücke**, -n parking space (7)
der **Parkplatz**, ⁻e car park, parking lot (6)

die **Parole**, -n slogan
das **Partizip**, -ien participle
der **Partner**, - / die **Partnerin**, -nen partner (12)
die **Partnerschaft**, -en partnership (12)
die **Party**, -s party (1, 2); **auf eine Party gehen** to
   go to a party (1)
der **Pass**, ⁻e passport (7)
der **Passant**, -en (*wk.*) / die **Passantin**, -nen
   passerby
passen, **gepasst** (+ *dat.*) to fit; to suit (6, 11); (**zu**
   + *dat.*) to go (with), fit in (with); **das passt**
   gut that fits well (11)
passend fitting; proper
passieren, **passiert** to happen (4)
die **Pasta** pasta
der **Patient**, -en (*wk.*) / die **Patientin**, -nen
   patient (5)
der **Patrizier**, - patrician
die **Pause**, -n recess, break (1); **Pause machen** to
   take a break
der **Pazifik** Pacific Ocean
der **Pazifist**, -en (*wk.*) / die **Pazifistin**, -nen
   pacifist
das **Pech** bad luck
peinlich embarrassing (12)
der **Pelz**, -e fur
das **Penizillin** pencillin (4)
per per, by means of
perfekt perfect(ly)
das **Perfekt**, -e perfect (tense)
die **Person**, -en person, individual (A, 1)
der **Personalausweis**, -e (personal) ID card (1)
die **Personalien** (*pl.*) personal data (12)
das **Personalpronomen**, - personal pronoun
personell relating to staff or personnel
der **Personenzug**, ⁻e passenger train (7)
persönlich personal(ly); in person; **persönliche**
   Daten biographical information (1)
die **Perspektive**, -n perspective
die **Perücke**, -n wig (11)
die **Pfalz** Palatinate
die **Pfanne**, -n (frying) pan (5)
der **Pfarrer**, - / die **Pfarrerin**, -nen minister;
   parish priest
der **Pfeffer**, - (black) pepper (8)
das **Pferd**, -e horse (2, 9)
der **Pfifferling**, -e chanterelle (*type of mushroom*)
das **Pfingsten**, - Pentecost
der **Pfirsich**, -e peach (8)
die **Pflanze**, -n plant (3, 6)
die **Pflanzenheilkunde** herbal medicine
das **Pflaster**, - adhesive bandage (11)
der **Pflasterstein**, -e cobblestone
die **Pflaume**, -n plum (8)
pflegen, **gepflegt** to attend to; to nurse; to
   nurture (5)
die **Pflicht**, -en duty; requirement; obligation (3)
pflichtbewusst conscious of one's obligations
das **Pflichtfach**, ⁻er required subject
die **Pflichtschulzeit**, -en required school time
der **Pflichtunterricht** required instruction

pflücken, **gepflückt** to pick (9)
die **Pforte**, -n gate
pfui Teufel! (*interj.*) ugh! yuck!
das **Pfund**, -e pound; 500 grams (5)
die **Phantasie**, -n imagination
das **Phantom**, -e phantom
die **Physik** physics (1)
das **Picknick**, -s picnic (4)
das **Piercing**, -s piercing (2)
der **Pilot**, -en (*wk.*) / die **Pilotin**, -nen pilot (5)
der **Pilz**, -e mushroom (8)
die **Pinakothek**, -en painting gallery
der **Pinsel**, - paintbrush (12)
der **Piranha**, -s piranha (10)
die **Pizza**, -s pizza (2)
der **PKW**, -s = der **Personenkraftwagen**, -
   automobile; passenger car
das **Plakat**, -e poster
der **Plan**, ⁻e plan (3)
planen, **geplant** to plan (7)
die **Platte**, -n plate; sheet; board; record
der **Platz**, ⁻e place; seat; room, space; square (3);
   Platz nehmen to take a seat
plötzlich sudden(ly) (9)
plus plus
(das) **Polen** Poland (B)
die **Politik** politics (5)
der **Politiker**, - / die **Politikerin**, -nen politician
politisch political(ly) (4)
die **Polizei** police; police station (5); **auf der**
   Polizei at the police station (5)
der **Polizist**, -en (*wk.*) / die **Polizistin**, -nen
   police officer (5)
(das) **Polnisch** Polish (*language*)
die **Polonistik** *study of Polish language and culture*
die **Pommes (frites)** (*pl.*) French fries (8)
populär popular(ly)
der **Porsche** *make of car*
das **Portal**, -e portal
das **Porträt**, -s portrait
(das) **Portugal** Portugal (B)
(das) **Portugiesisch** Portuguese (*language*) (B)
positiv positive(ly)
das **Possessivpronomen**, - possessive pronoun,
   possessive adjective
die **Post**, -en mail; post office (5); **auf der Post** at
   the post office (5); **auf die Post gehen** to go to
   the post office
der/die **Postangestellte**, -n (ein Postangestellter)
   postal employee (5)
der **Postbeamte**, -n (ein Postbeamter) / die
   Postbeamtin, -nen postal employee
das **Poster**, - poster (6)
das **Postfach**, ⁻er post office box
die **Postkarte**, -n postcard (2)
prächtig splendid(ly)
prädestiniert predestined
die **Präferenz**, -en preference (1)
das **Präfix**, -e prefix
prägen, **geprägt** to shape
pragmatisch pragmatic(ally)

V-24

das **Praktikum, Praktika** practical training
praktisch practical(ly) (5); **praktische Ausbildung** practical (career) training (5)
die **Präposition, -en** preposition
das **Präsens, Präsentia** present (tense)
präsentieren, präsentiert to present
der **Präsident, -en** (*wk.*) / die **Präsidentin, -nen** president (5)
das **Präsidium, Präsidien** police station
die **Präteritumsform, -en** preterite (tense) form
der **Preis, -e** price; prize (7, 12)
preisgünstig at a favorable price; inexpensive
die **Prellung, -en** bruise
pressen, gepresst to press, squeeze
das **Prestige** prestige (5)
der **Priester, -** / die **Priesterin, -nen** priest (5)
prima great (6)
der **Prinz, -en** (*wk.*) / die **Prinzessin, -nen** prince/princess (9)
privat private(ly)
pro per (3); **pro Woche** per week
die **Probe, -n** test; rehearsal
der **Probeschluck, -e** test sip, taste
probieren, probiert to try; to taste (3)
das **Problem, -e** problem
das **Produkt, -e** product
die **Produktion, -en** production
der **Professor, -en -** / die **Professorin, -nen** professor (A, B)
das **Profil, -e** profile
progressiv progressive(ly) (B)
das **Projekt, -e** project
der **Promoter, -** / die **Promoterin, -nen** promoter
das **Pronomen, -** pronoun
das **Propagandadelikt, -e** propaganda offense
protestieren (gegen + *acc.*), protestiert to protest (against) (12)
das **Prozent, -e** percent (4)
der **Prozentsatz, -e** percentage
die **Prozentzahl, -en** percentage
prüfen, geprüft to test; to examine; to certify
die **Prüfung, -en** test, exam (1)
die **Prüfungskommission, -en** examination committee
die **Prügel** (*pl.*) beating(s)
prügeln, geprügelt to beat
der **Psychiater, -** / die **Psychiaterin, -nen** psychiatrist (11)
psychisch mental(ly); psychological(ly)
die **Psychologie** psychology
der **Pudding, -s** pudding
der **Pudel, -** poodle
der **Puder, -** powder
der **Pulli, -s** = der **Pullover** (2)
der **Pullover, -** pullover; sweater (2)
der **Punkt, -e** point (3); dot
pünktlich punctual(ly); on time (4)
die **Puppe, -n** doll (9)
der **Purzelbaum, -e** somersault
das **Putenschnitzel, -** turkey cutlet
der **Putz** plaster

putzen, geputzt to clean (3, 6); **sich die Zähne putzen** to brush one's teeth (11)
der **Putzlappen, -** cloth, rag (for cleaning) (6)
die **Pyramide, -n** pyramid

qm = der **Quadratmeter, -** square meter (6)
das **Quadrat, -e** square
die **Quadratmeile, -n** square mile
der **Quadratmeter, -** square meter (6)
quaken, gequakt to quack; to croak
quälen, gequält to torment
die **Qualifikation, -en** qualification
die **Qualität, -en** quality
der **Quark** *type of creamy cottage cheese* (8)
die **Quelle, -n** source
die **Querflöte, -n** transverse flute (12)
die **Quickcard** *Austrian debit card*
quietschend screeching
die **Quittung, -en** receipt, check (8)

das **Rad, -er** wheel (7); bicycle; **Rad fahren** to ride a bicycle (6)
radeln, ist geradelt to ride a bicycle
der **Radfahrer, -** / die **Radfahrerin, -nen** bicyclist (7)
das **Radieschen, -** radish
das **Radio, -s** radio (2)
das **Radium** radium
die **Radtour, -en** bicycle tour (9)
der **Radweg, -e** bicycle path; bike lane (7)
ragen, geragt to rise, tower up
der **Rahmen, -** frame; framework; context
die **Rakete, -n** rocket (7)
der **Rand, -er** edge; margin; brim
die **Rangfolge, -n** ranking; order of importance
die **Rangliste, -n** ranking list
der **Ranzen, -** schoolbag; knapsack; satchel
der **Rasen, -** lawn (5)
der **Rasenmäher, -** lawnmower (6)
der **Rasierapparat, -e** shaver, (electric) razor
(**sich**) **rasieren, rasiert** to shave (11)
die **Rasierklinge, -n** razor blade
das **Rasierwasser** aftershave lotion
rasseln, gerasselt to rattle
rassistisch (*adj.*) racist
der **Rat** advice (5)
raten (rät), riet, geraten to guess; (+ *dat.*) to advise (*s.o.*) (5)
das **Ratespiel, -e** guessing game; quiz
das **Rathaus, -er** town/city hall (1, 6); **auf dem Rathaus** at the town/city hall (1)
der **Ratschlag, -e** (piece of) advice (5)
das **Rätsel, -** puzzle, riddle (9); **ein Rätsel lösen** to solve a puzzle/riddle (9)
die **Ratte, -n** rat (10)
der **Raub** robbery
rauchen, geraucht to smoke (3)
der **Raucher, -** / die **Raucherin, -nen** smoker (10)
der **Raum, -e** room; space; area
raus = **heraus** out
rauschen, gerauscht to rustle

raus·drücken, rausgedrückt = **heraus·drücken** to squeeze out
raus·gehen (geht ... raus), ging ... raus, ist rausgegangen = **heraus·gehen** to go out
reagieren, reagiert to react
die **Reaktion, -en** reaction
der **Realismus, Realismen** realism
realistisch realistic(ally)
der **Realschulabschluss, -e** vocational school diploma
die **Rechenart, -en** arithmetical operation
recherchieren, recherchiert to research
rechnen, gerechnet to do arithmetic
die **Rechnung, -en** bill; check (*in restaurant*) (4)
recht- (*adj.*); **rechts** (*adv.*) right; on the right (7, 10); **von rechts** from the right
das **Recht, -e** right; law
recht haben (hat ... recht), hatte ... recht, recht gehabt to be right (2)
rechtlich legal(ly)
der **Rechtsanwalt, -e** / die **Rechtsanwältin, -nen** lawyer
das **Rechtschreiben** spelling
der **Rechtschreibtest, -s** spelling test
die **Rechtschreibung** spelling; orthography
rechtsextrem extreme right-wing
der **Rechtsextremismus** right-wing extremism
der **Rechtsextremist, -en** (*wk.*) right-wing extremist (12)
rechtsextremistisch extreme(ly) right-wing
rechtsradikal radical(ly) right-wing
der **Rechtsradikalismus** right-wing radicalism
rechtzeitig timely, on time (12)
die **Rede, -n** speech, talk; discourse
reden, geredet to speak, talk
das **Referat, -e** report; (term) paper (3); **ein Referat halten** to give a paper/oral report (4)
das **Reflexivpronomen, -** reflexive pronoun
das **Regal, -e** bookshelf, bookcase (2)
die **Regel, -n** rule
regelmäßig regular(ly) (11)
regeln, geregelt to regulate
die **Regelung, -en** regulation
der **Regen, -** rain (7); **bei Regen** in rainy weather (7)
der **Regenschirm, -e** umbrella (5)
die **Regierung, -en** government
das **Regime, -** regime
regimetreu loyal to a/the regime
die **Region, -en** region
regional regional(ly)
der **Regisseur, -e** / die **Regisseurin, -nen** stage/film director (9)
registrieren, registriert to register; **sich registrieren lassen** to get registered (11)
regnen, geregnet to rain; **es regnet** it's raining (B)
die **Reibe, -n** grater
reiben (reibt), rieb, gerieben to rub
reich rich(ly)
das **Reich, -e** empire; kingdom; realm; **das Dritte Reich** the Third Reich (Nazi Germany)

reichen, gereicht to be enough
der Reifen, - tire (7)
die Reifenpanne, -n flat tire (7)
die Reihe, -n row; series
die Reihenfolge, -n sequence, order (2, 4)
das Reihenhaus, -̈er row house, town house (6)
der Reim, -e rhyme
(sich) reimen, gereimt to rhyme
rein = herein in
die Reinigung, -en dry cleaner's (6)
rein·kommen (kommt ... rein), kam ... rein, ist reingekommen = herein·kommen to come in
der Reis rice (8)
die Reise, -n trip, journey (7); auf Reisen sein to be on a trip (7)
das Reisebüro, -s travel agency (6)
das Reiseerlebnis, -se travel experience (7)
der Reiseführer, - travel guidebook (5)
reisen, ist gereist to travel (1, 10)
der/die Reisende, -n (ein Reisender) traveler (10)
der Reisepass, -̈e passport (10)
der Reisescheck, -s traveler's check (7)
reiten (reitet), ritt, ist geritten to ride horse-back; to go horseback riding (1); Wellen reiten to ride the waves, surf
der Reiter, - / die Reiterin, -nen (horseback) rider
rekonstruieren, rekonstruiert to reconstruct
rekrutieren, rekrutiert to recruit
relativ relative(ly) (5)
die Religion, -en religion (1)
religiös religious(ly) (B)
die Renaissance, -n Renaissance
rennen (rennt), rannte, ist gerannt to run (7)
renovieren, renoviert to renovate
die Rente, -n pension
das Rentnerpaar, -e retired couple
die Reparatur, -en repair
reparieren, repariert to repair (1)
der Reporter, - / die Reporterin, -nen reporter, journalist (4)
der Repräsentant, -en (wk.) / die Repräsentantin, -nen representative
repräsentativ representative(ly)
die Republik, -en republic
republikanisch Republican (adj.)
reservieren, reserviert to reserve (7)
die Residenz, -en residence
die Resonanz, -en resonance
der Rest, -e remainder, rest
das Restaurant, -s restaurant (2, 8); im Restaurant at the restaurant (8)
restaurieren, restauriert to restore
das Resultat, -e result
retten, gerettet to save; to rescue
die Rettichscheibe, -n radish slice
die Rettung rescue; salvation
die Revolution, -en revolution
das Rezept, -e recipe; prescription (11)
die Rezeption, -en reception desk (10)
der Rhein Rhine (River)

das Rheinland Rhineland
(das) Rheinland-Pfalz Rhineland-Palatinate
der Rhythmus, Rhythmen rhythm
richten, gerichtet to direct; to turn; sich richten (nach + dat.) to depend (on); to comply (with)
der Richter, - / die Richterin, -nen judge (5)
richtig right(ly), correct(ly) (2)
die Richtung, -en direction (7)
riechen (riecht), roch, gerochen to smell (11)
der Riese, -n (wk.) giant (9)
die Riesenschildkröte, -n giant tortoise
die Riesenschlange, -n boa constrictor; python (10)
riesig gigantic; tremendous(ly)
die Rinderlende, -n beef loin
das Rindfleisch beef (8)
der Ring, -e ring (2)
der Rinnstein, -e gutter
das Risiko, -en risk; jeopardy
der Rock, -̈e skirt (A); (sg. only) rock music
der Rock 'n' Roll rock 'n' roll
die Rockband, -s rock band
das Rockkonzert, -e rock concert (9)
roh raw
die Rolle, -n role; part (4)
das Rollenspiel, -e role-play
die Rollenverteilung, -en assignment of roles
die Rollerblades (pl.) roller-blades
das Rollschuhlaufen roller-skating
(das) Rom Rome
der Roman, -e novel (3, 5)
der Römer, - / die Römerin, -nen Roman (person)
römisch Roman (adj.)
röntgen, geröntgt to X-ray (11)
rosa pink (A)
der Rosenkohl Brussels sprouts (8)
die Rösti coarsely grated fried potatoes
rostig rusty (8)
rot red (A)
die Röteln (pl.) German measles
(das) Rotkäppchen Little Red Riding Hood
die Roulade, -n braised meat roll filled with bacon and onions
der Ruck, -e jerk, jolt
der Rücken, - back (B)
die Rückfahrt, -en return journey; die Hin- und Rückfahrt round trip (10)
der Rucksack, -̈e backpack (2)
rufen (ruft), rief, gerufen to call, shout (7, 11)
(das) Rügen island in the Baltic Sea
die Ruhe silence; peace
ruhen, geruht to rest
ruhig quiet(ly), calm(ly) (B)
das Rührei, -er scrambled egg
rühren, gerührt to stir; to move
(das) Rumänien Romania (B)
(das) Rumpelstilzchen Rumpelstiltskin
das Rumpsteak, -s rump steak (8)
rund round; around; approximately; rund um around

der Rundgang, -̈e (walking) tour
runter·bringen (bringt ... runter), brachte ... runter, runtergebracht = herunter·bringen to bring down
der Rüssel, - trunk (of an elephant) (10)
russisch Russian (adj.) (12)
(das) Russisch Russian (language) (B)
(das) Russland Russia (B)
rustikal country-style, rustic
rutschen, ist gerutscht to slide, slip (9)

die Sache, -n thing; cause (2)
sachlich objective(ly), matter-of-fact
(das) Sachsen Saxony
(das) Sachsen-Anhalt Saxony-Anhalt
sächsisch Saxon (adj.)
der Saft, -̈e juice (8)
sagen, gesagt to say; to tell (A, 5)
die Sahara Sahara (Desert)
das Sakko, -s sports jacket (A)
die Salami, - salami
der Salat, -e salad; lettuce (8)
die Salatschüssel, -n salad (mixing) bowl (5)
die Salbe, -n ointment, salve
das Salz salt (8)
salzig salty (7)
die Salzkartoffeln (pl.) boiled potatoes (8)
sammeln, gesammelt to collect; to gather (10)
das Sample-Institut polling institute
der Samstag, -e Saturday (1); am Samstag on Saturday (2)
samstags on Saturday(s)
der Sand, -e sand (7)
die Sandale, -n sandal
die Sandburg, -en sandcastle (4)
der Sarg, -̈e coffin (9)
satt full; well-fed; satt werden to get full, get enough to eat
der Satz, -̈e sentence (3)
die Satzklammer, -n sentence bracket
die Satzstellung, -en word order
der Satzteil, -e part of sentence, clause
sauber clean (B); sauber machen to clean (3)
sauer sour (8); angry, cross, annoyed (5); saure Gurken (pl.) pickles (8)
der Sauerbraten, - sauerbraten (marinated beef roast)
das Sauerkraut sauerkraut, pickled cabbage (7)
saugen, gesaugt to vacuum; Staub saugen to vacuum (6)
die Sauna, -s sauna (11)
der S-Bahnanschluss, -̈e city and suburban railway connection
das Schach chess (1)
die Schachtel, -n box
schade! too bad! (3)
schaden (+ dat.), geschadet to be harmful (to) (6)
der Schaden, -̈ damage (11)
schaffen (schafft), schuf, geschaffen to create
schaffen, geschafft to manage; jemanden aus dem Weg schaffen to get someone out of the way
der Schafskäse, - cheese made with sheep's milk

der Schal, -s scarf (2)

schälen, geschält to peel, skin

die Schallplatte, -n (phonograph) record

der Schalter, - ticket booth, ticket window (5);
am Schalter at the ticket booth/window (5)

der Schatten, - shadow; shade (9)

der Schatz, ⁻e treasure (9)

schätzen, geschätzt to value; to estimate; to reckon

schauen (an/auf + *acc.*), geschaut to look (at) (A)

schaufeln, geschaufelt to shovel (11)

das Schauspiel, -e play (12)

der Schauspieler, - / die Schauspielerin, -nen
actor/actress (9)

der Scheck, -s check

die Scheibe, -n pane, windowpane (7); slice

der Scheibenwischer, - windshield wiper (7)

scheiden (scheidet), schied, geschieden to leave;
to divorce

die Scheidung, -en divorce (12)

der Schein, -e bill, note (*of currency*) (8)

scheinen (scheint), schien, geschienen to shine;
to seem, appear

schenken, geschenkt to give (as a present) (5)

die Schere, -n scissors (8)

schick chic, stylish(ly), smart(ly) (2)

schicken, geschickt to send (2); sich schicken to
be proper

das Schicksal, -e fate, destiny

schieben (schiebt), schob, geschoben to push;
to shove

schief gehen (geht ... schief), ging ... schief, ist
schief gegangen to go wrong

die Schiene, -n train track (10)

schießen (schießt), schoss, geschossen to shoot

das Schiff, -e ship

der Schiffer, - boatman

das Schild, -er sign (7)

das Schildchen, - small sign

schildern, geschildert to describe; to portray

die Schildkröte, -n turtle; tortoise (10)

der Schilling, -e schilling (*former Austrian monetary
unit*) (7); zwei Schilling two schillings (7)

schimpfen, geschimpft to cuss, curse; to scold
(9)

der Schinken, - ham (8)

der Schlaf sleep (9)

der Schlafanzug, ⁻e pajamas

schlafen (schläft), schlief, geschlafen to sleep
(2); lange schlafen to sleep late

der Schlafsack, ⁻e sleeping bag (2)

der Schlafwagen, - sleeping car (4)

das Schlafzimmer, - bedroom (6)

der Schlag, ⁻e strike (*of a clock*); (heart)beat; blow

schlagen (schlägt), schlug, geschlagen to beat,
strike, hit (8, 11)

die Schlagsahne whipped cream; whipping
cream

das Schlagzeug drums; percussion
instruments (12)

die Schlange, -n snake (10)

schlank slender, slim (B)

schlapp run-down; listless

das Schlauchboot, -e inflatable dinghy (10)

schlecht bad(ly) (2)

schleichen (schleicht), schlich, ist geschlichen to
creep, sneak

die Schleife, -n ribbon; bow

(das) Schleswig Schleswig

(das) Schleswig-Holstein Schleswig-Holstein

schleudern, geschleudert to hurl

schlicht simple, simply; plain(ly)

schließen (schließt), schloss, geschlossen to
close, shut (A)

schließlich finally; after all (7)

schlimm bad (11)

die Schlinge, -n sling

der Schlitten, - sled (2); Schlitten fahren to go
sledding

der Schlittschuh, -e ice skate (3); Schlittschuh
laufen to go ice-skating (3)

das Schloss, ⁻er castle (9)

der Schlossgang, ⁻e castle walkway

das Schlump *name of a building in Hamburg*

die Schlumper (*pl.*) group of artists named after the
Schlump

der Schluss, ⁻e end (8); conclusion; am Schluss
in the end; jetzt aber Schluss finish up now;
zum Schluss in the end, finally (8)

der Schlüssel, - key (9)

schmal narrow; thin

schmecken (+ *dat.*), geschmeckt to taste good
(to) (6)

schmelzen (schmelzt), schmolz, ist geschmolzen
to melt

der Schmerz, -en pain (11)

schmerzlos painless(ly)

sich schminken, geschminkt to put makeup on (11)

schmoren, geschmort to braise

der Schmuck jewelry (2)

schmutzig dirty (A)

der Schnaps, ⁻e spirit; schnapps

die Schnecke, -n snail (10)

der Schnee snow (9)

(das) Schneewittchen Snow White

schneiden (schneidet), schnitt, geschnitten to
cut (3); Haare schneiden to cut hair (3); sich
schneiden to cut oneself (11)

schneien, geschneit to snow; es schneit it is
snowing (B)

schnell quick(ly), fast (3)

das Schnitzel, - (veal/beef/pork) cutlet (8); das
Wiener Schnitzel breaded veal cutlet

der Schnupfen, - cold (*with a runny nose*), sniffles
(11)

die Schnupftabakdose, -n snuffbox

die Schnur, ⁻e string (8)

der Schnurrbart, ⁻e moustache (A)

schnurstracks (*coll.*) straight, directly

der Schock, -s shock (11)

schocken, geschockt to shock

die Schokolade, -n chocolate

schon already (2, 4); indeed; ich glaube schon I
think so; schon wieder once again (3); warst
du schon einmal ...? were you ever . . . ? (4)

schön pretty, beautiful (B); nice; bitte schön
help yourself; there you go; bitte schön? yes
please? may I help you? (7); ganz schön quite
pretty; ganz schön viel quite a bit (3)

die Schönheit, -en beauty

der Schrank, ⁻e closet; cupboard; cabinet; wardrobe (2, 6)

der Schreck, -e fright; terror; shock

schrecklich terrible, terribly; horrible, horribly

der Schrei, -e cry; shout; scream

schreiben (schreibt), schrieb, geschrieben to
write; to spell (A); (an + *acc.*) to write to;
(über + *acc.*) to write about; (von + *dat.*) to
write of/about; wie schreibt man das? how do
you spell that? (A)

die Schreibmaschine, -n typewriter

der Schreibtisch, -e desk (2)

das Schreibwarengeschäft, -e stationery store (6)

das Schreibzeug writing materials

schreien (schreit), schrie, geschrien to scream,
yell (3)

die Schrift, -en script; (hand)writing

schriftlich written, in writing (10)

der Schriftsteller, - / die Schriftstellerin, -nen
writer (5)

der Schritt, -e step; Schritt für Schritt step by
step

die Schublade, -n drawer (5)

schüchtern shy(ly) (B)

der Schuh, -e shoe (A)

das Schuhgeschäft, -e shoe store (6)

der Schulabschluss, ⁻e *degree received after completing
secondary school*

der Schulalltag, -e daily routine at school

die Schulbildung education, schooling (5)

schuld: schuld sein (an + *dat.*) to be at fault (for)

die Schuld, -en debt; fault; guilt (12)

schulden, geschuldet to owe

die Schule, -n school (A, 1, 3, 4, 5); in die / zur
Schule to school; in der Schule at school (5)

der Schüler, - / die Schülerin, -nen student;
pupil (1)

das Schulfach, ⁻er school subject (1)

der Schulfreund, -e / die Schulfreundin, -nen
school friend

der Schulhof, ⁻e schoolyard, playground

die Schulinspektion, -en school inspection

schulisch school (*adj.*), scholastic(ally)

das Schuljahr, -e school year

das Schulkind, -er schoolchild

die Schulklamotten (*pl., coll.*) school clothes

die Schulleistung, -en scholastic achievement

die Schulleistungsstudie study of scholastic
achievement

der Schulleiter, - / die Schulleiterin, -nen
principal, headmaster

der Schulmeister, - / die Schulmeisterin, -nen
schoolmaster

die **Schulnote, -n** grade, mark (*in school*)

die **Schulstunde, -n** school period

das **Schulsystem, -e** school system

der **Schultag, -e** school day

die **Schultasche, -n** book bag

die **Schulter, -n** shoulder (B)

die **Schuluniform, -en** school uniform

die **Schulzeit** school days

die **Schummelhilfe, -n** (*coll.*) cheating aid

die **Schüssel, -n** bowl (8)

schütteln, geschüttelt to shake; **die Hand
  schütteln** to shake hands (A); **sich schütteln**
  to shake (*o.s.*)

schützen, geschützt to protect

schwach weak(ly)

der **Schwager, ⸚** / die **Schwägerin, -nen**
  brother-/sister-in-law

der **Schwamm, ⸚e** sponge; eraser (*for blackboard*)
  (B)

der **Schwan, ⸚e** swan

schwanger pregnant

schwanken, geschwankt to sway; to rock

schwarz black (A); **das schwarze Brett** bulletin
  board

das **Schwarzbier, -e** *very dark beer*

schwarzhaarig black-haired (9)

der **Schwarzwald** Black Forest

(das) **Schweden** Sweden (B)

(das) **Schwedisch** Swedish (*language*) (B)

schweifen, ist geschweift to wander

schweigen (schweigt), schwieg, geschwiegen to
  become silent; to be silent, say nothing

das **Schweigen** silence

das **Schwein, -e** pig (9)

der **Schweinebraten, -** pork roast

das **Schweinefleisch** pork (8)

die **Schweinerei, -en** (*coll.*) mess

der **Schweinestall, ⸚e** pigpen (5)

die **Schweiz** Switzerland (B)

Schweizer Swiss (*adj.*)

der **Schweizer, -** / die **Schweizerin, -nen** Swiss
  (*person*) (B)

die **Schwellung, -en** swelling

schwer heavy, heavily; hard; difficult (3); **schwer
  verletzt** critically injured (11); **zu schwer** too
  heavy (4)

schwer·fallen (+ *dat.*) **(fällt ... schwer), fiel ...
  schwer, ist schwergefallen** to be difficult for

die **Schwester, -n** sister (B)

schwierig difficult (2)

die **Schwierigkeit, -en** difficulty

das **Schwimmbad, ⸚er** swimming pool (1, 5);
  im Schwimmbad at the swimming pool (5);
  ins Schwimmbad fahren to go/drive to the
  swimming pool (1)

**schwimmen (schwimmt), schwamm, ist/hat
  geschwommen** to swim; to float (7); **im
  Meer schwimmen** to swim in the sea (1);
  schwimmen gehen to go swimming (1)

der **Schwimmstar, -s** swimming star

schwitzen, geschwitzt to sweat, perspire

Se (*dial. for. sg./pl.*) = **Sie** you

sechs six (A); **um sechs (Uhr)** at six o'clock (1)

sechst- sixth (4)

sechsundzwanzig twenty-six (A)

sechzehn sixteen (A)

sechzig sixty (A)

der **See, -n** lake (7)

die **See, -n** sea

das **Seebad, ⸚er** seaside bathing resort

seekrank seasick (7)

die **Seele, -n** soul (12)

segeln, ist/hat gesegelt to sail (1)

sehen (sieht), sah, gesehen to see (2)

sehr very (B); **bitte sehr** there you go; **so sehr** so
  much; **zu sehr** too much

der **Sehtest, -s** eye test

das **Seidenkleid, -er** silk dress

die **Seife, -n** soap (6)

die **Seilbahn, -en** cable railway (7)

der **Seiltänzer, -** / die **Seiltänzerin, -nen**
  tightrope walker

sein (ist), war, ist gewesen to be (A, 4)

sein(e) his, its (1, 2)

seit (*prep.*) since, for (4, 11); **seit mehreren Tagen**
  for several days (11); **seit zwei Jahren** for two
  years (4)

seitab off to the side

die **Seite, -n** side; page (6)

der **Sekretär, -e** fold-out desk

der **Sekretär, -e** / die **Sekretärin, -nen** secretary (5)

der **Sekt, -e** sparkling wine

die **Sekunde, -n** second (1)

selber, selbes, selbe same

selbst even; oneself, myself, yourself, himself, herself, itself; ourselves, yourselves,
  themselves; by (one)self; **selbst gemacht**
  homemade (8)

selbstbewusst self-confident(ly)

der **Selbstmord, -e** suicide

die **Selbstmordrate, -n** suicide rate

das **Selbstporträt, -s** self-portrait

selbstständig independent(ly) (12)

selbstverständlich of course (10)

selten rare(ly), seldom (8)

seltsam strange(ly)

das **Semester, -** semester (1)

die **Semesterferien** (*pl.*) semester break

das **Seminar, -e** seminar

die **Semmel, -n** (bread) roll

senden (sendet), sandte, gesandt to send

der **Sendetermin, -e** broadcast time

der **Senf** mustard (8)

der **September** September (B)

(das) **Serbien** Serbia

servieren, serviert to serve

die **Serviette, -n** napkin (8)

servus! hello! good-bye! (*infor.; southern Germany,
  Austria*) (A)

der **Sessel, -** armchair (2, 6)

setzen, gesetzt to put, place, set (*in a sitting position*) (7); **sich setzen** to sit down (A, 11)

das **Shampoo, -s** shampoo

sich oneself, himself, herself, itself, yourself;
  themselves, yourselves

sicher safe(ly); sure(ly) (1)

der **Sicherheitsgurt, -e** safety belt (7)

die **Sicherheitskontrolle, -n** safety checkpoint

sicherlich certainly (3)

die **Sicht, -en** sight; view

sichtbar visible, visibly (11)

sie she, it; they

Sie (*for. sg./pl.*) you

sieben seven (A)

siebenundzwanzig twenty-seven (A)

siebt- seventh (4)

siebzehn seventeen (A)

siebzig seventy (A)

der **Sieg, -e** victory

signalisieren, signalisiert to signal; to
  indicate

silbern silver (*adj.*), silvery

(das) **Silentium** quiet time

singen (singt), sang, gesungen to sing (1); **wir
  singen gern** we like to sing (1)

sinken (sinkt), sank, ist gesunken to sink

der **Sinn, -e** sense; **aus dem Sinn kommen** to
  forget; **im Sinne** (+ *gen.*) in the sense of

die **Sinologie** *study of Chinese language and culture*

die **Situation, -en** situation

der **Sitz, -e** seat (7)

sitzen (sitzt), saß, gesessen to sit; to be in a
  sitting position (4); **sitzen bleiben (bleibt ...
  sitzen), blieb ... sitzen, ist sitzen geblieben**
  to be held back a grade

(das) **Skandinavien** Scandinavia

das **Skateboard, -s** skateboard (3); **Skateboard
  fahren** to skateboard (3)

der **Ski, -er** ski (3); **Ski fahren** to ski (3)

die **Skihütte, -n** ski lodge (6)

der **Skorpion, -e** scorpion (10)

die **Skulptur, -en** sculpture (12)

die **Slowakei** Slovakia (B)

(das) **Slowenien** Slovenia (B)

die **SMS** SMS (= short message service: *text
  messaging by cell phone or other electronic device*)

so so; such; that way (A); **das stimmt so** that's
  right; keep the change (8); **so viel** so much; **so
  viele** so many; **und so weiter** and so forth

sobald (*subord. conj.*) as soon as

die **Socke, -n** sock (2)

das **Sofa, -s** sofa, couch (6)

sofort immediately (3)

der **Soft-Rock** soft rock music

sogar even

sogenannt so-called

der **Sohn, ⸚e** son (B)

(der) **Sokrates** Socrates

solange (*subord. conj.*) as long as; while

das **Solarium, Solarien** tanning salon (11)

solcher, solches, solche such

der **Soldat, -en** (*wk.*) / die **Soldatin, -nen** soldier

sollen (soll), sollte, gesollt to be supposed to (3)

der **Sommer, -** summer (B); **im Sommer** in the summer; **letzten Sommer** last summer (4)

der **Sommerkurs, -e** summer school (3)

der **Sommertreffpunkt, -e** summer meeting place

sondern but (rather/on the contrary) (A, 11)

das **Songbuch, ⸚er** songbook (2)

der **Sonnabend, -e** Saturday

die **Sonne, -n** sun (1); **in der Sonne liegen** to lie in the sun (1)

sich **sonnen, gesonnt** to sunbathe (11)

sonnenbaden gehen (geht ... sonnenbaden), ging ... sonnenbaden, ist sonnenbaden gegangen to go sunbathing (10)

der **Sonnenbrand, ⸚e** sunburn (10)

die **Sonnenbrille, -n** sunglasses (1, 2)

die **Sonnenmilch** suntan lotion (10)

der **Sonnenschein** sunshine; **etwas ist eitel Sonnenschein** something is positive/happy

der **Sonnenschirm, -e** sunshade; parasol (10)

sonnig sunny (B)

der **Sonntag, -e** Sunday (1)

sonst otherwise (B); **sonst noch etwas?** anything else? (5)

sonstig other; **Sonstiges** other things (9)

sorgen (für + *acc.***), gesorgt** to take care (of) (12)

die **Soße, -n** gravy; sauce; (salad) dressing (8)

das **Souvenir, -s** souvenir (7)

sowie as well as

sowieso anyway

sozial social(ly)

der **Sozialismus** socialism

der **Sozialist, -en** (*wk.*) / die **Sozialistin, -nen** socialist (*person*)

die **Sozialkunde** social studies (1)

die **Sozialpädagogik** social education

die **Soziologie** sociology (1)

die **Spaghetti** (*pl.*) spaghetti (7)

die **Spalte, -n** column

(das) **Spanien** Spain (B)

spanisch Spanish (*adj.*)

(das) **Spanisch** Spanish (*language*) (B)

die **Spannweite, -n** wingspan

sparen, gespart to save (*money*) (7); (**auf** + *acc.*) to save up for

das **Sparkonto, -konten** savings account (12)

der **Spaß, ⸚e** fun; **Spaß haben** to have fun; **Spaß machen** to be fun; **viel Spaß!** have fun! (A)

spät late (1); **wie spät ist es?** what time is it? (1)

die **Spätzle** (*pl.*) spaetzle (*kind of noodles*)

spazieren gehen (geht ... spazieren), ging ... spazieren, ist spazieren gegangen to go for a walk (1)

der **Spaziergang, ⸚e** walk (10)

der **Speck** bacon (8)

die **Spedition, -en** transport

die **Speditionsfirma, -firmen** trucking company

speichern, gespeichert to store

die **Speise, -n** food, dish

die **Speisekarte, -n** menu (8)

der **Speisewagen, -** dining car

spekulieren, spekuliert to speculate

der **Sperrmüll** bulk refuse (heap)

die **Spezialität, -en** speciality

der **Spiegel, -** mirror (6)

sich **spiegeln, gespiegelt** to be reflected

das **Spieglein, -** (*diminutive form of* der **Spiegel**) little mirror

das **Spiel, -e** game; match

spielen, gespielt to play (1); **Klavier spielen** to play the piano; **wann spielt die Geschichte?** when does the story take place?

der **Spieler, -** / die **Spielerin, -nen** player

der **Spielfreund, -e** / die **Spielfreundin, -nen** playmate

der **Spielkamerad, -en** (*wk.*) / die **Spielkameradin, -nen** playmate

der **Spielplatz, ⸚e** playground (9)

das **Spielzeug, -e** toy

der **Spinat, -e** spinach (8)

der **Spion, -e** / die **Spionin, -nen** spy

spitz pointed

der **Spitzbart, ⸚e** goatee

die **Spitze, -n** tip; top

der **Spitzel, -** informer

der **Spitzname, -n** (*wk.*) nickname (1)

der **Sport** sport(s); physical education (1); **Sport treiben** to do sports (2)

die **Sporthose, -n** tights; sports pants (2)

sportlich athletic (B)

der **Sportplatz, ⸚e** sports field; playing field

der **Sportschuh, -e** athletic shoe (A)

die **Sportverletzung, -en** sports injury

die **Sprache, -n** language (B)

das **Sprachlabor, -s** language laboratory (4)

sprachlos speechless(ly)

sprechen (spricht), sprach, gesprochen to speak, talk (B); (**über** + *acc.*) to talk about; **er/sie spricht ...** he/she speaks . . . (B)

der **Sprecher, -** / die **Sprecherin, -nen** speaker

die **Sprechsituation, -en** conversational situation (A)

die **Sprechstunde, -n** office hour (3)

die **Sprechstundenhilfe** (doctor's) receptionist

sprengen, gesprengt to water, sprinkle

das **Sprichwort, ⸚er** proverb, saying

springen (springt), sprang, ist gesprungen to jump, spring (A)

die **Spritze, -n** shot, injection (11)

sprühen, gesprüht to spray

spucken, gespuckt to spit

das **Spülbecken, -** sink (5)

die **Spüle, -n** sink

spülen, gespült to wash; to rinse (4); **Geschirr spülen** to wash the dishes (4)

das **Spülwasser** dishwater

der **Spürsinn** intuition

das **Squash** squash (*game*) (1)

der **Staat, -en** state; nation (10)

staatlich state, government (*adj.*)

die **Staatsangehörigkeit, -en** nationality, citizenship (1)

die **Staatsbürgerschaft** citizenship

der **Staatschef, -s** / die **Staatschefin, -nen** head of state

das **Staatsexamen, -** *final university examination*

die **Staatssicherheit** national security; *East German secret police*

die **Stadt, ⸚e** town, city (2, 6, 10); **in der Stadt** in town, in the city (6, 10)

der **Stadtpark, -s** municipal park (10)

der **Stadtplan, ⸚e** city street map (10)

der **Stadtrand, ⸚er** city limits (6)

die **Stadtrundfahrt, -en** tour of the city (7)

der **Stadtrundgang, ⸚e** walking tour of the city

der **Stadtteil, -e** district, neighborhood (6)

das **Stadtviertel, -** quarter, district, neighborhood (6)

die **Staffelei, -en** easel (12)

stammen (aus + *dat.***), gestammt** to come (from), originate (from)

standhaft steadfast(ly)

der **Standort, -e** location

stark strong(ly); heavy, heavily (11); severe(ly); **echt stark!** (*coll.*) great! cool!

starren (auf + *acc.***), gestarrt** to stare (at)

der **Start, -s** start; beginning

starten, ist gestartet to start; to take off

die **Stasi** = die **Staatssicherheit** (*East German secret police*)

die **Station, -en** station

die **Statistik, -en** statistics

statt (+ *gen.*) instead of (12)

stattdessen instead (of that)

statt·finden (findet ... statt), fand ... statt, stattgefunden to take place (5)

das **Statussymbol, -e** status symbol

der **Stau, -s** traffic jam (7)

der **Staub** dust; **sich aus dem Staub machen** (*coll.*) to scram; to get lost; to go; **Staub saugen** to vacuum (6); **Staub wischen** to (wipe) dust

der **Staubsauger, -** vacuum cleaner (6)

die **Stauchung, -en** compression

das **Staunen** amazement

das **Steak, -s** steak

stechen (sticht), stach, gestochen to prick; to sting; to bite (*of insects*) (10)

der **Steckbrief, -e** personal description; personal details

stecken, gesteckt to stick; to put; to be; **stecken bleiben (bleibt ... stecken), blieb ... stecken, ist stecken geblieben** to get stuck (11)

der **Stefansdom** St. Stephen's Cathedral

stehen (steht), stand, gestanden to stand (*be in a vertical position*) (2, 6); to be (situated); to stop, come to a standstill; (+ *dat.*) to suit (6); **das steht / die stehen dir gut** that looks / they look good on you (2)

stehlen (stiehlt), stahl, gestohlen to steal (9)

steigen (steigt), stieg, ist gestiegen to climb; to ascend; to increase

der **Stein, -e** stone (12)

steinern (*adj.*) (made of) stone

die **Steinzeit** Stone Age (12)

die **Stelle, -n** position; place

stellen, gestellt to stand up, put, place (*in a vertical position*) (3, 5); **eine Frage stellen** to ask a question (A, 5); **gerade stellen** to straighten (3)

das **Step-Aerobic** step aerobics

sterben (stirbt), starb, ist gestorben to die (9)

die **Stereoanlage, -n** stereo system (6)

das **Sternzeichen, -** star sign, sign of the zodiac

das **Steuer, -** steering wheel

die **Steuer, -n** tax

der **Steward, -s** / die **Stewardess, -en** flight attendant (5)

der **Stichpunkt, -e** main point (12)

das **Stichwort, -̈er** keyword

der **Stiefel, -** boot (A)

die **Stiefmutter, -̈** stepmother (9)

der **Stiefvater, -̈** stepfather (9)

der **Stift, -e** pen, pencil (A, B)

der **Stil, -e** style

still quiet(ly); silent(ly)

die **Stille** quiet; silence

das **Stillleben, -** still life

die **Stimme, -n** voice (12)

stimmen, gestimmt to be right (8); **(das) stimmt!** that's right! (4); **das stimmt so** that's right; keep the change (8)

die **Stimmung, -en** mood; atmosphere

das **Stipendium, Stipendien** scholarship (1)

die **Stirn, -en** forehead

das **Stirnband, -̈er** headband (A)

der **Stock, -̈e** stick; walking stick

der **Stock, -** floor, story (6); **im ersten Stock** on the second floor (6)

das **Stockwerk, -e** floor, story (6)

stolpern, ist gestolpert to trip, stumble (9)

stolz proud(ly)

stop (*interj.*) stop, halt

der **Stopp, -s** stop

stoppen, gestoppt to stop

stören, gestört to disturb (3)

stoßen (stößt), stieß, gestoßen to shove; to push

der **Stoßzahn, -̈e** tusk (10)

stottern, gestottert to stutter

Str. = die **Straße, -n** street

die **Straftat, -en** criminal offense

der **Strafzettel, -** (parking or speeding) ticket

der **Strand, -̈e** beach, shore (4, 7)

der **Strandkorb, -̈e** basket chair (*for the beach*) (10)

die **Strandpromenade, -n** (beach) promenade

die **Straße, -n** street, road (6)

die **Straßenbahn, -en** streetcar (7)

der **Straßenjunge, -n** (*wk.*) street urchin

sich **sträuben, gesträubt** to stand on end, bristle (*hair*); to resist

strebsam ambitious; industrious

strecken, gestreckt to stretch

streichen (streicht), strich, gestrichen to paint

das **Streichholz, -̈er** match (8)

die **Streife, -n** patrol; **Streife gehen** to be on patrol

streiten (streitet), stritt, gestritten to argue, quarrel (9)

streng strict(ly); severe(ly); disciplined (9)

stricken, gestrickt to knit (3)

der **Strom, -̈e** stream; current; electricity, power (8)

die **Strömung, -en** current

die **Strophe, -n** strophe; verse

die **Struktur, -en** structure

die **Strumpfhose, -n** tights; pantyhose

das **Stück, -e** piece; slice (8)

das **Stückchen, -** little piece

der **Student, -en** (*wk.*) / die **Studentin, -nen** student (A, B)

das **Studentenheim, -e** dorm (2, 6)

das **Studentenleben** student life (4)

die **Studie, -n** study

der **Studienabschluss, -̈e** completion of one's studies

der **Studienanfänger, -** / die **Studienanfängerin, -nen** beginning student

das **Studienfach, -̈er** academic subject (1)

der **Studiengang, -̈e** course of study

die **Studiengebühr, -en** registration fee, tuition

der **Studientag, -e** day of study

studieren, studiert to study; to attend a university/college (1)

der/die **Studierende, -n (ein Studierender)** student

das **Studierzimmer, -** study (room)

das **Studium, Studien** university studies (1, 3)

der **Stuhl, -̈e** chair (B, 2)

die **Stunde, -n** hour (2)

stundenlang for hours

der **Stundenlohn, -̈e** hourly wage

der **Stundenplan, -̈e** schedule (1)

stundenweise by the hour

stürmen, gestürmt to storm; to attack

der **Sturz, -̈e** fall

stürzen, ist gestürzt to fall

das **Subjekt, -e** subject

das **Substantiv, -e** noun

subtrahieren, subtrahiert to subtract

die **Suchanzeige, -n** housing-wanted ad (6)

die **Suche, -n** search

suchen, gesucht to look for (1)

(das) **Südafrika** South Africa (B)

(das) **Südamerika** South America (B)

süddeutsch Southern German (*adj.*)

(das) **Süddeutschland** Southern Germany

der **Süden** south

südlich (von + *dat.***)** south (of) (7)

südöstlich (von + *dat.***)** southeast (of) (7)

südwestlich (von + *dat.***)** southwest (of) (7)

der **Südwind** south wind

super super

der **Superbowl** Super Bowl

der **Supermarkt, -̈e** supermarket (5); **im Supermarkt** at the supermarket (5)

superschnell superfast (7)

die **Suppe, -n** soup (8)

das **Surfbrett, -er** surfboard (2)

surfen, gesurft to surf, go surfing

der **Sushi** sushi

süß sweet(ly) (4)

die **Süßigkeit, -en** sweet, candy (9)

der **Swimmingpool, -s** swimming pool

das **Symbol, -e** symbol

symbolisieren, symbolisiert to symbolize

sympathisch congenial(ly), appealing(ly); sympathetic(ally)

das **Symphonieorchester, -** symphony orchestra

das **Symptom, -e** symptom (11)

syrisch Syrian (*adj.*)

die **Szene, -n** scene

das *SZ-Magazin* = *Süddeutsche Zeitung Magazin* magazine section of Sunday edition of *SZ*

---

der **Tabak, -e** tobacco

die **Tabelle, -n** table; list

die **Tablette, -n** tablet, pill (11)

die **Tafel, -n** blackboard (A, B)

der **Tag, -e** day (1); **an welchem Tag?** on what day? (4); **den ganzen Tag** all day long, the whole day (1); **eines Tages** one day; **guten Tag!** good afternoon! hello! (*for.*) (A); **seit mehreren Tagen** for several days (11); **Tag für Tag** day after day; **vor zwei Tagen** two days ago (4); **welcher Tag ist heute?** what day is today? (1)

das **Tagebuch, -̈er** diary (4)

der **Tagesablauf, -̈e** daily routine; course of (one's) day

das **Tageslicht** daylight

der **Tageslichtprojektor, -en** overhead projector

die **Tageszeit, -en** time of day

die **Tageszeitung, -en** daily newspaper (5)

täglich daily (9)

der **Taktverkehr** regularly scheduled transportation

das **Tal, -̈er** valley (7)

das **Talent, -e** talent (3)

der **Tank, -s** tank (7)

tanken, getankt to fill up (with gas) (5)

die **Tankstelle, -n** gas station (5); **an der Tankstelle** at the gas station (5)

die **Tante, -n** aunt (B)

tanzen, getanzt to dance (1)

der **Tänzer, -** / die **Tänzerin, -nen** dancer

die **Tanzschule, -n** dance school

die **Tapete, -n** wallpaper

tapfer brave(ly) (9)

die **Tasche, -n** (hand)bag; purse; pocket (1)

das **Taschengeld, -er** pocket money, allowance

die **Taschenlampe, -n** flashlight (9)

das **Taschentuch, -̈er** handkerchief (3)

die **Tasse, -n** cup (2, 5)

die **Tat, -en** act; deed

der **Täter, -** / die **Täterin, -nen** perpetrator

tätig active

die **Tätigkeit, -en** activity (5)

der **Tatort, -e** scene of a crime

tätowieren, tätowiert to tattoo

der **Tätowierer**, - / die **Tätowiererin**, -nen tattoo artist

die **Tauchausrüstung** diving equipment

tauchen, hat/ist getaucht to dive (3)

tausend thousand

tausendmal a thousand times

das **Taxi**, -s taxi (3, 7)

der **Taxifahrer**, - / die **Taxifahrerin**, -nen taxi driver (5)

die **Technik**, -en technology (12)

technisch technical(ly); technological(ly)

der **Technische Überwachungsverein (TÜV)** Technical Control Board (*German agency that checks vehicular safety*)

die **Technologie**, -n technology

der **Teddy**, -s / der **Teddybär**, -en (*wk.*) teddy bear (A, 9)

der **Tee**, -s tea (4)

die **Teekanne**, -n teapot (8)

der **Teekessel**, - tea kettle (8)

der **Teil**, -e part, portion (7)

sich **teilen**, geteilt to split; to be divided

teil·nehmen (an + *dat.*) (nimmt ... teil), nahm ... teil, teilgenommen to participate (*in s.th.*)

das **Telefon**, -e telephone (A, 2); **am Telefon** on the phone (2)

das **Telefonat**, -e telephone call

telefonieren, telefoniert to telephone, talk on the phone (4)

die **Telefonkarte**, -n telephone card (2)

die **Telefonnummer**, -n telephone number (1)

die **Telefonzelle**, -n telephone booth (2)

das **Telegramm**, -e telegram (2)

der **Teller**, - plate (8)

die **Temperatur**, -en temperature

das **Tennis** tennis (1)

der **Tennisschläger**, - tennis racket

der **Tennisspieler**, - / die **Tennisspielerin**, -nen tennis player (9)

der **Teppich**, -e carpet, rug (2)

der **Termin**, -e appointment (5, 11); **sich einen Termin geben lassen** to get an appointment (11)

der **Terminkalender**, - appointment calendar (11)

die **Terrasse**, -n terrace, deck (6)

der **Test**, -s test

testen, getestet to test

der **Tetanus** tetanus (11)

teuer expensive(ly) (2)

der **Teufel**, - devil (12); **pfui Teufel!** (*interj.*) ugh! yuck!

das **Teufelszeug** (*coll.*) terrible stuff

der **Teutoburger Wald** *mountainous forest in North Rhine-Westphalia*

der **Text**, -e text (12)

das **Theater**, - theater (4)

das **Thema**, Themen theme, topic, subject (4)

die **Theologie** theology

theoretisch theoretical(ly)

die **Theorie**, -n theory

der **Thunfisch**, -e tuna

(das) **Thüringen** Thuringia

das **Ticket**, -s ticket

tief deep(ly) (7)

das **Tiefland**, -̈er lowlands

das **Tier**, -e animal (3, 7, 9, 10)

der **Tierarzt**, -̈e / die **Tierärztin**, -nen veterinarian (11)

der **Tierpfleger**, - / die **Tierpflegerin**, -nen animal keeper

der **Tipp**, -s tip

tippen, getippt to type (3, 6)

(das) **Tirol** Tyrol

Tiroler (*adj.*) Tyrolean

der **Tisch**, -e table (B); **den Tisch abräumen** to clear the table (3); **den Tisch decken** to set the table (3)

der **Tischler**, - / die **Tischlerin**, -nen carpenter

das **Tischtennis** table tennis (3)

der **Titel**, - title

der **Toaster**, - toaster (8)

die **Tochter**, -̈ daughter (B)

der **Tod**, -e death (12)

die **Toilette**, -n toilet (6)

das **Toilettenpapier** toilet paper (4)

die **Toilettentasche**, -n cosmetic bag

tolerant tolerant(ly) (B)

toll (*coll.*) great, neat (2); **das hört sich toll an** that sounds great (4); **einfach toll** simply great

die **Tollwut** rabies (10)

die **Tomate**, -n tomato (8)

der **Ton**, -e clay (12)

der **Topf**, -̈e pot, (sauce)pan (5)

die **Töpferei**, -en pottery; ceramic art (12)

die **Töpferscheibe**, -n potter's wheel (12)

der **Topflappen**, - potholder (5)

das **Tor**, -e gate

die **Torte**, -n pie

der **Tortenheber**, - cake server

tot dead (9); **das Tote Meer** the Dead Sea

total total(ly) (4)

der/die **Tote**, -n (ein **Toter**) dead person

töten, getötet to kill (9)

der **Totengang**, -̈e path of the dead

der **Totenkopf**, -̈e skull; death's head

die **Tour**, -en tour; trip

der **Tourismus** tourism (10)

der **Tourist**, -en (*wk.*) / die **Touristin**, -nen tourist

die **Touristenklasse** tourist class (5)

das **Touristenmenü**, -s (set) meal for tourists

die **Tradition**, -en tradition (4, 12)

traditionell traditional(ly)

tragen (trägt), trug, getragen to carry; to wear (A); **er/sie trägt ...** he/she is wearing (A); **trägst du ...?** are you wearing . . . ? (A) **trägst du gern ...?** do you like to wear . . . ? (A)

der **Träger**, - / die **Trägerin**, -nen recipient (*of a prize*) (12)

die **Tragödie**, -n tragedy (12)

der **Trailer**, - trailer

der **Trainingsanzug**, -̈e sweats

trampen, ist getrampt to hitchhike (10)

der **Tramper**, - / die **Tramperin**, -nen hitchhiker

die **Transaktion**, -en transaction

transkontinental transcontinental

transportieren, transportiert to transport, carry (7)

das **Transportmittel**, - means of transportation; vehicle (7)

die **Trauer** grief; mourning

der **Traum**, -̈e dream

träumen (von + *dat.*), geträumt to dream (of/about) (9)

traurig sad(ly) (B)

(sich) **treffen** (trifft), traf, getroffen to meet (2); to hit; **eine Entscheidung treffen** to make a decision; **treffen wir uns ...** let's meet . . . (2)

treiben (treibt), trieb, getrieben to drive; to carry out, do; **Sport treiben** to do sports (2)

trennbar separable

(sich) **trennen**, getrennt to separate, break up (*people*) (7); to divide

die **Treppe**, -n stairway (6)

das **Treppenhaus**, -̈er stairwell (10)

treten (tritt), trat, ist getreten to step

treu loyal(ly); faithful(ly); true (9)

die **Treue** loyalty

trinken (trinkt), trank, getrunken to drink (1)

das **Trinkgeld**, -er tip (8)

trivial trivial(ly)

trocken dry(ly) (11)

die **Trompete**, -n trumpet (12)

der **Tropfen**, - drop

trotz (+ *gen.*) in spite of (12)

trotzdem in spite of that; nonetheless (9)

(das) **Tschechien** Czech Republic (B)

tschechisch (*adj.*) Czech

tschüss! (*infor.*) bye! (A)

das **T-Shirt**, -s T-shirt (2)

tun (tut), tat, getan to do (A)

(das) **Tunesien** Tunisia (B)

der **Tunnel**, - tunnel

die **Tür**, -en door (A)

der **Türke**, -n (*wk.*) / die **Türkin**, -nen Turk (12)

die **Türkei** Turkey (B)

türkisch Turkish (*adj.*)

(das) **Türkisch** Turkish (*language*) (B)

der **Turm**, -̈e tower

der **Turnschuh**, -e gym shoe

die **Türschwelle**, -n threshold

der **Türspalt**, -e crack of the door

die **Tüte**, -n (paper or plastic) bag (11)

der **TÜV** = der **Technische Überwachungsverein** Technical Control Board (*German agency that checks vehicular safety*)

der **Typ**, -en (*coll.*) character, person, guy

typisch typical(ly)

tyrannisieren, tyrannisiert to tyrannize

die **U-Bahn**, -en = **Untergrundbahn** subway (7)

üben, geübt to practice; to exercise

über (+ *dat./acc.*) over, above; about; across (4); **übers Wochenende** over the weekend (4) überall everywhere (12)

überdenken, überdacht to think over

übereinander on top of one another

überfahren (überfährt), überfuhr, überfahren to run over (11)

überfliegen (überfliegt), überflog, überflogen to skim

überfordern, überfordert to overtax

überhaupt anyway; at all

überlegen, überlegt to consider, think about

übermäßig excessive(ly)

übermorgen the day after tomorrow (9)

übermütig in high spirits, cocky

übernachten, übernachtet to stay overnight (6)

übernehmen (übernimmt), übernahm, übernommen to take on, take over, adopt (12)

überprüfen, überprüft to check, inspect

überraschen, überrascht to surprise

überreden, überredet to convince, persuade

die Überredungskunst, ⸚e powers of persuasion

überrollen, überrollt to overrun

übers = über das over/about the

der Überschwang exuberance

das Überseegebiet, -e overseas territory

übersetzen, übersetzt to translate (9)

die Übersetzung, -en translation

überwachen, überwacht to watch; to monitor

überweisen (überweist), überwies, überwiesen to transfer (money) (12)

die Überweisung, -en transfer (of money) (12)

überzeugt convinced; staunch

überziehen (überzieht), überzog, überzogen to overdraw (12)

der Überziehungskredit, -e overdraft protection (12)

üblich usual; customary

übrig remaining, left over

die Übung, -en exercise (A)

die Übungsfahrt, -en practice drive

die Uhr, -en clock (B); watch; bis acht Uhr until eight o'clock (2); bis um vier Uhr until four o'clock (4); erst um vier Uhr not until four o'clock (4); um wie viel Uhr ...? at what time . . . ? (1); wie viel Uhr ist es? what time is it? (1)

die Ukraine Ukraine (B)

der Ukrainer, - / die Ukrainerin, -nen Ukrainian (person)

(das) Ukrainisch Ukrainian (language)

ultramodern ultramodern

um around; about; at; for; bis um vier Uhr until four o'clock (4); erst um vier Uhr not until four o'clock (4); (gleich) um die Ecke (right) around the corner (5, 6); um halb drei at two thirty (1); um sechs (Uhr) at six (o'clock) (1); um sieben Uhr zwanzig at seven twenty (1); um so lauter all the louder; um Viertel vor vier at a quarter to four (1); um wie viel Uhr ...? at what time . . . ? (1); um zwanzig nach fünf at twenty after/past five (1); ums Leben kommen to lose one's life

um ... zu (+ inf.) in order to (12)

um·bauen, umgebaut to rebuild

um·bringen (bringt ... um), brachte ... um, umgebracht to kill

(sich) um·drehen, umgedreht to turn around

um·fallen (fällt ... um), fiel ... um, ist umgefallen to fall over (9)

die Umfrage, -n survey (4)

der Umgang contact

die Umgebung, -en surrounding area, environs (5)

um·hängen, umgehängt to hang somewhere else

umher·schwimmen (schwimmt ... umher), schwamm ... umher, ist umhergeschwommen to swim around

um·kippen, ist/hat umgekippt to turn over; to knock over (11)

umklammern, umklammert to clutch, grasp

die Umkleidekabine, -n dressing room (5)

um·knicken, ist umgeknickt to twist one's ankle

der Umlaut, -e umlaut

der Umsatz, ⸚e sales, returns

sich um·schauen, umgeschaut to look around

der Umschlag, ⸚e cover; envelope; warmer Umschlag warm compress, poultice

sich um·sehen (sieht ... um), sah ... um, umgesehen to look around

der Umstand, ⸚e circumstance

um·steigen (steigt ... um), stieg ... um, ist umgestiegen to change (from one vehicle to another)

die Umwelt, -en environment

die Umweltkunde environmental studies

um·werfen (wirft ... um), warf ... um, umgeworfen to knock over/down

um·ziehen (zieht ... um), zog ... um, ist umgezogen to move (to another residence); (sich) umziehen, hat umgezogen to change clothes

der Umzug, ⸚e move

unangenehm unpleasant(ly)

unbedingt without fail; absolute(ly)

unbegabt untalented (12)

unbestimmt indefinite(ly)

und and (A, 11); und so weiter (usw.) and so forth (5)

unerwartet unexpected(ly)

der Unfall, ⸚e accident (4, 11)

der Unfallbericht, -e accident report (11)

die Unfallstelle, -n scene of the/an accident (11)

unfreiwillig involuntary, involuntarily

unfreundlich unfriendly

ungarisch Hungarian (adj.)

(das) Ungarn Hungary (B)

ungeduldig impatient(ly) (11)

ungefähr approximate(ly) (7)

ungelernt unskilled

ungenau inaccurate(ly); imprecise(ly)

ungenügend insufficient; unsatisfactory

ungerecht unjust(ly); unfair(ly)

ungestört undisturbed

ungewöhnlich unusual(ly)

ungezogen naughty, naughtily; badly behaved

unglaublich incredible, incredibly (5)

das Unglück, -e misfortune

unhöflich impolite(ly)

die Uni, -s (coll.) = die Universität, -en university (B, 1); auf der Uni sein to be at the university (1); zur Uni gehen to go to the university (1, 2)

die Uniform, -en uniform

die Union, -en union

die Universität, -en university (1, 4, 5); auf der Universität at the university (5)

die Unizeitung, -en university newspaper (4)

unklug unwise(ly)

unkonzentriert lacking in concentration

das Unkraut weeds

unlängst not long ago; lately, recently

unmöglich impossible, impossibly

die UNO UN (United Nations)

unordentlich untidy, untidily

unpraktisch impractical(ly)

unruhig restless(ly); uneasy, uneasily

uns us (acc./dat.)

die Unschuld innocence

unser(e) our (2)

unsereins (coll.) people like us

der Unsinn nonsense (12)

unsympathisch uncongenial(ly); disagreeable, disagreeably; unpleasant(ly)

unten (adv.) below; down; downstairs; nach unten down(ward)

unter (+ dat./acc.) under, underneath; below, beneath; among (5, 6); (adj.) lower; unter anderem among other things; unter dem Fenster under the window (5)

die Untergrundbahn, -en (U-Bahn) subway (7)

sich unterhalten (unterhält), unterhielt, unterhalten to converse (9)

die Unterhaltung, -en conversation; entertainment (3)

das Unterhemd, -en undershirt (2)

die Unterhose, -n underpants (2)

die Unterkunft, ⸚e lodging (10)

der Unterlass: ohne Unterlass incessantly

der Untermieter, - / die Untermieterin, -nen subletter

unternehmen (unternimmt), unternahm, unternommen to undertake

das Unternehmen undertaking; enterprise; company

der Unterricht class, instruction (B)

unterrichten, unterrichtet to teach, instruct (5)

unterscheiden (unterscheidet), unterschied, unterschieden to distinguish; sich unterscheiden to differ, be different

der Unterschied, -e difference

unterschiedlich different; various(ly)

unterschreiben (unterschreibt), unterschrieb, unterschrieben to sign (1); unterschreib bitte hier (infor.) sign here, please (A)

die Unterschrift, -en signature (1)

unterstreichen (unterstreicht), unterstrich, unterstrichen to underline

unterstützen, unterstützt to support

die Unterstützung support

untersuchen, untersucht to investigate; to examine (5)

der Untertitel, - subtitle

unterwegs underway; on the road (4, 9); **geschäftlich unterwegs sein** to be away on business

unterzeichnen, unterzeichnet to sign

unwichtig unimportant

unzufrieden dissatisfied

uralt very old, ancient

der Uranus Uranus (4)

der Urlaub, -e vacation (4, 5); **im Urlaub** on vacation; **in Urlaub fahren** to go (away) on vacation; **Urlaub machen** to take a vacation

der Urlauber, - / **die Urlauberin, -nen** vacationer

ursprünglich original(ly)

(die) USA (*pl.*) U.S.A. (B)

US-amerikanisch American (from the U.S.A.) (*adj.*)

usw. = und so weiter and so forth

die Utopie, -n utopia

v. Chr. = vor Christus B.C.

der Valentinstag Valentine's Day (4)

der Vampir, -e vampire

die Vase, -n vase (3)

der Vater, ⸚ father (B)

die Vaterstadt, ⸚e hometown

der Vati, -s dad, daddy

die Vatikanstadt Vatican City

der Vegetarier, - / **die Vegetarierin, -nen** vegetarian (*person*)

sich verabreden, verabredet to make a date, make an appointment; (**mit** + *dat.*) to agree to meet (with)

die Verabredung, -en appointment; date (11)

sich verabschieden, verabschiedet to say good-bye

das Verabschieden leave-taking (A)

verachten, verachtet to despise

die Veränderung, -en change

die Veranstaltung, -en public event

die Verantwortung, -en responsibility (12)

verantwortungslos irresponsible, irresponsibly

das Verb, -en verb

der Verband, ⸚e bandage (11)

die Verbendung, -en verb ending

verbessern, verbessert to improve; to correct

verbinden (verbindet), verband, verbunden to connect (A)

das Verbot, -e prohibition (7)

verboten (*p.p. of* **verbieten**) forbidden, prohibited (8)

verbrennen (verbrennt), verbrannte, verbrannt to burn (11); **sich (die Zunge) verbrennen** to burn (one's tongue) (11)

verbringen (verbringt), verbrachte, verbracht to spend, pass (*time*) (3)

verdammt damned

verdienen, verdient to earn (4)

der Verdienst, -e earnings

verdrängen, verdrängt to drive out, displace

verdüstern, verdüstert to darken

verdutzt taken aback

der Verein, -e organization; association; club

vereinigen, vereinigt to unite

verfallen (auf + *acc.*) **(verfällt), verfiel, verfallen** to think of, come up with

die Verfassung, -en constitution; **körperliche und geistige Verfassung** physical and mental state

verfassungsfeindlich hostile to the constitution

verfehlen, verfehlt to miss; not to notice (10)

verfolgen, verfolgt to persecute (12)

die Vergebung, -en forgiveness

vergehen (vergeht), verging, ist vergangen to pass, go by (*time*)

vergessen (vergisst), vergaß, vergessen to forget (2)

vergiften, vergiftet to poison (9)

der Vergleich, -e comparison

vergleichbar comparable

vergleichen (vergleicht), verglich, verglichen to compare (7)

das Vergnügen pleasure; entertainment (2)

sich verhalten (verhält), verhielt, verhalten to behave, act

das Verhalten behavior

das Verhältnis, -se relationship

verharren, verharrt to remain

verheimlichen, verheimlicht to conceal

sich verheiraten (mit + *dat.*)**, verheiratet** to get married (to) (12)

verheiratet married (1, 12)

verhungern, ist verhungert to starve

der Verkauf, ⸚e sale

verkaufen, verkauft to sell (2, 5); **zu verkaufen** for sale

der Verkäufer, - / **die Verkäuferin, -nen** salesperson (5)

verkaufsoffen open for business

der Verkehr traffic (7, 11)

das Verkehrsmittel, - means of transportation; **die öffentlichen Verkehrsmittel** (*pl.*) public transportation (7)

das Verkehrsschild, -er traffic sign (7)

verkleiden, verkleidet to disguise

verlassen (verlässt), verließ, verlassen to leave; to abandon (11)

sich verletzen, verletzt to get hurt, injure o.s. (11)

verletzt injured (11); **schwer verletzt** critically injured (11)

der/die Verletzte, -n (ein Verletzter) injured person (11)

sich verlieben (in + *acc.*)**, verliebt** to fall in love (with) (9, 12); **verliebt sein** to be in love (4, 12)

verlieren (verliert), verlor, verloren to lose (7)

sich verloben (mit + *dat.*)**, verlobt** to get engaged (to) (12); **verlobt sein** to be engaged (12)

der Verlobungsring, -e engagement ring

vermieten, vermietet to rent (out) (6)

der Vermieter, - / **die Vermieterin, -nen** landlord/landlady (6)

vermischen, vermischt to mix (8)

das Vermögen, - fortune

vernehmen (vernimmt), vernahm, vernommen to question, interrogate

vernünftig sensible, sensibly

veröffentlichen, veröffentlicht to publish

die Veröffentlichung, -en publication

verpassen, verpasst to miss (9)

verraten (verrät), verriet, verraten to betray; to disclose, give away (*a secret*)

verreisen, ist verreist to go on a trip (3)

verrücken, verrückt to move; to shift

verrückt crazy, crazily (B)

verrühren, verrührt to mix together

der Vers, -e verse

(sich) versammeln, versammelt to assemble, gather

verschieden different(ly); various(ly) (8)

verschlafen (verschläft), verschlief, verschlafen to sleep in, oversleep

verschlingen (verschlingt), verschlang, verschlungen to devour, swallow up

verschlossen reserved; taciturn

verschlucken, verschluckt to swallow

verschmutzen, verschmutzt to pollute

verschollen lost; missing

verschütten, verschüttet to spill

verschwinden (verschwindet), verschwand, ist verschwunden to disappear (12)

versetzen, versetzt to promote (*to next grade in school*) (3)

die Versetzung, -en promotion (*to next grade in school*)

versichern, versichert to insure

die Versicherung, -en insurance (5)

die Version, -en version

die Verspätung, -en lateness; delay (9)

versperren, versperrt to block; to obstruct

versprechen (verspricht), versprach, versprochen to promise (7)

die Verständigung, -en understanding; communication

das Verständnis, -se understanding

verstauen, verstaut to stow (7)

das Versteck, -e hiding place

(sich) verstecken, versteckt to hide (9)

verstehen (versteht), verstand, verstanden to understand (4)

der Verstoß, ⸚e violation

verstummt speechless

versuchen, versucht to try, attempt (4)

verteidigen, verteidigt to defend

verteilen, verteilt to distribute

der Vertrag, ⸚e contract (12)

vertrauen (+ *dat.*)**, vertraut** to trust

vertreten (vertritt), vertrat, vertreten to represent; to plead for

verunsichert insecure; unsure of oneself

verurteilen, verurteilt to sentence; to condemn

vervollständigen, vervollständigt to complete

die Verwaltung, -en administration

verwandeln, verwandelt to convert, transform; sich verwandeln (in + *acc.*) to change (into) (9)

der/die Verwandte, -n (ein Verwandter) relative (2)

verwanzt (*p.p. of* verwanzen) bugged

verwechseln, verwechselt to confuse

verwenden, verwendet to use

verwundern, verwundert to surprise

verwunschen cursed, enchanted (9)

verwünschen, verwünscht to curse, cast a spell on (9)

verzaubert (*p.p. of* verzaubern) bewitched

verzeichnen, verzeichnet to list; to record

die Verzeihung forgiveness

verzichten (auf + *acc.*), verzichtet to do without, renounce (*s.th.*)

verziehen (verzieht), verzog, verzogen: keine Miene verziehen not to bat an eyelid

der Vetter, -n (male) cousin (B)

das Video, -s video (9)

der Videorekorder, - video recorder (A)

das Videospiel, -e video game (2)

viel (*sg.*) much, a lot (of) (A); viele (*pl.*) many (A); ganz schön viel quite a bit (3); um wie viel Uhr ...? at what time . . . ? (1); viel Glück! lots of luck! good luck! (3); viel Spaß! have fun! (A); vielen Dank many thanks (10); wie viel ...? how much . . . ?; wie viel Uhr ist es? what time is it? (1); wie viele ...? how many . . . ?

vielfältig diverse

vielleicht perhaps, maybe (2)

vier four (A)

viermal four times

viert- fourth (4)

das Viertel, - quarter; um Viertel vor vier at a quarter to four

die Viertelstunde, -n quarter hour (6)

vierundzwanzig twenty-four (A)

vierzehn fourteen (A)

vierzehnt- fourteenth

vierzig forty (A)

vierzigst- fortieth

die Villa, Villen mansion (6)

der Villenbewohner, - / die Villenbewohnerin, -nen mansion resident

die Visakarte, -n Visa card

die Vision, -en vision

visualisieren, visualisiert to visualize

das Visum, Visa visa (7, 12)

das Vitamin, -e vitamin

der Vogel, ⸚ bird (10)

volkseigen state-owned

das Volksfest, -e public festival; fair

der Volkstanz, ⸚e folk dance

volkstümlich popular; of the people

voll full; full of; fully (10)

der Vollbart, ⸚e (full) beard

vollenden, vollendet to complete, finish

der Volleyball, ⸚e volleyball (1)

völlig fully, completely

vollkommen perfect(ly); flawless(ly); complete(ly) (12)

vollständig complete(ly)

voll·tanken, vollgetankt to fill up (with gas) (5)

vom = von dem of/from/by the

von (+ *dat.*) of; from (A, 10); by (*authorship*); von allein on one's own; von außen on the outside; von der Arbeit from work (3); von nebenan from next door (5); von selber by oneself; was sind Sie von Beruf? what's your profession? (1)

voneinander from each other

vor (+ *dat./acc.*) before; in front of; ago (4); because of; um Viertel vor vier at a quarter to four (1); vor allem above all; vor Christus (v. Chr.) B.C.; vor kurzem a short time ago; vor Lachen from laughing (so hard); vor zwei Tagen two days ago (4)

die Voraussetzung, -en prerequisite

voraussichtlich expected; probably

vorbei past, over (9); an ... vorbei past, by (10)

vorbei·gehen (an + *dat.*) (geht ... vorbei), ging ... vorbei, ist vorbeigegangen to go by (10)

vorbei·kommen (kommt ... vorbei), kam ... vorbei, ist vorbeigekommen to come by; to visit (3); komm mal vorbei! come on over! (11)

vorbei·schauen, vorbeigeschaut to drop in; to come over

(sich) vor·bereiten, vorbereitet to prepare

das Vorbild, -er role model, idol (9)

vorerst for now; for the time being

der Vorfahre, -n (*wk.*) ancestor (10, 12)

die Vorfahrt, -en right-of-way (7)

vor·finden (findet ... vor), fand ... vor, vorgefunden to find

die Vorgängergeneration, -en preceding generation

die Vorgeschichte prehistory

vorgestern the day before yesterday (4)

der Vorhang, ⸚e drapery, curtain (6)

vorher before, previously

die Vorhersage, -n prediction

vor·kommen (kommt ... vor), kam ... vor, ist vorgekommen to occur; (+ *dat.*) to seem (to *s.o.*)

vor·legen, vorgelegt to present, produce (*documents*) (10)

vor·lesen (liest ... vor), las ... vor, vorgelesen to read aloud (9)

die Vorlesung, -en lecture (4)

der Vormittag, -e late morning (4); am Vormittag in the morning

vormittags in the morning(s)

vorn at the front; nach vorn(e) to the front, forward

der Vorname, -n (*wk.*) first name (A, 1)

vornehm noble, nobly

vors = vor das in front of the

der Vorsatz, ⸚e intention

der Vorschlag, ⸚e suggestion (5)

vor·schlagen (schlägt ... vor), schlug ... vor, vorgeschlagen to suggest, propose (5)

das Vorschulalter preschool age

vorsichtig careful(ly)

vor·singen (singt ... vor), sang ... vor, vorgesungen to sing (*s.th.*) to (*s.o.*) (5)

die Vorspeise, -n appetizer (8)

vor·spielen, vorgespielt to perform

(sich) vor·stellen, vorgestellt to introduce (*o.s.*); to present (*o.s.*) (6); sich (*dat.*) etwas vorstellen to imagine (*s.th.*) (6, 10)

das Vorstellungsgespräch, -e job interview

der Vorteil, -e advantage (7)

der Vortrag, ⸚e talk; lecture; presentation

das Vorurteil, -e prejudice (12)

das Vorwort, -e preface

vor·zeigen, vorgezeigt to show

der Vulkan, -e volcano

der VW = Volkswagen *make of car*

wach awake; wach werden to wake up

wach·rütteln, wachgerüttelt to rouse

das Wachs, -e wax

wachsen (wächst), wuchs, ist gewachsen to grow (9)

der Wachtmeister, - (police) constable

wagen, gewagt to dare; to risk

der Wagen, - car (7)

der Waggon, -s train car (7)

die Wahl, -en choice; election

wählen, gewählt to choose, select; to elect

wahlfrei optional

der Wahlpflichtunterricht compulsory class

der Wahn delusion

der Wahnsinn insanity, madness

wahnsinnig crazy, crazily; insane(ly) (12)

wahr true (3); nicht wahr? isn't it so?

während (+ *gen.*) during (11); (*subord. conj.*) while

die Wahrheit, -en truth

wahrscheinlich probable, probably (1)

die Währung, -en currency (12)

der Wald, ⸚er forest, woods (2, 7); im Wald laufen to run in the woods (2)

der Walkman, Walkmen Walkman (2)

die Walpurgisnacht Walpurgis Night (*the witches' sabbath, April 30*)

der Walzer, - waltz (3)

die Wand, ⸚e wall (B); das Bild an die Wand hängen to hang the picture on the wall (3)

die Wandergans, ⸚e migratory goose

wandern, ist gewandert to hike (1); in den Bergen wandern to hike in the mountains (1)

der Wanderschuh, -e hiking shoe (2)

die Wanderung, -en hike (7)

die Wange, -n cheek

wann when (B, 1); wann sind Sie geboren? when were you born? (1)

der Wannsee *lake in Berlin*

warm warm(ly) (B); (*of room/apartment*) heated, heat included (6)

warnen, gewarnt to warn (7)

(das) **Warschau** Warsaw

die **Wartburg** *famous castle in Thuringia*

warten (auf + *acc.*), **gewartet** to wait (for) (7); **ein Auto warten** to do maintenance on a car

das **Wartezimmer, -** waiting room

warum why (3)

was what (B); **was für** what kind of; **was sind Sie von Beruf?** what's your profession? (1); **was zeigen Ihre Bilder?** what do your pictures show? (A)

das **Waschbecken, -** (wash) basin (6)

die **Wäsche, -n** laundry (4)

(sich) **waschen (wäscht), wusch, gewaschen** to wash (o.s.) (2, 11)

der **Wäschetrockner, -** clothes dryer (8)

die **Waschküche, -n** laundry room (6)

die **Waschmaschine, -n** washing machine (6)

der **Waschsalon, -s** laundromat (10)

das **Wasser** water

der **Wasserhahn, ⸚e** faucet (5)

der **Wasservogel, ⸚** water fowl (10)

der **Wechselkurs, -e** exchange rate

wechseln, gewechselt to change; **Geld wechseln** to exchange money

wecken, geweckt to wake (s.o.) up (9)

der **Wecker, -** alarm clock (2)

weg away; **wie weit weg?** how far away? (6)

der **Weg, -e** way; road; path; **den Weg beschreiben** to give directions; **nach dem Weg fragen** to ask for directions; **sich auf den Weg machen** to go on one's way, set off

weg·bringen (bringt ... weg), brachte ... weg, weggebracht to take out; to take away (5)

wegen (+ *gen.*) on account of; because of; about (6)

weg·fahren (fährt ... weg), fuhr ... weg, ist weggefahren to drive off, leave

weg·gehen (geht ... weg), ging ... weg, ist weggegangen to go away, leave (4)

weg·laufen (läuft ... weg), lief ... weg, ist weggelaufen to run away

weg·legen, weggelegt to put away; to put down

weg·nehmen (nimmt ... weg), nahm ... weg, weggenommen to take away

weg·stellen, weggestellt to put away (5)

weg·tragen (trägt ... weg), trug ... weg, weggetragen to carry away (9)

weg·trampen, ist weggetrampt to hitchhike away

weg·ziehen (zieht ... weg), zog ... weg, ist weggezogen to move away

das **Weh** pain; longing

wehen, geweht to blow

weh·tun (tut ... weh), tat ... weh, wehgetan to hurt (11)

(das) **Weihnachten** Christmas (4)

das **Weihnachtsgeschenk, -e** Christmas present (5)

weil (*subord. conj.*) because (3, 11)

die **Weile, -n** while

der **Wein, -e** wine (7)

weinen, geweint to cry (3)

der **Weinkeller, -** wine cellar (6)

das **Weinregal, -e** wine rack (6)

die **Weintraube, -n** grape (8)

weisen (weist), wies, gewiesen to show; to point

weiß white (A)

die **Weiße: die Berliner Weiße** *light, fizzy beer served with raspberry syrup*

(das) **Weißrussisch** Byelorussian (*language*)

(das) **Weißrussland** Belarus (B)

die **Weißwurst, ⸚e** veal sausage

weit far (6); **wie weit weg?** how far away? (6)

weiter (*adj.*) additional; (*adv.*) farther; further; **und so weiter (usw.)** and so forth

weiter·erzählen, weitererzählt to continue telling

weiter·fahren (fährt ... weiter), fuhr ... weiter, ist weitergefahren to keep on driving (10)

weiter·gehen (geht ... weiter), ging ... weiter, ist weitergegangen to keep on walking (10)

weiter·helfen (hilft ... weiter), half ... weiter, weitergeholfen to help along

weiter·lesen (liest ... weiter), las ... weiter, weitergelesen to keep on reading

weiter·schreiben (schreibt ... weiter), schrieb ... weiter, weitergeschrieben to keep on writing

weiter·verfolgen, weiterverfolgt to pursue further

welch- which, what (B); **ab welchem Alter** from what age; **an welchem Tag?** on what day? (4); **welche Farbe hat ...?** what color is . . . ? (A); **welcher Tag ist heute?** what day is today? (1); **welches Datum ist heute?** what is today's date? (4)

die **Welle, -n** wave (10); **Wellen reiten** to ride the waves, surf

der **Wellensittich, -e** budgerigar

die **Welt, -en** world (7)

der **Weltkrieg, -e** world war; **im Zweiten Weltkrieg** in World War II

die **Weltkunde** *field of study encompassing history, social studies, and geography*

die **Weltmeisterschaft, -en** world championship

wem whom (*dat.*) (4)

wen whom (*acc.*) (4)

die **Wende, -n** change

(sich) **wenden (wendet), wandte/wendete, gewandt/gewendet** to turn

wenig (*sg.*) little; **wenige** (*pl.*) few; **am wenigsten** the least (8)

wenn (*subord. conj.*) if; when(ever) (2, 11); **wenn ja** if so

wer who (A, B)

das **Werbeplakat, -e** advertising poster

die **Werbung, -en** advertisement

werden (wird), wurde, ist geworden to become (5)

werfen (wirft), warf, geworfen to throw (3); **Bomben werfen** to drop bombs

das **Werk, -e** work; product (9)

die **Werkstatt, ⸚en** workshop; repair shop, garage (5)

das **Werkzeug, -e** tool (8)

der **Wert, -e** value

wertvoll valuable, expensive (2)

weshalb why

wessen whose

West west

westdeutsch West German (*adj.*)

(das) **Westdeutschland** (*former*) West Germany

der **Westen** west

(das) **Westfalen** Westphalia

westlich (*adj.*) western; (**von** + *dat.*) west of (7)

das **Wetter, -** weather

Whg. = die **Wohnung, -en** apartment

wichtig important (2)

widersprechen (+ *dat.*) **(widerspricht), widersprach, widersprochen** to contradict

widmen, gewidmet to dedicate

wie how (B); **um wie viel Uhr ...?** at what time . . . ? (1); **wie bitte?** excuse me?; could you repeat that?; **wie fühlst du dich?** how do you feel? (3); **wie geht es dir?** (*infor.*) / **wie geht es Ihnen?** (*for.*) how are you?; **wie heißen Sie?** (*for.*) / **wie heißt du?** (*infor.*) what's your name? (A); **wie schreibt man das?** how do you spell that? (A); **wie spät ist es?** what time is it? (1); **wie viel ...?** how much . . . ?; **wie viel Uhr ist es?** what time is it? (1); **wie viele ...?** how many . . . ? (A); **wie weit weg?** how far away? (6)

wieder again (3); **schon wieder** once again (3); **wieder hören** to hear again (6)

wieder·finden (findet ... wieder), fand ... wieder, wiedergefunden to find again; to regain

wieder·geben (gibt ... wieder), gab ... wieder, wiedergegeben to give back; to repeat; to render

wiederholen, wiederholt to repeat (10)

die **Wiederholung, -en** repetition

das **Wiederhören: auf Wiederhören!** good-bye! (*on the phone*); until I hear from you again! (6)

wieder·kommen (kommt ... wieder), kam ... wieder, ist wiedergekommen to come back (5)

das **Wiedersehen: auf Wiedersehen!** good-bye! until we see each other again! (A)

die **Wiedervereinigung, -en** reunification

(das) **Wien** Vienna

Wiener Viennese (*adj.*); **das Wiener Schnitzel** breaded veal cutlet

die **Wiese, -n** meadow, pasture (7)

wieso why

wild wild(ly)

die **Wildnis, -se** wilderness

der **Wildpark, -s** game park

das **Wildschwein, -e** wild boar (10)

der **Wille** will

willkommen welcome

die **Wimperntusche** mascara

der **Wind, -e** wind (9)

windig windy (B)

die **Windpocken** (*pl.*) chicken pox

windsurfen gehen (geht ... windsurfen), ging ... windsurfen, ist windsurfen gegangen to go windsurfing (1)

der **Winter, -** winter (B)

wir we

wirken, gewirkt to work, take effect (11); to look

wirklich real(ly) (B)

die **Wirklichkeit, -en** reality

der **Wirt, -e** / die **Wirtin, -nen** host/hostess; innkeeper; barkeeper (10)

die **Wirtschaft, -en** economy; economics (1)

die **Wirtschaftskunde** economics

wischen, gewischt to wipe (7); **Staub wischen** to (wipe) dust

wissen (weiß), wusste, gewusst to know (*as a fact*) (2)

das **Wissen** knowledge

die **Wissenschaft, -en** science

der **Wissenschaftler, -** / die **Wissenschaftlerin, -nen** scientist (9)

der **Witz, -e** joke (3); **Witze erzählen** to tell jokes (3)

wo where (B); **wo willst du denn hin?** where are you going? (A)

die **Woche, -n** week (1); **in der Woche** during the week (1); **jede Woche** every week (3); **letzte Woche** last week (4); **pro Woche** per week

das **Wochenende, -n** weekend (1); **am Wochenende** over the weekend (1); **letztes Wochenende** last weekend (4); **übers Wochenende** over the weekend (4)

das **Wochenendhaus, -̈er** weekend cabin/cottage

wochentags on weekdays

wodurch through what

wofür what for (8)

wogegen against what

woher from where; whence (B)

wohin where to; whither (3)

wohl probably (12); well; **sich wohl fühlen** to feel well (11)

wohlbekannt well-known

wohlig pleasant; with pleasure

der **Wohnblock, -s** residential block, apartment complex

wohnen (in + *dat.*), gewohnt to live (in) (B)

die **Wohngemeinschaft, -en** shared housing (6)

das **Wohnhaus, -̈er** residential building

das **Wohnheim, -e** state-subsidized apartment building; dorm

die **Wohnmöglichkeit, -en** living arrangements (6)

der **Wohnort, -e** place of residence (1)

die **Wohnung, -en** apartment (1, 2, 6)

das **Wohnviertel, -** residential district

der **Wohnwagen, -** mobile home; travel trailer

das **Wohnzimmer, -** living room (6)

der **Wolf, -̈e** wolf (9)

die **Wolga** Volga (River)

wollen (will), wollte, gewollt to want (to); to intend (to); to plan (to) (3); **wo willst du denn hin?** where are you going? (A)

womit with what, by what means

woran at/on/of what

worauf on/for what

woraus from what, out of what

das **Wort, -̈er/-e** word; **Worte** words (*connected discourse*); **Wörter** words (*individual vocabulary items*) (A)

das **Wörterbuch, -̈er** dictionary (2)

der **Wortkasten, -̈** word box

der **Wortschatz, -̈e** vocabulary (A)

worüber about what

worum about/around what

wovon about what

wozu to/for what

die **Wunde, -n** wound (11)

das **Wunder, -** miracle, wonder; **kein Wunder** no wonder

wunderbar wonderful(ly)

wundersam strange

wunderschön exceedingly beautiful (10)

der **Wunsch, -̈e** wish

wünschen, gewünscht to wish (for)

der **Wunschzettel, -** wish list (*of things one would like to have*)

die **Wurst, -̈e** sausage; cold cuts (8)

das **Würstchen, -** sausage; frank(furter); hot dog (8)

würzen, gewürzt to season (8)

die **Wüste, -n** desert (7)

wütend angry (3)

das **Ypsilon, -s** the letter Y

z. B. = **zum Beispiel** for example (3)

die **Zahl, -en** figure, number (A)

zahlen, gezahlt to pay (for) (5); **Miete zahlen** to pay rent; **zahlen, bitte** the check, please

zählen, gezählt to count (A)

das **Zahlenrätsel, -** number puzzle

die **Zahlung, -en** payment

das **Zahlungsmittel, -** means of payment (12); **gesetzliches Zahlungsmittel** legal tender

zahm tame(ly) (10)

der **Zahn, -̈e** tooth (11); **sich die Zähne putzen** to brush one's teeth (11)

der **Zahnarzt, -̈e** / die **Zahnärztin, -nen** dentist (5)

die **Zahnschmerzen** (*pl.*) toothache (11)

die **Zange, -n** pliers; tongs (8)

zart tender(ly) (8)

der **Zauber, -** magic; charm

der **Zaum, -̈e** bridle; **im Zaum halten** to control

der **Zaun, -̈e** fence (9)

das **Zebra, -s** zebra (10)

der **Zebrastreifen, -** crosswalk (10)

die **Zehenspitze, -n** tiptoe

zehn ten (A)

zehnt- tenth (4)

die **Zeichensprache, -n** sign language

der **Zeichentrickfilm, -e** cartoon, animated film

zeichnen, gezeichnet to draw (3, 5)

die **Zeichnung, -en** drawing

der **Zeigefinger, -** index finger

(sich) **zeigen, gezeigt** to show (o.s.); **was zeigen Ihre Bilder?** what do your pictures show? (A)

die **Zeile, -n** line

die **Zeit, -en** time (4); **in letzter Zeit** recently; **lange Zeit** (for) a long time; **zu welcher Zeit** at what time; **zur Zeit** at present

der **Zeitgenosse, -n** (*wk.*) / die **Zeitgenossin, -nen** contemporary

die **Zeitung, -en** newspaper (2); **Zeitung lesen** to read the newspaper (1)

das **Zelt, -e** tent (2, 5)

zelten, gezeltet to camp (1)

der **Zeltplatz, -̈e** campsite

der **Zentimeter, -** centimeter

zentral central(ly) (10)

die **Zentralheizung, -en** central heating (6)

das **Zentrum, Zentren** center

der **Zeppelin, -e** zeppelin, dirigible (7)

zerbrechen (zerbricht), zerbrach, hat/ist zerbrochen to break into pieces

zerreißen (zerreißt), zerriss, zerrissen to tear (to pieces) (9)

zerstören, zerstört to destroy

das **Zeug** stuff

der **Zeuge, -n** (*wk.*) / die **Zeugin, -nen** witness (11)

das **Zeugnis, -se** report card

Zi. = das **Zimmer, -** room

der **Ziegel, -** clay tile

ziehen (zieht), zog, ist gezogen to move (2); (*p.p. with* **haben**) to pull (8)

das **Ziel, -e** goal; destination (10)

zielorientiert goal-oriented

ziemlich rather (2); **ziemlich groß** pretty big (2)

die **Zigarette, -n** cigarette (4)

die **Zigarre, -n** cigar (7)

das **Zimmer, -** room (1, 2)

die **Zimmersuche, -n** search for a room (*to rent*)

das **Zinn** tin

die **Zinsen** (*pl.*) interest (12)

zirka circa, about, approximately

der **Zirkus, -se** circus (9)

das **Zitat, -e** quotation

die **Zitrone, -n** lemon (8)

der **Zivilisationskritiker, -** / die **Zivilisationskritikerin, -nen** cultural critic

der **Zoll, -̈e** customs duty

der **Zoo, -s** zoo (10)

zool. Garten = der **zoologische Garten** zoological garden, zoo

zu (*adj.*) closed; (*adv.*) too (4); **zu schwer** too heavy (4); **zu viel** too much

zu (+ *dat.*) to; for (*an occasion*); for the purpose of (2, 10); (+ *inf.*) to; **bis zu** as far as; up to (10); **noch zu haben** still available; **um ... zu** (+ *inf.*) in order to (12); **zu Abend essen** to dine, have dinner (4); **zu Fuß** on foot (3); **zu Hause** at home (A, 1, 10); **zu Mittag essen** to eat lunch (3); **zu zweit** in pairs; **zum Arzt** to the doctor (3); **zum Beispiel (z. B.)** for example

(3); **zum ersten Mal** for the first time (4); **zum Geburtstag** for someone's birthday (2); **zum Mittagessen** for lunch (3); **zum Schluss** in the end, finally (8); **zur Arbeit gehen** to go to work (1); **zur Uni** to the university (1, 2); **zur Zeit** at present

zu·bereiten, zubereitet to prepare (*food*) (8)

die Zubereitung, -en preparation (8)

zu·betonieren, zubetoniert to cover with concrete

zu·binden (bindet ... zu), band ... zu, zugebunden to tie shut (8)

zücken, gezückt to take out, draw

der Zucker sugar (8)

zu·decken, zugedeckt to cover (*with a blanket*) (11)

zu·drücken, zugedrückt to squeeze shut; **ein Auge zudrücken** to look the other way

zuerst first (4, 7)

der Zufall, ⸚e chance; coincidence

zufällig accidental(ly) (9)

der Zug, ⸚e train (7, 10); draught

der Zugang, ⸚e access (12)

die Zugfahrkarte, -n train ticket (6)

die Zugspitze *highest mountain in Germany*

zu·hören (+ *dat.*), **zugehört** to listen (to) (6); **hören Sie zu** listen (A)

die Zukunft, ⸚e future

zukünftig future (*adj.*)

zulässig permissible

zu·legen, zugelegt: sich einen Künstlernamen zulegen to adopt a pseudonym

zuletzt finally (10)

zum = zu dem to/for the

zu·machen, zugemacht to close, shut (3)

zunächst at first

der Zuname, -n (*wk.*) surname, last name

die Zunge, -n tongue (11)

zu·ordnen (+ *dat.*), **zugeordnet** to relate (to); to assign (to)

zur = zu der to/for the

(das) **Zürich** Zurich

zurück back (9); **hin und zurück** there and back; round-trip (5, 10)

zurück·bekommen (bekommt ... zurück), bekam ... zurück, zurückbekommen to get back

zurück·bringen (bringt ... zurück), brachte ... zurück, zurückgebracht to bring back

zurück·geben (gibt ... zurück), gab ... zurück, zurückgegeben to give back, return; to reply

zurück·gehen (geht ... zurück), ging ... zurück, ist zurückgegangen to go back

zurück·kehren, ist zurückgekehrt to come back, return

zurück·kommen (kommt ... zurück), kam ... zurück, ist zurückgekommen to come back, return (6)

zurück·rufen (ruft ... zurück), rief ... zurück, zurückgerufen to call back

sich zurück·ziehen (zieht ... zurück), zog ... zurück, zurückgezogen to withdraw

zusammen together (2); **alles zusammen** all together, one check

die Zusammenarbeit, -en collaboration

zusammen·brechen (bricht ... zusammen), brach ... zusammen, zusammengebrochen to collapse

der Zusammenbruch, ⸚e breakdown; collapse

zusammen·falten, zusammengefaltet to fold up

zusammen·fassen, zusammengefasst to summarize

die Zusammenfassung, -en summary

zusammen·gehören, zusammengehört to go together; to belong together

das Zusammenleben life together

zusammen·packen, zusammengepackt to pack up

zusammen·passen, zusammengepasst to go together

zusammen·sitzen (sitzt ... zusammen), saß ... zusammen, zusammengesessen to sit together

zusammen·stoßen (stößt ... zusammen), stieß ... zusammen, ist zusammengestoßen to crash (11)

zu·schauen, zugeschaut to watch

zu·schnüren, zugeschnürt to tie up; to constrict

zuschulden: sich (*dat.*) **etwas zuschulden kommen lassen** to do something wrong

zu·treffen (trifft ... zu), traf ... zu, zugetroffen to be correct; (**auf** + *acc.*) to pertain to, apply to

die Zutat, -en ingredient (8)

(**sich**) **zu·wenden (wendet ... zu), wandte ... zu, zugewandt** to turn toward

zwanzig twenty (A)

der Zwanzigeuroschein, -e twenty-euro note (8)

zwanzigst- twentieth (4)

zwar to be sure

zwei two (A)

zweifeln (an + *acc.*)**, gezweifelt** to doubt

zweimal twice (5)

zweit: zu zweit in pairs; **zu zweit leben** to live together (*two people*)

zweit- second (4)

zweiundzwanzig twenty-two (A)

der Zwerg, -e dwarf (9)

die Zwiebel, -n onion (8)

zwinkern, gezwinkert to blink; to wink

zwischen (+ *dat./acc.*) between; among (7)

zwölf twelve (A)

zwölft- twelfth (4)

(das) **Zypern** Cyprus

Vokabeln

Englisch-Deutsch

This list contains the words from the chapter vocabulary lists.

to abandon **verlassen (verlässt), verließ, verlassen** (11)

able: to be able (to) **können (kann), konnte, gekonnt** (3)

about **wegen** (+ *gen.*) (6)

above (*prep.*) **über** (+ *dat./acc.*) (4); (*adv.*) **oben** (10)

abroad **im Ausland** (6); center for study abroad **das Auslandsamt, ⸚er** (1)

academic subject **das Fach, ⸚er** (1); **das Schulfach, ⸚er** (1); **das Studienfach, ⸚er** (1)

access **der Zugang** (12)

accident **der Unfall, ⸚e** (4, 11); accident report **der Unfallbericht, -e** (11); scene of the accident **die Unfallstelle, -n** (11)

accidental(ly) **zufällig** (9)

accordion **das Akkordeon, -s** (4)

account: bank account **das Konto, Konten** (5); to open a bank account **ein Konto eröffnen** (5); checking account **das Girokonto, -konten** (12); savings account **das Sparkonto, -konten** (12); on account of **wegen** (+ *gen.*) (6)

acquainted: to get acquainted with **kennen·lernen, kennengelernt** (1)

across **gegenüber** (+ *dat.*) (6); across from **gegenüber von** (+ *dat.*) (10); right across the way **gleich gegenüber** (6)

activity **die Tätigkeit, -en** (5); favorite activity **die Lieblingsbeschäftigung, -en** (5)

actor/actress **der Schauspieler, - / die Schauspielerin, -nen** (9)

actually **eigentlich** (3)

ad **die Anzeige, -n** (6); housing-wanted ad **die Suchanzeige, -n** (6)

addition: in addition **dazu** (8); in addition to **neben** (+ *dat./acc.*) (3)

address **die Adresse, -n** (1); **die Anschrift, -en** (11)

adhesive bandage **das Pflaster, -** (11)

admissions ticket **die Eintrittskarte, -n** (5)

advantage **der Vorteil, -e** (7)

advice **der Rat, Ratschläge** (5)

to advise (*a person*) **raten** (+ *dat.*) **(rät), riet, geraten** (5)

afraid: to be afraid **Angst haben** (3); to be afraid of **sich fürchten vor** (+ *dat.*), **gefürchtet** (10)

Africa **(das) Afrika** (B)

Afro-German (*adj.*) **afro-deutsch** (12)

after **nach** (+ *dat.*) (3); at twenty after five **um zwanzig nach fünf** (1)

afternoon **der Nachmittag, -e** (4); afternoons, in the afternoon **nachmittags** (4); good afternoon (*for.*) **guten Tag!** (A)

afterward **nachdem** (9, 11); **danach** (10)

again **wieder** (3); to hear again **wieder hören, wieder gehört** (6); once again **schon wieder** (3)

against **gegen** (+ *acc.*) (9)

age **das Alter** (1)

agent: train agent **der/die Bahnangestellte, -n (ein Bahnangestellter)** (10)

ago **vor** (+ *dat.*) (4); two days ago **vor zwei Tagen** (4)

agreement: in agreement **einverstanden** (12); to be in agreement with **einverstanden sein mit** (+ *dat.*) (12); prenuptial agreement **der Ehevertrag, ⸚e** (12)

ahead: straight ahead **geradeaus** (10)

air **die Luft** (7); air mattress **die Luftmatratze, -n** (10)

airplane **das Flugzeug, -e** (7)

airport **der Flughafen, ⸚** (6)

alarm clock **der Wecker, -** (2)

Albania **(das) Albanien** (B)

albatross **der Albatros, -se** (10)

Algeria **(das) Algerien** (B)

alive: to be alive **am Leben sein** (9)

all: all day long **den ganzen Tag** (1); all night long **die ganze Nacht** (3); all together **alles zusammen** (5); by all means **auf jeden Fall** (4)

allergic **allergisch** (11)

alley **die Gasse, -n** (10)

almost **fast** (5)

along **entlang** (10); to go along **entlang·gehen (geht ... entlang), ging ... entlang, ist entlanggegangen** (10)

aloud: to read aloud **vor·lesen (liest ... vor), las ... vor, vorgelesen** (9)

alphabet **das Alphabet** (3)

Alps **die Alpen** (*pl.*) (7)

already **schon** (2, 4)

also **auch** (A)

although (*subord. conj.*) **obwohl** (11)

always **immer** (3)

ambulance **der Krankenwagen, -** (11)

America **(das) Amerika** (B)

American (*person*) **der Amerikaner, - / die Amerikanerin, -nen** (B)

among **unter** (+ *dat./acc.*) (6)

amount (*of money*) **die Höhe, -n** (12)

ancestor **der Vorfahre, -n** (*wk.*) (10, 12)

and (*coord. conj.*) **und** (A, 11); and so forth **und so weiter** (5)

angry **wütend** (3); **sauer** (5); to get angry **sich ärgern, geärgert** (11)

animal **das Tier, -e** (3, 7, 9, 10)

to annoy **ärgern, geärgert** (3)

another: one another **einander** (3)

answer **die Antwort, -en** (A); to answer **antworten** (+ *dat.*), **geantwortet** (4, 10); **beantworten, beantwortet** (7)

any (+ *n.*) **irgendwelch-** (5); in any case **jedenfalls** (11)

anything **etwas** (5); anything else? **sonst noch etwas?** (5)

apartment **die Wohnung, -en** (1, 2, 6)

appendix **der Blinddarm, ⸚e** (11)

appetizer **die Vorspeise, -n** (8)

apple juice **der Apfelsaft** (8)

appliance **das Gerät, -e** (8)

to apply for **beantragen, beantragt** (12)

appointment **der Termin, -e** (5, 11); **die Verabredung, -en** (11); appointment calendar **der Terminkalender, -** (11); to get an appointment **sich einen Termin geben lassen** (11)

apprenticeship **die Lehre, -n** (5)

approximately **ungefähr** (7)

April **der April** (B)

Arabic (*language*) **(das) Arabisch** (B)

architect **der Architekt, -en** (*wk.*) / **die Architektin, -nen** (5)

area **die Gegend, -en** (10); **der Bereich, -e** (12)

to argue **streiten (streitet), stritt, gestritten** (9)

arm **der Arm, -e** (B); to break one's arm **sich den Arm brechen** (11)

armchair **der Sessel, -** (2, 6)

army: German army **die Bundeswehr** (5); in the German army **bei der Bundeswehr** (5)

around the corner **um die Ecke** (5)

to arrive **an·kommen (kommt ... an), kam ... an, ist angekommen** (1)

art die Kunst, ⸚e (1, 12); art history die Kunstgeschichte (1); ceramic art die Töpferei (12)
as als (5); as . . . as possible möglichst (+ adv.)
(6); as far as bis zu (+ dat.) (10); as well auch
(A); as what? als was? (5)
Asia (das) Asien (B)
to ask (for) bitten (um + acc.) (bittet), bat,
gebeten (9); to ask a question eine Frage
stellen (A, 5); to ask about sich erkundigen
nach (+ dat.), erkundigt (10)
asleep: to fall asleep ein·schlafen (schläft ... ein),
schlief ... ein, ist eingeschlafen (7)
aspirin das Aspirin (3, 11)
assignment die Aufgabe, -n (4); homework
assignment die Hausaufgabe, -n (A)
at an (+ dat.) (2); bei (+ dat.) (2, 6, 10); in
(+ dat.) (4); at a bank bei einer Bank (6);
at home zu Hause (A, 1, 10); daheim (9); at
Monika's bei Monika (2); at night nachts
(4); at noon mittags (2); at six (o'clock) um
sechs (Uhr) (1); at the café im Café (4); at the
courthouse auf dem Gericht (5); at the gas
station an der Tankstelle (5); at the moment
im Moment (1); at what time . . . ? um wie
viel Uhr ...? (1); at your parents' bei deinen
Eltern (6); at your place bei dir (3)
athletic sportlich (B); athletic shoe der
Sportschuh, -e (A)
to attack an·greifen (greift ... an), griff ... an,
angegriffen (12)
to attempt versuchen, versucht (4)
to attend to pflegen, gepflegt (5)
attention die Achtung (7); to pay attention
auf·passen, aufgepasst (3); to pay attention to
achten auf (+ acc.), geachtet (11)
attitude die Einstellung, -en (12)
attractive attraktiv (6)
August der August (B)
aunt die Tante, -n (B)
Australia (das) Australien (B)
Australian (person) der Australier, - / die
Australierin, -nen (B)
Austria (das) Österreich (B)
Austrian (person) der Österreicher, - / die Österreicherin, -nen (B)
authority: public authority die Behörde, -n (12)
automatic teller machine (ATM) der Geldautomat,
-en (wk.) (12)
autumn der Herbst, -e (B)
available: is this seat/place available? ist hier
noch frei? (8)
away: how far away? wie weit weg? (6); right
away gleich (4); to carry away weg·tragen
(trägt ... weg), trug ... weg, weggetragen (9);
to go away weg·gehen (geht ... weg), ging ...
weg, ist weggegangen (4); to put away
weg·stellen, weggestellt (5)

baby das Baby, -s (7); baby carriage der Kinderwagen, - (7)
back (n.) der Rücken, - (B)

back (adv.) zurück (9); back then damals (9);
there and back hin und zurück (10); to come
back wieder·kommen (kommt ... wieder),
kam ... wieder, ist wiedergekommen (5)
backpack der Rucksack, ⸚e (2)
bacon der Speck (8)
bad schlecht (2); schlimm (11); too bad schade! (3)
bag die Tasche, -n (1); (paper or plastic) die Tüte,
-n (11); sleeping bag der Schlafsack, ⸚e (2)
baggage das Gepäck (10)
to bake backen (bäckt), backte, gebacken (5)
bakery die Bäckerei, -en (5); at the bakery in der
Bäckerei (5)
balance: bank balance das Guthaben (12)
balcony der Balkon, -e (6)
ball der Ball, ⸚e (A, 1); soccer ball der Fußball,
⸚e (A, 1)
ballerina die Ballerina, -s (9)
ballet class der Ballettunterricht (9)
ballpoint pen der Kugelschreiber, - (4)
Baltic Sea die Ostsee (B)
banana die Banane, -n (8)
bandage der Verband, ⸚e (11); adhesive bandage
das Pflaster, - (11)
bandanna das Halstuch, ⸚er (1)
bank die Bank, -en (5); at a bank bei einer Bank
(6); at the bank auf der Bank (5); bank account das Konto, Konten (5); to open a bank
account ein Konto eröffnen (5); bank balance
das Guthaben (12); bank employee der/die
Bankangestellte, -n (ein Bankangestellter) (5)
bar die Kneipe, -n (3)
barely knapp (6)
barkeeper der Wirt, -e / die Wirtin, -nen (10)
baseball team die Baseballmannschaft, -en (9)
basement der Keller, - (4, 6)
basin das Waschbecken, - (6)
basketball der Basketball, ⸚e (2)
bat die Fledermaus, ⸚e (10)
bath, bathroom das Bad, ⸚er (6)
to bathe (sich) baden, gebadet (3, 11)
bathing suit der Badeanzug, ⸚e (5)
bathrobe der Bademantel, ⸚ (2)
bathtub die Badewanne, -n (6)
bay die Bucht, -en (6, 7)
to be sein (ist), war, ist gewesen (A, 4)
beach der Strand, ⸚e (4, 7); beach chair der
Strandkorb, ⸚e (10)
bean die Bohne, -n (8)
bear: teddy bear der Teddybär, -en (wk.) (A)
beard der Bart, ⸚e (B)
to beat schlagen (schlägt), schlug, geschlagen (8)
beautiful schön (B); exceedingly beautiful
wunderschön (10)
because (subord. conj.) weil (3, 11); (coord. conj.)
denn (9, 11); because of wegen (+ gen.) (6)
to become werden (wird), wurde, geworden (5)
bed das Bett, -en (1, 6); bed-and-breakfast
(inn) das Gästehaus, ⸚er (10); to get up on
the wrong side of bed mit dem linken Fuß
auf·stehen (4); to go to bed ins Bett gehen (1)

bedroom das Schlafzimmer, - (6)
bedside table der Nachttisch, -e (6)
bee die Biene, -n (10)
beef das Rindfleisch (8); ground beef das
Hackfleisch (8)
beer das Bier, -e (2)
before (subord. conj.) bevor (11)
to begin beginnen (beginnt), begann, begonnen
(1); an·fangen (fängt ... an), fing ... an,
angefangen (4)
Belarus (das) Weißrussland (B)
Belgium (das) Belgien (B)
to believe glauben, geglaubt (2)
belly der Bauch, ⸚e (B)
to belong to gehören (+ dat.), gehört (6); to
belong to (an organization) an·gehören,
angehört (12)
beloved female friend die Geliebte, -n (3)
below unter (+ dat./acc.) (6)
belt der Gürtel, - (2); safety belt der Sicherheitsgurt, -e (7)
beneath unter (+ dat./acc.) (6)
beside neben (+ dat./acc.) (3)
besides außerdem (5, 10)
best: like (to do s.th.) best am liebsten (7)
better besser (2)
between zwischen (+ dat./acc.) (7)
beverage das Getränk, -e (8)
bicycle das Fahrrad, ⸚er (2, 7); to bicycle Rad
fahren (fährt ... Rad), fuhr ... Rad, ist Rad
gefahren (6); bicycle helmet der Fahrradhelm,
-e (5); bicycle path der Radweg, -e (7); bicycle
tour die Radtour, -en (9); bicyclist der
Radfahrer, - / die Radfahrerin, -nen (7)
big groß (B); pretty big ziemlich groß (2)
bikini der Bikini, -s (5)
bill die Rechnung, -en (4); (of currency) der
Schein, -e (8); der Geldschein, -e (12)
biographical information persönliche Daten (pl.) (1)
biology die Biologie (1)
bird der Vogel, ⸚ (10)
birthday der Geburtstag, -e (1, 2); birthday card
die Geburtstagskarte, -n (2)
bit: not a bit gar nicht (3); quite a bit ganz schön
viel (3)
to bite beißen (beißt), biss, gebissen (9); to bite (of
insects) stechen (sticht), stach, gestochen (10)
black schwarz (A); black-haired schwarzhaarig (9)
blackboard die Tafel, -n (A, B)
blanket die Decke, -n (11)
to bleed bluten, geblutet (11)
blond blond (B); blond hair blondes Haar (B)
blood das Blut (9, 11); blood pressure der
Blutdruck (11); to have low/high blood
pressure niedrigen/hohen Blutdruck haben
(11); to take blood Blut ab·nehmen (11)
blouse die Bluse, -n (A)
to blow-dry (one's hair) sich (die Haare) föhnen,
geföhnt (11)
blue blau (A); blue eyes blaue Augen (B); blue
whale der Blauwal, -e (10)

boa constrictor die Riesenschlange, -n (10)

boar: wild boar das Wildschwein, -e (10)

to board ein·steigen (steigt ... ein), stieg ... ein, ist eingestiegen (3, 10)

boat das Boot, -e (2)

body der Körper, - (B, 11)

boiled gekocht (8); boiled eggs gekochte Eier (pl.) (8); boiled potatoes die Salzkartoffeln (pl.) (8)

book das Buch, ̈er (A, B, 2); to book buchen, gebucht (7)

bookcase, bookshelf das Regal, -e (2)

bookstore der Buchladen, ̈ (6)

boot der Stiefel, - (A)

booth: telephone booth die Telefonzelle, -n (2); ticket booth der Schalter, - (5)

bored: to be bored Langeweile haben (3)

boredom die Langeweile (3)

boring langweilig (2)

born geboren (1); when were you born? wann sind Sie geboren? (1)

Bosnia (das) Bosnien (B)

bottle die Flasche, -n (5); bottle opener der Flaschenöffner, - (8)

boutique die Boutique, -n (6)

bowl die Schüssel, -n (8); salad (mixing) bowl die Salatschüssel, -n (5)

to box boxen, geboxt (1)

boyfriend der Freund, -e (A)

bracelet das Armband, ̈er (2)

brain das Gehirn, -e (11)

brake die Bremse, -n (7); to brake bremsen, gebremst (11)

brave tapfer (9)

Brazil (das) Brasilien (B)

bread das Brot, -e (8); farmer's bread das Bauernbrot, -e (5)

break die Pause, -n (1); to break brechen (bricht), brach, gebrochen (11); to break one's arm sich den Arm brechen (11)

breakfast das Frühstück, -e (2, 8); breakfast room das Frühstückszimmer, - (10); to eat breakfast frühstücken, gefrühstückt (1)

to breathe atmen, geatmet (11)

bride die Braut, ̈e (9)

bridge die Brücke, -n (10)

to bring bringen (bringt), brachte, gebracht (2); to bring along mit·bringen (bringt ... mit), brachte ... mit, mitgebracht (3)

broiled gebraten (8)

broken kaputt (A)

broom der Besen, - (6)

brother der Bruder, ̈ (B); brothers and sisters die Geschwister (pl.) (B)

brown braun (A); to brown bräunen, gebräunt (8)

brush die Bürste, -n (6); to brush (one's teeth) sich (die Zähne) putzen, geputzt (11)

Brussels sprouts der Rosenkohl (8)

building das Gebäude, - (6); high-rise building das Hochhaus, ̈er (6); office building das Bürohaus, ̈er (6)

Bulgaria (das) Bulgarien (B)

bureau: tourist bureau das Fremdenverkehrsamt, ̈er (10)

burglar der Einbrecher, - / die Einbrecherin, -nen (9)

to burn brennen (brennt), brannte, gebrannt (11); verbrennen (verbrennt), verbrannte, verbrannt (11); to burn one's tongue sich die Zunge verbrennen (11)

bus der Bus, -se (2, 7); bus stop die Bushaltestelle, -n (6)

bush der Busch, ̈e (9)

business hours die Öffnungszeiten (pl.) (8); business letter der Geschäftsbrief, -e (10); business trip die Geschäftsreise, -n (7)

businesspeople die Geschäftsleute (pl.) (7)

busy beschäftigt (3)

but aber (A, 11); but (rather, on the contrary) sondern (A, 11)

butcher shop die Metzgerei, -en (6)

butter die Butter (8); herb butter die Kräuterbutter (8)

to buy kaufen, gekauft (1)

by an ... vorbei (10); by all means auf jeden Fall (4); to go by vorbei·gehen (an + dat.) (geht ... vorbei), ging ... vorbei, ist vorbeigegangen (10)

bye (infor.) tschüss! (A)

cabbage der Kohl (8)

cable railway die Seilbahn, -en (7)

café das Café, -s (4); at the café im Café (4); ice cream café das Eiscafé, -s (8)

cafeteria: student cafeteria die Mensa, Mensen (2)

cage der Käfig, -e (10)

cake der Kuchen, - (5)

calendar: appointment calendar der Terminkalender, - (11)

to call rufen (ruft), rief, gerufen (7, 11); to call on the telephone telefonieren, telefoniert (4); to call up an·rufen (ruft ... an), rief ... an, angerufen (1)

called: to be called heißen (heißt), hieß, geheißen (A)

calm ruhig (B)

calorie: calorie-conscious kalorienbewusst (8); low in calories kalorienarm (8)

camera die Kamera, -s (2)

to camp zelten, gezeltet (1)

camping das Camping (10)

campsite der Campingplatz, ̈e (10)

can (n.) die Dose, -n (8); can opener der Dosenöffner, - (8); garbage can der Mülleimer, - (8); watering can die Gießkanne, -n (6)

can (v.) können (kann), konnte, gekonnt (3)

Canada (das) Kanada (B)

Canadian (person) der Kanadier, - / die Kanadierin, -nen (B)

candle die Kerze, -n (3)

candy die Süßigkeit, -en (9)

canoe das Kanu, -s (10)

canoeing: to go canoeing Kanu fahren (fährt ... Kanu), fuhr ... Kanu, Kanu gefahren (10)

cap die Mütze, -n (5)

capital city die Hauptstadt, ̈e (3)

car das Auto, -s (A, 7); der Wagen, - (7); car phone das Autotelefon, -e (2); car radio das Autoradio, -s (7); sleeping car der Schlafwagen, - (4); train car der Waggon, -s (7); used car der Gebrauchtwagen, - (7)

card die Karte, -n (1, 2); birthday card die Geburtstagskarte, -n (2); Eurocheque Card die Euroscheckkarte, -n (12); identification card der Ausweis, -e (10); telephone card die Telefonkarte, -n (2)

care: to care for mögen (mag), mochte, gemocht (3); to take care of sich kümmern um (+ acc.), gekümmert (12); sorgen für (+ acc.), gesorgt (12); to be equally responsible for taking care of mit·versorgen, mitversorgt (12)

career der Beruf, -e (5); das Berufsleben (12); career counselor der Berufsberater, - / die Berufsberaterin, -nen (5)

carpet der Teppich, -e (2)

carriage: baby carriage der Kinderwagen, - (7)

carrot die Karotte, -n (8)

to carry away weg·tragen (trägt ... weg), trug ... weg, weggetragen (9); to carry out aus·führen, ausgeführt (12)

case: in any case jedenfalls (11)

cash das Bargeld (12); cash-free bargeldlos (12)

cast (plaster) der Gips (11)

to cast a spell on verwünschen, verwünscht (9)

castle das Schloss, ̈er (9)

cat die Katze, -n (2)

to catch a cold sich erkälten, erkältet (11)

cathedral der Dom, -e (10)

cauliflower der Blumenkohl (8)

CD die CD, -s (A, 3); CD player der CD-Spieler, - (2)

ceiling die Decke, -n (B)

to celebrate feiern, gefeiert (5)

celebration die Feier, -n (9); family celebration das Familienfest, -e (4)

cellar der Keller, - (4, 6); wine cellar der Weinkeller, - (6)

cellular phone das Handy, -s (2)

Celsius Celsius (B)

center: center for study abroad das Auslandsamt, ̈er (1); shopping center das Einkaufszentrum, -zentren (10)

central heating die Zentralheizung (6)

ceramic art die Töpferei (12)

certainly bestimmt (3); sicherlich (3)

chair der Stuhl, ̈e (B, 2); beach chair der Strandkorb, ̈e (10); deck chair der Liegestuhl, ̈e (4)

chalk die Kreide, -n (B)

chance die Chance, -n (12)

change: keep the change das stimmt so (8)

to change ändern, geändert (9); to change (into) sich verwandeln (in + acc.), verwandelt (9)

chaos das Chaos (5)

chapter das Kapitel, - (A)

character der Charakter, -e (12)

to charge **berechnen** (+ *dat.*), **berechnet** (8)

chauvinist **der Chauvi, -s** (12)

cheap **billig** (2)

check (*in restaurant*) **die Rechnung, -en** (4); **die Quittung, -en** (8); one check **alles zusammen** (5); separate checks **getrennt** (5); traveler's check **der Reisescheck, -s** (7)

to check the oil **das Öl kontrollieren** (5)

checking account **das Girokonto, -konten** (12)

cheese **der Käse** (8); (*type of*) creamy cottage cheese **der Quark** (8)

cheetah **der Gepard, -e** (10)

chemistry **die Chemie** (1)

cherry **die Kirsche, -n** (8)

chess **das Schach** (1)

to chew **kauen, gekaut** (11)

chic **schick** (2)

child **das Kind, -er** (B)

childhood **die Kindheit** (9)

chili **der Chili** (11)

China **(das) China** (B)

Chinese (*language*) **(das) Chinesisch** (B)

chisel **der Meißel, -** (12)

chocolate: hot chocolate **der Kakao** (8)

choir **der Chor, ⸚e** (1)

to chop **auf·schneiden (schneidet ... auf), schnitt ... auf, aufgeschnitten** (8)

Christmas **(das) Weihnachten** (4); Christmas present **das Weihnachtsgeschenk, -e** (5)

church **die Kirche, -n** (5); (*religious denomination*) **die Konfession, -en** (12); at church **in der Kirche** (5)

cigar **die Zigarre, -n** (7)

cigarette **die Zigarette, -n** (4)

cinema **das Kino, -s** (1)

circus **der Zirkus, -se** (9)

citizen **der Bürger, - / die Bürgerin, -nen** (10)

citizenship **die Staatsangehörigkeit, -en** (1)

city **die Stadt, ⸚e** (2, 6, 10); capital city **die Hauptstadt, ⸚e** (3); city limits **der Stadtrand, ⸚er** (6); city park **der Stadtpark, -s** (10); city street map **der Stadtplan, ⸚e** (10); in the city **in der Stadt** (6, 10); tour of the city **die Stadtrundfahrt, -en** (7)

class **der Kurs, -e** (A, 1); **der Unterricht, -e** (B); **die Klasse, -n** (5, 10); ballet class **der Ballettunterricht** (9); class reunion **das Klassentreffen, -** (9); tourist class **die Touristenklasse** (5); to travel first class **erster Klasse fahren** (5, 10)

classical **klassisch** (12)

clay **der Ton** (12)

clean **sauber** (B); to clean **putzen, geputzt** (3, 6); **sauber machen, sauber gemacht** (3); to clean (up) **auf·räumen, aufgeräumt** (1)

cleaner: dry cleaner's **die Reinigung, -en** (6)

cleaning: spring cleaning **der Frühjahrsputz** (6)

to clear **ab·räumen, abgeräumt** (3); to clear the table **den Tisch ab·räumen** (3)

clerk **der/die Angestellte, -n (ein Angestellter)** (7)

to climb **besteigen (besteigt), bestieg, bestiegen** (7); **klettern, ist geklettert** (9); to climb down **herunter·klettern, ist heruntergeklettert** (11)

clock **die Uhr, -en** (B); alarm clock **der Wecker, -** (2); kitchen clock **die Küchenuhr, -en** (5)

to close **schließen (schließt), schloss, geschlossen** (A); **zu·machen, zugemacht** (3)

close (*adj./adv.*) **nah** (6)

closed **geschlossen** (4)

closet **der Schrank, ⸚e** (6); clothes closet **der Kleiderschrank, ⸚e** (6)

cloth (*for cleaning*) **der Putzlappen, -** (6)

clothes **die Kleidung** (A, 2); clothes closet **der Kleiderschrank, ⸚e** (6); clothes dryer **der Wäschetrockner, -** (8)

clown **der Clown, -s** (9)

coast **die Küste, -n** (7)

coat **der Mantel, ⸚** (A)

cocoa **der Kakao** (8)

coffee **der Kaffee** (1); coffee filter **der Kaffeefilter, -** (4); coffee grinder **die Kaffeemühle, -n** (8); coffeemaker **die Kaffeemaschine, -n** (5)

coffin **der Sarg, ⸚e** (9)

cold (*adj.*) **kalt** (B); ice-cold **eiskalt** (8)

cold (*n.*) (*head cold*) **die Erkältung, -en** (11); cold (*with a runny nose*) **der Schnupfen, -** (11); to catch a cold **sich erkälten, erkältet** (11)

to collect **sammeln, gesammelt** (10)

college prep school **das Gymnasium, Gymnasien** (4); college-prep-school degree **das Abitur** (5)

color **die Farbe, -n** (A, 1); color of eyes **die Augenfarbe, -n** (1); color of hair **die Haarfarbe, -n** (1); favorite color **die Lieblingsfarbe, -n** (A); what color is . . . ? **welche Farbe hat ...?** (A)

to comb **kämmen, gekämmt** (3); to comb (one's hair) **sich (die Haare) kämmen, gekämmt** (11)

to combine **kombinieren, kombiniert** (3)

to come (from) **kommen (aus + dat.) (kommt), kam, ist gekommen** (B); to come back **wieder·kommen (kommt ... wieder), kam ... wieder, ist wiedergekommen** (5); **zurück·kommen (kommt ... zurück), kam ... zurück, ist zurückgekommen** (6); to come by **vorbei·kommen (kommt ... vorbei), kam ... vorbei, ist vorbeigekommen** (3); to come in this way **herein·kommen (kommt ... herein), kam ... herein, ist hereingekommen** (10); come on over **komm mal vorbei!** (11); to come out this way **heraus·kommen (kommt ... heraus), kam ... heraus, ist herausgekommen** (10); to come this way **her·kommen (kommt ... her), kam ... her, ist hergekommen** (10); does it come with a . . . ? **ist ein(e) ... dabei?** (6)

comfortable **bequem** (2); **gemütlich** (12)

common **gemeinsam** (11)

company **die Firma, Firmen** (3); computer company **die Computerfirma, -firmen** (4)

to compare **vergleichen (vergleicht), verglich, verglichen** (7)

to complain (to) **sich beschweren (bei + dat.), beschwert** (8)

to complete **ergänzen, ergänzt** (4)

computer **der Computer, -** (2); computer company **die Computerfirma, -firmen** (4); computer science **die Informatik** (1)

concert **das Konzert, -e** (1); concert ticket **die Konzertkarte, -n** (5); rock concert **das Rockkonzert, -e** (9); to go to a concert **ins Konzert gehen** (1)

concrete **konkret** (12)

conductor (*of an orchestra*) **der Dirigent, -en** (*wk.*) / **die Dirigentin, -nen** (5)

to congratulate **gratulieren** (+ *dat.*), **gratuliert** (2)

to connect **verbinden (verbindet), verband, verbunden** (A)

to conquer **besiegen, besiegt** (7)

conservative **konservativ** (B)

to consider **nach·denken (über + *acc.*) (denkt ... nach), dachte ... nach, nachgedacht** (7)

conspicuous **auffällig** (10)

construction worker **der Bauarbeiter, - / die Bauarbeiterin, -nen** (5)

contract **der Vertrag, ⸚e** (12)

contrary: on the contrary **doch!** (4)

conversational situation **die Sprechsituation, -en** (A)

to converse **sich unterhalten (unterhält), unterhielt, unterhalten** (9)

cook **der Koch, ⸚e / die Köchin, -nen** (5)

to cook **kochen, gekocht** (1)

cooked **gekocht** (8)

cool **kühl** (B); **grell** (2)

copy shop **der Kopierladen, ⸚** (10)

corkscrew **der Korkenzieher, -** (8)

corner **die Ecke, -n** (5); around the corner **um die Ecke** (5)

correct **richtig** (2)

to correct **korrigieren, korrigiert** (4)

cost: extra costs (*e.g. utilities*) **die Nebenkosten** (*pl.*) (6)

to cost **kosten, gekostet** (2, 6)

costume **das Kostüm, -e** (9)

couch **das Sofa, -s** (6)

cough **der Husten, -** (11); cough drop **das Hustenbonbon, -s** (11); cough syrup **der Hustensaft, ⸚e** (11)

counselor: career counselor **der Berufsberater, - / die Berufsberaterin, -nen** (5)

to count **zählen, gezählt** (A)

country **das Land, ⸚er** (B, 6); foreign countries **das Ausland** (6); in the country (*rural*) **auf dem Land** (6)

course **der Kurs, -e** (A, 1); course of studies **das Studium, Studien** (3); of course! **klar!** (2); **selbstverständlich** (10)

courthouse **das Gericht, -e** (5); at the courthouse **auf dem Gericht** (5)

cousin: female cousin **die Kusine, -n** (B); male cousin **der Vetter, -n** (B)

to cover **decken, gedeckt** (3); **zu·decken, zugedeckt** (11)

cozy **gemütlich** (12)

crash: stock market crash der Börsenkrach, -e (12)

to crash (*airplane*) ab·stürzen, ist abgestürzt (11); (*cars*) zusammen·stoßen (stößt ... zusammen), stieß ... zusammen, ist zusammengestoßen (11)

crazy verrückt (B); wahnsinnig (12)

crisis die Krise, -n (12)

critically injured schwer verletzt (11)

Croatia (das) Kroatien (B)

crocodile das Krokodil, -e (10)

croissant das Hörnchen, - (8)

croquette die Krokette, -n (8)

crosswalk der Zebrastreifen, - (10)

cruel grausam (9)

to cry weinen, geweint (3)

Cuba (das) Kuba (B)

cucumber die Gurke, -n (8)

culture die Kultur, -en (12)

cup die Tasse, -n (2, 5); der Becher, - (9)

cupboard der Schrank, -̈e (6)

to cure heilen, geheilt (5)

curious neugierig (12)

currency die Währung, -en (12)

to curse verwünschen, verwünscht (9); fluchen, geflucht (11)

cursed verwunschen (9)

curtain der Vorhang, -̈e (6)

to cuss schimpfen, geschimpft (9)

custodian der Hausmeister, - / die Hausmeisterin, -nen (5)

customer der Kunde, -n (*wk.*) / die Kundin, -nen (5)

to cut schneiden (schneidet), schnitt, geschnitten (3); to cut hair Haare schneiden (3); to cut off ab·schneiden (schneidet ... ab), schnitt ... ab, abgeschnitten (8); to cut oneself sich schneiden (schneidet), schnitt, geschnitten (11); to cut through durch·schneiden (schneidet ... durch), schnitt ... durch, durchgeschnitten (8)

cutlery das Besteck (5)

cutlet das Schnitzel, - (8)

Czech Republic (das) Tschechien (B)

daily täglich (9); daily newspaper die Tageszeitung, -en (5); daily routine der Alltag (4)

damage der Schaden, -̈ (11)

to dance tanzen, getanzt (1)

dangerous gefährlich (10)

dark dunkel (6)

data: electronic data processing die EDV = elektronische Datenverarbeitung (12); personal data die Personalien (*pl.*) (12)

date das Datum, Daten (4); die Verabredung, -en (11); what is today's date? welches Datum ist heute? (4)

daughter die Tochter, -̈ (B)

day der Tag, -e (1); all day long, the whole day den ganzen Tag (1); day after tomorrow übermorgen (9); day before yesterday vorgestern (4); on what day? an welchem Tag? (4); to take the day off blau machen,

blau gemacht (3); what day is today? welcher Tag ist heute? (1)

dead tot (9)

dear lieb (7); geehrt (10); dear Mr. sehr geehrter Herr (10); dear Ms. sehr geehrte Frau (10)

death der Tod, -e (12)

debt die Schuld, -en (12)

decade das Jahrzehnt, -e (4)

December der Dezember (B)

deception die List, -en (9)

to decide entscheiden (entscheidet), entschied, entschieden (10)

deck chair der Liegestuhl, -̈e (4)

deep tief (7)

definitely bestimmt (3)

degree der Grad, -e (B); college-prep-school degree das Abitur (5)

delay die Verspätung, -en (9)

to deliver aus·tragen (trägt ... aus), trug ... aus, ausgetragen (5); to deliver newspapers Zeitungen austragen (5)

Denmark (das) Dänemark (B)

denomination: religious denomination die Konfession, -en (12)

dentist der Zahnarzt, -̈e / die Zahnärztin, -nen (5)

to depart ab·fahren (fährt ... ab), fuhr ... ab, ist abgefahren (4); ab·reisen, ist abgereist (10)

department store das Kaufhaus, -̈er (5); at the department store im Kaufhaus (5); fire department die Feuerwehr (11)

deposit: security deposit die Kaution, -en (6)

depressed deprimiert (11)

to describe beschreiben (beschreibt), beschrieb, beschrieben (11)

description die Beschreibung, -en (B)

desert die Wüste, -n (7)

desire die Lust, -̈e (2)

desk der Schreibtisch, -e (2)

dessert die Nachspeise, -n (8)

destination das Ziel, -e (10)

devil der Teufel, - (12)

diary das Tagebuch, -̈er (4)

dictionary das Wörterbuch, -̈er (2)

to die sterben (stirbt), starb, ist gestorben (9)

different verschieden (8)

difficult schwierig (2); schwer (3)

to dine zu Abend essen (4)

dinghy: inflatable dinghy das Schlauchboot, -e (10)

dining room das Esszimmer, - (6)

dinner das Abendessen (8); to have dinner zu Abend essen (4)

diphtheria die Diphtherie (11)

direction die Richtung, -en (7)

director der Regisseur, -e / die Regisseurin, -nen (9)

dirty schmutzig (A)

disadvantage der Nachteil, -e (7)

to disappear verschwinden (verschwindet), verschwand, ist verschwunden (12)

disco die Disko, -s (3)

to discover entdecken, entdeckt (4)

to discriminate diskriminieren, diskriminiert (12)

to discuss diskutieren, diskutiert (4)

dish das Gericht, -e (8); dish of ice cream der Eisbecher, - (8); dishes das Geschirr (4, 5); to wash the dishes Geschirr spülen (4)

dishwasher die Geschirrspülmaschine, -n (5)

to disinfect desinfizieren, desinfiziert (11)

district der Stadtteil, -e (6); das Stadtviertel, - (6)

to disturb stören, gestört (3)

to dive tauchen, hat/ist getaucht (3)

divorce die Scheidung, -en (12)

to do tun (tut), tat, getan (A); to do sports Sport treiben (treibt ... Sport), trieb ... Sport, Sport getrieben (2)

doctor der Arzt, -̈e / die Ärztin, -nen (3, 5, 11); doctor's office die Arztpraxis, -praxen (11); eye doctor der Augenarzt, -̈e / die Augenärztin, -nen (11); family doctor der Hausarzt, -̈e / die Hausärztin, -nen (11); to the doctor zum Arzt (3)

dog der Hund, -e (2); dog food das Hundefutter (5)

doll die Puppe, -n (9)

dollar der Dollar, -s (7); two dollars zwei Dollar (7)

dolphin der Delfin, -e (10)

dominant dominant (12)

door die Tür, -en (A); next door nebenan (5); from next door von nebenan (5)

dorm das Studentenheim, -e (2, 6)

double room das Doppelzimmer, - (10)

down (*toward the speaker*) herunter (11); to climb down herunter·klettern, ist heruntergeklettert (11); to fall down hin·fallen (fällt ... hin), fiel ... hin, ist hingefallen (11); to lie down sich hin·legen, hingelegt (11); to sit down sich setzen, gesetzt (A, 11)

downtown die Innenstadt, -̈e (6)

dragon der Drache, -n (*wk.*) (9)

drapery der Vorhang, -̈e (6)

to draw zeichnen, gezeichnet (3, 5)

drawer die Schublade, -n (5)

to dream träumen, geträumt (9)

dress das Kleid, -er (A)

dressed: to get dressed sich an·ziehen (zieht ... an), zog ... an, angezogen (11)

dresser die Kommode, -n (6)

dressing: salad dressing die Soße, -n (8)

dressing room die Umkleidekabine, -n (5)

to drink trinken (trinkt), trank, getrunken (1)

to drive fahren (fährt), fuhr, ist/hat gefahren (2); to drive off los·fahren (fährt ... los), fuhr ... los, ist losgefahren (4, 9); to keep on driving weiter·fahren (fährt ... weiter), fuhr ... weiter, ist weitergefahren (10)

driver der Fahrer, - / die Fahrerin, -nen (7); driver's license der Führerschein, -e (4); taxi driver der Taxifahrer, - / die Taxifahrerin, -nen (5) driveway die Einfahrt, -en (11)

drop (*candy*) das Bonbon, -s (11); cough drop das Hustenbonbon, -s (11)

drugstore die Drogerie, -n (6)

drum das Schlagzeug, -e (12)

dry (*adj.*) trocken (11); dry cleaner's die Reinigung, -en (6)

to dry (dishes) ab·trocknen, abgetrocknet (6); to dry oneself off sich ab·trocknen, abgetrocknet (11)

dryer: clothes dryer der Wäschetrockner, - (8)

dumb dumm (6)

dumpling der Knödel, - (8)

during während (+ *gen.*) (11); during the week in der Woche (1)

Dutch (*adj.*) holländisch (8)

duty die Pflicht, -en (3)

DVD player der DVD-Spieler, - (2, 3)

dwarf der Zwerg, -e (9)

each jeder, jedes, jede (3, 5); each other einander (3); next to each other nebeneinander (8); with each other miteinander (3)

eagle der Adler, - (10)

ear das Ohr, -en (B)

earache die Ohrenschmerzen (*pl.*) (11)

early früh (1)

to earn verdienen, verdient (4)

earring der Ohrring, -e (A, 2)

earth science die Erdkunde (1)

easel die Staffelei, -en (12)

east (of) östlich (von + *dat.*) (7)

easy leicht (6)

to eat essen (isst), aß, gegessen (2, 4); to eat (*said of an animal*) fressen (frisst), fraß, gefressen (9); to eat breakfast frühstücken, gefrühstückt (1)

economics die Wirtschaft (1)

educated ausgebildet (12)

education die Ausbildung, -en (9); die Schulbildung (5)

effect: to take effect wirken, gewirkt (11)

egg das Ei, -er (8); boiled eggs gekochte Eier (*pl.*) (8); fried eggs gebratene Eier (*pl.*) (8)

Egypt (das) Ägypten (B)

eight acht (A)

eighteen achtzehn (A)

eighth acht- (4)

eighty achtzig (A)

electric(al) elektrisch (8)

electricity der Strom (8)

electronic data processing die EDV = elektronische Datenverarbeitung (12)

elegant elegant (8)

elementary school die Grundschule, -n (4)

elephant der Elefant, -en (*wk.*) (9)

elevator der Aufzug, ̈-e (6)

eleven elf (A)

eleventh elft- (4)

embarrassing peinlich (12)

to emigrate aus·wandern, ist ausgewandert (4, 12)

employee die Arbeitskraft, ̈-e (12); bank employee der/die Bankangestellte, -n (ein Bankangestellter) (5); postal employee der/die Postangestellte, -n (ein Postangestellter) (5)

empty (*adj.*) leer (8)

to empty aus·leeren, ausgeleert (3)

enchanted verwunschen (9)

end der Schluss, ̈-e (8); in the end zum Schluss (8)

engaged: to be engaged verlobt sein (12); to get engaged to sich verloben mit (+ *dat.*), verlobt (12)

engineer der Ingenieur, -e / die Ingenieurin, -nen (5)

engineering: mechanical engineering der Maschinenbau (1)

England (das) England (B)

English (*language*) (das) Englisch (B); (*person*) der Engländer, - / die Engländerin, -nen (B)

enough genug (4)

to enrich bereichern, bereichert (12)

entertainment die Unterhaltung, -en (3)

environs die Umgebung, -en (5)

equal egal (6)

eraser (*for blackboard*) der Schwamm, ̈-e (B)

to establish fest·stellen, festgestellt (10)

euro der Euro, - (7)

Eurocheque Card die Euroscheckkarte, -n (12)

Europe (das) Europa (B)

even noch (B)

evening der Abend, -e (1, 4); evening meal das Abendessen, - (1); evenings abends (4); good evening guten Abend! (A); in the evening am Abend (4); this evening heute Abend (2)

ever: were you ever . . . ? warst du schon einmal ...? (4)

every jeder, jedes, jede (3); every week jede Woche (3)

everything alles (2); everything possible alles Mögliche (2)

everywhere überall (12)

evil böse (9)

exactly genau (B)

to examine untersuchen, untersucht (5)

example das Beispiel, -e (3); for example zum Beispiel (z. B.) (3)

exceedingly beautiful wunderschön (10)

excellent ausgezeichnet (3)

exchange: stock exchange die Börse, -n (12)

excited: to get excited sich auf·regen, aufgeregt (11)

to excuse entschuldigen, entschuldigt (5); excuse me Entschuldigung! (3); entschuldigen Sie! (5)

to execute aus·führen, ausgeführt (12)

exercise die Übung, -en (A)

exotic exotisch (7)

to expect erwarten, erwartet (12)

expensive teuer (2); wertvoll (2)

experience das Erlebnis, -se (4); travel experience das Reiseerlebnis, -se (7)

to experience erleben, erlebt (10)

to explain erklären, erklärt (5)

extra costs (*e.g. utilities*) die Nebenkosten (*pl.*) (6)

extremist: right-wing extremist der Rechtsextremist, -en (*wk.*) (12)

eye das Auge, -n (B); blue eyes blaue Augen (B); color of eyes die Augenfarbe, -n (1); eye doctor der Augenarzt, ̈-e / die Augenärztin, -nen (11)

face das Gesicht, -er (B)

factory die Fabrik, -en (6)

Fahrenheit Fahrenheit (B)

to faint in Ohnmacht fallen (fällt), fiel, ist gefallen (11)

fairy die Fee, -n (9); fairy tale das Märchen, - (9)

fall der Herbst, -e (B)

to fall fallen (fällt), fiel, ist gefallen (9); to fall asleep ein·schlafen (schläft ... ein), schlief ... ein, ist eingeschlafen (7); to fall down hin·fallen (fällt ... hin), fiel ... hin, ist hingefallen (11); to fall in love (with) sich verlieben (in + *acc.*), verliebt (9, 12); to fall over um·fallen (fällt ... um), fiel ... um, ist umgefallen (9)

family die Familie, -n (B); family celebration das Familienfest, -e (4); family doctor der Hausarzt, ̈-e / die Hausärztin, -nen (11); family member das Familienmitglied, -er (10); family name der Familienname, -n (*wk.*) (A, 1); single-family home das Einfamilienhaus, ̈-er (6)

famous berühmt (7)

fanatic der Fanatiker, - (12)

far weit (6); as far as bis zu (+ *dat.*) (10); how far away? wie weit weg? (6)

farmer's bread das Bauernbrot, -e (5)

farmhouse das Bauernhaus, ̈-er (6)

fast schnell (3); superfast superschnell (7)

fat dick (B); fettig (8)

father der Vater, ̈ (B)

faucet der Wasserhahn, ̈-e (5)

favorite Lieblings- (A); favorite activity die Lieblingsbeschäftigung, -en (5); favorite color die Lieblingsfarbe, -n (A); favorite name der Lieblingsname, -n (*wk.*) (A); favorite subject das Lieblingsfach, ̈-er (5)

fax das Fax, -e (2)

fear die Angst, ̈-e (3)

February der Februar (B)

to feed füttern, gefüttert (9)

to feel (sich) fühlen, gefühlt (3, 11); do you feel like it? hast du Lust? (2); how do you feel? wie fühlst du dich? (3); I feel . . . ich fühle mich ... (3); to feel well sich wohl fühlen (11)

feeling das Gefühl, -e (3)

fellow student der Mitstudent, -en (*wk.*) / die Mitstudentin, -nen (A)

fence der Zaun, ̈-e (9)

to fetch holen, geholt (9)

fever das Fieber (11)

few: a few ein paar (2)

field **das Feld, -er** (7)

fifteen **fünfzehn** (A)

fifth **fünft-** (4)

fifty **fünfzig** (A)

to fight **kämpfen, gekämpft** (9)

figure **die Figur, -en** (12)

to figure **aus·rechnen, ausgerechnet** (8)

to fill in the blanks **ergänzen, ergänzt** (4); to fill out **aus·füllen, ausgefüllt** (1); to fill up (*with gas*) **voll·tanken, vollgetankt** (5)

film **der Film, -e** (2); horror film **der Gruselfilm, -e** (2); TV film **der Fernsehfilm, -e** (12)

filter: coffee filter **der Kaffeefilter, -** (4)

finally **schließlich** (7); **zum Schluss** (8); **endlich** (9); **zuletzt** (10)

to find **finden (findet), fand, gefunden** (2)

fine **fein** (8)

finger **der Finger, -** (11)

fingernail **der Fingernagel, ⸚** (11)

finished **fertig** (3)

Finland **(das) Finnland** (B)

fire **das Feuer, -** (9); fire department **die Feuerwehr** (11)

firm **die Firma, Firmen** (3)

first (*adj.*) **erst-** (4); (*adv.*) **zuerst** (4, 7); first name **der Vorname, -n** (*wk.*) (A, 1); first of October **der erste Oktober** (4); for the first time **zum ersten Mal** (4); on the first of October **am ersten Oktober** (4); to travel first class **erster Klasse fahren** (5, 10)

fish **der Fisch, -e** (8)

to fit **passen** (+ *dat.*), **gepasst** (6, 11); that fits well **das passt gut** (11)

five **fünf** (A)

flashlight **die Taschenlampe, -n** (9)

flat tire **die Reifenpanne, -n** (7)

flawless **vollkommen** (12)

flea market **der Flohmarkt, ⸚e** (2)

to flee **flüchten, ist geflüchtet** (11)

flexible **flexibel** (5)

flight **der Flug, ⸚e** (7)

to float **schwimmen (schwimmt), schwamm, ist geschwommen** (7)

floor **der Boden, ⸚** (B); **der Stock, Stockwerke** (6); on the second floor **im ersten Stock** (6)

to flow **fließen (fließt), floss, ist geflossen** (7)

flower **die Blume, -n** (3); to water the flowers **die Blumen gießen** (3)

flu **die Grippe** (11)

flute: transverse flute **die Querflöte, -n** (12)

fly **die Fliege, -n** (8)

to fly **fliegen (fliegt), flog, ist/hat geflogen** (1)

food: dog food **das Hundefutter** (5)

foot **der Fuß, ⸚e** (B); on foot **zu Fuß** (3)

for (*prep.*) **für** (+ *acc.*) (2); **seit** (+ *dat.*) (4, 11); **zu** (+ *dat.*) (2); (*coord. conj.*) **denn** (9, 11); do you have something for it (*illness*)? **haben Sie etwas dagegen?** (11); for example **zum Beispiel (z. B.)** (3); for lunch **zum Mittagessen** (3); for several days **seit mehreren Tagen** (11); for someone's birthday **zum Geburtstag**

(2); for the first time **zum ersten Mal** (4); for two years **seit zwei Jahren** (4); what for? **wofür?** (8)

forbidden **verboten** (8)

foreign **ausländisch** (12); foreign countries **das Ausland** (6); foreign language **die Fremdsprache, -n** (9)

foreigner **der Ausländer, -** / **die Ausländerin, -nen** (12); hostility toward foreigners **der Ausländerhass** (12)

forest **der Wald, ⸚er** (2, 7)

to forget **vergessen (vergisst), vergaß, vergessen** (2)

fork **die Gabel, -n** (8)

form **das Formular, -e** (12)

formality **die Formalität, -en** (12)

forth: and so forth **und so weiter** (5)

forty **vierzig** (A)

fountain **der Brunnen, -** (9)

four **vier** (A)

fourteen **vierzehn** (A)

fourth **viert-** (4)

fowl: water fowl **der Wasservogel, ⸚** (10)

franc: Swiss franc **der Franken, -** (7)

France **(das) Frankreich** (B)

frank(furter) **das Würstchen, -** (8)

free (*adj.*) **frei** (3)

to free **erlösen, erlöst** (9)

freeway **die Autobahn, -en** (7)

freezer **die Gefriertruhe, -n** (8)

French (*language*) **(das) Französisch** (B); (*person*) **der Franzose, -n** (*wk.*) / **die Französin, -nen** (B); French fries **die Pommes (frites)** (*pl.*) (8)

fresh **frisch** (8)

Friday **der Freitag** (1)

fried **gebraten** (8); fried eggs **gebratene Eier** (*pl.*) (8)

friend **der Freund, -e** / **die Freundin, -nen** (A)

friendly **freundlich** (B)

fries: French fries **die Pommes (frites)** (*pl.*) (8)

frog **der Frosch, ⸚e** (9)

from **von** (+ *dat.*) (A, 10); **aus** (+ *dat.*) (10); from next door **von nebenan** (5); from where **woher** (B); from work **von der Arbeit** (3)

frustrated **frustriert** (3)

to fry **braten (brät), briet, gebraten** (8); **bräunen, gebräunt** (8)

fun **lustig** (12); have fun **viel Spaß!** (A)

funny **lustig** (12); **komisch** (12)

furnished **möbliert** (6)

furniture **die Möbel** (*pl.*) (6); piece of furniture **das Möbelstück, -e** (6)

game: video game **das Videospiel, -e** (2)

garage **die Werkstatt, ⸚en** (5); **die Garage, -n** (6)

garbage **der Müll** (6); garbage can **der Mülleimer, -** (8)

garden **der Garten, ⸚** (4, 6); garden hose **der Gartenschlauch, ⸚e** (6); in the garden **im Garten** (4)

garlic **der Knoblauch** (8)

gas station **die Tankstelle, -n** (5); at the gas station **an der Tankstelle** (5)

gasoline **das Benzin** (6)

gaudy **grell** (2)

gear **der Gang, ⸚e** (7)

gentleman **der Herr, -en** (*wk.*) (A)

geography **die Erdkunde** (1); **die Geografie** (7)

German (*language*) **(das) Deutsch** (B); (*person*) **der/die Deutsche, -n (ein Deutscher)** (B); German army **die Bundeswehr** (5); German class/course **der Deutschkurs, -e** (A); German-speaking **deutschsprachig** (9); I am German **ich bin Deutscher/Deutsche** (B)

Germany **(das) Deutschland** (B)

to get **bekommen (bekommt), bekam, bekommen** (3); to get acquainted with **kennen·lernen, kennengelernt** (1); to get in this way **herein·kommen (kommt ... herein), kam ... herein, ist hereingekommen** (10); to get information about **sich erkundigen nach** (+ *dat.*), **erkundigt** (10); to get up **auf·stehen (steht ... auf), stand ... auf, ist aufgestanden** (A, 1); to get up on the wrong side of bed **mit dem linken Fuß auf·stehen** (4); to (go) get **holen, geholt** (9)

giant **der Riese, -n** (*wk.*) (9)

gifted **begabt** (9)

giraffe **die Giraffe, -n** (10)

girl **das Mädchen, -** (9)

girlfriend **die Freundin, -nen** (A)

to give **geben (gibt), gab, gegeben** (A, 6); to give (as a present) **schenken, geschenkt** (5); to give a paper / oral report **ein Referat halten (hält), hielt, gehalten** (4)

glacier **der Gletscher, -** (7)

gladly **gern** (1, 5)

glass **das Glas, ⸚er** (5, 9); (*made of glass*) **gläsern** (9)

glasses (pair of) **die Brille, -n** (A)

glove **der Handschuh, -e** (2)

to go **gehen (geht), ging, ist gegangen** (A); **laufen (läuft), lief, ist gelaufen** (A); to go along **entlang·gehen (geht ... entlang), ging ... entlang, ist entlanggegangen** (10); to go away **weg·gehen (geht ... weg), ging ... weg, ist weggegangen** (4); to go by **vorbei·gehen (an +** *dat.*) **(geht ... vorbei), ging ... vorbei, ist vorbeigegangen** (10); to go canoeing **Kanu fahren (fährt ... Kanu), fuhr ... Kanu, Kanu gefahren** (10); to go for a walk **spazieren gehen (geht ... spazieren), ging ... spazieren, ist spazieren gegangen** (1); to go home **nach Hause gehen** (1); to go in this way **herein·kommen (kommt ... herein), kam ... herein, ist hereingekommen** (10); to go on a trip **verreisen, ist verreist** (3); to go out **aus·gehen (geht ... aus), ging ... aus, ist ausgegangen** (1); to go out (*power*) **aus·fallen (fällt ... aus), fiel ... aus, ist ausgefallen** (8); to go over that way **hinüber·gehen (geht ... hinüber), ging ... hinüber, ist hinübergegangen** (10); to go shopping **einkaufen gehen (geht ... einkaufen), ging ... einkaufen, ist einkaufen gegangen** (1, 5); to go that way **hin·gehen** (geht ... hin), ging ... hin, ist hingegangen (10); to go to a party **auf eine Party gehen** (1); to go to bed **ins Bett gehen** (1); to go to the mountains **in die Berge gehen** (1); to go to the movies **ins Kino gehen** (1); to go to the swimming pool **ins Schwimmbad fahren** (1); to go to work **zur Arbeit gehen** (1); to go up that way **hinauf·gehen (geht ... hinauf), ging ... hinauf, ist hinaufgegangen** (10); where are you going? **wo willst du denn hin?** (A)

god **der Gott, ⸚er** (12)

goldfish **der Goldfisch, -e** (11)

golf **das Golf** (1)

good **gut** (A); good afternoon (*for.*) **guten Tag!** (A); good evening **guten Abend!** (A); good luck **viel Glück!** (3); good morning **guten Morgen!** (A); it looks good **es sieht gut aus** (2); that looks / they look good on you **das steht / die stehen dir gut** (2)

good-bye **auf Wiedersehen!** (A); (*infor.; southern Germany, Austria*) **servus!** (A); (*on the phone*) **auf Wiederhören!** (6)

to grab **greifen (greift), griff, gegriffen** (11)

grade (*level*) **die Klasse, -n** (9); (*mark*) **die Note, -n** (3, 9)

graduation **der Abschluss** (9)

grammar **die Grammatik, -en** (A)

granddaughter **die Enkelin, -nen** (5)

grandfather **der Großvater, ⸚** (B)

grandma **die Oma, -s** (3)

grandmother **die Großmutter, ⸚** (B)

grandparents **die Großeltern** (*pl.*) (B)

grandson **der Enkel, -** (5)

grape **die Weintraube, -n** (8)

to grasp **greifen (greift), griff, gegriffen** (11)

gravy **die Soße, -n** (8)

gray **grau** (A); grayish green **graugrün** (7)

greasy **fettig** (8, 11)

great **toll** (2); great! **prima!** (6); that sounds great **das hört sich toll an** (4)

Great Britain **(das) Großbritannien** (B)

Greece **(das) Griechenland** (B)

green **grün** (A); grayish green **graugrün** (7)

to greet **grüßen, gegrüßt** (11)

greeting **das Begrüßen** (A); **der Gruß, ⸚e** (10)

grill **der Grill, -s** (8)

grilled **gegrillt** (8)

grinder: coffee grinder **die Kaffeemühle, -n** (8)

grocery store **das Lebensmittelgeschäft, -e** (6)

gross **eklig** (9)

ground beef (or pork) **das Hackfleisch** (8)

to grow **wachsen (wächst), wuchs, ist gewachsen** (9); to grow up **auf·wachsen (wächst ... auf), wuchs ... auf, ist aufgewachsen** (12)

guidebook: travel guidebook **der Reiseführer, -** (5)

guided tour **die Führung, -en** (10)

guinea pig **das Meerschweinchen, -** (10)

guitar **die Gitarre, -n** (1)

hair **das Haar, -e** (B, 11); black-haired **schwarzhaarig** (9); blond hair **blondes Haar** (B); to blow-dry one's hair **sich die Haare föhnen** (11); color of hair **die Haarfarbe, -n** to comb one's hair **sich die Haare kämmen** (11); to cut hair **Haare schneiden** (3); (1); short hair **kurzes Haar** (B); with the short/long hair **mit dem kurzen/langen Haar** (A)

haircut **der Haarschnitt, -e** (2)

hairdresser **der Friseur, -e / die Friseurin, -nen** (5)

half **die Hälfte, -n** (10)

hall: town hall **das Rathaus, ⸚er** (1, 6); at the town hall **auf dem Rathaus** (1)

ham **der Schinken** (8)

hammer **der Hammer, ⸚** (8)

hamster **der Hamster, -** (10)

hand **die Hand, ⸚e** (B); hand towel **das Handtuch, ⸚er** (5); to shake hands **die Hand schütteln** (A)

handkerchief **das Taschentuch, ⸚er** (3)

handy **handwerklich** (12)

to hang (*be in a hanging position*) **hängen (hängt), hing, gehangen** (3); to hang the picture on the wall **das Bild an die Wand hängen** (3); to hang (up) **hängen, gehängt** (3); **auf·hängen, aufgehängt** (12)

hangover **der Kater, -** (11)

to happen **passieren, ist passiert** (4)

happiness **das Glück** (3)

happy **glücklich** (B); to be happy about **sich freuen über** (+ *acc.*), **gefreut** (11)

harbor **der Hafen, ⸚** (10)

hard **schwer** (3)

hardware store **das Eisenwarengeschäft, -e** (6)

harmful: to be harmful to **schaden** (+ *dat.*), **geschadet** (6)

harmonica **die Mundharmonika, -s** (12)

hat **der Hut, ⸚e** (A)

to hate **hassen, gehasst** (9)

to have **haben (hat), hatte, gehabt** (A); to have to **müssen (muss), musste, gemusst** (3)

head **der Kopf, ⸚e** (B)

headache **die Kopfschmerzen** (*pl.*) (11); headache tablet **die Kopfschmerztablette, -n** (11)

headband **das Stirnband, ⸚er** (A)

to heal **heilen, geheilt** (5)

health **die Gesundheit** (11)

healthy **gesund** (11)

to hear **hören, gehört** (1); to hear again **wieder hören, wieder gehört** (6)

heart **das Herz, -en** (11)

heartache **die Herzschmerzen** (*pl.*) (11)

to heat **erhitzen, erhitzt** (8)

heated, heat included **warm** (6)

heating: central heating **die Zentralheizung** (6)

heavy **schwer** (3); **stark** (11)

height **die Größe, -n** (1); **die Höhe, -n** (12)

hello (*for.*) **guten Tag!** (A); (*for.; southern Germany, Austria*) **grüß Gott!** (A); (*infor.; southern Germany, Austria*) **servus!** (A)

helmet: bicycle helmet **der Fahrradhelm, -e** (5)

help **helfen** (+ *dat.*) **(hilft), half, geholfen** (6); help! **Hilfe!** (11); may I help you? **bitte schön?** (7)

her (*adj.*) **ihr(e)** (1, 2)

herb butter **die Kräuterbutter** (8)

herbs **die Kräuter** (*pl.*) (8)

here **hier** (A)

herring salad **der Heringssalat, -e** (8)

Herzegovina **(das) Herzegowina** (B)

hi (*infor.*) **hallo!** (A); (*Switzerland*) **grüezi!** (A); to say hi to **grüßen, gegrüßt** (11)

to hide **sich verstecken, versteckt** (9)

high **hoch** (6); to have high blood pressure **hohen Blutdruck haben** (11)

high school **das Gymnasium, Gymnasien** (4)

highlight **der Höhepunkt, -e** (7)

high-rise building **das Hochhaus, ⸚er** (6)

highway: interstate highway **die Autobahn, -en** (7); rural highway **die Landstraße, -n** (7)

hike **die Wanderung, -en** (7); to hike **wandern, ist gewandert** (1); to hike in the mountains **in den Bergen wandern** (1)

hiking shoe **der Wanderschuh, -e** (2)

hill **der Hügel, -** (7)

him (*acc.*) **ihn** (2), (*dat.*) **ihm**

his **sein(e)** (1, 2)

history **die Geschichte** (1); art history **die Kunstgeschichte** (1)

to hit **schlagen (schlägt), schlug, geschlagen** (11)

to hitchhike **trampen, ist getrampt** (10)

hobby **das Hobby, -s** (1)

hole **das Loch, ⸚er** (9)

holiday **der Feiertag, -e** (4); national holiday **der Nationalfeiertag, -e** (4)

Holland **(das) Holland** (B)

home **das Haus, ⸚er** (2); **die Heimat, -en** (12); at home **daheim** (9); to be at home **zu Hause sein** (A, 1); to go home **nach Hause gehen** (1, 10); single-family home **das Einfamilienhaus, ⸚er** (6)

homeland **das Heimatland, ⸚er** (12); **die Heimat, -en** (12)

homemade **selbst gemacht** (8)

homemaker **der Hausmann, ⸚er / die Hausfrau, -en** (12)

homesick: to be homesick **Heimweh haben** (3)

homesickness **das Heimweh** (3)

hometown **die Heimatstadt, ⸚e** (6); **die Heimat, -en** (12)

homework (assignment) **die Hausaufgabe, -n** (A)

honey **der Honig** (8)

to honk **hupen, gehupt** (7)

honored **geehrt** (10)

hood **die Motorhaube, -n** (7)

hook **der Haken, -** (8)

to hope **hoffen, gehofft** (3)

horn **die Hupe, -n** (7)

horror film **der Gruselfilm, -e** (2)

horse **das Pferd, -e** (2, 9)

hose: garden hose **der Gartenschlauch, ⸚e** (6)

hospital **das Krankenhaus, ⸚er** (3, 5, 11); in the hospital **im Krankenhaus** (5) host der Wirt, -e / die Wirtin, -nen (10)

hostel: youth hostel die Jugendherberge, -n (10)

hostility toward foreigners der Ausländerhass (12)

hot heiß (B); hot chocolate der Kakao (8); hot dog das Würstchen, - (8)

hotel das Hotel, -s (2, 5); at the hotel im Hotel (5)

hour die Stunde, -n (2); business hours die Öffnungszeiten (pl.) (8); office hour die Sprechstunde, -n (3); quarter hour die Viertelstunde, -n (6)

house das Haus, ̈er (1, 2, 6); farmhouse das Bauernhaus, ̈er (6); house key der Hausschlüssel, - (9); house number die Hausnummer, -n (1); row house, town house das Reihenhaus, ̈er (6); tree house das Baumhaus, ̈er (6); vacation house das Ferienhaus, ̈er (4)

houseboat das Hausboot, -e (6)

household der Haushalt (8, 9); in the household im Haushalt (8)

housemate der Mitbewohner, - / die Mitbewohnerin, -nen (2)

housewife die Hausfrau, -en (12)

housing: shared housing die Wohngemeinschaft, -en (6); housing-wanted ad die Suchanzeige, -n (6)

how wie (B); how do you feel? wie fühlst du dich? (3); how do you spell that? wie schreibt man das? (A); how far away? wie weit weg? (6); how many wie viele (A)

humid feucht (B)

hummingbird der Kolibri, -s (10)

hundred, one hundred hundert (A)

hundredth hundertst- (4)

Hungary (das) Ungarn (B)

hunger der Hunger (3)

hungry hungrig (9); to be hungry Hunger haben (3)

hunter der Jäger, - (9)

hurry die Eile (3); to be in a hurry in Eile sein (3); es eilig haben (10); to hurry sich beeilen, beeilt (8)

to hurt weh·tun (tut ... weh), tat ... weh, wehgetan (11)

husband der Mann, ̈er (B)

hygiene: personal hygiene die Körperpflege (11)

ice das Eis (2); dish of ice cream der Eisbecher, - (8); ice-cold eiskalt (8); ice cream parlor das Eiscafé, -s (8); ice skate der Schlittschuh, -e (3); to go ice-skating Schlittschuh laufen (läuft ... Schlittschuh), lief ... Schlittschuh, ist Schlittschuh gelaufen (3)

idea die Idee, -n (10)

ideal ideal (12)

identification card der Personalausweis, -e (1); der Ausweis, -e (10)

idol das Vorbild, -er (9)

if (subord. conj.) wenn (2, 11); ob (6)

igloo das Iglu, -s (6)

illegal illegal (12)

illness die Krankheit, -en (11)

to imagine (s.th.) sich (etwas) vor·stellen, vorgestellt (6, 10)

immediately sofort (3)

immigrant der Einwanderer, - (4, 12)

to immigrate ein·wandern, ist eingewandert (12)

impatient ungeduldig (11)

important wichtig (2)

in (prep.) in (+ dat./acc.) (A, 4); an (+ dat./acc.) (4); (adv.) hinein (9); in addition dazu (8); in any case jedenfalls (11); in it drin/darin (6); in January im Januar (B); in love verliebt (4); in order to um ... zu (12); in spite of trotz (+ gen.) (12); in spite of that trotzdem (9); in the afternoon nachmittags (4); in the city in der Stadt (6, 10); in the country (rural) auf dem Land (6); in the end zum Schluss (8); in the evening am Abend (4), abends (4); in the middle mitten (9); in the middle of the night mitten in der Nacht (9); in the morning früh (4); in the spring im Frühling (B); in this way herein (10)

included inbegriffen (10); (utilities) inklusive (6)

income das Einkommen (12)

incredible unglaublich (5)

indeed ja (4)

independent selbstständig (12)

industrious fleißig (12)

inexpensive billig (2)

infection die Entzündung, -en (11); kidney infection die Nierenentzündung (11)

inferior minderwertig (12)

inflatable dinghy das Schlauchboot, -e (10)

influenza die Grippe (11)

to inform oneself about sich informieren über (+ acc.), informiert (10)

information die Information, -en (4); biographical information persönliche Daten (pl.) (1); to get information about sich erkundigen nach (+ dat.), erkundigt (10)

ingredient die Zutat, -en (8)

injection die Spritze, -n (11)

to injure oneself sich verletzen, verletzt (11)

injured verletzt (11); critically injured schwer verletzt (11); injured person der/die Verletzte, -n (ein Verletzter) (11)

inn: bed-and-breakfast inn das Gästehaus, ̈er (10)

innkeeper der Wirt, -e / die Wirtin, -nen (10)

insane wahnsinnig (12)

instead of (an)statt (+ gen.) (12)

to instruct unterrichten, unterrichtet (5)

instruction die Aufforderung, -en (A); der Unterricht, -e (B)

instructor der Lehrer, - / die Lehrerin, -nen (A, 1)

instrument das Instrument, -e (12)

insurance die Versicherung, -en (5)

integration die Integration (12)

intelligence die Intelligenz (12)

intelligent intelligent (B)

to intend (to) wollen (will), wollte, gewollt (3)

interest das Interesse, -n (5); (money) die Zinsen (pl.) (12); to be interested in Interesse haben

an (+ dat.) (5); sich interessieren für (+ acc.) (5); to interest interessieren, interessiert (5)

interesting interessant (7)

intersection die Kreuzung, -en (7)

interstate highway die Autobahn, -en (7)

interview das Interview, -s (4); to interview interviewen, interviewt (12)

to introduce vor·stellen, vorgestellt (6)

introduction die Einführung, -en (A)

to invent erfinden (erfindet), erfand, erfunden (4)

to investigate untersuchen, untersucht (5)

invitation die Einladung, -en (2)

to invite ein·laden (lädt ... ein), lud ... ein, eingeladen (2)

inward hinein (9)

Ireland (das) Irland (B)

iron das Bügeleisen, - (6); to iron bügeln, gebügelt (6)

island die Insel, -n (7)

Israel (das) Israel (B)

it is . . . es ist ... (B)

Italian (language) (das) Italienisch (B)

Italy (das) Italien (B)

its ihr(e) (2); sein(e) (2)

ivory das Elfenbein (10)

jacket die Jacke, -n (A); sports jacket das Sakko, -s (A)

jail das Gefängnis, -se (6)

jam die Marmelade, -n (8); traffic jam der Stau, -s (7)

January der Januar (B)

Japan (das) Japan (B)

Japanese (adj.) japanisch (8); (language) (das) Japanisch (B); (person) der Japaner, - / die Japanerin, -nen (B)

jealous eifersüchtig (3)

jeans die Jeans (pl.) (2)

jewelry der Schmuck (2)

joke der Witz, -e (3); to tell jokes Witze erzählen (3)

journey die Reise, -n (7)

joy die Freude, -n (9)

judge der Richter, - / die Richterin, -nen (5)

juice der Saft, ̈e (8); apple juice der Apfelsaft (8); orange juice der Orangensaft (8)

July der Juli (B)

to jump springen (springt), sprang, ist gesprungen (A)

June der Juni (B)

jungle der Dschungel, - (7)

just knapp (6); that's just it! das ist es ja! (4)

kangaroo das Känguru, -s (10)

to keep: keep the change das stimmt so (8); to keep on driving weiter·fahren (fährt ... weiter), fuhr ... weiter, ist weitergefahren (10); to keep on walking weiter·gehen (geht ... weiter), ging ... weiter, ist weitergegangen (10)

kettle: tea kettle der Teekessel, - (8)

key der Schlüssel, - (9); house key der Hausschlüssel, - (9)

kidney die Niere, -n (11); kidney infection die
Nierenentzündung (11)

to kill töten, getötet (9)

kiln der Brennofen, ÷ (12)

kilometer der Kilometer, - (2)

kind die Art, -en (2)

kindergarten der Kindergarten, ÷ (6)

king der König, -e (9)

kiss der Kuss, ÷e (4); to kiss küssen, geküsst (9)

kitchen die Küche, -n (5); in the kitchen in der
Küche (5); kitchen clock die Küchenuhr,
-en (5); kitchen lamp die Küchenlampe, -n
(5); kitchen scale die Küchenwaage, -n (5);
kitchen table der Küchentisch, -e (5); kitchen
work die Küchenarbeit, -en (5)

knife das Messer, - (8)

to knit stricken, gestrickt (3)

to knock over um·kippen, umgekippt (11)

to know kennen (kennt), kannte, gekannt (B);
wissen (weiß), wusste, gewusst (2)

knowledge about a field die Kenntnisse (pl.) (5)

labor die Arbeitskraft, ÷e (12)

laboratory: language laboratory das Sprachlabor,
-s (4)

lake der See, -n (7)

lamp die Lampe, -n (B); kitchen lamp die
Küchenlampe, -n (5)

land mammal das Landsäugetier, -e (10)

landlord/landlady der Vermieter, - / die Vermieterin, -nen (6)

language die Sprache, -n (B); foreign language
die Fremdsprache, -n (9); language
laboratory das Sprachlabor, -s (4)

large dick (B)

last letzt- (4); last Monday letzten Montag (4);
last night gestern Abend (4); last summer
letzten Sommer (4); last week letzte Woche
(4); last weekend letztes Wochenende (4);
the last time das letzte Mal (4)

to last dauern, gedauert (4)

late(r) spät(er) (1); late morning der Vormittag,
-e (4)

Latin (language) das Latein (1)

to laugh lachen, gelacht (3)

laundromat der Waschsalon, -s (10)

laundry die Wäsche (4); laundry room die
Waschküche, -n (6)

lawn der Rasen, - (5)

lawnmower der Rasenmäher, - (6)

lawyer der Anwalt, ÷e / die Anwältin, -nen (5)

lazy faul (3)

to learn lernen, gelernt (1)

least: the least am wenigsten (8)

to leave verlassen (verlässt), verließ, verlassen (11)

leave-taking das Verabschieden (A)

lecture die Vorlesung, -en (4)

left links (4, 10)

leg das Bein, -e (B)

leisure time die Freizeit (1)

lemon die Zitrone, -n (8)

to lend leihen (leiht), lieh, geliehen (5)

to let lassen (lässt), ließ, gelassen (11)

letter der Brief, -e (1); business letter der
Geschäftsbrief, -e (10)

lettuce der Kopfsalat (8)

liberal liberal (6)

librarian der Bibliothekar, -e / die Bibliothekarin, -nen (5)

library die Bibliothek, -en (2)

license: driver's license der Führerschein, -e (4);
license plate das Nummernschild, -er (7); license plate number die Autonummer, -n (11)

to lie liegen (liegt), lag, gelegen (1); to lie down
sich hin·legen, hingelegt (11); to lie in the sun
in der Sonne liegen (1)

Liechtenstein (das) Liechtenstein (B)

life das Leben, - (9); professional life das
Berufsleben (12); student life das Studentenleben (4)

light (n.) das Licht, -er (3); (adj., color) hell (6);
(adj., weight) leicht (6); to light an·zünden,
angezündet (3)

to like mögen (mag), mochte, gemocht (1, 3); I
like it es gefällt mir (6); I would like . . . ich
hätte gern ... (5); like (to do s.th.) best am
liebsten (7); to be to one's liking gefallen (gefällt), gefiel, gefallen (6); we like to sing wir
singen gern (1); would like (to) möchte (2, 3)

limit: city limits der Stadtrand, ÷er (6)

line die Linie, -n (10)

linguistics die Linguistik (1)

lion der Löwe, -n (wk.) (10)

lip die Lippe, -n (11)

list die Liste, -n (5)

to listen (to) zu·hören (+ dat.), zugehört (6)

liter der Liter, - (7)

literature die Literatur, -en (1, 12)

little: a little (bit) ein bisschen (B)

to live leben, gelebt (3); to live (in) wohnen
(in + dat.) (B)

liver die Leber, -n (11)

living arrangements die Wohnmöglichkeiten
(pl.) (6); living room das Wohnzimmer, - (6)

loathsome eklig (9)

lobster der Hummer, - (8)

locomotive die Lokomotive, -n (7)

lodge: ski lodge die Skihütte, -n (5)

lodging die Unterkunft, ÷e (10)

logical logisch (12)

loner der Einzelgänger, - (12)

long lang (B); all day long den ganzen Tag (1);
all night long die ganze Nacht (3); long hair
langes Haar (B); with the long hair mit dem
langen Haar (A)

to look schauen, geschaut (A); aus·sehen
(sieht ... aus), sah ... aus, ausgesehen (2);
it looks good es sieht gut aus (2); to look
at an·schauen, angeschaut (2); an·sehen
(sieht ... an), sah ... an, angesehen (3); to

look for suchen, gesucht (1); to look up
nach·sehen (sieht ... nach), sah ... nach,
nachgesehen (10); that looks / they look good
on you das steht / die stehen dir gut (2)

to lose verlieren (verliert), verlor, verloren (7);
to lose weight ab·nehmen (nimmt ... ab),
nahm ... ab, abgenommen (8, 11)

lot: a lot viel (A)

lotion: suntan lotion die Sonnenmilch (10); to put
lotion on sich ein·kremen, eingekremt (11)

lots of luck viel Glück! (3)

lottery die Lotterie, -n (5); to win the lottery in
der Lotterie gewinnen (5)

loud laut (3)

lounge der Aufenthaltsraum, ÷e (10)

lovable lieb (10)

to love lieben, geliebt (2); to be in love verliebt
sein (4, 12); to fall in love with sich verlieben
(in + acc.), verliebt (9, 12)

lover der/die Geliebte, -n (ein Geliebter) (3)

lovesickness der Liebeskummer (11)

low: to have low blood pressure niedrigen Blutdruck haben (11); low in calories kalorienarm (8)

loyal treu (9)

lozenge das Bonbon, -s (11); throat lozenge das
Halsbonbon, -s (11)

luck das Glück (3); lots of luck, good luck viel
Glück! (3)

luggage das Gepäck (10)

lunch das Mittagessen (3, 8); for lunch zum Mittagessen (3)

lung die Lunge, -n (11)

machine: automatic teller machine (ATM) der
Geldautomat, -en (wk.) (12); washing
machine die Waschmaschine, -n (6)

magical magisch (12)

main point der Stichpunkt, -e (12)

makeup: to put makeup on sich schminken,
geschminkt (11)

mammal: land mammal das Landsäugetier, -e (10)

man der Mann, ÷er (A, B); man! (coll.) Mensch! (2)

manager der Geschäftsführer, - / die Geschäftsführerin, -nen (8)

mansion die Villa, Villen (5)

many viele (A); many thanks vielen Dank (10)

map die Landkarte, -n (7); city street map der
Stadtplan, ÷e (10)

March der März (B)

marital status der Familienstand (1)

mark (former German monetary unit) die Mark, - (7)

to mark markieren, markiert (11)

market der Markt, ÷e (10); flea market der Flohmarkt, ÷e (2); market square der Marktplatz,
÷e (6)

marmalade die Marmelade, -n (8)

marriage die Ehe, -n (12)

married: to be married verheiratet sein (1, 12); to
get married to sich verheiraten mit (+ dat.),
verheiratet (12)

to marry heiraten, geheiratet (5)

match das Streichholz, ⸚er (8)

material das Material, -ien (12)

mathematics die Mathematik (1)

matter: it doesn't matter to me das ist mir egal (6); to be the matter with (s.o.) fehlen (+ dat.), gefehlt (11)

mattress: air mattress die Luftmatratze, -n (10)

May der Mai (B)

may (v.) dürfen (darf), durfte, gedurft (3); können (kann), konnte, gekonnt (3)

mayonnaise die Mayonnaise (8)

meadow die Wiese, -n (7)

meal die Mahlzeit, -en (8); evening meal das Abendessen, - (1); midday meal das Mittagessen (3)

mean böse (9)

means: by all means auf jeden Fall (4); means of payment das Zahlungsmittel, - (12); means of transportation das Transportmittel, - (7)

meat das Fleisch (8)

mechanical engineering der Maschinenbau (1)

medical medizinisch (11)

medicine das Medikament, -e (11); medicine for ein Medikament gegen (+ acc.) (11)

Mediterranean Sea das Mittelmeer (B)

to meet treffen (trifft), traf, getroffen (2); begegnen (+ dat.), ist begegnet (6); let's meet . . . treffen wir uns . . . (2)

member das Mitglied, -er (6); family member das Familienmitglied, -er (10)

memory die Erinnerung, -en (4)

menu die Speisekarte, -n (8)

meter: square meter (m²) der Quadratmeter, - (qm) (6)

Mexican (adj.) mexikanisch (8); (person) der Mexikaner, - / die Mexikanerin, -nen (B)

Mexico (das) Mexiko (B)

midday der Mittag, -e (3); midday meal das Mittagessen (3)

middle: in the middle mitten (9); in the middle of the night mitten in der Nacht (9)

mileage der Kilometerstand (7)

milk die Milch (8)

million die Million, -en (7)

mineral water das Mineralwasser (8)

mirror der Spiegel, - (6)

to miss (not catch) verpassen, verpasst (9); (not notice) verfehlen, verfehlt (10)

missing: to be missing fehlen (+ dat.), gefehlt (6)

to mix vermischen, vermischt (8)

mixed gemischt (8)

mixer die Küchenmaschine, -n (8)

modern modern (6)

Moldavia, Moldova (das) Moldawien (B)

moment der Moment, -e (1); at the moment im Moment (1)

Monday der Montag (1); last Monday letzten Montag (4)

money das Geld (2)

month der Monat, -e (B)

to mop (up) auf·wischen, aufgewischt (6)

more mehr (3)

morning: good morning guten Morgen! (A); in the morning früh (4); in the morning, mornings morgens (3); late morning der Vormittag, -e (4); until four in the morning bis um vier Uhr früh (4)

Morocco (das) Marokko (B)

mosquito die Mücke, -n (10)

mostly meistens (8)

mother die Mutter, ⸚ (A, B); Mother's Day der Muttertag (4)

motif das Motiv, -e (12)

motorcycle das Motorrad, ⸚er (1, 7); to ride a motorcycle Motorrad fahren (1)

mountain der Berg, -e (1); to go to the mountains in die Berge gehen (1); to hike in the mountains in den Bergen wandern (1); mountain range das Gebirge, - (7)

mountaintop der Gipfel, - (7)

mouse die Maus, ⸚e (10)

mouth der Mund, ⸚e (B); (of an animal) das Maul, ⸚er (9)

to move ziehen (zieht), zog, ist gezogen (2)

movie: to go to the movies ins Kino gehen (1); movie theater das Kino, -s (1); movie ticket die Kinokarte, -n (2); TV movie der Fernsehfilm, -e (12)

to mow mähen, gemäht (5)

mower: lawnmower der Rasenmäher, - (6)

MP3 player der MP3-Spieler, - (5)

Mr. der Herr, -en (wk.) (A)

Mrs., Ms. die Frau, -en (A)

much viel (A)

mug der Becher, - (9)

muscle: sore muscles der Muskelkater, - (11)

museum das Museum, Museen (1); to go to the museum ins Museum gehen (1)

mushroom der Pilz, -e (8)

music die Musik (1)

mussel die Muschel, -n (8)

must müssen (muss), musste, gemusst (3)

mustache der Schnurrbart, ⸚e (A)

mustard der Senf (8)

my mein(e) (A, 2)

nail der Nagel, ⸚ (8)

name der Name, -n (wk.) (A, 1); family name der Familienname, -n (wk.) (A, 1); favorite name der Lieblingsname, -n (wk.) (A); first name der Vorname, -n (wk.) (A, 1); my name is . . . ich heiße . . . (A); what's your name? wie heißen Sie? (for.) / wie heißt du? (infor.) (A)

named: to be named heißen (heißt), hieß, geheißen (A)

napkin die Serviette, -n (8)

narrow eng (12); narrow street die Gasse, -n (10)

national holiday der Nationalfeiertag, -e (4)

nationality die Herkunft, ⸚e (B); die Staatsangehörigkeit, -en (1)

natural science die Naturwissenschaft, -en (9)

naturally natürlich (2)

nature die Natur (9)

near bei (+ dat.) (10)

neat toll (2); grell (2)

neck der Hals, ⸚e (9)

necklace die Halskette, -n (2, 5)

to need brauchen, gebraucht (1)

neighbor der Nachbar, -n (wk.) / die Nachbarin, -nen (4)

neighborhood der Stadtteil, -e (6); das Stadtviertel, - (6)

neo-Nazi der Neonazi, -s (12)

nephew der Neffe, -n (wk.) (B)

nervous nervös (B)

nest das Nest, -er (10)

Netherlands die Niederlande (pl.) (B)

never nie (2)

new neu (A)

New Zealand (das) Neuseeland (B)

news die Nachrichten (pl.) (7)

newspaper die Zeitung, -en (2); daily newspaper die Tageszeitung, -en (5); to deliver newspapers Zeitungen austragen (5); to read the newspaper Zeitung lesen (1); university newspaper die Unizeitung, -en (4)

next to neben (+ dat./acc.) (9); next to each other nebeneinander (8); next door nebenan (5); from next door von nebenan (5)

nice nett (B); (weather) schön (B)

nickname der Spitzname, -n (wk.) (1)

niece die Nichte, -n (B)

night die Nacht, ⸚e (3); all night long die ganze Nacht (3); at night, nights nachts (4); in the middle of the night mitten in der Nacht (9); last night gestern Abend (4)

nightshirt das Nachthemd, -en (2)

nine neun (A)

nineteen neunzehn (A)

ninety neunzig (A)

ninth neunt- (4)

no nein (A); kein(e) (2); no one niemand (2)

nobody niemand (2)

noise das Geräusch, -e (9)

none kein(e) (2)

nonsense der Unsinn (12)

nonsmoker der Nichtraucher, - / die Nichtraucherin, -nen (10)

noodle die Nudel, -n (8)

noon der Mittag, -e (3); at noon mittags (2)

normal normal (5)

normally normalerweise (8)

north (of) nördlich (von + dat.) (7)

North Sea die Nordsee (B)

northeast (of) nordöstlich (von + dat.) (7)

Northern Ireland (das) Nordirland (B)

northwest (of) nordwestlich (von + dat.) (7)

Norway (das) Norwegen (B)

nose die Nase, -n (11)

no-stopping zone das Halteverbot, -e (7)

not nicht (A); not a bit gar nicht (3); not at all kein bisschen (3); gar nicht (9); not until erst (4); not until four o'clock erst um vier Uhr (4)

note (*of currency*) der Schein, -e (8); der Geld-schein, -e (12); twenty-euro note der Zwan-zigeuroschein, -e (8);

notebook das Heft, -e (B)

nothing nichts (9)

notice: not to notice verfehlen, verfehlt (10)

noticeable: to be noticeable auf·fallen (fällt ... auf), fiel ... auf, ist aufgefallen (12)

novel der Roman, -e (3, 5); romance novel der Liebesroman, -e (9)

November der November (B)

now jetzt (3)

number die Zahl, -en (A); die Nummer, -n (1); house number die Hausnummer, -n (1); license plate number die Autonummer, -n (11); ordinal number die Ordinalzahl, -en (4); telephone number die Telefonnummer, -n (1)

nurse der Krankenpfleger, - / die Krankenpfle-gerin, -nen (5); to nurse pflegen, gepflegt (5)

nut die Nuss, ¨-e (8)

obligation die Pflicht, -en (3)

o'clock: at six o'clock um sechs Uhr (1); until four o'clock bis um vier Uhr (4)

October der Oktober (B)

Octoberfest (*festival held yearly during late September and early October*) das Oktoberfest, -e (7)

of von (+ *dat.*) (A, 3, 10); aus (+ *dat.*) (10)

of course! klar! (2); selbstverständlich (10)

off: to cut off ab·schneiden (schneidet ... ab), schnitt ... ab, abgeschnitten (8); to drive off los·fahren (fährt ... los), fuhr ... los, ist losge-fahren (4, 9); to take the day off blau machen, blau gemacht (3)

office das Büro, -s (5); at the office im Büro (5); doctor's office die Arztpraxis, Arztpraxen (11); office building das Bürohaus, ¨-er (6); office hour die Sprechstunde, -n (3); *office to register town residents* das Einwohnermeldeamt, ¨-er (12)

often oft (B)

oh boy! (*coll.*) Mensch! (2)

oil das Öl (5, 8); to check the oil das Öl kontrol-lieren (5); oil paint die Ölfarbe, -n (12)

old alt (A); old part of town die Altstadt, ¨-e (10)

olive die Olive, -n (8)

omelet das Omelett, -s (8)

on an (+ *acc./dat.*) (2, 4); on foot zu Fuß (3); on Saturday am Samstag (2); on the contrary sondern (11); on the first of October am ersten Oktober (4); on the phone am Telefon (2); on the road unterwegs (4, 9); on time pünktlich (4); rechtzeitig (12); on what day? an welchem Tag? (4); to turn on ein·schalten, eingeschaltet (11)

once einmal (4); once again schon wieder (3)

one eins (A); one another einander (3); one-way street die Einbahnstraße, -n (7); one-way trip die einfache Fahrt (10)

onion die Zwiebel, -n (8)

only nur (3)

open (*adj.*) offen (3); to open öffnen, geöffnet (A); auf·machen, aufgemacht (3); eröffnen, eröffnet (9); to open a bank account ein Konto eröffnen (5); out in the open (country) in freier Natur (10)

opener: bottle opener der Flaschenöffner, - (8); can opener der Dosenöffner, - (8)

open-face sandwich das belegte Brot, die beleg-ten Brote (8)

opposite gegenüber (6)

optimistic optimistisch (B)

or (*coord. conj.*) oder (A, 11)

oral report: to give an oral report ein Referat halten (4)

orange (*n.*) die Apfelsine, -n (8); orange juice der Orangensaft (8)

orange (*adj.*) orange (A)

orchestra conductor der Dirigent, -en (*wk.*) / die Dirigentin, -nen (5)

order die Reihenfolge, -n (2); in order to um ... zu (12); to order (*food*) bestellen, bestellt (8)

ordinal number die Ordinalzahl, -en (4)

organ (*musical instrument*) die Orgel, -n (12)

origin die Herkunft, ¨-e (B)

other: each other einander (3); next to each other nebeneinander (8); other things Sonstiges (9); with each other miteinander (3)

otherwise sonst (B)

our unser(e) (2)

out: out of aus (+ *dat.*) (10); out in the open (country) in freier Natur (10); out this way heraus (10); to go out aus·gehen (geht ... aus), ging ... aus, ist ausgegangen (1); to go out (*power*) aus·fallen (fällt ... aus), fiel ... aus, ist ausgefallen (8)

outside draußen (11); outside of außerhalb (+ *gen.*) (12)

oven der Backofen, ¨- (5)

over (*prep.*) über (+ *dat./acc.*) (4); (*adv.*) vor-bei (9); over that way hinüber (10); over the weekend am Wochenende (1), übers Wochenende (4)

overcoat der Mantel, ¨- (A)

overdraft protection der Überziehungskredit, -e (12)

overnight: to stay overnight übernachten, über-nachtet (6)

own eigen (6)

to pack packen, gepackt (7); to pack up ein·packen, eingepackt (1)

package das Paket, -e (8)

pact der Pakt, -e (12)

page die Seite, -n (6)

pain der Schmerz, -en (11)

to paint malen, gemalt (12)

paintbrush der Pinsel, - (12)

painting das Gemälde, - (12); die Malerei (12)

Palestine (das) Palästina (B)

palm tree die Palme, -n (6)

pan die Pfanne, -n (5); der Topf, ¨-e (5)

pants die Hose, -n (A); sports pants die Sporthose, -n (2)

paper das Papier, -e (B); paper towel das Pa-piertuch, ¨-er (5); to give a paper ein Referat halten (4); toilet paper das Toilettenpapier (4)

parents die Eltern (*pl.*) (B)

park der Park, -s (1); city park der Stadtpark, -s (10); to park parken, geparkt (7); to walk in the park im Park spazieren gehen (1)

parking lot der Parkplatz, ¨-e (6); parking space die Parklücke, -n (7)

parlor: ice cream parlor das Eiscafé, -s (8)

parrot der Papagei, -en (10)

part der Teil, -e (7)

to participate mit·machen, mitgemacht (10)

particularly besonders (3)

partner der Partner, - / die Partnerin, -nen (12); work with a partner arbeiten Sie mit einem Partner (A)

partnership die Partnerschaft, -en (12)

party die Party, -s (1, 2); die Feier, -n (9); to go to a party auf eine Party gehen (1)

passenger train der Personenzug, ¨-e (7)

passport der Pass, ¨-e (7); der Reisepass, ¨-e (10)

past (*adv.*) vorbei (9); at twenty past five um zwanzig nach fünf (1)

pasture die Wiese, -n (7)

path: bicycle path der Radweg, -e (7)

patient (*n.*) der Patient, -en (*wk.*) / die Patientin, -nen (5)

patient (*adj.*) geduldig (12)

to pay zahlen, gezahlt (5); to pay (for) bezahlen, bezahlt (4); to pay attention auf·passen, aufgepasst (3); to pay attention to achten auf (+ *acc.*), geachtet (11); to pay off ab·zahlen, abgezahlt (12)

payment: means of payment das Zahlungsmittel, - (12)

pea die Erbse, -n (8)

peach der Pfirsich, -e (8)

pear die Birne, -n (8)

pedestrian der Fußgänger, - / die Fußgängerin, -nen (7); pedestrian mall die Fußgängerzone, -n (10)

pen der Stift, -e (A, B); ballpoint pen der Kugel-schreiber, - (4)

pencil der Bleistift, -e (A, B)

penicillin das Penizillin (4)

peninsula die Halbinsel, -n (7)

people die Leute (*pl.*) (7)

pepper der Pfeffer (8)

per pro (3)

percent das Prozent, -e (4)

perfect vollkommen (12)

perfume das Parfüm, -e (5)

perhaps vielleicht (2)

perm (permanent wave) die Dauerwelle, -n (11)

permit: residence permit die Aufenthaltserlaub-nis, -se (12); work permit die Arbeitserlaub-nis, -se (12); to permit erlauben, erlaubt (7) permitted: to be permitted (to) **dürfen (darf), durfte, gedurft** (3)

to persecute **verfolgen, verfolgt** (12)

person **die Person, -en** (A, 1); **der Mensch, -en** (*wk.*) (2); personal data **die Personalien** (*pl.*) (12); personal hygiene **die Körperpflege** (11)

pet **das Haustier, -e** (10)

pharmacist **der Apotheker, - / die Apothekerin, -nen** (11)

pharmacy **die Apotheke, -n** (6, 11)

photo **das Foto, -s** (1)

to photograph **fotografieren, fotografiert** (4)

physician **der Arzt, ⸚e / die Ärztin, -nen** (3, 5, 11)

physics **die Physik** (1)

piano **das Klavier, -e** (2)

to pick **pflücken, gepflückt** (9); to pick (*s.o.*) up (from a place) **ab·holen, abgeholt** (1)

pickle **die saure Gurke, die sauren Gurken** (8)

picnic **das Picknick, -s** (4)

picture **das Bild, -er** (2); to hang the picture on the wall **das Bild an die Wand hängen** (3); what do your pictures show? **was zeigen Ihre Bilder?** (A)

piece **das Stück, -e** (8); piece of furniture **das Möbelstück, -e** (6)

piercing **das Piercing, -s** (2)

pig **das Schwein, -e** (9)

pigpen **der Schweinestall, ⸚e** (5)

pill **die Tablette, -n** (11)

pillow **das Kopfkissen, -** (6)

pilot **der Pilot, -en** (*wk.*) **/ die Pilotin, -nen** (5)

PIN: secret PIN **die Geheimzahl, -en** (12)

pink **rosa** (A)

piranha **der Piranha, -s** (10)

pizza **die Pizza, -s** (2)

place **der Ort, -e** (1, 4); **der Platz, ⸚e** (3); **die Lage, -n** (10); at your place **bei dir** (3); is this seat/place available? **ist hier noch frei?** (8); to place (*in a sitting position*) **setzen, gesetzt** (7); to place (*in an upright position*) **stellen, gestellt** (3, 5); to take place **statt·finden (findet ... statt), fand ... statt, stattgefunden** (5)

plan **der Plan, ⸚e** (3); to plan **planen, geplant** (7); to plan (to) **wollen (will), wollte, gewollt** (3)

plant **die Pflanze, -n** (3, 6)

plate **der Teller, -** (8); license plate **das Nummernschild, -er** (7); license plate number **die Autonummer, -n** (11)

play **das Schauspiel, -e** (12); to play **spielen, gespielt** (1)

player: CD player **der CD-Spieler, -** (2); DVD player **der DVD-Spieler, -** (2, 3); MP3 player **der MP3-Spieler, -** (5); soccer player **der Fußballspieler, - / die Fußballspielerin, -nen** (9); tennis player **der Tennisspieler, - / die Tennisspielerin, -nen** (9)

playground **der Spielplatz, ⸚e** (9)

playwright **der Dramatiker, - / die Dramatikerin, -nen** (9)

pleasant **angenehm** (6)

please **bitte** (A); to please **gefallen (+ *dat.*)**

(**gefällt**), **gefiel, gefallen** (6); yes please? **bitte schön?** (7)

pleasure **das Vergnügen** (2); **die Freude, -n** (9); with pleasure **gern** (1)

pliers **die Zange, -n** (8)

plum **die Pflaume, -n** (8)

pneumonia **die Lungenentzündung** (11)

pocket **die Tasche, -n** (1)

poem **das Gedicht, -e** (3)

point **der Punkt, -e** (3); main point **der Stichpunkt, -e** (12)

to poison **vergiften, vergiftet** (9)

poisonous **giftig** (9)

Poland **(das) Polen** (B)

police officer **der Polizist, -en** (*wk.*) **/ die Polizistin, -nen** (5); police station **die Polizei** (5); at the police station **auf der Polizei** (5)

political(ly) **politisch** (4)

politics **die Politik** (5)

pool: swimming pool **das Schwimmbad, ⸚er** (1, 5); at the swimming pool **im Schwimmbad** (5); to go to the swimming pool **ins Schwimmbad fahren** (1)

poor **arm** (9)

popular **beliebt** (3)

pork **das Schweinefleisch** (8); ground pork **das Hackfleisch** (8)

port **der Hafen, ⸚** (10)

Portugal **(das) Portugal** (B)

Portuguese (*language*) **(das) Portugiesisch** (B)

position **die Lage, -n** (10)

possessions **der Besitz** (2)

possibility **die Möglichkeit, -en** (5)

possible: as . . . as possible **möglichst ...** (6); everything possible **alles Mögliche** (2)

post office **die Post** (5); at the post office **auf der Post** (5)

postal employee **der/die Postangestellte, -n (ein Postangestellter)** (5)

postcard **die Postkarte, -n** (2)

poster **das Poster, -** (6)

pot **der Topf, ⸚e** (5)

potato **die Kartoffel, -n** (8); boiled potatoes **die Salzkartoffeln** (*pl.*) (8)

potholder **der Topflappen, -** (5)

potter's wheel **die Töpferscheibe, -n** (12)

poultry **das Geflügel** (8)

pound **das Pfund, -e** (5)

to pour **gießen (gießt), goss, gegossen** (8)

power **der Strom** (8)

practical **praktisch** (5); practical (career) training **praktische Ausbildung** (5)

to practice **aus·üben, ausgeübt** (12)

preference **die Präferenz, -en** (1)

prejudice **das Vorurteil, -e** (12)

prenuptial agreement **der Ehevertrag, ⸚e** (12)

preparation **die Zubereitung, -en** (8)

to prepare (*food*) **zu·bereiten, zubereitet** (8)

prescription **das Rezept, -e** (11)

present **das Geschenk, -e** (2); Christmas present **das Weihnachtsgeschenk, -e** (5); to

present **vor·stellen, vorgestellt** (6); to present (*documents*) **vor·legen, vorgelegt** (10)

president **der Präsident, -en** (*wk.*) **/ die Präsidentin, -nen** (5)

pressure: blood pressure **der Blutdruck** (11); to have low/high blood pressure **niedrigen/hohen Blutdruck haben** (11)

prestige **das Prestige** (5)

pretty **hübsch** (A, 2); **schön** (B); pretty big **ziemlich groß** (2)

price **der Preis, -e** (7)

priest **der Priester, - / die Priesterin, -nen** (5)

prince **der Prinz, -en** (*wk.*) (9)

princess **die Prinzessin, -nen** (9)

principal **der Direktor, -en** (*wk.*) **/ die Direktorin, -nen** (9)

prison **das Gefängnis, -se** (6)

prize **der Preis, -e** (12)

probably **wahrscheinlich** (1); **wohl** (12)

processing: electronic data processing **die EDV = elektronische Datenverarbeitung** (12)

to produce (*documents*) **vor·legen, vorgelegt** (10)

profession **der Beruf, -e** (1, 5); what's your profession? **was sind Sie von Beruf?** (1)

professional life **das Berufsleben** (12)

professor **der Professor, -en / die Professorin, -nen** (A, B)

progressive **progressiv** (B)

prohibition **das Verbot, -e** (7)

to promise **versprechen (verspricht), versprach, versprochen** (7)

to promote **fördern, gefördert** (12)

promoted (*to next grade in school*) **versetzt** (3)

protected **geborgen** (12)

protection: overdraft protection **der Überziehungskredit, -e** (12)

protector **der Beschützer, - / die Beschützerin, -nen** (12)

to protest **protestieren, protestiert** (12)

proximity **die Nähe** (7)

psychiatrist **der Psychiater, - / die Psychiaterin, -nen** (11)

public: public authority **die Behörde, -n** (12); public transportation **die öffentlichen Verkehrsmittel** (*pl.*) (7)

to pull **ziehen (zieht), zog, gezogen** (8)

pullover **der Pullover, - (der Pulli, -s)** (2)

punctual **pünktlich** (4)

pupil **der Schüler, - / die Schülerin, -nen** (1)

purple **lila** (A)

purse **die Tasche, -n** (1)

to put (*in a sitting position*) **setzen, gesetzt** (7); to put (*in an upright position*) **stellen, gestellt** (3, 5); to put (into) **geben (in + *acc.*) (gibt), gab, gegeben** (8); to put away **weg·stellen, weggestellt** (5); to put on **an·legen, angelegt** (10); to put on (*clothes*) **an·ziehen (zieht ... an), zog ... an, angezogen** (3)

puzzle **das Rätsel, -** (9)

python **die Riesenschlange, -n** (10)

to quarrel **streiten (streitet), stritt, gestritten** (9)

quarter: at a quarter to four **um Viertel vor vier** (1); quarter hour **die Viertelstunde, -n** (6)

queen **die Königin, -nen** (9)

question **die Frage, -n** (A); to ask a question **eine Frage stellen** (A, 5)

quick **schnell** (3)

quiet(ly) **ruhig** (B); **leise** (9)

quite **ganz** (2); quite a bit **ganz schön viel** (3)

rabies **die Tollwut** (10)

radio **das Radio, -s** (2); car radio **das Autoradio, -s** (7)

rag (*for cleaning*) **der Putzlappen, -** (6)

railroad **die Bahn, -en** (7)

railway: cable railway **die Seilbahn, -en** (7)

rain **der Regen** (7)

raining: it is raining **es regnet** (B)

rainy: in rainy weather **bei Regen** (7)

range of mountains **das Gebirge, -** (7)

rare(ly) **selten** (8)

rat **die Ratte, -n** (10)

rather **ziemlich** (2); **lieber** (2); **eher** (12); I'd rather go . . . **ich gehe lieber ...** (2)

rattlesnake **die Klapperschlange, -n** (10)

to reach **erreichen, erreicht** (12)

to read **lesen (liest), las, gelesen** (A, 1); to read aloud **vor·lesen (liest ... vor), las ... vor, vorgelesen** (9); to read the newspaper **Zeitung lesen** (1)

ready **fertig** (3)

real(ly) **echt** (2); really **wirklich** (B)

receipt **die Quittung, -en** (8)

to receive **bekommen (bekommt), bekam, bekommen** (3)

recently **neulich** (9)

reception **die Rezeption, -en** (10)

recess **die Pause, -n** (1)

recipient (*of a prize*) **der Träger, -** (12)

recorder **die Blockflöte, -n** (12)

recreation room **der Aufenthaltsraum, ⁼e** (10)

to recuperate **sich erholen, erholt** (11)

red **rot** (A)

refrigerator **der Kühlschrank, ⁼e** (5)

refugee **der Flüchtling, -e** (12)

regards **mit freundlichen Grüßen** (10)

to register **sich an·melden, angemeldet** (12); to get registered **sich registrieren lassen** (12); *office to register town residents* **das Einwohnermeldeamt, ⁼er** (12)

regularly **regelmäßig** (11)

relative **relativ** (5)

relatives **die Verwandten** (*pl.*) (2)

religion **die Religion** (1)

religious **religiös** (B); religious denomination **die Konfession, -en** (12)

to remain **bleiben (bleibt), blieb, ist geblieben** (1)

to remember **sich erinnern (an + *acc.*), erinnert** (9)

remembrance **die Erinnerung, -en** (4)

to remove **ab·nehmen (nimmt ... ab), nahm ... ab, abgenommen** (11)

rent **die Miete, -n** (6); to rent **mieten, gemietet** (6); to rent out **vermieten, vermietet** (6)

renter **der Mieter, - / die Mieterin, -nen** (6)

to repair **reparieren, repariert** (1); repair shop **die Werkstatt, ⁼en** (5)

to repeat **wiederholen, wiederholt** (10)

report **das Referat, -e** (3); accident report **der Unfallbericht, -e** (11); to give an oral report **ein Referat halten** (4)

reporter **der Reporter, - / die Reporterin, -nen** (4); TV reporter **der Fernsehreporter, - / die Fernsehreporterin, -nen** (5)

requirement **die Pflicht, -en** (3)

to rescue **erlösen, erlöst** (9)

to reserve **reservieren, reserviert** (7)

residence **der Wohnort, -e** (1); residence permit **die Aufenthaltserlaubnis, -se** (12)

resident: *office to register town residents* **das Einwohnermeldeamt, ⁼er** (12)

responsibility **die Verantwortung, -en** (12)

to rest **sich aus·ruhen, ausgeruht** (11)

restaurant **das Restaurant, -s** (2, 8); **die Gaststätte, -n** (5); at the restaurant **im Restaurant** (8); **in der Gaststätte** (5)

to return **zurück·kommen (kommt ... zurück), kam ... zurück, ist zurückgekommen** (6)

reunion: class reunion **das Klassentreffen, -** (9)

rice **der Reis** (8)

riddle **das Rätsel, -** (9); to solve a riddle **ein Rätsel lösen** (9)

to ride **reiten (reitet), ritt, ist geritten** (1); **fahren (fährt), fuhr, ist/hat gefahren** (2); to ride a motorcycle **Motorrad fahren** (1); to ride off **los·fahren (fährt ... los), fuhr ... los, ist losgefahren** (9)

right (*adj.*) **richtig** (2); (*adv.*) **rechts** (10); right across the way **gleich gegenüber** (6); right away **gleich** (4); that's right **stimmt!** (4); **das stimmt so** (8); to be right **recht haben (hat ... recht), hatte ... recht, recht gehabt** (2); to be right **stimmen, gestimmt** (8); to the right **rechts** (7)

right-of-way **die Vorfahrt, -en** (7)

right-wing extremist **der Rechtsextremist, -en** (*wk.*) (12)

ring **der Ring, -e** (2)

to ring **klingeln, geklingelt** (2)

to rinse **spülen, gespült** (4)

river **der Fluss, ⁼e** (7)

road **die Straße, -n** (6); on the road **unterwegs** (4, 9)

roast **der Braten, -** (8)

roasted **gebraten** (8)

rock concert **das Rockkonzert, -e** (9)

rocket **die Rakete, -n** (7)

role **die Rolle, -n** (4); role model **das Vorbild, -er** (9)

roll **das Brötchen, -** (8)

romance novel **der Liebesroman, -e** (9)

Romania **(das) Rumänien** (B)

roof **das Dach, ⁼er** (6)

room **das Zimmer, -** (1); bedroom **das Schlafzimmer, -** (6); breakfast room **das Frühstückszimmer, -** (10); dining room **das Esszimmer, -** (6); double room **das Doppelzimmer, -** (10); dressing room **die Umkleidekabine, -n** (5); laundry room **die Waschküche, -n** (6); living room **das Wohnzimmer, -** (6); recreation room **der Aufenthaltsraum, ⁼e** (10); single room **das Einzelzimmer, -** (5); TV room **das Fernsehzimmer, -** (10)

roommate **der Mitbewohner, - / die Mitbewohnerin, -nen** (2)

roundabout: traffic roundabout **der Kreisverkehr, -e** (10)

round-trip **hin und zurück** (5, 10); **die Hin- und Rückfahrt** (10)

routine: daily routine **der Alltag** (4)

row: in a row **hintereinander** (3); row house **das Reihenhaus, ⁼er** (6)

rump steak **das Rumpsteak, -s** (8)

to run **laufen (läuft), lief, ist gelaufen** (A, 2); **rennen (rennt), rannte, ist gerannt** (7); to run in the woods **im Wald laufen** (2); to run over **überfahren (überfährt), überfuhr, überfahren** (11)

rural highway **die Landstraße, -n** (7)

rushed **eilig** (10)

Russia **(das) Russland** (B)

Russian (*adj.*) **russisch** (12); (*language*) **(das) Russisch** (B)

rusty **rostig** (8)

sad **traurig** (B)

safety belt **der Sicherheitsgurt, -e** (7)

to sail **segeln, ist/hat gesegelt** (1)

salad **der Salat, -e** (8); herring salad **der Heringssalat, -e** (8); salad (mixing) bowl **die Salatschüssel, -n** (5); salad dressing **die Soße, -n** (8)

salesperson **der Verkäufer, - / die Verkäuferin, -nen** (5)

salon: tanning salon **das Solarium, Solarien** (11)

salt **das Salz** (8)

salted **gesalzen** (8)

salty **salzig** (7)

same **egal** (6)

sand **der Sand** (7)

sandcastle **die Sandburg, -en** (4)

sandwich: (open-face) sandwich **das belegte Brot, die belegten Brote** (8)

Saturday **der Samstag** (1); on Saturday **am Samstag** (2)

sauce **die Soße, -n** (8)

sauerkraut **das Sauerkraut** (7)

sauna **die Sauna, -s** (11)

sausage **die Wurst, ⁼e** (8)

to save (*money*) **sparen, gespart** (7)

savings account **das Sparkonto, -konten** (12)

to say **sagen, gesagt** (A, 5); to say hi to **grüßen, gegrüßt** (11)

scale: kitchen scale **die Küchenwaage, -n** (5)

scar die Narbe, -n (1)

scarf der Schal, -s (2)

scene of the accident die Unfallstelle, -n (11)

schedule der Stundenplan, ⸚e (1)

schilling (*former Austrian monetary unit*) der Schilling, -e (7); two schillings zwei Schilling (7)

scholarship das Stipendium, Stipendien (1)

school die Schule, -n (A, 1, 3, 4, 5); at school in der Schule (5); elementary school die Grundschule, -n (4); high school, college prep school das Gymnasium, Gymnasien (4); school principal der Direktor, -en (*wk.*) / die Direktorin, -nen (9) summer school der Sommerkurs, -e (3)

schooling die Schulbildung (5)

science: computer science die Informatik (1); earth science die Erdkunde (1); natural science die Naturwissenschaft, -en (9)

scientist der Wissenschaftler, - / die Wissenschaftlerin, -nen (9)

scissors die Schere, -n (8)

to scold schimpfen, geschimpft (9)

scorpion der Skorpion, -e (10)

to scream schreien (schreit), schrie, geschrien (3)

sculptor der Bildhauer, - / die Bildhauerin, -nen (12)

sculpture die Skulptur, -en (12); die Bildhauerei (12)

sea das Meer, -e (1, 7); to swim in the sea im Meer schwimmen (1); to the sea ans Meer (2)

seagull die Möwe, -n (10)

seasick seekrank (7)

to season würzen, gewürzt (8)

seasoning das Gewürz, -e (8)

seat der Sitz, -e (7); is this seat/place available? ist hier noch frei? (8)

second (*n.*) die Sekunde, -n (1)

second (*adj.*) zweit- (4)

secret (*n.*) das Geheimnis, -se (5)

secret (*adj.*) heimlich (9); secret PIN die Geheimzahl, -en (12)

secretary der Sekretär, -e / die Sekretärin, -nen (5)

sector der Bereich, -e (12); die Branche, -n (12)

security deposit die Kaution, -en (6)

to see sehen (sieht), sah, gesehen (2); see you soon bis bald! (A)

seldom selten (8)

to select aus·wählen, ausgewählt (8)

to sell verkaufen, verkauft (2, 5)

semester das Semester, - (1)

to send schicken, geschickt (2)

sentence der Satz, ⸚e (3)

to separate trennen, getrennt (7)

separately; separate checks (*in restaurant*) getrennt (5)

September der September (B)

sequence die Reihenfolge, -n (2, 4)

serious ernsthaft (B)

servant der Diener, - / die Dienerin, -nen (9)

service die Bedienung (8)

to set decken, gedeckt (3); setzen, gesetzt (7); to set the table den Tisch decken (3); to set up auf·stellen, aufgestellt (11)

seven sieben (A)

seventeen siebzehn (A)

seventh siebt- (4)

seventy siebzig (A)

several mehrere (10); several times mehrmals (5)

shade, shadow der Schatten, - (9)

to shake hands die Hand schütteln (A)

share (*of stock*) die Aktie, -n (12)

shared housing die Wohngemeinschaft, -en (6)

shark der Hai, -e (10)

to shave sich rasieren, rasiert (11)

shirt das Hemd, -en (A); T-shirt das T-Shirt, -s (2)

shock der Schock (11)

shoe der Schuh, -e (A); athletic shoe der Sportschuh, -e (A); hiking shoe der Wanderschuh, -e (2); shoe store das Schuhgeschäft, -e (6)

shop: copy shop der Kopierladen, ⸚ (10); repair shop die Werkstatt, ⸚en (5); to shop, to go shopping einkaufen gehen (geht ... einkaufen), ging ... einkaufen, ist einkaufen gegangen (1, 5)

shopping center das Einkaufszentrum, -zentren (10)

shore der Strand, ⸚e (7)

short klein (B); kurz (B); short hair kurzes Haar (B); with the short hair mit dem kurzen Haar (A)

shot die Spritze, -n (11)

shoulder die Schulter, -n (B)

to shout rufen (ruft), rief, gerufen (7)

to shovel schaufeln, geschaufelt (11)

to show: what do your pictures show? was zeigen Ihre Bilder? (A)

shower die Dusche, -n (5); to shower, to take a shower (sich) duschen, geduscht (1, 11)

shrill grell (2)

shrimp die Krabbe, -n (8)

to shut schließen (schließt), schloss, geschlossen (A); tied shut zugebunden (8)

shy schüchtern (B)

siblings die Geschwister (*pl.*) (B)

sick krank (3)

sickness die Krankheit, -en (11)

side die Seite, -n (6)

sidewalk der Fußgängerweg, -e (7)

to sightsee besichtigen, besichtigt (7)

sign das Schild, -er (7); traffic sign das Verkehrsschild, -er (7); to sign unterschreiben (unterschreibt), unterschrieb, unterschrieben (1); sign here, please unterschreib bitte hier (A)

signature die Unterschrift, -en (1)

sill: windowsill die Fensterbank, ⸚e (5)

silverware das Besteck (5)

similar ähnlich (A)

simple, simply einfach (2)

since seit (+ *dat.*) (4, 11)

to sing singen (singt), sang, gesungen (1); to

sing (*s.th.*) to (*s.o.*) vor·singen (singt ... vor), sang ... vor, vorgesungen (5); we like to sing wir singen gern (1)

single room das Einzelzimmer, - (5)

single-family home das Einfamilienhaus, ⸚er (6)

sink das Spülbecken, - (5)

sister die Schwester, -n (B); brothers and sisters die Geschwister (*pl.*) (B)

to sit sitzen (sitzt), saß, gesessen (4); to sit down sich setzen, gesetzt (A, 11)

situation: conversational situation die Sprechsituation, -en (A)

six sechs (A)

sixteen sechzehn (A)

sixth sechst- (4)

sixty sechzig (A)

skate: ice skate der Schlittschuh, -e (3); to go ice-skating Schlittschuh laufen (läuft ... Schlittschuh), lief ... Schlittschuh, ist Schlittschuh gelaufen (3)

skateboard das Skateboard, -s (3); to skateboard Skateboard fahren (fährt ... Skateboard), fuhr ... Skateboard, ist Skateboard gefahren (3)

ski der Ski, -er (3); to ski Ski fahren (fährt ... Ski), fuhr ... Ski, ist Ski gefahren (3); ski lodge die Skihütte, -n (5)

skills die Kenntnisse (*pl.*) (5)

skin die Haut, ⸚e (3, 11)

skirt der Rock, ⸚e (A)

sled der Schlitten, - (2)

sleep der Schlaf (9); to sleep schlafen (schläft), schlief, geschlafen (2)

sleeping bag der Schlafsack, ⸚e (2); sleeping car der Schlafwagen, - (4)

slender schlank (B)

slice das Stück, -e (8)

to slide rutschen, ist gerutscht (9)

slim schlank (B)

to slip rutschen, ist gerutscht (9); aus·rutschen, ist ausgerutscht (11)

Slovakia die Slowakei (B)

Slovenia (das) Slowenien (B)

small klein (B); eng (12)

to smell riechen (riecht), roch, gerochen (11)

to smoke rauchen, geraucht (3)

smoked geräuchert (8)

smoker der Raucher, - / die Raucherin, -nen (10)

snail die Schnecke, -n (10)

snake die Schlange, -n (10)

sniffles der Schnupfen, - (11)

snow der Schnee (9)

snowing: it is snowing es schneit (B)

so so (A); also (2); and so forth und so weiter (5); so long bis bald! (A); so that (*subord. conj.*) damit (11)

soap die Seife, -n (6)

soccer: soccer ball der Fußball, ⸚e (A, 1); soccer player der Fußballspieler, - / die Fußballspielerin, -nen (9); soccer stadium das Fußballstadion, -stadien (10) social studies **die Sozialkunde** (1)

sociology **die Soziologie** (1)

sock **die Socke, -n** (2)

sofa **das Sofa, -s** (6)

sold out **ausverkauft** (5)

to solve a puzzle/riddle **ein Rätsel lösen, gelöst** (9)

somebody, someone **jemand** (3)

something **etwas** (2, 4, 5); something interesting/new **etwas Interessantes/Neues** (4)

sometimes **manchmal** (B)

son **der Sohn, ⸚e** (B)

song **das Lied, -er** (3)

songbook **das Songbuch, ⸚er** (2)

soon **bald** (9); see you soon **bis bald!** (A); soon thereafter **bald darauf** (9)

sore muscles **der Muskelkater, -** (11); sore throat **die Halsschmerzen** (*pl.*) (11)

sorry: to be sorry **leid·tun (tut ... leid), tat ... leid, leidgetan** (5); I'm sorry **tut mir leid** (4, 5)

soul **die Seele, -n** (12)

sound **das Geräusch, -e** (9)

to sound (like) **klingen (wie) (klingt), klang, geklungen** (11); that sounds great **das hört sich toll an** (4)

soup **die Suppe, -n** (8)

sour **sauer** (8)

south (of) **südlich (von + *dat.*)** (7)

South Africa **(das) Südafrika** (B)

South America **(das) Südamerika** (B)

southeast (of) **südöstlich (von + *dat.*)** (7)

southwest (of) **südwestlich (von + *dat.*)** (7)

souvenir **das Souvenir, -s** (7); **das Andenken, -** (10)

space: parking space **die Parklücke, -n** (7)

spaghetti **die Spaghetti** (*pl.*) (7)

Spain **(das) Spanien** (B)

Spanish (*language*) **(das) Spanisch** (B)

to speak **sprechen (spricht), sprach, gesprochen** (B)

speaking: German-speaking **deutschsprachig** (9)

specialized training **die Ausbildung** (5)

spell: to cast a spell on **verwünschen, verwünscht** (9)

to spell **schreiben (schreibt), schrieb, geschrieben** (A); how do you spell that? **wie schreibt man das?** (A)

to spend (*money*) **aus·geben (gibt ... aus), gab ... aus, ausgegeben** (3); to spend (*time*) **verbringen (verbringt), verbrachte, verbracht** (3)

spice **das Gewürz, -e** (8)

spinach **der Spinat** (8)

spite: in spite of **trotz (+ *gen.*)** (12); in spite of that **trotzdem** (9)

spoon **der Löffel, -** (8)

sports **der Sport** (1); to do sports **Sport treiben (treibt ... Sport), trieb ... Sport, Sport getrieben** (2); sports jacket **das Sakko, -s** (A); sports pants **die Sporthose, -n** (2)

spouse **der Ehepartner, - / die Ehepartnerin, -nen** (12)

spring **der Frühling, -e** (B); in the spring **im Frühling** (B); spring cleaning **der Frühjahrsputz** (6)

to sprinkle **bestreuen, bestreut** (8)

square: market square **der Marktplatz, ⸚e** (6); square meter (m^2) **der Quadratmeter, - (qm)** (6)

squash (*game*) **das Squash** (1)

stadium: soccer stadium **das Fußballstadion, -stadien** (10)

stairway **die Treppe, -n** (6)

stairwell **das Treppenhaus, ⸚er** (10)

stamp **die Briefmarke, -n** (5)

to stand **stehen (steht), stand, gestanden** (2, 6); to stand up **auf·stehen (steht ... auf), stand ... auf, ist aufgestanden** (A)

state **der Staat, -en** (10)

station: train station **der Bahnhof, ⸚e** (4, 5); at the train station **auf dem Bahnhof** (5)

stationery store **das Schreibwarengeschäft, -e** (6)

to stay **bleiben (bleibt), blieb, ist geblieben** (1); to stay overnight **übernachten, übernachtet** (6)

steak: rump steak **das Rumpsteak, -s** (8)

to steal **stehlen (stiehlt), stahl, gestohlen** (9)

steering wheel **das Lenkrad, ⸚er** (7)

stepfather **der Stiefvater, ⸚** (9)

stepmother **die Stiefmutter, ⸚** (9)

stereo system **die Stereoanlage, -n** (6)

still **noch** (B)

to sting **stechen (sticht), stach, gestochen** (10)

stock **die Aktie, -n** (12); stock exchange **die Börse, -n** (12); stock market crash **der Börsenkrach, ⸚e** (12)

stomach **der Bauch, ⸚e** (B); **der Magen, ⸚** (11)

stomachache **die Magenschmerzen** (*pl.*) (11)

stone **der Stein, -e** (12); Stone Age **die Steinzeit** (12)

stop **die Haltestelle, -n** (10); bus stop **die Bushaltestelle, -n** (6); to stop **an·halten (hält ... an), hielt ... an, angehalten** (7); **halten (hält), hielt, gehalten** (7); to stop (*doing s.th.*) **auf·hören (mit + *dat.*), aufgehört** (1)

store **das Geschäft, -e** (2); department store **das Kaufhaus, ⸚er** (5); at the department store **im Kaufhaus** (5)

story (*of a building*) **der Stock, Stockwerke** (6)

stove **der Herd, -e** (5)

to stow **verstauen, verstaut** (7)

straight ahead **geradeaus** (10)

to straighten **gerade stellen** (3)

strange **komisch** (12)

strawberry **die Erdbeere, -n** (8)

street **die Straße, -n** (6); city street map **der Stadtplan, ⸚e** (10); narrow street **die Gasse, -n** (10); one-way street **die Einbahnstraße, -n** (7)

streetcar **die Straßenbahn, -en** (7)

strict **streng** (9)

string **die Schnur, ⸚e** (8)

stuck: to get stuck **stecken bleiben (bleibt ... stecken), blieb ... stecken, ist stecken geblieben** (11)

student **der Student, -en** (*wk.*) / **die Studentin, -nen** (A, B); fellow student **der Mitstudent, -en** (*wk.*) / **die Mitstudentin, -nen** (A); student life **das Studentenleben** (4)

study: course of studies, university studies **das Studium, Studien** (1, 3); to study **studieren, studiert** (1)

stupid **dumm** (6)

stylish **schick** (2)

subject **das Thema, Themen** (4); academic subject **das Fach, ⸚er** (1); academic subjects **Schul- und Studienfächer** (1); favorite subject **das Lieblingsfach, ⸚er** (5)

subway **die U-Bahn (Untergrundbahn), -en** (7)

to suck **lutschen, gelutscht** (11)

suddenly **plötzlich** (9)

sugar **der Zucker** (8)

to suggest **vor·schlagen (schlägt ... vor), schlug ... vor, vorgeschlagen** (5)

suggestion **der Vorschlag, ⸚e** (5)

suit **der Anzug, ⸚e** (A); bathing suit **der Badeanzug, ⸚e** (5); to suit **stehen (+ *dat.*) (steht), stand, gestanden** (6)

summer **der Sommer, -** (B); last summer **letzten Sommer** (4); summer school **der Sommerkurs, -e** (3)

sun: to lie in the sun **in der Sonne liegen** (1)

to sunbathe **sich sonnen, gesonnt** (11)

sunbathing: to go sunbathing **sonnenbaden gehen** (10)

sunburn **der Sonnenbrand, ⸚e** (10)

Sunday **der Sonntag** (1)

sunglasses **die Sonnenbrille, -n** (1, 2)

sunny **sonnig** (B)

sunshade **der Sonnenschirm, -e** (10)

suntan lotion **die Sonnenmilch** (10)

superfast **superschnell** (7)

supermarket **der Supermarkt, ⸚e** (5); at the supermarket **im Supermarkt** (5)

supper **das Abendessen, -** (1)

supposed: to be supposed to **sollen (soll), sollte, gesollt** (3)

sure **sicher** (1)

surface **die Fläche, -n** (7)

surfboard **das Surfbrett, -er** (2)

surrounding area **die Umgebung, -en** (5)

survey **die Umfrage, -n** (4)

to swear **fluchen, geflucht** (11)

sweater **der Pullover, - (der Pulli, -s)** (2)

Sweden **(das) Schweden** (B)

Swedish (*language*) **(das) Schwedisch** (B)

to sweep **fegen, gefegt** (5)

sweet (*adj.*) **süß** (4); **lieb** (10); (*n.*) **die Süßigkeit, -en** (9)

to swim **schwimmen (schwimmt), schwamm, ist geschwommen** (7); to swim in the sea **im Meer schwimmen** (1)

swimming: to go swimming **schwimmen gehen (geht ... schwimmen), ging ... schwimmen, ist schwimmen gegangen** (1); swimming pool **das Schwimmbad, ⸚er** (1, 5); at the swimming pool im Schwimmbad (5); to go to the swimming pool ins Schwimmbad fahren (1); swimming pool attendant der Bademeister, - / die Bademeisterin, -nen (5); swimming trunks die Badehose, -n (5)

Swiss (*person*) der Schweizer, - / die Schweizerin, -nen (B)

to switch on an·machen, angemacht (3)

Switzerland die Schweiz (B)

symptom das Symptom, -e (11)

syrup: cough syrup der Hustensaft, ⁼e (11)

table der Tisch, -e (B); bedside table der Nachttisch, -e (6); to clear the table den Tisch ab·räumen (3); kitchen table der Küchentisch, -e (5); to set the table den Tisch decken (3); table tennis das Tischtennis (3)

tablet die Tablette, -n (11); headache tablet die Kopfschmerztablette, -n (11)

to take nehmen (nimmt), nahm, genommen (A); to take (*a course*) belegen, belegt (3); to take along mit·nehmen (nimmt ... mit), nahm ... mit, mitgenommen (3); to take away, take out weg·bringen (bringt ... weg), brachte ... weg, weggebracht (5); to take blood Blut ab·nehmen (11); take care (*infor.*) mach's gut! (A); to take effect wirken, gewirkt (11); to take off (*clothes*) aus·ziehen (zieht ... aus), zog ... aus, ausgezogen (3); to take on (*responsibility*) übernehmen (übernimmt), übernahm, übernommen (12); to take out (*loan*) auf·nehmen (nimmt ... auf), nahm ... auf, aufgenommen (12); to take place statt·finden (findet ... statt), fand ... statt, stattgefunden (5); to take the day off blau machen, blau gemacht (3)

tale: fairy tale das Märchen, - (9)

talent das Talent, -e (3)

tall groß (B)

tame zahm (10)

tank der Tank, -s (7)

tanning salon das Solarium, Solarien (11)

to taste probieren, probiert (3); to taste good to schmecken (+ *dat.*), geschmeckt (6)

tavern die Kneipe, -n (3)

taxi das Taxi, -s (3, 7); taxi driver der Taxifahrer, - / die Taxifahrerin, -nen (5)

tea der Tee (4); tea kettle der Teekessel, - (8)

to teach unterrichten, unterrichtet (5)

teacher der Lehrer, - / die Lehrerin, -nen (A, 1)

team die Mannschaft, -en (9); baseball team die Baseballmannschaft, -en (9)

teapot die Teekanne, -n (8)

to tear zerreißen (zerreißt), zerriss, zerrissen (9)

to tease ärgern, geärgert (3)

technology die Technik (12)

teddy bear der Teddybär, -en (*wk.*) (A); der Teddy, -s (9)

telegram das Telegramm, -e (2)

telephone das Telefon, -e (A, 2); on the telephone am Telefon (2); telephone booth die

Telefonzelle, -n (2); telephone card die Telefonkarte, -n (2); telephone number die Telefonnummer, -n (1); to telephone telefonieren, telefoniert (4)

to tell erzählen, erzählt (3, 5); sagen, gesagt (A, 5); to tell jokes Witze erzählen (3)

teller: automatic teller machine (ATM) der Geldautomat, -en (*wk.*) (12)

ten zehn (A)

tender zart (8)

tennis das Tennis (1); table tennis das Tischtennis (3); tennis player der Tennisspieler, - / die Tennisspielerin, -nen (9)

tent das Zelt, -e (2, 5)

tenth zehnt- (4)

terrace die Terrasse, -n (6)

terrible furchtbar (4)

test die Prüfung, -en (1)

tetanus der Tetanus (11)

text der Text, -e (12)

thank you danke (A)

thanks: many thanks vielen Dank (10)

that (*dem. pron.*) dieser, dieses, diese (4); (*subord. conj.*) dass (11); that is . . . das ist ... (B); that sounds great das hört sich toll an (4); that way hin (10); over that way hinüber (10); up that way hinauf (10); that's right stimmt! (4); das stimmt so (8); that's why deshalb (4)

theater das Theater, - (4)

their ihr(e) (2)

theme das Thema, Themen (4); das Motiv, -e (12)

then dann (A); back then damals (9)

there da (2); dort (7); there (*to a specific place*) dorthin (10); there and back hin und zurück (10); there is/are . . . es gibt ... (6); is/are there . . . ? gibt es ...? (A, 6)

thereafter: soon thereafter bald darauf (9)

therefore deshalb (4)

these diese (2, 4); these are . . . das sind ... (B)

thing das Ding, -e (2); die Sache, -n (2); other things Sonstiges (9)

to think (about) nach·denken (über + *acc.*) (denkt ... nach), dachte ... nach, nachgedacht (7); to think (of) denken (an + *acc.*) (denkt), dachte, gedacht (4); to think of halten von (+ *dat.*) (hält), hielt, gehalten (12)

third dritt- (4)

thirst der Durst (3)

thirsty: to be thirsty Durst haben (3)

thirteen dreizehn (A)

thirteenth dreizehnt- (4)

thirty dreißig (A)

this dieser, dieses, diese (2, 4); this evening heute Abend (2); this is . . . das ist ... (B); this way her (10); in this way herein (10); out this way heraus (10)

thorn der Dorn, -en (9)

those diese (4); those are . . . das sind ... (B)

three drei (A); three times dreimal (3)

throat der Hals, ⁼e (9); sore throat die Halsschmerzen (*pl.*) (11); throat lozenge das Halsbonbon, -s (11)

through durch (+ *acc.*) (7); to cut through durch·schneiden (schneidet ... durch), schnitt ... durch, durchgeschnitten (8)

to throw werfen (wirft), warf, geworfen (3)

Thursday der Donnerstag (1)

thus also (2)

ticket die Fahrkarte, -n (4); admissions ticket die Eintrittskarte, -n (5); concert ticket die Konzertkarte, -n (5); movie ticket die Kinokarte, -n (2); ticket booth der Schalter, - (5); at the ticket booth am Schalter (5); ticket window der Fahrkartenschalter, - (7); train ticket die Zugfahrkarte, -n (6)

tie die Krawatte, -n (A)

to tie to binden an (+ *acc.*) (bindet), band, gebunden (12)

tied shut zugebunden (8)

tight eng (12)

tights die Sporthose, -n (2)

time die Zeit, -en (4); das Mal, -e (4); at what time . . . ? um wie viel Uhr ...? (1); for the first time zum ersten Mal (4); last time das letzte Mal (4); leisure time die Freizeit (1); on time pünktlich (4); rechtzeitig (12); several times mehrmals (5); three times dreimal (3); what time is it? wie spät ist es? wie viel Uhr ist es? (1)

timely rechtzeitig (12)

tip das Trinkgeld, -er (8)

tire der Reifen, - (7); flat tire die Reifenpanne, -n (7)

tired müde (3)

to an (+ *acc./dat.*) (2); zu (+ *dat.*) (2, 10); nach (+ *dat.*) (3, 10); to a specific place dorthin (10); to the doctor zum Arzt (3); to the sea ans Meer (2); to the university zur Uni (2); up to bis zu (+ *dat.*) (10); where to wohin (3)

toaster der Toaster, - (8)

today heute (B); what day is today? welcher Tag ist heute? (1); what is today's date? welches Datum ist heute? (4)

together zusammen (2); gemeinsam (11); all together alles zusammen (5)

toilet die Toilette, -n (6); toilet paper das Toilettenpapier (4)

tolerant tolerant (B)

tomato die Tomate, -n (8)

tomorrow morgen (2); the day after tomorrow übermorgen (9)

tongs die Zange, -n (8)

tongue die Zunge, -n (11); to burn one's tongue sich die Zunge verbrennen (11)

too auch (A); zu (4); too bad schade! (3); too heavy zu schwer (4)

tool das Werkzeug, -e (8)

tooth der Zahn, ⁼e (11); to brush one's teeth sich die Zähne putzen (11)

toothache die Zahnschmerzen (*pl.*) (11)

topic das Thema, Themen (4)

to total (up) aus·rechnen, ausgerechnet (8)

total(ly) total (4)

tour of the city die Stadtrundfahrt, -en (7); bicycle tour die Radtour, -en (9); guided tour die Führung, -en (10)

tourism der Tourismus (10)

tourist bureau das Fremdenverkehrsamt, ̈er (10); tourist class die Touristenklasse (5)

towel: hand towel das Handtuch, ̈er (5); paper towel das Papiertuch, ̈er (5)

town der Ort, -e (4); die Stadt, ̈e (6); old part of town die Altstadt, ̈e (10); town hall das Rathaus, ̈er (1, 6); at the town hall auf dem Rathaus (1); town house das Reihenhaus, ̈er (6)

track: train track die Schiene, -n (10); (set of) train tracks das Gleis, -e (10)

tradition die Tradition, -en (4, 12)

traffic der Verkehr (7, 11); traffic jam der Stau, -s (7); traffic roundabout der Kreisverkehr, -e (10); traffic sign das Verkehrsschild, -er (7)

tragedy die Tragödie, -n (12)

train der Zug, ̈e (7, 10); passenger train der Personenzug, ̈e (7); train agent der/die Bahnangestellte, -n (ein Bahnangestellter) (10); train car der Waggon, -s (7); train station der Bahnhof, ̈e (4, 5); at the train station auf dem Bahnhof (5); train ticket die Zugfahrkarte, -n (6); train track die Schiene, -n (10); (set of) train tracks das Gleis, -e (10)

training: practical (career) training praktische Ausbildung (5); specialized training die Ausbildung (5)

transfer (of money) die Überweisung, -en (12)

to translate übersetzen, übersetzt (9)

to transport transportieren, transportiert (7)

transportation: means of transportation das Transportmittel, - (7); public transportation die öffentlichen Verkehrsmittel (pl.) (7)

transverse flute die Querflöte, -n (12)

trash der Müll (6)

to travel reisen, ist gereist (1, 10); to travel first class erster Klasse fahren (10); travel agency das Reisebüro, -s (6); travel experience das Reiseerlebnis, -se (7); travel guidebook der Reiseführer, - (5)

traveler der/die Reisende, -n (ein Reisender) (10); traveler's check der Reisescheck, -s (7)

traveling: to be traveling through auf der Durchreise sein (7)

treasure der Schatz, ̈e (9)

tree der Baum, ̈e (9); tree house das Baumhaus, ̈er (6)

trick die List, -en (9)

trip die Reise, -n (7); die Fahrt, -en (10); business trip die Geschäftsreise, -n (7); one-way trip die einfache Fahrt (10); round-trip hin und zurück (5, 10), die Hin- und Rückfahrt (10); to be on a trip auf Reisen sein (7); to go on a trip verreisen, ist verreist (3)

to trip stolpern, ist gestolpert (9)

trouble der Ärger (9)

trout die Forelle, -n (8)

truck der Lastwagen, - (7)

true wahr (3); treu (9)

trumpet die Trompete, -n (12)

trunk (of a car) der Kofferraum, ̈e (7); (of an elephant) der Rüssel, - (10)

trunks: swimming trunks die Badehose, -n (5)

to try probieren, probiert (3); versuchen, versucht (4)

T-shirt das T-Shirt, -s (2)

Tuesday der Dienstag (1)

Tunisia (das) Tunesien (B)

Turk der Türke, -n (wk.) / die Türkin, -nen (12)

Turkey die Türkei (B)

Turkish (language) (das) Türkisch (B)

to turn ab·biegen (biegt ... ab), bog ... ab, ist abgebogen (10); to turn off aus·machen, ausgemacht (3); to turn on an·machen, angemacht (3); ein·schalten, eingeschaltet (11)

turtle die Schildkröte, -n (10)

tusk der Stoßzahn, ̈e (10)

tutoring die Nachhilfe (3)

TV movie der Fernsehfilm, -e (12); TV reporter der Fernsehreporter, - / die Fernsehreporterin, -nen (5); TV room das Fernsehzimmer, - (10); TV set der Fernseher, - (2); to watch TV fern·sehen (sieht ... fern), sah ... fern, ferngesehen (1)

twelfth zwölft- (4)

twelve zwölf (A)

twentieth zwanzigst- (4)

twenty zwanzig (A)

twenty-one einundzwanzig (A)

twice zweimal (5)

two zwei (A)

type die Art, -en (2)

to type tippen, getippt (3, 6)

U.S.A. die USA (pl.) (B)

ugly hässlich (2)

Ukraine die Ukraine (B)

umbrella der Regenschirm, -e (5)

uncle der Onkel, - (B)

unconsciousness die Ohnmacht (11)

under, underneath unter (+ dat./acc.) (5); under the window unter dem Fenster (5)

underpants die Unterhose, -n (2)

undershirt das Unterhemd, -en (2)

to understand verstehen (versteht), verstand, verstanden (4)

to undress, get undressed sich aus·ziehen (zieht ... aus), zog ... aus, ausgezogen (11)

unemployed arbeitslos (5)

unfortunately leider (B)

university die Universität, -en (1, 4, 5); (coll.) die Uni, -s (B, 1); at the university auf der Universität (5); to be at the university auf der Uni sein (1); to go to the university zur Uni gehen (1); university newspaper die Unizei-tung, -en (4); university studies das Studium, Studien (1)

unmarried ledig (1)

untalented unbegabt (12)

until (prep.) bis (+ acc.) (2, 4, 11); (subord. conj.) bis (11); not until erst (4); not until four o'clock erst um vier Uhr (4); until eight o'clock bis acht Uhr (2); until four in the morning bis um vier Uhr früh (4)

up to bis zu (+ dat.) (10); up that way hinauf (10)

upset: to get upset sich auf·regen, aufgeregt (11)

Uranus der Uranus (4)

urgent(ly) dringend (2)

use der Gebrauch, ̈e (12)

to use brauchen, gebraucht (1); benutzen, benutzt (7)

used: to get used to sich gewöhnen an (+ acc.), gewöhnt (11); used car der Gebrauchtwagen, - (7)

useful nützlich (10)

usually meistens (8)

vacation die Ferien (pl.) (1); der Urlaub, -e (4, 5); vacation house das Ferienhaus, ̈er (4)

to vaccinate against impfen gegen (+ acc.), geimpft (10)

to vacuum Staub saugen, Staub gesaugt (6)

vacuum cleaner der Staubsauger, - (6)

Valentine's Day der Valentinstag (4)

valley das Tal, ̈er (7)

valuable wertvoll (2)

various verschieden (8)

vase die Vase, -n (3)

vegetable das Gemüse, - (8)

vehicle das Fahrzeug, -e (11)

very sehr (B)

veterinarian der Tierarzt, ̈e / die Tierärztin, -nen (11)

vicinity die Nähe (6); in the vicinity in der Nähe (6)

video das Video, -s (9); video game das Videospiel, -e (2); video recorder der Videorekorder, - (A)

view der Ausblick, -e (6)

vinegar der Essig (8)

violence die Gewalt (12)

violin die Geige, -n (3)

visa das Visum, Visa (7, 12)

visible sichtbar (11)

visit der Besuch, -e (3); to visit besuchen, besucht (1); zu Besuch kommen (3); vorbei·kommen (kommt ... vorbei), kam ... vorbei, ist vorbeigekommen (3); besichtigen, besichtigt (7)

vocabulary der Wortschatz, ̈e (A)

voice die Stimme, -n (12)

volleyball der Volleyball, ̈e (1)

to wait warten, gewartet (7)

waiter/waitress der Kellner, - / die Kellnerin, -nen (8); die Bedienung (8) to wake up **auf·wachen, ist aufgewacht** (4); to wake (*s.o.*) up **wecken, geweckt** (9)

walk **der Spaziergang, ⸚e** (10); to go for a walk **spazieren gehen (geht ... spazieren), ging ... spazieren, ist spazieren gegangen** (1); to keep on walking **weiter·gehen (geht ... weiter), ging ... weiter, ist weitergegangen** (10); to walk **gehen (geht), ging, ist gegangen** (A); to walk in the park **im Park spazieren gehen** (1)

Walkman **der Walkman, Walkmen** (2)

wall **die Wand, ⸚e** (B); to hang the picture on the wall **das Bild an die Wand hängen** (3)

waltz **der Walzer, -** (3)

to want **wollen (will), wollte, gewollt** (3)

wardrobe **der Schrank, ⸚e** (2); **der Kleiderschrank, ⸚e** (6)

warm **warm** (B)

to warn **warnen, gewarnt** (7)

wash basin **das Waschbecken, -** (6)

to wash **waschen (wäscht), wusch, gewaschen** (2, 11); **spülen, gespült** (4); to wash oneself **sich waschen (wäscht), wusch, gewaschen** (11); to wash the dishes **Geschirr spülen** (4)

washing machine **die Waschmaschine, -n** (6)

wastebasket **der Papierkorb, ⸚e** (3)

watch **die Armbanduhr, -en** (A)

to watch **an·sehen (sieht ... an), sah ... an, angesehen** (3); to watch out **auf·passen, aufgepasst** (3); to watch out for **achten auf (+ acc.), geachtet** (11); to watch TV **fern·sehen (sieht ... fern), sah ... fern, ferngesehen** (1)

water: mineral water **das Mineralwasser** (8); water fowl **der Wasservogel, ⸚** (10); to water **gießen (gießt), goss, gegossen** (3); to water the flowers **die Blumen gießen** (3)

watering can **die Gießkanne, -n** (6)

wave **die Welle, -n** (10)

to wear **tragen (trägt), trug, getragen** (A)

weather **das Wetter, -** (B); in rainy weather **bei Regen** (7)

Wednesday **der Mittwoch** (1)

week **die Woche, -n** (1); during the week **in der Woche** (1); every week **jede Woche** (3); last week **letzte Woche** (4)

weekend **das Wochenende, -n** (1); last weekend **letztes Wochenende** (4); over the weekend **am Wochenende** (1); übers Wochenende (4)

weight: to lose weight **ab·nehmen (nimmt ... ab), nahm ... ab, abgenommen** (8, 11)

well (*n.*) **der Brunnen, -** (9)

well (*adv.*): that fits well **das passt gut** (11); to feel well **sich wohl fühlen** (11)

well (*interj.*) **also** (2); **na** (3)

west (of) **westlich (von + dat.)** (7)

wet **nass** (3)

whale: blue whale **der Blauwal, -e** (10)

what **was** (B); at what time . . . ? **um wie viel Uhr ...?** (1); on what day? **an welchem Tag?** (4); what day is today? **welcher Tag ist heute?** (1); what do your pictures show? **was zeigen Ihre Bilder?** (A); what for? **wofür?** (8); what is today's date? **welches Datum ist heute?** (4); what time is it? **wie spät ist es? wie viel Uhr ist es?** (1); what's your profession? **was sind Sie von Beruf?** (1)

wheel **das Rad, ⸚er** (7); potter's wheel **die Töpferscheibe, -n** (12); steering wheel **das Lenkrad, ⸚er** (7)

when **wann** (B, 1); (*subord. conj.*) **als** (5, 11); when(ever) (*subord. conj.*) **wenn** (2, 11); when I was eight years old **als ich acht Jahre alt war** (5); when were you born? **wann sind Sie geboren?** (1)

whenever (*subord. conj.*) **wenn** (2, 11)

where **wo** (B); from where **woher** (B); where are you going? **wo willst du denn hin?** (A); where to **wohin** (3)

whether **ob** (6, 10, 11)

which **welcher, welches, welche** (B)

white **weiß** (A)

who **wer** (A, B)

whole **ganz** (2); the whole day **den ganzen Tag** (1)

whom (*dat.*) **wem** (4); (*acc.*) **wen** (4)

why **warum** (3); that's why **deshalb** (4)

wife **die Frau, -en** (B)

wig **die Perücke, -n** (11)

wild boar **das Wildschwein, -e** (10)

willingly **gern** (1)

to win **gewinnen, gewonnen** (4); to win the lottery **in der Lotterie gewinnen** (5)

wind **der Wind, -e** (9)

window **das Fenster, -** (B); ticket window **der Fahrkartenschalter, -** (7); under the window **unter dem Fenster** (5)

windowpane **die Scheibe, -n** (7); **die Fensterscheibe, -n** (9)

windowsill **die Fensterbank, ⸚e** (5)

windshield wiper **der Scheibenwischer, -** (7)

windsurfing: to go windsurfing **windsurfen gehen (geht ... windsurfen), ging ... windsurfen, ist windsurfen gegangen** (1)

windy **windig** (B)

wine **der Wein, -e** (7); wine cellar **der Weinkeller, -** (6)

winter **der Winter, -** (B)

to wipe **wischen, gewischt** (7); to wipe clean **ab·wischen, abgewischt** (6)

witch **die Hexe, -n** (7, 9)

with **mit (+ dat.)** (A); **bei (+ dat.)** (2, 6, 10); does it come with a . . . ? **ist ein(e) ... dabei?** (6); with

each other **miteinander** (3); with me **mit mir** (3); with your parents **bei deinen Eltern** (6)

witness **der Zeuge, -n** (*wk.*) / **die Zeugin, -nen** (11)

wolf **der Wolf, ⸚e** (9)

woman **die Frau, -en** (A, B)

wood **das Holz, ⸚er** (12)

woods **der Wald, ⸚er** (2, 7); to run in the woods **im Wald laufen** (2)

word **das Wort, ⸚er** (A)

work **die Arbeit, -en** (1); (*product*) **das Werk, -e** (9); from work **von der Arbeit** (3); kitchen work **die Küchenarbeit, -en** (5); to go to work **zur Arbeit gehen** (1); to work **arbeiten, gearbeitet** (1); to work (*take effect*) **wirken, gewirkt** (11); work permit **die Arbeitserlaubnis, -se** (12); work with a partner **arbeiten Sie mit einem Partner** (A)

workbook **das Arbeitsbuch, ⸚er** (3)

worker **der Arbeiter, -** / **die Arbeiterin, -nen** (5); construction worker **der Bauarbeiter, -** / **die Bauarbeiterin, -nen** (5)

world **die Welt, -en** (7)

would like (to) **möchte** (2, 3)

wound **die Wunde, -n** (11)

to write **schreiben (schreibt), schrieb, geschrieben** (A); to write down **auf·schreiben (schreibt ... auf), schrieb ... auf, aufgeschrieben** (11)

writer **der Schriftsteller, -** / **die Schriftstellerin, -nen** (5)

written **schriftlich** (10)

wrong **falsch** (2); to be wrong with (*s.o.*) **fehlen (+ dat.), gefehlt** (11); to get up on the wrong side of bed **mit dem linken Fuß auf·stehen** (4)

to X-ray **röntgen, geröntgt** (11)

year **das Jahr, -e** (2)

to yell **schreien (schreit), schrie, geschrien** (3)

yellow **gelb** (A)

yes (*on the contrary*) **doch!** (4); yes please? **bitte schön?** (7)

yesterday **gestern** (4); the day before yesterday **vorgestern** (4)

you (*acc.*) **dich** (2)

young **jung** (B)

your (*infor. sg.*) **dein(e)** (B, 2); (*infor. pl.*) **euer, eure** (2); (*for.*) **Ihr(e)** (B, 2)

youth **die Jugend** (9); youth hostel **die Jugendherberge, -n** (10)

Yugoslavia **(das) Jugoslawien** (B)

zebra **das Zebra, -s** (10)

zeppelin **der Zeppelin, -e** (7)

zoo **der Zoo, -s** (10)

Index

This index is divided into three subsections: Culture, Grammar, and Vocabulary. The notation "n" following a page number indicates that the subject is treated in a footnote on that page. Reading titles are included in the Culture section.

Culture

Grammar

INDEX

with **als,** 327
with **möchte,** 101
with **nachdem,** 334–335
with **(nicht) gern,** 71
with prepositions for giving directions, 365
with separable-prefix verbs, 75, 231
with **wann** in indirect questions, 330
würde, 428
w-word questions, 161

yes/no questions, 77, 161

zu, 230, 361–362, 362 *margin*
zu Hause, 230
zwischen. *See* two-way prepositions.

Vocabulary

academic subjects, 53, 67
accidents, 383, 386, 393
activities. *See* childhood and childhood activities;
   daily life and routine; leisure activities.
animals, 325, 352, 359–360
apartments and apartment hunting, 204, 212,
   222–223
appliances, 275, 291–292
artists' tools and materials, 417
asking directions, 342, 359
auto parts, 246, 254

banking, 414, 423
beach activities, 349
belongings, 80, 83, 95
biographical information, 61, 67
birthdays and anniversaries, 150
body care, 378, 393
body parts, 29, 38, 378, 383, 392
buildings, 190–191, 207, 209, 212, 222

calendar and dates, 150
car parts, 246, 254
childhood and childhood activities, 304, 307, 324
chores, 216, 304
city vocabulary, 359
classroom vocabulary, 18, 26, 38, 67, 128, 159
clothing and accessories, 8, 17, 87, 96
colors, 10, 17
commands, 4, 17
continents, 39
cooking, 280–281, 291
countries, 39

daily life and routine, 56, 67–68, 140, 154, 378, 393
descriptions, 27, 38
directions, 342, 359

fairy tales, 316, 324–325
family life, 404, 422
family relationships, 30, 38
favors and gifts, 172
feelings, 123, 128
finances, 414, 423
food and drink, 270–271, 290–291
   cooking, 280–281, 291
   preparation, 291
   shopping, 280–281
furnishings, 95

gender roles, 404, 422
geography, 238, 254
gifts, 83, 172, 191
giving directions, 342, 359
greeting and leave-taking, 12, 17

health and health care, 374, 383, 392–393
holidays, 159
home furnishings, 95
household appliances, 275, 291–292
household chores, 216, 304
household items, 291–292
housing, 204, 212, 222–223

illness, 374, 383, 392

kinship terms, 30, 38
kitchen items, 184, 191

landscape features, 238
languages, 39
leisure activities, 50, 67, 92, 110, 115, 128, 140, 145
living arrangements, 223
living spaces, 204, 222–223

married life, 404, 422
meals, 270–271, 290–291
   restaurant, 285
money, 414, 423
multiculturalism, 407, 422–423
musical instruments, 417

nationalities, 35, 39
nature, 325
neighborhoods, 207, 209, 222
numbers, cardinal, 14, 17

objects, 80, 83, 95
obligations, 115, 128
occupations, 176, 190
offices and stores, 190–191
ordinal numbers, 159

personal descriptions, 27, 38
personal hygiene, 393
personal information, 61, 67
pharmacy and hospital, 392–393
physical and mental states, 123, 128
places, 67
plans, 110, 128
pleasures, 92
politeness formulas, 119
possessions, 80, 83, 95

questions, 18

restaurant expressions, 285, 291
rooms, 204, 222–223
routine activities, 56, 67–68, 140, 154, 378, 393

school subjects, 53, 67
school vocabulary, 128. *See also* classroom
   vocabulary.
seas, 39
seasons and weather, 32, 38
shopping, 190–191, 280–281
states of being, 123, 128
stores, 207, 209, 222
subjects, academic, 53, 67

talents, 110, 128
time expressions, 158–159
transportation, 242, 246
travel, 158, 250, 254–255, 338–339, 359

vacations, 145, 158, 250, 254–255, 338–339, 349,
   359
vehicles, 242, 246, 254

weather and seasons, 32, 38
workplaces, 180, 190–191

Credits

Grateful acknowledgment is made for use of the following photographs, realia, and readings.